WORK AND ORGANIZATIONAL BEHAVIOUR

WORK and ORGANIZATIONAL BEHAVIOUR

UNDERSTANDING the WORKPLACE

John BRATTON

Militza CALLINAN

Carolyn FORSHAW

Peter SAWCHUK

First published 2007 by
PALGRAVE MACMILLAN
Houndmills, Basingstoke, Hampshire RG21 6XS and
175 Fifth Avenue, New York, N.Y. 10010
Companies and representatives throughout the world

PALGRAVE MACMILLAN is the global academic imprint of the Palgrave
Macmillan division of St. Martin's Press, LLC and of Palgrave Macmillan Ltd.
Macmillan® is a registered trademark in the United States, United Kingdom
and other countries. Palgrave is a registered trademark in the European
Union and other countries.

ISBN-13: 978-1-4039-1114-8
ISBN-10: 1-4039-1114-2

This book is printed on paper suitable for recycling and made from fully
managed and sustained forest sources.

A catalogue record for this book is available from the British Library.

A catalog record for this book is available from the Library of Congress

10   9   8   7   6   5   4   3   2   1
16 15 14 13 12 11 10 09 08 07

Printed and bound in China

Contents in brief

Contents

part 1   Work and organizational behaviour   1

chapter 1   The nature of organizational behaviour   3

figures

Plates

Tables

John Bratton   *Militza Callinan*   *Carolyn Forshaw*   *Peter H. Sawchuk*

About the authors

John Bratton is Professor of Sociology at Thompson Rivers University, Kamloops, Canada. He was the first Director of the Workplace Learning Research Unit at the University of Calgary. He has served on the faculties of Leeds Business School at Leeds Metropolitan University, the University of Bradford and the Open University, England. His research interests focus on the politics of technology, leadership and workplace learning. He is a member of the editorial board of the *Journal of Workplace Learning and Leadership*. In addition to co-authoring this book, he is co-author (with Jeff Gold) of *Human Resource Management: Theory and practice*, now in its fourth edition; co-author (with Peter Sawchuk, J. Helms-Mills and T. Pyrch) of *Workplace Learning: A critical introduction* (2004), co-author (with Keith Grint and Debra Nelson) of *Organizational Leadership* (2005), author of *Japanization of Work: Managerial studies in the 1990s*, and co-author (with Jeremy Waddington) of *New Technology and Employment* (1981).

Militza Callinan lectures in organizational behaviour and human resource management at Leeds Business School, England. Her main research interests are in the area of individual differences, particularly personality and work behaviour, as well as the related area of employee selection and development. Currently she is engaged in a project funded by the ESRC, investigating conscious deception by job applicants during selection procedures. A second project, funded by the Leverhulme Trust, is exploring the accuracy with which personality measures can predict people's behaviour. A third area of research involves the effect of personality in groups.

Carolyn Forshaw lectures in professional writing at Thompson Rivers University. She has had over 25 years' experience in the field in Britain and Canada. Her research interests include gender and language, post-colonial literary theory and Canadian and Caribbean literature.

Peter H. Sawchuk is cross-appointed to the Sociology of Education and Industrial Relations departments at the University of Toronto. He teaches, researches and writes in the areas of technology, learning, work and the labour movement. His latest books include *Adult Learning and Technology in Working-Class Life* (Cambridge, 2003), *Workplace Learning: A critical introduction* (Garamond, 2004), *Hidden Dimensions of Knowledge: Organized labour in the Information Age* (co-authored with D. Livingstone; Rowman and Littlefield, 2004), and most recently *Critical Perspectives on Activity: Explorations of education, work and everyday life* (co-edited with N. Duarte and M. Elhammoumi; Cambridge 2006).

Message to students

Dear student,

Thank you for buying *Work and Organizational Behaviour*. This textbook provides an accessible but critical introduction to organizational behaviour that will equip you with a comprehensive knowledge and understanding of the latest relevant theories and applications of the subject. Importantly, by 'critical' we mean to help set the stage for the type of learning that will support your thinking about how (and eventually your efforts) to make workplaces more effective in a variety of ways: more productive, more satisfying, more developmental and, we would add, more equitable as well. That is a tall order to say the least. But remember, change does not happen on its own, and better understanding of the workplace is a vital starting point.

The book is structured in five parts which are described in detail in the Preface. Each chapter follows a similar structure in order to help you navigate the text easily. At the beginning of each chapter we offer quotes from academics or practitioners to show the direct relevance of the chapter topic. The chapter outline and chapter objectives which follow summarize the key concepts that will be covered and the knowledge you will gain.

The main text introduces you to key organizational behaviour concepts and offers critical comment as well as discussing competing perspectives. 'Stop and reflect' questions encourage you to think critically about key issues and consider broader consequences of human action and processes on the behaviour of people at work. We have included a feature we call 'OB in focus' to illustrate current developments or practices in organizational behaviour so you can see the practices applied in the real world. 'Critical insights' is intended to help you formulate questions about the subject, and 'OB web links' to help you research topics further.

At the end of each chapter you will find a summary of the chapter content and a list of key concepts. These can be used alongside the chapter outlines and chapter objectives to ensure you have understood the key issues. If you need to recap on any topics, page references are provided to enable you to find the relevant section. There is also an extensive glossary at the back of the book. We provide details of further reading sources to enable you to explore the subject further, and case studies to reinforce learning and apply organizational behaviour theory. Finally, the 'Web-based assignments' develop your research skills and provide further examples of OB applied in the workplace, and the 'OB in films' exercise offers entertaining insights into the behaviour of people in the workplace.

The companion website to this text can be accessed at **www.palgrave.com/ business/brattonOB** and provides multiple choice questions, a film guide exploring organizational behaviour through popular film, summary notes for each chapter, web links, a skill development guide to help with essays, reports and presentations and a searchable online glossary to check on definitions of key terms.

We hope the learning features will help you to make maximum use of this book, and be successful in your organizational behaviour course. We would welcome any feedback on the text and any suggestions on how we can improve the next edition; please contact us via our email addresses on the companion website.
Good luck with your studies.

John Bratton
Militza Callinan
Carolyn Forshaw
Peter Sawchuk

Message to lecturers

Dear lecturer,

Thank you for adopting *Work and Organizational Behaviour*. This new textbook incorporates material and pedagogical features we have used in teaching our own courses, and comments from nine anonymous reviewers of the manuscript. As you perhaps already know, there are several sections and components that are unique to texts in the field, and that have been added in order to expand the scope of our thinking in undergraduate offerings in key ways.

The book has been written specifically to fulfil the needs of students completing an introductory undergraduate organizational behaviour course, and as such it assumes no previous knowledge of the discipline by the student. Our approach to explaining organizational behaviour is to examine the traditional core introductory material, but we depart from traditional texts by introducing business students to unfamiliar theories and research from the sociology of work. Further, we emphasize six core themes: competing standpoints, change in the workplace, relation between the self and society, diversity/equity, power and globalization. In many ways, it is these core themes that constitute and support what we understand as a 'critical' approach. That is, these core themes encourage a pluralistic or multi-voiced perspective on organizational behaviour, leading to a more holistic and nuanced awareness of forces and processes shaping the behaviour of people in the workplace. The book also includes an eclectic selection of academic material and behaviour practices drawn from the European Union, North America and parts of Asia, to help you provide your students with a global appreciation of organizational behaviour.

Work and Organizational Behaviour embraces an 'educative' approach to studying OB in that it seeks to challenge students to question and to develop their own understanding of organizational behaviour. This is also an important element of our notion of a 'critical' approach. With this in mind, the 'Stop and reflect' questions, 'OB in focus' and 'Critical insight' features are designed to prompt your students to reflect on ideas, competing perspectives and implications of organizational behaviour. The student website for the text provides further learning resources which we hope will encourage your students to discover more about OB on their own.

The publishers provide a variety of supporting materials to help you prepare and present the material in this new textbook. The companion website at **www.palgrave. com/business/ brattonOB** offers downloadable teaching supplements including lecture notes and enhancement ideas, a sample course outline, a testbank including multiple choice questions and a sample final exam paper, a film guide exploring organizational behaviour through popular film and PowerPoint lecture slides for each chapter.

To add more value for your students using *Work and Organizational Behaviour*, we suggest that you make reference to the book during your lectures, for instance identifying relevant sections of the chapter, referring to the 'OB in focus' and other pedagogic features, as well as asking students to attempt the end-of-chapter case study in preparation for your seminar or in-class discussion.

We would welcome any feedback on these features or any suggestions on how we can improve the next edition. Please contact us via our email addresses.

Best wishes,

John Bratton
Militza Callinan
Carolyn Forshaw
Peter Sawchuk

Preface

Welcome to *Work and Organizational Behaviour: Understanding the workplace.* This book has been written specifically to fulfil the needs of introductory undergraduate courses for an accessible analysis of behaviour in work organizations, which draw from the two major human sciences of psychology and sociology. It assumes no previous knowledge of psychology or sociology by the student, practitioner or general reader.

Context

Since 1985, when the first edition of Huczynski and Buchanan's text *Organizational Behaviour* was published, the world of work and the way it is studied have changed. The major changes include the ascendancy of neo-liberalism, the implosion of Soviet and East European communism and South African apartheid, the expansion of the European Union and North America Free Trade zone, the positioning of the People's Republic of China and India as major economic players, and the economic reverberations in the other Asian economies and beyond. The widespread application of microelectronics has seen the emergence of the Internet, the virtual knowledge-based organization, and the virtual or postmodern organization.

The earlier predictions of a 'leisure society' resulting from new technology have not materialized. Many managers and non-managers alike still work long hours, are electronically connected, through email, mobile phones and BlackBerries, and appear to be suffering increased levels of work-related stress. And in addition to movements of capital and goods, many people have migrated to Western Europe and North America, making the diverse workforce a reality. New management paradigms have come and gone: the ebb and flow of concepts associated with the 'Japanization' of work organization, the 'reengineered organization' and the 'learning organization' to name just three major developments.

A major issue for academics and practitioners is the effect of globalization on aspects of organizational behaviour (OB) ranging from individual work motivation to organizational governance. As the globalization of world markets continues apace, there has been growing interest in studying whether managerial behaviour in work organizations outside North America is converging on the US way of doing things. Over the last decade, therefore, a major theme in the literature has been the convergence in managerial behaviour, affecting production, marketing, information technology, finance and employment policies and practices in different regions of the world.

The convergence debate has a solid and deep-rooted background in neoclassical economic theory. However, its detractors emphasize the existence of varieties of capitalism, and of divergence in organizational behaviour, which offers different ways to preserve the quality of life and effective ways to compete globally. The 'divergence' school tends to be sceptical of claims that convergence is occurring, believing that local cultures, social values and norms, and national business systems are strong forces against convergence. It would seem the variations in the forms of capitalism that are found make it difficult, if not impossible, to extract management practices founded on OB theory and research from one particular national setting and implant it in a different culture and matrix, and have them achieve the same results.

When it comes to organizational behaviour there are no universal prescriptions. One size doesn't fit all. Additionally, the behaviour of corporate executives and corporate governance have come under close scrutiny following the exposure of fraudulent accounting practices, and the job and pension losses that occurred as a result, at Enron, WorldCom and other prominent US corporations in the early twenty-first century, and this has reduced the appeal of US-centred convergence.

The last 25 years have not only seen major changes in the global economy, society and the workplace. They have also seen some of the people who study the workplace – organizational theorists – abandoning the application of the rules of physical science to the study of social phenomena. The traditional approach to researching organizational behaviour can loosely be describe as 'positivism'. In the context of postmodernism, it has been challenged by 'constructivists'. The core argument of the constructivists is that organizational reality does not have an objective existence, but is constructed by people with power in the organizations, and by organizational behaviour theorists themselves. The constructivist view challenges researchers to re-examine their frame of reference, and their ideas about the research process itself and the production of knowledge.[1]

In some academic circles postmodernism has fallen out of fashion in the analysis of organizational behaviour, in a similar manner to the Japanese management model which was popular a few years earlier. The favoured theoretical foundation of today's discourse and research is the 'societal effects' approach, which argues that human behaviour in work organizations is socially embedded.[2] Scholars adopting this approach argue that work organizations are not 'free agents' able to design their own employment and governance practices, unfettered by social institutions and values. Rather, they argue, societal effects are central to the shaping of organizational practices. For example, the widespread demonstrations in France in spring 2006 against non-standard or precarious employment – with the slogan 'Non à la précarité!' – can be seen as confirmation of this.

Despite these global changes and rival intellectual traditions, which lead to competing research perspectives among those studying organizations, most OB textbooks, at least for the undergraduate market, only expose students to the dominant orthodoxy in the subject, which is built on an extremely narrow set of theoretical assumptions. In general they concentrate on the positivist-functionalist point of view: how to foster commitment, cooperation, integration, and ultimately improve organizational performance. Rival perspectives are rarely explored, and the textbooks have little, if anything, to say about gender, race, ethnicity, disability and social class, or about competing views of the workplace.[3] Most of the popular textbooks are written from a managerial perspective, and largely ignore competing views of organizational behaviour presented by critical and feminist writers. They have a distinctly 'psychological' tone, and draw heavily on psychological studies of human behaviour. More pointedly, few encourage their readers to call into question the dominant assumptions underpinning US-centric management theory and practice.

Our approach

Our approach to explaining human behaviour in the workplace is rather different. We cover the three levels of analysis – individual, group and organizational – found in traditional organizational behaviour textbooks, and examine the concepts and issues that comprise the core of an introductory course in the subject. However, we depart from 'mainstream' texts on organizational behaviour in three important respects.

First, we attempt to take the student of organizational behaviour into realms rarely explored in most undergraduate courses in management. We try to offer an intellectual journey, which draws on familiar areas from workplace psychology, but also takes readers to unfamiliar paradigms and research from the realm of sociology. Our approach to studying organizational behaviour privileges the idea that history and the interplay of people and society matter – that the work organization is embedded in the particularities of time and society, and in the dynamics of the local and the global. Our intention is to draw upon both mainstream and critical perspectives, as a requirement for generating a more eclectic inter-disciplinary dialogue. It is hardly an original orientation,[4] but in adopting a more critical perspective, we believe this book embraces a more educative approach to studying OB. It seeks to challenge students to question, to debate, to seek multi-causality and to develop their own understanding of organizational behaviour.

Second, this book emphasizes six core themes: competing standpoints, change in the workplace, the relationship between the self and the social, diversity/equity, power and globalization. These core themes provide a holistic view of organizational behaviour, and help differentiate *Work and Organizational Behaviour* from the dominant psychologically based OB texts.

Third, we have brought together an eclectic selection of academic material and behaviour practices from the European Community, North America and parts of Asia, to offer students a more global appreciation of behaviour at work. Thus, in an increasingly globalized world in which managers and the managed are increasingly expected to be sensitive to cultural diversity, to be independent thinkers and to be creative, *Work and Organizational Behaviour* offers students an accessible alternative to the more psychological, managerialist-oriented texts on the market.

Content

Work and Organizational Behaviour is divided into five major parts, based on the traditional division of behavioural studies. These parts are of course interconnected, but we believe the division provides a convenient heuristic (teaching) device to guide the reader through the learning material.

Part 1 explains the meaning of organizational behaviour, the psychological and sociological perspectives, developments in the design of paid work, and the classical and contemporary approaches to studying work.

Part 2 focuses on the context of organizational behaviour, including the role of management and the nature of managerial leadership.

Part 3 explores how various individual differences affect employee behaviour. The study of personality and perception, and learning and motivation, helps us understand how differences between individuals (for example in their personality), and processes within individuals (such as learning), are made manifest in workplace behaviour. We also consider the enduring social phenomenon of inequality, and the role of gender, race, disability and class in employment.

Part 4 examines the social processes that take place in the context of work groups and teams. Group dynamics, face-to-face communications, decision making in groups, and power relations and conflict are of special interest to us.

Part 5 shifts the focus to developed accounts of the functioning of modern large-scale work organizations in a global economy, how organizations are designed, the motive and affects of technological change, and how human resources are managed to improve organizational performance.

Teaching aspects of the book

Work and Organizational Behaviour includes a number of features that are designed to complement, supplement and reinforce the main text. These features are designed to help students learn the relevance of OB to understanding life at work, and to promote self-awareness and critical thinking:

▷ Introduction to show the relevance of each OB topic to readers.
▷ Chapter outline and chapter objectives.
▷ Graphic exhibits to help explain OB concepts.
▷ Self-reflective questions in the body paragraphs.
▷ Websites located in the body paragraphs to give readers access to Internet resources.
▷ 'Critical insight' to promote dialogue.
▷ 'OB in focus' boxes which illustrate or supplement the textual material.
▷ Chapter summary.
▷ End-of-chapter discussion questions.
▷ End-of-chapter case study to illustrate major concepts of the chapter.
▷ Further reading.
▷ End-of-book glossary.
▷ Web-based assignments to bring OB to life.
▷ 'OB in films' illustrates and explores OB concepts and issues as well as entertains.

Acknowledgements

To write a critical book on organizational behaviour is an audacious undertaking. The four-year journey of taking *Work and Organizational Behaviour* from an idea to a finished book has had diversions and hold-ups, and at times it has been frustrating. It has however also been exhilarating, and I have thoroughly enjoyed working with Militza Callinan, Carolyn Forshaw, Peter Sawchuk and Justine Wheeler, Librarian at the University of Calgary, who produced the Instructor's guide. I am deeply indebted to Lori Rilkoff, Senior Human Resource Manager at the City of Kamloops and lecturer in HRM at Thompson Rivers University, who contributed three chapter case studies and edited, polished and doubled-checked several other case studies in this book.

I would also like to extend sincere thanks to the lecturers and practitioners in Britain and Canada who contributed cases to *Work and Organizational Behaviour*:

Dan Haley, Thompson Rivers University, Canada
Len Hutt, Thompson Rivers University, Canada
Gill Musson, University of Sheffield, England
Lori Rilkoff, Thompson Rivers University, Canada
Ian Roper, University of Middlesex, England
Susanne Tietze, University of Bradford, England

My research assistants, Andrew Bratton, Amy Bratton, and Sabrina Weeks, have typed material and retrieved articles and data that make up this book's many tables and figures. Palgrave Press subjected the manuscripts to an extensive and welcome peer review process, and we are very grateful to the nine anonymous reviewers who made valuable suggestions for improving the content and style of this book. We are also grateful to the copyright holders who permitted us to reprint the extracts, diagrams and photographs.

I am also grateful to the talented and dedicated editorial team at Palgrave who have given encouragement and support for the project since 2002: Ruth Lake, Sarah Brown, Helen Bugler, Ursula Gavin and Lee Ann Tutton. Thanks too to Susan Curran of Curran Publishing Services, who copy-edited and indexed the book, and Jim Weaver who designed and typeset it.

My greatest debt is to my partner, Carolyn Forshaw, who for years has spent many hours helping to evolve the ideas in this book, accompanied me on numerous research trips, and given me support and, in the final phase of the project, encouragement to be totally consumed in putting this book together. Finally, my thanks to my family – Amy, Andrew and Jennie – who continue to be an important part of my life.

John Bratton

Like John, I would like to thank my co-authors and Palgrave for their creativity, commitment and hard work. As always, my partner Jill deserves my acknowledgement and thanks for her generous sharing of our time with these pages

Peter Sawchuk
September 2006

Notes

1 Clegg and Hardy (1999), Charmaz (2005), Grey (2005), Legge (2005).
2 Jacoby (2005), Wright Mills (1959/2000).
3 Burrell and Morgan (1979), Anderson and Collins (2004), Wilson (2003), Mills, Simmons and Helms Mills (2005).
4 See Arblaster (1970) and Godard (1992).

Acknowledgements

This book has been improved and developed with the help of comments and suggestions from reviews of the manuscript at various stages. We are particularly grateful to the reviewers: Dr Dorota Dobosz-Bourne, Queen Mary, University of London; Judith Chapman, University of Western Sydney, Australia; Dr Melissa Tyler, Loughborough University; Astrid Kaufmann, the Norwegian School of Management, Norway; Dr Susanne Tietze, Bradford University School of Management; Dr Donald Hislop, Loughborough University Business School; Dr Ian Roper, Middlesex University Business School; Dr Damian Hodgson, University of Manchester; Dr Titus Oshagbemi, Queen's University Belfast; Maeve Houlihan, University College Dublin; Dr Frank Carr, University of Bedfordshire; Dr Alan Tuckman, Nottingham Trent University; Dr Keith Thomas, the University of New South Wales at Australian Defence Force Academy; Dr Christian Waldstrøm, Aarhus School of Business, Denmark; Lanni Füssel, Copenhagen Business School, Denmark; Professor Karen Legge, Warwick Business School; Charles Malone, Dundee Business School; Dr Louise Preget, Bournemouth University; Aarti Vyas-Brannick, Manchester Metropolitan University; Mairi Gudim, Paisley University; Steve Holman, Staffordshire University; Martin Gammell, University of Luton; Gillian Forster, Northumbria University; Dr Annie Pye, University of Bath; Paul Stokes, Sheffield Hallam University; Ian Steers, Thames Valley University; and Dr Chris Martin, University of South Australia. We have endeavoured to incorporate their insights and criticisms to improve this text.

The authors and publishers are grateful to the following for permission to reproduce copyright material:

Emerald Group Publishing Limited for the figure 'A model of work-related learning' from Hoeve, A. and Nieuwenhuis, L. (2006) 'Learning Routines in Innovation Processes', *Journal of Workplace Learning*, Vol. 18, Issue 3, p. 175.

Professors Andrew Pettigrew and Chris Hendry for the 'Warwick Model of HRM', which was published in *International Journal of Human Resource Management* (1990), Routledge, Vol. 1, No. 1, p. 26.

Harvard Business School Publishing for the exhibit 'An alternate conception of the diversified firm' from Hamel, G. and Prahalad, C. K. (1994) *Competing for the Future*, Boston, Mass.: Harvard Business School Press, p. 279.

People Management and Dr Martin Clarke, Lecturer in Management Development, Cranfield School of Management, UK, for the extract from 'Critical condition' by Dr Clarke and published in *People Management*, 1 September 2005.

The H. J. Eysenck Memorial Fund for the figure 'Eysenck's major personality dimensions' from Eysenck, H. (1973) *The Inequality of Man*, London: Temple Smith.

John Wiley & Sons, Inc., for permission to use the figure 'The Fombrun, Tichy and Devanna Model of HRM' from Fombrun C. J., Tichy, N. M. and Devanna, M. A. (1984) *Strategic Human Resource Management*, New York: John Wiley & Sons. © John Wiley & Sons, Inc. 1984.

Michael Beer and Bert Spector for 'The Harvard Model of HRM' as published in Beer, M., Spector B., Lawrence, P. R., Mills, D. Q. and Walton, R. E. (1984) *Managing Human Assets*, New York: Free Press.

Guardian News & Media Limited for the article, 'Why women are poor at science, by the president of Harvard' by Suzanne Goldenberg, published in the *Guardian*, 18 January 2005. Copyright Guardian News & Media Ltd 2005.

The Globe and Mail for extracts of the following articles: 'Kilimanjaro's global warming: a wake-up call to the G8' by Jeremy Lovell, 15 March 2005, pp. 1, 15; 'Restructuring Ford Motor Company' by Karen Howlett, 11 January 2002, pp. B1–B4; and 'A culture of overwork exacts an extreme price' by Geoffrey York, 21 August 2006, p. A2.

University College London for the illustration of the Panopticon (Figure 2.1).

Canadian HR Reporter for the extract from the article, 'Psychometric testing: ensuring the right fit', by Shawn Bakker, a psychologist at Psychometrics Canada, 27 March 2006, p. 7.

Sage Publications Ltd for the figure, 'Differing concepts of leadership competencies' from Bolden, R. and Gosling, J. (2006) 'Leadership competencies: time to change the tune?' *Leadership*, **2** (2).

Blackwell Publishing for use of the figure, 'Wrong on influence and power' from Wrong (1979) *Power: Its Forms, Bases and Uses*.

Every effort has been made to trace all copyright holders, but if any have been inadvertently overlooked, the publishers would be pleased to make the necessary arrangements at the first opportunity.

The authors and publishers are also very grateful to the following suppliers of the images in the book: Getty Images, Fotosearch, Torstar Syndication Services, SCORE*Golf*, a division of CCMC (Canadian Controlled Media Communications), Marxists Internet Archive, Bruce Jackson, University of Buffalo, New York, the Bridgeman Art Library Ltd., Scott Deming of Scott Deming's ESP (Extraordinary Sales Presentations), London Fire Brigade, EMPICS, Nick Hedges and Nicholas P. Tutton.

The structure of the book

This book is divided into five major parts. These parts are interconnected as shown by a feedback loop that connects the distinct levels of analysis.

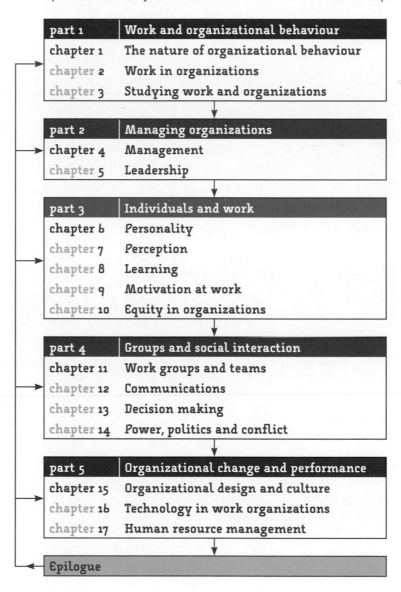

part 1	Work and organizational behaviour
chapter 1	The nature of organizational behaviour
chapter 2	Work in organizations
chapter 3	Studying work and organizations

part 2	Managing organizations
chapter 4	Management
chapter 5	Leadership

part 3	Individuals and work
chapter 6	Personality
chapter 7	Perception
chapter 8	Learning
chapter 9	Motivation at work
chapter 10	Equity in organizations

part 4	Groups and social interaction
chapter 11	Work groups and teams
chapter 12	Communications
chapter 13	Decision making
chapter 14	Power, politics and conflict

part 5	Organizational change and performance
chapter 15	Organizational design and culture
chapter 16	Technology in work organizations
chapter 17	Human resource management

Epilogue

Key features

Chapter outline and
chapter objectives

Introduction to show you the
relevance of each OB topic

'OB in focus' boxes: extra
insight into special issues

'Stop and reflect' questions
for you to think about

Photos to help explain
OB concepts

Website addresses
for you to explore

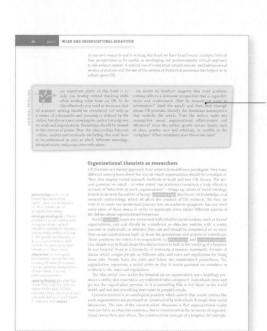

'Critical insight' to show
what others have thought

Chapter summary

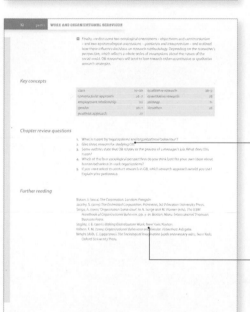

End-of-chapter
discussion questions

Case study illustrating
some of the major
concepts discussed

Further reading

'OB in films' entertainingly
illustrates and explores
OB concepts and issues

Web-based assignments
to bring OB to life

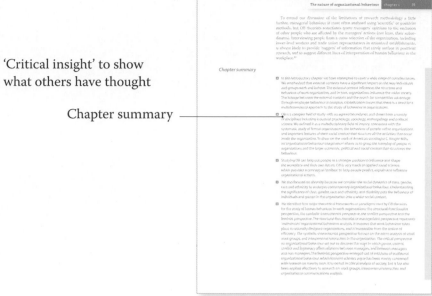

WORK AND ORGANIZATIONAL BEHAVIOUR

In this part of the book we examine the nature of organizational behaviour, and give a summary of the historical dimensions of paid work, and present concepts and theories. This provides a basis for evaluating the competing perspectives on what determines and influences the behaviour of people in organizations.

In Chapter 1 we explain that organizational behaviour is a multi-disciplinary field of study. We emphasize that external contexts have a significant impact on the way people work and behave. As an introduction to what follows, we discuss how the social dynamics of class, gender, disability, race and ethnicity underpin contemporary organizational behaviour.

In Chapter 2, we explore the continuities as well as the discontinuities in paid work over time. We highlight diversity and equity issues in the workplace in order to counterbalance the conventional preference for male history. Our interpretation of the past leads us to conclude that employment is inherently and irreducibly constructed, interpreted and organized through social actions and social discourse.

In Chapter 3, we explain how the three founders of the sociology of work – Marx, Durkheim and Weber – all continue to have contemporary supporters and detractors. Organizational theorists have used different theoretical approaches to exploring work organizations – technical, human relations, neo-human relations, systems thinking, contingency, cultures, learning, control, feminist, social action, political and postmodern – and these are also examined.

chapter 1
The nature of organizational behaviour

chapter 2
Work in organizations

chapter 3
Studying work and organizations

chapter 1
The nature of organizational behaviour

The productivity of the knowledge worker is likely to become the center of the management of people .... This will require, above all, very different assumptions about people in organizations and their work.[1]

With corporations at the center of globalization, they can be blamed for much of its ills as well as given credit for many of its achievements.[2]

chapter outline

▷ Introduction
▷ The meaning of organizational behaviour
▷ A framework for studying organizational behaviour
▷ The multidisciplinary nature of organizational behaviour
▷ Why study organizational behaviour?
▷ The influence of class, gender, race, ethnicity and disability on organizational behaviour
▷ Researching organizational behaviour
▷ Chapter summary
▷ Key concepts
▷ Chapter review questions
▷ Further reading
▷ Chapter case study: Tuition reimbursement for studying OB?
▷ Web-based assignment
▷ OB in films
▷ Notes

chapter objectives

After completing this chapter, you should be able to:

▷ explain work organizations, their basic characteristics and their connections to the wider social context
▷ define the term 'organizational behaviour' and describe the contribution to the field of organizational behaviour of three disciplines: psychology, sociology and anthropology
▷ describe the evolution of organizational behaviour as a field of research and learning
▷ explain an integrated framework for conceptualizing organizational behaviour
▷ describe the challenges of conducting research on organizational behaviour.

Introduction

Most mornings, we turn the front doorhandle of our homes and set off to work in formal organizations such as banks, insurance offices, retail stores, garages, schools, universities, hospitals, sports centres, police stations, hotels and factories. In work settings like these, people engage in a host of work-related activities, communicate and interact, and learn with and from each other. For example, members of the organization may operate a computer, serve customers, teach students, diagnose patients, coach athletes, apprehend and arrest criminals, cook meals for guests or build cars. The way these work-related activities are designed, and the regularities displayed by the people in the workplace, are only partly the result of individual preferences or psychologies. People are exposed to a multitude of organizational processes and control systems, which limit, influence or determine their behaviour in work organizations. Work organizations are simply physical and legal structures within which people undertake paid work – and it is the people who 'behave', and not, of course, the organizations.

Formal organizations pervade our modern world. Their presence affects our economic, cultural, political and ecological environment, providing employment, producing goods and services, lobbying politicians and policy makers, and infecting the ecosystem. Richard Scott observed, 'Ours is an organizational society.'[3] We sell to organizations our mental or physical skills, and we buy the goods or services organizations provide, usually for profit. Our 'experience' of work organizations, as employees, customers or stakeholders, may be good, bad or indifferent.

People acquire identities and roles in organizations as they interact socially. 'Identities' refers to both the names we give ourselves – female, male, adult, colleague, professional, leader – and how others see us. People play out organized scripts, in the form of specific duties and obligations that are attached to positions in the organization, which are called roles.

For employees, the employment relationship might offer exceptional career opportunities, provide a high salary, require high levels of skill and personal development, and provide high security of tenure. In contrast, it could offer low pay, require low levels of skill and provide low security of tenure. Users or customers will find their experience of the organization affected by whether employees are adequately staffed, trained, motivated and supervised. Both employees and customers might have an experience of the organization that is different again if they are disabled, non-white, a member of an ethnic group or a visible minority, or female. Visible minorities have experienced widespread employment discrimination in Britain and elsewhere.

Our experience of work organizations can be analysed and explained using a variety of contextual, individual, group or organizational processes. The study of

organizational behaviour (OB):
the systematic study of form
organizations and of what
people think, feel and do in
and around organizations

social interaction: the process
by which people act toward
or respond to other people.

organizational behaviour (OB) centres on how the behaviour of organizational members evolves and adapts, how employee behaviour is shaped by group dynamics and social interaction, and how work organizations are structured in different ways. It looks at why organizational controls occur in the way they do, and how organizational processes have an impact on societal and ecological stability or instability.

Most North American textbooks on OB adopt a 'managerialist' approach. The emphasis is on how an understanding of human behaviour underscores management practices, and results in organizational efficiency and effectiveness. A managerialist approach to OB emphasizes that the turbulent business climate, caused by increased global price competitiveness, changing technologies, changing employment legislation and changing work force composition, is challenging organizational leaders to use their managers and non-managers more effectively to gain competitive advantage. As our opening quote suggests, the case for behaviourial studies in modern management education is strengthened by the change towards more knowledge-based work, and the growing acknowledgement that people are the key to sustainable competitive advantage.

The meaning of organizational behaviour

capitalism: an economic system
characterized by private ownership
of the **means of production**,
from which personal profits
can be derived through market
competition and without
government intervention

means of production: an analytical
construct that contains the forces
of production and the relations
of production, which combined
define the socioeconomic
character of a society

work organization: a deliberately
formed social group in which
people, technology and
resources are deliberately co-
coordinated through formalized
roles and relationships to
achieve a division of labour
designed to attain a specific set
of objectives efficiently. Also
known as formal organization.

society: a large social grouping
that shares the same geographical
territory and is subject to the
same political authority and
dominant cultural expectations

sociology: the systematic
study of human society
and social interaction

This book is about work–life; particularly it is about people in work organizations in capitalist societies. It has two broad aims. First it aims to help the student of OB understand how people undertake paid work, and how they interact with each other in the workplace; and how the organization, or more precisely the decisions made by people controlling the organization, affects the people in it. Second, it aims to help the reader learn to influence processes and shape events within organizations.

What are organizations?

Individual or group behaviour occurs in organizations. A work organization is a socially designed unit, or collectivity, that engages in activities to accomplish a goal or set of objectives, has an identifiable boundary, and is linked to the external society. Work organizations can be distinguished from other social entities or collectivities – such as a family, a clan or tribe, or a complex society – by four common characteristics.

First, when we state that an organization is 'a socially designed unit or collectivity', we mean that one essential property is the presence of a group of people who have something in common, and who deliberately and consciously design a structure and processes. We use the term 'social structure' to refer to those activities, interactions and relationships that take on a regular pattern. Work organizations have some form of hierarchy. There are standard methods of doing things, norms, communications and control techniques that are coordinated and repeated every day. Organizations are made up of people, and they form relationships with each other and perform tasks that help attain the organization's goals. In sociology, we refer to this as the 'formal social structure'. Many aspects of the formal social structure are explicitly defined in organizational charts, job descriptions and appraisal documents. However, human activities, relationships and interactions emerge in the workplace that are not expressed in charts or written job descriptions. This covers an array of human behaviour including the communication of rumours – the 'grapevine' – destructive behaviour such as the sabotaging of a computer or machine by a disgruntled employee, and trade union action. These activities are referred to as the 'informal social structure'. The formal and informal social structures are the basic building blocks of an organization.

plate 1 Today, our lives revolve around diverse work organizations, universities, banks, hospitals, and factories. Work organizations are structures and groups of people organized to achieve goals efficiently. For-profit work organizations have financial goals, normally profit maximization. Non-profit work organizations, such as Friends of the Earth, organize their activities around raising public awareness and lobbying politicians and governments to protect the environment, wildlife, and to reduce greenhouse gas emissions.

Source: Nicholas P. Tutton

The second common characteristic of organizations is that human activity is directed towards accomplishing 'a goal or set of objectives'. For-profit organizations have financial goals: specific targets towards which human action is oriented, normally of profit maximization. For Bakan, the modern for-profit organization is a 'pathological institution' which strives for profit and power and primarily exists 'to pursue, relentlessly and without exception, its self-interest, regardless of the often harmful consequences it might cause to others'.[4] This means that making money is the first priority for for-profit businesses. They survive by minimizing their costs in any way they can within the law. As Stiglitz explains, the modern multinational corporation avoids paying taxes when possible and many try to avoid spending on cleaning up the pollution they create; the cost is picked up by the governments in the countries where they operate.[5] Benevolent non-profit organizations have goals such as helping the destitute, educating students, caring for the sick or promoting the arts. In addition, most organizations have survival as a goal.

The third common characteristic is the existence of an 'identifiable boundary' that establishes common membership, distinguishing between the people who are inside and outside the organization.

The fourth element of our definition connects the organization to the 'external society', and draws attention to the fact that organizational activities and action influence the environment or larger society. The impacts or 'outcomes' on society may include consumer satisfaction or dissatisfaction, political lobbying, pollution of the ecosystem, and other by-products of the organization's activities. In Western capitalist economies, argues Stiglitz, big corporations have used their economic muscle to protect themselves from bearing the full social consequences of their actions.[6] Despite the rhetoric about organizations being 'socially responsible', the law 'compels executives to prioritize the interests of their companies and shareholders above all others and forbids them from being socially responsible – at least genuinely so'.[7]

Multiple types of work organization are possible. Organizations vary in their size, the product or services they offer, their purpose, ownership and management. An organization's size is normally defined in terms of the number of people employed, which can vary from fewer than ten people to over 100,000. We are all familiar with very small organizations such as independent newsagents, grocery stores and hotels. Larger work organizations include the Ford Motor Company, the Royal Bank of Scotland, Volvo and governments.

Organizations can be grouped into four major categories according to their products. The first category grows food and extracts raw material. They include family farms, market gardens, corporate agro-operations, forestry and mining organizations. The second category manufactures a vast array of commodities, such as apparel, construction items, cars and mobile phones. The third category provides services, such as hairstyling, car repairs, train and air transportation. The fourth category of work organizations supplies and processes information, offering services such as market and public opinion research. The growth in numbers of people employed in the service and information category of organizations has been characterized as the post-industrial society.

post-industrial economy:
an economy that is based
on the provision of services
rather than goals

Work organizations can also be categorized into those that operate for profit, and not-for-profit institutions. The purpose of for-profit organizations is to make money, and they are judged primarily by how much money is made or lost: the bottom line. Not-for-profit organizations, such as registered charities, many children's nurseries, public libraries, art galleries and swimming pools, and most hospitals, measure their success or failure not by profit but in some other way. A university, for example, might measure its success by the total number of students graduating or obtaining grants from research bodies.

The primary purpose of an organization is linked to who owns and manages the organization. Many organizations are owned by one person, one family or a small group of people. An individual may own and manage a small business, employing a few other people. Not all businesses are incorporated (that is, they are companies), but many companies too are owned by only a few individuals. It is estimated that one-third of US *Fortune* 500 companies (the top 500 companies in the United States) are family-controlled. Privately owned organizations are a large part of the British and North American economy. They include many household names, such as General Motors, Honda, London Life Insurance and Kraft Foods. Private companies may have corporate shares (that is, they are part-owned by other companies), but the shares are not traded publicly on a stock market.

In contrast, publicly held organizations issue shares that are traded freely on a stock market and are owned by a large number of people. These organizations normally pay dividends – a proportion of their profits – to their shareholders. The owners of the organization are its principals, and these individuals either manage the activities of the organization themselves or employ agents (the managers) to manage it on their behalf. Privately and publicly owned organizations have the rights, privileges and responsibilities of a 'person' in the eyes of the law. But because a company is not actually a 'person', its director or directors are held responsible for its actions, and directors have been fined and even jailed for crimes committed by 'the organization'.

Now we have reviewed the basic characteristics and types of work organizations, we can look more directly at the meaning and scope of organizational behaviour.

What is organizational behaviour?

As a field of study, organizational behaviour is not easy to define because it is an extremely complex and wide-ranging area which draws upon numerous theoretical frameworks and research traditions. These are themselves derived from a variety of disciplines and sub-disciplines, including psychology, sociology and management theory. Within this field there is a collection of 'conversations' – from individuals with different standpoints on organizational theories – each with a different perspective and offering a competing theory and interpretation of organizational behaviour.

Traditionally, OB textbooks begin with a single definition of the subject, and tend to emphasize the contentious relationship between OB and management theory and practice. One popular North American text, for example, explains that organizational behaviour involves the systematic study of attitudes and behaviours of individuals and groups in organizations, and provides insight about '*effectively managing* [italics added] and changing them.'[8]

Organizations are arenas of situated social behaviour (that is, places in which particular kinds of social behaviour take place), which are both explicitly organized by management theory and practices, and fashioned consciously and unconsciously by values, beliefs, community of practices, gender, ethnicity, and national employment relations systems and practices.[9] Organizational behaviour, in other words, is embedded in the wider social, cultural and institutional fabric of society. Organizational behaviour is best understood as a series of complex active processes in which people participate formally and informally, at several levels including the micro, macro and global (see Figure 1.1), in ways shaped by organizational roles and power.

theory: a set of logically interrelated statements that attempts to describe, explain, and (occasionally) predict social events. A general set of propositions that describes interrelationships among several concepts

perspectives: an overall approach to or viewpoint on some subject

plate 2 Organizational behaviour is an interdisciplinary field concerned with studying the behaviour of people in the workplace, why things happen the way they do, what purposes they serve, and what effects change or transformation have on people

Source: Getty Images

conflict: the process in which one party perceives that its interests are being opposed or negatively affected by another party

conflict perspective: the sociological approach that views groups in society as engaged in a continuous power struggle for control of scarce resources.

microstructures: the patterns of relatively intimate social relations formed during face-to-face interaction

macrostructures: overarching patterns of social relations that lie outside and above a person's circle of intimates and acquaintances

A wider, more inclusive definition would recognize the importance of 'social embeddedness', and external as well as internal forces that affect the behaviour of people in organizations. We can define OB as *a multidisciplinary field of inquiry, concerned with the systematic study of formal organizations, the behaviour of people within organizations, and important features of the social context that structures all the activities that occur inside the organization*. Workplace behaviour for this purpose includes face-to-face communicating, decision making, ethical practice, leadership style, and cooperation over work processes, learning and innovation. Behaviour also includes cognitive behaviour, such as thinking, feeling or perceiving, and values. Further, behaviour includes power struggles, alienation, absenteeism, bullying, racial, ethnic and gender discrimination, sabotage and other forms of conflict and resistance between managers, and between managers and workers.

The organization's microstructures and processes must be analysed and explained by reference to events and developments outside it. Macrostructures, composed of class relations, cultural, patriarchal, economic and political systems – the external environment – represent the 'macrocosm' or the immediate outer world that affects organizational life and behaviour. *Global structures* composed of international organizations such as the World Bank, the International Monetary Fund (IMF) and the International Labour Organization (ILO), and patterns of global communications, trade and travel also surround and permeate work organizations.

These three levels of social structure surround people and shape their work behaviour. Global, macro and micro social structures are also interrelated: they are shaped by each other, and action or change in one stimulates or affects action in the others. Consider, for example, a change in the patterns of global trade and investment. In France, the change might cause the government to amend 'macro' public policy by increasing the length of the working week, with politicians claiming this will improve labour productivity and France's international competitiveness. The change in macrostructure generates action inside the organization, the microcosm zone, as workers stop work and take to the streets to protest against the government policy. We can think of these three levels of social structures – global, macro and micro – surrounding and permeating the workplace and influencing behaviour as concentric circles radiating out from people in the workplace, as shown in Figure 1.1.

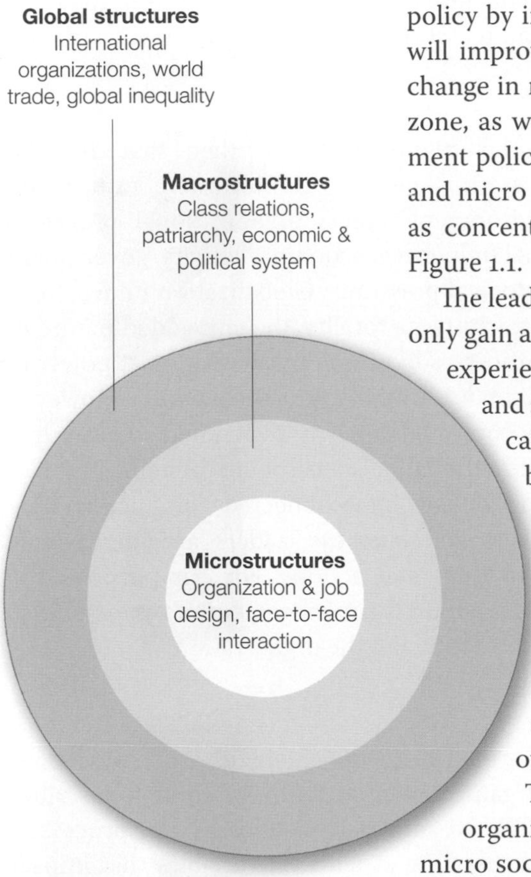

The leading American sociologist C. Wright Mills (1916–1962) argued that we can only gain a full understanding of human experience when we look beyond individual experiences and locate those experiences within the larger economic, political and social context that structures them. Mills wrote in 1959 that the 'sociological imagination allows us to grasp the interplay of man [sic] and society, of biography and history, of self and world'.[10] We agree with Mills here, and suggest that the behaviour of owners and managers, and the agency of individuals and work groups, cannot fully be understood without reference to the outer organizational context or macrocosm. The workplace is therefore an arena of competing social forces – owners, managers and workers – which mirror and generate paradox, tension, conflict and change. The focus here on the organization as an 'arena' provides a theoretical framework for examining the behaviour of managers and other employees in relation to politics, power and ideology.[11]

There are many valid ways of studying the behaviour of people in work organizations, but by recognizing the interplay between global, macro and micro social dimensions we are led to acknowledge the dynamic linkages between external economic, political and social forces on the one hand, and internal management processes, power and political activities, and individual and group agency on the other.

Global structures
International organizations, world trade, global inequality

Macrostructures
Class relations, patriarchy, economic & political system

Microstructures
Organization & job design, face-to-face interaction

figure 1.1 The three levels of social structure surrounding the organization

OB is a multi-faceted and interdisciplinary study of:

▷ the behaviour of individuals and groups
▷ organizational design and technology in which human behaviour takes place
▷ control processes over resources, people and work activities
▷ management processes, for example the recruitment and training of workers, and the rewards they receive
▷ interactions between the organizational, external and evaluative contexts
▷ the relationship between organizational agency and societal stability or instability at large (see Figure 1.2).

A framework for studying organizational behaviour

The manifestations of behaviour outlined above provide parameters within which a number of interrelated dimensions can be identified. These collectively control and shape the behaviour of people in organizations. We offer here a simple integrative or 'open' framework for studying organizational behaviour. Like the 'congruence model' presented by the theorists Nadler and Tushman,[12] our model is divided into four components. They are:

▷ environmental forces as external context inputs
▷ processes for converting the inputs into outputs in an individual group managerial context
▷ the evaluation of organizational processes as outputs
▷ a feedback loop which links the organizational processes and external environmental forces, with the feedback flowing into the organization and from the organization into the external environmental context (see Figure 1.2).

The external context

In examining the 'external inputs', we shall highlight a few of them that are most crucial for the study of OB. This discussion is meant to be illustrative, rather than exhaustive, of how the external environment affects organizational processes through, for example, cultural and social influences, economic activity, government policies, technological change and ecological pressures. Globalization underscores the need to examine the organization within its totality, the embedded nature of organizational behaviour and the processes by which those with most power in the organization respond to the demands of the external context.[13] (However, globalization itself is a thoroughly contested concept, depending whether it is viewed as primarily an economic, political or social phenomenon.) The fact that work organizations operate in a globally interconnected world has become a cliché. Academics, policy makers and business leaders are increasingly addressing globalization in their writings and actions. For our purpose, the main issues are the effects of globalization on the management of opportunities and constraints, and on the strategic choices facing the organization.

How have external environment factors impacted on work organizations you, or members of your family or friends, have worked for? How did these external factors influence the behaviour of people in the organization?

STOP AND REFLECT

The organizational context

The structure of the organization is formed from the interaction of individuals, groups and organizational controls. Organizational structure or context describes the regular, patterned nature of work-related activities, technology and processes, which is repeated day in and day out. There are at least six variables that impact on the active interplay of people within the structure of the formal organization: strategy, structure, work, technology, people and control processes.

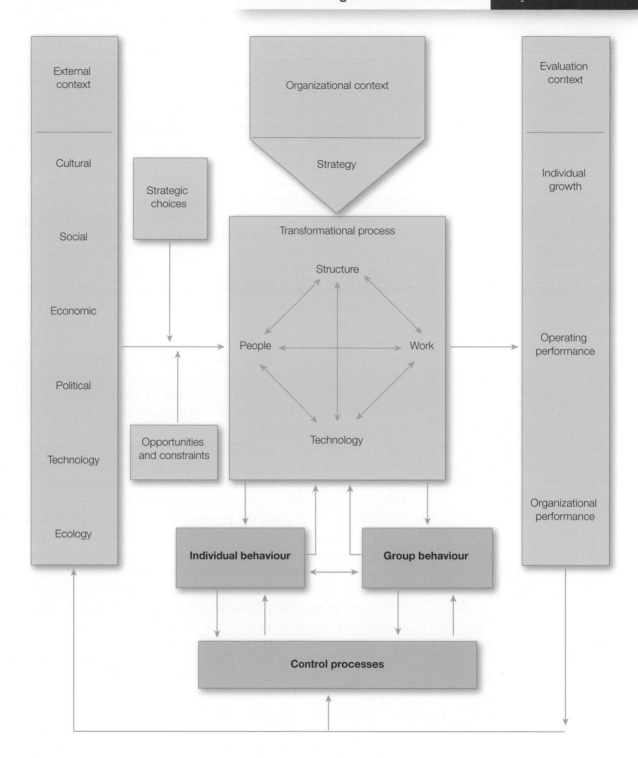

figure 1.2 An integrated framework for studying organizational behaviour

strategy: the long-term planning and decision-making activities undertaken by managers related to meeting organizational goals

The word 'strategy' comes from the Greek noun 'strategus', meaning 'commander in chief'. In an organizational context, strategy refers to what senior managers do to accomplish an organization's goals. Strategy can be viewed as a pattern of behaviour over time to achieve performance goals. A narrow view of strategy tends to dominate prescriptive management textbooks. The emphasis in their approach is on strategic formulation, which involves senior managers evaluating the interaction of factors, making choices, and acting to transform the organization's processes. The 'transformational processes' include the type of structure, standard work activities, the technology used and people employed to meet organizational goals. Strategic choice is examined in depth in Chapter 4, but we need to outline our own perspective here. We would suggest that it is the behaviour of organizational members at critical points in the process of organizational change that is critical in shaping organizational processes and outcomes.

organizational structure: the formal reporting relationships, groups, departments, and systems of the organization

bureaucracy: an organizational model characterized by a hierarchy of authority, a clear division of labour, explicit rules and procedures, and impersonality in personnel matters

Organizational structure is defined as the manner in which an organization divides up its specific work activities, and achieves coordination and control of these activities. The structure of formal organizations can take many forms. For example, a 'mechanistic' organizational structure resembles a bureaucracy, in that it is characterized by highly specialized tasks, a hierarchical authority and control configuration, and communications that primarily take the form of orders and decisions issued by top managers to subordinates. In contrast, an 'organic' structure focuses on low specialization, a 'flat' authority and control configuration, and decentralized flows of communication.[14] Chapter 15 examines the relationship between organizational design, and individual and group behaviour.

The way individuals and groups interact within the formal organization will be strongly influenced by the way work is designed. For example, managers working for the organization decide how work-related tasks are divided into various jobs, and how they relate to other tasks and other jobs, depending on the different modes of production and technology. Managers also make decisions about the training of workers, the formation of work teams, and the nature of the reward system. Thus, the way work is designed affects both the experience and the behaviour of individuals and groups.

technology: a broad concept referring to the application of knowledge and skills to create and use products, services and information

Within the organization, technology affects the behaviour of individuals, groups and operating processes. Early research on the impact of technology suggested a relationship between types of technology and organizational structure, and by extension the behaviour of organizational members.[15] Here we would just emphasize that organizational structure and technology are both multidimensional concepts, and the literature on technological change reflects a very varied body of research. Consequently, we cannot relate technology to structure and behaviour in any simple manner. All the theories about the relationship have their strengths and weaknesses. Chapter 16 provides insights into the technology–behaviour relationship.

Because much of this book focuses on the behaviour of people, we can afford to be brief in outlining this element of the model in Figure 1.2. *People* are a central feature of organizational behaviour, and a necessary part of any social interaction, whether it is performed in an individual capacity or as a member of a work group, and whether it was prompted by external forces or by organizational expectations and processes of control. People differ on a number of dimensions that are relevant to organizational behaviour. Demographic variations, such as age, education, experience, skills, abilities and learning styles, are just a few of the variables that can affect how individuals and groups behave and relate to each other in the workplace.

Visit www.fastcompany.com and see short articles on management strategy. You will also find articles that analyse the strategies of various organizations.

WEB LINK

The individuals who enter the organization bring with them different attitudes and values about work, parenthood, leisure, notions of 'fairness' and organizational loyalty. Demographics determines the 'mix' of a work team as well as its dynamics. Individuals' internal needs can influence group dynamics and employment relations. Members of work groups influence each other in different ways, and work groups or teams may develop their own norms and leaders, which can shape the behaviour and performance of individual members either positively or negatively. Chapter 11 provides an important dimension to behaviourial studies by examining group dynamics.

The issues of gender, class, race, ethnicity and disability in the workplace arise in relation to both individual needs and group dynamics. Studies of the gendering of work organizations and sexuality in the paid workplace emphasize that gender and sexuality make an overwhelming difference to the organizational reality.[16] Globalization encourages people from many different ethnic and religious backgrounds to work in organizations abroad, and this creates cultural diversity in the many workplaces. The 'people' aspects of our model of OB can never be examined in isolation. The need to adopt a multidimensional approach is emphasized by this observation from Clegg, Hardy and Nord:

> The time-honored distinctions between three levels of analysis – the individual, the organization, and the environment – are clearly breaking down. The previous certainty of discrete, self-contained individuals, fully informed by their roles in organizations, has been shattered. Now identity is far more complex matter formed inside and outside organizations, enduring multiple commitments and ties and only partially formed by organizational scripts.[17]

The *control* processes in the organizational context of our integrated model refer to the ability of organizational members to promote their own objectives, and to resist other people's objectives when they do not suit them. Managerial behaviour revolves around a range of managerial policies, procedures, rules and mechanisms concerned with regulating individual and group behaviour. These control processes draw attention to the exploitative character of organizations. They can be seen as 'class' systems, in which people are unequal because of the uneven distribution of resources and power. Numerous sociologists have observed that formal organizations are in essence 'structures of control'.[18] If we accept this premise, the question is, how exactly is this control exercised, by whom, and why is control necessary?

As we noted earlier, people at work do tasks that are specialized to varying degrees, whether they are working in isolation or in a work group. The differentiation of work (by giving different people different sets of tasks) has the effect of enhancing organizational control. Even among organizations where people have a high amount of discretion in how they do their work, sometimes considerable control is exercised by the use of technology. When work activities (particularly in manual work, such as factory work) have been redesigned on a team basis, in a way that is claimed to give workers a relatively high degree of autonomy, sometimes that has not been the case because they are actually closely monitored using microprocessor-based technology. As a result, what is presented as a move to more autonomy leads to increased managerial control.

Technological changes, and changes in work organization that result from them, are not the only way in which more control is exercised. A wide range of human resource management (HRM) techniques, covering all aspects of the employment relationship from an employee's entry into the organization to his or her exit from it, aim to make people's behaviour and performance predictable and 'controllable'. Selection instruments such as personality tests serve to ensure that new employees are compatible and are a good 'fit' with the organization style and personality, that they have appropriate skills, and that they are thoroughly socialized into appropriate value and behaviour patterns. An array of rewards – both direct rewards such as basic pay and bonuses, and indirect rewards like increased status – is also important in influencing employees' performance and behaviour. If selection, training and rewards fail to make employees comply with managerial directives, a system of progressive discipline is designed precisely to achieve this. So HRM policies and practices influence the mix of individuals entering the organization, and once they are inside it, HRM practices shape, control and determine their behaviour.[19] The role HRM plays in influencing employees' behaviour is discussed in Chapter 17.

The evaluative context

An essential aspect of the integrative model of organizational behaviour is the recognition that strategy and organizational processes are not an end in themselves, but are explicitly related to the organization's goals. The *evaluative context* addresses the question, why is control necessary? OB is a body of theory that provides information that can be applied to management problems and used to improve organizational effectiveness. Does OB really matter? Do certain organizational behaviours actually lead to high-performance organizations? Much of the current interest in the OB literature revolves around questions like these, especially for managers who are looking for direction in today's competitive climate. Our model therefore ends with a brief look at the evaluative context, or at 'outputs'. The outputs of individual, group, organizational and control processes can be classified into three components: individual performance, operating performance and financial performance.

Individual performance refers to skills and skill development. We can make a distinction between technical skills and soft skills, which is relevant for understanding the importance of skill development in organizational behaviour. Technical skills generally refer to craft and computer skills. Soft skills generally refer to interpersonal or people skills, such as communicating and adapting to co-workers from different cultures.

Operating performance refers to internal measurements of efficiency, such as units produced per shift, the quality of output, and sales per employee.

Financial performance refers to financial outputs such as return on investment, market share, profits and share price. Information on these variables is needed if we are to evaluate the behaviour of individuals and groups in formal organizations. While there is growing evidence that certain organizational behaviours are associated with positive outcomes, the link between OB and organizational performance is by no means proven.

The multidisciplinary nature of organizational behaviour

OB as a body of knowledge and field of inquiry is multidisciplinary in nature. It has no agreed boundaries and sources in the manner of other management fields such as accounting or economics. Researchers engaged in the field of OB gather and analyse data using either quantitative or qualitative methods, or a combination of both. OB also draws on theory and findings from a number of other disciplines, including psychology, sociology, anthropology and political science.

Psychology

The origin of 'psycho' is the Greek word for 'mind', and the origin of 'ology' is the Greek for 'science', so the word 'psychology' literally means 'the science of the mind'. Early in the development of the discipline, psychologists conceived of the mind as an independent, free-floating spirit. Later, they described it as a characteristic of a functioning brain whose ultimate function was to control behaviour. In other words, the focus turned from the mind, which cannot be directly observed, to behaviour, which can. As a result, psychology can be defined as the systematic study of human behaviours and mental processes.[20]

Although we cannot directly observe mental processes (at least in the sense that we cannot readily tie what we can see of brain activity to behaviour of complex kinds), we have concepts for a wide range of them: for instance, thinking, imaging and learning. Psychologists concern themselves with studying and attempting to address one key question: why did this individual behave in this way?

Social psychology is a branch of psychology which involves the study of social interactions, stereotypes, prejudices, conformity and group behaviour. Social psychology has as its basic unit of analysis the social group. Social psychologists concern themselves with answering such questions as why we use stereotypes, and how group norms affect individual behaviour. They bring to the workplace knowledge of how groups form, how people act within a group or team, and how groups interact. Studies have shown that the behaviour of individuals is affected by their membership of groups. For example group members have a tendency to conform to the norms of the group, either because they are coerced into doing so, or because they unconsciously try to 'fit in'.

Industrial psychologists are a subclass of social psychologists who concentrate on the behaviour of people at work. They concern themselves with explaining why a particular work behaviour occurred in a specific situation, but they also attempt to offer a theory of the mental processes that led to the behaviour. If we develop a theory, we can predict what will happen in similar situations in the future. Industrial psychologists have helped to shape HRM practices – their work informs aspects such as personality testing, workplace learning and payment systems – and the management of work teams.

WEB LINK

Go to the following sites for information and a list of resources on industrial psychology and social psychology: www.socialpsychology.org/ and www.socialpsychology.org/io.htm

Sociology

Sociology is the systematic study of the pattern of social relationships that develop between human beings, with a particular focus on the analysis of industrialized societies. Whereas psychologists focus their professional work on the individual, sociologists spend their professional lives trying to understand social life. As in any modern academic discipline, a diversity of perspectives exists in sociology, but an essential feature of the sociological approach is ultimately to relate the social phenomenon being studied back to the way society as a whole is organized.

Industrial and organizational sociologists have made their greatest contribution to organizational behaviour through their study of formal and complex organizational structures, technologies, control processes, power, social interactions and work-based groups. They have explored the relationship between organizational actions and societal stability or instability, and analysed the role of global and macro-structures in buttressing or undermining organizational structures and processes.

The sociology of work as a field of study focuses on three main issues. The first is the nature of the social relations involved in the production of goods and services, broadly to determine whether these are harmonious or conflictual. Second is the gendering of work, with particular emphasis on why men and women are concentrated in different types of jobs, based on prevailing cultural understandings of what is 'male' and 'female' work. Third, sociologists look at whether the paid work that is performed in the workplace provides for the satisfaction of human needs.

WEB LINK

Go to the following site for further information and resources related to the sociology of work: www.sosig. ac.uk/roads/subject-listing/World-cat/sociowork.html

Sociological analysis recognizes that working life involves conflicting interests, and that conflict in the workplace is not always the result of personality conflicts or poor communications, nor is it necessarily irrational. Conflict must be examined and explained by analysing the employment relationship between the employer and workers, and many sociologists read this relationship in terms of social class.

Anthropology

Anthropology is the scientific study of humanity, and especially of societies and customs. Anthropologists spend their professional lives studying human beings and their activities, fundamental values, attitudes, beliefs, customs and rituals.

There are differences both within and between national cultures and organizational cultures. Societal or national cultures differ chiefly on the values level, whereas organizational cultures differ at the levels of heroes, symbols and rituals: what is collectively known as 'practices'.

In terms of OB, much of the work on understanding organizational culture, the differences between national cultures, and international HRM is the result of the work of anthropologists or those organizational theorists using their concepts and research methodologies. Organizational culture is a term used for analysing complex work organizations, with the emphasis revolving around the development of shared assumptions, meanings, beliefs and values, which shape and are reinforced by people's behaviour at work.[21] Employers and managers attempt to engineer and manage a 'strong' organizational culture that encapsulates and supports an organization's identity and business strategy.

organizational culture: a generic term to describe the set of beliefs, norms, artifacts and values that represents the characteristics of an organization, and provides the context for behaviour within it

Political science

Political science is the study of individual and group behaviour within a political system. The essence of politics involves not only making and executing decisions for society, but choosing between competing demands in the midst of social conflict. Politics, therefore, might be defined as the struggle for power and the management of conflict. It is often viewed as a junior discipline in terms of its influence on OB, but in recent years the work of political scientists, or their concepts and methodologies, has made a significant contribution to the understanding of managerial behaviour in organizations.

table 1.1 Towards a multidisciplinary approach to OB

Social science	Contribution	Levels of analysis
Psychology	Personality	Individual
	Perception	
	Learning	
	Motivation	
	Communication	
	Leadership	
	Group processes	
Sociology	Class relations	Group organization
	Power	
	Bureaucracy	
	Conflict	
	Group interaction	
	Control processes	
	Gendering of work	
	Technology processes	
Anthropology	Comparative attitudes	Group organization
	Comparative beliefs & values	
	Organizational culture	
	Organizational environment	
	Cross-cultural analysis	
Political science	Conflict	Organization
	Power	
	Decision-making	

The political science approach has focused attention specifically on the concept of power, which is often defined in political science as the ability of one individual to impose his or her will on another, through coercion, material inducements or force of personality. In the workplace, researchers have analysed the distribution of power, and how individuals and groups manipulate power for self-interest. Additionally, others have used the metaphor of 'political systems' to describe the behaviour of people in the organization. In this context, the workplace is characterized as a complex social network of competing and cooperating individuals and alliances, in which conflict is the natural occurrence.[22]

Recognizing the relevant work of psychologists, sociologists, anthropologists and political scientists aids our ability to accurately explain and predict the behaviour of people in organizations. This multidisciplinary framework and the major contributions to the study of OB are shown in Table 1.1.

OB IN FOCUS

Is OB a science?

Can we really study behaviour in formal work organizations? The word 'science' refers to the use of systematic methods of empirical investigation, the analysis of data, theoretical thinking, and the logical assessment of arguments to develop a body of knowledge about a particular subject matter. Using this definition, OB is a scientific activity. OB involves the use of systematic methods of empirical investigation, the analysis of data, and the assessment of theories based on evidence and logical argument. Does this mean that OB is a science which can consistently and accurately predict human behaviour?

The answer is, not really. Studying the behaviour of people is different from studying events in the physical world, and OB should not be compared to a natural science such as chemistry. Unlike matter in chemistry, people are self-aware human beings who confer meaning and purpose on what they do. Accordingly, it is impossible even to describe with any accuracy (let alone understand) the social world of work unless we first grasp the concepts that people apply in their behaviour.

The study of the behaviour of people in work organizations is different from that of the natural world for another reason. Through their actions, people are constantly creating and recreating the societies and organizations in which they live and perform paid work. The work organization

is a dynamic or changing social collective. OB concerns itself with the study of human agency, not inert objects, and therefore the relationship between OB and its subject matter is necessarily different from that between natural scientists and the physical world.

There are many questions about human behaviour that remain unanswered, there is much research that is contradictory, and theories of human behaviour that are currently in vogue will be replaced by new ones. Any study of OB would be generally acknowledged to be contestable or incomplete, not least because of the two research traditions or perspectives – the quantitative and qualitative approaches – in the social sciences, of which OB is a part.

Quantitative approaches represent the mainstream in a wide variety of social sciences, including OB. Quantitative research methods emphasize numerical precision, a detached stance on the investigator's part and a **deductive approach**. In contrast, qualitative research methods emphasize non-numerical data, a belief that theory should be grounded in the day-to-day realities of the people being studied, and use an inductive perspective.

Caution: the quantitative–qualitative distinction is more than an abstract set of principles debated by academics. These two approaches affect how people do research, and are fundamental to understanding and evaluating any research you read on OB.

Sources: Palys (2003) and Giddens (2001).

deductive approach: research in which the investigator begins with a theory and then collects information and data to test the theory

Why study organizational behaviour?

ethics: the study of moral principles or values that determine whether actions are right or wrong and outcomes are good or bad

OB is more than just an intellectual exercise. Much OB theory is an applied social science closely allied to management practice. Learning about people, groups, decision making, power, politics, ethics, culture, and how work and organizations are designed – in short, how the workplace is organized – can put people in a stronger position to influence and shape the workplace and their own future. It is, therefore, an applied social science with practical, everyday management uses.

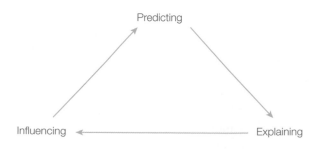

figure 1.3 Reasons for studying organizational behaviour

What can be called classical or orthodox OB is best understood as a set of intellectual tools designed to help people pursue a particular agenda. It helps people predict, explain and influence organizational activities. (See Figure 1.3.)

Both outside and inside the organization, predicting the behaviour of other people is an inherent requirement of everyday life. In other words, we want to be able to say, if X happens, then Y will occur. Our lives are made easier by our ability to predict when people will respond favourably to a request, when workers will respond favourably to a new payment system, or when managers are telling the truth about a case of sexual harassment at work. So-called 'common-sense', and uneducated predictions of human behaviour in work organizations, are often unreliable. The science of OB makes generalizations and predictions of organizational behaviour as systematically as possible in the light of available research and theory. Studying OB will help you further develop your knowledge of human behaviour, and so help you more accurately predict human behaviour within work organizations.

While it is important to predict human behaviour, it is also vital to understand and *explain* the behaviour of people in complex organizations. Prediction and explanation are not the same. Normally accurate prediction precedes understanding and explanation. Through observation and experience we are all capable of predicting the downward direction of an apple when it falls off a tree, but unless we have knowledge of the theory of gravity developed by the English mathematician and physicist Isaac Newton (1642–1727), we cannot fully explain *why* the apple falls to the ground. In the work context, organizational research will help us explain (for instance) why people are less or more motivated when certain aspects of their work tasks or form of rewards are redesigned or changed.

Explanation of human behaviour in organizations is complicated, however, because a particular action might have multiple causes, and the underlying causes of some particular action or behaviour can change over time. For example, an organization might be experiencing a large number of employee resignations. This might be because employees are dissatisfied with their pay, or they might have suffered from sexual harassment by a supervisor, or they might be unhappy about a perceived change in the organization's values. Whatever the reason, both the causes and the behaviour that results are affected by situational factors, such as whether unemployment is high or low in the locale.

The ability to understand human behaviour is a necessary prerequisite for making informed choices and for influencing organizational actions. According to Chris Grey, 'Theory is a weapon used to bludgeon others into accepting practice.'[23] As we have explained already, work organizations are social structures, designed and created by people who have the capacity to shape and change them. An important reason

plate 3 The ability to understand behaviour in the workplace is a necessary prerequisite for making informed choices and for influencing organizational action

for studying OB theory is to provide a conceptual 'toolbox' to at best understand and at worst justify organizational actions.

STOP AND REFLECT

Can you think of other reasons for studying OB?

While it can defend the status quo as being necessary, OB theory potentially can help others – who might be workers, consumers or informed citizens – to understand better the effects of organizational actions, the alternative ways in which work can be designed, rewarded and managed, and the determinants and implications of organizational actions and ideologies for society at large. For example, while many mainstream OB textbooks recognize the importance of 'diversity' in the contemporary workplace, they often see it from a managerialist perspective. In contrast, we have chosen diversity and equity as a core theme in this book. We add 'equity' to show that we recognize the importance of this social phenomenon, but we are also seeking to highlight power imbalances in the workplace and to challenge the status quo.

We suggest that studying OB is a requirement for active citizenship in advanced capitalist societies that are subject to periodic turbulence and change. We need to go to the root of the nature and tendencies of work organizations, and to exercise our sociological imaginations by presenting options for changing the way organizations function in society.

Most students of OB not only wish to predict and understand work behaviour, they also wish to influence or manage it. If prediction and explanation constitute theory, then management constitutes practice. Management can be defined as a system of authority and administration, and there is certainly no shortage of textbooks explaining how understanding OB can make managers more effective and improve an organization's effectiveness. Learning about OB can be characterized as a journey of self-enlightenment: a search for a magic elixir that will unleash the 'motivation genie', gained from understanding human behaviour.

At a more concrete level, over the last decade there has developed a substantive body of literature demonstrating a relationship between 'clusters', organizational behaviours, competitive advantage and superior performance. For example, Jeffrey Pfeffer argued that sustained economic success can no longer be achieved through traditional organizational strategies, such as economies of scale, new technology and access to financial resources. The real source of sustainable competitive advantage, he persuasively suggests, is derived from the workforce: 'the culture and capabilities of your organization that derive from how you manage your people'.[24] In other words, competitive advantage increasingly comes from understanding and managing organizational behaviour.

The influence of class, gender, race, ethnicity and disability on organizational behaviour

Anyone who takes even a cursory look inside a contemporary organization will mostly likely see a diverse workforce. Although different groups will be segregated into specific jobs, the presence of women and visible minorities will be evident. Together, people of Afro-Caribbean, Bangladeshi, Pakistani, Asian, Chinese and East European origin account for an increasing proportion of the British workforce, and the same is true in many other EU states and other countries that have expanded their populations through immigration, such as Australia and Canada. Studying diversity is not simply a matter of learning about other people's cultures: it involves discovering how social class, gender, disability, race and ethnicity frame people's life chances and work experience. It may come as a surprise, therefore, to learn that academic journals and most mainstream textbooks in the OB field show little interest in social class, gender, disability, race and ethnicity. Why is this? We address this serious question more fully in Chapter 10, but to frame our discussion at the outset, we suggest that class relationships, for example, are so deeply embedded in capitalist employment relations as to become all but invisible.

We focus on diversity and equity here not because it is an interesting yet benign fact of the modern workplace, but because we consider that the social dynamics of class, gender, race, ethnicity and disability underpin contemporary organizational behaviour. To understand the significance of class, gender, race, ethnicity and disability is to give emphasis to power imbalances, and to put the behaviour of individuals and groups in the organization into a wider social context. However, no book can contain everything: the material we have chosen inevitably not only reflects our personal bias but is highly selective. Though we draw mainly from the narrow field of workplace psychology and sociology, we cannot cover everything, even in a cursory fashion.

In every society inequalities exist between individuals and groups, with some people having more money, wealth, schooling and power than others. Sociologists use the term 'social stratification' to refer to a system by which each society ranks people in a hierarchy. One type of stratification is the class system. A social class is defined as a large group of people in a given society who have a similar degree of access to a material resource such as income, wealth or property. The sociological analysis of class has been strongly influenced by the work of Karl Marx (1818–1883) and Max Weber (1864–1920). In Marx's view, class is rooted in people's relationship to the means of production – the means by which they gain an economic livelihood. Under industrial capitalism, capitalists – who are also known as the bourgeoisie – hire and exploit workers – also known as the proletariat – who sell their productive labour for wages. Marx believed that these class relations generate perpetual social conflict.

Weber expanded upon Marx's theory of class by arguing that in addition to a division between the bourgeoisie and the proletariat, there are internal divisions within each group, based on status, social prestige and power. For Weber, people's position in the class hierarchy derives not from only their ability (or inability) to control the means of production, but from their 'market position', which is determined by the possession of skills and qualifications. Weber's more complex, multidimensional view of class also led him to believe that a person's market position strongly influences her or his overall 'life chances'.

The concept of class can be used in constructing theories about observable regularities in social organization and work behaviour. In the contemporary workplace, class translates into the employment relationship between the employer or agent (manager) and workers. The analysis of the employment relationship in class terms has been important in allowing us to predict, explain and manage work-based conflict.

Traditionally, studies of organizational behaviour have devoted little attention to the question of gender. Gender refers to the attitudes, feelings and behaviours members of a society typically associate with being male or female. Gender is a dimension of social organization, affecting how we interact with others, how we think about our identity, and what social behaviours and roles are expected of men and women in society in general, and the workplace in particular. Gender involves hierarchy, because men and women tend to be found in different social positions, as judged by their access to resources and power.

The feminist movement has produced a body of literature that offers various explanations for gender inequality. Radical feminism, for example, looks for explanations of gender inequality through the analysis of patriarchy: the systematic domination of women by men. From this perspective, men's power characterizes all relationships between the sexes, including those in the public world of organizational activity, and is sustained by the whole of our culture.[25]

---

class: the relative location of a person or group within a larger society, based on wealth, power, prestige or other valued resources

bourgeoisie (or capitalist class): Karl Marx's term for the class comprised of those who own and control the means of production

proletariat (or working class): Karl Marx's term for those who must sell their labour because they have no other means to earn a livelihood.

life chances: Weber's term for the extent to which persons have access to important scarce resources such as food, clothing, shelter, education and employment

gender: the culturally and socially constructed differences between females and males found in meanings, beliefs and practices associated with 'femininity' and 'masculinity'

Gender is embedded in the modern workplace. Organizational structures and hierarchies are characterized by gender segregation, in which women predominantly occupy jobs that are part-time, low-skilled and low-paid, whereas men occupy full-time, high-skilled, high-pay positions and are allowed to climb the corporate ladder to senior management. A career in management is typically viewed as a 'male career'. Some feminists emphasize that patriarchal society confuses sex and gender, deeming appropriate for women only those occupations associated with the feminine personality. So in Western societies, for example, young women are encouraged to enter child care, nursing and elementary school teaching, and discouraged, or even barred, from entering such 'masculine' jobs as mining or working on oil rigs.

The gendering of work and organizations in 'malestream' OB textbooks is normally discussed – if at all – in the context of the benefits to the organization (in economic terms) of a 'diverse' workforce. As Fiona Wilson correctly argues, 'women and issues about their work have been considered by many as less important than that of men'.[26] In our view, one of the most important consequences of acknowledging the crucial role of gender analysis in OB studies is its power to question OB research findings and analysis that segregates studies of work behaviour from occupational gender segregation, 'dual role' work–family issues, the consideration of patriarchal power, and issues of gender inequality.

Race and ethnicity are complex sociological concepts to introduce in OB. Race can be understood as a socially constructed community composed of people who share biological characteristics that members of a given society consider important. Typically, people in Britain attach more meaning to skin colour and hair texture than, for instance, do people in Cuba. The variety of racial traits found in Britain and the European Union today is the product of European colonialism and subsequent migration, so that genetic traits once common to a single place are now found in all EU member states.

Go to the following sites for more information and resources on race, ethnicity and human rights in the workplace: www.ethnos.co.uk/ is the site of a consulting company that researches ethnic minorities in the United Kingdom. www.coe.int/t/E/human_rights/ecri/ (the Council of Europe's site on human rights) www.businessweek.com/magazine/content/01_31/b3743084.htm for an article on the subject.

WEB LINK

While the concept of 'race' implies something biological and permanent, 'ethnicity' is purely social in meaning.[27] It refers to the shared cultural practices and heritage of a given category of people that set them apart from other members of society. Britain is a multi-ethnic society in which English is the official language, yet many people speak other languages at home including Hindu, Punjabi and Mandarin. Ethnic differences are learned, and for many people ethnicity is central to individual identity.

The concepts of race and ethnicity are fundamental to an awareness of racism and discrimination in society and the workplace. Prejudice is an attitude that judges a person on her or his group's real or imagined characteristics. Racism refers to the prejudices held by members of one group towards another based on socially important traits. In Weberian sociology, race appears to have a major influence on life chances. Discrimination is a behaviour affecting all minorities in work organizations. Discrimination can be direct or indirect, and takes many forms. Direct discrimination at work involves, but is not limited to, cases whereby individuals of a particular race, ethnic group or sex are treated less favourably than other members of the organization. In the United Kingdom, such behaviour is disallowed and is unlawful under the Race Relations Act 1976 (amended in 2000) and the Sex Discrimination Act 1975 (amended in 1986).

discrimination: actions or practices of dominant group members (or their representatives) that have a harmful impact on members of a subordinate group

While it is important to assess class, gender and ethno-racial issues in the workplace in order to generate a broad and critical view of organizational behaviour, here we wish to introduce another important under-researched area of inequality and disadvantage in the workplace: disability. Theoretical and empirical OB or sociological research on disability has been extremely limited, as disability has tended to be analysed primarily within a 'medical model'. Disability is viewed as a specialized medical condition requiring the intervention of qualified medical professionals; disabled people and their families are viewed as passive recipients of care who have no informed opinion and therefore need not be consulted about matters that directly concern them; disabled people's needs are seen as special and different from everyone else's.[28] The common assumptions about disability focus on disabled people's lack of abilities. In the United Kingdom, for example, more than 2.4 million people are disabled, and disabled people are three times more likely to be unemployed than others. A critical perspective on disability draws to our attention how the capitalist mode of production is itself disabling for some people, and calls for the 'normalization' of the disabled as socially valued members of society, and the end to inequitable treatment in the workplace.[29]

In our view, the various permutations of relationships at work stemming from the variables of class, gender, race, ethnicity and disability are necessary factors in explaining the social world of work and contemporary organizational behaviour. We do not suggest that this book single-handedly redresses the imbalance in research and writing on these topics, and here we can do little more than skim the surface, but we hope that by adding class, gender, race and ethnicity, and disability to the work behaviour equation, we can encourage more OB lecturers to give major coverage to these important issues, and support more students in asking serious questions about diversity/equity issues.

STOP AND REFLECT

Have you experienced or observed discrimination in the workplace based on class, gender, race or ethnicity, or disability? What form did it take? How did management handle the discrimination?

Researching organizational behaviour

We feel that even when all possible scientific questions have been answered, the problems of life remain completely untouched.[30]

We have already alluded to an important issue that underpins all social science research: how researchers approach their subject of study depends on their life experiences, and a whole series of assumptions they make about people and society. Much debate in OB stems from competing theoretical perspectives, which we can define for our purposes as frameworks of interconnected beliefs, values and assumptions that guide thinking and research on the nature of the social world. In OB these rival perspectives or ideologies tend to be reflected in different schools of thought, each of which disseminates its research findings through particular academic journals.[31]

When people ask, 'What's your perspective on this?' they might just as well be asking, 'What is your bias on this?' because each perspective reflects a particular bias, based on our life experience, how we see an issue, and our vested interests. Thus, perspectives are theoretical 'lenses' or 'road maps' we use to view the social world. When we refer to a perspective on OB, we are therefore speaking of an interconnected set of beliefs, values and intentions that legitimize academic and organizational behaviours. Before we continue further with our educational journey in OB, it is worth considering two fundamental questions. What major perspectives do academics adopt when studying organizational behaviour? And to what extent can OB theorists construct a truly objective account of behaviour in work organizations?

Major theoretical perspectives on organizational behaviour

OB theorists using one or more theoretical perspectives or 'lenses' view what goes on in organizations in different ways. Some see work organizations basically as enduring stable social arrangements. They are impressed with the degree of cooperation and consensus among individuals and groups in organizations. To other scholars, work organizations consist of social groups in constant conflict over how work is done and controlled, and how resources are distributed. To yet other researchers, the most fascinating aspect of organizational life is the everyday routine interactions among people, and to others, the focus must be placed on the significance of such factors as gender and patriarchy when examining the relations and inequalities in organizations and society.

At the risk of glossing over a multiplicity of schools of thought which OB theorists identify with and defend with passion, it is possible to identify four competing ideological camps, into which many, or most, theorists fall. They are the managerialist, the conflict, the symbolic interactionist and the feminist camps. These perspectives or theoretical paradigms will serve as useful points of reference for understanding the competing views and organizational practices discussed throughout the remainder of the book.

paradigm: a term used to describe a cluster of beliefs that dictates for researchers in a particular discipline what should be studied, how research should be conducted and how results should be interpreted

The managerialist perspective

The managerialist perspective is also referred to as the structural functionalist perspective in sociology, and is adhered to by most organizational behaviour theorists. The managerialists view society and organizations within them as complex systems whose parts work together to promote consensus and stability. The managerialists are interested in order, consensus, integration, commitment and performance issues, with a partisan preference for the managers rather than the managed. Though there are variations and tensions, managerialists make a number of core assumptions, or statements, about the nature of organizational behaviour.

In their view, managerial and non-managerial behaviour takes place in rationally designed organizations, typically formal work organizations, to accomplish collective goals. The organization is characterized as a paragon of rational decision making. The basic concern of managers is to mobilize other employees for formal organizational ends, which are ultimately concerned with profit maximization. The managerialist perspective, therefore, becomes inseparable from the notion of efficiency. Most managerialist thinking also assumes that work organizations are harmonious bodies, tending towards a state of equilibrium and order. The focus of much of the research endeavour is about finding the 'winning formula', so that more managers can become 'successful' in achieving prescribed goals by successfully shaping the behaviour of other employees.

Common to all variations of the managerialist paradigm is a failure to connect organizational behaviour to internal power relations, the dialectics of control and the larger dominant political economic paradigm of neo-liberalism. Our view is that organizational behaviour cannot be understood without appreciating that organizations are more than social entities for maximizing profit. They are also places where those with power determine what work is done, how it is done and how people are affected – through issues such as job and pension losses, deskilling, work-related stress, health and safety – by getting work done in a certain way. We think these are really important issues that should be examined and debated in OB courses.

The managerialist perspective is 'mainstream' and dominates most OB textbooks, which in part is the reason we wrote this book.

The critical perspective

The critical perspective views capitalism and work organizations as an arena of inequality and exploitation that generates conflict and change. The word 'critical' comes from the Greek root *krinein*, meaning 'to estimate the value of something'. Thus, a critical thinker is a critic of thought. One of the most foremost critical thinkers in the discipline of sociology was Karl Marx (1818–1883). His analysis of industrial capitalism maintained that the interests of 'capital', as represented by those who own and manage work organizations, and 'labour', as represented by workers, are on the whole diametrically opposed. Contemporary critics argue that this clash of interests is especially apparent in organizations, where the attempts to extract the maximum of effort from workers for minimum cost is the primary cause of social behaviour.

Critical theorists are interested in power, control, the degradation of work, inequality and conflict, with a partisan preference for the less powerful, the managed rather than the managers. They attempt to discover the ways in which asymmetrical power relations affect the social relations between employers and workers. Critical theorists also believe, to varying degrees, in a positive role for government in the economy and in the rights of workers to organize into trade unions.

As is the case with the mainstream managerialist perspective, the critical perspective is based on numerous theoretical ideas. Obviously, the starting point is criticism itself: that is, the identification of the limitations, paradoxes, contradictions and ideological functions of the orthodox standpoint.[32] In critical theory, historical and contextual considerations are underscored. Consequently OB theory and practice can only be understood as something in process and located within a structural setting.

dialectic: refers to the movement of history through transcendence of internal contradictions that in turn produce new contradictions, themselves requiring solutions

In addition, critical theorists put more substance into the notion of a **dialectical** process as a means of explaining social interactions in the workplace. Typically, a dialectical process refers to a two-way interaction, between management systems and people, or between conflicting employee groups. This approach means more analysis of economic forces, political cultures and communities; it calls for multidimensional causal explanations. Critical research involves paradox. Although the critics provide analytical accounts of the workplace, generally research *of* management rather than *for* management, they are less likely to be awarded research grants and have the results of their research published in the 'right' academic journals, with consequences for academic appointments and promotions. This and the politics surrounding academic publishing and research grants mean that critical scholars tend to be far more marginal than their managerialist colleagues in the business schools where most OB is taught.[33]

The symbolic-interactionist perspective

Managers and other employees interacting in work teams, on the job or in committees: these are the typical social behaviours that catch the attention of symbolic interactionists. Whereas managerialist and conflict theorists both analyse macro-level patterns of behaviour, the symbolic-interactionist perspective generalizes about everyday forms of individual-level social interaction in order to understand society as a whole.

The European philosopher Georg Simmel (1858–1918) is credited with the development of small-group research and symbolic interactionism. Simmel was interested in how individuals interact with one another, and wrote about the 'web of group affiliations', aspects of social reality that are invisible in Marx's more macro-sociological analysis. George Herbert Mead (1863–1931), Charles Cooley (1864–1929) and other American sociologists developed Simmel's ideas on the nature of interactionism. Charles Cooley, for example, introduced the notion of the 'looking-glass self' we form by looking into the reactions of people around us. If everyone treats us as intelligent, for instance, we conclude that we are.

Mead focused on the role of communications in social behaviour. He argued that most social interactions revolve around individuals reaching a shared understanding through the use of language, non-verbal cues, gestures and attitudes – hence the term symbolic interactionism. The symbolic-interactionist paradigm is captured in Karl Weick's notions of 'enactment' and 'sense-making'.[34] Organization controllers frame workplace activities and stimuli that are commonly understood and widely shared, in order to generate commitment and motivate social action. A sense of mission, organizational objectives and a language are constructed and communicated (or 'enacted') so that employees can make sense of what it is they do, and explain what it is they have accomplished. Managers and other employees are embedded in a symbolic context.

The feminist perspective

feminism: the belief that all people – both women and men – are equal and that they should be valued equally and have equal rights

The feminist perspective emerged out of criticisms of traditional organizational behaviour research, which feminist scholars argued has been mainly concerned with research *on* men *by* men. The feminist perspective depends on more than criticizing the tendency to use masculine pronouns and nouns (see Chapter 12). It is rooted in a critical analysis of society, and has drawn attention to aspects of organizational life that other perspectives do not reveal. In part, feminist perspectives and research have focused on gender differences and how they relate to leadership styles, interpersonal communications, discrimination, and inequality of opportunities in paid work. Feminist perspectives not only reveal employment discrimination or the experience of oppression, they often point to limitations in how other aspects of organizational behaviour are examined and understood. Feminist perspectives have also provided important insights into the leadership style of women holding senior management positions. As Judy Wajcman argues:

> The literature on women's management style … has been concerned with the issue of whether women manage in the same way as men or have a distinct style of their own …. We are asked to celebrate an idealized femininity as demonstrated by women's greater caring, intuitive qualities. The trouble is that the qualities, characteristics and culture ascribed to women originate from the historical subordination of women. Despite attempts to reclaim these values, they lie at the heart of traditional and oppressive conceptions of womanhood. My study shows that, in practice, senior women managers manage in much the same way as senior men within the same specific context. This is because styles of management are shaped more by organizational imperatives than by the sex or personal style of specific individuals.[35]

Which perspective should a student use in studying organizational behaviour: managerialist, conflict, symbolic-interactionist or feminist? Each offers unique insights into organizational behaviour (see Table 1.2). We do not aim to privilege a singular perspective, but rather to provide a frame of reference against which readers can learn and develop their own understanding of organizational behaviour.

***table* 1.2** Comparing major perspectives on organizational behaviour

Topic	Managerialist	Conflict	Symbolic-interactionist	Feminist
View of society	Stable Well integrated	Unstable Tension	Dynamic	Inequality
Key concepts	Functions Dysfunctions	Capitalism Power	Symbols Communications	Patriarchy
Primary focus	Management practices Performance	Conflict Control	Sense-making	Gender equality
Prescriptions	Better practices Greater cooperation	Employee ownership and control	Create space Dialogue	Law reforms
Proponents	Emile Durkheim Talcott Parsons	Karl Marx Richard Hyman	George Mead Karl Weick	Mary Wollstonecraft Kate Millett

In our own research and in writing this book we have found some concepts from all four perspectives to be useful, in developing our predominantly critical approach to the subject matter. A critical use of contextual considerations, multidimensional modes of analysis and the use of the notion of dialectical processes has helped us to reflect upon OB.

An important object of this book is to help you develop critical thinking skills when reading other texts on OB. To do this effectively you need to be aware that all academic writing should be considered not only as a source of information and meaning as defined by the author, but also as a text revealing the author's standpoint on work and organizations. Knowledge should be viewed in the context of power. Thus, the relationships between writers, readers and textbooks (including this one) have to be understood as sites at which different meanings, interpretations and perspectives take place.

An article by Reinharz suggests that most academic writing reflects a dominant perspective that is capitalist, racist and androcentric (that is, focused on men) in orientation.[36] Read the article and then look through recent OB journals. Identify the dominant assumptions that underlie the article. Does the author make any assumption about organizational effectiveness and efficiency? Does the author ignore certain issues, such as class, gender, race and ethnicity, or conflict in the workplace? What standpoint does the writer take?

Organizational theorists as researchers

OB theorists not merely approach their subject from different paradigms; they make different assumptions about the way in which organizations should be investigated. They also employ varied research methods to build and test OB theory. The second question we asked – to what extent can academics construct a truly objective account of behaviour in work organizations? – brings up issues of social ontology (which deals with the nature of being), epistemology (the theory of knowledge) and research methodology, which all affect the conduct of OB research. We have no wish to re-route our intellectual journey into an academic quagmire, but you need some sense of these issues in order to appreciate some rather different aspects of the debate about organizational behaviour.

Social ontology issues are concerned with whether social entities, such as formal organizations, can and should be considered as objective entities with a reality external to individuals, or whether they can and should be considered as no more than social constructions built up from the perceptions and actions of individuals. These positions are referred to respectively as objectivism and constructionism. One simple way to think about this distinction is to look at the working of a hospital. In any hospital there is a hierarchy of authority, a mission statement, division of labour which assigns people to different jobs, and rules and regulations for doing those jobs. People learn the rules and follow the standardized procedures. The organization represents a social order in that it exerts pressure on members to conform to the rules and regulations.

The 'objectivist' view is that the hospital (as an organization, not a building) possesses a reality that external to any individual who occupies it. Individuals come and go, but the organization persists, so it is something that is 'out there' in the social world, and not just something that exists in people's minds.

Constructionism is an ontological position which asserts that social entities like work organizations are produced or constructed by individuals through their social interaction. The core of the 'constructivist' discourse is that organizational reality does not have an objective existence, but is constructed in the accounts of organizational researchers and others. The constructivist concept of a hospital, for example,

epistemology: a theory of knowledge, particularly used to refer to a standpoint on what should pass as acceptable knowledge

ontology, ontological: a theory of whether social entities such as organizations, can and should be considered objective entities with a reality external to the specific social actors, or as social constructions built up from the perceptions and behaviour of these actors

objectivism: an *ontological* position that asserts that the meaning of social phenomena have an existence independent of individuals; compare with *constructionism*

constructionism: the view that researchers actively construct reality on the basis of their understandings, which are mainly culturally fashioned and shared. It contrasts with *realism*.

is one of a 'social order'. The hospital does not just encompass the formal rules, it is concerned with informal rules and activities as well. For instance, the official rules may state that only a doctor can increase a patient's medication, but unofficially, nurses are routinely given the power to do this. Both these understandings become part of the researcher's construction of the hospital.

The social order of any work organization is characterized as an outcome of agreed-upon patterns of actions among the different social actors involved, and the social order is in a constant state of change because the informal agreements are being constantly established, revoked or revised.[37] The notion that knowledge and truth are created, not objectively discovered by researchers, means that constructionists are more inclined to challenge researchers to re-examine their perspectives, the research process itself and the whole process of the production of knowledge.

An epistemological issue concerns the question of what is (or should be) regarded as acceptable knowledge in the social sciences. For example, what forms of knowledge can be collected, and what is to be regarded as 'true' or 'false'? An important issue in this context is whether organizational behaviour can and should be investigated according to the same principles and methods as the physical sciences. The doctrine of positivism affirms the importance of modelling social science research on the physical sciences.

The French social theorists Auguste Comte (1798–1857) and Emile Durkheim (1858–1917) were early leaders in embracing positivist approaches to understanding human behaviour. There are five working assumptions that 'positivists' make in approaching their research. First, knowledge is arrived at through the gathering of social facts, which provide the basis for generalizations or laws by which human behaviour operates. Second, the purpose of theory is to generate hypotheses that can be tested, and this allows explanations of laws to be assessed. Third, only phenomena and regularities confirmed by the senses (that is, by for example sight or hearing) can genuinely be warranted as knowledge. Fourth, research can and must be conducted in a way that is value-free. And finally, social science must distinguish between 'scientific' statements and normative statements.[38] This means the social science deals with 'what is', not with what 'should be'.

It is a common mistake to equate positivism with the 'scientific'. Many social scientists differ fundamentally over how best to characterize scientific practice. An alternative term to describe the nature of social 'science' practice is realism.[39] This epistemological position shares two features with positivism: a belief that the social sciences can and should use the same approach to the collection of data and to its analysis, and a commitment to an external reality.

Two forms of realism can be identified. Empirical realism simply asserts that, using appropriate methods, social reality can be understood. Critical realism is a philosophy of and for the social sciences. It distinguishes between the social world and people's experience of it, but also between the real, the actual and the empirical. It maintains that deeper social structures and generative processes lie beneath the surface of observable social structures and patterns. For empirical realists, a social scientist is only able to understand the social world – and so change it – if the structures at work that generate human activity are identified.

An example of the application of both symbolic interactionism and critical realism is the work of Yrjö Engeström on informal workplace learning (discussed in Chapter 8, page 230). Individual and small group learning is understood as an observable social process – the 'tip of the iceberg' – but learning is also embedded in an interlocking human activity system – the 'submerged part of the iceberg' – consisting of a community of practice, rules and division of labour.

The doctrine of interpretivism is a contrasting epistemology to positivism. The interpretivists' preference is for an empathetic 'understanding' and interpretation

---

positivism: a view held in quantitative research in which reality exists independent of the perceptions and interpretations of people; a belief that the world can best be understood through scientific inquiry

realism: the idea that a reality exists out there independently of what and how researchers think about it. It contrasts with constructionism.

critical realism: a realist epistemology that asserts that the study of the human behaviour should be concerned with the identification of the structures that generate that behaviour in order to change it

interpretivism: the view held in many qualitative studies that reality comes from shared meaning among people in that environment

of human behaviour. For them it is important to examine how people define their situation, how they make sense of their lives, and how their sense of self develops in interaction with other people. The interpretive approach has its intellectual roots in Max Weber's concept of understanding, or *Verstehen*. [*Verstehen* is a German word that can be translated as 'human understanding.'] In Weber's view, the social scientist should try to imagine how a particular individual perceives social actions, and understand the meaning an individual attaches to a particular event. The symbolic interactionist perspective attempts to provide an empathetic understanding of how individuals see and interpret the events of their everyday work experiences.

The purpose of this brief discussion of epistemological issues in social research is to point out that over the last 25 years or so, some organizational theorists have abandoned the application of the canons of physical science – positivism – to the study of human inquiry. The ontological and epistemological issues we outlined above have direct implications for research methodology.

Research methodologies can be broadly classified as either **quantitative** or **qualitative**. Each strategy reflects differences in ontological and epistemological considerations: differences in the types of questions asked, the kinds of evidence considered appropriate for answering a question, the degree to which the analysis is done by converting observations to numerical or non-numerical data, and the methods used to process this data.

Quantitative research can be defined as a research strategy that emphasizes numerical data and statistical analyses, and that entails deductive theorizing. It incorporates the practices and norms of positivism, is oriented towards aggregated data which compiles responses from many respondents so that general patterns are visible (a process called nomothetic analysis), and embodies a view of social reality as a relatively constant, objective reality.

Qualitative research, on the other hand, can be defined as a research strategy that emphasizes non-numerical data, entails inductive theorizing, rejects positivism, is

qualitative research: refers to the gathering and sorting of information through a variety of techniques, including interviews, focus groups, and observations, and inductive theorizing

quantitative research: refers to research methods that emphasize numerical precision, and deductive theorizing

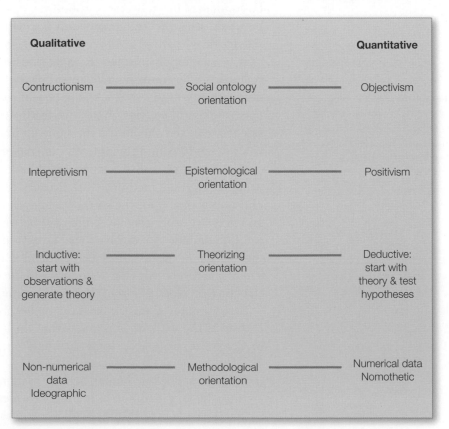

figure 1.4 A scheme for comparing quantitative and qualitative research strategies

Source: Burrell and Morgan (1979)

Source: Getty Images

plate 4 OB researchers use quantitative and qualitative methods to investigate what goes on in the workplace

oriented towards case studies (a process called ideographic analysis), and embodies a view of social reality as the product of individual thought.

Figure 1.4 compares the differences between quantitative and qualitative, at least as they have historically been associated with different assumptions. At first glance, the quantitative–qualitative distinction seems to be about whether quantitative researchers employ more 'hard' measurements than qualitative researchers do, but there is in fact much more to it. These two approaches affect how social scientists do research, and are fundamental to understanding any inquiry on organizational behaviour.

Drawing on the elements in Figure 1.1, you should now be better able to account for the misrepresentation of social reality by researchers. First, researchers make different ontological assumptions that affect how they attempt to investigate and obtain 'knowledge' about organizational behaviour. For example, if a researcher subscribes to the view that organizations are objective social entities that shape individual behaviour, then the research endeavour is likely to focus upon an analysis of the formal properties and regularities between the various elements of the organization. Alternatively, if the researcher subscribes to a view that emphasizes the dynamic nature of organizational life, then the researcher will focus on the active participation of individuals in reality construction.

Second, the epistemological assumptions researchers make about the social world affect how they attempt to investigate and obtain 'knowledge' about organizational behaviour. As we have discussed, at the heart of epistemology are questions such as 'What is the relation between seeing and knowing?' and 'Whose knowledge is produced in surveys and interviews?' For the positivists, the challenge is to discover the laws of human behaviour, and perhaps then predict future social action. The constructivists reject the notion that we can ever have an objective account of the phenomenon under investigation, because all such accounts are 'linguistic reconstructions'.

As we have seen, the constructivist approach recognizes that the researcher and those being researched create the data. Researchers' data do not discover social reality; rather the 'discovery' arises from the interactive process (between the researcher and the organization) and the political, cultural and structural contexts. Traditionally the interview, for example, is viewed as an opportunity for knowledge to be transmitted between, for instance, a manager and a researcher. Yet, through the interactional process the viewed and the viewer are active *makers of meaning*, assembling and modifying their questions and answers in response to the dynamics of the interview. The researcher is not simply a conduit for information, but rather is deeply implicated in the production of knowledge.[40]

The constructivist approach suggests that what the manager and the situation actually are is a consequence of various accounts and interpretations. From this perspective, managers act as 'practical authors' of their own identities. Further, some interpretations are more equal than others. For example, one account of British Prime Minister Tony Blair's leadership performance following the 11 September 2001 attack on the World Trade Center might describe it as 'Churchillian eloquence'. Others could interpret his speeches as populist rhetoric. The point here is that if more powerful 'voices' (including the popular press and television news channels) support Blair, 'the Churchillian' view will prevail, and the negative voice will carry little weight. The constructivist conclusion in this case is that what is important is not what the leader (or the organization) is 'really' like, but the processes by which he or she (or it) is perceived, and defined as a success or failure. In terms of managerial behaviour, what constitutes a 'good' manager does not rest on an objective evaluation but on criteria generated by the social setting.[41]

This does not mean that knowledge is impossible. Rather, it means that the knowledge that is produced on what people in organizations allegedly do cannot be an objective narrative about their workplace activities. We must maintain a healthy scepticism as we read what researchers have to say about OB.

Third, there are different research strategies, or general orientations to the conduct of the inquiry. The different research designs – such as questionnaire surveys, interviews and observational studies – may capture distortions of reality. For example, the mail survey (a questionnaire sent out to employees or customers) is favoured by quantitative researchers, but it can at best only provide a 'snapshot' of managerial and employee workplace activities. It cannot hope to provide an accurate picture of the subtleties and the dynamics of employment relations, or how individuals perceive social actions. The sample size may vary considerably, and if small samples of organizational members are surveyed, one or more atypical participants could unduly influence the findings.

Case studies and direct observational techniques, favoured by qualitative researchers, often provide 'rich' data on workplace activities, but may not capture cognitive processes. For example, a manager or group leader who is captured sitting in his or her office staring through the window could be either reflecting on a long-term plan, or simply admiring the spring blossom.

Finally, we should be aware that management is embedded in the social structure, and is highly political. This means that it involves power relationships between managers and non-managers, and between managers and other managers. As a result, political issues will rarely be far removed from the research process.[42] Consequently, the data gathered by researchers might not provide a 'reality report' on what managers do inside the organization, but rather reflect the diversity of managers, and their need for self-justification, perhaps in connection with complex internal power struggles.

STOP AND REFLECT

According to the constructivist approach to knowledge making, language does not transmit truth, rather it produces what we come to regard as truth. What are your views of the constructivist model? What are the implications of this view for understanding behavioural studies?

To extend our discussion of the limitations of research methodology a little further, managerial behaviour is most often analysed using 'scientific' or positivist methods, but OB theorists sometimes quote managers' opinions to the exclusion of other people who are affected by the managers' actions (not least, their subordinates). Interviewing people from a cross-selection of the organization, including lower-level workers and trade union representatives in unionized establishments, is always likely to provide 'nuggets' of information that rarely surface in positivist research, and to suggest different lines of interpretation of human behaviour in the workplace.[43]

Chapter summary

- ☐ In this introductory chapter we have attempted to cover a wide range of complex issues. We emphasized that external contexts have a significant impact on the way individuals and groups work and behave. The external context influences the structure and behaviour of work organization, and in turn, organizations influence the wider society. The linkage between the external contexts and the search for competitive advantage through employee behaviour is complex. Globalization means that there is a need for a multidimensional approach to the study of behaviour in organizations.

- ☐ OB is a complex field of study with no agreed boundaries, and draws from a variety of disciplines including industrial psychology, sociology, anthropology and political science. We defined it as a multidisciplinary field of inquiry, concerned with the systematic study of formal organizations, the behaviour of people within organizations, and important features of their social context that structure all the activities that occur inside the organization. To draw on the work of American sociologist C. Wright Mills, an 'organizational behaviour imagination' allows us to grasp the interplay of people in organizations and the larger economic, political and social context that structures the behaviour.

- ☐ Studying OB can help put people in a stronger position to influence and shape the workplace and their own future. OB is very much an applied social science, which provides a conceptual 'toolbox' to help people predict, explain and influence organizational actions.

- ☐ We also focused on diversity because we consider the social dynamics of class, gender, race and ethnicity to underpin contemporary organizational behaviour. Understanding the significance of class, gender, race and ethnicity, and disability puts the behaviour of individuals and groups in the organization into a wider social context.

- ☐ We identified four major theoretical frameworks or paradigms used by OB theorists for the study of human behaviour in work organizations: the structural-functionalist perspective, the symbolic-interactionist perspective, the conflict perspective and the feminist perspective. The structural-functionalist or managerialist perspective represents 'mainstream' organizational behaviour analysis. It assumes that work behaviour takes place in rationally designed organizations, and is inseparable from the notion of efficiency. The symbolic-interactionist perspective focuses on the micro analysis of small work groups, and interpersonal interaction in the organization. The critical perspective on organizational behaviour set out to discover the ways in which power, control, conflict and legitimacy affect relations between managers, and between managers and non-managers. The feminist perspective emerged out of criticisms of traditional organizational behaviour, which feminist scholars argue has been mainly concerned with research on men by men. It is rooted in critical analysis of society, but it has also been applied effectively to research on work groups, interpersonal interaction and organizational communications analysis.

❑ Finally, we discussed two ontological orientations – objectivism and constructionism – and two epistemological orientations – positivism and interpretivism – and outlined how these influence decisions on research methodology. Depending on the researcher's perspective, which reflects a whole series of assumptions about the nature of the social world, OB researchers will tend to lean towards either quantitative or qualitative research strategies.

Key concepts

class	19–20	qualitative research	28–9
constructivist approach	26–7	quantitative research	28
employment relationship	20	strategy	11
gender	20–1	*Verstehen*	28
positivist approach	27		

Chapter review questions

1. What is meant by 'organizations' and 'organizational behaviour'?
2. Give three reasons for studying OB.
3. Some authors state that OB relates to the process of a manager's job. What does this mean?
4. Which of the four sociological perspectives do you think best fits your own ideas about human behaviour in work organizations?
5. If you were asked to conduct research in OB, which research approach would you use? Explain your preference.

Further reading

Bakan, J. (2004) *The Corporation*. London: Penguin

Jacoby, S. (2005) *The Embedded Corporation*. Princeton, NJ: Princeton University Press.

Sorge, A. (1997) 'Organization behaviour', in A. Sorge and M. Warner (eds), *The IEBM Handbook of Organizational Behavior*, pp. 3–21. Boston, Mass.: International Thomson Business Press.

Stiglitz, J. E. (2006) *Making Globalization Work*, New York: Norton.

Wilson, F. M. (2003) *Organizational Behaviour and Gender*, Aldershot: Ashgate.

Wright Mills, C. (1959/2000) *The Sociological Imagination* (40th anniversary edn), New York: Oxford University Press.

Chapter case study: *Tuition reimbursement for studying OB?*

Background

The skilled labour shortage, predicted for many years, appears to have arrived for many in the global economy. In a survey of 33,000 employers in 23 countries, an average of 40 per cent of employers admitted to challenges in filling vacancies. The survey also found that the three countries with the highest number of employers struggling with this issue were Mexico, Japan and Canada. In Canada, the Director of the Conference Board's Research Centre remarked that 'strong economic conditions, coupled with the effects of an aging workforce, are setting the stage for increased competition for talent in Canada's labour market'.

The Company: Tournament Projects, Inc.

Tournament Projects, Inc. is a medium-sized Canadian employer located in the province of British Columbia. The company manufactures promotional materials and equipment for sports tournaments and other entertainment events, and employs a variety of skilled workers, including carpenters and electricians. Established in 1992, the company had no difficulty in recruiting or retaining its workforce in its early years. However, in the last year, with the province and the country's economies heating up, demand for the company's product has increased dramatically. For the first time, the company could find workers needed for its key positions, including in trades and management. It found it was not alone. In fact, 150 employers compete for every 100 new entrants into the British Columbia job market.

To reduce the need to recruit externally, the company decided to introduce a training programme, including a component for leadership skills development. It was hoped that the programme would grow the skills the company needed then and for the future with the staff it currently had, and hoped to retain.

Tuition reimbursement policy

One of the first aspects to be introduced was a new tuition reimbursement policy, which outlined the process for employees to apply for financial assistance for work-related education offered outside the organization. Reimbursement was available for a range of learning activities, including correspondence courses, technical or vocational programmes, and computer or video/CD-based training and would cover costs for tuition and reimbursement fees, books and materials. Upon successful completion, reimbursement of 25–100 per cent of the training and education costs would be paid to the employee. A management committee was formed to review the applications for reimbursement. Members of the committee were asked to consider the following before approving funding:

- The programme provided specific job-related skills that the employee required.
- The programme fulfilled a competence/productivity need as determined in the employee's development action plan.
- The programme fulfilled developmental needs that applied generally to the employee's position or that were required for further movement in the department or organization.
- The employee had demonstrated commitment and contribution to the organization and a willingness to use knowledge and skills in the workplace learned from past training and development programmes.
- The employee specifically indicated what he/she hoped to learn from the programme and how the knowledge and skills gained would be used back in the workplace.
- In the case of supervisory and management development programmes, the employee was currently in a supervisory or management position or he/she had demonstrated potential that would warrant consideration for a future supervisory or management position.

▶

In the first six months, over a dozen employees were provided financial assistance through the policy.

Application review meeting

At the most recent monthly meeting to review the tuition reimbursement requests, the committee was presented with only one application. Ed Loeffler, a long-service employee, requested funding for a course in organizational behaviour he had taken at the local university. Stephen Gill, a supervisor who worked in Ed's area, explained to the group that Ed had been identified as a possible future manager, and that he would support the application.

Not everyone agreed with Stephen's position. A recent appointee to the committee, Carol Nishimura, remarked 'I don't see how a potential manager taking a course in organizational behaviour can help us with our turnover or help him manage his staff. Isn't it all theory, without any practical application?' After some debate, HRD manager Dianne Smith, who was chairing the meeting, asked Stephen to provide a written summary detailing the reasons for his support of the application.

Task

Provide a written recommendation supporting the funding application for specifically a course in organizational behaviour, referring to the company's tuition reimbursement policy guidelines provided.

Sources of additional information

For more information on Canada's labour shortage, visit http://www.workopolis.com. Search the archives in the Resource Centre for articles.

Willocks, P. (2006) 'A looming labour crisis: B.C. needs to act now', *PeopleTalk* 9 (2), pp. **9**-12.

Visit the official Government of Canada website at www.canada.gc.ca/main_e.html.

Note

This case study was written by Lori Rilkoff, MSc, CHRP, Senior Human Resources Manager at the City of Kamloops, and part-time lecturer in HRM at Thompson Rivers University, BC, Canada.

Web-based assignment

To help you develop your understanding of the subject, we have developed an activity that requires you to maintain a learning journal or log. A learning journal is a simple and straightforward way to help you integrate content, process, personal thoughts and personal work experience of OB. Learning logs operate from the stance that people learn from reflection and through writing.

We suggest you make an entry in your log after each completed week of class. Properly understood and used, learning journals assist the learning process by becoming a vehicle for understanding the complex nature of human behaviour in the workplace. Visit the website http://olc.spsd.sk.ca/DE/PD/instr/strats/logs/ for information on the value of learning journals.

Learning journals are concise, objective factual and impersonal in tone. The following questions could be used to guide you in making thoughtful entries in your learning journal about OB:

- What did I learn in class this week?
- What did I find interesting?
- How well does the material connect with my work experience?
- How well does the OB material connect to my other management courses?
- What questions do I have for the instructor about what I learned?

Later in the book we shall be asking you to use your completed learning journal to help evaluate your studies of OB.

OB in films

In the film *Working Girl* (1988), Tess McGill (played by Melanie Griffith) is employed as a secretary to Katherine Parker (played by Sigourney Weaver). When her boss breaks her leg in a skiing accident, Tess has an opportunity to implement some of her own ideas for new business ventures. An investment banker, Jack Trainer (played by Harrison Ford) helps Tess to present her proposal to a group of senior business executives. The film humorously illustrates the meaning of gender harassment and organizational politics.

Watch the early scenes in the film. How is Tess treated by her male co-workers? What does the film tell us about the gendering of organizations? When Tess is presenting her proposal, what is her power base, and does this shift in the scenes near the end of the film?

Notes

1   Drucker (1999: 21).
2   Stiglitz (2006: 188).
3   Scott (2003: 3).
4   Bakan (2004: 1–2).
5   Stiglitz (2006).
6   Stiglitz (2006: 209).
7   Bakan (2004: 35).
8   Johns and Saks (2001: 8).
9   Clegg and Hardy (1999: 3).
10 Wright Mills (1959/2000: 4).
11 For early literature on this, see Giddens (1979), Clegg and Dunkerley (1980) and Esland and Salaman (1980).
12 Nadler and Tushman (1997).
13 Scholte (2005); Hoogvelt (2001); Stiglitz, (2002); Saul (2005).
14 Burns and Stalker (1961).
15 For example, Woodward (1965) and Perrow (1970).
16 See Alvesson and Due Billing (1997), Mills and Tancred (1992), Hearn et al. (1989), Wilson (2003) and Wajcman (1998).
17 Clegg, Hardy and Nord (1999: 9).
18 See for instance Clegg and Dunkerley (1980), Salaman (1979) and Thompson and McHugh (2002).
19 See Bratton and Gold (2007).
20 For more information on the development, definition and scope of psychology, see for example Plotnik (2005) or Carlson et al. (2005).
21 See for example Hofstede (1998) and Morgan (1997).
22 See Dyck (2000) and Lee and Lawrence (1991).
23 Grey (2005: 14).
24 Pfeffer (1998a: 5).
25 See Millett (1985), Bryson (2003) and Wilson (2003).
26 Wilson (2003: 3).
27 See Tong (1998) and Giddens (2001).
28 Camilleri (1999), also quoted in Bilton et al. (2002: 91).
29 See Oliver (1996).
30 Wittgenstein (1922) quoted by Sayer (1992: 12).
31 Burrell and Morgan (1979) and Mills et al. (2005).
32 Thompson and McHugh (2006).
33 See Grey (2005) and Mills et al. (2005).

34 Weick (1995).

35 Wajcman (1998: 158–9).

36 Reinharz (1988).

37 See Palys (2003), Neuman (2007) and Schwandt (1994).

38 Bryman and Teevan (2005).

39 Bhaskar (1989), Sayer (2000).

40 Charmaz (2005).

41 See Grint (1995) and Bratton, Grint and Nelson (2005).

42 Easterby-Smith et al. (1991).

43 Nichols (1986) quoted in Bratton (1992: 14).

chapter 2

Work in organizations

The craftsman is engaged in tasks where the capacity for original thought is exercised …. His work creates a feeling of self-reliance.[1]

Work is the blank patch between one brief evening and the next.[2]

The new high-technology revolution could mean fewer hours of work and greater benefits for millions. For the first time in modern history, large numbers of human beings could be liberated from long hours of labor in the formal marketplace, to be free to pursue leisure-time activities.[3]

chapter objectives

After completing this chapter, you should be able to:

▷ explain the function and meaning of work

▷ explain the relationship between work and an individual's personal and social identity

▷ be able to summarize the historical dimensions of work, pre-industry, the factory system, trade unions, government intervention, occupational changes, and the emergence of knowledge work in the virtual worksite.

chapter outline

Introduction

It is a paradox of life that its recognizable features are often the most difficult to understand. This observation is highly relevant to the topic of this chapter: work. Benjamin Franklin said that 'in this world nothing can be said to be certain, except death and taxes'. He was wrong. There is another certainty for most of us, and that is work. It may be called a profession or a career, but work itself is constant even though the nature of work, the workplace and the workforce have changed enormously over the last 200 years.

de-industrialization: a term to describe the decline of the manufacturing sector of the economy

occupation: a category of jobs that involve similar activities at difference work sites

The trend at the beginning of the nineteenth century was for people to gravitate from agricultural employment to the new factories. In response to competitive forces factories became more capital-intensive, and work more subject to intensification and routinization. By the early twentieth century, the spread of 'scientific management' resulted in tighter discipline of workers and a lessening of traditional craft skills and control. There are many examples of craft workers' resistance to managerial control. Scientific management principles for fragmenting and routinizing work were conceived for manual labour, but were eventually also incorporated into clerical labour and professional work.

During the last century, another noticeable trend has been a shift in the United Kingdom out of manufacturing – the process of de-industrialization – into the service sector: from physical labour to clerical functions, or what we now call 'knowledge work'. Increased employment in the service sector is to be found across most developed economies. Among the top ten countries, the International Labour Organization (ILO) reports that service employment increased from 127.4 million to 216 million between 1970 and 1994. Modern telecommunications and the Internet mean that knowledge workers are no longer constrained by place or time. In the nineteenth century, working-class women found employment in the new factories, but in the last third of the twentieth century the growing presence of women in virtually all occupations was a significant development in paid work. In the United Kingdom, however, women are still significantly under-represented in senior management in all sectors of employment, and over-represented in both part-time and low-skilled work.

If paid work is one of the most familiar facts of life, it is an extremely complex human activity. Writing about the 'transformation of work' might be described as a cottage industry. Since the late 1970s many books and research articles have been published, offering optimistic and pessimistic accounts of the effects of technological change on the nature of work, organizations and employment. The optimistic scenario focuses on the liberating effect of information technology, as is seen in one of our opening quotes. André Gorz in 1982 predicted 'the liberation of time and the abolition of work'.[4] For more than a decade Gorz set the trend for polemical 'future of work' books.[5] More recently, economist Jeremy Rifkin has argued that sophisticated 'Information Age' technologies are fundamentally transforming the nature of work, thus 'freeing up' the talent of men and women to create social capital in local communities. Similarly, Microsoft's Bill Gates has argued that computers allow us to reduce our work hours and increase leisure time.[6] Jeremy Rifkin and Bill Gates write very persuasively, and their material has reached a wide audience.

The reduction in traditional work is associated with other post-traditional movements. In the context of the shift from machine to knowledge dependence to improve competitiveness, work is no longer about producing tangible goods or providing a service, but is concerned with the centrality of knowledge and learning at all levels of the organization.[7] There used to be vertical divisions of labour in organizations, determined by people's specialization in doing particular types of work, creating a pyramid of bureaucracy. They are being replaced by horizontal coordination and team working,[8] as the imperatives of knowledge work create a 'web of enterprise'.

The optimistic predictions of economists and management gurus are only one view of work in the Information Age. Sociologists offer strikingly different accounts of work. They argue that the new patterns of work organization, new technology, and the latest idiom of flexibility create regimes that lead to the intensification of work, deskilling, tighter managerial control over work activities, and work-based inequalities.[9] At the society level, communication technologies have produced occupational restructuring and widespread unemployment. Rifkin does not acknowledge the new exploitation that is a feature in the globalization of work, or the fact that for millions of redundant workers in the developed economies, unemployment is more of a curse than a liberation. With a particular eye to the gendering of work, it is argued that 'Where the goal of most employers throughout the world is to get the work of one full-time male done for one part-time female at a fraction of the cost, talk of the new liberation from toil can sound offensive.'[10]

Psychologists have offered alternative insights into the nature of work, which focus on the relationships between work and an individual's personal and social identity, work or job designs that encourage or discourage work motivation, and models that seek to explain the connections between personality and occupational choices for work and leisure. It is sometimes argued that who we are is best understood by knowing what work we do. In essence, the suggestion is that people form their identities through their daily work occupations. George Herbert Mead championed our understanding of the relationship between paid work and identity (see Chapter 7) based on symbolic interactionism. The connection between paid work and identity is understood implicitly in the phrase 'we are known by what we do'.

Psychologically based theories of the fit between the individual and the situation, such as Maslow's ideas on self-actualization,[11] support the importance of work for shaping identity (see Chapter 10). The self-determination theory is a reformulated needs-based approach to work motivation that attempts to explain work motivation from the standpoint of people who seek to develop their identities as competent, relationship-oriented and autonomous individuals.[12]

Research on personality traits and types has also shown that people with similar personality types usually share preferences for various types of occupational work. John Holland's theory of vocational choice[13] is based on known relationships between personality traits, vocational choice and leisure preferences. As we discuss in Chapter 10, psychological research on the relationship between the design of work and motivation has shaped the way in which organization controllers design work structures and rewards.

For example, a popular model seeks to diagnose the interrelations between core characteristics of work and the critical psychological processes acting on individuals

---

flexibility: action in response to global competition, including employees performing a number of tasks (functional flexibility), the employment of part-time and contract workers (numerical flexibility), and performance-related pay (reward flexibility)

STOP AND REFLECT

Look at the quotes on the nature of work at the beginning of this chapter. What is your own view of the effects of information technology on work? Is it liberating or a curse?

and their immediate work groups. The nature of the work and how managers organize work is a critical internal issue which affects worker and managerial behaviour in the workplace (see Figure 1.2). The use of work teams, job enrichment tasks and inverting the shape of organizational hierarchies all affect the pattern of entry into the organization.[14] The new skills associated with work teams and decentralized decision making shape the kind of workplace learning people need (Chapter 8). And new ways of organizing work influence the design of HR systems (Chapter 17).

In this chapter we explain contemporary Western definitions of work. We then move on to trace the evolution of work from early capitalism to post-industrial times. In keeping with the educational philosophy underpinning this book, we look at the historical dimension of work in the belief that present problems associated with work are the outcome of the past, and the problems of the future are embedded in the social relations of work designed in the present. The broader context of work provides an essential background for understanding the connection between work, occupation, identity and behavioural decisions in the workplace, and the implications for managing the employment relationship.

Work and non-work

social structure: the stable pattern of social relationships that exist within a particular group or society

'What kind of work do you do?' is such a classic question that it is asked repeatedly in social conversation. This question is significant because it underscores the fact that paid work – employment – is generally considered to be a central defining feature of our identity. It is also one important means by which we judge others. Adults with paid jobs usually name their occupation by way of an answer, but we can see this question in a wider sense too. It invites us to explore the nature of work in relation to time, space and social structure.

Consider this everyday scene in any Western town or city. It is two o'clock in the afternoon and a neighbourhood park is busy with adults and children enjoying themselves. Some are walking quickly through the park, perhaps going back to their office or store after their lunch break. A city employee is pruning roses in one of the flower beds. Near the bandstand, three musicians are playing a saxophone, a clarinet and a violin. Two people are playing tennis. Others are watching young children play. A man sitting on a bench is reading a book, a woman is using a mobile phone, and a teenager is completing a printed form.

This scene draws attention to the blurred boundary between work and non-work activity. It gives us an entry point for answering the question, what is work?

If we try to define some of these individual activities as work, the confusion and ambiguity about the meaning of work will become apparent. For example, the people walking back to their offices or to the shops might prune the roses in their gardens at the weekend, but they are unlikely to see the task in the same way as the gardener who is employed to do tasks like pruning. The three musicians might be playing for amusement, or they might be rehearsing for an evening performance for which they will be paid. An amateur who plays tennis for fun and fitness does not experience or think of the game in the same way as a professional tennis player. Similarly, a parent keeping an eye on a child playing does not experience child-minding in the same way as a professional nanny. The person using the cell phone might be talking to a friend; but she could be, say, a financial adviser phoning a client. The person filling in the form might be applying for a student grant, or a clerical worker catching up with an overdue job during his lunch hour. We can see from these examples that work cannot be defined simply by the activities that are carried out.

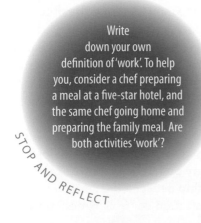

STOP AND REFLECT

Write down your own definition of 'work'. To help you, consider a chef preparing a meal at a five-star hotel, and the same chef going home and preparing the family meal. Are both activities 'work'?

So what is work, exactly? 'Work' can be contrasted with 'labour'. According to Williams, labour has a 'strong medieval sense of pain and toil',[15] and 'work' can be distinguished from 'occupation', which is derived from a Latin word meaning 'to occupy or to seize'.[16] The terms 'work', 'occupation' and 'job' have become interchangeable: work is not just an activity, something one *does*, but something a person *has*.[17] Conventionally, to 'have work' or to 'have a job' is to use a place (or space) and sell time.

A substantial number of people have an *instrumental* orientation to work. They work for economic rewards in order to do non-work or leisure activity they 'really enjoy'. For these people, life begins when work ends. Different occupations provide different levels of pay, and so those doing them have different life chances and opportunities in terms of health, education, leisure pursuits and quality of life. Among people who 'have work', it is not simply the case that people need to work in order to have enough money to live on. People do paid work to earn money to acquire 'consumer power'. Thus paid work for many is a means to an end: commodity consumption (buying designer clothes, fast cars, stereos, mobile phones and so on) or social consumption (such as drinking, dining out and holidaying). The central differentiating feature between people 'out of work' and those 'in work' is that the latter have much higher levels of consumer power and more choice about their lifestyle.

However, pay is only part of the equation. Research suggests that many people do paid work not primarily for extrinsic rewards (such as pay), but for the intrinsic rewards work can bring, such as self-esteem, enjoyment and the social purpose of work. Traditionally, people occupying higher positions in an organization's hierarchy obtain more prestige and self-esteem than those in lower positions, and most people get satisfaction from participating in activities that demonstrably contribute to human well-being.[18]

plate 5 Work in the service sector often requires workers to provide more than physical labour. Jobs such as flight attendants, shop assistants and waiting at tables require workers to manage their feelings in order to create a publicly observable facial display: what Hochschild calls 'emotional labour'

Source: Getty Images

We can begin to understand the complexity of 'work' and its social ramifications by exploring the following definition of work:

> Work refers to physical and mental activity that is carried out at a particular place and time, according to explicit or implicit instructions, in return for remuneration.

This definition draws attention to some central features of work. First, the most obvious purpose of work is an economic one. The notion of 'physical and mental' suggests that the activities of both a construction worker and a computer systems analyst can be considered as work. The 'mental activity' also includes the commercialization of human feeling, or what is called 'emotional labour'.

Second, work is related to place (or space) and time, and for much of the twentieth century it was typically carried out away from home and at set periods of the day or night. Thus 'place and time' locates work within a social context. However, in the Information Age of the Western capitalist economies, there are new expectations of spatial mobility and temporal flexibility.[19] The mass timetable of the '8 to 5' factory world, of the '9 to 5' office world, and of recreational Sundays, has given way to a flexi-place, flexi-time world. The Internet means that the timing of the working day may be shaped by working times in a number of time zones.

Third, work always involves social relations between people: between employer and employee, between co-workers, between management and trade unions, and between suppliers and customers. Social relations in the workplace can be cooperative or conflictual, hierarchical or egalitarian. When a parent cooks dinner for the family, he or she does tasks similar to those performed by a cook employed by a hospital to prepare meals for patients. However, the social relations involved are quite different. Hospital cooks have more in common (in this sense) with factory or office workers than with parents, because their activities are governed by rules and regulations. They accept 'instructions' from the employer or the employer's agent, a manager. Obviously, then, it is not the nature of the activity that determines whether it is considered 'work', but rather the nature of the social relations in which the activity is embedded. Thus, to be 'in work' is to have a definite relationship with some other who has control of the time, place and activity.

Finally, work is remunerated (that is, there is a reward for it). There are two types of reward, **extrinsic** and **intrinsic**. The worker provides physical effort and/or mental application, and accepts fatigue and the loss of control over his or her time. In return, the extrinsic work rewards he or she usually receives consist of (primarily) wages and bonuses. The intrinsic rewards he or she might get from the job include status and recognition from his or her peers.

Although our definition helps us to identify key features of work, it is too narrow and restrictive. First, not all work, either physical or mental, is remunerated. We cannot assume there is a simple relationship in which 'work' means a paid employment or occupation, 'real' work which is remunerated. Our definition obscures as much as it reveals. Most people would agree that some activities that are unpaid count as work. This work can be exhilarating or exhausting. Some of it is household-based work – cooking, child-rearing, cleaning and so on – and some of it is done voluntarily, for the good of society – for instance, working for the Citizen's Advice Bureau. The activities that are done in the course of this unpaid or 'hidden' work are identical to those in some paid jobs, such as working in a nursery or advising people on their legal rights. Is it fair to exclude it simply because it is not paid?

Further, whether an activity is experienced as work or non-work or leisure is dependent on social relations, cultural conditions, social attitudes, and on how

extrinsic reward: a wide range of external outcomes or rewards to motivate employees

intrinsic reward: inner satisfaction following some action (such as recognition by an employer or co-workers) or intrinsic pleasures derived from an activity (such as playing a musical instrument for pleasure)

Go to the following websites for more information on employment trends: in Britain (www.statistics.gov.uk), Canada (www.statcan.ca/start.html and the Canadian Labour Force Development Board www.hrmguide.net/canada/), the European Union (www.eiro.eurofound.ie), the United States (www.bls.gov and www.workindex.com), and South Africa (www.statssa.gov.za).

WEB LINK

various activities are perceived by others. So, for example, 'an active women, running a house and bringing up children, is distinguished from a women who works: that is to say, takes paid employment'.[20] Historically, unpaid work is undertaken disproportionately by one-half of the population: women. This book concentrates on paid work, and as a consequence we largely omit the critically important area of women's unpaid work in the household, but that is not to suggest that we see it as unimportant.

Second, our definition of paid work says little about how employment opportunities are shaped by gender, ethnicity, age, and abilities or disabilities. For example, when women do have access to paid work they tend to receive less pay than men doing similar work. Women are disproportionately represented in paid work that involves tasks similar to those they carry out in their domestic life – catering, nursing, teaching, clerical and retail employment. Ethnic and racially defined minorities experience chronic disadvantage in paid work because of racism in organizations and in recruitment. The likelihood of participating in paid work varies with age and certain types of work. For example, young people are disproportionately represented in more physically demanding paid work. Disabled adults, especially disabled young adults, experience higher levels of unemployment and under-employment than do the able-bodied.[21]

Third, paid work can be dangerous and unhealthy, but the hazards are not distributed evenly. Manual workers face more work-related hazards, and have more accidents at work, than do (for example) office workers. It has been argued that this unequal distribution of work-related accidents is not only related to the risks the individuals face, it is also influenced by values and economic pressures.

Our approach to understanding the issue of inequality surrounding work involves an analysis of the differential treatment of people based on class, gender and race. We need to look at who does what job, analysing the social and sexual division of labour. We need to consider what sort of occupations there are, and who exercises power or control over the social institutions.

Fourth, our definition obscures an important element of the employment relationship: the psychological contract.[22] The 'psychological contract' is a metaphor that captures a wide variety of largely unwritten expectations and understandings of the two parties (employer and employee) about their mutual obligations. Denise Rousseau defines it as 'individual beliefs, shaped by the organization, regarding terms of an exchange agreement between individuals and their organization'.[23] Most commentators view the concept as a two-way exchange of perceived promises and obligations. The concept has been around since the early 1960s, but in recent years it has become a 'fashionable' framework within which to study aspects of the employment relationship.

One reason for this interest in the psychological contract is the degree of organizational restructuring that has taken place. Organizations are looking for two qualities from their employees, flexibility and employee commitment, which are fundamentally incompatible. The restructuring of many corporations has led to an increase in 'non-standard' forms of employment such as temporary, part-time and contract work. There is a 'no guarantees' attitude in many organizations. At the same time competitive advantage appears to come from making the most of managerial and knowledge workers' intellectual assets, and this involves investing in employees and maximizing their commitment. This fundamental problem emphasizes the importance of managing the psychological contract. In Chapter 7 we examine this contemporary concept more fully.

Finally, and perhaps most importantly for understanding behaviour in the workplace, it clear that work inside and outside the organization is affected by the processes of globalization, technological change and managerial strategies. The

value: a collective idea about what is right or wrong, good or bad, and desirable or undesirable in a particular culture

values: stable, long-lasting beliefs about what is important in a variety of situations

corporation: a large-scale organization that has legal powers (such as the ability to enter into contracts and buy and sell property) separate from its individual owner or owners

emergence of 'knowledge work' helps to capture these changes in work. As we discuss more fully below and in Part 3, the shift from traditional work to knowledge work shapes managerial behaviour, how the employment relationship is managed, and has important implications for personal satisfaction, for relations between men and women, and for social life at work.[24]

The development of work

Do you think that managers need to manage the employment relationship differently for knowledge workers and for manual industrial workers? Why and how?

STOP AND REFLECT

Industrial Revolution: the relatively rapid economic transformation that began in Britain in the 1780s. It involved a factory and technology-driven shift from agriculture and small cottage-based manufacturing to manufacturing industries and the consequences of that shift for virtually all human activities.

the economy: the social institution that ensures the maintenance of society through the production, distribution and consumption of goods and services

The structure of the labour market and paid work is not static. It reflects patterns of substantial change in the ways that work is organized in specific industrial sectors. This is the essence of industrialization and a new emerging form of life, modernity. In this section, we trace the emergence of new work forms, starting with the Industrial Revolution in Britain and finishing with a look at employment in what has been called 'post-industrial' work.

We provide this brief historical overview of paid work because, in our view, it provides a perspective on contemporary work problems, which often result from decisions made in the past. For example, to divide work into simple tasks each performed by one worker, which each take only a few seconds to complete, might appear irrational today, but it made sense when it was first introduced in a work regime very different from many of those found today. The managerial need it reflected was to improve productivity on car assembly lines, and 'scientific management' (as it is known) did achieve that objective.

In addition, when we look at how work forms have developed, it becomes apparent that most 'new' work forms have deep historical roots. New management gurus might claim to have 'discovered' the importance of 'communities of practice' and informal learning for competitive advantage, but these issues were recognized and tackled in the apprenticeship system of pre-industrial Europe. They may have 'discovered' that 'virtual' home-based work reduces the need for office space and provides greater flexibility, but this was well understood by employers in the eighteenth century who operated the 'putting-out' system of home working (discussed on page 46). Developments in work forms might be claimed as 'new', 'revolutionary', or offering evidence of 'innovation', but when viewed through a historical lens, they might be a rediscovery of past practices which had been forgotten or abandoned.

Before we retrace the organization of work in the economy, we need to understand the concepts of the economy and of social organization, and we need to take a moment to highlight some challenges this task presents.

The economy is the social process of providing and distributing sufficient goods and services for the material well-being of society. The social organization of work is the set of relations among the people who work to produce and distribute those goods and services. Much of the sociology of work is concerned with the methods used by employers and managers to control the content and pace of work. It considers the effect of these control strategies on workers, the responses of workers to the strategies, and gender inequality in the social organization of work.

The history of the nature of work emphasizes that work is a social activity, not an individual one. Even those who work alone do so within a socially constructed network of relations, among people associated with the pursuit of economic activity. The history of work tends to contradict the suggestion that divisions on the basis of class, ethnicity, gender and race are systematic features created by the organization of work, and found solely in industrial capitalism. The social inequality of work long predates the rise of capitalism.

Industrial capitalism also fosters the image of work as a predominantly male activity, separate from, and unrelated to, the home. However this is historically atypical: 'home and the place of work have always been, and still are, intimately connected by a seamless web of social interdependence'.[25]

However, to study work and organizational forms from a historical perspective is problematic and ambiguous, for a number of reasons. First, by its very nature such an exercise involves a compression of time periods and of different modes of social organization and work designs. As Eric Hobsbawm wrote, 'The past is a permanent dimension of the human consciousness, an inevitable component of institutions, values and other patterns of human society'.[26] The problem for social theorists is to avoid presenting the emergence of new work forms as a coherent, orderly and inevitable process of change. Looking back from the vantage point of the early twenty-first century, it might seem reasonable to talk of the emergence of the factory, or of new forms of management control. But as others have pointed out, the development of new work forms and social relations took place piecemeal, sporadically and slowly – and frequently they were resisted. Many features of work in the pre-industrial economy (the period before 1750) survived until late into the nineteenth century, and similarly many nineteenth-century work forms (for example, the subcontracting of labour) survived into the last century. If we outline general trends, this not only compresses wide variations and collapses time periods, it also attaches a coherent pattern to these changes, which they did not show in reality.[27]

The second problem is also one that is found in any historical account. How do we differentiate between establishable fact and fiction, and how do we separate the actual developments from the theoretical perspectives that have been developed in order to explain them?[28] The facts of economic history cannot exist in a 'pure form'. How historians assemble and interpret a chosen sample of facts will depend mainly on what methods are chosen, how the data are analysed, and the kinds of interpretation the historian is looking to put on them. Different methods and theoretical perspectives generate different kinds of data, and 'the facts of history … are always refracted through the mind of the recorder …. By and large, the historian will get the kind of facts he [sic] wants'.[29] Each of the classical theorists, such as Marx, Weber and Durkheim, and the contemporary theorists, such as Mayo, Braverman and Foucault, chooses and exaggerates the features that he or she considers most significant.

As the postmodernist argument goes, we cannot claim that any particular work design is good or bad, because each work form is an intellectual construction: it is a categorization of individual instances, on lines chosen by the categorizer. And how we evaluate each work form we have categorized is a product of the social context.[30] In short, there is no clear dividing line between facts and interpretation of the facts. We cannot invent the facts. A question such as whether early factory owners employed child labour can be answered unambiguously on the basis of evidence. But how do we interpret that fact, and how do we fit it into the wider context of economic development? Here there is no equally unambiguous right answer.

The rest of this section examines pre-industrial work, the transition to factory forms of work, the significance of concentrated production, the rise of trade unions, and the interventions of the state.[31]

Pre-industrial work

In the middle of the eighteenth century the most striking feature of the economy in England, and the rest of Europe, was the importance of agriculture as a basic human activity. Agricultural and industrial work was also characterized by low productivity. Generally the work was performed by people who were unskilled, uneducated in a formal way, and frequently undernourished. The rising population

To what extent does a 'good' or 'bad' work design depend on which approach we use and which theorist we believe?

STOP AND REFLECT

labour power: the potential gap between a worker's capacity or potential to work and its exercise

created an ever-growing class of landless labourers who were compelled to sell their labour power and buy their food. Urbanization was another stimulus to agricultural production. These forces eventually led to new farming techniques, new machinery, and the reorganization of farms in what is known as the enclosure movement. It is impossible to measure the precise economic impact of these agricultural changes, but we do know that the growth in the population, and particularly the urban population, was possible because of the agrarian revolution and the resulting increased agricultural productivity. By 1750, as far as England was concerned subsistence agriculture no longer existed.[32]

Before 1780, most manufacturing in England operated on a small scale, employed labour-intensive methods, and used little fixed capital. Given the size of the market and the nature of manufacturing technology, extensive investment in buildings and machinery was unnecessary. The English economy was also characterized by regulation. Craft gilds in the towns regulated all activities related to their trade, including conditions of apprenticeships, control of raw materials, and supervision of standards of work. The central government played a major indirect role as a regulator of the economy. The Statute of Artificers of 1563, for example, set the level of wages, conditions of employment, regulated the mobility of labour (as the government did during the Second World War, 1939–45), demanded a seven-year apprenticeship for workers in the garment trades, and intervened extensively to protect and promote domestic manufacturing and trade. The navigation acts assisted the growth of English shipbuilding. But by the early eighteenth century, the state had dismantled the legal restrictions on trade and industry.

putting-out system: a pre-industrial home-based form of production in which the dispersed productive functions were coordinated by an entrepreneur

Away from the town-based gilds, the rural-based putting-out system was a feature of a wide range of manufacturing in pre-Industrial Revolution England. It was used especially for woollen goods, footwear, and many branches of metal working. The putting-out system was a decentralized method of manufacturing which was based on the division of labour. In the manufacture of woollen cloth, for example, the various processes of sorting the wool, combing, spinning, weaving and shearing were usually distinct occupations performed by different workers, mostly in their cottages. Many of the workers were also farmers or farm labourers.

Such a form of work organization had profound consequences for the social organization of work and the nature of workers' reactions to the Industrial Revolution:

> It could not be used in industries requiring bulky plant and power-driven machinery. Neither was it suitable for crafts demanding a high degree of skill or which needed close supervision; nor where production processes had to flow without interruption from one stage to another. Even when technical conditions were favourable to the use of out-workers, high costs of distribution and losses arising from pilfering and fraud by the workers were serious weaknesses.[33]

So although the system was useful in its time, it contained considerable rigidities and inefficiencies, which were apparent when markets expanded and there was a greater economic need for planning and integration.

Gender-based patterns of work predate industrial capitalism. In the pre-industrial European family, both men and women both produced goods for the household and were engaged in paid work as part of the putting-out system, but depending on local norms and customs there were 'rather strict ideas about women's work and men's work within the specific community'.[34] In France, for example, milking cows was exclusively regarded as women's work until the twentieth century. In towns the craft gilds placed severe restrictions on women's membership.

In pre-industrial Europe, the rhythms of work depended on the variation of the seasons or the weather. Later on, choices of work and non-work times were constrained by the clock and the pace of factory work.

Diversity and dependence are words that summarize work in pre-Industrial Revolution England. Before the dawn of the factory system, paid work was small-scale, does not appear to have been conducted by a mass of skilled craft workers, and its allocation was affected by gender. Moreover, work was not simply an economic activity but 'a social activity circumscribed by custom and traditions that went deeper than the cash nexus'.[35] In short, work was not regarded as separate from private life; it was an end in itself, not a means to an end.

Factory-based work

In the final quarter of the eighteenth century, the traditional work rhythms and practices of pre-industrial society tended to give way to the specialization and discipline of the factory system. The Industrial Revolution in England, which occurred between about 1780 and 1830, did not just denote an acceleration of economic growth, or even the concentration of manufacturing into factories. The transformation of economic activity was slower than literary metaphors like 'revolution' suggest: that term implies a precision in dating which was not in fact true. The tendencies of the Industrial Revolution were still being completed at end of the nineteenth century.[36] We can describe it as a fundamental change in the structure of the economy, in which the capitalists' pursuit and accumulation of profit guided the mode of organizing work, harnessing technology and determining the social relations of work.

The Industrial Revolution was characterized by the rise of the factory, a combination of power technology and specialized machines with specialized occupations. The conventional view is that the economic rationality of large-scale production, particularly using water and steam technology, demanded the factory system. It gave capitalist factory owners more power to coordinate and control their workers. The significance of the concentration of workers lay in the potential for extending the division of labour, installing machines, regulating the flow of raw materials, and moulding workers' behaviour in the workplace.

Here the focus is on the division of labour within the factory organized by the owner. The putting-out system divided up work, but the factory offered the opportunity to improve each specialized task through the use of innovative technology, to a greater degree than was possible with the decentralized putting-out system: 'The very division of labour ... prepared the ground from which mechanical invention could eventually spring.'[37] Factory production also had the advantage that it enabled a tighter control of the work in process than was possible with the domestic system. With the putting-out system, merchant-manufacturers found it difficult to control the behaviour of cottage-based workers because they had 'no way of compelling his workers to do a given number of hours of labour; the domestic weaver or craftsman was master of his time, starting and stopping when he [sic] desired'.[38] The factory system, with its specialized machines tended by specialized operatives, provided new opportunities for controlling the pace and quality of work by the 'discipline of mechanization' – the actual speed of the machine – and by a hierarchy of control over the work in process.

Theories on the way work is organized, and on employment relations, occupy a major place in the discussion of social change by social scientists. Early contributors to the debate include Adam Smith (1723–1790), Charles Babbage (1791–1871) and Karl Marx (1818–1883).

Adam Smith, the founder of modern economics, studied the newly emerging industrial division of labour in eighteenth-century England. For Smith, the separation of manual tasks was central to his theory of economic growth. Smith argued that this division of labour leads to an improvement of economic growth in three ways. First, output per worker increases because of enhanced dexterity.

factory system: a relatively large work unit that concentrated people and machines in one building that enabled the specialization of productive functions and, at the same time, enabled a closer supervision of employees than the pre-industrial putting-out system. Importantly, the factory system gave rise to the need for new conception of time and organizational behaviour.

division of labour: the allocation of work tasks to various groups or category of employee

Second, work preparation and changeover time is reduced; and third, specialization stimulates the invention of new machinery. In his book *The Wealth of Nations* Smith described the manufacture of pins, and gave an early example of job design:

> Man draws out the wire; another straightens it; a third cuts it; a fourth points it; a fifth grinds it at the top for receiving the head … the important business of making a pin is, in this manner, divided into eighteen distinct operations. [39]

In the nineteenth century Charles Babbage, often referred to as the 'father of computing' for his contributions to the basic design of the computer, pointed out that the division of labour gave the employer a further advantage: by simplifying tasks and allocating fragmented tasks to unskilled workers, the employer could pay a lower wage. Braverman's account of the division of labour (written in 1974) presents management's strategy for 'cheapening' craft labour in its starkest terms.[40]

The emergence of the industrial division of labour gave rise to a more radical theory of social change. Karl Marx argued that changes in the way work is organized and capitalist 'relations' of production – the economic 'infrastructure' – are the prime movers of social change. He asserted that the factory and the new work patterns constituted a form of systematic exploitation, and that workers were alienated from the product of their labour because of capitalist employment relations and the loss of autonomy at work: 'factory work does away with the many-sided play of the muscles, and confiscates every atom of freedom, both in bodily and intellectual activity'.[41] In short, Marx believed that under nineteenth-century capitalist class relations, the division of labour and machinery played a key role in the alienation of workers. He saw these inner processes of work organization and class relations as forces for social change.

Historians have also debated the role of technology in factory work organization. For example, it is argued that the origins of management within capitalist production lie not in the extended division of labour created by technical developments, but in the desire for social control on the part of capitalists, so that levels of exploitation could be increased.[42] The term control is used as a synonym for a managerial network of rules and the capacity to exercise power. Thus factories were constructed to maximize control; they were not the inevitable results of technical change, nor were they the inexorable results of the search for simple efficiency.

Indeed, this perspective sees the development of the factory system in terms of the need for disciplined workers in the capitalist production system. The architecture of the new factories had much in common with the new prisons. The utilitarian philosopher Jeremy Bentham coined the term 'panopticon' in 1816 to describe a circular building that could provide 'hierarchical observation' and 'normalizing judgement' (see Figure 2.1). Observing Victorian public architecture and Bentham's idea of a panopticon, a twentieth-century philosopher, Michel Foucault, asked, 'Is it surprising that prisons resemble factories, schools, barracks, hospitals, which all resemble prisons?'[43] In essence, the suggestion is that the factory with its specialization and logical flows of processes provided capitalists with a formal role as managers or coordinators.

There is an alternative interpretation of the factory system, which also sees it as a means to increase control over workers, but maintains that capitalists did not need to create a role for themselves, or suffer from any crisis of legitimacy. In this interpretation, to account for the factory system we must consider the full cycle of business: purchase of capital equipment and labour, surplus from the work process, and profit from marketing the finished goods.

Thus, there is no sound theoretical reason for granting most importance to one part in this cycle, the employer–employee relation. The emergence of factories has to be sought in the development of markets, and not solely by reference to the issue

control: the collection and analysis of information about all aspects of the work organization and the use of comparisons, which are either historical and/or based on benchmarking against another business unit

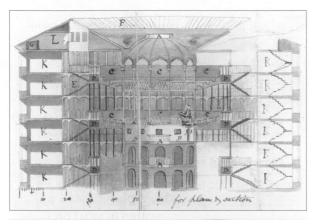

figure 2.1 The panopticon building

work ethic: a set of values which stress the importance of work to the identity and sense of worth of the individual and encourages an attitude of diligence in the mind of people

of control. According to this argument, it was the inadequacy of the family-based putting-out system in the face of expanding markets for some products that led capitalists to find new forms of organizing work.[44]

The new factory system transformed the social organization of work. Investment in new technology and work divided into separate tasks required management and a disciplined workforce. In this lay another key development associated with factory-based work, the shaping of workers' behaviour by the employers based on new concepts of commitment and time. In the early period of industrialization, the changing workers' behaviour had a number of aspects: both entering the factory itself, and work behaviour or discipline. (This is sometimes known as the new work ethic.) Although the pay in the new factories tended to be higher than in the putting-out sector, people were reluctant to enter the factories, with their unaccustomed rules and discipline. Workers, particularly men, felt this 'because in doing so men lost their birthright, independence.'[45]

Recruitment into the new factories was such a problem that in 1838 less than a quarter of textile factory workers were adult men. The majority of workers were women and children, who were more pliant and easier to manage. Once in the factory, the employers had to develop 'appropriate' and 'responsible' behaviour that met the needs of the new work regime. This involved the management instilling in them attitudes of obedience to factory regulations and punctuality. What the new factory owners required was a 'new breed of worker' whose behaviour reacted favourably to the exorable demands of the pace-setting machine, factory rationality, and the 'tyranny of the clock'. The process took several generations: 'by the division of labour; the supervision of labour; fines; bells and clocks; money incentives; preaching and schooling; the suppression of fairs and sports – new labour habits were formed, and a new time-discipline was imposed.'[46] From the preoccupation with workers' work motivation and behaviour there eventually emerged a specialized branch of management: personnel or human resource management.

Gender, work and trade unions

Gender-based patterns of work and gender inequality were universal in industrial capitalism. In 1838 over 70 per cent of factory textile workers were adult women and children. Family labour, with women and their children working together, was a feature of employment relations in the new factory system. The factory owner did not accept direct responsibility for the conditions of employment or supervision of the workforce, but subcontracted these people-management functions to an intermediary. Factory owners negotiated with the heads of families for the whole family unit. There is evidence that the worst conditions of employment under industrial capitalism existed in these circumstances. Child labour began at the age of four, in some cases in order to oblige parents, but most child workers started between the ages of seven and ten. An adult man entered the new textile factories with his family, and the 'fact that discipline was imposed on the children largely by their own parents made the harshness of the new disciplines socially tolerable.'[47]

After 1850, with the exception of waged work in domestic service and textiles, industrial capitalism not only witnessed the decline of agricultural work, but also tended to create a clear distinction between the paid work opportunities of women (particularly married women) and men. With the spread of the factory system, the need for cheap labour power provided opportunities for working-class women to do waged work in areas unrelated to their former work in the home. Large-scale food processing factories – for example, bakeries – were female-dominated in the late nineteenth century. In working-class families women often remained in the labour market to support the family income. When middle-class women married, they were primarily expected to withdraw from paid employment to take care of the house and children. Reinforcing the belief that work and family life were two separate spheres, the stereotypes of men as strong and competitive and women as frail and nurturing began to emerge: 'images that depicted men as naturally suited to the highly competitive nineteenth-century workplace and women as too delicate for the world of commerce.'[48]

From 1850, another feature of industrial capitalism developed: trade unions. The growth of trade unions illustrates the assumption originally made by Max Weber of a *paradox of consequences* in the world of work. The intended initiative of concentrating women and men into factories to improve productivity also had unintended consequences. The new factories helped to develop awareness among the concentrated workforce of their common conditions of employment, and of the inequalities that occurred. Skilled male workers were the first to organize effective trade unions. They had a more privileged position in the labour process, and were determined to influence the wage–effort bargain and retain their traditional forms of employment.

A mixture of old and new skilled workers – the 'aristocracy of labour' – led the revival of trade unionism in the 1850s. In 1851 the Amalgamated Society of Engineers (ASE), referred to as a 'new model' union, had a membership of almost 12,000. During the 1850s, employers began to consider seriously the possibility of coming to an agreement with unions, and the ASE won recognition from the employers to negotiate. Union development varied considerably within each industry, as a result of differences in local circumstances. The leaders of the engineers, carpenters, iron founders, bricklayers and boot and shoe operatives – the 'Junta' – led the campaign for the legal recognition of unions, and secured this in legislation passed in 1871 and 1875.[49]

The years from the 1880s saw a significant growth of trade unionism, in both numbers of members and scope of activities. Large numbers of unskilled workers were organized, and this 'new unionism', as various labour historians have suggested, represented an ideological and political 'sharp turn to the left.'[50] In 1892, 1233 trade unions had a combined membership of 1,576,000, or just over 11 per cent of the British workforce. The purpose of trade unionism was, as it remains today, to secure better terms for the sale of labour power through collective negotiation. Exclusionary practices against working-class women and unskilled men persisted, however, and trade unionism was dominated by skilled male workers throughout most of the nineteenth century.

Gender-based patterns of work changed when war broke out in Europe in 1914. The First World War was the first 'mass' war in the sense that it required the mobilization of massive quantities of products and people. While Napoleon waged war against Prussia in 1806 using no more than 1500 rounds of artillery shells, in 1917 the French munitions industry had to produce 200,000 shells a day: 'Mass war required mass production.'[51] It also made it necessary to rethink the social organization of work. As Britain mobilized 12.5 per cent of its able-bodied men for the armed forces, the government encouraged women to enter the munitions and engineering factories, and this led to a revolution in waged work for women outside the household.

trade union: An organization whose purpose is to represent the collective interest of workers.

aristocracy of labour: a term used to describe nineteenth-century trade unions representing craft/skilled workers

WEB LINK

Go to the following websites for more information on the history of trade unions and current statistics on trade union organization: www.tuc.org.uk; www.icftu.org/; www.cosatu.org.za.

It resulted in several occupations turning permanently into female preserves, including offices, hotels, shops, cinemas, and to a lesser extent transport. In other occupations, such as engineering, men were reabsorbed in 1919 and women went back to pre-war patterns of paid or unpaid work.

Did industrial capitalism segregate the home from work and allocate women to the former and men to the latter? Gender-based patterns of work, and family-located sites of work, are forms that predate capitalism: they are not the results of social changes induced by capitalism. Women's work tended to be concentrated around six human activities that predate capitalism: to bear children, to feed them and other members of the family, to clothe the family, to care for the young and old when sick, to educate children, and to take care of the home.[52] Explanations why some work was men's and some was women's are almost as various as the patterns of wages that have existed. In the pre-Industrial Revolution period there is some evidence that women did a much greater variety of jobs, but even then gender influenced the allocation and reward of work. A disproportionate number of women undertook the most menial, poorly paid and domestically related jobs.

Evidence about work-related gender relations before the nineteenth century is sparse. Contemporary accounts emphasize that the gender division of work is socially constructed, and work tended to be labelled female or male on the basis of socially changeable expectations about how to view, judge and treat the two sexes. Part of the long historical process of gender inequality at work can be explained by the activities of the pre-industrial craft gilds and the trade unions. The town-based craft gilds, the forerunners of trade unions, tended to be exclusively male-oriented, with severe restrictions on women's membership. In the context of competitive pressure to reduce labour costs and the economic effect of female workers in depressing wages, male-dominated trade unions worked hard to maintain or restore wage levels and traditional employment privileges.[53]

Source: Nick Hedges, from the cover of P. Thompson, The Nature of Work, Palgrave Macmillan

plate 6 The First World War (1914–18) saw large numbers of women finding employment in the munitions and engineering factories.

OB IN FOCUS

Worn-out middle managers may get protection

Many Canadian middle managers and supervisors are struggling under increased workloads and long hours. Policy makers are beginning to listen to the cries of exhaustion from these employees who are not currently covered by Canadian labour standards legislation. Laws designed for the nine-to-five world of the 1960s do not provide adequate protection for many 'overworked and overwhelmed employees who, because of global com-petition and technological advances, are expected to be available 24-7', Federal Labour Minister Joe Fontana said last month in launching a sweeping review of the Canada Labour Code, with a view to expanding its reach.

Among the issues open to discussion: Should managers and supervisors be protected by labour code restrictions on hours of work, with entitlement to overtime pay or time off in lieu if they exceed the standard workweek? Or do long hours come with the territory?

Source: Virginia Galt, *Globe and Mail*, 3 January 2005, p. B1.

Trade union bargaining strategies developed gender-based occupational segregation. One function of trade unionism, according to one union leader, was 'to bring about a condition … where wives and daughters would be in their proper sphere at home, instead of being dragged into competition for livelihood against the great and strong men of the world'.[54] Prior to 1858, women participated in medicine quite widely, but thereafter, as in other traditional professions, the work became a male preserve. With the exception of midwifery and nursing, a combination of government legislation and male tactics excluded middle-class women from all medical practices.[55] Feminist critiques of the sociology of work have demonstrated in important ways the manner in which both the theory and practice of work and work behaviour have excluded women as subjects, as well as their experiences and voices.[56]

To sum up, married women were systematically removed from waged work after the initial phase of the Industrial Revolution. The new factory system proved beneficial to working-class women, particularly unmarried women, providing waged work outside the grossly exploitative decentralized putting-out system. Throughout the nineteenth century and well into the twentieth century, men managed to effectively exclude working-class and middle-class women from participating in many trade and professional occupations, by retaining old 'skills' or monopolizing new ones, using their professional privilege and power, using strategies of closure and demarcation, and encouraging the concepts of 'skill' and 'profession' to be seen as male property.[57]

WEB LINK
Go to the following websites for more information and statistics on women employed in advanced capitalist societies: www.europa.eu.int/; www.statistics.gov.uk; www.iegd.org/

Taylorism and Fordism

In this section we turn to what others call 'classical' work organization, Taylorism and Fordism. They are considered classical partly because they represent the earliest contributions to modern management theory, but they are also classical because they identify ideas and issues that keep occurring in contemporary organizational behaviour and management literature, although writers now tend to use a different vocabulary.[58] We now consider each of these influential classical approaches to work organization.

Taylorism

The American Frederick W. Taylor (1856–1915) pioneered the scientific management approach to work organization, hence the term 'Taylorism'. Taylor developed his ideas on work organization while working as superintendent at the Midvale Steel Company in Pennsylvania, USA. Taylorism represents both a set of management practices and a system of ideological assumptions.[59] The autonomy (freedom from control) of craft workers was potentially a threat to managerial control. For the craft worker the exercise of control over work practices was closely linked to his personality, as this description of 'craft pride' suggests:

Taylorism: a process of determining the division of work into its smallest possible skill elements, and how the process of completing each task can be standardized to achieve maximum efficiency. Also referred to as scientific management.

> [The craftsman] is engaged in tasks where the capacity for original thought is exercised: he has refined and critical perceptions of the things pertaining to his craft. His work creates a feeling of self-reliance … he lives a full and satisfying life.[60]

As a first-line manager, not surprisingly Taylor viewed the position of skilled shop-floor workers differently. He was appalled by what he regarded as inefficient working practices, and the tendency of his subordinates not to put in a full day's work, what Taylor called 'natural soldering'. He believed that workers who did manual work were motivated solely by money – the image of the 'greedy robot' – and were too stupid to develop the most efficient way of performing a task – the 'one best way'. The role of management was to analyse 'scientifically' all the tasks to be undertaken, and then to design jobs to eliminate time and motion waste.

Taylor's approach to work organization and employment relations was based on the following five principles:

▷ maximum job fragmentation
▷ separate planning and doing
▷ separate 'direct' and 'indirect' labour
▷ minimization of skill requirements
▷ minimize handling component parts and material.

The centrepiece of scientific management is the separation of tasks into their simplest constituent elements – 'routinization of work' (the first principle). Most manual workers were viewed as sinful and stupid, and therefore all decision-making functions had to be removed from their hands (the second principle). All preparation and servicing tasks should be taken away from the skilled worker (direct labour), and, drawing on Charles Babbage's principle, performed by unskilled and cheaper labour (indirect labour, in the third principle). Minimizing skill requirements to perform a task reduces the worker's control over work activities or the labour process (the fourth principle). Finally, management should ensure that the layout of the machines on the factory floor minimizes the movement of people and materials to shorten the time taken (the fifth principle).

While the logic of work fragmentation and routinization is simple and compelling, the principles of Taylorism reflect the class antagonism that is found in employment relations. When Taylor's principles were applied to work organization they led to the intensification of work: to 'speeding up', 'deskilling' and new techniques to control workers, as shown in Figure 2.2. And since gender, as we have discussed, is both a system of classification and a structure of power relations, it should not surprise us that Taylorism contributed to the shift in the gender composition of engineering firms. As millions of men were recruited into the armed forces for the First World War (1914–18), job fragmentation and the production of standardized items such as rifles, guns and munitions enabled women 'dilutees' to be employed in what had previously been skilled jobs reserved exclusively for men.[61]

Some writers argue that Taylorism was a relatively short-lived phenomenon, which died in the economic depression of the 1930s: 'Some Taylorians invested a great effort to gain its acceptance among American employers but largely failed.'[62] However, others have argued that this view underestimates the spread and influence of Taylor's principles on work organization: 'the popular notion that Taylorism has been "superseded" by later schools of "human relations", that it "failed" … represents a woeful misreading of the actual dynamics of the development of management.'[63] Similarly, others have made a persuasive case that, 'In general the direct and indirect influence of Taylorism on factory jobs has been extensive, so that in Britain job design and technology design have become imbued with neo-Taylorism.'[64]

Can you think of jobs in the retail and service sector that would support the charge that work systems in the modern workplace continue to be affected by neo-Taylorism?

STOP AND REFLECT

A TAYLOR SYSTEM MACHINIST "UP-TO-DATE"

An argument without words

figure 2.2 A craft union response to Taylorism

Fordism

Henry Ford (1863–1947) applied the major principles of scientific management in his car plant, and also installed specialized machines and added a crucial innovation to Taylorism: the flow-line principle of assembly work. This kind of work organization has come to be called Fordism. The moving assembly line had a major impact on employment relations. It exerted greater control over how workers performed their tasks, and it involved the intensification of work and labour productivity through ever-greater job fragmentation and short task-cycle times. In 1922, Henry Ford stated his approach to managing shopfloor workers: 'The idea is that man ... must have every second necessary but not a single unnecessary second.'[65]

The speed of work on the assembly line is determined by the technology itself rather than by a series of written instructions. Management's control of the work process was also enhanced by a detailed time and motion study inaugurated by Taylor. Work study engineers attempted to discover the shortest possible task-cycle time. Recording job times meant that managers could monitor more closely their subordinates' effort levels and performance. Task measurement therefore acted as the basis of a new structure of control.

Fordism is also characterized by two other essential features. The first was the introduction of an interlinking system of conveyor lines that feed components to different work stations to be worked on, and the second was the standardization of commodities to gain economies of scale. Thus, Fordism established the long-term principle of the mass production of standardized commodities at a reduced cost.

Ford's production system was, however, not without its problems. Workers found the repetitive work boring and unchallenging, and their job dissatisfaction was expressed in high rates of absenteeism and turnover. In 1913, for example, Ford required about 13,500 workers to operate his factories at any one time, and in that year alone the turnover was more than 50,000 workers. The management techniques developed by Ford in response to these employment problems serve further to differentiate Fordism from Taylorism. Ford introduced the 'five dollar day' – double the pay and shorter hours for those who qualified. Benefits depended on a factory worker's lifestyle being deemed satisfactory, which included abstaining from alcohol. Ford's style of paternalism attempted to inculcate new social habits, as well as new labour habits, that would facilitate job performance. Taylorism and Fordism became the predominant approach to job design in vehicle and electrical engineering – the large-batch production industries – in the United States and Britain.[66]

Post-Fordism and modern management

As a work organization and employment relations strategy, Taylorism and Fordism had limitations even when the workforce accepted them. First, work simplification led to boredom and dissatisfaction, and tended to encourage adversarial industrial relations and conflict, including frequent work stoppages. Second, Taylor-style work organization involves control and coordination costs. With extended specialization, indirect labour costs increase as the organization employs an increasing number of production planners, supervisors and quality control inspectors. The economies associated with the division of labour tend to be offset by the diseconomies of management control costs.

Third, Taylorism and Fordism affect what might be called 'cooperation costs'. As management's control over the quantity and quality of workers' performance increases, workers experience increased frustration and dissatisfaction, which leads to a withdrawal of their commitment to the organization. The relationship between controller and controlled can deteriorate so much that it results in a further increase in management control. The principles of Taylorism and Fordism thus reveal a basic

---

Fordism: a term used to describe mass production using assembly-line technology that allowed for greater division of labour and time and motion management, techniques pioneered by the American car manufacturer Henry Ford in the early twentieth century

paradox, 'that the tighter the control of labour power, the more control is needed'.[67] The adverse reactions to the extreme division of labour led to the development of new approaches to work organization that attempted to address these problems.

The 'human relations' movement attempted to address the limitations of Taylorism and Fordism by shifting attention to the perceived psychological and social needs of workers. The movement grew out of the Hawthorne experiments conducted by Elto Mayo in the 1920s. Mayo set up an experiment in the relay assembly room at the Hawthorne Works in Chicago, USA, which was designed to test the effects on productivity of variations in working conditions (lighting, temperature and ventilation). The Hawthorne research team found no clear relationship between any of these factors and productivity. However, the study led the researchers to develop concepts that might explain the factors affecting worker motivation. They concluded that more than just economic incentives and the work environment motivated workers: recognition and social cohesion were important too. The message for management was also quite clear: rather than depending on management controls and financial incentives, it needed to influence the work group by cultivating a climate that met the social needs of workers. The human relations movement advocated various techniques such as worker participation and non-authoritarian first-line supervisors, which would, it was thought, promote a climate of good human relations in which the quantity and quality needs of management could be met.

Criticisms of the human relations approach to work organization and employment relations were made by numerous writers. Human relations detractors charged managerial bias and the fact that the human relations movement tended to play down the basic economic conflict of interest between the employer and employee. Critics also pointed out that when the techniques were tested, it became apparent that workers did not inevitably respond as predicted. Finally, the human relations approach has been criticized because it neglects wider socioeconomic factors.[68] Despite these criticisms, however, the human relations approach to job design began to have some impact on management practices in the post-Second World War environment of full employment. Running parallel with the human relations school of thought, though, came ideas about work that led to the quality of working life (QWL) movement.

In the 1970s and 1980s, new approaches to work organization stressed the principles of closure, whereby the scope of the job is such that it includes all the tasks to complete a product or process, and task variety, whereby the worker acquires a range of different skills so that job flexibility is possible and the worker can personally monitor the quantity and quality of the work. New approaches to work organization spawned new techniques such as 'job enrichment', which gave the worker a wider range of tasks to perform and some discretion over how those tasks are done. For example, in the context of a fast food outlet, instead of an employee's job being limited to grilling burgers, the job would be enlarged to grilling the burgers, preparing the salad, ordering the produce from the wholesaler and inspecting the quality of the food on delivery.

Some theorists have been critical of these new work designs. An influential study argues that although job enrichment techniques may increase job satisfaction and commitment, the key focus remains managerial control. While work organization strategies such as job enrichment result in individuals or groups of workers being given a wider measure of discretion over their work, or 'responsible autonomy', the strategy is a 'tool of self-discipline' and a means of maintaining or even intensifying managerial control.

With the growth of call centres over the past decade, critical organizational research has drawn attention to 'new' forms of Taylorism. It is alleged that sophisticated electronic eavesdropping on salesperson–client conversations, and peer group scrutiny, have created 'electronic sweatshops' or a form of 'electronic Taylorism'.[69]

Work teams and self-management

The favoured work configuration over the last two decades has been teamworking. The focus on work teams has grown out of, drawn upon, and sometimes reacted against Taylorism and Fordism.[70] The centrepiece of teamworking is functional flexibility, with members undertaking a wide range of tasks with a high degree of autonomy.

In the 1980s, Japanese work organization and employment relations was held up as a model for the struggling UK and North American manufacturing sectors.[71] The Japanese management model has three notable elements: flexibility, quality control and minimum waste. Flexibility is achieved by arranging machinery in a group – what is known as 'cellular technology' – and by employing a multiskilled workforce. Thus, the work organization is the opposite of that of 'Taylorism': a generalized, skilled machinist with flexible job boundaries is a substitute for the specialized machinist operating one machine in one particular workstation. Higher quality standards is achieved by making quality every worker's responsibility. Minimum waste, the third element of the Japanese model, is achieved by just-in-time (JIT) techniques. As the name suggests, this is a hand-to-mouth mode of manufacture that aims to produce no more than the necessary components, in the necessary quantities, of the necessary quality and at the necessary time.

Japanese work organization and employment relations also has a cultural and social dimension. The practices aim to generate social cohesion and a 'moral commitment' to common organizational goals. From the culture management perspective, self-managed work teams are 'a socialization device' aimed at solving the classical management problem of empowering employees to release creativity, synergy and commitment without reducing management control of the labour process.[72] We examine work teams in more detail in Chapter 11.

Go to the 2004 Workplace Employee Relations Survey website www.dti.gov.uk/er/emar/2004wers.htm for more information on trends in work organization.

WEB LINK

In the 1980s, many US and European manufacturing companies strived to introduce cellular production, quality circles, just-in-time methods, and union–management cooperation. The managerial mantra of the 1980s and early 1990s was flexibility and multi-tasking, although various terms were used to describe these tendencies: flexible specialization or 'flex-spec', 'lean' production, 'reengineering' and 'high performance work systems' are well established in the literature.

Much of the rationale for new work structures has been found in alleged shifts towards 'market-oriented' considerations. Two US gurus, Hammer and Champy, for example, inform us that 're-engineering' is necessary because the world is a different place.[73] To respond more rapidly to global changes workers must have many tasks, some autonomy, be paid according to individual effort, and be attuned to the needs of customers. By the late 1990s, with Japan and the European Union, especially Germany, experiencing slow economic growth, low productivity and record high levels of unemployment, US work organization was again held up as the exemplar. Thereafter the big debate focused on the consequences of globalization, and whether a 'bundle' of 'best' work organization practices and more market-oriented employment relations could be implanted in a different national business matrix (see Chapters 4 and 17).

Post-industrial work

The Information Revolution, which we date from 1980 with the development of the silicon chip, marks a fundamental transformation of human activity like the Industrial Revolution two hundred years earlier. One theme running through this chapter has been the continuities as well as the discontinuities across time. There is no doubt that for many people paid work has changed profoundly during the Information Age, but these changes must be set in a historical context if we are to appreciate their significance and relevance.

 As you study organizational behaviour you should look at less orthodox material – expanding voices – as well as the established experts in the field. Leslie Salzinger's book *Genders in Production* is an example of the kind of other voices it is useful to consider.[74] Through case studies of employment and management in four different transnational factories, the author provides a sophisticated analysis of gender relations in the workplace. She explains the variability and flexibility of concepts of femininity and masculinity, and the fact that they are context-dependent behaviours.

As Salzinger asserts, in a globalized world the creation of 'cheap labour' is central to the economic process. However, although the young women at the factories she studied are generally perceived to be intrinsically 'cheap, docile, and dextrous', she comments that 'Panoptimex, like all effective arenas of production, makes not only TVs but workers.'

Obtain a copy of Salzinger's book and read Chapter 2, 'Producing women – femininity on the line'. What does Salzinger mean when she states that Panoptimex makes not only TVs but also workers?

table 2.1 The nature of traditional work and knowledge work

	Traditional work	**Knowledge work**
Skill/knowledge sets	Narrow and often functional	Specialised and deep, but often with diffuse peripheral focuses
Locus of work	Around individuals	In groups and projects
Focus of work	Tasks, objectives, performance	Customers, problems, issues
Skill obsolescence	Gradual	Rapid
Activity/feedback cycles	Primary and of an immediate nature	Lengthy from a business perspective
Performance measures	Task deliverables Little (as planned), but regular and dependable	Process effectiveness Potentially great, but often erratic
Career formation	Internal to the organization through training, development, rules and prescriptive career schemes	External to the organization, through years of education and socialisation
Employee's loyalty	To organization and his or her career systems	To professions, networks and peers
Impact on company success	Many small contributions that support the master plan	A few major contributions of strategic and long-term importance

Source: adapted from Despres and Hiltrop (1995) and Boud and Garrick (1999)

knowledge work: paid work that is of an intellectual nature, non-repetitive, result-orientated, and engaging scientific and/or artistic knowledge demanding continuous learning and creativity

The emergence of 'knowledge work' – intellectual capital – and 'knowledge worker' – employees who carry knowledge as a powerful resource which they, rather than the organization, own – is closely associated with the contemporary sophisticated Internet-based information technologies. Defining the notion of knowledge work and knowledge worker has proven problematic. Following Horwitz et al., however, we can say knowledge work is characterized as 'ambiguity intensive', and a knowledge worker is an individual with the ability to communicate and apply professional knowledge, as well as manage other employees.[75]

The nature of knowledge work is said to be fundamentally different from what we have traditionally associated with the 'machine age' and mass production, and hence it requires a different order of employment relations. It should not be confused with routine clerical work. It requires knowledge workers to learn a broad range of skills and knowledge, often with a focus around problems or customers, and to work in small groups or project teams to co-create new insights. It also requires a different employment relationship, with a psychological contract that has implications for employee commitment and career trajectory.

These differences in the nature of traditional work and knowledge work are spelled out in Table 2.1. In the Information Age, when an organization's wealth and ability to compete may exist 'principally in the heads of its employees' and that human competitiveness can effectively 'walk out the gates' every day, it is not surprising that organizations are concerned with 'better' human resource practices and 'knowledge management'.[76] Information technology, new employment contracts and knowledge work have changed the 'spatiality' of work: some people do paid work at home, and others undertake more short-term work assignments as organizations reduce their 'core' employees and contract work out.[77]

Emotional work

With the growth of routinized service work – such as work with fast food, tourism, hotels, and in call centres – new kinds of social relations and aspects of the self have developed and come under scrutiny. As the service workforce has grown in importance, there has been a growing interest in what sociologists call 'emotional work' or 'emotional labour'. It was the pioneering work of Arlie Hochschild[78] that drew attention to the significance of social interaction as a crucial element of service provision. She considered emotional labour as part of the employment contract when 'the emotional style of offering the service is part of the service itself'.[79]

Although servers in restaurants have always been trained to 'serve with a smile', there has been growing recognition that emotional labour is far more significant for a larger proportion than this of service employees, as management theorists emphasize 'customer service' as a vital aspect of business competitiveness. Emotional labour exists when workers are required, as part of the wage–effort bargain, to show emotions with the specific aim of causing customers or clients to feel and respond in a particular way. They might do this by verbal means – 'Good morning, sir/madam' – or non-verbal means, for example by smiling. It is important to understand that emotional labour, like physical and intellectual labour, is bought by the employer for a wage. It requires a specific set of behaviours, and it can be a potential source of stress and alienation. Emotional labour 'carries the potential for individuals to become self-estranged – detached from their own "real" feelings – which in turn might threaten their sense of their own identity'.[80]

Our brief history of work organization suggests that when an economy enjoys economic success, its work and management practices will often be regarded as a model by slower-growing economies.[81] Consistent with this prediction, British and other European organizations adopted US management ideas for most of the twentieth century, and adopted Japanese management practices in the 1980s, including team working, team briefings and employee involvement schemes. Evidence for each of these trends is readily available. The 2004 Workplace and Employee Relations Survey (WERS) showed how these work design practices are commonly applied in UK work organizations.

Much of the literature on newly emerging work structures simplifies the analysis to a polar comparison between 'traditional' Fordist, and new or 'post-Fordist' work team characteristics. But though it looks elegant to draw up lists of opposite characteristics, that is not a good reflection of reality.[82] As in other periods of workplace transformation, we can today still witness old work forms existing alongside new work configurations. If post-industrial capitalism created highly skilled knowledge

A major theme of this section has been the continuities as well as the discontinuities across time in paid work. Can you see any similarities between knowledge work in home-based distributed environments and the putting-out system? Look at Plate 5 (page 41), showing a scene of customers and a server. What does the picture reveal about emotional labour? Have you ever been in a situation at work where you had to manage your feelings before customers? If so, what did it do to your sense of self?

STOP AND REFLECT

work, work organization designs reminiscent of the industrial era still remain. Work is still divided up and routinized in both the manufacturing and the service sectors. In many workplaces the common feature of paid work is limited task variety, low or no skill requirements and close managerial control, reminiscent of Frederick Taylor's philosophy of a century ago. All this suggests that the design of work organization is not a smooth transition from one model to another. New work regimes are most likely to resemble a hybrid configuration, with elements from the old work organization design and parts of the new.

> WEB LINK
>
> Go to the following websites for more information and statistics on economic trends and gender relations in the workplace: www.statistics.gov.uk; www.eiro.eurofound.ie; www.un.org/womenwatch/; www.isreview.org (search for Eleanor Burke Leacock).

Work in organizations: an integration of ideas

Earlier in this chapter, we described the transformation of work thesis, and how changes influence the quality of work, identity and the psychological contract, which then influence behaviour in the workplace. In discussing post-Fordist or 'post-bureaucratic' work organizations, we emphasized competing claims over whether new forms of work organization lead to an enrichment of work or the degradation of work. Optimists argue that new work structures empower employees, and celebrate the claim that managerial behaviour has shifted from the 'management of control' to the 'management of commitment'.[83] Pessimists argue that some new work arrangements are 'electronic sweatshops', and that employee-empowering work regimes are basically a euphemism for work intensification. To capture the new realities of the modern workplace, critics often use the term 'McWorld', meaning that a vast amount of work experience, especially for young people, women and workers of colour, involves menial tasks, part-time contracts, close monitoring of performance and entrenched job insecurity.[84]

In Figure 2.3, we draw together the developments in work organization and employment relationships over the last 200 years, by highlighting four paradigms or distinctive approaches: craft/artisan, Taylorism/Fordism, neo-Fordism and post-Fordism. Paid work is shown to vary along two dimensions: the *variety of work* – the

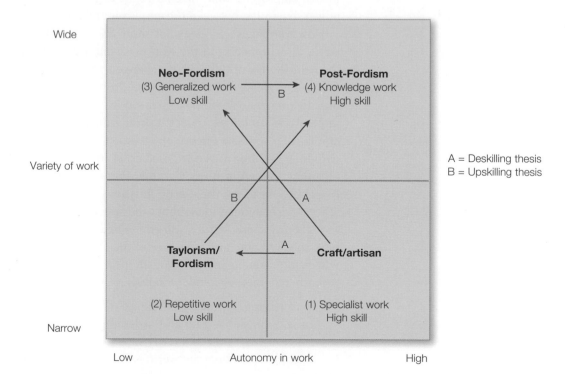

figure 2.3 Development of work organization and employment relationships

extent to which employees have an opportunity to do a range of tasks using their various skills and knowledge – and the *autonomy in work* – the degree of initiative that employees can exercise over how their immediate work is performed.

Here, *craft/artisan* means the types of work organization that are based on craft-based skills and often associated with a narrow range of specialized tasks, a high level of skill and a high degree of autonomy. Taylorism/Fordism means the adoption of basic scientific management principles and the assembly-line methods pioneered by Henry Ford. Neo-Fordism refers to a work configuration that has modified the core principles of Fordism through flexible working practices to fit contemporary operations. In contrast to the craft/artisan paradigm, the Taylorism/Fordism and neo-Fordism paradigms are often associated with a narrow variety of tasks, a low level of skill and a low degree of autonomy in work. Post-Fordism refers to work organizations that do not rely on the principles of Taylorism or Fordism, and is often associated with 'high-performance work systems', with self-management, and with knowledge work involving a wide variety of professional activities with a high degree of autonomy in work.

As others have mentioned, the strength of this conceptual model is as a heuristic device – a teaching aid – to help us summarize the complex development of work organization and employment relations. The research literature on the trends in work design suggests that Taylorism and Fordism have dominated managerial approaches to work organization.

In addition to the four broad classifications of work organization, the model shows two trends proposed by the proponents of the 'deskilling' and 'upskilling' theses. The deskilling thesis maintains that in Western capitalist economies there is a general trend in paid work towards a narrow variety of tasks and low autonomy. The solid arrow marked 'A' represents this trend in the diagram. The upskilling thesis suggests an opposite trend towards a wide variety of tasks and high autonomy in work. The solid arrow marked 'B' represents this trend. It is important to understand that different regimes of work organization affect the nature of the employment relationship, whether or not this is explicitly acknowledged in the writings of organizational theorists. For example, if work is reorganized to deskill or upskill employees, this will change the degree of interdependency, and typically the power dynamics, between the employer and employee.

However, Figure 2.3 does not show the persistence of gender ideologies on paid work, discrimination in the workplace and the sexual division of paid work. While the realities of workplaces have changed, ideas about them have lagged far behind.[85] Many Europeans and North Americans still believe in the 'traditional' male breadwinner/female homekeeper model, even though household lives and financial imperatives no longer reflect it. In Germany, for example, the traditional sense of family roles remains strong, and women who do anything other than stay at home with their children are considered cruel and unnatural. They are called *rabenmutter*, meaning a raven mother. Commenting on German social values in 2006, Reiner Klingholz, head of the Berlin Institute for Population and Development, said, 'These old-fashioned ideas about the sexes aren't really part of mainstream German thought any more, but it's still embedded in the neurons of our brains that women have to stay home and take care of the children.'[86] Balancing paid work and family will enable women and men to live the lives they say they want to live. As one man recently reflected on gender ideologies:

> It's amazing. I grew up thinking a man was someone who was gone most of the time, then showed up and ordered people around and, aside from that, never said a word. I don't want my sons to have to deal with that kind of situation or to think that's how the world is.[87]

neo-Fordism/post-Fordism: the development from mass production assembly lines to more flexible manufacturing processes

Some of the more recent empirically based literature offers a context-sensitive understanding of the development of work, and rejects a general tendency towards either deskilling or upskilling. The 'context-sensitive' view makes the point that new work structures do not have uniform outcomes, but are likely to be 'mixed' and contingent on a number of variables, such as business strategy, the nature of new technology, the degree of employee involvement in decision making, union involvement in the change process, and the extent to which 'bundles' of HR practices support the new work regime. Another issue is whether the work is in the private or public sector.[88] In sum, the identification of potential benefits and costs for workers from new work configurations provides a more complex picture, one that strongly supports the hypothesis that changes in the nature and organization of work can strengthen or threaten the 'psychological contract'.

In very broad terms, these are the major tendencies and developments of paid work over the last 200 years. The shift from craft work to relatively unskilled routine work is well documented. The Tayloristic principles for fragmenting and routinizing work were conceived for manual labour but were eventually incorporated into clerical labour. During the last century, there has been a shift from physical labour to clerical functions, or what we now call knowledge work. The development of an informational economy and the emergence of the Internet-based 'network society' mean that knowledge workers are no longer constrained by place or time. Despite the persistence of gender ideologies, the growing presence of women in the paid workforce is a significant change in the last third of the twentieth century. How these developments in paid work have been conceptualized and theorized is examined in the next chapter.

hypotheses: statements making empirically testable declarations that certain variables and their corresponding measure are related in a specific way proposed by theory

hypothesis: in search studies, a tentative statement of the relationship between two or more concepts or variables

Chapter summary

- One of the major themes running through the approach has been the continuities as well as the discontinuities across time. There is no doubt that changes occur all the time, but these must be contextualized adequately if we are to appreciate their relevance. Thus, we can only really talk about a rise in instrumental orientations to work if we know what existed previously.

- Trying to summarize the experience of work over several millennia is a difficult task. There is so much material to cover that no text of conventional size would be able to deal adequately with the complexities. However, this chapter has been written on the assumption that some knowledge is preferable to complete ignorance, especially if to understand the present we have to situate it against the past. It has tended to highlight gender issues in the workplace to balance out the conventional preference for male history.

- The complexity of the experience of work defies any simple assumptions about the significance of work. However, perhaps we can salvage from the past a conclusion that illuminates the significance of the social. Work, like other institutions, is inherently and irreducibly constructed, interpreted and organized through social actions and social discourse.

discourse: a way of talking about and conceptualizing an issue, presented through concepts, ideas and vocabulary that recur in texts

Key concepts

McDonaldization (also known as 'McWork' or 'McJobs'): a term used to symbolize the new realities of corporate-driven globalization which engulf young people in the twenty-first century, including simple work patterns, electronic controls, low pay, part-time and temporary employment

aristocracy of labour	50	Industrial Revolution	46–7
cellular technology	56	knowledge work	57–8
control	52–3	labour power	56
division of labour	47–8	McJobs	59
emotional labour	58–9	putting-out system	47
factory system	47	trade unions	50
gender-based patterns of work	49–53	work	42

Chapter review questions

1. What is work?
2. What were the advantages and disadvantages of the putting-out system?
3. Why were men reluctant to enter the new factories during the Industrial Revolution?
4. Why were male trade unionists so hostile to women entering traditional occupations?
5. Explain the importance of 'control' in a factory system.
6. How does knowledge work different from traditional work?
7. How does emotional labour differ from traditional paid work?

Further reading

Bolton, S. and Boyd, C. (2003) 'Trolley dolly or skilled emotion manager? Moving on from Hochschild's managed heart.' *Work, Employment and Society* **17** (2), pp. 289–308.

Hardill, I. and Green, A. (2003) 'Remote working – altering the spatial contours of work and home in the new economy.' *New Technology, Work and Employment,* **18** (3), pp. 212–22.

McIvor, A. (2001) *A History of Work in Britain, 1880–1950.* Basingstoke: Palgrave Macmillan.

Noon, M. and Blyton, P. (2002) *The Realities of Work,* Basingstoke: Palgrave Macmillan.

Salzinger, L. (2003). *Genders in Production,* University of California Press.

Case study: Homeworking at Matherdom City Council

Background

Matherdom City Council (MCC) (a fictional body) is a local council which provides a wide range of services and is a major employer in the region. It has the ambition to establish itself as a 'progressive and modern employer', which takes the concern of its workforce seriously and cares about their well-being. Therefore, its managers considered a series of work–life balance initiatives. These included the introduction of permanent home-based teleworking in some parts of the council. The initiatives were guided and overseen by a senior corporate human resource manager, who had always taken an interest in making the council more 'employee friendly'. The operational technicalities were overseen by a more junior human resource officer, who saw her leadership of the 'home-working initiative' as 'a great opportunity for my career and a huge step forward'. Other motivations for council managers were a serious lack of suitable office space, with old and partly decrepit buildings, and a growing work force.

The initiative

The staff of the local taxation and benefits section were selected as the 'guinea pigs', in agreement with their management, and home-working was introduced in some of the teams. The staff involved worked on processing tax and benefit forms, and evaluating applications for tax relief and benefits. Their work involved providing advice to external telephone callers. The more senior staff mentored the less experienced staff, and many jobs – in particular time-consuming report reading and the checking of outgoing mail – were spread out evenly to all staff on a rota system.

The home workers had a variety of reasons for volunteering to take part. They welcomed the opportunity to avoid commuting, they expected to be able to deal better with domestic responsibilities and make time for hobbies while becoming increasingly productive in their work performance, and they were keen to avoid the incessant interruptions they experienced in the office open-plan environment. Their team leaders were overall supportive, but also wary of the operational consequences. They felt the scheme would mean making new arrangements to communicate with their staff, it would involve reallocation of tasks, it was not clear how the home workers could be supervised, and so on. The service manager and the general manager of the taxation and benefits section, however, were quite enthused about this initiative, since their accommodation problems were pressing and the section's office was cramped and uncomfortable. They also stressed the potential to increase performance (through processing more forms). An IT specialist was called in to advise on, arrange to purchase, and monitor the use of equipment such as laptop computers, and the necessary software. This enabled the home workers to access the council's IT systems, and they started to work from home.

At first there was a phenomenal increase in the performance of home workers (measured in terms of forms completed), and the initiative was hailed a large success. However, over time performance levelled out, though it remained much improved. The IT member of staff had a difficult time at the beginning. She had to deal with systems failures, downtime, and some IT training needs which only became apparent during the pilot. When they had been in the office, staff could ask a colleague if they were stuck with a computing task, but they now had to rely on themselves, and asking advice via phone or email proved to be cumbersome.

Overall, however, the home workers reported great satisfaction with their choice, with family members and co-residents mainly being supportive. But there were conflicts in some households, as the home was rearranged to provide a workspace, and family members felt that work was intruding into a private space and time. A typical comment was that a home worker had to work hard at 'keeping the family happy because of my increased presence ▶

in the house – presence as a council employee, not as a mother!'. Another home worker reported that he liked being able to process many more forms, but was conscious that the variety of his work had been reduced.

The colleagues of the home workers who had stayed in the office were less happy. Particularly when they were in small teams, they felt they were landed with many more of the 'so-called little jobs' that needed doing as back-up to the form filling. They also commented upon the fact that many of the home workers were experienced staff, and they missed being able to call readily on their knowledge. When they had small queries, they had to go to the team leader or find someone else to ask. They also had to collect, check and post the letters prepared and emailed by the home workers, and this was an additional burden in an already busy schedule.

Members of one small team complained particularly, because it dealt with a large number of phone calls and enquiries. These used to be shared out between five people, but were now answered by two. The staff involved were frustrated and stressed, and felt that they had been given the 'rough end of the stick'. One went on extended 'stress leave' a month after the introduction of the home-working initiative.

Some team leaders were sympathetic to complaints about home working, because it also made their working life harder. For example, they had to stay in touch by phone or electronically rather than just 'popping in and having a quick chat' with someone, and managing office cover was becoming an increasingly difficult task. On the other hand, other team leaders welcomed the additional space they gained in their office, and the 'culture of independence' which they associated with home working.

After a period of three months the home-working initiative was reviewed, and it was decided to continue and expand this particular form of flexible work.

Task

Working either alone or in a small group, prepare a briefing document for MCC's neighbouring council. This council wants to introduce permanent home working, but is concerned how its introduction might affect the organization. Your report should address these questions:

1. Which organizational and non-organizational groups are affected by the introduction of home working?
2. Which different organizational agendas are these groups pursuing?
3. What recommendations would you make in order to ensure a smooth introduction of permanent home working?

Sources of additional information

Felstead, A. and Jewson, N. (2000) *In Work, At Home*, London: Routledge.

Tietze, S. and Musson, G. (2005) 'Recasting the home-work relationship: a case of mutual adjustment?' *Organization Studies* 26 (9), pp. 1331–52.

Department of Trade and Industry: www.dti.gov.uk/er/fw_wlb.htm

Telework Association: www.tca.org.uk/

Work Foundation: www.employersandwork-lifebalance.org.uk/

Note

This case study was written by Dr Susanne Tietze, Senior Lecturer in Organizational Analysis, University of Bradford, and Dr Gill Musson, Senior Lecturer in HRM and Organizational Behaviour, University of Sheffield, England.

Web-based assignment

Central to the advance of organizational behaviour as a field of critical inquiry is an openness to expanding our understanding of both work and the 'workplace'. We believe it is important to understand that work expands beyond the boundaries of 'paid work', and importantly, the place where work is performed extends beyond the formal organization. The notion of work–life balance has increasing relevance to workers, particularly to women, in the early twenty-first century.

On an individual basis, or working in a small group, visit the following websites and write a brief report of the research and practical issues associated with (a) home-working and (b) work–life balance.

www.dti.gov.uk/er/fw_wlb.htm

www.tca.org.uk/

www.employersandwork-lifebalance.org.uk/

OB in films

The film *Modern Times* (1936) features Charlie Chaplin in a scathing portrayal of North American assembly-line work. The first 15 minutes of the film humorously illustrate the meaning of Taylorism and the stress associated with working on an assembly line. The film led Charlie Chaplin to be banned from the United States, and some of the actors to be investigated by the FBI.

Watch the first 15 minutes of the film. What does the film tell us about Taylorism? How would you rate Chaplin's job in terms of 'job enrichment' techniques?

Notes

1 A passage from the trade journal *Machinery* in 1915 and quoted by James Hinton (1973: 97).
2 A female munitions worker, 1943 quoted in Grint (1998: 1).
3 Jeremy Rifkin (1996: 13).
4 Gorz (1982: 1).
5 Rifkin (1996) and Pahl (1988).
6 Gates (1996).
7 See for example Boud and Garrick (1999), Despres and Hiltrop (1995), Hamel and Prahalad (1994) and Drucker (1999).
8 Procter and Mueller (2000), Reich (1991), Thompson and Warhurst (1998).
9 See Pahl (1988), Wood (1982), Zuboff (1988), Hearn et al. (1989), Littler and Salaman (1984), Mills and Tancred (1992), Thompson (1989).
10 Pahl (1988: 752).
11 Maslow (1954).
12 Christiansen and Townsend (2004).
13 Holland (1985).
14 See for example Felstead and Ashton (2000).
15 Williams (1983: 335).
16 Christiansen and Townsend (2004: 2).
17 Gorz (1982).
18 See Noon and Blyton (2002) and Rinehart (2006).
19 Hardill and Green (2003), Coyle-Shapiro et al. (2005).
20 Williams (1983: 335).
21 Barnes (1996).
22 See Guest and Conway (2002), Herriot (1998), Kramer and Tyler (1996), Rousseau (1995).
23 Rousseau (1995: 9).
24 See Sveiby (1997) and Hodson and Sullivan (2002).

25 Grint (1998: 46).

26 Hobsbawm (1997: 10).

27 See Littler (1982) and Salaman (1981).

28 Hobsbawm (1997).

29 Carr (1961: 22–3).

30 Grint (1995).

31 Hobsbawm (1997).

32 Hobsbawm (1968: 24). See also Clarkson (1971: 70).

33 Clarkson (1971: 102).

34 Alvesson and Due Billing (1997: 55).

35 Grint (1998: 52).

36 See Mathias (1969), Kumar (1978).

37 Dobb (1963: 145).

38 Landes (1969: 59).

39 Smith (1982: 109).

40 Braverman (1974).

41 Quoted in Nichols (1980: 69).

42 M245.8arglin (1982).

43 Foucault (1977) quoted in Salaman (1981: 30).

44 Kelly (1985).

45 Hobsbawm (1968: 51).

46 Thompson (1967: 90).

47 Mathias (1969: 202).

48 Reskin and Padavic (1994: 21), and quoted by Alvesson and Due Billing (1997: 58).

49 For an extended account of early trade union history, see Mathias (1969) and Pelling (1963).

50 Lovell (1977: 20).

51 Hobsbawm (1994: 45).

52 Alvesson and Due Billing (1997), Berg (1988).

53 Bradley (1986).

54 Turner (1962: 185) and quoted in Grint (1998: 72).

55 Witz (1986).

56 Sydie (1994).

57 Knights and Willmott (1986).

58 Grey (2005).

59 Littler (1982: 51).

60 A passage from the trade journal *Machinery* in 1915, quoted by James Hinton (1973: 97).

61 Hinton (1973).

62 Rose (1988: 56).

63 Braverman (1974: 56).

64 Littler and Salaman (1984: 73).

65 Quoted in Beynon (1984: 33).

66 Beynon (1984), Littler and Salaman (1984).

67 Littler and Salaman (1984: 36–7).

68 See Thompson (1989) for an excellent critical analysis of this approach to work organization.

69 See Friedman (1977), Thompson (1989), Callaghan and Thompson (2001) and Sewell (1998).

70 Grey (2005).

71 See Bratton (1992), Elger and Smith (1994), Thompson and McHugh (2006), Womack et al. (1990), Oliver and Wilkinson (1992).

72 See Etzioni (1988), Findlay et al. (2000), Geary and Dobbins (2001), Grey (2005), Procter and Mueller (2000) and Thompson and Wallace (1996).

73 Hammer and Champy (1993).

74 Salzinger (2003).

75 This definition is based on Horwitz et al.'s review of the literature (2003: 31).

76 Boud and Garrick (1999: 48).

77 Hardill and Green (2003).

78 Hochschild (2003).

79 Hochschild (2003).

80 Noon and Blyton (2002: 193).

81 Jacoby (2005).

82 See Jaffee (2001), Vallas (1999).

83 Walton (1985).

84 See Sewell (1998), Hyman and Mason (1995), Reiter (1992), Ritzer (2000) and Leidner (1993) for a good critical review of this trend.

85 See Kimmel (2004).

86 Quoted by Doug Saunders, 'Politician-mom seeks to change dated German social values', *Globe and Mail*, 22 June 2006, p. A3.

87 Quoted in Kimmel (2004: 209).

88 Bratton (1992), Edwards et al. (2001), Gallie et al. (2004), Geary and Dobbins (2001), Milkman and Pullman (1991) and Marchington et al. (1992).

chapter 3
Studying work and organizations

The unexamined life is not worth living.[1]

Durkheim reminds us that it is intellectually naïve to celebrate differences as though it could exist apart from community, for contemporary societies require both, which must be founded to a great extent on rational discussion.[2]

[Managers] are theoreticians – they use theory every day. They just don't know they are using it.[3]

chapter outline

▷ Introduction
▷ Classical approaches to studying work
▷ Contemporary theories of work organizations
▷ The value of theory about contemporary organizational behaviour
▷ Chapter summary
▷ Key concepts
▷ Further reading
▷ Chapter review questions
▷ Chapter case study: Research at Aeroprecision AB
▷ Web-based assignment
▷ OB in films
▷ Notes

chapter objectives

After completing this chapter, you should be able to:

▷ explain the classical approaches to studying work through the ideas of Marx, Durkheim and Weber
▷ explain contemporary theories of work organizations and the importance of theory to understanding work, and behaviour in the workplace.

Introduction

This chapter examines classical and contemporary approaches to studying work and work organizations. We begin by considering the classical social theories about paid work through the ideas of Marx, Weber and Durkheim. They can be described as classical partly because they had their roots in European industrialization and culture – from about 1800 through to the early 1900s – and also because in their response to industrial capitalism, the early social theorists set out a series of themes, concepts, assumptions, problems and ideas which continue to exercise an enormous influence over contemporary organization theory. As others have pointed out, both the perspectives of analysis which are clearly set out in the works of the classical theorists, and the characteristic focuses of those traditions, continue to dominate study of the sociology of work.[4]

As we discussed in Chapter 1, over the last three decades not only have organizations fundamentally changed how they organize work, new approaches and concepts have also been developed for studying work organizations. In the 1970s, the orthodox consensus on organization theory focused on 'functionalism', which emphasized consensus and coherence rather than asymmetrical power relations and conflict.[5] The key concept is that of the organization as a 'system' which functions effectively if it achieves explicit goals, which are formally defined through 'rational' decision making. Alternative theoretical approaches have since challenged the supremacy of functionalism.

A multitude of contemporary theories of formal organizations exist, so we cannot hope to do justice to the complexities of such a wide-ranging debate. We therefore seek here to highlight the major distinguishing themes related to work and organizations. Drawing on the work of Keith Grint,[6] we review 12 competing theoretical perspectives or 'conversations' in organization theory: the technical, human relations, neo-human relations, systems thinking, contingency, cultures, learning, control, feminist, social action, political and postmodernist perspectives.

Classical approaches to studying work

Do contemporary organizational behaviour (OB) theorists have anything to learn from the classical sociologists such as Marx, Durkheim and Weber?

STOP AND REFLECT

Marx, Durkheim and Weber each analysed the new work forms, but also placed their analysis within a wider discourse on modern society and social change. While Karl Marx focused on social fragmentation, conflict and social change, Emile Durkheim concerned himself with social fragmentation and the nature of order, and Max Weber developed his theory of rationality and bureaucracy.

Karl Marx (1818–1883)

Marx believed that industrialization was a necessary stage for the eventual triumph of human potential, but that the mainspring of this social formation was capitalism,

Source: Marx/Engels Image Library

plate 7 Karl Marx

objectification: Karl Marx's term to describe the action of human labour on resources to produce a commodity, which under the control of the capitalist remains divorced from and opposed to the direct producer

and not industrialism as such. It is only capitalism that carries within it the seeds of its own destruction. For Marx, the human species is different from all other animal species, not because of its consciousness but because it alone produces its own means of subsistence.

Marx's argument is that what distinguishes humans from other animals is that our labour creates something in reality that previously existed only in our imagination:

> We presuppose labour in a form that stamps it as exclusively human .... But what distinguishes the worst architect from the best bees is this, that the architect raises his structure in imagination before he erects it in reality. At the end of every labour process we get a result that existed in the *imagination* [our emphasis] of the labourer at its commencement. He not only effects a change of form in the material on which he works, but he also realizes a purpose.[7]

Marx calls this process where humans create external objects from their internal thoughts objectification. This labour does not just transform raw materials or nature; it also transforms humans, including human nature, people's needs and their consciousness. We can begin to understand Marx's concept of objectification by thinking of the creative activity of an artist. The artist's labour is a representation of the imagination of the artist: 'the art work is an objectification of the artist'.[8] In addition, through the labour process, the artist's ideas of the object change, or the experience may prompt a new vision or creativity that needs objectification. Labour, for Marx, provides the means through which humans can realize their true human powers and potential. By transforming raw materials we transform ourselves, and we also transform society. Thus, according to Marx, the transformation of the individual through work and the transformation of society are inseparable.

Marx's discussion of work under capitalism focuses on the nature of employment relationships. Under capitalism the aim is to buy labour at sufficiently low rates to make a profit. Marx is careful to distinguish between 'labour' and 'labour power'. Human labour is the actual physical or mental activity incorporated in the body of the worker. Labour power, on the other hand, refers to the *potential* of labour to add use value to raw materials or commodities. This labour power is bought by the capitalist at a value less than the value it creates. In purchasing the worker's potential or capacity to labour and add use values to materials, at a wage level less than the value created by the worker's labour, the capitalist is able to make a profit.

We can begin to appreciate the significance of Marx's use of the term 'labour power' when we think of it as a promise: it is therefore indeterminate and there may be a gap between the potential or promise of labour, and the actual labour. This distinction between 'labour' and 'labour power' allowed Marx to locate the precise mechanism which creates profit in capitalist societies. It also gives rise to the creation of two classes that are potentially, if not always in practice, in conflict with each other.

Capitalism involves the work relationship between buyers and sellers of labour power. Marx's concept of surplus value is rooted in this social relationship. Surplus value is the value remaining when the worker's daily costs of subsistence have been subtracted from the value that she or he produces for the capitalist. As such, it is unpaid, and 'goes to the heart of the exploitation of the worker'.[9]

surplus value: the portion of the working day during which workers produce value that is appropriated by the capitalist

In the workplace the primacy of profit and conflict relationships gives rise to three broad necessary features of activity and change. Each of these involves substantial shifts in the work performed. Most significant is the need for the capitalist to centralize the labour power that is purchased, and to discipline the interior of the factory, by organizing space, time and the behaviour of workers whose commitment is unreliable. The aim is to close or minimize the gap between potential labour power and actual labour power. For Marx, the accumulation of profit is inevitably and irrevocably mediated by managerial control strategies. It is the inevitable outcome of capitalism: 'The directing motive, the end and aim of capitalist production, is to extract the greatest possible amount of surplus-value, and consequently to exploit labour-power to the fullest possible extent.'[10]

The second broad plane of activity changing the nature of work is the **division of labour**. To increase control and surplus value for the capitalist, extensive division of labour takes place within the factory. According to Marx, 'Division of labour within the workshop implies the undisputed authority of the capitalist over men that are but parts of a mechanism that belong to him.'[11] As an example, Marx described the manufacture of horse carriages. In pre-capitalist production, the manufacture of carriages involved the simple cooperation of various trades: coach construction, ironwork, upholstery and wheelwright work. Each of these trades was regulated by gilds in order to maintain their specialization and control over these operations. In capitalist production, simple cooperation gives way to what Marx described as 'complex cooperation', as individual trades lose their specialized skills and workers perform operations that are disconnected and isolated from one another, and carried out alongside each other. According to Marx and his colleague Engels, this mode of production also creates a hierarchy of managers and supervisors:

> Modern industry has converted the little workshop of the patriarchal master into the great factory of the industrial capitalist. Masses of labourers, crowded into the factory, are organized like soldiers. As privates of the industrial army they are placed under the command of a perfect hierarchy of officers [managers] and sergeants [supervisors].[12]

Marx examined the impact of technological change on employment relationships. He argued that machinery is used by the capitalist to increase surplus labour by cheapening labour, to deskill workers and thus make it easier to recruit, control and discipline workers. Machinery, he argued, led to the progressive reduction of skills:

> On the automatic plan skilled labour gets progressively superseded. The effect of improvements in machinery [results] in substituting one description of human labour for another, the less skilled for the more skilled, juvenile for adult, female for male, [and] causes a fresh disturbance in the rate of wages.[13]

Machinery allows the capitalist to transfer the knowledge and skill in production from the worker to reliable agents of capital – that is, managers. Marx described the process like this: 'Intelligence in production expands in one direction, because it vanishes in many others. What is lost by the detail labourers, is concentrated in the capital that employs them.'[14] Machinery also increases the capitalist's control over workers' work activities. In what Marx referred to as the despotism of the factory, machinery sets the pace of work and embodies powerful mechanisms of control: 'the technical subordination of the workman to the uniform motion of the instruments of labour [machinery] … gave rise to a barrack discipline'. He continued: 'To devise and administer a successful code of factory discipline, suited to the necessities of factory diligence, was the Herculean enterprise, the noble achievement of Arckwright!'[15]

These characteristics of work in industrial capitalism have two major consequences: the **alienation** of the workers, and conflict resulting ultimately in social change. Whereas objectification embodies the worker's creativity, work under capitalism is devoid of the producer's own potential creativity and sensuousness. Because workers' labour is not their own, it no longer transforms them. Hence, the unique quality of human beings – their ability to control the forces of nature and produce their own means of existence, to realize their full creative capacity through work – is stultified by capitalism.

division of labour: the allocation of work tasks to various groups or categories of employee

alienation: a feeling of powerlessness and estrangement from other people and from oneself

Drawing on the 1807 work by Georg Hegel, *The Phenomenology of Mind*, Marx developed the theory of alienation. In essence, alienation ruptures the fundamental connection human beings have to the self-defining aspect of their labouring activity.[16] Marx broke down the formulation of alienation into four conceptually discrete but related spheres. First, workers are alienated (or separated) from the product of their labour. The product – its design, quality, quantity and how it is marketed and disposed of – is not determined by those whose labour is responsible for its manufacture. Second, workers are alienated from productive activity. Marx emphasized the tendency for machinery to deskill work:

> Owing to the extensive use of machinery and to division of labour, the work of the proletarians has lost all individual character, and, consequently, all charm for the workman. He becomes an appendage of the machine, and it is only the most simple, most monotonous, and most easily acquired knack, that is required of him.[17]

Thus work offers no intrinsic satisfaction. Workers only work for the money; workers only work because they have to. Marx called this the 'cash nexus'. Accordingly, work takes on an instrumental meaning: it is regarded simply as a means to an end.

The third type of alienation discussed by Marx is alienation from the human species. Marx contended that self-estrangement develops because of the 'cash nexus'. In order to be clear on Marx's meaning, we need to know that Marx believed that people were essentially creative and that individuals expressed creativity through their work. Work, according to Marx, is the medium for self-expression and self-development. It is through work that people should be able to shape themselves and their communities in accordance with their own needs, interests and values. Under alienating conditions, however, work becomes not a social activity that personifies life, but simply a means for physical survival: people become detached from their true selves.

The fourth type of alienation discussed by Marx is alienation from fellow human beings and from the community. This results when the sole purpose of life is competition, and all social relations are transformed into economic relations. Workers and managers are alienated from each other. This economic relationship, between those who are controlled and the controllers, is an antagonistic one. And this asymmetry of social relationships in the workplace creates the foundation for a class structure that necessitates sharp differences in power, income and life chances.

Marx's analysis of the social organization of work is that people express themselves through their work, and in so far as their labour is merely a commodity to be paid for with a wage, they are alienated. Alienation is characteristic of a certain kind of organization of work – industrial capitalism – that is predicated on a set of socioeconomic conditions. In short, then, capitalism destroys the pleasure associated with labour, the distinctively human capacity to shape and reshape the world.

The second major consequence of work in capitalism, that relations between capitalists and workers are in constant conflict, is the engine of social change. Impelled by its internal contradictions, the reverberation of work under capitalism helps the development of class consciousness among the workers or proletariat. The defining features of work – deskilling, intensification of work, constant pressure to lower the wages allocated to labour – encourage the development of class conflict. Marx and Engels explain the logic whereby capitalism develops and then destroys itself. In their search for profits, capitalists closely control and discipline workers.[18]

Capitalism creates new contradictions, such as the concentration of workers into factories. As workers are concentrated under one roof they become aware of their common exploitation and circumstances. As a result, over time workers begin to resist capitalist controls, initially as individuals, then collectively as groups. Gradu-

contradictions: contradictions are said to occur within social systems when the various principles that underlie these social arrangements conflict with each other

class consciousness: Karl Marx's term for awareness of a common identity based on a person's position in the means of production

class conflict: a term for the struggle between the capitalist class and the working (proletariat) class

ally the workers become organized, through trade unions, and increasingly they become more combative and engage the ruling class in wider social struggles, which Marx believed would culminate in replacing the rule of the bourgeoisie and ridding society of capitalism: 'What the bourgeoisie therefore produce above all, is its own gravediggers. Its fall and the victory of the proletariat are equally inevitable.'[19] Thus, those selling their labour power, the workers, are exposed to such exploitation and degradation that they begin to oppose capitalists, in order to replace the system.

Marx provides a sophisticated theory of capitalism, with the working class as the embodiment of good, but his concentration on the extraction of surplus value in the labour process inhibits him from considering managerial and government strategies that serve to develop consent and cooperation. The capitalist mode of production is not characterized solely by the conflict between employer and labour: it is also marked by competition between organizations and economies. To put it another way, profits are realized by gaining a competitive advantage, and the need to gain workers' cooperation undermines the contradictory laws that promote constant conflict and crises. Thus, Marx systematically underestimates the possibility that management may need to organize on the basis of consent as well as coercion.

The reconceptualization of management as necessarily engaged in consent building also suggests that Marx's zero-sum theory of power is insufficient. Critics argue that while the interests of labour and capital do not coincide, the assumption that they are irreconcilably and utterly antagonistic is misleading. Therefore, the inadequacy of Marx's account lies at the level of analysis. Marx emphasized the irreconcilable interests of social classes at the societal level, and this obscures the very real way in which, in the workplace, the interests of employers and employees may be very closely intertwined.

Go to the following websites for more information on Marx:
http://plato.stanford.edu/entries/marx
www.anu.edu.au/polsci/marx/classics/manifesto.html
www.marxists.org/

WEB LINK

Despite the strong criticisms of Marx's analysis of work on capitalism, his impact on the sociology of work is immense. His illumination of the politics of work and organizations – the relationship between work and the distribution of interests and power in the society outside the workplace, and the relationships of power and managerial strategies inside the workplace – still informs contemporary analyses of work and employment relations, as we shall see later in this chapter.

Emile Durkheim (1858–1917)

Emile Durkheim's contribution to our understanding of work is essentially derived from his book *The Division of Labour in Society*,[20] and its discussion of the relationship between individuals and society, and the conditions for social cohesion. Durkheim was preoccupied with the issue of social solidarity and unity during a time when France was subject to the profound revolutionary changes that created modern society. The popular belief of the time was that the collapse of social life was imminent, in response to the expansion of the division of labour, ever-increasing industrialization and urbanization, and the declining significance of traditional moral beliefs. This was described as the transition from *Gemeinschaft* or 'community' forms of society, to *Gesellschaft* or 'social' forms, representing mere 'associations' where social solidarity was disintegrating. Durkheim suggested that such fears were not just exaggerated but actually wrong. His thesis on social development held that solidarity and order were being reconstructed in a different form. Durkheim's position was that the interdependence resulting from the progressive differentiation and specialization of labour gave rise to a new form of social solidarity, which is the bond that unites individuals when there is no normative consensus.

Durkheim's prime question was, if pre-industrial societies were held together by shared understandings, ideas, norms and values, what holds a complex industrial

social solidarity: the state of having shared beliefs and values among members of a social group, along with intense and frequent interaction among group members

urbanization: the process by which an increasing proportion of a population lives in cities rather than in rural areas

plate 8   Emile Durkheim

mechanical solidarity: a term to describe the social cohesion that exists in pre-industrial societies, in which there is a minimal division of labour and people feel united by shared values and common social bonds

organic solidarity: a term for the social cohesion that exists in industrial (and perhaps post-industrial) societies, in which people perform very specialized tasks and feel untied by their mutual dependence

anomie: a state condition in which social control becomes ineffective as a result of the loss of shared values and a sense of purpose in society

society together? He believed that increasing division of labour has enormous implications for the structure of society. In pre-industrial society, social solidarity is derived from people's similarities, and the rather suffocating effects of uniformity of experience and thought. Such societies are held together through the collective consciousness at the direct expense of individuality: 'individual personality is absorbed into the collective personality', as Durkheim put it.[21] He called this form of social unity 'mechanical solidarity'. In contrast, the increasing division of labour causes a diminution of collective consciousness, and 'this leaves much more room for the free play of our imitative'.[22]

Complex industrial societies, with new work forms based on functional specialization, are held together by relations of exchange and people's reciprocal need for the services of many others. This symmetry of life Durkheim called 'organic solidarity'. He believed that in societies whose solidarity is organic, individuals are linked increasingly to each other rather than to society as a whole. The totality of the nature of these social links compels individuals to remain in contact with one another, which in turn binds them to one another and to society. Thus, each of us becomes aware of our dependence on others and of the new cultural norms that shape and restrain our actions.

For Durkheim, only the division of labour could furnish social solidarity and ethical individualism: 'Since the division of labour becomes the source of social solidarity, it becomes, at the same time, the foundation of moral order.'[23] In summary, he argued that there was no necessary correlation between increased division of labour and decreasing solidarity. On the contrary, it was not a source of disorder and conflict but of order and social solidarity. The nature of moral solidarity in industrial society has not disappeared, but changed.

Of course, Durkheim was not oblivious to the reality of industrialization in Western Europe, which might have been argued to show the opposite. Not least, there were intense class conflict and widespread labour strikes in France, often led by radical workers known as revolutionary syndicalists, in unions organized in the *Confédération Générale du Travail* (CGT). Durkheim explained the existence of instability and social fragmentation by analysing what he called 'abnormal' forms of the division of labour. These abnormal forms occur when the development of the division of labour is obstructed and distorted by various factors. He identified these as the anomic division of labour, the forced division of labour, and the mismanagement of operations.

The first abnormal effects can arise because of the 'anomic' condition of the division of labour. The word anomie comes from the Greek *anomia*, meaning 'without law'. For Durkheim, anomie results from a condition where social norms and/or moral norms are confused or simply absent. Generally, Durkheim believed that anomie results from widespread business failure, or when there is rapid and uneven economic development that has expanded ahead of the necessary developments in social regulation. In such circumstances, he suggests, breaches occur in the social solidarity existing between specialized occupations, causing tensions in social relationships and eroding social cohesion.

Durkheim also considered anomie as another 'pathology' of industrialization, but believed that such deviant behaviour could be 'cured' through the proper level of regulation. He argued that occupational associations centred within civil society are the most effective means of regulating anomie in modern society. Such collective institutions provide moral authority, which dominates the life of their members. They are also a method by which individualistic egotism can be subordinated harmoniously to the general interest.

Durkheim explained the importance of occupational groups like this: '[W]herever a group is formed, a moral discipline is also formed.' He continued:

> A group is not only a moral authority regulating the life of its members, but also a source of life *sui generis*. From it there arises warmth that quickens or gives fresh life to each individual, which makes him disposed to empathise, causing selfishness to melt away.[24]

Durkheim also warned that mere construction of consensually grounded goals without any associated provision of opportunities to achieve such goals would extend the form of social 'pathology' under which anomie prevailed.

The second factor causing abnormal development, according to Durkheim, is the 'forced division of labour'.[25] He emphasized that the division of labour is frequently not 'spontaneous' because of class and inherited privilege that operate to limit life chances. Durkheim, then, is considered to be a supporter of meritocracy. The normal division of labour would occur if social inequalities mirrored what Durkheim took to be personal inequalities:

> The division of labour only produces solidarity if it is spontaneous, and to the degree that it is spontaneous. But spontaneity must mean not simply the absence of any deliberate, formal type of violence, but of anything that may hamper, even indirectly, the free unfolding of the social force each individual contains within himself .... In short, labour only divides up spontaneously if society is constituted in such a way that social inequalities express precisely natural inequalities.[26]

Thus, Durkheim's 'normal' division of labour is a 'perfect meritocracy' produced by the eradication of personal inheritance.[27] For the division of labour to engender solidarity, society must allocate functions based on ability, not class or hereditary tendencies, so that 'The sole cause then determining how labour is divided up is the diversity of abilities.'[28]

The third factor responsible for 'abnormal' development of the division of labour is mismanagement of functions in society. Durkheim believed that when functions are faltering or are badly coordinated with one another, individuals are unaware of their mutual dependence, and this lessens social solidarity. Thus, if work is insufficient, as a result of mismanagement and organization, Durkheim argues that solidarity, 'is itself naturally not only less than perfect, but may even be more or less completely missing.'[29]

In addition, if class-based social inequalities are imposed on groups, it not only forces the division of labour but also undermines social linkages. It means that individuals are mismatched to their functions, linkages between individuals are disrupted, and this creates inequitable forms of exchange. In the absence of restraint from a centralized authority (either the state or the government), there is disequilibrium, which leads to instability and conflict. For Durkheim, most of the pathologies of the new industrial order were attributed to the prevalence of anomie.

In sum, while Marx's critique was directed at capitalism, Durkheim's critique was aimed not at the essence of capitalism but at industrialism. Whereas Marx is against fragmentation of work and for the reintegration of skills, Durkheim is for the expansion of specialization in line with individuals' 'natural' abilities. Although the concepts of alienation and anomie lead to significantly different analysis and political results, and are different too in their assumptions about human nature, the two concepts have been compared by sociologists. For Marx, alienation results from certain kinds of social control; on the other hand, according to Durkheim anomie results from the absence of social control. While Marx's solution to the crisis of capitalism is dependent on the state or government, Durkheim argued that centralized government was too far removed from the everyday experience of people to play this role. He believed mediating organizations would form the primary mode of social organization. For Durkheim, the crisis of modern society is a moral one, caused by a lack of social unity. The solution therefore is achieved by socially regulated institutions coupled with an ever-widening division of labour. He believed this would facilitate the development of individual potential, and create a future utopia. The process of social change was to be evolutionary, not revolutionary.

In this chapter we cannot provide a thorough critique of Durkheim's theory of the relationship between increasing differentiation and specialization of labour, and transformative social change. However we must critically assess some of his assumptions: for example, those about 'natural' inequalities. He regarded men as more intelligent than women, and industrial workers as more intelligent than farmers. Durkheim also assumed that the gender-based domestic division of labour was a good example of the social harmony generated when social inequalities were allowed to mirror 'natural' inequalities. His assumptions about gender relations provoked the beginnings of a critique of patriarchy.[30]

Go to the following website for more information on Durkheim:
www.relst.uiuc.edu/durkheim/summaries/forms.html

WEB LINK

plate 9 Max Weber
c.1896–97

By an unknown German photographer ©Private Collection/
Archives Charmet/The Bridgeman Art Library

Max Weber (1864–1920)

Max Weber's work is broad and wide-ranging, and has been much misrepresented. It is often assumed to be a dialogue with the ghost of Marx, but that does not do justice to it. He wrote on a wide range of topics including art, architecture and music; he examines the role of ideology in social change; and he explores the emergence and nature of modernity. His contribution to the study of work and work organizations is extensive. The main contributions he made are, first, his theory concerning the rise of capitalism; second, his arguments concerning rationality, the nature of bureaucracy and authority; third, his theory of social class and inequality; and fourth, his methodology and theory of knowledge.

The rise of capitalism and rationalization

Weber's interpretation of the rise of capitalism in the West is presented in his best-known work, *The Protestant Ethic and the 'Spirit' of Capitalism* (written in 1905),[31] which links the rise of modern capitalism to Protestant (or more precisely Calvinist) religious beliefs and practices. Briefly, he argued that a new attitude to work and the pursuit of wealth was linked to the rise of Calvinism. In this attitude, work became a means of demonstrating godliness, and Weber saw this cultural shift as associated with the rise of 'rational' capitalism itself.

According to Weber, while Catholics believed they could secure their place in heaven through (among other things) 'good works' on behalf of the poor or by performing acts of faith on earth, Calvinism developed a set of beliefs around the concept of predestination, which broke the hold of tradition. It was believed by followers of Calvin that it was already decided by God ('predestined') whether they would go to heaven (as one of the 'elect') or hell after their death. They had no means of knowing their ultimate destination, and also no means of altering it. This uncertainty led Calvinists to search for signs from God, since naturally they were anxious to be among the elect. Wealth was taken as a manifestation that they were one of God's elect, and this encouraged followers of Calvin to apply themselves rationally to acquiring wealth. They did this through their ascetic lifestyles and hard work.

The distinctive features of 'rational capitalism' that Weber identified – limits on consumption, especially luxury consumption, and a tendency to reinvest profits in order to systematically accumulate more wealth – had a clear similarity to the Calvinist lifestyle. While Weber did not believe Calvinism was the cause of the rise of industrial capitalism, he did believe that capitalism in part grew from Calvinism. Contrary to Marx, Weber argued that the development of rational capitalism cannot be explained through wholly material and structural forces; the rise of modern Western society was embedded in the process of rationalization.

Rationalization

Central to Weber's analysis of the rise of capitalism and new organizational forms is this concept of rationalization. But what did he mean by this term? Weber's use of rationality is complex and multifaceted. He used the term to describe the overall historical process 'by which nature, society and individual action are increasingly mastered by an orientation to planning, technical procedure and rational action'[32] For Weber, all societies exhibit rationality, in that all people can explain the basis of their behaviour, but only in the West does a particular type of rationality, based on capitalization, bureaucracy, and calculation, become dominant. The essence of the concept consisted of three facets: secularization, calculability and rational action.

Rationality means the decline of magical interpretations and explanations of the world. Scientific models of nature and human behaviour are good examples of this type of rationalization, which involves calculating maximum results at minimum cost. It means the replacement of 'traditional' action by 'rational' action. Rationalization depends on two types of activities: strategies of human action, and modification of the means and ends of action in the pursuit of goals. Rather than doing things for emotional reasons, people do things because they calculate that the benefits will outweigh the cost, or because they assess the action as the most efficient way to achieve their goals. Human actions are also guided by the use of rational decision making in pursuit of unlimited profit. Rules are obeyed because they appear to be built upon rational principles and common sense. In the business sphere, for example, technical and managerial rules are obeyed because they result in efficiency and profits.

Rationalization is different from rationality. Rationalization, the principal process of modernity, refers to the overall process by which reality is increasingly mastered by calculation and rational action, while rationality refers to the capacity of human action to be subject to calculation about means and ends.

Four types of rationality have been identified in Weber's work: practical, theoretical, formal and substantive:

▷ *Practical rationality* assumes there are no external mystical causes affecting the outcome of human actions, and sees reality in terms of what is given.
▷ *Theoretical or technical rationality* involves a cognitive effort to master the world through causality, logical deduction and induction. This type of rationality allows individuals to understand the 'meaning of life' by means of abstract concepts and conceptual reasoning.
▷ *Formal rationality* refers to the accurate calculation procedures that go into decisions, to ensure consistency of outcome and efficiency in attaining goals.
▷ *Substantive rationality* refers to the degree to which human action is guided or shaped by a value system, regardless of the outcome of the action. Accordingly, 'Where formal rationality involves a practical orientation of action regarding outcomes, substantive rationality involves an orientation to values.'[33]

While these four different rationalization processes can complement each other, they can also conflict. For example, the pursuit of efficiency and productivity by calculating the 'best' means to achieve a given end (formal rationality) sometimes conflict with ethical behaviour (substantive rationality). When examined through a substantive lens, formal rationality is often irrational. In his book, *The McDonaldization of Society*, George Ritzer makes a strong case that formal rationality, embodied in standardized fast-food products, undermines values of social responsibility and individualism in pursuit of efficiency. In the early

rationality: the process by which traditional methods of social organization, characterized by informality and spontaneity, are gradually replaced by efficiently administered formal rules and procedures – bureaucracy

corporate social responsibility
(CSR): an organization's moral
obligation to its stakeholders

bureaucratization: a tendency
towards a formal organization
with a hierarchy of authority,
a clear division of labour and
an emphasis on written rules

twenty-first century, rationalization shapes the subjective experiences of peoples, as they understand and evaluate climate change and global warming in terms of non-sustainable growth, profit maximization and corporate social responsibility.

Bureaucracy

According to Weber, bureaucratization is an inescapable development of modern society. Weber's analysis of the development of capitalism was similar to that of Marx, in that he believed that the rise of capitalism has been marked by the centralization of production, by increased specialization and mechanization, by the progressive loss by workers of the means of production, and an increase in the function and growth of management. With centralized production all human activity gives way to more systematic, rational and extensive use of resources, including labour, which is facilitated by calculable techniques like accounting. Weber's contention was that 'Where capitalist acquisition is rationally pursued, the corresponding action is oriented towards the calculation of capital. In other words, such action takes place within a planned utilization of material or personal output.'[34]

According to Weber, bureaucracies are goal-oriented organizations, administered by qualified specialists, and designed according to rational principles in order to efficiently attain the stated goals. In his *Economy and Society*, written in 1921, Weber explained that 'Bureaucracy ... is fully developed in the private economy only in the most advanced institutions of capitalism.'[35] He also noted that as the complexity of modern society increases, bureaucracies grow. He defined the bureaucratic 'ideal type' by these characteristics: business is continually conducted, there are stipulated rules, individual spheres of competence are structured in a hierarchy, offices (that is, positions at work) are not owned, selection and promotion is through proven ability, and rewards are commensurate with people's qualifications, ability and performance.

formalization: the degree to
which organizations standardize
behaviour through rules,
procedures, formal training
and related mechanisms

Two core ideas underscore Weber's concept of bureaucracy: formal rationality and formalized decision making. Formal rationality operates on the principles of expert knowledge and calculability, whereas formalized decision making operates on the basis of set procedures. This means decisions can be judged as correct or otherwise by reference to a body of rules. It would be a misrepresentation of Weber to assume that he was an avid supporter of bureaucracy. Weber was not unaware of the dysfunctions of any over-formalized work form. Bureaucracy removes workers from the decision-making process. It consists of rational and established rules, and restricts individual activity. As a result it can resemble an 'iron cage', and it can mean that organizational behaviour becomes less and less regulated by ethical principles, as these are replaced by technical means and ends.[36] Weber's argument is that because bureaucratic work forms remove workers, including white-collar and managerial staff, from ownership of the means of production, there is a loss of democracy in the workplace, and a panoply of managerial control measures are then necessary to keep the workers in line.[37]

Types of authority

All systems of work require a minimum of 'voluntary compliance', and some mechanism of coordination and control over the activity. This compliance, which is defined as 'an interest in obedience'[38] of the subordinate controlled (such as a worker) to the dominant controller (such as a manager), is based on the ulterior motives of the subordinate, which are governed by custom and a material calculation of advantage, and her or his perception of the employment relationship.

Weber's analysis of authority relations provides another insight into the changing structure of work systems. Weber used the terms 'domination' and 'authority' interchangeably in *Economy and Society*. Both derive from the German term *Herrschaft*, which points to leadership, and his theory of domination does have direct relevance to theories of organizational leadership (see Chapter 11). However, Weber did make a distinction between power and domination. He defined power as the ability to impose one's will on others in a given situation, even when the others resist. Domination, or authority, is the right of a controller to issue commands to others and expect them to be obeyed. Underscoring Weber's study of authority is his concern for 'legitimacy'. Essentially, he was interested in knowing on what basis subordinates actively acknowledge the validity of authority figures in an established order, and give obedience to them, and on what basis men and women claim authority over others.

> **power:** A term defined in multiple ways, involving cultural values, authority, influence and coercion as well as control over the distribution of symbolic and material resources. At its broadest power is defined as a social system which imparts patterned meaning.

Subordinates and the controlled obey dominant controllers by custom and for material advantage and reward, but a belief in legitimacy is also a prerequisite. Weber pointed out that each authority system varies '[a]ccording to the kind of legitimacy which is claimed, the type of obedience, the kind of administrative staff developed to guarantee it, and the mode of exercising authority.'[39] He then went on to propose three types of legitimate authority: traditional, rational-legal and charismatic. All types of authority, however, require a managerial system characterized by efficiency and continuity.

Traditional authority is based on the sanctity of tradition and the legitimacy of those exercising authority under such regimes. It is usually acquired through inheritance: for example, this is the kind of authority held by kings and queens in monarchies. Compliance rests on a framework of obligations that bind followers to leaders by personal loyalties.

Rational-legal authority is derived from the rationality of the authority. For example, car drivers usually obey traffic laws because they appear to make sense, not because police officers have some inherited authority or are charismatic.

Charismatic authority refers to an attribute or exceptional quality possessed by an individual. In charismatic domination, the leader's claim to legitimacy originates from his or her followers' belief that the leader is to be obeyed because of her/his extraordinary attributes or powers of inspiration and communication.

Weber's typology of authority is important in understanding why individuals behave as they do in the workplace. He was one of the earliest social theorists who saw domination as being characteristic of the relationship between leaders and followers, rather than an attribute of the leader alone.

Social class, inequality and types of class struggle

Authority is equated to possessing power, and difference in the degree of power is one factor that gives rise to differentiated social classes. Weber's description of social class was similar to Marx's, in that he defined a social class by property ownership and by market relations. He stated that:

> a class is a number of people having in common a specific causal component of their life chances. This component is represented exclusively by economic interests in the possession of goods and opportunities for income, under the conditions of the commodity or labour markets.[40]

However, whereas Marx had proposed that individuals carry forward their class interests by virtue of dominant economic forces, Weber argued that the 'mere differentiation of property classes is not "dynamic", that is, it need not result in class struggles and revolutions'.[41] He argued instead that the complex and multi-dimensional nature of social stratification in modern society necessarily inhibits the acquisition of the degree of class consciousness that is necessary for a revolution to occur.

In this argument, people who experience inequality and who have a degree of political consciousness are much more likely to form to rational associations (such as trade unions and social democratic political parties) that would thrust them to the forefront of political activity, than to start a revolution. Under these conditions there are no class interests as such, only the 'average interests' of individuals in similar economic situations, and therefore the class struggle and revolution predicted by Marx are extremely unlikely to happen. Instead, the nature of class conflict changes in a modern society in two fundamental ways. First, there is a shift from direct confrontation between the owners of capital and workers to mediated pay disputes, and second, conflicts between social classes are resolved through the courts and legal means.

Weber's methodology

Between 1902 and 1903, Weber wrote two papers which were central to shaping his views about the nature of doing research in the social sciences, and which continue to influence contemporary inquiry into work and behaviour in the workplace. Let us look at two concepts he developed, ideal types and *Verstehen*.

ideal type: an abstract model that describes the recurring characteristics of some phenomenon

empiricism: an approach to the study of social reality that suggests that only knowledge gained through experience and the senses is acceptable

The ideal type is one of Weber's best-known contributions to contemporary organizational theory. At its most basic level, an ideal type is a theoretical abstraction constructed by a social scientist, who draws out important characteristics and simultaneously suppresses less important characteristics. It can be viewed as a measuring rod or yardstick, whose function is to compare empirical reality with preconceived notions of a reality. Weber put it like this: 'It functions in formulating terminology, classifications, and hypotheses, in working out concrete causal explanation of individual events.'[42] As a methodological construction, ideal types are neither ideal nor typical. That is, they are not ideal in any evaluative sense, nor are they typical because they do not represent any norm. They merely approximate reality. To put it differently, ideal types are heuristic devices (teaching aids) which are used to study slices of reality and to enable us to compare empirical forms. Organizational theorists refer for example to an 'ideal type of bureaucracy' or 'ideal flexibility'.

Verstehen: method of understanding human behaviour by situating it in the context of an individual's or actor's meaning

The second concept, *Verstehen*, we introduced when we discussed research methods in Chapter 1. Weber believed that social scientists must look at the actions of individuals and examine the meanings attached to these behaviours. His approach to understanding human behaviour suggests that observational language is never theoretically independent of the way the observer sees a phenomenon, and the questions he or she asks about the action. As a consequence, an individual researcher's interpretation of human activity is an inherent aspect of knowledge about organizational behaviour. Weber's 'interpretative' methodology is based on *Verstehen*, meaning 'human understanding'. Human subjects, in contrast to the objects studied in the natural sciences, always rely on their 'understanding' of each other's behaviour and on the 'meanings' they assign to what they and others do.

This interpretive approach to studying reality is best illustrated by distinguishing between someone walking in a park as a pleasurable leisure experience, and someone walking in a park in an aimless way to kill time because he or she is unemployed and bored. The outer behaviour is exactly the same but the inner state of the two people is different. It is difficult for a researcher to understand and explain the fundamental distinction between the inner states of the employed and unemployed (in this case) just by observing their outer states, or behaviour. We need an interpretive understanding in order to give a convincing analysis of what is seen.

Weber's theories have been challenged. For instance, it is argued that the earliest examples of rational capitalism are not restricted to Calvinist

Go to this website for more information on Weber:
www.marxists.org/reference/archive/Weber

WEB LINK

or even Protestant nations. Some Calvinist countries, such as Scotland, failed to 'take off' as capitalist industrialized nations, and some Catholic nations, such as Belgium, were among the market leaders.

As our review of the theories of work moves from the classical sociological theories of the 'big three' – Marx, Durkheim and Weber – to contemporary perspectives on work organizations, we will be better equipped to see how these classical theories continue to inform contemporary theories of work, organizational design and managerial behaviour.

Contemporary theories of work organizations

Organizational studies constitute a discipline in itself, with a plethora of alternative theoretical perspectives. In recent years, different theoretical approaches to studying work and organizations have forced organizational theorists to re-examine and be more reflexive about organizational 'knowledge'. With these changes, as Clegg and Hardy put it, 'Gone is the certainty about what organizations are; gone, too, is the certainty about how they should be studied.'[43] In this chapter we cannot hope to do justice to the complexities of the bewildering variety of perspectives, and we shall therefore seek to highlight what Clegg and Hardy call the major 'conversations' in organizational studies.

How we represent these conversations always involves a choice concerning what theories we wish to represent and how we represent them. To help, we have drawn a schema of organizational theories. The competing theories are plotted along two interlocking axes: the horizontal critical-managerial axis and the vertical positivist-interpretivist axis (see Figure 3.1).

The critical-managerial axis represents the political left/right continuum (see Chapter 1). At one extreme, the managerial pole positions those perspectives that are essentially concerned with issues of organizational efficiency and performance.

Can you think of any workplace studies that have based their findings on data gathered through observing people in the workplace? How should the interpretative method affect your evaluation of the studies?

STOP AND REFLECT

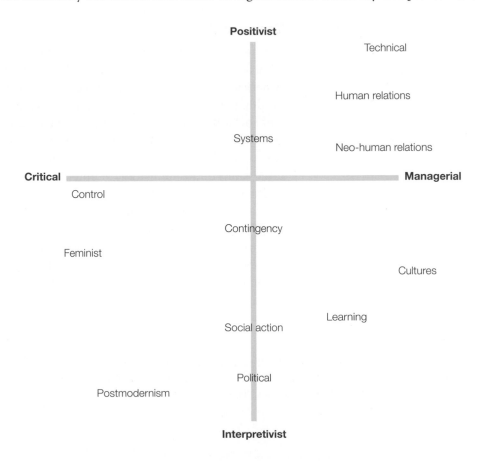

figure 3.1 Contemporary theories of work organizations

Thus, researchers adopting this approach have tended to develop theoretical frameworks and generate empirical data aimed at understanding organizational structures, work arrangements and social processes that can improve labour productivity and organizational effectiveness, or can help solve people-related 'problems' in the workplace. As we explained in Chapter 1, this particular framework is often viewed as mainstream thinking in OB texts. At the other extreme, the critical pole, are critical explanations of work and organizational behaviour that have traditionally been concerned with issues of exploitation and the alienating effects of dividing and routinizing paid work. Researchers adopting this perspective tend to conceptualize organizational structures and management behaviour as control mechanisms that function to fulfil economic imperatives.

The positivist-interpretivist axis affirms the importance of epistemological considerations when conducting research: what is (or should be) regarded as acceptable knowledge in organizational behaviour theory. The axis distinguishes between the doctrines of 'positivism' and 'interpretivism'. The positivist epistemological position is generally taken to involve the application of natural science research methods to the study of work organizations, as we saw in Chapter 1. It puts emphasis on the scientific and technical way in which organizational activities can be studied and assessed (using goals, efficiency ratios, rational decision making, productivity measures and so on). In contrast, the interpretivist position maintains that human behaviour is not fully controllable, and therefore a research strategy for organizational behaviour must respect the differences between people and inanimate objects. For interpretivists, the role of the social scientist is to grasp the subjective meaning of behaviour or social action. Researchers focus on the indeterminate and contingent nature of social reality, the unintended consequences of human action, and the influence of interpretation. Where these 12 conversations or theories are plotted on the 'map' is clearly a matter of interpretation and subject to dispute; here the map's function is to act as a heuristic device.

Technical

The 'technical' approach to studying work organizations is most closely associated with the work of Fredrick Winslow Taylor (1865–1915). Taylor, an engineer at an American steel mill, experimented with work arrangements to improve labour productivity. Taylor's work configuration rests upon the principle of the technical and social division of mental and manual labour. The technical division of labour generally refers to how a complex task is broken down into component parts. Adam Smith's classic observations on pin manufacturing[44] give us one of the first discussions of this in relation to potential increases in labour productivity.

The social division of labour refers to issues of which individuals occupy specific positions in the technical division of labour, how, why and for how long. In addition, scientific management, or Taylorism (as it became known), involved the following five principles: maximum job fragmentation, the separation of planning and doing, the separation of direct and indirect labour, minimum skill requirements and minimum material handling (see Chapter 2). These five job design principles gave to management 'the collective concept of control'.[45]

scientific management: involves systematically partitioning work into its smallest elements and standardizing tasks to achieve maximum efficiency

Other important theorists contributing to this organization studies genre were Henry Gantt (1856–1915), a protégé of Taylor, who designed the Gantt chart, a straight-line chart to display and measure planned and completed work as time elapsed, Frank Gilbreth (1868–1924), who helped to improve labour productivity

Go to the following websites for more information on Taylorism and Fordism: www.onepine.info/ptaylor.htm; www.nationmaster.com/encyclopedia/Taylorism; www.nosweat.org.uk; http://nationmaster.com/encyclopedia/Fordism

WEB LINK

through pioneering use of time and motion techniques, and Henry Ford (1863–1947), who perfected the application of the principles of scientific management to assembly-line production, an approach others would later call 'Fordism'. For most of the twentieth century the essential principles of Taylorism and Fordism represented a 'common-sense' management strategy in North America and Western Europe.[46]

Human relations

human relations: a school of management thought that emphasizes the importance of social processes in the organization

Disenchantment with the technical approach to work and organizational design led to the development of the human relations school of thought. Data gathered at the Hawthorne plant of the Western Electric Companies – subsequently known as the Hawthorne studies – suggested a positive association between labour productivity and management styles. The phenomenon can be explained like this: 'The determinants of working behaviour are sought in the structure and culture of the group, which is spontaneously formed by the interaction of individuals working together.'[47]

Elton Mayo is most closely associated with the Hawthorne studies. Another pioneering management theorist, Mary Parker Follet, is associated with the early human relations management (HRM) movement. She contended that traditional authority as an act of subordination was offensive to an individual's emotions, and therefore could not serve as a good foundation for cooperative relations in the workplace. Instead, Follet proposed an authority function, whereby the individual has authority over her or his own job area.[48]

The Hawthorne studies have been criticized at both the technical and political levels. Technically, it has been contended that the researchers used a 'rudimentary' research design and their analysis of the data was faulty. At a political level, charges of managerial bias, insularity from wider socioeconomic factors, neglect of workers' organization (that is, trade unions) and organizational conflict were effectively levelled against the researchers. The critique included the charge that human relations theorists conceptualized the 'normal' state of the work organization in 'romantic' and harmonious terms, and neglected workplace conflict because of their pro-management bias.[49]

Despite the criticisms, the Hawthorne studies provided the impetus for a new 'common-sense' management strategy – 'neo-human relations' – which focused on a paternalistic style of management, emphasizing workers' social needs as the key to harmonious relations and better performance, albeit this was narrowly conceived. Prominent contributors to human relations theory were Abraham Maslow (1908–1970) with his idea of 'self-actualization' needs, and Douglas McGregor (1906–1964), with his Theory X and Theory Y approach to work motivation (see Chapter 9). These contributions to organizational studies promoted five principles of 'good' work design: closure, whereby the scope of the job includes all the tasks to complete a product or process; task variety, whereby the worker learns a wider range of skills to increase job flexibility; self-regulation, allowing workers to assume responsibility for scheduling the work and quality control; social interaction to allow cooperation and reflectivity; and continuous work-based learning.[50]

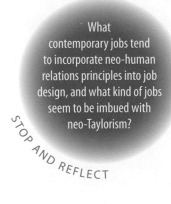

What contemporary jobs tend to incorporate neo-human relations principles into job design, and what kind of jobs seem to be imbued with neo-Taylorism?

STOP AND REFLECT

Systems theory

Systems theory has played, and continues to play, an influential part in attempts to analyse and explain work organizations. Systems theory involves providing holistic explanations for social phenomena, with a tendency to 'treat societies or social wholes as having characteristics similar to those of organic matter or organisms'.[51] It shows the relationships and interactions between elements, and these in turn are claimed to explain the behaviour of the whole. The notion of 'system' is associated with 'functionalism', and the work of Talcott Parsons (1902–1972). Parsons used a system model that was designed to demonstrate how formal organizations carry out a necessary set of functions to ensure survival.[52] The Parsonian model was also adopted by Dunlop to explain rule-bound behaviour among all major actors within the industrial relations system: unions, management and government.[53] Peter Senge's elaboration of systems thinking provides insight into 'personal mastery', team learning and 'shared vision'.[54] A systems perspective is also used to examine the multidimensional and changing nature of the work context.[55]

Figure 3.2 shows a systems model, with a set of interrelated and interdependent parts configured in a manner that produces a unified whole. That is, any working system takes inputs, transforms them, and produces some output. Systems may be classified as either 'closed' or 'open' to their environment. Work organizations are said to be open systems, in that they acquire inputs from the environment (such as materials, energy, people, finance), transform them into services or products, and discharge outputs in the form of services, products and sometimes pollutants to the external environment.

open systems: organizations that take their sustenance from the environment, and in turn affect that environment through their output

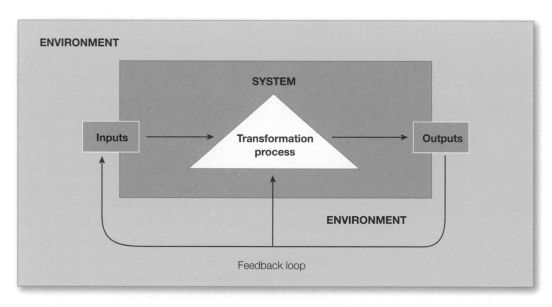

figure 3.2
An open system

The open-system model emphasizes that management action is not separate from the world but is connected to the wider context. That is, 'The existing internal structure, strategy, and success of an organization is heavily influenced by environmental forces in which it operates and with which it interacts and competes.'[56] However, it is too simple to regard the influence of context as a one-way flow only. Systems thinking is closely linked to the Weberian notion of the paradox of consequences in organizational life. A systems approach can illustrate how managerial behaviour and actions designed to advance a goal or solve a problem have unintended consequences which undermine or exacerbate the problem.[57]

This kind of systems or functionalist thinking highlights the apparent functions of different work organizations. But the system has its critics. Detractors emphasize that systems analysis reifies organizations: in other words, it treats a concept as if it was a real thing. To assert that organizations make decisions implies that organizations have an existence beyond their human members, but it can be argued that this is not so: organizations are merely legal constructs. (See the discussion on page 7.) So when we talk of organizations 'making decisions' we really mean that some or all of the dominant controllers of an organization make the decisions.

Second, systems theory suggests a greater degree of stability and order in organizations than might actually exist across time. Third, systems theories tend

Can you think of an example from your own work experience of the paradox of consequences? What did management do, and what was the unintended outcome(s)?

STOP AND REFLECT

to downplay the significance of historical developments to explain contemporary organizational phenomena. And finally, the essential thrust of functionalism or systems analysis is towards consensus. It is inherently deterministic: it 'is not only technocratic in its denial of conflicting ideologies and material interests but also deterministic in its pursuit of the correct prediction of behaviour through an analysis of organizational rules'.[58]

Contingency theory

Contingency theory focuses on the three-way relationship between structure, contingency and outcomes, and has proved to be one of the most influential of all organizational theories. Contingency, as it applies to work organizations, means that the effectiveness of a particular strategy, structure or managerial style depends on the presence or absence of other factors or forces. Accordingly, there are no absolutely 'one best' strategies, structures or styles. Instead, whether an action is 'best' must be gauged relative to the context, the circumstances or the other factors.

The most noted contingency research was conducted over 40 years ago.[59] Joan Woodward, for example, found there was no best way of organizing production, but that a particular organizational design and managerial style of behaviour was most appropriate for each technological situation (for example, worker-oriented production as found in car assembly compared with process production as found in a chemical plant). She reported that organizations differed not only in the general character of their structure and technology, but also in such detailed respects as managerial behaviour, methods of inter-management communication, and interactions. In some organizations studied, 'it was not always easy to distinguish between those who gave and those who took orders'.[60]

The British writers Burns and Stalker suggested that organizational structures and managerial behaviours differed according to a range of environments differentiated by their degree of predictability and stability. Management styles would tend to be different in what they called 'mechanistic' or 'organic' systems. The American researchers Lawrence and Lorsch developed contingency analysis, by showing the importance of establishing integrative mechanisms to counter the centrifugal forces that differentiate and fragment managers and non-managers alike.

For dominant controllers of work organizations, the appeal of a contingency perspective is in part because the 'if-then' formula represents an explicit fracture with the simpler 'one best way' approach, while offering persuasive normative guidelines for what organizational leaders should do to sustain organizational performance. Where the contingency approach is most vulnerable to criticism is in its construction of independent variables, and this is why it is positioned close to the determinist line. The various studies argue that although some degree of contingency exists, in so far as controllers can choose between different forms of organizational structure, only those who chose the most 'appropriate' structure are likely to be successful. Others have noted the role of 'environmental determinism', and the removal of contingency by specifying the external conditions under which success can be determined: 'environments are not only given determinate power ... but they are literally reified through the language of environments acting on passive organizations'.[61]

Culture theory

The notion of applying 'cultural' thinking to organizational studies is derived from Durkheimian concerns for organizational solidarity through ideological consensus, and from Mayo's pronouncements on the connections between the emotional needs of individuals and the organizational need for integration. Organizational culture consists of the shared beliefs, values and assumptions that exist in an organization. Typically the approach is interpretive to the extent that managers are free to interpret and develop a specific form of organizational culture.

This approach tends to be normative: that is, it is intended to explain not so much what the contemporary culture of an organization is, but what it should be. Thus, it may well persuade managers to act as if the preferred cultural attributes already existed, so the acting out of a cultural myth becomes the organizational reality.[62] A less manipulative approach to the significance of organizational cultures is provided by Gareth Morgan.[63] According to Morgan, the study of organizational behaviour uses metaphors. The use of metaphors is one of a number of well-established techniques used by sociologists to conceptualize a complex social reality and to engage their audiences.[64]

Morgan believes that how we define, understand and conceptualize organizations depends on our images or mental models of the essential shape, artefacts and features of organizations. He has argued that most definitions and theories of work organizations can be associated with a particular organizational metaphor. The most common metaphors view organizations as cultures, organisms, an iron cage, machines, networks or learning systems. These metaphors are embedded in various theories of organizational behaviour.

Charles Handy has suggested that 'role cultures', which are typically found in large bureaucracies, exude rationality, specialization, routines and rule following.[65] Generally speaking, he suggests that the larger an organization, the more expensive its technology, and the more routine its environment, the more likely it will be to adopt a role culture.

Edgar Schein identifies three levels of organizational culture, shown in Table 3.1.[66] The first level of culture is the artefacts that can be seen, heard and touched – in other words, sensory perception. For example, artefacts include the architecture, observable rituals (for instance, in universities the ritual of graduating at a convocation ceremony) and language. The second level of culture is the espoused values, which refer to the normative aspects of the organization. They communicate to organizational members and users what ought to be rather than what is. (For instance, universities claim to be 'student-centred' and/or 'research-intensive' institutions, and companies claim they believe in 'life-long learning'.)

table **3.1** Schein's levels of organizational culture

Level	Definition	Examples
Artefacts	Tangible and observable aspects of the workplace	Display cabinets, dress code
Espoused values	Beliefs about what should happen in the organization	Mission statement and goals
Basic assumptions	Taken-for-granted thinking and ways of accomplishing organizational goals	Standard administrative procedures, presumed methods of efficiency or effectiveness

The third level of culture, according to Schein, consists of the core assumptions or the taken-for-granted premises that shape behaviour in the organization. For example, in some universities a basic assumption is made that face-to-face teaching in a classroom is the best learning experience. The whole teaching-learning process revolves around this assumption, and it guides institutional planning and course delivery. Universities specializing in distance and 'open' learning operate around a different assumption, however.

The cultural perspective converges with popular HRM models, which highlight the importance of 'contextual relations' and organizational 'climate' to generate employee commitment.[67] Although the use of metaphor has entered popular culture, we need to be aware of the common error of treating metaphors as literal descriptions of social reality.[68] See Chapter 15 for more discussion on organizational culture, and Chapter 12 on the use of metaphors in organization communications.

Learning theories

The 'learning organization' and 'workplace learning' are two popular, and relatively new, metaphors in organizational studies. A learning organization is one that 'facilitates the learning of all its members and continually transforms itself'.[69] Proponents of management and workplace learning equate the learning organization with organizational economic success.[70] Typically the learning organization approach is interpretive, because it is more closely related to the concept of organizational culture than to something tangible. The focus in a learning organization is on creating an environment that fosters learning through strategies that promote a 'growth-oriented workplace'.[71]

The concept of organizational learning is an influential organizational theory that has attracted scholars from various disciplines. Its origins lie in the work of Argyris and Schon, Cyert, and most recently, it has been popularized in North America by the work of Peter Senge.[72] Learning is driven by external competitive demands, and a learning organization can be understood in terms of its espoused values and operating principles, which seek competitive advantage not only through unique organizational processes but through superior intellectual capital. A learning organization is normally understood as one that is 'good' at learning because of the types of activities it employs. Learning organizations are understood as places where individuals can be 'creative' and where people 'learn how to learn together'. We discuss workplace learning further in Chapter 8.

WEB LINK

Go to the following website for more information on organizational learning: http://www.bond.org.uk/pubs/ol.htm

Social action theory

The most influential contributions to social action theory were those of Silverman.[73] He provided a powerful critique of the reification embodied in systems thinking, and advocated a view of organizations as the product of individuals pursuing their own ends with the available means. He argued that social reality did not just happen, but had to be made to happen. The implication of this was that through social interaction people could modify and possibly even transform social meanings, and therefore any explanation of human activity had to take into account the meanings that those involved assigned to their actions. For example, whether a failure to obey a manager's instruction is a sign of worker insubordination or militancy, or caused by the beginnings of deafness, depends not on what managers or researchers observe to happen, but on what the worker involved means by her or his behaviour. This approach drew from Weber's work on the methodology and theory of knowledge action.

The social action approach involves examining six interrelated areas:

▷ the nature of the role system and pattern of interaction that has developed in the organization
▷ the nature of involvement of 'ideal-typical' actors and the characteristic hierarchy of ends they pursue
▷ the actors' present definitions of their situation within the organization, and their expectations of the likely behaviour of others
▷ the typical actions of different actors, and the meaning they attach to their actions

▷ the nature and source of the intended and unintended consequences of action
▷ any changes in the involvement and ends of the actors and in the role system.[74]

This method of analysing workplace behaviour is influenced by the work of George Herbert Mead (1863–1931) and symbolic interactionism (see Chapter 2). The approach assumes that human beings act towards things on the basis of subject meanings, and these meanings are the product of social interaction in human society. Organizational study, therefore, involves notions of 'symbolic meaning' and 'sense-making' so that individuals can make sense of what they do. Critics have stressed that the micro-level approach of symbolic interactionism does not give sufficient attention to the 'big picture', and the inherent conflict of interest between the key actors representing capital and labour.

Political theory

The political approach to understanding work organizations characterizes the workplace as a purposive miniature society, with politics pervading all managerial work. By politics we mean the power relationships between managers and relevant others, and in turn the capacity of an individual manager to influence others who are in a state of dependence. It refers to those social processes that are not part of a manager's formal role, but that influence (perhaps not directly) the distribution of resources for the purpose of promoting personal objectives.

Developing organizational learning in the UK National Health Service

Learning has been identified as a central concern for a modernized British National Health Service (NHS). Continuing professional development has an important role to play in improving learning, but there is also a need to pay more attention to collective (organizational) learning. Such learning is concerned with the way organizations build and organize knowledge.

The recent emphasis within the NHS has been on the codification of individual and collective knowledge – for example, in guidelines and National Service Frameworks. This needs to be balanced by more personalized knowledge management strategies, especially when dealing with innovative services that rely on tacit knowledge to solve problems. Having robust systems for storing and communicating knowledge is only one part of the challenge. It is also important to consider how such knowledge gets used, and how routines become established in organizations to structure the way in which knowledge is deployed.

In many organizations these routines favour the adaptive use of knowledge, which helps organizations to achieve incremental improvements to existing practice However, the development of organizational learning in the NHS needs to move beyond adaptive (single-loop) learning, to foster skills in generative (double-loop) learning and meta-learning. Such learning leads to a redefinition of the organization's goals, norms, policies, procedures or even structures. However, moving the NHS in this direction will require attention to the cultural values and structural mechanisms that facilitate organizational learning.

Source: Sandra M. Nutley and Huw T. O. Davies.[75]

Politics in organizations is simply a fact of life. However, as others have observed, in many studies of work organizations the political quality of the management practice is 'denied' or 'trivialized'. And although individual managers might privately question the moral value and integrity of their actions, 'Caught in the maelstrom of capitalist organization, managers are pressured to emulate and reward all kinds of manipulative and destructive behaviours.'[76] This perspective to studying organizations offers an approach that examines individual managers as 'knowledgeable human agents' functioning within a dynamic arena where both organizational resources and outcomes can be substantially shaped by their actions. It also reinforces the theoretical and practical importance attached to building alliances and networks of cooperative relationships among organizational members. These negotiating processes shape, and in turn are shaped by, organizational dynamics (see Chapter 14).

An early study of management adopting a political perspective was undertaken by Dalton in 1959.[77] Building on work by Fox,[78] Graham Salaman pronounced the political approach most clearly. Power relations that reflect the social inequality prevailing in the wider society determine the structure of work organizations. Organizations are not independent bodies but embedded into a wider (again political) environment. Further, notions of identity and the part played by organizational life in the construction of both individual and group identity are important.

The political perspective has also drawn attention to the role of 'strategic choice' in shaping organizational structures and management behaviour.[79] The strategic choice approach emphasizes the importance of the political power of dominant coalitions and ideological commitments in explaining variations in managerial policies and behaviour, and ultimately explaining variations in managerial effectiveness and organizational outcomes. The political perspective has been criticized for failing to offer little or no explanation of the asymmetrical nature of power, which is the essence of the 'radical' control perspective on management.

Control theories

At the critical pole of the managerial-critical continuum lie the 'control' theories. Much of this work has its roots in Marx's analysis of capitalism. This approach to work and management has come to be associated with the seminal work of Harry Braverman.[80] Organizational theorists approaching the study of work and organizations from this perspective stress the inherent source of tension in organizations arising from technological rationality.[81] A related focus is the labour process approach, which conceptualizes organizational managers as controlling agents who serve the economic imperatives imposed by capitalist market relations. Managerial control is thus *the* central focus of management activity. According to this perspective, organizational structures and employment strategies are instruments and techniques to control the labour process, to secure high levels of labour productivity and corresponding levels of profitability.

The control perspective views work organizations as hierarchical structures in which workers are deskilled by scientific management techniques and new technology. Managerial behaviour is characterized primarily as control relations: 'organizations are structures of inequality and control'.[82] Such an approach recognizes the existence of inconsistent organizational designs and management practices, and these paradoxical tendencies provide the source of further management strategies that attempt to eradicate the tensions caused by them. The most important of these paradoxes is considered to be the simultaneous desire for control over workers, and cooperation and commitment from them.

The control perspective has also attracted much criticism from both critical and mainstream management theorists. For example, critiques of the deskilling and control thesis draw attention to moderating factors such as markets, worker resistance and batch size.[83]

labour process: the process whereby labour is applied to materials and technology to produce goods and services which can be sold in the market as commodities. It is typically applied to the distinctive labour processes of capitalism in which owners/managers design, control and monitor work tasks so as to maximize the extraction of surplus value from the labour activity of workers

Learning organizations and organizational learning

For a critical review and evaluation of the literature on learning organizations and organizational learning, see

Chapter 4 of *Workplace Learning: A critical introduction*, by John Bratton, Jean Helms Mills and Peter Sawchuk.[84] A review of this literature is also given by Thomas Garavan in an article 'The learning organization: a review and evaluation'.[85]

Feminist theory

Until relatively recently, studying the workplace using a 'feminist' approach has not been a major topic of inquiry. The organizational discourse is still, in the main, a masculine endeavour to illuminate organizational behaviour. For radical feminists, science is not sexless: on the contrary, 'the attributes of science are the attributes of males'.[86] Research about work organizations tends to be both androcentric (focused on males) and ethnocentric (focused on the white Anglo-Saxon culture). One interpretation is that it has focused on the management agenda, and up to now this has consisted largely of 'important' white men in one field (academia) talking to, reflecting on and writing about 'important' white men in another field (organizations).[87]

Theoretically, one of the most important consequences of gender analysis in organizational studies is its power to question research findings that segregate OB from the larger structure of social and historical life. Accordingly, much of the recent work most directly related to the feminist approach requires us to look at the interface between social context and work. It is argued that this shapes and reshapes the employment relationship. We need to look at gender divisions in the labour market, patriarchal power, issues of sexuality and inequality in society and at work, and the interface between home and work (the 'dual role' syndrome). More importantly however, incorporating gender development in the study of organizational studies would represent the life experience of both men and women in a more comprehensive and inclusive way.

Postmodernism

postmodernism: the sociological approach that attempts to explain social life in modern societies that are characterized by post-industrialization, consumerism and global communications

A new focus for organization theory is postmodernism. While traditional writings of organization theory tend to view work organizations as fine examples of human rationality, postmodernists such as Michel Foucault regard organizations as more akin to defensive reactions against inherently destabilizing forces.[88] The postmodernist perspective has its roots in the French intellectual tradition of poststructuralism, an approach to knowledge which puts the consideration of 'reflexivity' and how language is used at the centre of the study of all aspects of human activity. Thus, postmodern perspectives question attempts to 'know' or 'discover' the genuine order of things (what is known as representation). Researchers must possess the ability to be critical of their own intellectual assumptions (that is, exercise reflexivity).

This approach plays down the notion of a disinterested observer, and instead stresses the way in which people's notion of who and what they are – their agency, in other words – is shaped by the discourses which surround them. This is known as decentring the subject. Postmodernists also believe that researchers are materially involved in constructing the world they observe through language (by writing about it). Thus, where modernists perceive history as a grand narrative of human activity, rationality and progress, postmodernists reject the grand narrative and the notion of progressive intent. Clegg and Hardy frame the postmodern approach this way: 'They are histories, not history. Any pattern that is constituted can only be a series of assumptions framed in and by a historical context.'[89]

Michel Foucault's relevance to organizational theory lies in several related spheres.[90] First, he argues that contemporary management controls human behaviour neither by consensus nor by coercion, but rather by systems of surveillance and HRM techniques. Second, he suggests that although an organization is 'constructed by power', its members do not 'have' power. Power is not the property of any individual or group. While modernists see the direction of power flowing downwards against subordinates, and its essence as negative, Foucault argues that power should be configured as a relationship between subjects. It has 'capillary' qualities which enable it to be exercised '*within* the social body, rather than *above* it'.[91] Third, with the ever-increasing expansion of electronic surveillance in the workplace, Foucault offers his own image of an 'iron cage' in the form of the extended panopticon – hidden surveillance.

Postmodernism is a useful way to study work organizations. In particular, the notion of power as a 'web' within which managers and non-managers are held has much to offer. However, its critics have described postmodernism as a reactionary intellectual trend, which amounts to a 'fatal distraction' from engagement with important issues in the increasingly globalized world.[92]

The value of theory about contemporary organizational behaviour

In this chapter we have reviewed the main themes and arguments of both classical and contemporary theories of work. As we explained, the classical theories are derived from the works of Karl Marx, Emile Durkheim and Max Weber, and are an intellectual response to the transformation of society caused by industrial capitalism. A legitimate question for students of OB is, 'Why bother studying sociological classics – three "dead white men"?' We believe an understanding of the classical accounts of work is important because, as others have also argued, the epistemological, theoretical and methodological difficulties that were identified and debated by Marx, Durkheim and Weber remain central to the conduct of contemporary research on organizational behaviour.[93] Those of us who study contemporary work organizations are informed by the 'canonical' writers, and constantly return to them for ideas and inspiration.

In terms of understanding what goes on in the workplace, theory cannot be separated from management practice. It is used both to defend existing management practices and to validate new ways of organizing work, or *doing*. The nature of the employment relationship is clearly an issue of central importance to understanding human behaviour in work organizations. The classical sociologists developed a body of work which directly or by inference provides an account of the relations between employers and employees.

For Marx, conflict is structured into the employment relationship and is, for most of the time, asymmetrical. That is, the power of the employer or agent (manager) typically exceeds that of the workers. Durkheim's work influenced how theorists have studied organizations, and he reminds us that there are multiple ways in which society imposes itself upon us and shapes our behaviour. A number of Weber's concepts also continue to have much relevance in the early twenty-first century. For example, his concept of charismatic domination is prominent in contemporary leadership theories. In addition, Weber's concepts of bureaucracy and rationalization have been applied to the fast-food sector, and exposed the irrationality associated with the paradigm of McDonaldization. Weber's interpretive method, and in particular the researcher's capacity to assign different meanings to shared reality, gives a postmodern ring to his theory. Finally, classical theories enter the contemporary debates on work organization and management practices by reinforcing the message that understanding the nature of the employment relationship necessarily involves considering organizational culture, societal values and norms as well as national institutions. It is through these that individuals acquire a self-identity and the mental, physical and social skills that shape their behaviour both outside and inside the work organization.

Chapter summary

The three founders of the sociology of work all continue to have their contemporary adherents and detractors.

☐ Marx's fascination with class, conflict and the labour process formed the basis for the most popular new approach throughout much of industrial sociology, from the late 1960s to the 1980s. It spawned a complete school of thought in the labour process tradition; but its limitations became more evident as the approach attempted to explain all manner of social phenomena directly through the prism of class.

☐ Durkheim's moral concerns continue to pervade the market economy, and make predictions about human actions that are based on amoral, economically rational behaviour less than convincing. Perhaps where Durkheim has been most vigorously criticized has been in relation to the allegedly cohering effects of an extended division of labour. The mainstream of managerial theories does not support Durkheim on this point: dependency does not generate mutual solidarity.

☐ Weber's theories of rationalization and bureaucracy have never been far from the minds of those analysing the trend towards larger and larger organizations, and the recent movement towards more flexible work organization patterns. Again, however, Weber's over-rationalized approach underestimated the significance of destabilizing and sectional forces within work organizations.

☐ This chapter has reviewed 12 theoretical approaches or conversations on organizational studies: the technical, human relations, neo-human relations, systems thinking, contingency, cultures, learning, control, feminist, social action, political and postmodernist approaches. It adopted a particular form of differentiating between the various theories through an organizational grid based on two axes, managerial-critical and determinist-interpretative. This is a heuristic way of structuring the various possibilities.

Key concepts

alienation	71–2	labour power	70
androcentrism	90	paradox of consequences	50
anomie	74	rationality	77–8
ideal type	80	strategic choice	89

Chapter review questions

1. To what extent has the decline of communism undermined the utility of Marx's ideas?
2. Why was Weber so pessimistic about work when Durkheim and Marx were so optimistic?
3. Do we need theory to explain the way organizations work?

Further reading

Grint, K. (1998) *The Sociology of Work* (2nd edn), Cambridge: Polity Press. Chapters 3 and 4.

Jaffee, D. (2001). *Organization Theory: Tension and change,* Boston, Mass.: McGraw-Hill. Chapters 1 and 2.

Rowlinson, M. (2004) 'Challenging the foundations of organization theory.' *Work, Employment and Society* **18** (3), pp. 607–20.

Swingewood, A. (2000) *A Short History of Sociological Thought.* New York: St. Martin's Press. Chapters 2, 3 and 4.

Chapter case study: Research at Aeroprecision AB

Background

The 11 September 2001 attacks on the World Trade Center and subsequent threats to bomb commercial aircraft caused chaos and delays at public airports throughout Europe and North America. While the costs of extra security affected European airports, not all air travel was equally affected by the events. Increasingly frequent flyers, mostly business executives, are using private aircraft operating from small airports which are devoid of any burdensome security checks and long queues. The fractional ownership of small aircraft has appealed to business executives and the wealthy since 2001. Similar in concept to a holiday timeshare, it involves owners buying a fraction of a plane and sharing it with others. Each owner has the rights to use the plane up to his or her time limit, while a fleet manager handles scheduling details and maintenance. Growth in the fractional jet business has increased the market for small jet aircraft in Europe and North America.

The company

Aeroprecision AB is a medium-sized Swedish company located in Uddevalla, 80 km north of Gothenburg, Sweden. The company has 194 employees, and manufactures fuselage and wing components for companies producing 14-seat and 19-seat jet aircraft. Most shop-floor workers are members of the Swedish Metalworkers' Union (SMU). The company wants to increase production to take advantage of strong demand for its products. Finding skilled workers to implement its plan, however, is the key challenge that Aeroprecision shares with other aerospace companies in this market.

Rumours had been swirling for over a year that Aeroprecision would move out of Uddevalla. The company responded publicly with a statement that it still might invest €2 million to refurbish the plant or expand – if the plant met its productivity and cost-reduction goals.

It was against this backdrop that Yrjö Carlgren, the director of production, sent an illustrated report printed on glossy paper to all local managers. Entitled *'Teams Now and Survive'*, it offered a point-by-point comparison between Aeroprecision and a similar aero parts operation in Poland. It stated that the Aeroprecision operation was a good example of how not to operate, and argued that it would not be possible to implement the plan to meet the productivity goals. 'Low productivity and skill shortages mean it is not financially viable,' Carlgren's report argued. 'With global competition we can no longer assume that the aircraft makers will buy our parts. Cost and quality issues must be managed successfully if we are to avoid outsourcing the work.'

The CEO, Erik Engeström, called for a top-level meeting of the senior management team and representatives of SMU to discuss the productivity plan and Carlgren's report.

Management-union meeting

At this meeting, Carlgren went through some of the main points of the report. He added that the general perception of managers and supervisors was of a motivated workforce enthusiastic about the advantages of working for a quality company. However, there was a culture of 'that's not my job', an attitude that Aeroprecision owed its employees something, and a tendency to take extended breaks and to slack off once quotas were met. 'People are not giving a full day's work for a full day's pay,' he said. He added, 'It's a humbling experience to visit other similar-sized operations abroad and see them outperforming us on nearly every front.'

Erik Engeström explained that the company was exploring ways to reduce costs and improve productivity by introducing work teams. As part of this process, the company had hired a consulting firm to survey the workforce on employees' mental readiness to work in small self-regulated teams. Figure 3.3 shows sample questions the consultants planned to use in the employee survey.

survey: a research method in which a number of respondents are asked identical questions though a systematic questionnaire or interview

►

1 Respondent details

  a) Name ....

  b) Age ....

  c) Trade ....

  d) Supervisor ....

2 Directions: Respond to each statement on the following scale: SD, strong disagree; D, disagree; N, neutral; A, agree; SA, strongly agree

		Amount of agreement				
a.	Employees should make the majority of decisions related to their work	SD	D	N	A	SA
b.	It is possible for employees to take as much pride in their work as if it were their own business	SD	D	N	A	SA
c.	Groups can work effectively without a clear-cut centre of authority	SD	D	N	A	SA
d.	It is worth sacrificing some specialization of labour to give workers a chance to develop multiple skills	SD	D	N	A	SA
e.	Having authority over people is not as important to me as being part of a smooth-working team	SD	D	N	A	SA
f.	Given the opportunity, many workers could manage themselves without much supervision	SD	D	N	A	SA

Scoring and interpretation: Score the answers as 1 through 5, with SD being 1 and SA being 5. Add the numerical value you assigned to each statement and total your scores. The closer your score is to 50, the higher your degree of mental readiness to lead or participate on a work team. If you score is 30 or less, attempt to develop a more optimistic view of the capabilities and attitudes of workers. Start by looking for evidence of good accomplishments by skilled and semi-skilled workers.

Figure 3.3 Aeroprecision AB: Employee attitude survey

Eva Axlid, the HR manager, explained that the completed questionnaire was to be handed into each employee's supervisor's office. 'We see this survey as integral to good HRM practice,' she claimed.

The chief shop steward, Göran Johnsson, accused Aeroprecision of trying to destroy employee morale. He said, 'Every worker knows Swedish business plays the "lower East European wages" card for more profits and to threaten or bully the workforce. We know management wants to beat the workers down.' The second SMU steward accompanying Johnsson, Debbie Deresh, accused the company of using bogus researchers: 'These consultants are paid by you and will take management's side all the time. If you want a real partnership between the union and management in solving the company's problems, let's look at it together.'

Task

Working individually, or in groups, provide a written report for the SMU of the research issues related to the workforce survey.

1. Why might the proposed employee survey raise ethical concerns?
2. How do you think employees will perceive the survey in terms of trust and motivation?
3. How could an academic inquiry on work teams at Aeroprecision AB be conducted?
4. In what ways are politics and power manifested in researching the world of work? ▶

Sources of additional information

Whitfield, K. and Strauss, G. (eds) (1998) *Researching the World of Work*, New York: Cornell University Press.

Visit these websites for guidance on the ethics of conducting workplace research:
www.dhhs.gov (search for workplace ethics)
www.asanet.org (search for ethics)
www.apa.org/ethics/

Visit http://en.wikipedia.org/wiki/Swedish_Industrial_Union for information on trade unions in Sweden.

Note

This case study was written by John Bratton, Thompson Rivers University, Kamloops, Canada.

Web-based assignment

How are we to make sense of the competing assortment of theoretical approaches to organizational behaviour? We address this question here with reference to the classical accounts of sociology and contemporary approaches to studying formal organizations. Our collective experience in teaching and researching aspects of OB has made it clear that the contemporary student of OB cannot understand the discipline without an appreciation of the works of Marx, Weber and Durkheim. In their own way, each addressed the following two fundamental questions:

- What is the source of societal and organizational conflict?
- What is the relationship between consciousness (the 'self' or 'inside') and society or social structure (the 'outside')?

On an individual basis, or working in a small group, visit the following websites and write a brief summary of how Marx, Weber and Durkheim have fundamentally shaped the modern debate about work and organizations.

http://plato.stanford.edu/entries/marx/
www.relst.uiuc.edu/durkheim/summaries/forms.html
www.marxists.org/reference/archive/weber/

OB in films

The film *Roger & Me* (1989), directed by Michael Moore, is a documentary about the closure of General Motors' car plant at Flint, Michigan, which resulted in the loss of 30,000 jobs. The film provides insight into corporate restructuring and US deindustrialization, and details the attempts of the film maker to conduct a face-to-face interview with General Motors chief executive officer Roger Smith. The film also raises questions about values, politics and practical considerations of doing OB research.

Values reflect the personal beliefs of a researcher. Gaining access to organizations, particularly to top managers, is a political process. Access is usually mediated by gatekeepers concerned not only about what the organization can gain from the research, but also about the researcher's motives.

Watch the documentary, and consider these questions:

- Can OB researchers be value-free and objective in their research?
- Who are the gatekeepers in *Roger & Me*? How can gatekeepers influence how the inquiry will take place?

Practical considerations refer to issues about how to carry out OB research: for example, choices of research design or method need to be dovetailed with specific research questions.

- What alternative methods could a researcher use to investigate the closure of General Motors' factory at Flint?

Notes

1   Socrates.
2   Tucker (2002:150).
3   Clayton Christensen, Harvard Business School, quoted by Gordon Pitts, 'Guru puts his theories into practice', *Globe and Mail*, 6 December 6 2003, p. B1.
4   See Salaman (1981), Turner (1999) and Hurst (2005).
5   Clegg and Hardy (1999).
6   Grint (1998).
7   Marx (1867/1970: 178).
8   Ritzer and Goodman (2004: 137).
9   Morrison (1995: 81).
10 Marx (1867/1970: 331).
11 Marx (1867/1970: 356).
12 Marx and Engels (1848/1967: 227).
13 Marx (1867/1970: 433).
14 Marx (1867/1970: 361).
15 Marx (1867/1970: 423–4).
16 Morrison (1995).
17 Marx and Engels (1848/1967: 227).
18 Marx and Engels (1848/1967).
19 Marx and Engels (1848/1967: 46).
20 Durkheim (1893/1997).
21 Durkheim (1893/1997: 85).
22 Durkheim (1893/1997: 85).
23 Durkheim (1893/1997: 333).
24 Durkheim (1893/1997: lii).
25 Durkheim (1893/1997: 310).
26 Durkheim (1893/1997: 313-313).
27 Grint (1998: 97), Salaman (1981: 45).
28 Durkheim (1893/1997: 313).
29 Durkheim (1893/1997: 326).
30 Grint (1998).
31 Weber (1922/1968)
32 Morrison (1995: 218).
33 Morrison (1995: 222).
34 Weber (1905/2002: 359).
35 Weber (1922/1968: 956).
36 Morrison (1995: 297).
37 Weber (1922/1968: 1002).
38 Weber (1922/1968: 212).
39 Weber (1922/1968: 213).
40 Weber (1922/1968: 927).
41 Weber (1922/1968: 303).
42 Weber (1922/1968: 21).
43 Clegg and Hardy (1999: 3).
44 Smith (1776/1982).

45 George (1972: 97).

46 See Braverman (1974), Littler and Salaman (1984), Thompson and McHugh (2006).

47 Mouzelis (1967: 99), quoted by Clegg and Dunkerley (1980: 128).

48 George (1972).

49 Clegg and Dunkerley (1980), Thompson (1989).

50 Bratton et al. (2003).

51 Cohen (1968: 14), quoted in Brown (1992: 41).

52 Parsons (1960).

53 Dunlop (1958).

54 Senge (1990).

55 Scott (2003).

56 Jaffee (2001: 209).

58 Grint (1998: 132–3).

59 Woodward (1958, 1965), Burns and Stalker (1961) and Lawrence and Lorsch (1967).

60 Woodward (1965: 27).

61 Thompson and McHugh (2002: 63).

62 Lopez (2003).

63 Morgan (1997)

64 See Bratton, Grint and Nelson (2005).

65 Handy (1985).

66 Schein (1992).

67 See Rigney (2001) and Crow (2005).

68 For early literature on this, see Etzioni (1988).

69 Lopez (2003).

70 Pedler et al. (1988: 2).

71 See Fenwick (1998), Garavan (1997) and Bratton et al. (2004).

72 Argyris and Schön (1978), Cyert and March (1963), Senge (1990).

73 Silverman (1970).

74 Brown (1992: 158).

75 Nutley and Davies (2001: 35).

76 Alvesson and Willmott (1996: 39).

77 Dalton (1959).

78 Fox (1971).

79 See Child (1972), Pettigrew (1973), Kotter (1979), Kochan et al. (1986).

80 Braverman (1974).

81 Alvesson (1987), Alvesson and Willmott (1992), Clegg and Dunkerley (1980), Habermas (1970, 1971) and Marcuse (1964, 1969).

82 Littler and Salaman (1984).

83 Kelly (1985), Wood (1982) and Bratton (1992).

84 Bratton et al. (2003).

85 Garavan (1997).

86 Sydie (1994: 207).

87 See Townley (1994), Collins (2002).

88 See Grint (1998), Hassard and Parker (1993).

89 Clegg and Hardy (1999: 2).

90 Foucault (1977, 1979).

91 Sheridan (1980: 39), quoted in Grint (1998: 140).

92 Thompson (1993).

93 See Turner (1999), Ray (1999), Craib (1997); Delaney (2004), Smart (2003) and Goodwin and Scimecca (2006).

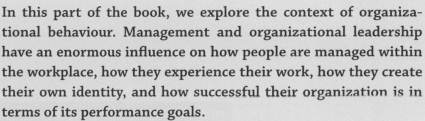

MANAGING ORGANIZATIONS

In this part of the book, we explore the context of organizational behaviour. Management and organizational leadership have an enormous influence on how people are managed within the workplace, how they experience their work, how they create their own identity, and how successful their organization is in terms of its performance goals.

In Chapter 4 we explore the issue of management through a three-dimensional management model that, for analytic purposes, separates management activities and behaviours from contingencies. The issues are grouped into three broad categories: external context, business strategy and organizational design. This model acts as a heuristic device – something to help us understand the world – but it should not be taken as a model of the world itself. It does, however, help us to understand that managers and other employees are not isolated from the rest of society but are deeply embedded in it.

Chapter 5 explains that leadership in organizations is a dialectical process wherein an individual persuades others to do things they would not otherwise do. This is a result of the interaction of the leader and followers in a specific context, and is equated with power. We explain that leadership is not the same as management. Whereas management is associated with certain activities, the leadership process produces change or significant movement.

chapter 4
Management

chapter 5
Leadership

chapter 4
Management

The manager is the dynamic, life-giving element in every business. Without his [sic] leadership the 'resources of production' remain resources and never become production... the quality and performance of the managers determines the success of a business, indeed they determine its survival.[1]

I really do wonder what my bloody job is sometimes .... I'm in charge of this office ... but then I ask whether I'm really in charge of even myself when it comes down to it. I get told to jump here, jump there, sort this, and sort that, more than I ever did before I was even a section leader.[2]

chapter outline

▷ Introduction
▷ The meaning of management
▷ Major perspectives on management
▷ The process of management
▷ Managerial rationality
▷ An integrated model of management
▷ The behaviour of successful managers
▷ Chapter summary
▷ Key concepts
▷ Chapter review questions
▷ Further reading
▷ Chapter case study: Managing changing at Eastern University
▷ Web-based assignment
▷ OB in films
▷ Notes

chapter objectives

After studying this chapter, you should be able to:

▷ define management and explain the main activities of management
▷ explain the competing perspectives on management, including the science, political, labour process and practical perspectives
▷ demonstrate knowledge of why managerial behaviour may vary because of the organization's strategy, structure and environment
▷ explain the meaning of strategic management and describe the three levels of strategy formation
▷ explain how globalization affects management decision making, work and organizational behaviour
▷ understand the significance of managerial work for improving organizational performance.

Introduction

How people behave inside an organization is strongly influenced and shaped by executive management decisions, as well as what happens outside the boundaries of the organization. We saw in Chapter 2 that since the Industrial Revolution, work organization and employment relations have changed profoundly because of decisions by the owners of capital or their agents. As factory owners adopted new work practices and organizations became more bureaucratic, a new occupational group emerged: executives, managers and administrators.

While the term 'executive' refers to an individual who is at the very top of a workplace bureaucracy, typically called the chief executive officer (CEO), and 'administrators' are typically people who perform coordination and leadership roles in government or non-profit organizations, here we use the generic term 'manager' to refer to an occupational group that organizes and coordinates, and makes decisions about what work is done, how it is done, by whom, and all matters relating to production, finance, marketing and human resources.

The development of capitalist production and services and the bureaucratic complexity of the work organization, often with a shareholder-oriented corporate governance structure, encouraged the growth of managers and the professionalization of management. Managers, and especially executives, make decisions based on what is happening in their organization and the external environment. Such decisions affect organizational behaviour. For example, when executives at the electrical giant Philips Electronics make a decision to downsize and lay off workers, managers and other employees who are faced with unemployment might be prepared to change the way they perform their jobs, even if it means an intensification of work and stress. It is important, therefore, to understand there is a relationship between economic stability or instability, management decision making and organizational behaviour.

stress: an individual's adaptive response to a situation that is perceived as challenging or threatening to the person's well-being

The locatedness of managerial work – what the manager acquires from occupying a particular organizational position – is a central theme for some industrial sociologists. The external context, the business strategy pursued by the organization, structural design and control processes, the abilities and attitudes of others in the organization, all affect the way the manager performs managerial activities. Different competitive strategies often require different work configurations, knowledge, learning and practices. And the manager's decisions may be affected by organizational and social factors such as technology, the availability of skilled workers, and past experiences. The manager can adopt a wide array of means to accomplish tasks. These may range from common processes such as communicating, motivating and coercing, to complex technologies. Together, these processes constitute the manager's repertoire for 'getting things done through people', and each individual manager may be more or less skilled in or disposed towards using a particular process.

This example allows us to formulate three key questions that are central to analysing the management process. If management is instrumental, what do managers do? If managerial behaviour is contingent, what affects what they do? And if it is processual, how do managers do it?

Each question has been the focus for research, and will be examined in this chapter. The chapter aims to provide a short overview of the nature of management, and to consider how, with ever-increasing globalization, managerial behaviour affects the behaviour of other employees. (The behaviour of other employees is discussed in other chapters.) We clarify what we mean by the term 'management', and assess the causal connections between 'strategic management' decisions and managerial behaviour in a globalized world. We discuss some recent studies of managerial work that have unsettled the old certainties about the role managers play in organizations, as illustrated by our opening quote from Peter Drucker's seminal text *The Practice of Management*.

STOP AND REFLECT

Go back to Chapter 1 and look at Figure 1.2, 'An integrated framework for studying organizational behaviour' (page 11). Can you think of some recent economic and political events that significantly influence the world of work?

The meaning of management

It is important to note that there are no agreed definitions of the terms 'manager' and 'managerial behaviour'. The definitional problem arises from the difficulties in defining the nature of managerial work in terms of tasks performed. For example, is a home maker a manager?[3] The words 'manage' and 'manager' are derived from the Italian word *maneggiare* – to handle or train horses.[4] To manage suggests taking care of, leading, arranging and so forth. Henri Fayol (1841–1925), regarded as the 'father of modern management', provided the classic definition of management as a series of four key activities that managers must continually perform: planning, organizing, directing and controlling (see Figure 4.1).

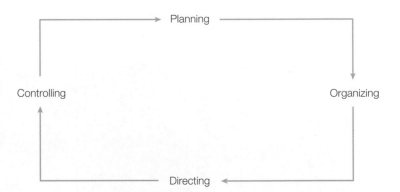

figure 4.1 The classic Fayolian management cycle

Fayol's management cycle presents the job of the manager in a positive way, and to this day, all mainstream management textbooks present management as having four central functions: plan, organize, direct and control – the PODC tradition. For Fayol, planning meant to study the future and draw up a plan of action. Organizing meant coordinating both the material and the people aspects of the organization. Directing refers to ensuring that all efforts focus on a common goal, and controlling means that all workplace activities are to be done according to specific rules and orders.

In a number of ways Fayol's and Frederick Taylor's principles (see Chapter 2) complement each other. For example, they both shared the assumption that employment relations were essentially adversarial – 'a state of war' between employers and employees. While Fayol admonished Taylor against the excesses of specialization and organization of work in minute detail, Fayol's writing lends itself to abusive interpretation, and his work was presented as close to a universal scientific truth.[5]

In Drucker's *The Practice of Management*, management is seen as both a function and a social group. The emergence of management as a social group is seen as one of the most significant events in modern history: 'The emergence of management as an essential, a distinct and a leading institution is a pivotal event in social history.'[6] Management, according to Drucker, is specifically 'charged with making resources productive' in society. Indeed:

> Management expresses basic beliefs of modern Western society. It expresses the belief in the possibility of controlling man's [sic] livelihood through the systematic organization of economic resources. It expresses the belief that economic change can be made into the most powerful engine for human betterment and social justice … its competence, its integrity and its performance will be decisive both to the United States and to the free world.[7]

Management, therefore, takes place within formal organizations, and managers have prescribed roles depending upon whether they have line or staff responsibility. A line manager supervises other employees directly in the production of goods or services. A staff manager, on the other hand, supervises a service – for example, the human resource department – that is necessary to the organization but is not the organization's core strategic or business activity.

As in any area of the social sciences, we find multiple approaches to studying the phenomenon of management, each with a preferred model. For traditional management theorists, such as Peter Drucker, management is a central process through which the organization achieves the semblance of congruence and direction. Sociological studies of management conceptualize management as a process designed primarily to control work activities, which leaves room in the process for uncertainties, paradoxes and conflicts. Sociological writings stress that management is embedded in a hierarchy of power relations, and regard control in organizations as *the* central process relevant to the analysis of management.[8] They take the view that the answer to the question, 'Who is a manager?' depends not on the tasks a

line manager: a manager who is responsible for supervising other employees directly responsible for providing a service or manufacturing goods, such as a production manager. Also known as operating managers.

staff manager: a manager who is responsible for supervising other employees in a department or business unit that services and/or supports line managers and their subordinates, such as an HR manager

plate 10 Mainstream management textbooks present management as having four main functions: planning, organizing, directing and controlling

Source: Getty Images

person undertakes but on his or her social position in the organization's hierarchy. A manager is an organizational member who is 'institutionally empowered to determine and/or regulate certain aspects of the actions of others'.[9] The term 'managerial behaviour' is used here to describe the behaviour or activities of managers, as 'what managers do'.

Major perspectives on management

To study the complex and contradictory nature of management, sociologists have developed various theoretical perspectives. Drawing on our discussion of Figure 3.1 and the work of Watson and Reed,[10] this section explores different analytical approaches to the study of management which will inform our review of the practice of management.

Figure 4.2 shows four major perspectives on management: the science, political, control and practice perspectives.

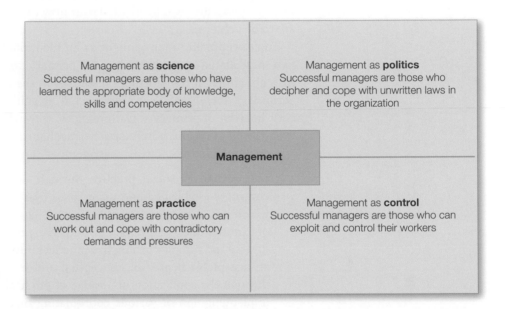

figure 4.2 Four major perspectives on management

The *science perspective* is articulated in the works of Frederick Taylor and Henri Fayol. Management is identified a distinct body of knowledge and managerial activities, from planning to controlling. It offers an idealized image of management as a rationally designed and operationalized tool for the realization of organizational goals. Also, by focusing on the knowledge and skills possessed by an individual manager, management can be analysed as if it was separate from the social context in which it is embedded, leading to the conception of the 'universal manager' performing a set of generalized skills independent of any specific organizational or national context.[11]

The *political perspective* provides a view of management that characterizes the workplace as a purposive miniature society, with politics pervading all managerial work. By 'politics' we mean the power relationships between managers and relevant others, and in turn, the capacity of an individual manager to influence others who are in a state of dependence. This perspective examines individual managers as 'knowledgeable human agents' functioning within a dynamic arena where both resources and outcomes can be substantially shaped by their actions. It reinforces the importance attached to building alliances and networks of cooperative relationships among other managers.

The *control perspective* conceptualizes management as a controlling agent that serves the economic imperatives imposed by capitalist market relations. Managerial control is thus the central focus of management activity. It recognizes the existence of inconsistent organizational designs and managerial behaviour, and these paradoxical tendencies provide the source of further management strategies which attempt to eradicate the tensions these paradoxes cause. The most important of these paradoxes is considered to be the simultaneous desire for control over workers, and cooperation and commitment from them.

The *practice perspective* conceptualizes management as an activity aimed at the continual improvement of diverse, fragmented and usually contested complex practices. It seeks to address the limitations of the first three perspectives by recognizing that management is indeed a science, but at the same time it involves both a political process and control mechanisms. It further acknowledges that organizations 'generate both structural and processual contradictions that will be reflected within management practice'.[12] Managers will be called upon, therefore, to secure subordinates' discipline and consent simultaneously, and given the varied nature of management, they will be divided over how these mutually incompatible objectives are to be achieved.

To conceptualize management as an identifiable 'practice' requires us to define two interrelated 'social practices', the primary and secondary. *Primary social practices* are aimed at transforming resources in the production of goods and services. *Secondary social practices* are directed at achieving the overall integration and coordination of primary social practices, through the design, implementation and monitoring of various administrative mechanisms.

Considered in these terms, management can be defined as:

> that secondary social practice through which administrative regulation and control is established and maintained over those activities and relationships in which non-managerial practitioners are engaged by virtue of their membership of communities of primary productive practice. It is directed at assembling diverse and complex productive practices into institutional structures that exhibit an acceptable degree of conceptual and material coherence. This is achieved through the application of a range of physical and symbolic resources, and the implementation of various coordinating mechanisms through which incipient fragmentation and decay can be temporarily resisted. Consequently, management constitutes both a mechanism through which conflict over the possession and control of resources necessary for primary productive activity can be, at least temporarily, regulated and a process which provides a medium for struggle over the institutional arrangements through which this regulation is achieved.[13]

The theoretical advantage of the practice perspective is that it synthesizes the three key aspects of management – science, process and control – by conceptually reworking and integrating these elements within a model of management as a social unit of reciprocal interaction, which is geared to the job of assembling productive practices through various organizational structures and processes. Within these structures and processes, a system of bureaucratic practices and supporting rationales is constructed to provide the mechanisms by which managers strive to secure control over, and commitment from, organizational members. In other words, they work to ensure that employees are manageable. Managerial behaviour, therefore, inevitably reflects the tension that necessarily arises between maintaining the long-term economic viability of the organization, and the viability of the organization's control techniques on which managers rely to sustain its long-term survival.

What do you think of these four perspectives of management? Go back to Figure 3.1 in Chapter 3. Where would you place the 'practice' perspective on the conceptual schema? Do these four perspectives help us to understand managerial work, and the uncertainties and conflicts found in managing people?

STOP AND REFLECT

Table 4.1 provides a summary of the theoretical perspectives discussed in this section. Taken together, these four distinct perspectives of management suggest that those who attempt to define and describe the management process will find uncertainties, paradoxes and conflicts. Managers cannot avoid these paradoxes; indeed the very nature of managerial work is a manifestation of the contingent and paradoxical quality of managerial behaviour. This analysis reaffirms the need to explore the different dimensions of the management processes.

table 4.1 Theoretical perspectives on management

	Subject matter	**Explanatory model**	**Policy strategy**
1. Science perspective	Rationally designed tool for the realization of instrumental objectives	Systems theory	Enhanced effectiveness of structural design
2. Political perspective	Negotiated social process for the regulation of interest group conflict	Action theory	Improved negotiating skills for practitioners
3. Control perspective	Control mechanism geared to the extraction of maximum surplus value	Marxist theory	Liberate practitioners from distorted view of social reality
4. Practice perspective	Mediating between internal pressures and external demands	Social practice theory	Improved social skills for coping with contradictory demands and pressures

Source: Based on Reed (1989)

The process of management

The purpose of this section is to explore two related questions, 'What do managers do?' and 'Why do managers do what they do?' The third related question, 'How do managers do what they do?' is only briefly explored because it is examined throughout the rest of the book.

The nature of managerial work is an important but amorphous topic in the literature. It is not easy to describe because unlike a professional, for example a medical doctor, who shares common credentials and training with other members of the profession, managers do not necessarily share a common base knowledge, and are defined principally in relation to their employing organization. Management is essentially an integrating and coordinating activity.

Sociologists have developed several ways to study the practice of management, one of which is the behavioural approach. This micro-level approach relies on researchers' observations of how managers choose to carry out their roles, given the diverse range of activities required of them. In order to study the highly complex nature of managerial work, therefore, we draw upon a wide range of competing theoretical perspectives. We examine managerial behaviour and the contingencies affecting managerial behaviour. After reviewing the studies of managerial behaviour, we proceed to answer the more controversial question, 'Why do managers do what they do'? The aim here is to develop a more in-depth understanding of the factors that shape managerial work, and the rationale underlying the adoption of different policies and behaviours.

Since the mid-twentieth century, studies on what managers do have contributed to a comprehensive picture of managerial work. Many studies are in the Fayolian genre: that is, managerial behaviour is represented as a rational, technical, and morally and politically neutral activity. Others present a more nuanced account of the nature of management. Managers seem to have little time for long-term strategic planning because of constant interruptions from others, spend much time building and maintaining a reciprocal network of social relationships, have many brief meetings lasting five minutes or less, managerial work is very contextually specific, and typically managers' work is characterized by brevity, fragmentation and variety. The Swedish researcher Sune Carlson conducted an early European study of managerial work in 1951, when he asked nine Swedish executives to keep a diary of how they spent their time over a period of four weeks.[14] Carlson found that the managing directors had little time for long-term strategic planning because of constant interruptions from subordinates. Another well-known study found that the defining characteristic of managerial work is ad hoc superficiality:

> In effect, the manager is encouraged by the realities of his [sic] work to develop a particular personality – to overload himself with work, to do things abruptly, to avoid wasting time, to participate only when the value of participation is tangible, to avoid too great an involvement with any one issue. To be superficial is, no doubt, an occupational hazard of managerial work. In order to succeed, the manager must, presumably, become proficient in his superficiality.[15]

Studies of what managers actually do during their long, frequently interrupted work days provide us with a clearer picture of the context within which they perform their managerial duties. The best known aspect of Henry Mintzberg's studies[16] is his classification of managerial work into ten roles within three organized sets of behaviours: interpersonal, informational and decisional (see Figure 4.3). 'Role' here refers to a set of behaviours that individuals are expected to perform because of the position they hold within the organization. Mintzberg usefully distinguished three different interpersonal roles – figurehead, leader and liaison – which arise directly from the manager's formal authority.

By virtue of these interpersonal encounters, with both other managers and non-managers, the manager acts as a 'nerve centre' for the dissemination of information. The manager's three informational roles – monitor of information, disseminator of information and spokesperson – flow from the interpersonal roles. Finally, the interpersonal and informational roles enable the manager to perform four decision-making roles: entrepreneur, disturbance handler, resource allocator and negotiator.

The extent to which managers perform these functions will depend upon their position in the organization's hierarchy and their specific functional responsibilities. According to Mintzberg,[17] production managers give relatively more attention to the decisional roles, because of their concern with efficient workflow. Marketing managers spend relatively more time in the interpersonal roles, because of the

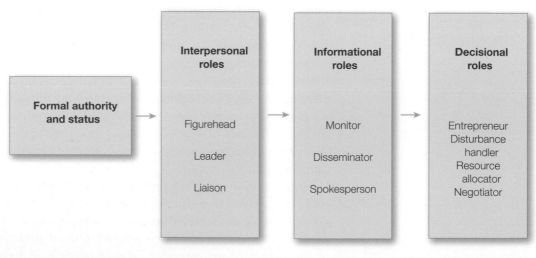

figure 4.3 The manager's ten roles

Source: adapted from Mintzberg (1975)

extrovert nature of the marketing activity. The time spent on interpersonal roles will be influenced by the manager's position, with the figurehead role being less significant for first or middle-line managers than for the most senior managers, as the behaviour of managers at lower levels is more focused and short-term in outlook. Major surveys of managerial practices in Britain reveal significant differences in managerial behaviour. For example, we would expect HR managers to give relatively more attention to the disturbance-handling and negotiating roles, given the nature of the work (see Chapter 17).

Another well-known study of managerial work[18] found that general managers do not follow the famous Fayolian management cycle (planning, organizing, directing, controlling). After studying 15 general managers in different organizations, using documentary material, interviews, questionnaires and observations, the study concluded that managerial work is contextually specific. Consequently, general managers are unlikely to be able to transfer successfully from one setting to another.

The study determined that two sets of demands account for the work of all general managers: demands associated with *task responsibilities*, and demands associated with *relationships*. Demands associated with task responsibilities include setting goals, allocating and stewarding resources, meeting targets, and identifying and solving problems, or 'firefighting'. Demands associated with relationships include obtaining information, cooperation and support from other managers, and motivating and supervising subordinates. Two important managerial behaviours were particularly logged by the researchers: agenda setting and network building. General managers were expected to implement their agendas despite great complexity and uncertainty. Moreover, they had to implement their agendas by persuading a diverse group of others over whom they had little direct control, hence the importance of network building.

Unsurprisingly perhaps, recent studies have found that the relative importance of managerial tasks varied with not only the respondent's position in the management hierarchy but also the level of education of the co-workers. Research suggests that monitoring the external business environment is more important to senior managers at the apex of the organization, while activities to promote horizontal linkages across teams or departments are more important to middle-level managers, and instructing other employees and managing individual performance are more important to first-line managers than the other two groups.[19] Interestingly, managerial work in 'creative milieus' may not follow the conventional concerns for 'command and control' of work activities. For example, managerial work in research-intensive pharmaceutical companies includes controlling and stewarding day-to-day work, but managers also act as scientists, play a major role in scaffolding the research project, and 'conventional management practices and managerial concerns come, at best, second'.[20]

Despite claims to the contrary, the surveys of observable managerial behaviour seem to confirm the longevity of Fayol's original formulation, even though new terms have replaced the old: for example, managers now 'set agendas' and engage in 'network building' rather than plan. Colin Hales drew up a composite list from six published studies of managerial work, which exhibits striking parallels with the classic Fayolian management cycle: see Table 4.2.[21]

Much of the earlier research on managerial work reflects an Anglo-American bias. Some more recent studies have challenged the universality of managerial behaviour, and emphasized the importance of factoring into the analysis gender and cross-cultural considerations.[22] Sally Helgesen, for example, replicated the research design used in Mintzberg's 1973 study, but came up with different findings. She

WEB LINK

Go to the 2005 Workplace Employee Relations Survey website, www.dti.gov.uk/er/emar/2005wers.htm for information on managerial work.

Source: Getty Images

found that her sample of female executives only matched Mintzberg's in the last two categories. Her female managers also preferred face-to-face communications and had developed complex social networks. However, unlike Mintzberg's male executives, the female managers reported that they fulfilled their role at a steady pace, with frequent breaks. They considered such unscheduled breaks to be a normal part of their work.

table 4.2 Summary of managerial work

Acting as a figurehead or leader of an organizational unit
Liaising with other managers
Monitoring, filtering and disseminating information
Allocating resources
Handling conflicts and maintaining workflows
Negotiating with other managers or representatives
Creative and innovative
Planning
Controlling and directing subordinates

Source: adapted from Hales (1986)

In addition, the female managers reported scheduling time to share information with their subordinates. Similarly, Rosener challenged the universality of managerial behaviour.[23] She describes female managers' behaviour as 'transformational and interactive' because they actively share information with their colleagues and subordinates, and encourage participation. The gender differences found between Mintzberg's study and that conducted by Helgesen can partly be attributed to the small sample size and the problem of generalizability. Nonetheless, such studies lead to suggestions that managerial behaviour is 'gendered'. Countering this argument is the view that both male and female managers' behaviour is largely determined by structural, control and market imperatives. Thus, there is no such thing as 'female' management behaviour.[24]

An alternative, less flattering picture of managerial behaviour is indicated through studies on workplace bullying. Though there are variations between the studies, with researchers adopting either psychological or sociological perspectives, several European studies suggest that in about 75 per cent of cases workplace bullying is a downward process, directed by someone in a managerial position at a subordinate. The studies, which were partly stimulated by debate on the quality of working life and informed by inquiry into bullying in schools, suggest workplace bullying can be conceptualized in terms of persistent behaviour and asymmetrical power relations. It may be defined, therefore, as occurring when one or several employees persistently over a period of time perceive themselves to be on the receiving end of negative actions from one or several managers or co-workers, and when, because of an imbalance in power relations, the victim has difficulty in defending her or himself against these actions.[25]

Workplace bullying and harassment is not a new phenomenon. The problem was highlighted some 60 years ago by Daniel Bell, who commented that 'our factories, hierarchical in structure, are, for all the talk of human relations programs, still places where certain men exercise arbitrary authority over others'.[26] Indeed, in the context of profit maximization and managerial control, bullying is part of the management repertoire of getting things done through people, and reflects the significance and dynamics of the unequal balance of power in typical workplaces. Shifts in power between managers and other co-workers arguably make workers more vulnerable to workplace bullying.

There is intellectual value in contextualizing workplace bullying within a work organization–management control framework. In terms of work organization, bullying may be more prevalent in an 'oppressive work regime': that is, when workers are subjected to alienating practices resulting from extensive division of labour, routinization and close control. Bullying may also be related to the type and extent of managerial control over the labour process: see Figure 4.4.

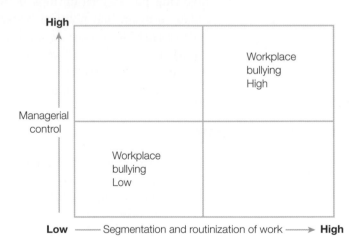

figure 4.4 Relationships between workplace bullying, work organization and control

The relationships between bullying and various forms of work organization and managerial control can be located along two interrelated dimensions of employment contexts: the work regime and managerial control axes. The work regime axis distinguishes between those work structures that emphasize segmentation and routinization, closely associated with Taylorist and Fordist management principles.

The vertical managerial control axis represents what may be called the managerial control continuum. A critical approach to workplace bullying suggests that it is more likely to be located in the upper right-hand quadrant of Figure 4.4. Accordingly, it is argued:

> a dynamic relationship between victimization of individual workers and oppressive work regimes, with the former possibly more likely to occur in the context of the latter … bullying might also be located on a continuum concerned with the various means of establishing and maintaining managerial control in the workplace.[27]

Analysing the complex nature of workplace bullying and the insidious effects it has on the victim and the perpetrators emphasizes the importance of going beyond asking the research question what managers do, to appreciating the importance of structural context in the analysis of management.

The characteristics of the *process* – 'How do managers do it?' – provide another dimension to studying management. The majority of management functions involve interacting with other people in the organization. Empirical studies found that managers spend over 70 per cent of their time in verbal interaction, and spend more than 20 per cent of every working day in some form of conflict-management activity.[28] This brings us to another aspect of managerial work: conflict management.

conflict management:
interventions that alter the level and form of conflict in ways that maximize its benefits and minimize its dysfunctional consequences

All managers are involved in a range of interventionist activities designed to alter the level and form of conflict, which inevitably arises when recalcitrant people enter into productive activity. The involvement of managers in negotiating social order is attributed to the social reality of managerial work, which views individual managers 'as practitioners of an art that requires the possession and application of skills enabling them to cope with the contradictory demands and pressures of resources that stubbornly resist efforts to contain them within prescribe limits'.[29] Thus, ensuring that conflict does not hinder organizational performance is a central managerial role.

Surveys of the content of managerial work expose the positive Fayolian image of the reflective strategist, organizer and planner as a myth. However, a larger question needs to be posed: to what extent do these studies actually describe managerial behaviour? The implications of recognizing that managerial behaviour is political, involving power relationships between managers and other people in the organization, mean that political issues will rarely be far removed from the research process (see Chapter 14). In summary, to return to the comments on the creation of knowledge in Chapter 1, we can say that the evidence on what managers allegedly do cannot be an objective narrative about managerial behaviour, as the research process itself is deeply influenced by the social milieu.

Managerial rationality

Many of the studies discussed thus far did not seek to answer the second and more controversial question of 'Why do managers do what they do?' Developing a fuller understanding of the management process requires a more in-depth look at the contingencies that affect managerial plans, policies and behaviour. There is a consensus among theorists that managerial behaviour is contingent upon, among other things, the external environment, pressures and constraints, competitive strategy, organizational design and technology, power relations and cross-cultural aspects. Scant attention has traditionally been given to these considerations in the management literature. Most are almost exclusively occupied with asking questions like 'how?' and rarely ask 'why?' The latter is often sidestepped, or dismissed with the excuse that it is a 'philosophical' issue, and so irrelevant.

In what follows, a number of competing theories are examined to give some insight into the 'why' question, the forces affecting what managers do. They are neoclassical theory, contingency theory, political theory, labour process theory and strategic choice theory. These theories form the theoretical foundation for the integrated model of managerial behaviour outlined later in the chapter.

neoclassical approach: a model of management which presupposes that managers have the sole right to shape activities, strategy and organize work and people

The neoclassical approach to managerial behaviour and causal explanations is based on the view that managers serve as 'agents' of owners and investors, and that, as agents, they strive to maximize the efficiency and profits of the company by minimizing the costs of factor inputs. In hiring and managing labour, this requires that managers offer the minimum remuneration necessary to attract qualified workers, and supervise subordinates in a way that maximizes their productivity.

Neoclassical theory underscores the importance and operations of the market to rational managerial behaviour. Managers do what they do because the imperatives of the markets (regarding products and labour) require that it be done. Those managers who do not manage in this way are deemed to be 'unsuccessful' and have limited career advancement.

This traditional account of managerial rationality has been criticized in a number of ways:

▷ It provides no insight into the authority structure of the organization through which efficiency is maximized.
▷ It presents management as a homogeneous body, viewing managers simply as agents of ownership interests.
▷ It ignores the politics of production and labour–management relations.
▷ It does not recognize the role of managerial values, culture and choice processes.

These criticisms of the neoclassical theory are largely addressed by the other competing theories.[30]

contingency approach: the idea that a particular action may have different consequences in different situations

The contingency approach focuses largely on the internal authority structure of the organization. Weber's account of managerial rationality[31] emphasizes different modes of legitimacy, and argues that managers with knowledge and expertise are obeyed because the workers recognize that it is rational to obey them.

plate 12 Information overload can lead to poor decisions and work-related stress

Source: Getty Images

Other theorists later suggested that bureaucracy is the most effective organizational configuration when managers are facing low variability and uncertainty. This is typically the case for large organizations characterized by large-batch production and operating in stable product markets (such as US car manufacturers in the 1950s and 1960s).

A contingency approach to managerial behaviour can be seen in Joan Woodward's influential study of manufacturing technology (see Table 4.3).[32] Woodward classified organizational structure and management behaviour according to the technical complexity of the manufacturing process. Technical complexity represents the extent of mechanization of the manufacturing process. Low technical complexity means that workers play a larger role in the production process; high technical complexity means that most of the work is performed by machines. Woodward classified technology into three groups: small-batch, large-batch and continuous process production. Small-batch production is not highly mechanized and relies heavily on the human operator (as in making hand-crafted furniture). Large-batch production is a manufacturing process characterized by long production runs of standard products (such as car assembly). In continuous process production, the entire process is mechanized from start to finish (as happens in a chemical plant).

table 4.3 The relationship between technical complexity and structural/managerial behavioural characteristics

Structural/behavioural characteristics	Technology		
	Small-batch	Large-batch	Continuous process
Number of management levels	3	4	6
Supervisor span of control	23	48	15
Direct/indirect labour ratio	9:1	4:1	1:1
Formalized procedures	Low	High	Low
Centralization	Low	High	Low
Overall structure	Organic	Mechanistic	Organic
Amount of verbal communication	High	Low	High
Amount of written communication	Low	High	Low

Source: based on Woodward (1965)

Woodward looked at the relationship between organizational structure and types of technology. Using her classification of technology and data, she contended that there was a relationship between the management hierarchy and elements of managerial behaviour, and technical complexity. The number of management levels and the manager/total follower ratio, for example, increased as technical complexity increased from small-batch to continuous production. The span of control, formalized procedures, centralization and the amount of written communication are high for large-batch production but low for other technologies, because the work is standardized. Overall, the management systems in both small-batch and continuous process technology are more flexible and adaptive, with fewer procedures, standardization and decentralized decision making. Two organizational theorists have used the term 'organic' to characterize this type of management structure. Large-batch technology, on the other hand, has a high degree of standardization, formalized procedures and centralized decision making. The term 'mechanistic' is used to characterize this type of management structure.[33] Small-batch and continuous process technologies require managers to engage in high amounts of verbal communications. Different technologies, depending upon their complexity, strongly explain managerial behaviour and impose different kinds of demands on people and organizations.[34]

Contingency theory is helpful for understanding variations in organizational structures and, ultimately, managerial policies and behaviour in the workplace; managers do what the structure and technology requires of them. However, even if it is true, contingency theory at best only provides a partial theory of management action; it focuses primarily on structural and technical determinants, and neglects the 'political' side of management.

While both the neoclassical and contingency theories emphasize the technical side of management, the political approach focuses upon pressures, constraints and power relationships as causal explanations of managerial behaviour. Rather than presenting an image of managers as simple agents of owners, stakeholder theory views managers as having to respond to pressures from various stakeholder groups such as shareholders, consumers and employees. The organization is viewed as a coalition of stakeholder groups.[35]

This suggests that managerial behaviour is explained by the need to ensure a continual supply of resources from the various stakeholder groups – finance, revenue and labour – by satisfying the competing demands of these groups. The formulation of managerial behaviour in different functional areas of the operation may be subject to a multitude of competing pressures and constraints. The extent to which managers attempt to satisfy the demands of a stakeholder group is a function of that group's power, according to the proponents of resource dependency theory.[36] Managerial behaviour is explained by the organization's dependence upon a particular group relative to other groups; the most powerful group will have the most influence upon managerial behaviour. In essence, resource dependency theory explains the interaction between managers and others in the workplace not so much in terms of differences in personal attributes, but by variation in the relational power of workers and other managers, and the market power of the organization.

The labour process theory views capitalism as a system that is both economically exploitative and socially alienating. Profit is achieved not so much through the attainment of efficiency in the technical sense, but rather by extracting a maximum of output from workers at a minimum cost. Indeed, one objective might very well be to reduce dependency on a particular group of employees, and therefore managers may attempt to reduce skill levels in order to make employees more easily replaceable. According to labour process theorists, managers attempt to reduce the indeterminacy resulting from the unspecified nature of the employment relationship by exerting control over all work activities or the labour process. They do so by monopolizing all relevant knowledge within the organization, by redesigning work to create a sharp divide between 'thinking' and 'doing', and finally, by deskilling workers. This leads to structured antagonism in the workplace because of the conflicting priorities embedded in capitalist relations. These embedded conflicts largely shape managerial behaviour in the workplace, and so it is critical to explain why they vary across organizations and over time.

So far, the contested theoretical perspectives we have considered have characterized managerial behaviour as rational, or as maximizing profit through various modes of control. Yet this assumption that managers act rationally has been the subject of much criticism for over 30 years. Managerial rationality may be limited

stakeholders: shareholders, customers, suppliers, governments, and any other groups with a vested interest in the organization.

by managers' impaired 'cognitive capacity', the limited time in which to make decisions and the imperfect information available to managers to assist rational decision making. Much of what managers do reflects embedded routines and assumptions, and is reactive and frenetic. In the critical area of strategic action, for example:

> Strategic decisions are characterized by the political hurly-burly of organizational life with a high incidence of bargaining, a trading off of costs and benefits of one interest group against another, all within a notable lack of clarity in terms of environmental influences and objectives.[37]

Although political theories of decision making provide us with important insights into the complexities of day-to-day managerial behaviour, they do not address the notion of strategic choice.

strategic choice: the idea that an organization interacts with its environment rather than being totally determined by it

Strategic choices (see Chapter 1, Figure 1.2) are activities that managers can do but do not have to do. The notion of strategic choices stresses that management is a social process, and choices on various issues are taken by a power-dominant group of leaders within the organization. Managerial behaviour can be explained in terms of a demands, constraints and choices model.[38] External and internal demands, constraints and strategic choices exist in different areas of management. Depending on the choice of competitive strategy, the amount and type of work managers delegate to subordinates, and the time they spend on supervision, will vary. For example, we can contrast the type of work managers do in team-based and traditional non-team organizations (see Chapter 11).

Strategic management

The strategic choice approach alert us to the complex nature of managerial behaviour, and enables us to move beyond the simple rationalistic approach to one in which we can recognize that managerial rationality is 'bounded' by such factors as cognitive capacity, time constraints, imperfect information, organizational politics, strategic business decisions, worker resistance, and managerial beliefs, values and philosophies. The focus here is on how strategic management affects work organization and employment relations. In management the word 'strategy' is used for a specific pattern of behaviour undertaken by the upper echelon of the organization in order to accomplish performance goals. In descriptive and prescriptive management texts, strategic management appears as a cycle in which several activities follow and feed upon one another. The strategic management process is typically broken down into five steps:

▷ mission and goals
▷ environmental analysis
▷ strategic formulation
▷ strategy implementation
▷ strategy evaluation.

Figure 4.5 shows the links between the five steps.

▷ The *mission and goals* give direction to the organization. A mission statement describes the organization's values and aspirations; it is the organization's DNA. Goals are the desired ends sought through the operating procedures, and typically describe short-term measurable outcomes.
▷ An *environmental analysis* looks at the internal strengths and weaknesses of the organization, and the external opportunities and threats. This process can be summarized by the acronym SWOT: strengths, weaknesses, opportunities and threats.
▷ *Strategic formulation* involves senior managers evaluating the SWOT analysis

Based on your own work experience, or that of family or friends, which approach to explaining managerial behaviour do you think represents reality? Think of examples to support your answer.

STOP AND REFLECT

and then making strategic choices that enable the organization to meet its goals. The process, as described here, draws on the strategic choice, and draws attention to strategic management as a political process, in which decisions and actions on issues are taken by a 'power-dominant' group of managers in the organization. Indeed, managerial behaviour cannot be understood without appreciating that management is an arena for conflicts over what strategic choices to pursue and how. These disputes over strategic choices are:

> partly the result of a Machiavellian jockeying for power inside the organization, power that brings with it perquisites and organizational status, but they also represent disagreements over how best to pursue competitive strategy – whether to emphasize financial goals, market share, product cost, or employee talent.[39]

It is necessary, therefore, to consider 'where power lies, how it comes to be there, and how the outcome of competing power plays and coalitions within senior management are linked to employee relations.'[40]

▷ *Strategy implementation* is an area of managerial function that focuses on the techniques used by managers to implement their strategies. In particular, it refers to activities that deal with leadership style (see Chapter 5), the design of the organization (see Chapter 15), information and technology systems (see Chapter 16), and the management of human resources (see Chapter 17).

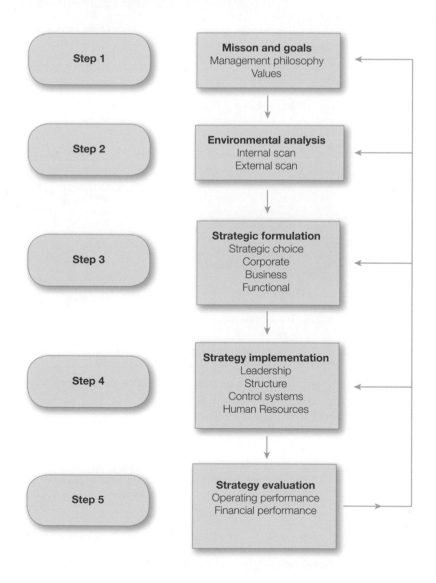

figure 4.5 The strategic management model

> *Strategy evaluation* is an activity that determines to what extent the actual change and performance match the desired change and performance.

As with all traditional accounts of management, the strategic management model shows the five major activities forming a rational and linear process. It is, however, important to note that it is a normative model: that is, it shows how strategic management *should* be done rather than describing what is *actually* done by managers. As we have already noted, the notion that strategic management is a political process implies a potential gap between the theoretical model and reality.

Hierarchy of strategy

Another aspect of strategic management in the multidivisional organization concerns the level to which strategic issues apply. Conventional wisdom identifies several different levels, or a hierarchy of strategy (see Figure 4.6):

> corporate
> business
> functional.

Corporate-level strategy describes the executive's overall direction in terms of its general philosophy about the growth and management of the organization's various business units. Such strategies determine the types of business a corporation wants to be involved in, and what business units should be acquired, modified or sold. This

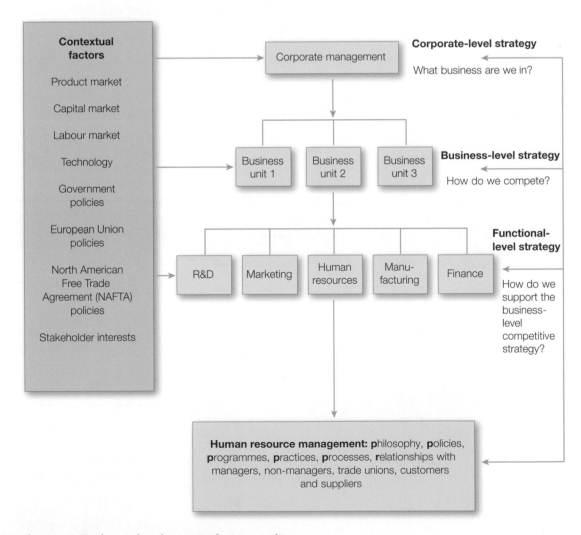

figure 4.6 The hierarchy of strategic decision making

type of managerial decision making addresses the key question, 'What business are we in?'

Business-level strategy deals with decisions and actions related to each business unit, the main objective of a business-level strategy being to make the unit more competitive. This level of strategy addresses the question, 'How do we compete?' Although business-level strategy is guided by 'upstream' corporate-level strategy, business unit managers must craft a strategy that is appropriate for their own operating situation.

Three popular competitive strategies are described in mainstream management texts: cost leadership, differentiation and focus.[41] The *low-cost leadership* strategy attempts to increase the organization's market share by having the lowest unit cost and price compared with competitors. A *differentiation* strategy assumes that managers distinguish their services and products from those of their competitors by providing distinctive levels of service or product, or higher quality, such that the customer is prepared to pay a premium price. The *focus* strategy attempts to make the organization competitive in the global marketplace by focusing on a specific buyer group or regional market. This gives the notion of niche markets, markets which are very narrow or focused.

Functional-level strategy refers to the major functional operations within the business unit, including research and development (R&D), marketing, manufacturing, finance and human resources (HR). This strategy level is typically primarily concerned with maximizing resource productivity, and addresses the question, 'How do we support the business-level competitive strategy?'

These three levels of strategy – corporate, business and functional – form a hierarchy of strategy within large multidivisional corporations. Strategic management literature emphasizes that the strategies at different levels must be fully integrated. The need to integrate business strategy and employment strategy has received much attention from the HR academic community, particularly because of the accelerated effects of globalization.

Global capitalism and managerial behaviour

The fact that we live in a globally interconnected world has become a cliché. As part of this interconnected world, the acceleration of the globalization of economic activity is one of the defining political economic paradigms of our time. In Chapter 1, we discussed how the term 'globalization' has several meanings, and without doubt, in the early twenty-first century globalization has been used to capture a range of developments in the world economy. These developments have been the subject of different interpretations by scholars, organizational leaders and policy makers.

The effects of globalization on income levels, climate change, local cultures and employment, to name just a few areas, are readily apparent. Globalization is arguably about the unfettered pursuit of profit.[42] Global organizations can realize even higher profits by applying their core competencies in foreign markets, where either there is no competition, or local competitors lack similar competencies. For example, following the implosion of soviet communism, the McDonald's Corporation expanded rapidly in Eastern Europe to exploit its distinctive competencies in managing fast-food operations.[43]

globalization: when an organization extends its activities to other parts of the world, actively participates in other markets, and competes against organizations located in other countries

STOP AND REFLECT

How does increasing globalization of markets impact on managerial behaviour?

WEB LINK

For further information on cultural and world trade issues, go to: www.ncf.edu/culture/; www.unesco.org; www.fairtradewatch.org

Kilimanjaro's global warming: a wake-up call to the G8

The stark image of Africa's tallest mountain without snow will be used as a dramatic warning of the harmful effects of climate change as the Group of Eight rich nations, the environment and energy ministers from 20 countries meet in London, England.

Steve Howard of the Climate Group said, 'This is a wake-up call and an unequivocal message that a low-carbon global economy is necessary, achievable, and affordable.' The ten hottest years on record have occurred during the past 15 years. Margaret Beckett, British Secretary of State for Environment, Food and Rural Affairs, and Patricia Hewitt, Secretary of State for Trade and Industry, said, 'Climate change is the greatest environmental challenge facing the international community today ... It's now widely accepted by most independent scientists that climate change is taking place as a result of human activity releasing greenhouse gases into the atmosphere.'

As the world's economy grows, energy demand will undoubtedly increase. In 2002, generation of energy and heat accounted for 40 per cent of worldwide carbon-dioxide emissions. In China, 80 per cent of the power plants that will be used by 2020 have yet to be built. Climate change is not just an environmental challenge; it is an economic challenge too. It has been estimated that the economic cost of global warming could double to US$150 billion each year in the next 10 years, hitting insurance companies with US$30–40 billion in annual claims.

'We must achieve increased awareness of the need for cleaner, more efficient technology in the short term, and R&D into new technologies in the longer term, but this doesn't remove the need for action now,' said Beckett and Hewitt. G8 members are reported to be already showing leadership, particularly on work towards a hydrogen economy, carbon dioxide capture and storage and renewable technologies. Climate change affects us all today, and will increasingly affect future generations and therefore cannot be viewed as a far-off, abstract, future inconvenience. The international community must act decisively now.

Source: Jeremy Lovell, *Globe and Mail*, 15 March 2005, p. 1, 15.

Numerous conferences and studies have directly and indirectly examined managerial behaviour in global organizations – that is, those operating across national frontiers. International business writings give accounts of how higher profits can be realized through economies of scale, which are consistent with the business strategy of low-cost leadership. The underlying assumption here is that organizations that are capable of supplying a global market from a single location are likely to realize economies of scale, and increased profit, faster than companies that restrict their marketing to a smaller local economy. Higher profits can also be achieved by exploiting the differences in a country's business environment. These are known in international management parlance as economies of location.

Organizations are embedded within their own economic, political, legal and social spheres. Levels of corporate taxation, employment standards and other 'business-friendly' incentives can affect profits. Since capital is portable (it can be employed in different countries), it is possible for global organizations to select their production location. Many indulge in an endlessly variable geometry of profit searching.[44] The logic of unfettered globalization means that any labour-intensive value-added activity is likely to migrate from high-wage to low-wage economies: that is to say, from the rich developed countries like the United States and Western Europe to the poorer developing countries like China, Bangladesh and India.

Managerial behaviour in global organizations is connected to the generic business-level strategies of cost leadership and differentiation we described above. A useful starting point to understand managerial behaviour on a global scale is a model developed by Bartlett and Ghoshal.[45] These two international business theorists suggest that managers in global corporations typically face tension from two types of business pressure. On the one hand, they face demands for global cost reductions, and on the other hand, they face demands for product differentiation to meet local tastes.

The demand to control costs and integrate has at its roots the argument from classical Taylor-Fayol management theory that there is 'one best way' to manage an organization. Managers in global organizations may strive for global efficiency by rationalizing their product lines, standardizing parts design, routinizing work, and integrating their global manufacturing and control systems. The consolidation of the European telecommunications industry, following the merger of Nokia Corp. and Siemens AG in June 2006, illustrates that the pressure for integration can be particularly high in technology-intensive sectors, or where the product is universal and requires minimal modification to local needs – for example, the steel industry, in which differentiation is difficult and price is the main competitive variable.

Countering the global prescriptions for standardization and lower costs are local realities and the pressures for local differentiation. Global managers need to satisfy consumer tastes in different places, and therefore competitive advantage is be derived from a differentiation strategy, one sensitive to national cultures and local tastes in the host countries where the global firm operates. For example, when the Swedish home furnishing company IKEA entered the US market it soon found that it had to be responsive to North American tastes and physiques. It had to manufacture larger beds and drinking glasses to accommodate American physiques and people's preference for adding ice to their drinks.[46]

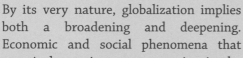

CRITICAL INSIGHT

By its very nature, globalization implies both a broadening and deepening. Economic and social phenomena that once affected a particular nation state or region in the European Union now have broader implications, and of necessity must include greater numbers of states and powerful actors. The globalization of economic activities has given rise to renewed interest in the actions of 'big business', and more specifically the managerial behaviour of large work organizations that operate in the global marketplace.

One part of the debate involves assessing the extent to which managerial behaviour is 'disembedded' from the domestic institutional and social contexts which affect management actions. It is argued that any understanding of the impact of globalization on organizational behaviour must recognize that managers and other actors are exposed to multiple and conflicting systematic constraints and opportunities, with no guarantee that the societal effects of the organization's home base will always prevail.

As an introduction to the debate about the effects of organizations being 'embedded' in society, obtain a copy of a book edited by Marc Maurice and Arndt Sorge, *Embedding Organizations*.[47] Consider its arguments, and ask yourself, does globalization mean that managerial behaviour will be universal? What are the counter forces to the implied 'convergence' of work and employment practices?

Another set of demands for local responsiveness arises from national regulatory regimes, for example on employment standards and product testing (for example, covering clinical trials of pharmaceutical products). Global organizations can be enticed to relocate by national governments that deregulate or offer lower safety, environmental or employment standards. In India, for example, the government recently deregulated the telecommunications industry and gave tax exemptions in order to increase foreign investment in call centres.[48] Given the immense pressure on governments to create employment, it will come as no surprise that managers in global organizations engage in 'negotiated strategies' with host governments.[49]

The point we wish to make here is that where an organization chooses to place itself on the strategic spectrum from cost-efficiency to product responsiveness may well depend on management's calculation about how best to exploit cross-national differences, including a country's social policies which are designed to safeguard the health and safety of its people and protect the planet.

These global realities mean people's interaction with an organization can be either positive or negative. Managerial behaviour is frequently the outcomes of complex strategic choices and negotiated processes, which profoundly shape our behaviour well beyond the boundaries of the organization.

An integrated model of management

The three related dimensions of management – activities, contingencies and behaviours – are brought together in the three-dimensional model shown in Figure 4.7. The vertical axis lists activities that answer the first question, 'What do managers do?' The horizontal axis shows the contingencies, and relates to the second question, 'Why do managers do what they do?' The diagonal axis represents the processes that managers use, and relates to the third question, 'How do managers do what they do?'

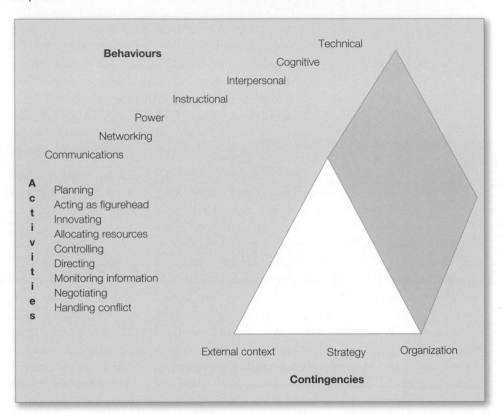

figure 4.7 An integrated model of management

The set of managerial activities draws on Hales's critical review of managerial behaviour,[50] and is strikingly similar to the classical theory of management. The contingencies are those forces and events, both outside and inside the organization, that affect management behaviour. They are grouped into three broad categories – external context, strategy and organization – as shown in our integrated OB model (see Figure 1.2). The third dimension, managerial behaviours, lists various means by which managers communicate ideas, gain acceptance of them, and motivate others to change in order to implement the ideas.

Managers use technical, cognitive and interpersonal processes and skills to accomplish their work. Power is included in the list because it is part of the influence process. Managers accomplish their role by teaching others to do things.[51] Management involves a mix of processes, and individuals will vary in terms of their capacity or inclination to use them, but ultimately these processes are about human interaction and relationships.

The model does not assign values to the relationships between the activities, contingencies and processes, and therefore it does not claim to be predictive. It is, however, a useful heuristic device that allows the different dimensions of management to be explored within a consistent, general framework.[52] The model suggests that management is a multidimensional integrating and controlling activity, which permeates every facet of workplace experience and shapes the employment relationship. It helps us explore how management functions are translated into means, such as leadership processes, and equally how various contingencies influence the process. We hope it will encourage students to view management with new eyes, and to research it with a higher level of understanding than would have been the case without the model.

The behaviour of successful managers

Despite considerable methodological challenges, most researchers – often responding to societal demands to demonstrate the relevance of their inquiries to the 'real world' – offer practical lessons for managers. Several studies claim that the behaviour of more successful managers differs from that of the less successful. While the management process is too complex to reduce to a simple formula, prescriptive texts offer principles that can be used to build a more nuanced and individualized conception of managerial work (see Figure 4.8).

A final word of caution is needed. Most of the orthodox theorists of managerial behaviour have spelled out the practical implications of their research for managerial effectiveness and success. However, we would emphasize that any predictions of a relationship between managerial behaviour and organizational performance are based on theories, rather than proof.

How do these different views of the nature of managerial behaviour and its relationship to organizational success help management practitioners? First, if the research presents an accurate picture of organizational life, then the recognition of the frenetic nature of the manager's work will help to change how potential and practising managers think about their managerial role and their own effectiveness.[53] Second, the studies reviewed in this chapter emphasize the importance of social relationships and the need for managers to be able to deal with other people adroitly. Since, as others have put it, 'managers get things done through people', these social interactions are the manager's work.[54] Thus, to be both effective and successful,

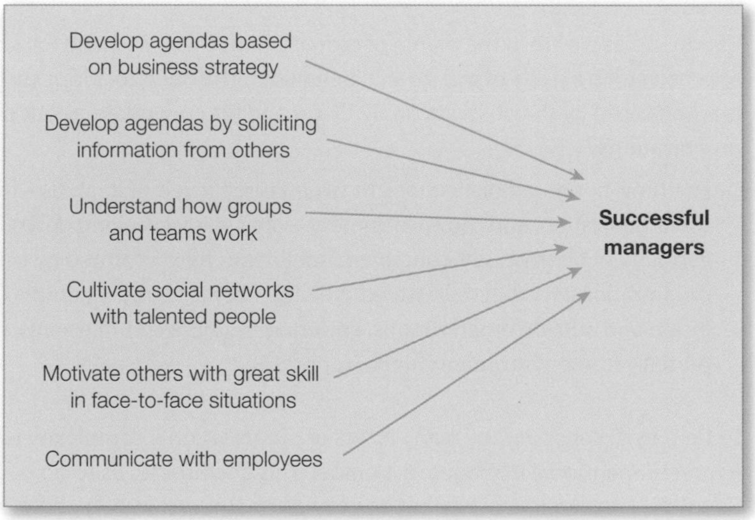

figure 4.8 Behaviour of successful managers

managers need to develop a high level of interpersonal as well as technical and cognitive skills.[55] Finally, the studies show consistently that an ability to understand the motives of others and develop a set of communication, networking and conflict resolution skills is essential for managerial effectiveness and success. However, the relative importance of these skills will depend upon the manager's position in the authority hierarchy of the organization. Cognitive skills for the strategic planning process, and interpersonal skills to persuade employees to implement the strategy, will be more important to senior managers than some technical skills.[56]

Chapter summary

☐ We have reviewed orthodox treatments of management – as a set of technical competences, functionally necessary tasks, and universal roles and processes found in any work organization.[57] For the traditionalist, managerial work is regarded as rational, morally and politically neutral, and its history and legitimacy are taken for granted. Mainstream texts obscure the politics of management. As Knights and Willmott put it, 'That the means as well as the ends of management practice might be radically contested, displaced or resisted by anything other than "irrational" forces is beyond the comprehension of the orthodox literature on management.'[58]

☐ We have also presented alternative accounts of management, in which managerial work is seen to be socially embedded in a politically charged arena of structured and contested power relationships.[59] The debates on management practices involve competing perspectives or ideologies, and central to all ideologies is that they obfuscate and try to refute contradictions and paradoxes.[60] By exposing the limits of orthodox formulations of management, we hope to give you a more critical and realistic approach to studying organizational behaviour in general, and managing the employment relationship in particular.

☐ We have emphasized that management studies must be able to deal with the new complexities and nuances. Strategic decisions typically change work organizations, employment relations and human behaviour. We explained that in multidivisional organizations, strategy formulation takes place at three levels – corporate, business and functional – to form a hierarchy of strategic decision making. Management strategies, as well as the national business system, dictate the choice of management policies and practices.

☐ Caught up as we are in the drama of globalization there is a need for a multidimensional approach to the study of managerial behaviour. The need to adopt such an approach is emphasized by the observation by Clegg and his co-workers about post-industrial organizations:

> The time-honoured distinctions between three levels of analysis – the individual, the organization, and the environment – are clearly breaking down. The previous certainty of discrete, self-contained individuals, fully informed by their roles in organizations, has been shattered. Now identity is far more complex matter formed inside and outside organizations, enduring multiple commitments and ties and only partially formed by organizational scripts.[61]

☐ To help us deconstruct the many facets of organizational complexity we have used a three-dimensional management model. This encourages us to go beyond simply describing managerial behaviour, to provide an understanding of the contingencies that explain why managerial policies and behaviour vary in time and space. Managers' behaviour does not follow the famous Fayolian management cycle. They are typically engaged in an assortment of frenetic, habitual, reactive, fragmented activities.

Key concepts

Chapter review questions

1. What, if any, do you see as the main difference between the nature of management in (a) for-profit enterprises and (b) non-profit organizations?
2. What are the connections, if any, between strategic management decisions and organizational behaviour?
3. How does globalization impact on work organizations?
4. Select one significant change in the external context, and describe how the change affects (a) managerial behaviour and (b) workers' behaviour, as shown in Figure 3.6.
5. How does the notion of strategic choice help us to understand managerial behaviour?

Further reading

Alvesson, M. and Willmott, H. (1996). *Making Sense of Management*, London: Sage.

McKinlay, A. and Starkey, K. (1998) *Foucault, Management and Organization Theory*, London: Sage.

Reed, M. (1989) *The Sociology of Management*, London: Harvester Wheatsheaf.

Watson, A. (2001) *In Search of Management,* London: Thomson Learning.

Chapter case study: Managing change at Eastern University

Setting

In Canadian universities, it is evident that there is a need for positive change, including in how they manage and lead their employees. Various reports emphasize that they compete not only for government and sponsorship funding, but also for the market share of potential students in the increasingly competitive local, provincial and international arenas. In a university setting, key factors in facing these challenges successfully are cooperative and collaborative relationships between administration and the unions representing the university's workers, including support and faculty employees. Publicly funded universities are under increasing pressure to thrive in an atmosphere of reduced funding and increased competition. Working collaboratively in the same direction can produce a viable enduring future.

Background to the case study

Eastern University College is located in Ontario, Canada, and has approximately 14,000 full and part-time students. It was recently granted full university status, enabling the institution to grant its own degrees. In addition, it was expanded to include a comprehensive distance learning programme as an alternative to traditional classroom learning. Resources for new research and developing postgraduate programmes are also planned for the near future. With these fresh opportunities, it was recognized that changes were needed in the institution's strategic direction, including in its management policies and practices.

The university's labour relations were a particular area of focus. Over the years, the university had developed an adversarial and confrontational relationship with the union representing the institution's 300 support workers. In a study undertaken by the administration to identify the drivers or resistors in creating a more positive alliance with the union, it was found that the university's hierarchical and bureaucratic organizational structure was one possible reason for the dysfunctional relationship. Agreements on issues became stalled as administrators were required to take items back to senior managers for their perusal. The union contributed to the delay of reaching resolutions as it referred back to its members for approval on any decisions to be made. In the process, each group sought to protect its own interests. The net result was loyalty to factions, departments, leaders and unions, rather than to the organization as a whole.

Management meeting: preparing for change

Lisa Chang, 28, was the new assistant human resource manager for Eastern University. Improving student services at the university was a high priority for Chang. Based on feedback from the students' union, one idea she had was to extend access to the computer labs so they would be available for student use seven days a week, 24 hours a day, except when they were being used by lecturers for teaching.

Chang visited the websites of several universities and downloaded details of their student computer services. She met with the manager of facilities, Doug Brown, the vice-president of student services, Dr. Susan Allen, and the head of campus security, Paul McGivern. Chang presented her proposal, which included the estimated cost, and was able to resolve the few questions the others had with examples and information acquired from other comparable universities. It was agreed that Chang would present her proposal to the next meeting of the Council of Deans.

The presentation to the deans went flawlessly. Chang was confident that the deans would agree to her proposal. But just as the meeting was to wrap up, the Dean of Arts said, 'Have the union agreed to this?' Alarm bells went off in Chang's head. 'Union?' she thought. 'Why wouldn't they agree to the new service?' She told the Dean she would discuss it with her boss Peter Webster, director of human resources.

At the next HR management meeting to discuss the labour relations situation, administrators were reviewing the most recent grievances, potential arbitrations and the generally poor relationship with the union representing the support staff. Peter Webster, a manager who had several years' experience in dealings with the union, sighed in frustration as he echoed a sentiment of many in the room. 'It seems to be impossible to work together collaboratively with this union! I think we may as well accept it.'

'It doesn't have to be this way,' said Chang, as she handed out copies of her proposed new student service. 'When I talked to one of the stewards last week he actually expressed the same desire for a more cooperative relationship. That is a sign of positive change already.'

After some discussion on what could be done to build upon this progress, the group asked Lisa Chang to prepare a detailed report for the next meeting outlining the next steps.

Tasks

Working either alone, or in a small group, prepare a report drawing on the material from this chapter addressing the following:

1. Thinking about the situation at Eastern University, how effective are Lisa Chang's and Peter Webster's performances in each of Mintzberg's managerial roles?
2. What recommendations would you make to the university's senior management? How would this help?

Sources of additional information

Mintzberg, H. (1990) 'The manager's job: folklore and fact', Harvard Business Review, March–April.

Kersley, B. et al. (2006) 'The management of employment relations,' pp. 36–70 in *Inside the Workplace*, London: Routledge.

*Visit www.change-management.org/ for information on change management.

Note

This case study was written by Dan Haley, MA, Assistant Director, Human Resources, Thompson Rivers University, Canada.

Web-based assignment

Enter the websites of British Airways and Canada's WestJet airline. Scan them to determine the key features of each organization's business strategy. In what ways are they similar? In what ways do they differ? How does each business strategy shape your expectation of how British Airways and WestJet's managers should behave towards other employees, and employees should behave towards customers?

OB in films

The film *Gung Ho!* (1986) features Hunt Stevenson – played by Michael Keaton – who travels to Japan to persuade the top management at Assan Motors to takeover and manage a closed US car factory. When Assan agrees and introduces Japanese management methods to the unionized American workers, there are notable differences in management style and culture clashes abound. This film provides some insight into alleged stereotyped differences in Japanese and American management styles.

Watch the first 30 minutes of the film, and consider these questions:

1. What elements of Japanese culture surprised Hunt Stevenson after arriving in Tokyo?
2. What are Assan's explicit and implicit objectives?
3. In what ways are Assan's management methods effective and ineffective?
4. Would you like to work for Assan Motors? Why? Why not?
5. What OB problems exist when a global company transfers part of its operations to another country?

Notes

1 Drucker (1954/1993: 3).
2 Steve, a manager quoted by Watson (2001: 29).
3 Hales (1986).
4 Williams (1983).
5 Aktouf (1996: 71).
6 Drucker (1954/1993: 3).
7 Drucker (1954/1993: 4).
8 See, for example, Alvesson and Willmott (1996), Knights and Willmott (1986), Reed (1989) and Thompson and McHugh (2006).
9 Willmott (1989: 350).
10 Watson (1986), Reed (1989).
11 Mintzberg (1973).
12 Reed (1989: 21).
13 Reed (1989: 23).
14 Carlson (1951).
15 Mintzberg (1973: 35).
16 Mintzberg (1973, 1989).
17 Mintzberg (1973).
18 Kotter (1982).
19 Kraut et al. (1989).
20 Sundgren and Styhre (2006).
21 Hales (1986).
22 See Willmott (1989), Knights and Willmott (1986), Alvesson and Willmott (1996), Stewart et al. (1994), Helgesen (1995).
23 Rosener (1990).
24 Wajcman (1998).
25 Hoel and Beale (2006: 240).
26 Bell (1948: 375), quoted in Fincham and Rhodes (2005: 330).
27 Hoel and Beale (2006: 256).
28 Bratton, Grint and Nelson (2005).
29 Reed (1989: 26).
30 Godard (2005).
31 Weber (1947).
32 Woodward (1965).
33 Burns and Stalker (1961).
34 Woodward (1965: vi).
35 Cyert and March (1963).
36 For example, Pfeffer and Salancik (1978).
37 Johnson (1987) cited in Purcell (1989: 72).
38 Stewart (1982).
39 Jacoby (2005: 3).
40 Purcell and Ahlstrand (1994: 45).
41 Porter (1980, 1985).

42 Hertz (2002).

43 Hill and Jones (2004), Royle (2005).

44 Castells (2000).

45 Bartlett and Ghoshal (1989).

46 Hill and Jones (2004).

47 Maurice and Sorge (2000).

48 Maitra and Sangha (2005).

49 Prahalad and Doz (1987: 251).

50 Hales (1986).

51 See Bratton, Grint and Nelson (2005), Yukl (2002).

52 Squires (2001).

53 Stewart (1998).

54 Mintzberg (1973).

55 Yukl (2002).

56 Katz and Katz (1978), quoted in Yukl (2002).

57 As discussed by, for example, Taylor (1911), Fayol (1949), Drucker (1954), Mintzberg (1973) and Kotter (1982).

58 Knights and Willmott (1986: 1).

59 As discussed by, for example, Bendix (1956), Braverman (1974), Clegg (1989), Nichols (1969), Knights and Willmott (1986) and Salaman (1981).

60 Godard (2005).

61 Clegg et al. (1999: 9).

chapter 5

Leadership

To be an effective leader, you must become yourself. To know how other people behave takes intelligence, but to know myself takes wisdom.[1]

Leadership finds our faults.[2]

Leadership is the art of accomplishing more than the science of management says is possible.[3]

Chapter outline

▷ Introduction
▷ The nature of leadership
▷ Leadership versus management
▷ A framework for studying organizational leadership
▷ Leadership theories
▷ Power and gender perspectives
▷ Is leadership important?
▷ Chapter summary
▷ Key concepts
▷ Chapter review questions
▷ Further reading
▷ Chapter case study: The challenge of evaluating leadership development training
▷ Web-based assignment
▷ OB in films
▷ Notes

Chapter objectives

After completing this chapter, you should be able to:

▷ explain the meaning of leadership and how it differs from management
▷ explain the three-dimensional model for conceptualizing organizational leadership
▷ explain the different approaches to studying organizational leadership
▷ demonstrate an understanding of how leadership influences organizational performance.

Introduction

In 1981 when Roger Smith was appointed chief executive officer (CEO) of US General Motors (GM), he was hailed as a bold and visionary leader. Yet a decade later when Japanese car sales penetrated North American markets and GM's market share plummeted, Roger Smith's reputation as a corporate leader spiralled downwards along the company's fortunes. When asked what went wrong, all Smith could say was, 'I don't know. It's a mysterious thing.'[4]

leadership: influencing, motivating and enabling others to contribute toward the effectiveness and success of the organizations of which they are members

How did GM's and other failing European car companies' leadership not see Japanese competition coming? Workers in the European car industry know to their cost that poor leadership has consequences. So do the thousands of workers and shareholders who lost their jobs, pensions and investments when the seventh largest company in the United States, Enron, declared bankruptcy in 2001. Enron's employees and shareholders became the casualty not of the effects of globalization but of corrupt and unethical leadership. In May 2006 Enron's former chairman Kenneth Lay, dubbed 'Mr Lie' by the US federal prosecutor, and former CEO Jeffrey Skilling, the two executives most responsible for the company's stunning collapse, were convicted of a total of 25 counts of securities fraud, lying to auditors and insider trading. The scale of the collapse and the illegal behaviour of its top leadership may ensure that Enron becomes the most analysed case study of leadership failure in corporate history.[5]

These examples of corporate failures emphasize that organizational leadership is more than a rhetorical issue. Leadership matters. On a day-to-day basis, organizational leaders profoundly affect where paid work is performed, how it is performed, how people are managed, how people experience their work, and how managers and co-workers interact and respond to each other.

Over the last century, there has been a plethora of research and scholarship devoted to 'leadership' and 'leaders'. One important reason for this interest is the very common assumption that leaders do shape events outside and inside the organization. Much of the debate, however, is framed by a familiar conception of the subject: the effective leader is a hero possessing a variety of traits or attributes, competencies and charismatic powers that enable him or her [mostly it is a him] to bring about transformative effects.[6]

A frequent antidote to a major financial or management crisis is to replace the leader – the CEO – in the hope that the newly appointed CEO will solve the problem, or at least satisfy shareholders' or the general public's demand for 'something to be done'. Essentially, these actions assume that every organization with a problem or facing a crisis needs new leadership, or more leadership, as leaders play a pivotal role in organizational performance.

Not surprisingly, a key question asked by researchers and practitioners alike is, 'What makes an effective leader?' Some suggest that one factor is the charisma and ability of an individual to inspire others to fulfil the vision and goals of the organization. Others emphasize that leadership of an organization is a collective phenomenon: every leader needs competent followers. Indeed, arguably organizations have had too much leadership and might need less leadership.[7] Leadership studies potentially offer a variety of explanations, including personal attributes, contingencies and the role of co-workers or subordinates.

This chapter examines the different ways academics have defined organizational leadership, and the difference between leadership and management. We explain a tri-axis model for conceptualizing leadership before reviewing the different approaches to studying leadership, and conclude by assessing the evidence on whether 'good' leadership can improve organizational performance.

The nature of leadership

Leadership has been studied since the emergence of civilization, but studies of organizational leadership have grown in tandem with the development of large-scale industrialization. During the last century, systematic research has also been driven by two world wars. In 1990 over 7000 entries on leadership were cited, and between January 1990 and January 2002 more than 11,000 articles were published in English-language management journals. The vast amount of scholarship has not resulted in a consensus about the substantive phenomenon itself, and the jury is still out on leadership effectiveness. The extensive research has prompted one respected scholar to acknowledge that 'leadership is one of the most observed and least understood phenomena on earth'.[8]

Leadership as a concept permeates and structures the theory and practice of work organizations, and hence the way we understand management. Leadership has been conceived as a matter of personality, as particular behaviour, as a matter of contingency, as a power relation, as the focus of group processes, and combinations of these variables.

Most definitions of managerial leadership reflect the assumption that it involves a process whereby an individual exerts influence upon others in an organizational context. The notion of influence is central to Gary Yukl's 2002 definition:

> Leadership is the process wherein an individual member of a group or organization influences the interpretation of events, the choice of objectives and strategies, the organization of work activities, the motivation of people to achieve the objectives, the maintenance of cooperative relationships, the development of skills and confidence by members, and the enlistment of support and cooperation from people outside the group or organization.[9]

Yukl's definition, while emphasizing many aspects of 'people skills', tends to focus on the dynamics and surface features of leadership as a social influence process. More critical accounts of leadership tend to focus on the hierarchical forms to which it gives rise, power relationships and gender dominance. Here leadership is viewed broadly as a dialectical process, in which an individual persuades others to do something they would not otherwise do. Leadership is socially constructed through the interaction of both leaders and followers, and is equated with power.

The concept of leadership has in recent times acquired extraordinary importance to work organizations concerned with developing a 'strong' workplace culture and building high-performance sustainable work practices. There is a search for an alternative to the traditional 'command and control' leadership model, which is variously labelled 'transformational leadership', 'charismatic leadership' or 'self-leadership'.[10] Managers are looking for a style of leadership that will develop the organization's human endowment, and generate worker commitment, flexibility, innovation and

WEB LINK

For information on organizational leadership, go to: www.ccl.org www.managementandleadershipcouncil.org

STOP AND REFLECT

Think about a position you have held in a voluntary organization or a work organization. To what extent were you a leader? To what extent were you a follower?

change. The general assumption is that leadership is a central aspect of strategic management, and to 'lead without leading' will result in higher productivity, quality and all-round performance. Interestingly, within this particular discourse, the terms 'subordinate' and 'follower' are often replaced by 'team member' or 'associate'. Language is never neutral, and this change in language reflects attempts by the protagonists to build a 'committed' workforce. Inevitably, our own subjectivity has crafted the definition and shaped our approach to leadership.

Leadership versus management

This chapter is about organizational leadership, but what are the differences between management and leadership? The word 'manage' came into English usage directly from the Latin and Italian *maneggiare*, meaning to handle and train horses, and from the sixteenth century it was extended to a general sense of taking charge or directing.[11] There are different approaches to studying management. Each approach conveys preferred models to explain the phenomenon of management. For some, management is the central process whereby work organizations achieve the semblance of congruence and direction. For others, it has been conceptualized as a process designed to coordinate and control productive activities. Within the latter, the management process contains uncertainties, paradoxes and conflicts.[12]

We can grasp the difference between leadership and management by examining the various roles carried out by managers. A role in an organizational setting is an expected set of activities or behaviours stemming from the position. Classical management theorists define the role of management in terms of planning, organizing, commanding, coordinating and controlling (see Chapter 4). Although this offers an idealized image of management, it emphasizes that leading is a subset of the roles performed by managers.

There are three different but interrelated dimensions to modern management: activities, contingencies and processes. The core of management activities includes the classical functions of planning, organizing, commanding, coordinating and controlling. These activities produce a degree of consistency, order and efficiency. The contingencies are those global and macro forces and events, both outside and inside the organization, that affect management behaviour (see Chapter 4). The managerial processes are the various means by which managers communicate ideas, gain acceptance of them, and motivate others to implement the ideas through change. These processes are about social relationships, and help to make the distinction between management and leadership.

Management is more associated with words like planning, organizing, order, controlling and efficiency, whereas leadership is associated with words such as vision, charisma and change agent. Managerial processes produce a degree of order and consistency in people's behaviour. Leadership processes produce significant change of behaviour or movement.[13] Some leadership theorists insist that leadership is fundamentally an interpersonal process, involving dyadic relationships (that is, relationships between two parties) and communications with followers. Others make the distinction by asserting that management is not a value-laden activity, whereas leadership is. One writer put it like this: 'What is important for the emerging age is that leaders have a foundation, an examined core of beliefs and values, that guides them during times of paradox, ambiguity, and chaotic change.'[14] Another suggestion is that managers 'do things right', whereas leaders 'do the right thing'. Whereas management is concerned with a set of contractual exchanges, 'you do this work for that reward', leadership is concerned with the reciprocal influence process that constitutes the 'psychological contract' (see Chapter 7). It is suggested

STOP AND REFLECT

Do you believe that managers and leaders exhibit fundamentally different personality types?

dyad: a group consisting of two members

that the differences between managers and leaders reflect fundamentally different personality types.

Prominent leadership theorist John Kotter argues that if work organizations are to survive, managers must be able to lead as well as manage. He identifies three important subprocesses that differentiate leadership from management. Leaders in complex work organizations must establish direction, align people with that vision, and motivate and inspire them to make it happen despite the barriers.[15]

The alleged difference between management and leadership is illustrated in Figure 5.1.

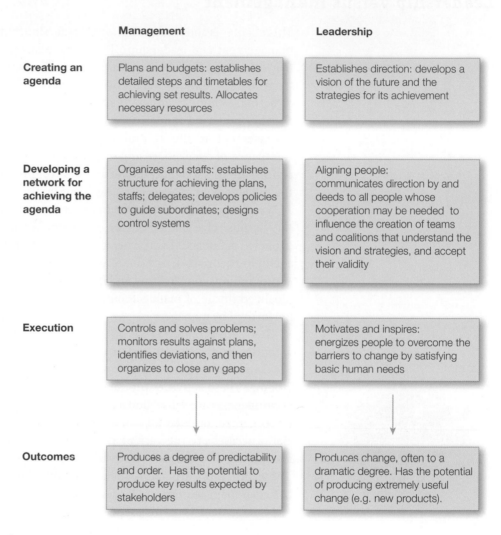

	Management	Leadership
Creating an agenda	Plans and budgets: establishes detailed steps and timetables for achieving set results. Allocates necessary resources	Establishes direction: develops a vision of the future and the strategies for its achievement
Developing a network for achieving the agenda	Organizes and staffs: establishes structure for achieving the plans, staffs; delegates; develops policies to guide subordinates; designs control systems	Aligning people: communicates direction by and deeds to all people whose cooperation may be needed to influence the creation of teams and coalitions that understand the vision and strategies, and accept their validity
Execution	Controls and solves problems; monitors results against plans, identifies deviations, and then organizes to close any gaps	Motivates and inspires: energizes people to overcome the barriers to change by satisfying basic human needs
Outcomes	Produces a degree of predictability and order. Has the potential to produce key results expected by stakeholders	Produces change, often to a dramatic degree. Has the potential of producing extremely useful change (e.g. new products).

figure 5.1 Management and leadership compared

According to Kotter, the 'engine that drives change' is leadership, and if a purely 'managerial mindset' is adopted, useful change in organizations via restructuring, restrategizing or re-engineering will inevitably fail, regardless of the quality of followers involved. In the popular management literature, a similar point is expressed when it is argued that leadership is critical in the re-engineering processes: 'most re-engineering failures stem from breakdowns in leadership'.[16] It is argued that the distinction between management and leadership is crucial in an era of turbulence and change, because 'successful transformation is 70 to 90 per cent leadership and only 10 to 30 per cent management'.[17] Indeed,

WEB LINK
For information on the role of leadership in organizational change, go to:
www.inspirelearning.com
www.change-management.com/
tutorial-change-leadership

plate 13 Early research on organizational leadership focused on the notion that successful entrepreneurs like Sir Richard Branson possess superior qualities or attributes compared with the traits possessed by non-leaders

Source: EMPICS

according to Kotter, the leader in organizational change of any magnitude plays a pivotal role in an eight-step sequential process (see Table 5.1).

table 5.1 Leaders creating major organizational change

1. Establish a sense of urgency
2. Creating the guiding coalition
3. Developing a vision and strategy
4. Communicating the change vision
5. Empowering broad-based action
6. Generating short-term wins
7. Consolidating gains and producing more change
8. Anchoring new approaches in the culture

Source: Kotter (1996a)

Recall an organization where you (or a relative or friend) have worked. To what extent were you a leader and a follower? Do managers where you work or have worked exhibit managerial or leadership behaviours? Explain your answer. Do you believe that managers and leaders reflect fundamentally different personality types?

STOP AND REFLECT

Building on Kotter's work, other leadership theorists draw another important distinction between management and leadership. Managers, by the very nature of their role, encourage compliance, whereas leaders encourage empowerment and a 'culture of pride'.[18] The leader creates a vision as well as the strategy to achieve the vision. In contrast, the manager's key role is to choose the means to implement the vision that the leader formulates. Modern management therefore involves a mix of both management and leadership processes, and individuals will vary in terms of their capacity or inclination to use each subprocess. As many observers of managerial behaviours have been quick to point out, not all managers lead and not all leaders manage. However, to negatively stereotype the manager as an administrator or bureaucrat mired in the status quo is to neglect empirically based evidence that shows successful managers to be good leaders, and successful leaders to be good managers.[19]

A framework for studying organizational leadership

Leadership is an elusive concept, though some would have you believe otherwise. From our perspective, organizational leadership is a process resulting from complex social interactions between a leader and co-workers in a specific context. This approach therefore conceptualizes leadership as a relational phenomenon, which resides in the context, and implies that a leader affects and is affected by other employees or followers and the situation in which he or she operates (see Figure 5.2).

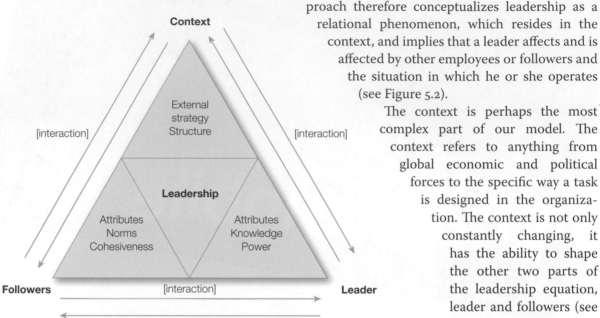

figure 5.2 Leadership as a process

The context is perhaps the most complex part of our model. The context refers to anything from global economic and political forces to the specific way a task is designed in the organization. The context is not only constantly changing, it has the ability to shape the other two parts of the leadership equation, leader and followers (see Chapter 1).

This chapter gives an overview of the leader part of our model, and examines what the leader contributes as an individual to the leadership process. It explores the personality traits and behavioural styles said to be required in a leader. It also recognizes the importance of power in the leadership equation. The perspective taken in this chapter is that followers are a critical component of the leadership process. We need some knowledge of the attributes and knowledge followers bring with them to the organization, how they learn, behave in work groups, and how communication processes affect leader–follower dynamics. We examine followers as individuals and as members of work groups, and the critical role communication plays in the leadership process, in Chapters 11 and 12.

Leadership theories

Leadership as a field of study has produced an inordinate amount of literature, concerned with both what leaders *should* do, and what leaders *actually* do. The former involves theories *for* leaders, while the latter involves theories *of* leadership. Theories for leaders are primarily normative, directed at providing *how to* prescriptions for improving leadership effectiveness. Theories of leadership, on the other hand, are primarily analytical, directed at better understanding leadership processes and explaining *why* they vary across time and space.

Leadership theories are a product of the historical and sociopolitical context in which their creators live and work. A leadership paradigm is a shared mindset that represents a fundamental way of thinking about, perceiving, researching and understanding leadership. As we review the major approaches or perspectives to leadership spanning the last hundred years or so, it is important to understand that leadership theorists necessarily take their view of their work in part from their view of the world and the context in which other people live and work.

Leadership theories are typically classified according to the types of variable emphasized in a theory or empirical study. These major research approaches include the trait, behaviour, contingency, power-influence, gender-influence, integrative and exchange approaches.

Richard Branson, chair of the Virgin Group since 1973, has attained cult status in England, the result of his business exploits, unique personal style and quests for high-risk adventure. By the late 1990s the Virgin brand had become one of the top 50 brands in the world, and a poll of British consumers at the time showed that 96 per cent had heard of Virgin.

Through Richard Branson's leadership, the Virgin Group has become a diversified grouping of more than 200 privately held companies. The largest of these are Virgin Atlantic Airways, the number two airline in the United Kingdom; Virgin Holidays, a vacation tour operator; Virgin Rail, the second largest UK train operator; the Virgin Retail Group, which operates numerous Virgin Megastores selling videos, music CDs and computer games; and Virgin Direct, which offers financial services. Although this is a disparate group of companies, under Branson's stewardship the Virgin brand has been associated with efficiency and high-quality services. According to Branson:

> Virgin is about doing things that really work, not just looking the part. We are passionate about running our businesses as well as we can, which means treating our customers with respect, giving them good value and high quality and making the whole process as much fun as it can be.

The Virgin Group has sales of over US$5 billion and employs 24,000 people.

Branson's entrepreneurial bent emerged during his childhood. At the age of 15 he started a magazine called *Student*, which sold 50,000 copies. The venture was so successful that Branson dropped out of school when he was 17 to run his business full time. In 1971 he opened a string of Virgin Record stores that was also successful. In 1984, Branson purchased a Boeing 747 and founded Virgin Atlantic Airways.

Virgin's success has been attributed to Branson's innovative entrepreneurial ideas and his leadership style, which was a radical departure from corporate norms in the 1980s. Branson operated his unwieldy holding company from his private boat, relying on telecommunications to keep him in touch with his managers. Branson's logic behind his remote office was that it gave his subordinates, spread out in more than 25 London buildings, greater autonomy. 'People always want to deal with the top person in the building. So somebody besides me takes complete responsibility. He becomes chairman of that company ... and I can be left to push the group forward into new areas.' Indeed, according to published accounts, one of Richard Branson's greatest virtues was his ability to delegate and allow managers to take control of the pet projects that he conceived and started.

For more information on Richard Branson and the Virgin Group visit Virgin's website at www.virgin.com.

Trait perspective: the search for 'giants'

Early research on leadership focused on the notion that individuals who occupy leadership positions possess superior qualities or attributes compared with the traits possessed by non-leaders. It was thought that leaders were endowed with more intelligence, self-confidence and determination, and were more sociable, than non-leaders. The so-called 'great man' theories therefore focused on identifying the innate qualities possessed by influential leaders among European monarchs, military generals or politicians. The subject matter for these studies was drawn from the social elite; little interest has been shown in identifying the traits of distinguished labour leaders. And despite the recorded histories of influential women, such as Joan of Arc and Rosa Luxemburg, the focus tended to be androcentric: these were 'great man' rather than 'great person' theories.

Replicating research published in 1948, US academic Ralf Stogdill reviewed 63 trait studies in 1974.[20] In his second major study, he noted the improvements in research methodology used to study leadership. The one-variable-at-a-time experiment had been replaced by multivariate experiments. He also suggested that other researchers had misinterpreted his earlier survey. The 1948 survey did not

WEB LINK

For information on leadership traits, go to
www.managementandleadershipcouncil.org.

personality: the relatively stable pattern of behaviours and consistent internal states that explain a person's behavioural tendencies

table 5.2 Selective leadership attributes according to Stogdill's 1948 and 1970 surveys

Attribute	Number of positive findings	
	1948	1970
Physical characteristics		
Energetic	5	24
Social background		
Social status	15	19
Cognitive ability		
Intelligence	23	25
Fluency of speech	13	15
Personality		
Dominant	11	31
Self-control	11	14
Self-confidence	17	28
Integrity	6	9
Task-related		
Determination	19	38
Social		
Sociability	14	35

Source: based on Stogdill (1974)

STOP AND REFLECT

What do you think makes an effective leader? List three leaders you know about who are alive today, and write down the special attributes you believe each of these people possesses. Compare your list of special qualities with that of your peers, and see whether you can agree on a 'master list'.

suggest that situational factors as such determined leadership status, but that personal traits and the requirements of the situation had to be incorporated into the leadership equation. The 1974 review found more consistent results. It found that leadership is based on complex groupings of traits and social interactions rather than on a single trait or a small cluster of traits (see Table 5.2).

The 1974 survey found that leaders tend to be endowed with a large supply of positive physical characteristics such as energy and stamina. Socioeconomic factors were found to be important variables in 19 studies. In terms of 'class position', few senior executives had fathers who were manual wage earners. Intelligence or cognitive ability is positively related to leadership. Having strong cognitive abilities and fluency in speech appears to make a person a better leader. Certain personality characteristics are positively related to leadership, including dominance, self-control, self-confidence and integrity. Task-related characteristics include such attributes as determination and the desire to excel.

The 1948 and 1970 reviews found that leaders tend to strive for achievement, and display initiative and enterprise. Social attributes, such as the ability to exhibit tact and diplomacy, and build cooperative relationships, are another cluster of traits that appear to be important characteristics of 'successful' leaders. Stogdill attempted to use these selective clusters of traits to differentiate leaders from followers, and effective from ineffective leaders. He concluded that considered singly, the traits have little diagnostic or predictive significance. However, specific 'patterns of traits' appear to interact in a complex way to give advantage to an individual seeking a leadership position.

In addition, Stogdill made an important epistemological point when he cautioned readers to interpret the data sceptically because his conclusions were based on *published studies*. Such studies may, he suggested, over-emphasize positive findings because academic journal editors tend to pursue fads and may be reluctant to publish negative findings.

The trait approach to studying leadership still flourishes. In recent years, there has been a resurgence of interest in the role of traits in effective leadership. For example, it has been asserted that 'it is unequivocally clear that leaders are not like other people',[21] and that eight major traits are positively associated with effective leadership (see Table 5.3).

Gary Yukl found that high energy level and a strong internal locus of control orientation appears to be related to leadership effectiveness.[22] Individuals with a strong internal locus of control orientation believe that their actions control events in their lives, rather than that events happen by chance. Self-confidence and emotional maturity are also found in effective leaders. Those leaders who consistently display integrity are more likely to retain the loyalty of followers, and most studies in the 1980s found a strong relationship between the need for power and leadership effectiveness. Achievement orientation refers to a set of needs and values related to the desire to excel and succeed, and although the achievement–leadership effectiveness linkage is 'very complex', a moderately high achievement orientation is associated with leadership effectiveness.

Finally, most recent studies report a negative correlation between leadership and a very high or very low need for social affiliation. A person with a very high need for affiliation is concerned primarily about relationships with colleagues rather than completing the task. On the other hand, a person who is very low in need for affiliation tends to be socially aloof, and therefore does not develop the kind of social network that is essential for an effective organizational leader. Thus, leadership effectiveness is associated with a 'moderately low' need for affiliation rather than a high or extremely low one.

table 5.3 Major traits predicting leadership effectiveness

| Energy |
| Internal locus of control |
| Self-confidence |
| Emotional maturity |
| Integrity |
| Power motivation |
| Achievement orientation |
| Low affiliation need |

Source: Based on Yukl (1998)

culture: the knowledge, language, values, customs and material objects that are passed from person to person and from one generation to the next in a human group or society

plate 14 Army NCOs (junior officers) exemplify individuals who are high in initiating structure. In training, they give orders and structure recruits' activities throughout the day. Emphasis on task accomplishments takes precedence over the recruits' personal needs.

Source: Getty Images

Evaluating the trait approach

Although the research findings on leadership traits have given top managers some benchmarks for selecting potential leaders, and offer would-be leaders insights into which traits and skills they need to improve, the trait perspective has several weaknesses.

The first criticism is that research on traits has largely neglected the context within which the leader and followers find themselves. A second criticism is that the trait approach celebrates 'inequality' between the leader and others, and does not recognize the importance of followership in the leadership process. The leader is only one of many individuals working cooperatively and pooling their intellectual or physical resources to accomplish some mutual goal.[23] As we emphasize throughout this book, followers vary in ability, motivation, role perceptions and emotional needs. The personality traits of followers, how followers learn in the workplace, and how followers behave in work groups all affect the leadership process and outcomes.

A third criticism is that to a large extent research on leadership traits is culturally determined. Culture can be viewed as the sum of the shared values and beliefs, shared assumptions and shared philosophies with which people identify. From this perspective it is apparent that Asian and Anglo-American scholars, for example, might not agree on what counts as a positive leadership trait. In spite of globalization, cultural differences are a major factor within as well as between regions. In Asia alone, for example, people speak at least seven different major languages (and a multitude of less widely spoken ones), and believe in a wide range of different religions and philosophies, ranging from Buddhism and Hinduism to Islam and Christianity. Personal characteristics such as 'strength of conviction', 'independence' and 'aggressiveness', which appear as 'positives' in Anglo-American trait research, might score negatively in cultures that value consensus, spirituality, collectivity and Confucian teachings.[24]

The behaviour perspective
Early theories: task and relationship behaviours

The effective critiques by Stogdill and others shifted the research focus away from personal traits in leadership – the notion that leaders are born – towards the investigation of the behaviour of leaders, and the relationship between leader behaviour and situational factors. The leadership behaviour perspective attempts to answer the question, 'What leadership style is most effective?' Theorists adopting this approach study what leaders do, and in particular how they behave towards subordinates.

This approach was influenced by the work of Edwin Fleishman.[25] Two US research programmes, the Michigan and Ohio State programmes, pioneered early research. The researchers distilled two clusters of leadership styles from more than 1800 leadership behaviour items. One cluster captures a leader's task-oriented behaviours, such as assigning work and job redesign activities. The other cluster represents people-oriented behaviours, such as showing respect and support for followers. The studies argue that an open, participative leadership style is more effective than an autocratic, non-participative style.

Despite the different names, the concepts were similar, and two analytical frameworks was developed for comparing different leadership styles based on two main types of behaviour:

task behaviour: focuses on the degree to which a leader emphasizes the importance of assigning followers to tasks, and maintaining standards: in other words, 'getting things done' as opposed to behaviours that nurture supportive relationships

relationship behaviour: focuses on manager's activities that shows concern for followers, looks after subordinates welfare and nurtures supportive relationships with followers as opposed to behaviours that concentrate on completing tasks

initiating: part of a behavioural theory of leadership which describes the degree to which a leader defines and structures her or his own role and the roles of followers toward attainment of the group's assigned goals

task behaviour and relationship behaviour. Task behaviour describes the extent to which the leader emphasizes productivity targets or goal accomplishment. These behaviours are also called 'production-centred' and task-oriented' leadership styles. Relationship behaviour describes the extent to which the leader is concerned about his or her followers as people: their needs, development and problems. These behaviours are also called 'employee-centred' and 'person-oriented' leadership styles. Four research studies provided the foundations of behavioural theories of leadership.

Similar to studies conducted by Lewin and his co-workers[26] and at the University of Michigan, the Ohio State University studies identified two dimensions of leadership behaviour, which the researchers called initiating and consideration structures. Initiating is leader behaviour aimed at defining and organizing work relationships and roles, as well as establishing clear patterns of communication and ways of completing tasks. In contrast, *consideration* is leader behaviour aimed at nurturing warm working relationships, and encouraging mutual trust and respect between the leader and his or her followers. The effective leader attempts to increase both the initiating and consideration structure, and to maintain a balance between the two.

The Ohio State researchers regarded the initiating and consideration structure as being two independent dimensions. Thus, leader behaviour was flexible and could be changed as situations warranted. Leaders could score highly on the initiating dimension and not on the consideration dimension, but equally could score high on both or low on both. This was the first time that leadership styles had been conceptualized as other than a continuum. The Ohio State researchers used these two dimensions to design a four-quadrant model for thinking about and characterizing leadership styles (see Figure 5.3).

The Ohio State approach measured both formal and informal variables. The Ohio research team was especially interested in the differences between the leader's formal responsibility and formal interaction with followers, on the one hand, and the informal elements of leadership activities performed and followers that the leader actually interacted with, on the other. One consequence of the research seemed to be that leadership could derive from individuals holding no formal position in the organization.[27]

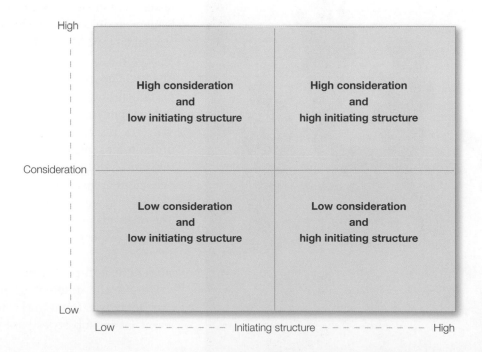

figure 5.3 Categorizing leadership styles

Evaluating the early behavioural approach

The behavioural approach to studying leadership does have its limitations. The first criticism of the approach is that it has not succeeded in doing what the trait approach did, and identifying a universal style of leadership that could be effective in the vast majority of situations. Second, it suggests that the most effective leadership style is the so-called 'high–high' style: that is, high production and high people-oriented behaviour. However, extensive research in Anglo-American countries found only limited support for the universal proposition that 'high–high' leaders are more effective. A third criticism is that it has not adequately demonstrated how leaders' behaviours are associated with performance outcomes. The behavioural leadership theorists have been unable to establish a consistent relationship between production and relationship behaviours and performance outcomes.

In his evaluation of behaviour taxonomies, Gary Yukl argues that 'like the trait approach, the behaviour research suffers from a tendency to look for simple answers to complex questions'.[28] Early behaviour taxonomies provided only a crude representation of a more complex reality. In the 'post-heroic' mid-1980s, however, researchers began to systematically examine leaders' behaviours as a response to the competencies that organizations prefer.

Modern theories: leadership competencies

competencies: the abilities, values, personality traits and other characteristics of people that lead to a superior performance

The concept of leadership competency has become ubiquitous in the field of management development and appraisal. Data derived from the analysis of work performance have been used to create a taxonomy (a classification) of either criterion-related behaviours, or standards of performance, which are referred to as competencies. Competency may be defined as 'the set of behaviour patterns that the incumbent needs to bring to a position in order to perform its tasks and functions with competence'.[29] A competency model applied to a leadership position specifies a set of desired values, behaviours and/or skills that organizational members feel their leaders need in order to be effective and to successfully meet current and future challenges.

Studies in the United Kingdom underscore the importance of competency frameworks in management and leadership development programmes. For example, in the United Kingdom competency frameworks were embraced in the National Occupational Standards (NOS) for management. In the 1990s, in identifying inadequate leadership as the first and fundamental barrier to successful team-based re-engineering projects, a competency framework identified a cluster of 11 leadership competencies that were considered necessary for the successful implementation and maintenance of 'high-performance work systems'. They were delegator, visionary, change agent, inspirer, high trust, coach, team builder, supporter, champion, facilitator and partner.[30]

The competency approach has been applied in three different ways:

▷ The management competence approach, derived from the appraisal of job roles to determine expected standards of behaviour, identifies specific sets of technical or functional competencies.
▷ The second approach focuses on behavioural competencies of effective managers that result in superior performance.
▷ The third approach identifies organizational competency, which underscores strategic competencies to enhance organizational performance.

Figure 5.4 indicates how different competency models applied to managers and leaders can be visualized, including as a cluster of individual competencies versus a series of shared or collective organizational competencies, or as a baseline standard – an acceptable standard of behaviour – versus an aspirational goal.

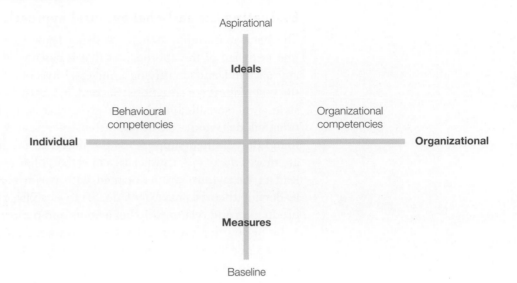

Aspirational

Ideals

Behavioural
competencies

Organizational
competencies

Individual ━━━━━━━━━━━━━━━━━━━━ Organizational

Measures

Baseline

figure 5.4 Differing concepts of
leadership competencies

Evaluating the competency approach

Competency approaches to leadership often drive selection, training, compensation
and performance appraisal. While competency models are apparently the most
dominant models for UK and US management and leadership development and
appraisal, the approach also has several shortcomings. The behavioural competencies
identified to promote an individual to a leadership role may be more likely to be
exhibited by a particular gender or ethnic group. This could be one factor explaining
the under-representation of women in senior leadership positions – the so-called
'glass ceiling effect.'[31]

Another criticism of the competency approach is the distinction between actual
and perceived competence. If an individual cultivates the correct 'office front', it may
enable a relatively incompetent individual to be perceived by co-workers as competent.[32] Perhaps the biggest drawback is that by restricting the analysis of leadership
to observable tangible behavioural or skill measurements, the competency model
inhibits a more nuanced understanding for the context and the complex relational
processes in which leaders find themselves.

To broaden the competency approach, organizations should value 'reflexivity'.
The use of a musical metaphor helps to underscore the point:

> Organizations should endeavour to develop opportunities for their members
> to articulate and explore the experience of leadership in all its richness .... We
> should encourage people in leadership roles to not only develop their music
> reading and basic playing skills (i.e. competencies) but also their interpretation,
> improvisation and performance abilities (i.e. emotion, intuition, moral
> judgement, experience and so on).[33]

This particular perspective on leadership behaviour emphasizes the dyadic
relationships between leaders and co-workers, and the importance of reflexivity and
social learning rather than the more exclusive individualistic notions of leadership.
By the mid-1960s, behaviour leadership theories had already become much more
complex by including the situation or contingency as a variable in the discussion of
leadership and leader.

social learning theory: a theory
stating that much learning occurs
by observing others and then
modelling the behaviours that
lead to favourable outcomes and
avoiding the behaviours that
lead to punishing consequences

The contingency perspective

Contingency leadership theories are based on the idea that the most effective
leadership style depends upon the leader, followers and situation. In other words,

whether a set of traits or behaviours will result in leadership success is contingent, or will depend upon the situational variables, including the characteristics of co-employees, the external and internal environments, and the nature of the work performed. The assumption is that different trait patterns (or behaviour patterns) will be effective in different situations, and that the same trait pattern (or behaviour pattern) is not optimal in all situations.

One aspect of this leadership research is to gain insights into the extent to which managerial behaviour is the same for different levels of management, and across different types of organization and culture. The research methodology is a comparative study of two or more situations, in which managerial behaviours are measured using questionnaires or by direct observation in various work situations.

Most contingency leadership theories assume that effective leaders must be flexible and able to adapt their behaviours and styles to match the situation. The least preferred co-worker theory, path–goal theory and the 'situational leadership' model provide three examples of leadership theories that diagnose contextual factors.

Fiedler's least preferred co-worker theory

Fiedler's contingency model: suggests that leader effectiveness depends on whether the person's natural leadership style is appropriately matched to the situation

Fred Fiedler's contingency theory of leadership proposes that the fit between the leader's need structure and the favourableness of the leader's situation determines the team's effectiveness in work accomplishment. This theory assumes that leaders are either task oriented or relationship oriented, and that leaders cannot change their orientations.[34] Task-oriented leaders are focused on accomplishing tasks and getting work done. Relationship-oriented leaders are focused on developing good, comfortable interpersonal relationships. The effectiveness of both types of leaders depends on the favourableness of the situation. The theory classifies the favourableness of the leader's situation according to the leader's position power, the structure of the team's task, and the quality of the leader–follower relationships.

Fiedler classifies leaders using the least preferred co-worker (LPC) scale.[35] The LPC scale is a projective technique through which a leader is asked to think about the person with whom he or she can work least well (the LPC). The leader is asked to describe this person using adjectives like pleasant versus unpleasant, and inefficient versus efficient. Leaders who describe their LPC in positive terms (that is, pleasant, efficient, cheerful and so on) are classified as high-LPC, or relationship-oriented, leaders. Those who describe their LPC in negative terms (that is, unpleasant, inefficient, gloomy and so on) are classified as low-LPC, or task-oriented, leaders.

The LPC score is a controversial element in contingency theory.[36] It has been criticized because it is a projective technique, with associated measurement biases and low measurement reliability. The leader's situation has three dimensions: task structure, position power and leader–member relations. Based on these three dimensions, the situation is either favourable or unfavourable for the leader.

Task structure refers to the number and clarity of rules, regulations and procedures for getting the work done. Position power refers to the leader's legitimate authority to evaluate and reward performance, punish errors and demote group members. The quality of leader–member relations is an indication of the positivity of the leader's relationship with the followers. A favourable leadership situation is one in which the task is highly structured, the leader has considerable position power, and the leader–member relations are good. The most unfavourable leadership situation is one with an unstructured task, weak position power for the leader, and poor leader–member relations. These three variables (task structure, position power and leader–member relations) combine in various ways to determine the favourableness of the situation, and occur between the extremes described above.

Contingency theory suggests that low and high-LPC leaders are each effective if placed in the right situation. Specifically, low-LPC (task-oriented) leaders are most effective in either very favourable or very unfavourable leadership situations. In contrast, high-LPC (relationship-oriented) leaders are most effective in situations of intermediate favourableness, as shown in Figure 5.4. What happens when a low-LPC leader is in a moderately favourable situation or when a high-LPC leader is in a highly favourable or highly unfavourable situation? Fiedler argued that leader orientation was difficult, if not impossible, to change, so he recommended that the leader's situation be changed to fit the leader's orientation.[37] A moderately favourable situation could be altered to be more favourable and a better fit for the low-LPC (task-oriented) leader. The highly favourable or highly unfavourable situation would be changed to one that is moderately favourable, and a better fit for the high-LPC (relationship-oriented) leader.

There is considerable debate about the validity of the LPC model. While a large number of studies have been conducted, not all of them have supported the model. In addition, the model has been better supported in lab studies than in field studies.[38] Another criticism surrounds the model's validity: that is, the LPC scale may not truly measure leadership style.[39]

STOP AND REFLECT

To what extent are contingency theories of leadership bound by culture?

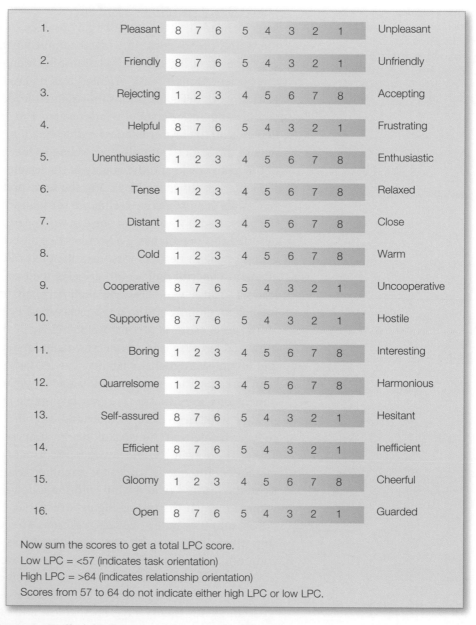

1.	Pleasant	8 7 6 5 4 3 2 1	Unpleasant
2.	Friendly	8 7 6 5 4 3 2 1	Unfriendly
3.	Rejecting	1 2 3 4 5 6 7 8	Accepting
4.	Helpful	8 7 6 5 4 3 2 1	Frustrating
5.	Unenthusiastic	1 2 3 4 5 6 7 8	Enthusiastic
6.	Tense	1 2 3 4 5 6 7 8	Relaxed
7.	Distant	1 2 3 4 5 6 7 8	Close
8.	Cold	1 2 3 4 5 6 7 8	Warm
9.	Cooperative	8 7 6 5 4 3 2 1	Uncooperative
10.	Supportive	8 7 6 5 4 3 2 1	Hostile
11.	Boring	1 2 3 4 5 6 7 8	Interesting
12.	Quarrelsome	1 2 3 4 5 6 7 8	Harmonious
13.	Self-assured	8 7 6 5 4 3 2 1	Hesitant
14.	Efficient	8 7 6 5 4 3 2 1	Inefficient
15.	Gloomy	1 2 3 4 5 6 7 8	Cheerful
16.	Open	8 7 6 5 4 3 2 1	Guarded

Now sum the scores to get a total LPC score.

Low LPC = <57 (indicates task orientation)

High LPC = >64 (indicates relationship orientation)

Scores from 57 to 64 do not indicate either high LPC or low LPC.

figure 5.5 Fiedler's least preferred co-worker (LPC) scale

Path–goal theory

Robert House developed the path–goal theory of leadership, with its roots in the expectancy theory of motivation.[40] In the expectancy theory of motivation, the linkages between effort and performance, and between performance and valued rewards, are critical to motivation. Chapter 10 explores this notion further in relation to the motivation of followers. In path–goal theory, the main task of the leader is to smooth the follower's path to the goal. The leader uses the most appropriate of four leader behavioural styles to help followers clarify the paths that lead them to work and personal goals, as shown in Figure 5.6.

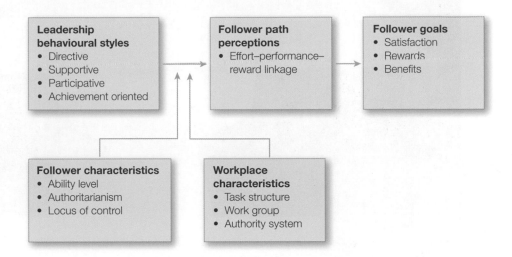

figure 5.6 The path–goal model

The four styles in the model are directive, supportive, participative and achievement-oriented. The directive style is used when the leader must communicate expectations, schedule work and maintain performance standards. The supportive style is used when the leader needs to express concern for followers and create a climate that demonstrates support. The participative style is used when the leader wants to share decision-making authority with followers. The achievement-oriented style is used when the leader must set challenging goals for followers, expect very high levels of performance, and show strong confidence in the followers.

The contingency variables in path–goal theory are the characteristics of the work environment (situation) and those of the followers. Research has focused on matching leader behaviours to follower characteristics and environment characteristics. For example, when tasks are ambiguous, directive leader behaviour is appropriate. When the environment is stressful, supportive leadership is appropriate. When followers are ready to be empowered, participative leadership is appropriate. When followers have high achievement orientations, achievement-oriented leadership is appropriate. These are just a few examples of the links between leader behaviour and the contingency variables. The leader selects the leader behavioural style that helps followers achieve their goals. Leaders can use several different styles, and can diagnose the situation and apply the appropriate style.

Evaluation of the path–goal theory

The research support for path–goal theory is quite mixed. In a meta-analysis of 120 field studies of path–goal theory, two researchers found mixed results, and very few carried out complete tests of the model.[41] Some of the relationships in the model have received support. The link between directive leader behaviour and satisfaction for low-ability subordinates received support. Supportive leadership was related to

plate 15 The entry of more women into management positions has generated more research on gender and leadership, questioning, among other things, whether women lead differently from men

subordinate satisfaction across situations. We can conclude that the full path–goal model has not been sufficiently tested.[42]

Situational leadership theory

The situational leadership model, developed by Paul Hersey and Kenneth Blanchard, suggests that the leader's behaviour should be adjusted to the maturity level of the followers.[43] The model employs two dimensions of leader behaviour as used in the Ohio State studies: one dimension is task or production oriented, and the other is relationship or people oriented. Follower maturity is categorized into four levels, as shown in Figure 5.7. Follower maturity is determined by the ability and willingness of the followers to accept responsibility for completing their work. Followers who are unable and unwilling are the least mature, and those who are both able and willing are the most mature. The four styles of leader behaviour associated with each level of follower maturity are shown in the figure as well.

According to the situational leadership model, a leader should use a telling style of leadership with immature followers who are unable and unwilling to take responsibility for completing their work. This style is characterized by high concern with the task and strong initiating structure behaviour, coupled with low concern with relationships and little consideration behaviour. As followers mature to the second level, the leader should use a selling style, in which there is high concern with both the task and relationships. Able but unwilling followers are the next most mature, and require a participating style from the leader. This style is characterized by high concern with relationships and low concern with the task. Finally, the most mature followers are ones who are both able and willing, and these require a delegating style of leadership. The leader employing this style of leadership shows low concern with both the task and relationships, because the followers accept responsibility.

One key limitation of the situational leadership model is the absence of central hypotheses that could be tested, which would make it a more valid, reliable theory of leadership. Some partial tests of the model have indicated support, but others

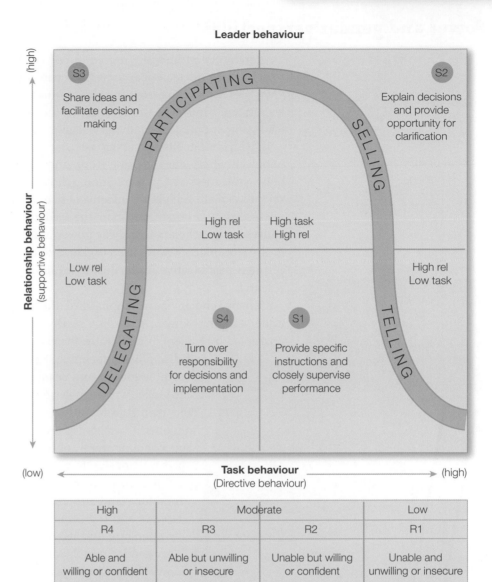

figure 5.7 The situational leadership model

have found no support at all.[44] However, the theory has intuitive appeal and is widely used for training and development in corporations. In addition, the theory focuses attention on followers as important participants in, if not determinants of, the leadership process.

CRITICAL INSIGHTS

The Hersey and Blanchard model is a widely used prescriptive approach to leadership. Read Chapter 8, 'Situational leadership' in their book *Management of Organizational Behaviour*.[45] What are the strengths and weaknesses of this model? Why do you think it is so popular among consultants and management trainers?

Obtain a copy of Mats Sundgren and Alexander Styhre's article, 'Leadership as de-paradoxification: leading new drug development work at three pharmaceutical companies'.[46] How, if at all, could the situational leadership model be used in a research-intensive creative work environment?

Power and gender perspectives

Leadership is intrinsically rooted in power. If leaders can persuade their followers to act, then leaders appear to be powerful. The new popular rhetoric on leadership envisages the shifting from the old 'command and control' style of leading to 'shared leadership'. Thus, it is argued that in the so-called knowledge economy much of leadership is paradoxical: managers gain power by giving it away.

power-influence approach: examines influence processes between leaders and followers, and explains leadership effectiveness in terms of the amount and type of power possessed by an organizational leader and how the power is exercised

Power is related to leadership because it is part of the influence process. But what is power, where does it come from, and what do we know about the relationship between leaders and power? Some scholars interested in power-influence theories seek to explain leadership effectiveness in terms of the amount and type of power possessed by a leader, and how the leader exercises that power. One major issue addressed by scholars is the way power is acquired and 'lost' by various individuals in the workplace. Team-based organizational designs and notions of power sharing through participative leadership styles have generated interest in power-influence research.

Others scholars have emphasized the primacy of language and discourse in understanding power. According to this perspective, power is not a commodity possessed by leaders, but operates through discourses, which produce knowledge, and disciplinary techniques that define and constrain the identities of both followers and leaders. Michel Foucault's work on power-knowledge, which suggests that followers are deeply enmeshed in their own subordination, is prominent in this approach to power-influence.[47] Chapter 14 provides further discussion on the traditional and contemporary approaches to power in the organization, and their relationship to work behaviour.

plate 16 Some argue that powerful economic and organizational imperatives do not permit opportunities for female managers to put into practice a 'feminist' style of leadership

HERE'S WHAT THE CORPORATE LADDER ACTUALLY LOOKS LIKE.

Source: SCOREGolf

Since the early 1990s, the topic of gender has entered leadership literature, and attracted much attention from academics, practitioners and the popular management press. The entry of more women into management positions has generated more research on gender and leadership, questioning, among other things, whether women lead differently from men. Several scholars argue that women managers have a more interactive style, which includes more people-oriented, knowledge-sharing and participative leadership. Feminist leadership characteristics that have been identified include consensus building, shared power and the promotion of diversity.

In addition, feminist analysis has focused on the way in which jobs, occupations and organizations are themselves gendered, arguing that the processes and practices of gendering within the organization consolidate men's power in the workplace, and marginalize and exclude women from management positions. This is popularly referred to as the 'glass ceiling'. As we have already noted, numerous writers have pointed out that most leadership models are based on male behaviour. Does gender make a difference? Do women managers have more people-oriented and participative leadership styles?

empathy: a person's ability to understand and be sensitive to the feelings, thoughts and situations of others

Whereas some observers proposed that feminine characteristics, such as warmth, caring and empathy, allow women to succeed in organizational leadership roles because they are associated with a 'transformative' or 'inspirational' leadership style,[48] sociologists analysing from a critical perspective have argued that the belief that women are 'naturally' more consensual could be 'the expression of a relative lack of power rather than a characteristic of womanhood per se'.[49] Data on practising managers suggests that workers tend to perceive female managers as having an 'inclusive' and 'soft' leadership style, and male managers as having a 'controlling' and 'hard' style. Some feminists argue that women leaders in organizations have the interactional leadership style needed to encourage and nurture worker commitment to organizational goals.

Sociological studies focus our attention on familiar antagonisms and imperatives, which avoid the tedious piety about female managers being inclusive and cooperative while male managers are competitive and controlling. Managers of both genders are competitive, and male managers are as capable of being inclusive as women. The choice between different leadership styles is usually dictated by the situation and by economic and organizational imperatives. The organizational dynamics and culture might not provide opportunities for female managers to put into practice a 'feminist' style of leadership, and compel them to 'manage like men'.

STOP AND REFLECT

How do you view feminist approaches to leadership? To what extent does the majority male culture of organizations shape gender relations in the workplace?

Is leadership important?

Is leadership intervention important to organizations? While the study of organizational leadership in mainstream OB is ultimately concerned with organizational performance, numerous writers reviewing and evaluating the modes of leadership interventions have concluded that that there is insufficient evidence to demonstrate the key to leadership effectiveness. To assess the merit of these competing claims, we should approach the issue of the leadership–performance link with a couple of key questions in mind. What types of performance data are available to measure the leadership–organizational performance link? Do leaders influence various organizational variables and organizational performance? In answering these questions, it is necessary to have not only an understanding of the relevant elements that measure performance, but also a sense of the methodological challenges of measuring leadership effectiveness.

WEB LINK

For information on leadership-performance links, go to: www.OrgDNA.com/Passive-Aggressive for an article on stimulating organizational performance through leadership.

What types of performance variables should be considered and measured? A variety of factors have been commonly employed to measure organizational performance and these are summarized in Figure 5.8.

This list is not exhaustive, and it is important to recognize that any assessment of an organization's performance is very much dependent upon, amongst other things, the perspective that is used.[50] For example, shareholders may evaluate the organization's performance solely in terms of financial outcomes such as profits, growth of sales and market share. Followers may judge the organization's performance in terms of whether the organization offers a healthy and safe working environment and job satisfaction. External groups, including neighbourhoods and local government, may focus on whether the organization complies with environmental regulations.

The argument that leaders actually influence organizational performance seems plausible, and is made by numerous writers. For example, one study found that 44 per cent of the profitability of the

figure 5.8 Components of organizational performance

organizations studied was accounted for by changing the leader,[51] while another study found that leadership is critical to mobilizing change in an organization.[52] Similarly, it has been asserted that the driving force behind any successful change process is 'leadership, leadership, and still more leadership'.[53] The counter-argument is that leadership is of little consequence to the performance of the organization: more influential are the forces in which the leader is situated. For example, the economic and political factors outside the leader's control have a greater effect on organizational performance than leadership behaviour does.[54]

A dramatic example of this principle is the 2001 downturn in the North American airline industry, which occurred even though the major airline carriers in the United States and Canada had not changed leadership. This unprecedented downturn in the market and the subsequent collapse of Canada's second largest airline, Canada 3000, resulted from the 11 September attack on the World Trade Center in New York. Other aspects of the 'leader is insignificant' hypothesis are that leaders have limited discretion in their strategic choices and behaviours, and ineffective leaders can be substituted by synergistic work teams, professional norms and information technology.[55]

Evaluating the leader–organizational performance link presents tough methodological challenges for researchers:

▷ Research on leadership outcomes requires management participation, and it also calls for disclosure of commercially sensitive information on performance indicators, which many managers are unwilling or unable to provide to an independent researcher. The researcher has therefore to use 'intermediate' performance indicators such as employee absenteeism and customer or client complaint rates.

▷ The use of a single composite criterion requires subjective judgements about how to assign weight to each measure, and multiple criteria are problematic when they are negatively correlated. For example, an increase in labour productivity may be achieved at the cost of higher accidents and injuries.

▷ How can relevant variables be isolated? Even if an apparently causal relationship between leadership and growth of market share is discovered, can it be assumed that nothing else has changed in the meantime? For example, exchange rates could significantly affect market share, and factors like this make it difficult to assess leadership effectiveness with complete confidence. Even if relevant indicators are made available to the researcher and the external variables are isolated, the problem of identifying the causal links remains a challenge. Moreover, the selection of appropriate criteria depends on the objectives and values of the person making the evaluation.[56]

▷ Measuring the leadership–organization performance link is problematic when better leadership behaviour and employment management are transferred and embedded in a different social environment.

As we assume that elements of potential conflict and active cooperation are both inherent in the employment relationship, and that it generates differences in relative power, the effectiveness of management practices in the multifaceted reality of corporate capitalism will be determined by the capability of leaders to create processes by which legitimate differences in stakeholder interests can be reconciled.[57] Therefore, if researchers and management practitioners wish to demonstrate the leadership factor in the organizational performance equation, there is a need for more case-study research that takes account of the 'societal effects' of management practices as they are transplanted around the globe and translated locally into workable social relations. It is difficult to evaluate the leader–organizational performance link when there are so many alternative measures of performance, when it is uncertain which criterion is most relevant, and when cultural and societal effects clearly give rise to distinctive leadership behaviours or styles.[58] Our perspective and understanding of leadership performance is more likely to be broadened when multiple conceptions of context and performance are adopted.

We started this section by asking the question, is leadership intervention important to organizations? Arguably in the twentieth century, there was popular enthusiasm for the transformative outcomes attributed to the charismatic or visionary leader. In the early twenty-first century, however, partly as a result of spectacular corporate failures – for instance, the Enron and WorldCom leadership debacles – enthusiasm for popular 'great men' theories of leadership has waned. Indeed, leadership theorists have shown the 'dark side' of charismatic leadership, and a number are scathing of heroic visionary leaders.[59]

Perhaps we need a model of organizational leadership that celebrates mutual equality between the actors. Leaders rely on followers to get things done, and leaders and followers are both interdependent and vulnerable to each other.[60] There is broad agreement that it is difficult to evaluate the leader–organizational performance link, as there are so many alternative measures of performance, and it is uncertain which criterion is most relevant. Our perspective and understanding of leadership as a *process* is more likely to provide a more realistic assessment of the role of leaders.

WEB LINK

Check the Birkbeck, University of London website at www.bbk.ac.uk/manop/research/mgesrc.shtml, from which you will be able to download various papers. For further information and research reports on evaluating the leader–performance linkage go to: www.nber.org/cgi-bin/author_papers.pl?author=casey_ichniowski http://people.few.eur.nl/paauwe/

In examining the totality of the employment relationship and relations between leaders and co-workers or followers, we can draw upon related HRM research to assess the leader–performance argument. The research suggests that organizational performance may be enhanced by adopting 'better' employment practices, with an emphasis on developing the organization's intellectual capital – a resource-based approach to competitive advantage (see Chapter 17). Organizations taking this approach to competitive advantage tend to create work regimes that encourage employee learning and, in turn, creativity and innovation.

In such cases, what behaviours would a leader need to display to be defined as effective? The research on leadership competencies supports the view that what is important in this particular context is not so much what leaders *are* but what they actually *do*. More specifically, it suggests that an important part of a leader's repertoire of competencies is the ability to facilitate informal learning and reflexivity – the ability of a work group or team to reflect critically on the way it performs tasks, how members relate to and work with one another, and ask themselves tough questions.[61] This involves an understanding of the dyadic exchange model between the leader and his or her co-workers, that leadership is a social activity embedded in a community of practices, and (more controversially perhaps) the notion that followers are *teachers* to the leader.

Challenging the traditional notion of leader–follower exchanges, Keith Grint argues, for example, that critical to successful leadership:

> is not a list of innate skills and competences, or how much charisma you have, or whether you have a vision or a strategy for achieving that vision, but whether you have *a capacity to learn from your followers* [our emphasis]. And that learning approach is inevitably embedded in a relational model of leadership.[62]

The challenge for researchers is to locate leadership in a wider social context, and to provide empirical evidence to substantiate the emerging theories on the interconnectedness of leadership, learning and creativity.

Chapter summary

☐ Leadership is a dialectical process in which an individual persuades others to do something they would not otherwise do. It is a result of the interaction of the leader and followers in a specific context, and is equated with power. Leadership is not the same as management. Management is associated with functions such as planning, organizing, controlling and efficiency, whereas leadership is associated with vision making and significant change. Management processes produce a degree of order and consistency in work behaviour. Leadership processes produce significant change or movement.

☐ To guide the reader through the immense terrain of leadership theory and practice, we provided a three-dimensional model that conceptualizes leadership as a relational phenomenon (Figure 5.2). We observed that leadership theories are typically classified according to the types of variables emphasized in a theory or empirical study.

☐ We reviewed the major perspectives of leadership, including the trait, behaviour, contingency, power and gender-influenced approaches. We showed how the systematic research on leadership has evolved from a narrow focus on the leader's traits to a multidimensional model of leadership, which looks at the exercise of leadership as a complex reciprocal process affected by the interaction among the leader, the followers, and the opportunities and constraints afforded by external and internal contexts in which they find themselves.

☐ We have drawn attention to the disadvantages of individualistic-oriented charismatic and visionary leadership models. In the context of twenty-first century corporate scandals and a single-minded focus on shareholder value, there is the danger that:

> Once people over-align themselves with a company, and invest excessive faith in the wisdom of its leaders, they are liable to lose their original sense of identity, tolerate ethical lapses they would have previously deplored, find a new and possibly corrosive value system taking root, and leave themselves vulnerable to manipulation by the leaders of the organization, and to whom they have mistakenly entrusted many of their vital interests.[63]

To help counter this phenomenon we have drawn attention to some of the emerging theories of leadership which focus on power, social relations and the importance of reflexivity.

☐ The study of organizational leadership in mainstream OB is ultimately concerned with organizational performance. Some research evidence supports the popular view that leaders, through their personal influence and behaviours, do make a difference to organizational performance. We emphasized that we should approach the issue of the leadership–performance link with at least one key question in mind: what types of performance data are available to measure the leadership–organizational performance link?

Key concepts

integrative approach: explains
the effectiveness of a leader in
terms of influence on the way
followers view themselves and
interpret the context and events

Chapter review questions

1. Are management and leadership diametrically opposed?
2. Is leadership irrelevant to most organizational outcomes?
3. Why might the model for understanding leadership presented in this text be considered multidimensional?
4. After reading this chapter, do you believe that leaders are born or made?
5. Can leadership make a difference to organizational performance?

Further reading

Bolden, R. and Gosling, J. (2006) 'Leadership competencies: time to change the tune?'
    Leadership **2** (2), p. 160.
Bratton, J., Grint, K. and Nelson, D. (2005) *Organizational Leadership*, Mason, Oh.: Thomson-
    South-Western.
Bryman, A. (1996) 'Leadership in organizations', pp. 276–92 in S. R. Clegg, C. Hardy and W. R.
    Nord (eds), *Handbook of Organizational Studies*, London: Sage.
Cunliffe, A. L. (2001) 'Managers as practical authors: reconstructing our understanding of
    management practice', *Journal of Management Studies* **38** (3), pp. 351–72.
Grint, K. (2005) *Leadership: Limits and possibilities*, Basingstoke: Palgrave Macmillan.
Storey, J. (ed.) (2003) *Leadership in Organizations: Current issues and key trends*, London:
    Routledge.
Sundgren, M. and Styhre, A. (2006) 'Leadership as de-paradoxification: leading new drug
    development work at three pharmaceutical companies', *Leadership* **2** (1) (February),
    pp. 31–51.

Chapter case study: The challenge of evaluating leadership development training

Setting

In 1999, Canadian local governments spent more than C$43 billion on providing services and managing the assets of local communities across the country. Typical municipal services include police, fire protection, road management, public transport, utility services, land use planning and development, taxation and local economic development.[64] Local governments provide more jobs than any other level of government in Canada, employing 350,717 people in 1999. In that year, local governments in British Columbia employed approximately 10 per cent of that total.[65]

In its 2002 study on the Canadian municipal sector and human resources entitled 'At the crossroads of change', the Federation of Canadian Municipalities (FCM) identified a number of the challenges facing local governments. These include remaining competitive in terms of attracting people and investment in a global economy, considering citizen demands for approaches to economic development that are environmentally sustainable, and responding to increasingly sophisticated taxpayer expectations regarding accountability and performance. In addition, the transferring of service responsibility from other levels of government, and financial pressures, have put immense pressures on local governments to review their corporate management. The consideration of innovative and alternative service delivery methods has also created a need for organizational change and staff development to meet the needs of local governments in this new environment. Leadership competencies were recognized as a skill set that had previously not been characteristic of the municipal sector, but that was vital for local governments to successfully face the new challenges.[66]

Kamloops is one of the largest cities in the central interior of British Columbia, with a city population base of 80,000. The local government, or what is known as the City of Kamloops, has over 500 full-time-equivalent employees. Approximately 60 per cent of the staff are represented by the Canadian Union of Public Employees (CUPE), and the rest is divided between firefighters represented by the International Association of Firefighters (IAFF) and management who are non-unionized. In the last two years, the organization experienced a major change in its senior management staffing, with a new city mayor, new chief administrative officer and new human resources director taking over from long-standing incumbents.

The 'Leading for Excellence' training programme

These organizational changes and a realization of the importance of developing leadership skills in existing staff led the City of Kamloops to hire a private consulting firm to develop and provide a customized leadership development training programme, 'Leading for Excellence'. The recognition of the importance that union supervisors play in dealing with staff on a regular basis, and a desire to promote unionized staff into management as vacancies occurred, prompted their inclusion in the training programme along with all the management staff.

Based on the needs identified by the Human Resources (HR) Department, the training programme's curriculum focused on three main areas:

- Module I: Self management – management roles, values, skills, and time and stress management (two days).
- Module II: Management of the team – interpersonal communication, coaching and performance management (two days).
- Module III: Management of the organization – understanding of the organization and how to create more inter-departmental collaboration (two days).

The fourth module, which was one day in length, focused on the integration of learning, motivation, learning from peers and creating successful daily habits. Module participants were divided into departmental groups of either management or union supervisory staff.

Managers or union supervisors attended the first three modules with their group, and joined their counterparts from the same department in the fourth module. A department's managers and its union supervisors were consciously kept apart for the first three modules in order to encourage open and honest discussion.

Challenge for the HR Department

The leadership skills development programme at the City of Kamloops was a highly visible initiative strongly supported by both senior management and union executive members. It also required a large amount of staff time and financial resources. Shortly after the training had taken place, Anne Setter, the City's human resources director, scheduled a meeting with her staff. The first item on the agenda was to discuss how to evaluate the training, and thus justify the expenditure for it in the department's budget.

At the meeting, Anne expressed a concern that evaluation of the training had not been considered when the programme was designed or developed. Colleen Sinclair, a junior HR advisor, was adamant that it was too late. She remarked, 'We don't have a baseline measure prior to the training to compare with changes after the program was completed.' Senior HR advisor Jeremy Edwards disagreed, saying it was still possible. He suggested, 'We can determine if desired behaviour has been brought back into the workplace by surveying those who work with the participants and who may observe changes in their behaviour. We can also see if there are any organizational changes resulting from this changed behaviour.'

Anne asked Jeremy to submit a proposal on how such an evaluation could be undertaken so that it could be given to senior management staff at their next meeting.

Tasks

Working either alone or in a small group, prepare a proposal for the evaluation, drawing on the material from this chapter, and addressing the following:

1. What challenges does the HR Department face in identifying the changes in management behaviour and at the organizational level resulting from the training?
2. What would be the most effective way to measure these changes?
3. What recommendations would you make in regard to evaluating future training programs?

Sources of additional Information

Blanchard, P.N. et al. (2000) 'Training evaluation: perspectives and evidence from Canada', *International Journal of Training and Development* **4** (4), pp. 1253–63.

Governance Network (2002) *At the Crossroads of Change: Human resources and the municipal sector*, Ottawa: Federation of Canadian Municipalities.

Kirkpatrick, D. (1994) E*valuating Training Programs: The four levels*, San Francisco: Berrett-Koehler.

McLean, S. and Moss, G. (2003) 'They're happy, but did they make a difference? Applying Kirkpatrick's framework to the evaluation of a national leadership program', *Canadian Journal of Program Evaluation* 18 (1), Spring, pp. 1–23.

Go to the City of Kamloops website at www.kamloops.ca.

Note

This case study was written by Lori Rilkoff, MSc, CHRP, senior human resources manager at the City of Kamloops, and lecturer in HRM at Thompson Rivers University, BC, Canada.

Web-based assignment

You can evaluate the extent that leadership research has influenced management education and training by visiting the Professional Associations Research Network at www.parn.org.uk/parn.cfm?sct=10&content=homepage2.cfm

Select a particular professional group, such as engineers. What leadership competencies do individuals need to display to be effective in the profession? Reading the competencies carefully, do any appear to have a gender bias? If so, why? Report your findings to your seminar group.

OB in films

The film *Master and Commander* (2004), directed by Peter Weir, tells the story of a British naval frigate, commanded by Captain 'Lucky' Jack Aubrey – played by Russell Crowe – sailing across two oceans to capture or destroy a French warship at any cost. The high-seas military adventure provides some insights into leadership and the importance of leader–follower relations. Watch it and consider the following questions:

1. Using any system of classifying leadership styles you choose, identify the dominant leadership style of Captain Aubrey.
2. What qualities make for a good leader, according to Aubrey?
3. Identify key traits and behaviours of Captain Aubrey, as illustrated in the film.

Notes

1 Lorraine Matusek, quoted in Avolio (1999: 33).
2 Jinkins and Jinkins (1998: 102).
3 Former US secretary of state and military commander Colin Powell, offering one of his leadership maxims (quoted in *Globe and Mail*, 2 August 2006, p. B2).
4 C. J. Loomis, 'Dinosaurs?' *Fortune,* 3 May 1993, p. 41, quoted in Bolman and Deal (1997: 3).
5 See Tourish and Vatcha (2005).
6 See Wood and Case (2006).
7 Mintzberg (2004).
8 Burns (1978: 2).
9 Yukl (2002: 5).
10 Tichy and Devanna (1986), Conger (1988), Manz and Sims (1989).
11 Williams (1983).
12 See for example Alvesson and Willmott (1996), Reed (1989).
13 Kotter (1990).
14 Apps (1994: 36).
15 Kotter (1990; 1996a).
16 Hammer and Champy (1993: 107).
17 Kotter (1996a: 26).
18 Bennis and Nanus (1997).
19 Yukl (2002).
20 Stogdill (1974).
21 Kirkpatrick and Locke (1991: 59).
22 Yukl (1998).
23 Harter, Ziolkowski and Wyatt (2006).
24 Granrose (2001).
25 Fleishman (1953).
26 Lewin et al. (1939).
27 Grint (1997).
28 Yukl (1998: 62).

29 Woodruffe (1992: 17), quoted in Bratton and Gold (2003: 227).

30 Oram (1998).

31 See Wajcman (1998: 80) for an explanation of the origin of this term.

32 Price and Garland (1981).

33 Bolden and Gosling (2006).

34 Fiedler (1964).

35 Fiedler (1970).

36 McMahon (1972), Peters, Hartke and Pohlman (1985).

37 Fiedler (1965).

38 Peters, Hartke and Pohlmann (1985).

39 Schriesheim and Kerr (1977).

40 House (1971), House and Mitchell (1974).

41 Wofford and Liska (1993).

42 Yukl (2002).

43 Hersey and Blanchard (1969), Hersey et al. (1977).

44 See for example, Vecchio (1987), Blank, Weitzel and Green (1990).

45 Hersey and Blanchard (1996).

46 Sundgren and Styhre (2006).

47 Foucault (1977).

48 Rosener (1990).

49 Wajcman (1998: 165).

50 See Gaertner and Ramnarayan (1983), Zammuto (1982).

51 Weiner and Mahoney (1981).

52 Burke et al. (1985).

53 Kotter (1996b: 31).

54 Pfeffer and Salancik (1977).

55 Howell et al. (1990).

56 Yukl (2002).

57 See, for example, Dobbin (2005), Konzelmann (2005), Sako (2005).

58 See Kakabade et al. (1997), Broadbeck, Frese and Akerblom (2000) and Jacoby (2005).

59 See, for example, Khurana (2002), Huy (2001), Morgan (2001) and Thomas (2003).

60 See Harter, Ziolkowski and Wyatt (2006).

61 Marsick and Watkins (1997).

62 Grint (2005a: 105).

63 Tourish and Vatcha (2005).

64 Governance Network (2002).

65 Governance Network (2002).

66 Governance Network (2002).

In this part of the book, we turn our attention to how various individual differences affect individual behaviour in the workplace. Individuals have different personalities, perceptions and learning styles. The chapters here emphasize that the work experiences of women, visible minorities and the disabled may be different from those of white male employees.

Chapter 6 examines personality, which we define as the distinctive and relatively enduring pattern of thinking, feeling and acting that characterizes a person's response to her or his environment.

In Chapter 7 we learn that perception, like personality, is interdependent with socialization, and impacts on people's behaviour in the workplace in complex ways. Understanding perception is important because the fundamental nature of perceptual processes means individuals usually interpret other people and situations differently, and so routinely hold different views of reality, which in turn strongly influence their attitudes and actions.

In Chapter 8 we explore learning in the workplace. Here we explain the growing interest in workplace learning, and how the quality of adult learning experience may depend upon how the organization is structured, how work is designed, and how individuals engage, interact and construct knowledge from their work situations.

In Chapter 9, we explain that motivation is the driving force in individuals that affects their direction, intensity and persistence of work behaviour in the interest of achieving organizational goals. We go on to explore two competing approaches to understanding motivation, the need-based and process theories of motivation.

We begin Chapter 10 with the claim that understanding issues of equity across the major social divisions of society is vital for a full understanding of organizational behaviour. We explore the general and specific tensions in organizations that make the issues of equity, inequity and justice relevant topics for learning and research. We ask, if the vast majority of people in our society experience systematic inequities in relation to work, why is it so difficult to realize significant, positive change?

chapter 6
Personality

To gain a comprehensive understanding of just one individual's personality ... one must know about developmental experiences (including cultural influences), genetic and other biological characteristics, perceptual and other information-processing habits and biases, typical patterns of emotional expression, and social skills.[1]

To be manageable, workers must be known; to be known, they must be rendered visible.[2]

chapter outline

chapter objectives

After completing this chapter, you should be able to:

▷ define personality and understand its importance in the workplace
▷ distinguish between the trait and psychodynamic theories of personality
▷ understand how cultural and life-long social experience shapes personality
▷ understand more of the main characteristics of your own personality
▷ apply the key findings of personality research to the workplace.

Introduction

At the morning coffee break, three nurses sat around a table in the hospital's cafeteria. Elizabeth spoke first. 'I'm really disappointed in Alan's behaviour. He became really excitable and loud again during the night shift when I asked him to assist in the emergency ward. He seems to be emotional and excitable whenever we have more than two or three critical cases in the ER. At the interview he came over as so confident and experienced.'

'And he had a wonderful CV,' Eleanor added.

'Interviews and good reference letters can't tell you about a person's personality, and how they will perform under stress,' said charge nurse Judy Finnigan. 'He's not easy to get along with either, especially in the mornings. You ask a question and he jumps down your throat.'

'Yet, you know, he can be totally different outside the ER. He's sociable and pleasant when we go to the pub or when things are quiet on the ward,' replied Elizabeth.

How is Alan able to be such a different person in different situations? Are certain personality types better adapted for certain job types? Why are some people loud and aggressive, while others are quiet and passive? Are certain personality types linked to job performance or career progress? Should managers try to recruit all employees with similar personalities? How does the personality characteristic influence motivation at work? Why do some people find it difficult to work in a team, while others excel as 'team players'? What personality types make for a 'good' team player?

Organizational behaviour theorists have long been interested in relationships between personality traits and job performance, and whether personality homogeneity (people having similar personalities) facilitates team integration. With the wave of interest in teamworking, 'new' individual-oriented employment contracts and performance-enhancing organizational cultures, more than ever managers are interested in the relationships between personality traits and job performance.

Many organizations have turned to psychometric testing to measure differences in candidates' agreeableness, conscientiousness, experience, extroversion, emotional stability and openness to experience in order to predict their job performance.[3] The use of psychometric testing to help predict job performance is an application of theory and research in personality psychology, but it is really only a more formal version of the process that most of us do when we meet someone new. We observe their behaviour, form impressions, and draw conclusions about how that person will behave at other times or under other situations. Like the employer or human resource manager, we look for clues to personality. As we shall see in this chapter, various personality theorists have attempted to understand human individuality and the reasons people behave as they do by investigating personality. We shall also understand how personality is an important factor shaping individual behaviour in the workplace.

In this chapter we present psychological and sociological perspectives that have made significant contributions to our understanding of personality, and some of the ways in which personality theory and research are being applied in the workplace. We begin by describing the psychological trait approach, which explores patterns of characteristic thoughts, feelings and behaviours that form individual personalities. Next we explain the social-cognitive approach, which focuses on the role of learning and social interaction in shaping individual behaviour and personality. We go on to explain the psychodynamic approach, developed by the Austrian neurologist Sigmund Freud (1856–1939), which focuses on the developmental processes that shape people's personalities from childhood. Finally, we present a sociological perspective with its emphasis on how culture and socialization mould human behaviour and personality.

Our overview of these varying approaches, which can only hope to provide a glimpse of their complexity and scope, is followed by a discussion of the connections between personality and job performance, personality and social integration, and personality and occupational stress, along with a critique of how personality tests are used in the workplace.

Go to www.queendom.com/tests.html and www.apa.org/science/testing.html for more information on personality testing instruments. In the UK, the British Psychological Society (www.bps.org.uk) assesses employment selection tests.

WEB LINK

What is personality?

The notion of personality permeates popular culture and discussion in the workplace. In Western cultures, the mass media – print, radio, television, films and other communication technologies – endlessly discuss 'cool' or 'nice' personalities. And like Alan in our opening vignette, we sometimes meet people at work who seem to have a personality that does not 'fit' with the job requirements or work group. We all use the term 'personality' quite often, and most people feel they understand it intuitively. But exactly what is personality? Although there is no universally accepted definition, we define personality here as a relatively enduring pattern of thinking, feeling and acting that characterizes a person's response to her or his environment.

There are several aspects of this definition that need further explanation.

▷ The concept of personality refers to notions of individuality; people differ significantly in the ways they routinely think, feel and act.

▷ Personality refers to an enduring set of characteristics and tendencies of a person. An individual's personality encapsulates her or his way of responding to their world. Personality rests on the observation that people seem to behave somewhat consistently over time and across different life situations. Thus, we would not characterize a person as having a shy personality if that individual tended to be dominantly shy and retiring only some of the time, and on other occasions was frequently observed to be very sociable and outgoing.

▷ Similarly, we need to be aware that individual behaviour is influenced by the social context. Individuals may be shy and retiring in a situation where they perceive the context to be unfavourable (such as meeting new people on the first day of employment), but outgoing when the situation is perceived as favourable. From this perceived consistency comes the notion of 'personality traits' that characterize individuals' customary ways of responding to their environment. Research suggests that stability or consistency becomes greater as we enter adulthood, but even in adulthood, there remains a capacity for meaningful personality change.[4]

▷ Finally, our definition of personality draws attention to the fact that in studying personality we are interested in factors within people that cause them to behave consistently as they do.

STOP AND REFLECT

What do you think of these typical observations of people that give rise to the concept of personality? Do they accurately reflect how you form an opinion of a person's 'personality'?

The patterns of thinking, feeling and actions that are viewed as reflecting a person's personality typically have three characteristics. First, they are seen as elements of identity that distinguish that individual from other people. Second, the individual's behaviours seem to 'interconnect' in a meaningful fashion, suggesting an inner element that shapes and directs behaviour. Third, the behaviours are viewed as being caused primarily by 'internal' rather than contextual factors.

In studying personality we need also to look at how social experience shapes personality. People develop a personality by internalizing – or taking in – their social experiences or surroundings. Without social experience personality cannot develop. Sociological research on the effects of social isolation on children points to the crucial role of social experience in forming personality.[5] Sociologists suggest that in the process of interacting with parents, siblings, family relatives, teachers and others, children develop an individual identity.

The precise meaning of the concept 'identity' is contested, but for the purposes of this discussion, we define identity as a complex fusion of the inner self and the outer social context. It is simultaneously located in the core of the individual and yet also in the core of her or his communal culture, and involves the interplay between cognition and social behaviour.[6] Over time, children identify social roles, first within their family and later in the community. They also develop an understanding of status differences, and the ways in which roles interact with class, gender, ethnicity and race to create complex patterns of social behaviour. This process of socialization is therefore affected by whether they are the son or daughter of a neurosurgeon or a hospital porter; whether they grow up in a two-parent or single-parent household; whether they grow up in London or Londonderry; whether they speak English or Hindu, and whether they worship at a mosque or a synagogue. As a result of socialization, most people acquire a set of attitudes, values, skills and behaviours that enable them to form and sustain close relationships with others, work cooperatively with co-workers, and avoid deviant behaviour. Figure 6.1 illustrates some perceived characteristics of behaviours that are seen as reflecting an individual's personality.

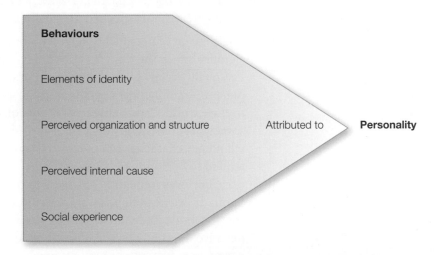

figure 6.1 Perceived characteristics of behaviours that are seen as reflecting an individual's personality

The trait, psychodynamic and sociocultural perspectives have guided the study of personality. These approaches provide very different conceptions of what personality is and how it functions. No doubt, as in other chapters of this book, you will find some of the theories more in accord with your own life views than others. Before we describe and evaluate each of the theories, we need to offer a few words of warning about personality in the workplace.

▷ As we have already said, there is no 'one best' personality type. Some personality characteristics are useful in certain situations, and organizations need to appreciate the value of diversity. When all employees hold similar personality traits and have similar values, studies suggest that fewer rules are needed to get things done. For many managers this may seem like a good thing. But, in some circumstances this same homogeneity could hinder the organization's ability to adapt to change.[7]

▷ Although many organizations consider personality an important criterion for employment, personality tests are still considered to be a relatively poor instrument for selecting people for key positions, such as management roles.

▷ Excessive 'classification' of personality types may prevent others from appreciating a person's potential to contribute to an organization.

▷ If we draw attention to the context and social experience, there is less likelihood of exaggerating the effect of personality on individual work-related behaviour. In highly structured situations – such as the armed forces – with clearly defined rules, roles and punishment contingencies, personality will have the least effect on work-related behaviour. In less structured situations – such as a volunteer community organization – personality will have the most effect on organizational behaviour.[8]

In what follows, we examine three approaches to the study of personality: the trait, psychodynamic and sociocultural approaches.

Trait theories of personality

Almost two thousand years ago, the ancient Greeks used the humoral theory to explain individual differences in personality.[9] The body was thought to contain four humours or fluids: black bile, blood, phlegm and yellow bile. The personality of individuals was classified according to the disposition supposedly produced by the predominance of one of these humours in their bodies. Optimistic or sanguine people, who had a preponderance of blood (*sanguis*), were cheerful and passionate. Melancholic people, who had an excess of black bile, had a pessimistic temperament. Phlegmatic individuals, whose body systems contained an excessive proportion of phlegm, were calm and unexcitable. Choleric individuals, on the other hand, had an excess of yellow bile and were bad-tempered and irritable. Although subsequent research discredited the humoral theory, the notion that people can be classified into different personality types has persisted to this day.

If you were to describe the personality of a close friend or relative, you would probably make a number of descriptive statements, for example, 'He is a real extrovert. He likes to be the focus of attention, is abrasive in debate, but also brilliant and charming. He works hard but he is generous with his time and he is a truly caring person. He will always try to help if he can.' In other words, you would describe others by referring to the kind of people they are ('extrovert') and to their thoughts ('caring' and 'brilliant'), feelings

plate 17 Observable traits, such as friendliness, are those traits that are obvious to others

Source: Getty Images

('attention'), and actions ('works hard'). Together, these statements describe personality traits, enduring personal characteristics that reveal themselves in a particular pattern of human behaviour in different situations.

The English dictionary contains approximately 18,000 words that could be used to describe personal traits, and obviously it would be impractical, even if it was possible, to describe people in terms of where they fall on some vast scale. Trait theorists therefore attempt to condense various descriptors into a manageable number of core personality traits that people display consistently over time, in order to understand and predict human behaviour.

Gordon Allport (1897–1967) pioneered research on personality traits. He believed that the set of words chosen to describe an individual reflects that person's central traits, personal characteristics that are apparent to others and that shape behaviour in a variety of environments. A central trait is equivalent to the descriptive terms used in a letter of reference (such as 'conscientious' or 'reliable'). Another aspect of what Allport called the 'building blocks' of personality is secondary traits, those that are more specific to certain situations and have less impact on behaviour. An example of a secondary trait is 'dislikes crowds.'[10]

factor analysis: a statistical technique used for large number of variables to explain the pattern of relationships in the data

Psychologists have used the statistical tool of factor analysis to identify clusters of specific behaviours that are correlated with one another so highly that they can be viewed as reflecting basic personality traits. Different people fall into these different clusters. For example, you might find that most people who are shy and socially reserved stay away from parties and enjoy solitary activities such as reading. At the other end of the spectrum are people who are talkative and outward-going, like parties and dislike solitary activities such as reading. These behavioural patterns define a dimension that we might label introversion–extroversion. At one end of the dimension are highly introverted behaviours, and at the other end are highly extroverted behaviours. As we describe below, studies have found introversion–extroversion to be a major dimension of personality.

Raymond Cattell (1965), a British psychologist, built upon Allport's investigations to develop his theory of personality. Cattell used a process of factor analysis to identify clusters of traits that he believed represented a person's central traits. He analysed questionnaire responses from thousands of people, and also obtained ratings from people who knew the participants well, and eventually identified 16 basic behaviour clusters, or factors. These 16 traits he called 'source traits' because, in his view, they were the building blocks upon which personality is built. From his data

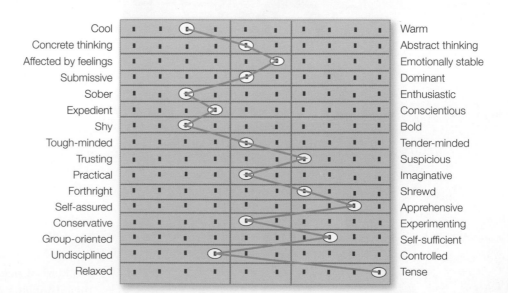

figure 6.2 Two hypothetical personality profiles using Cattell's 16PF test

Cattell developed a personality test called the 16 Personality Factor Questionnaires (16PF) to measure individual differences on each of the dimensions and provide a personality profiles for individuals and for groups of people. Figure 6.2 compares the personality profiles of two hypothetical individuals rated on Cattell's 16PF test.

Eysenck's three-factor model of personality

Hans J. Eysenck (1916–1997), another well-known British psychologist, also used factor analysis to devise his theory of personality. From his research, Eysenck concluded that normal personality can be understood in terms of three basic factors or dimensions: introversion–extroversion, stability–instability and psychoticism.[11] These factors are bipolar dimensions. Introversion is the opposite of extroversion, stability is the opposite of instability (sometimes called neuroticism), and psychoticism is the opposite of self-control.

Introversion refers to a reserved nature and the pursuit of solitary activities. Introverts tend to be shy, thoughtful, risk avoiders, and shun social engagements. **Extroversion** refers to the opposites of these human characteristics. Extroverts tend to be sociable, spontaneous, thrive on change and be willing to take risks. *Psychoticism* refers to an aggressive, egocentric and antisocial nature. People high on psychoticism display such attributes as aggression, coldness, moodiness, are fraught with guilt, and are unstable. People who score low on psychoticism do not show these attributes. Such people tend to be even-tempered and are characterized by emotional stability. Eysenck believed that the most important aspects of a person's personality are captured by the two-dimensional model (see Figure 6.3).

introversion: a personality dimension that characterizes people who are territorial and solitary

extroversion: a personality dimension that characterizes people who are outgoing, talkative, sociable and assertive

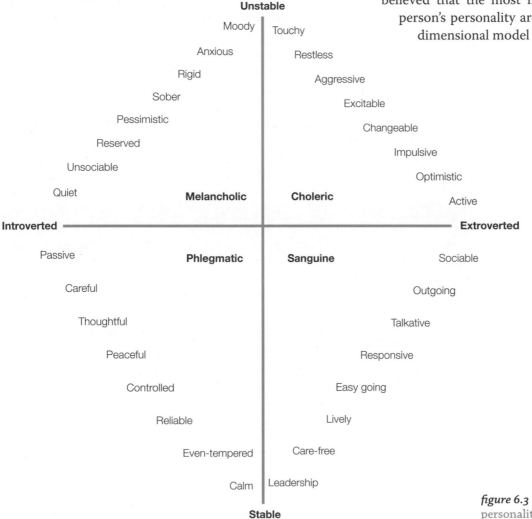

figure 6.3 Eysenck's major personality dimensions

Figure 6.3 illustrates the effects of various combinations of the three dimensions of introversion–extraversion, stability–instability and psychoticism, and relates them to the four personality types described by the Greek physician Galen in the second century AD. We should note that the two basic dimensions intersect at right angles (meaning that they are statistically uncorrelated or independent). Therefore, knowing how extrovert an individual is reveals little about a person's level of emotional stability; she or he could fall anywhere along the stability dimension. The secondary traits shown in the diagram reflect varying combinations of these two primary dimensions. Thus we can see that the emotionally unstable (neurotic) extrovert is touchy, restless and aggressive. In contrast, the stable extrovert is a carefree, lively individual who tends to seek out leadership roles. The unstable introvert is moody, anxious and rigid, but the stable introvert tends to be calm, even-tempered and reliable.

Eysenck's research produced data to show that test scores measuring these two basic personality dimensions can predict people's key personality patterns, including specific behaviour tendencies or disorders. Leaders, for example, are likely to be in the 'sanguine' quadrant and tend to display outgoing, sociable behaviour. Criminals, on the other hand, are likely to be in the 'choleric' quadrant and tend to display aggressive and impulsive behaviour. Eysenck's trait theory of personality has received considerable support because the three dimensions have been replicated in factor analyses performed by many different researchers.[12]

The five-factor model of personality

As we have seen, trait theorists tend to divide into those who suggest that personality is best captured by measuring a large number of basic traits, such as Gordon Allport and Raymond Cattell, and those who suggest that the basic structure of personality can be captured by grouping 'high-order' dimensions, such as Hans Eysenck. The Big Five model of personality trait structure proposes that personality is organized around only five core dimensions: openness, conscientiousness, extroversion, agreeableness and neuroticism.[13] These Big Five personality dimensions, represented by the handy acronym 'OCEAN' (or 'CANOE' if the words are reconfigured), are shown in Table 6.1.

table **6.1** The Big Five model of personality trait structure and the associated lower-order traits

Dimensions	Lower-order traits
Openness	Artistically sensitive, intellectual interests, reflective, insightful, curious, imaginative
Conscientiousness	Efficient, reliable, responsible, scrupulous, ethical, persevering, organized, self-disciplined
Extroversion	Talkative, outgoing, candid, adventurous, sociable, assertive, gregarious, energetic
Agreeableness	Good-natured, forgiving, generous, non-critical, warm, gentle, cooperative, trusting compassionate
Neuroticism	Anxious, self-pitying, nervous, tense, hostile, excitable, emotionally unstable, impulsive

Source: adapted from Bernstein et al. (2000)

Researchers using the Big Five model hold that when a person is placed at a specific point on each of these five core personality dimensions by means of a test or direct observations of behaviour, the essence of that person's personality is captured. These 'Big Five' personality dimensions may be universal, since they were found to be consistent in a study of women and men in diverse Asian, European and North American cultures.[14]

The research also shows evidence that some personality dimensions tend to be more stable than others over time. For example, introversion–extroversion tends to be quite stable from childhood into adulthood and across the adult years. When it comes to stability of behaviour across situations, personality again shows both a degree of stability and some capacity for change. For example, regarding the higher-order trait of 'conscientiousness', an employee might be highly conscientious in one situation (such as handing in class assignments on time to complete a college programme of studies) without being conscientious in another (such as coming to work on time).

Trait theorists have made an important contribution by focusing attention on the value of identifying, classifying and measuring stable and enduring personality characteristics. But as has been argued elsewhere, researchers need to pay more attention to how traits interact with one another to affect various behaviours if we are to capture the true personality. There is a tendency for researchers to make predictions on the basis of a single measured personality trait without taking into account other personality factors that also might influence the action in question.[15]

STOP AND REFLECT

Where would you place yourself on the personality scales? What is your reaction to the models? Are personality traits inherited or do they arise from social experience? What are the predictive advantages of the broad general traits and the narrow specific traits?

The psychodynamic theory of personality

Many social psychologists and organizational theorists believe that personality emerges from complex processes too dynamic to be captured by factor analysis. The Austrian physician Sigmund Freud (1856–1939) developed the influential psychoanalytic theory of personality, which claims that the dynamic interplay of inner psychological processes determines ways of thinking, feeling and acting. Freud's work introduced such terms as 'ego', 'fixation', 'libido', 'rationalization' and 'repression' into Western popular discourse, as well as having a profound effect on twentieth-century personality research. The significance of psychoanalytic theories of socialization pioneered by Freud has been recognized by sociologists.

When treating patients with the French neurologist Jean Charcot, Freud became convinced that conversion hysteria, a disorder in which physical symptoms such as paralysis and blindness appeared suddenly and with no apparent physical cause, was connected to painful memories, which were often sexual or aggressive in nature, and seemed to have been repressed by the patient. When his patients were able to re-experience these traumatic memories their physical symptoms often improved markedly or disappeared.

WEB LINK

Go to www.freud.org.uk, a site dedicated to Sigmund Freud and his work.

Freud experimented with various techniques to unearth the buried contents of the unconscious mind, including hypnosis and dream analysis. His research convinced him that personality develops out of each person's struggle to meet her or his basic needs in a world that often frustrates those efforts. Freud proposed that an individual's personality is determined by conscious, preconscious and unconscious brain activity, with the unconscious part of the mind exerting great influence on consciousness and behaviour. He proposed that most psychological events are located in what he termed the subconscious, a vast repository of traumatic events that a person apparently can no longer consciously recall without the use of hypnosis. The conscious mind, which consists of mental events people are presently aware of, represented just the 'tip of the iceberg' (see Figure 6.4).

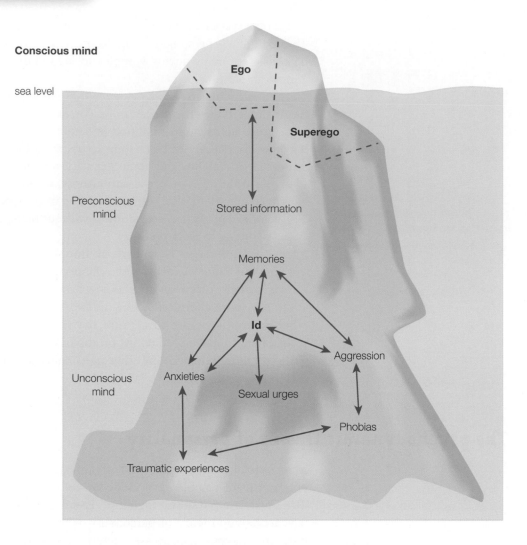

figure 6.4 Freud's conception of the personality structure: 'the Freudian iceberg'

The structure of personality: id, ego, and superego

According to Freud, personality is made up three separate but interacting parts: the id, the ego and the superego. In Figure 6.4, the pointed arrows inside the 'Freudian iceberg' are meant to show the connections and the dynamic nature of the structure of personality. Freud saw the **id** (Latin word for 'it') as the unconscious portion of the personality, where the libido, which is the primary source of life instincts, resides. The id is the only structure present at birth, and functions in a totally irrational manner. The id operates on the pleasure principle, seeking the immediate gratification of impulses produced by two innate drives, sex and aggression.

For Freud, the id is:

> [T]he dark, inaccessible part of our personality .... It is filled with energy reaching it from the instincts, but it has no organization, produces no collective will, but only a striving to bring about the satisfaction of the instinctual needs subject to the observance of the pleasure principle.[16]

The **ego** (Latin for 'I') is the thinking, organizing and protective self. It functions primarily at a conscious level, it controls and integrates behaviour, and it operates according to the reality principle. It negotiates a compromise among the pressures of the id and the demands of reality, deciding when and under what conditions the id can safely discharge its impulses and satisfy its needs. For example, the ego would seek sexual gratification within a consenting relationship rather than allow the pleasure principle to dictate an impulsive sexual assault.

id: Sigmund Freud's term for the component of personality that includes all of the individual's basic biological drives and needs that demand immediate gratification

ego: According to Sigmund Freud, the rational, reality-oriented component of personality that imposes restrictions on the innate pleasure-seeking drives of the id

superego: Sigmund Freud's term for the human conscience, consisting of the moral and ethical aspects of personality

The third component of personality is the superego (Latin meaning 'beyond' or 'above' the ego), which is subdivided into the conscience and the ego ideal, and tells us what we should and should not do. The superego, the moral arm of the personality, determines which actions are permissible and punishes wrongdoing with feelings of guilt. Like the ego, the superego strives to control the instincts of the id, particularly the sexual and aggressive impulses that are condemned by Western society. Whereas the id screams, 'I want!' the superego replies, 'Don't you dare! That would be wicked!' For the superego, moralistic principles take precedence over realist ones. Thus the superego might cause a person to experience intense guilt over sexual deviance.

The ego must achieve a compromise between the demands of the id, the constraints of the superego and the demands of reality. This mediating role has earned the ego the title 'executive of the personality'.[17]

Freud's theory of personality set the scene for a never-ending struggle between the id and the superego for control of the ego. When the ego confronts id drives that threaten to get out of control, anxiety results. Anxiety serves as a signal, and motivates the ego to deal with the problem. Freud proposed a number of defence mechanisms to enable people to cope with these conflicts. Examples of defence mechanisms are described in Table 6.2. The principal defence mechanism is repression.

Source: Getty Images

plate 18 Research into the genetic basis of personality suggests that traits such as extroversion may be inherited

table 6.2 Psychoanalytic defence mechanisms

Defence mechanism	Description	Example
Repression	An active defensive process through which anxiety-arousing impulses or memories are pushed into the unconscious mind.	An sports celebrity who was sexually abused in childhood develops amnesia for the event.
Denial	A person refuses to acknowledge anxiety-arousing aspects of the environment. The denial may involve either the emotions connected with the event or the event itself.	A young man who is told he has terminal cancer refuses to consider the possibility that he will not recover.
Displacement	An unacceptable or dangerous impulse is repressed, then directed at a safer substitute target.	A female employee who is harassed by her boss experiences no anger at work, then goes home and abuses her husband and children.
Rationalization	A person constructs a false but plausible explanation or excuse for an anxiety-arousing behaviour or event that has already occurred.	An employee caught stealing justifies the act by pointing out that the company can afford the loss and besides, other employees are stealing too.

Source: Adapted from Passer et al. (2003)

Freud believed that in repression, the ego uses some of its energy to prevent anxiety-arousing thoughts, feelings and impulses from entering consciousness. Defence mechanisms operate unconsciously, so people are unusually unaware that they are using self-deception to ward off anxiety.

In Freud's theory, personality develops through seven psychosexual stages: oral, anal, phallic, Oedipus, Electra complex, latency and genital – which involve seeking pleasure from specific parts of the body called erogenous zones. A major shortcoming of psychoanalytic theory is that many of its concepts are ambiguous, and difficult to define and measure operationally. A second major criticism is that Freud laid too much emphasis on the events of early childhood as determinants of adult personality.

STOP AND REFLECT

Have you ever found yourself using any of Freud's defence mechanisms? If so, what was the situation?

WEB LINK

Go to www.wynja.com/personality/theorists.html for books and theorists on personality and consciousness.

Sociocultural theories of personality

In this section we present an introduction to the work of prominent social psychologists and sociologists who, in different ways, are interested in understanding personality from a sociocultural perspective. According to the trait and psychodynamic approaches, personality consists of traits or inner dynamics that shape thoughts, feelings and actions. In contrast, those taking a sociocultural approach understand personality to be fundamentally rooted in life experience, communities of practice and relationships. It is acquired through learning in an immediate social milieu – the social setting that is directly open to an individual's personal experience.

Sociocultural researchers examine how personality is connected with social experience and the society in which people live: the culture, socialization and social dynamics of social interaction and situations. To illustrate this broad sociocultural perspective, we consider significant social-cognitive and phenomenological approaches to personality.

The *social-cognitive approach*, sometimes called the social learning approach, emphasizes the development of personality through people interacting with a social environment that provides learning experiences. The phenomenological approach to personality suggests that the way people perceive and interpret social experience forms their personalities and influences their thoughts, feelings and actions.

phenomenological approach: a philosophy concerned with how researchers make sense of the world around them whose adherents believe that the social researcher must "get inside people's heads" to understand how they perceive and interpret the world

The social-cognitive approach to personality

The most influential social-cognitive or social learning theories are those of Julian Rotter and Albert Bandura.[18] These theorists have developed an approach that views personality as the sum total of the cognitive habits and behaviours that develop as people learn through experience in their social setting.

Julian Rotter (pronounced like 'motor') argued that a person's decision to engage in a behaviour in a given situation is determined by two factors:

▷ what the person expects to happen following the action
▷ the value the person places on the outcome, which is called the reinforcement value.

expectancy theory: a motivation theory based on the idea that work effort is directed toward behaviours that people believe will lead to desired outcomes

Expectancy is our perception of how likely it is that certain consequences will occur if we engage in a particular behaviour within a specific situation. 'Reinforcement value' is basically how much we desire or dread the outcome that we expect the action to produce. For example, a candidate for a position may spend a lot of money on new clothes to attend a job interview because past learning leads him or her to expect that doing so will help secure the job, and s/he places a high value on having the job.

Rotter also argued that people learn general ways of thinking about their environment, in particular about how life's rewards and punishments are controlled. Differences in this generalized expectancy concerning the degree of personal control individuals have in their lives produced Rotter's influential concept of the internal–external locus of control. People with an internal locus of control believe that life outcomes are largely under personal control and depend on their own efforts. In contrast, people with an external locus of control believe that the environment is largely beyond their control, and their fate has less to do with their own efforts than with the influence of external factors, such as luck.

Research suggests that the locus of control people develop has important implications for personality in later life. For example, in the workplace there is evidence that internal locus of control is positively related to self-esteem and feelings of personal effectiveness, and the internally focused are less likely to experience depression or anxiety, and tend to cope with stress in a more active and problem-focused manner than do externally focused people.[19] One study has shown that because locus of control is fashioned by people's social experience, this aspect of personality can change.[20] In the workplace, for example, experiencing participative decision-making arrangements may cause a shift towards an internal locus of control in managers and non-managers alike.

According to Albert Bandura, neither personal traits nor the social context alone determines personality. Instead, he argues that the environment, the person, and the person's behaviour interacting in a pattern of two-way causal links determine personality. In short, personality is determined by what Bandura calls *reciprocal determinism* (see Figure 6.5).

> **locus of control:** a personality trait referring to the extent to which people believe events are within their control

Go to http://sociologyindex.com for major ideas in the sociological study of socialization.

WEB LINK

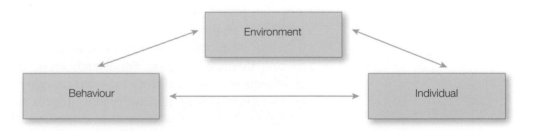

figure 6.5 Bandura's model of reciprocal determinism

One personal variable in this web of influence is particularly important in Bandura's view: self-efficacy refers to a person's beliefs about her or his ability to perform the actions needed to achieve desired outcomes. People whose self-efficacy is high have confidence in their ability to do what it takes to overcome obstacles and achieve their goals.

Self-efficacy not only determines whether a person will engage in a particular behaviour, it also determines the extent to which he or she will sustain that behaviour in the face of adversity. For example, if you believe that you are qualified for a job at the BBC, you are likely to apply for an interview. Even if you are turned down for the job, you are apt to apply for an interview at another TV company because you are confident of your abilities. High self-efficacy can facilitate both the frequency and the quality of behaviour–environment interactions, and low self-efficacy can hamper both.[21]

For Bandura self-efficacy beliefs are always specific to particular situations. Thus, we may have high self-efficacy in some situations and low self-efficacy in others. For example, those who have mastered sophisticated computer software skills do not

> **self-efficacy:** a person's belief that he or she has the ability, motivation and resources to complete a task successfully

feel more generally capable in all areas of their life, despite their enhanced computer abilities. Efficacy beliefs are strong predictors of future performance and accomplishment. In short, they become a kind of self-fulfilling prophecy. We present more of Bandura's work in Chapter 8.

Which environmental factors do you feel may be more important for shaping personality? What kinds of personality differences between males and females have you observed? Are these differences genuine or a product of your culture? How do you know?

STOP AND REFLECT

The phenomenological approach to personality

The most influential phenomenological theories, also known as humanistic theories, of personality are those of Abraham Maslow (1908–1970) and Carl Rogers (1902–1987). These theorists emphasize the positive, fulfilling experiences of life, and argue that the way people perceive and interpret their social experiences forms their personality. Maslow believed that human motivation is based on a hierarchy of needs, and to understand personality requires an understanding of this hierarchy of needs.[22] According to Maslow, personality is the expression of a basic human tendency towards growth and self-actualization. The innate drive for self-actualization, which is the realization of a person's true intellectual and emotional potential, is not specific to any particular culture. Maslow considered it as being a fundamental part of human nature: 'Man has a higher and transcendent nature, and this is part of his [sic] essence.'[23]

Like Maslow, Carl Rogers saw personality as the expression of a basic human tendency towards growth and self-actualization.[24] However, unlike Maslow he did not view personality development in terms of satisfying a hierarchy of needs. Rogers argued that personality development centres on a person's self-concept, the part of social experience that a person identifies as 'I' or 'me'. He believed that people who accurately experience the self – with all its preferences, approval, love, respect and affection – are en route to self-actualization.

The key to forming a psychologically positive personality is to develop a positive self-concept or image of oneself. How does a person do this? According to Rogers, people are happy if they feel that others are happy with them. Similarly, people are unhappy when others are dissatisfied or disappointed with them. People's feelings towards themselves depend significantly on what others think of them. From early childhood, we learn that there exist certain criteria or conditions that must be met before others give us positive regard. Rogers called these criteria 'conditions of worth'. In Rogers's view, rewards and punishment from others are important in personality development because they influence behaviour and shape self-perceptions. In short, personality is formed partly by the actualizing tendency and partly by others' evaluations.[25]

The social-self approach to personality

Socialization, the lifelong social experience by which people learn culture and develop their human potential, has great relevance for understanding personality. A century ago in 1902, sociologist Charles Cooley (1864–1929) introduced the phrase the 'looking-glass self' in *Human Nature and the Social Order*, to mean a conception of self based largely on how we imagine we appear to others, and imagine judgements likely to be made about that appearance.[26]

looking-glass self: Cooley's term for the way in which a person's sense of self is derived from the perceptions of others

Writing almost 30 years before the psychologist Carl Rogers, sociologist George Herbert Mead (1863–1931) developed the concept of the looking-glass self, and developed a theory to explain how personality is formed through social activity and interaction with other people. Mead's writings have some similarities to those of Maslow and Rogers. Central to Mead's theory of personality is the concept of the 'self', that part of a person's personality composed of self-awareness and self-image.[27] Mead believed that people form a personality by internalizing – or taking in – their locale. He rejected the notion that the self is inherited at birth and that personality is formed by biological inner impulses or drives, as argued by Sigmund Freud. According to Mead, the self develops only with social activity and social relationships, and if there is social isolation, as in the case of isolated children, the human body may develop but no self emerges.

After a self is formed, people usually, but not always, manifest it. For example, Daniel Defoe's Robinson Crusoe developed a self while he was living in his own culture, and he continued to have a self when he was alone on what he thought was a deserted island. Thus, Crusoe continued to have the ability to take himself as an object.

The self is dialectically related to the human mind. The body, therefore, is not a self and becomes a self only when the mind has developed and engaged in reflexiveness. While Freud concentrated on the denial of the id's drives as the mechanism that generates the self's objective side, Mead drew attention to the source of the 'me' – how we become self-aware – by taking 'the role of the other'. People are interpretative creatures who must make sense of the world they live in. We learn to play different roles in this process. We are at different times children, students, friends, workers, parents and so on, and we do not behave the same way in every situation. This process of role taking demonstrates that personality is a social product, and that 'group or collective action consists of aligning of individual actions, brought about by individuals' interpreting or taking into account each other's actions'.[28]

Language is an important aspect of socialization and the development of the self. As children learn to understand words and later to use them, they simultaneously learn to categorize their experience and evaluate their own behaviour and that of others. The first words many English or German children say is 'No' or 'Nein'. The use of language is one way individuals emphatically gauge different cultural meanings in disparate social situations and act accordingly. The self is reflexive, in that a person can become the object of her or his thought and actions. Language is central to the

OB IN FOCUS

Psychometric testing: ensuring the right fit

In spite of their best efforts, many organizations struggle with consistently finding and hiring successful job candidates. To make better selection decisions, many firms are turning to a less traditional tool: psychometric assessments. Psychometric assessments are scientifically designed to provide a standardized measure of a candidate's general intellectual ability, competencies and personality traits. While there are many different tests available, they can generally be classified into two broad types: ability and personality.

Ability is a measure of 'can do'. An ability assessment measures a person's current level of knowledge and her or his capability to acquire further knowledge and skills. It also reveals a candidate's capabilities and learning potential. Examples of assessments that fall in this area include measures of intelligence, verbal ability and mechanical aptitude. Ability assessments are among the best predictors of job performance.

Personality is a measure of 'will do'. A personality assessment measures typical behaviour, and discloses what candidates are likely to do on a daily basis. It is designed to measure a person's preference for behaving in certain ways. Personality measures also reveal whether the individual is easy to manage, works hard, offers innovative solutions and works well with others.

Psychometric tests are also used for assessing characteristics that cannot be developed through training but are acquired over long periods of time, such as personality traits or in-depth knowledge of a profession. The use of well-constructed assessments can improve organization fit and address counterproductive behaviours.

Shawn Bakker, a psychologist at Psychometrics Canada (www.psychometrics.com).
Source: *Canadian HR Reporter*, 27 March 2006, p. 7.

development of individual identity, the self. Moreover, 'the dynamics of the self and others are open to complex layers of interpretation and reflexive distancing'.[29]

Mead believed that the self has two parts: the 'I' (the unsocialized self) and the 'me' (the socialized self). The 'I' is the spontaneous, incalculable, impulsive, unsocialized and creative aspect of the self. Mead emphasized the 'I' because it is a key source of creativity in the social process, an individual's values are located in the 'I', it holds something all individuals seek – self-realization – and finally, as society develops people become increasingly dominated by the 'I' and less by the 'me'.

The 'me' is the social part of the self that is developed as the object of others' attitudes, beliefs and behaviour, including one's own reflections on one's self; it is 'the organized set of attitudes of others which one himself assumes'.[30] All social interaction has both parts: individuals initiate action (the 'I' phase of the self), and individuals continue their action based on how others respond to their behaviour (the 'me' phase of the self). While the 'I' is associated with creativity, change and reconstruction of the self, the 'me' has a self-control aspect, in that it serves to stabilize the self. The combining of the 'I' and the 'me' leads to the formation of individual personality.[31] This reflexive process is invariably a social one, in which people form their sense of self in the context of family, peers and the mass media.[32] Thus, a person's personality will change across her or his life course as s/he participates in a community and interacts with different pervasive agents of socialization – his or her family, school, peer group and the mass media.

Mead's concept of the 'I' and the 'me' should not be confused with Freud's concept of the id and superego. As others have pointed out, Freud believed that the id and superego were firmly embedded in the biological organism, while Mead, on the other hand, rejected any biological element of the self. Furthermore, while the id and superego are locked in constant struggle, the 'I' and the 'me' work cooperatively.

Detractors argue that Mead's theory of personality is completely social, neglecting any biological element at all. Moreover, Mead's analysis of personality is rooted in the tradition of symbolic interactionism, a sociological perspective that focuses on the subjective meanings people create through face-to-face communication in micro-level social settings. This was a perspective that resonated deeply in the North American individualistic culture and early US sociology.[33]

STOP AND REFLECT

Make a list of the personality traits you think characterize you. Share your list with others who know you well, and ask what they think. To what extent, if at all, do you think your own personality originates from the interaction between you and your environment? Can you give examples?

peer group: a group of people who are linked by common interests, equal social position and (usually) similar age

individualism: the extent to which a person values independence and personal uniqueness

Applying personality theories in the workplace

While policy makers and managers tend to think of diversity in terms of such factors as gender, ethnic origin, disability and race, the variety of personalities in the workplace is also important. As we have explained in this chapter, personality attributes determine how people interact with other workers, whether they can work on their own without supervision, whether they are conscientious or just do the minimum to 'get by', how they respond to change, whether they behave ethically or unethically, and much more. For example, researchers investigating the personality of individuals have demonstrated that four factors of personality – openness, agreeableness, emotional stability and extroversion – have an impact on work-related learning (see Chapter 8).[34]

For these reasons and others, organizations have developed an array of human resource management techniques to identify personality differences, to help them to admit the 'right' people into the organization. Once staff are selected, this knowledge will help with the design of employee training and development, and help identify those with the personality traits said to be required of an effective leader (see Chapter 5).

John Holland best articulated the view that organizations should consider aligning the requirements of the job and the characteristics of the workplace with personality characteristics.[35] In recent years, awareness that organizations should focus on the degree of congruence between the individual and her or his work environment has expanded because of the need for workers to change and adapt to new work structures and employment relations. These include teamworking, individual-oriented performance-related compensation and a 'learning-oriented' organizational culture. Holland's personality–job fit model identifies six personality types: realistic, investigative, social, conventional, enterprising and artistic. Each of the six personality types has a congruent occupational environment. He proposes that high congruence leads to satisfaction and the propensity to remain in that job or career. Table 6.3 defines these personality types, their personality attributes, and gives examples of congruent work environments.

Holland developed a model shaped like a hexagon which shows the relationships among occupational personality types, based on his Vocational Preference Inventory questionnaire, which contains 160 occupational titles. Respondents were asked to indicate which of the occupations they liked or disliked, and their answers were used to construct personality profiles. The closer two fields or orientations are in the hexagon, the more compatible they are. For example, the enterprising and social personality types are adjacent to each other in the hexagon model, so according to Holland's theory, the individuals with both enterprising and social personalities have high compatibility (see Figure 6.6).

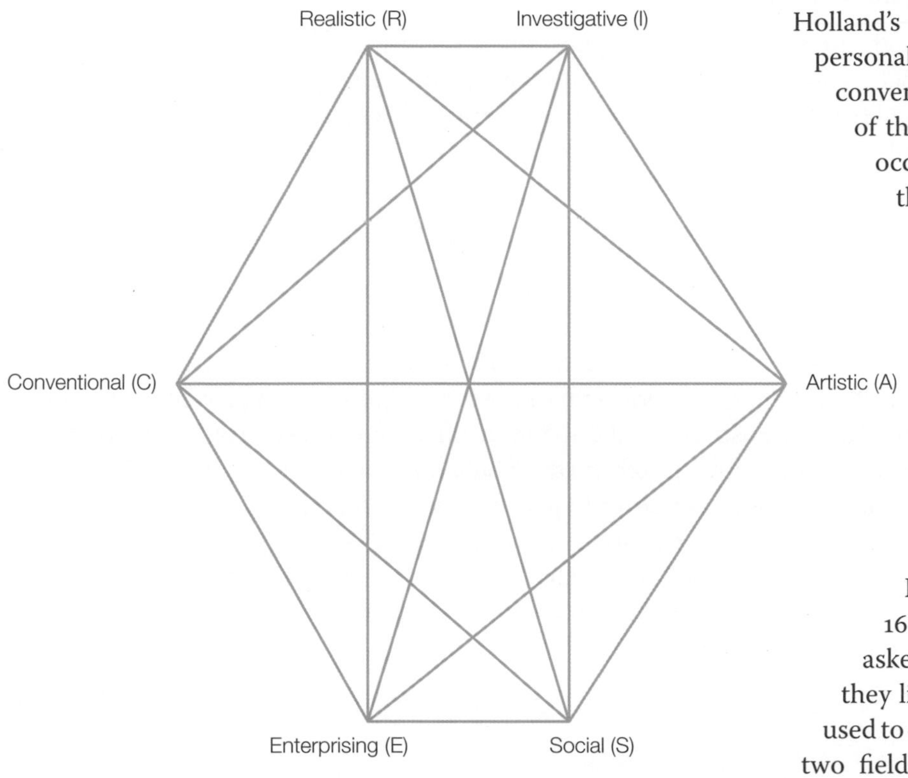

figure 6.6 Holland's individual–occupation hexagonal model

table 6.3 Holland's typology of personality and congruent work environments, and occupations

Personality type	Traits	Workplace characteristics	Congruent occupations
Realistic	Practical, shy, persistent, conforming, stable	Prefers physical activities that require skills and coordination	Mechanical engineer, farmer
Investigative	Analytical, creative, independent, reserved	Work involves thinking and analysing	Mathematician, biologist, systems analyst
Social	Sociable, friendly, outgoing, cooperative	Work involves helping and developing others	Social worker, teacher, counsellor, nurse
Conventional	Dependable, orderly, self-disciplined	Work is unambiguous, rule-regulated, orderly	Accountant, banker, administrator
Enterprising	Confident, ambitious, assertive, energetic	Prefers leading others, verbal activities, result-oriented setting	Lawyer, entrepreneur, salesperson, financial planner/consultant
Artistic	Creative, disorderly, impulsive	Thrives on ambiguous and unstructured activities	Musician, architect, painter, designer

Source: based on information from Holland (1985) and Greenhaus (1987)

There are three key points we should note about Holland's model:

▷ Intrinsic differences in personalities exist based on the restrictive Big Five personality model.
▷ Different types of occupations and work environments are better suited to certain personality types.
▷ Workers in workplaces and occupations congruent with their personality types should be more satisfied and more likely to remain with the organization than workers in incongruent occupations.

Research appears to strongly support the hexagonal model, but critics have pointed out that the model only incorporates the Big Five personality dimensions, and there are doubts whether the model can be generalized across cultures.[36]

With the resurgent interest in recruiting the 'right' people for the 'new' work regimes, and the 'discovery' of the Big Five personality model, research examining the relationships between personality traits and job performance, personality and social integration, and the efficacy of personality measuring instruments, has flourished. According to the new management parlance on knowledge work, workers are expected to create their own opportunities for innovation and positive change in the organization. Underlying the research on the relationship between personality traits and job performance is a presumption that a proactive personality – defined as a disposition to take action to influence one's environment – promotes job performance.[37] This is achieved by building a network of social relationships within an organization in order to gain access to information, wield influence and effect positive change – a process referred to as social capital . In short, the social capital approach advocates a view that individual power within a work organization is predicated on developing a network of relationships, which in turn enhances job performance (Figure 6.7).

social capital: the value of relationships between people, embedded in network links that facilitate trust and communication vital to overall organizational performance

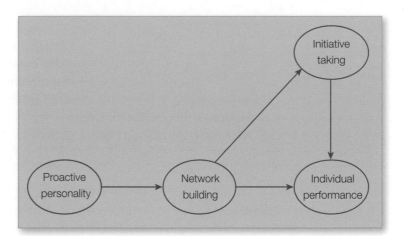

figure 6.7 A model of proactive personality and individual job performance

What do proactive employees do? By definition, employees with a proactive personality are inclined to construct their own environment. Proactive individuals are likely to seek ways to build a network of contacts in the organization that is conducive to their own self-interest. Proactive types, therefore, tend to seek allies and build alliances with other co-workers to support personal initiatives, and actively strive to become friends with people who occupy positions of influence and power. Thompson's quantitative study found a direct positive relationship between a proactive personality, network building and individual performance, suggesting that 'network building may occupy a critical stage in the process by which proactive personality engenders performance'.[38]

STOP AND REFLECT

If you were recruiting people to join you on an important work project, would you try to hire people with a similar personality profile similar to your own? If so, why? Can you think of advantages and disadvantages?

OB theorists have long been interested in the connection between personality and social integration. An important aspect of the current wave of interest in self-managed work teams is the cultural dimension. In addition to changing methods of job performance, work teams demand changes in workers' attitude and behaviour.[39] Accordingly, organizational theorists are devoting increased attention to whether people with similar personalities make up more effective work teams.

The argument is that similar personalities might facilitate social integration among team members, increase the likelihood that co-workers will cooperate with each other, and foster trust between team leaders and members. Employment recruitment practices that create a homogeneous workforce, of people with similar personalities and values, may appear ideal in a team-based environment. Studies suggest that when employees hold similar personality characteristics, few rules, regulations and formal decision-making processes are needed to get work done. As a consequence organizational leaders tend to choose people with personality traits similar to their own. The danger in top managers recruiting a workforce with similar personality traits is that homogeneity is a force potentially detrimental to change and long-term organizational survival.[40]

Personality testing

The increased focus given to personality attributes, and how such attributes predict job performance and social integration, has led to increased research on selection methods in general, and personality testing in particular. Recent studies, for example, have explored the predictive validity of the Big Five personality model in relation to job performance through a meta-analysis of 36 studies that related validity measures to personality factors.[41] The empirically based research concluded that 'conscientiousness and emotional stability showed most validity for job performance, and that openness to experience was valid for training proficiency.'[42]

If you were a manager and had the task of writing within a week a complete personality description of an applicant you did not know for an important position in your organization, what would you do? Most likely you would seek information in a variety of ways. You might start by interviewing the applicant to elicit information about her strengths and weaknesses, interests and opinions. Based on the theories we have reviewed in this chapter, what questions would you ask? Would you ask questions related to the kinds of traits embodied in the Big Five model? Would you want to know about the person's early childhood experiences? Would you ask how she sees herself with others? Would you be interested in knowing how she responds to problems in various situations? You might ask her to complete a questionnaire that indicates her values, interests and preferences. You might also want to ask other people who know her well and obtain their views of what she is like. Finally, you might decide to ask her to perform job-related tasks and observe how she behaves in a variety of situations. As a manager or potential manager, your answers to these questions would tend to reflect your own view of what is important in describing personality.

The major methods used by organizations to assess personality and predict work behaviour are shown in Figure 6.8. They consist of the interview, inventories, behaviour assessment, personality tests and e-assessment.

The task of devising valid and useful personality measures is anything but simple, and it has taxed the ingenuity of psychologists for nearly a century.[43] To be useful from a managerial perspective, personality tests must conform to the standards of reliability and validity. Reliability refers to the extent to which a technique achieves consistency in what it is claiming to measure over repeated use. For example, a selection test that measures a stable personality trait should yield similar scores

reliability: in sociological research, the extent to which a study or research instrument yields consistent results

validity: in sociological research, the extent to which a study or research instrument accurately measures what it is supposed to measure

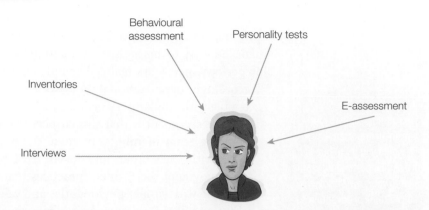

figure 6.8 Measurement approaches used to assess personality

when administered to the same individuals at different times (test-retest reliability). In addition, different managers should score and interpret the test in the same way (inter-judge reliability). Validity refers to the extent to which a test actually measures what it sets out to measure – in this case, the personality variable. A valid test allows us to predict a person's performance in work that is influenced by the personality variable being measured.

The interview is the oldest and most widely used method of personality assessment. For centuries, people have made judgements about others by talking with them and observing them. Structured selection interviews contain specific questions that are administered to every interviewee in order to obtain information about a candidate's thoughts, feelings and other internal states, as well as information about current and past relationships, experiences and behaviour.

Personality inventories, or scales, are used for assessing personality. These are usually self-completed questionnaires that include standard sets of questions, usually in a true–false or rating scale format, which are scored using an agreed-upon scoring key. Their advantages include the ability to collect data from many people at the same time, the fact that all people respond to the same items, and ease of scoring. Their major disadvantage is the possibility that some participants will 'fake' responses by choosing not to answer the items truthfully, in which case their scores will not be valid reflections of the trait being measured.[44]

Human resource practitioners can observe the behaviours they are interested in rather than ask participants about them. In behavioural assessment, psychologists devise an explicit coding system that contains the behavioural categories of interest. Then trained HR recruiters observe candidates until there is a high level of consensus (inter-judge reliability) about how to describe their behaviour.

Myers-Briggs Type Indicator (MBTI): A personality test that measures personality traits

On of the most widely used personality tests in North America is the Myers-Briggs Type Indicator (MBTI). The test contains 100 questions to participants about how they usually feel or act in certain situations. This personal test then labels participants as introverted or extroverted (I or E), intuitive or sensing (N or S), feeling or thinking (F or T), and perceiving or judging (P or J).

Online personality testing is also being used for personnel selection, a technique known as e-assessment. This form of assessment provides managers with the ability to conduct personality tests at any time and any place in the world, with the added advantage of the rapid processing of applicants.[45]

Whether the use of MBTI personality tests actually predicts accurately future work performance is problematic.[46] It has been argued, for example, that broad traits such as Eysenck's 'Big Two' and the Big Five may be useful instruments for predicting behaviour across a whole range of work situations, much as a wide-beamed floodlight illuminates a large area. However, like a narrowly focused and intense spotlight, specific traits such as Cattell's 16PF may be a better instrument in specific situations that call for the behaviours measured by the narrower traits.

For many managers, personality tests such as the Myers-Briggs Type Indicator are useful instruments for measuring personality variables and helping to select suitable candidates to join the organization. Read pages 239–42 in Chapter 7, 'Recruitment and selection' in John Bratton and Jeff Gold's *Human Resource Management: Theory and practice*,[47] for more information and discussion on psychometric testing. Also obtain a copy of Barbara Townley's *Reframing Human Resource Management: Power, ethics and the subject of work*,[48] and read pages 83–98. What role, if any, does psychometric testing play in making workers known and manageable? Do you think Townley overstates her case? If so, why?

Personality testing provides organizations with insights into people's thoughts, feelings and behaviour. In other words, it makes aspects of personality quantifiable, and this allows the inner feelings of workers to be transmitted into measurements, about which management decisions can be made.

Some critical organizational theorists argue that psychometric testing measures what is effectively a stereotype of an 'ideal' worker or manager. It provides management with new ways of 'knowing' and managing managers and non-managers alike. It also represents a shift in management practices from the coercion of bodies through, for instance, time and motion and other Tayloristic techniques, to the attempted construction of self-regulated minds.[49] It is argued, for example, that 'The minutiae of the human soul – human interactions, feelings, and thoughts, the psychological relations of the individual to the group – [has] emerged as a new domain for management.'[50] Finally, personality assessment based on limited information can be damaging to the organization. For example, the over-emphasis on traits to identify 'ideal' personality types in which employees 'fit' into the workplace potentially reinforces the notion that workplace problems are embedded only in the personality characteristics of people, rather than being embedded in the organization at large and the inner tensions associated with managing the employment relationship.

Chapter summary

☐ Personality is the distinctive and relatively enduring pattern of thinking, feeling and acting that characterizes a person's response to her or his environment. In this chapter, we have examined a number of different approaches to personality. Each of these theories offers a view of how personality forms.

☐ Trait theorists try to identify and measure personality variables. They disagree concerning the number of traits needed to adequately describe personality. Raymond Cattell suggested a 16-factor model to capture personality dimensions, Eysenck offered a two-factor model, and McCrae and Costa suggested the 'Big Five' factor model. Traits have not proved to be highly consistent across situations, and they also vary in consistency over time.

☐ We went on to examine Freud's psychoanalytic theory, which views personality as an energy system. He divided the personality into three structures, the id, ego and superego. According to Freud, the dynamics of personality involve a continuous struggle between impulses of the id and the counterforces of the ego and superego.

☐ Sociocultural theorists emphasize the social context, the subjective experiences of the individual, and deal with perceptual and cognitive processes. We examined the theory of Albert Bandura, a leading social-cognitive theorist, who suggests that neither personal traits nor the social context alone determine personality. A key concept is reciprocal determinism, relating to two-way causal relations between personal characteristics, behaviour and the environment.

☐ Phenomenological theories, also known as humanistic theories, of personality were also examined. Influential humanist theorists such as Abraham Maslow and Carl Rogers emphasize the positive, fulfilling experiences of life, and argue that the way people perceive and interpret their social experiences forms their personality. Self-actualization is viewed as an innate positive force that leads people to realize their positive potential, if they are not thwarted by the social context.

☐ The chapter examined Mead's theory of personality and his key concept of the 'self'. He argues that people develop a personality by internalizing – or taking in – their immediate environment. He rejected the notion that the self is inherited and that personality is the product of biological inner impulses or drives, as argued by Sigmund Freud. According to Mead, the self develops only with social activity and social relationships.

☐ Human resource professionals and managers use a variety of instruments and techniques to assess personality. These include the interview, inventories, behaviour assessment, personality tests and e-assessment. We noted also that to be useful to the organization, personality assessment instruments must conform to the standards of reliability and validity.

Key concepts

extroversion	167	introversion	167	personality traits	165
factor analysis	166	personality	163–5		
Freudian iceberg	170	personality types	168		

Chapter review questions

1. What is personality, and why is the concept difficult to define?
2. What is meant by the trait theory of personality? Choose one trait theory, and explain the strengths and weaknesses of this approach to personality assessment.
3. Drawing on your knowledge of Freud's psychoanalytic theory, explain why the ego is sometimes referred to as the 'executive of the personality'. What do you understand by 'defence mechanism', and what relevance has this concept to understanding behaviour in the workplace?
4. Assess critically the importance of understanding the terms 'social-self' and 'socialization', and explain how attitudes and values are developed and changed. Discuss the power of agents of socialization and managerial and trade union attitudes. Use examples from your work experience, family or workplaces you have studied.

Further reading

Arthur, W., Woehr, D. J. and Graziano, W. (2001) 'Personality testing in employment settings.' *Personnel Review* **30** (6), pp. 657–76.

Bandura, A. (1997b) *Self-Efficacy: The exercise of control*, New York: Freeman.

Giberson, T. R., Resick, C. and Dickson, M. (2005) 'Embedding leader characteristics: an examination of homogeneity of personality and values in organizations.' *Journal of Applied Psychology* **90** (5), pp. 1002–10.

Institute of Personnel and Development (IPD) (1997) *Key Facts: Psychological testing*, London: IPD.

Sternberg, R. (1999) 'Survival of the fit test.' *People Management* **4** (24), pp. 29–31.

Tucker, K. H. (2002) 'Freud, Simmel, and Mead: aesthetics, the unconscious, and the fluid self,' pp. 193–227 in *Classical Social Theory*, Oxford: Blackwell.

Wiggins, J. S. (ed.) (1996) *The Five-Factor Model of Personality: Theoretical perspectives*. New York: Guilford.

Chapter case study: *Building Anna's self-esteem*

Company setting

Flockmann's is an exclusive department store located in the centre of Helsinki, Finland. The store is family-owned, and highly successful. It has four main floors, with various departments situated adjacent to each other on each floor. In the early spring, there was a decline in sales volume experienced by most departments in the store. Most employees attributed the slowdown in sales to the economic downturn affecting the entire region.

Background

Each department in the store has a sales supervisor who reports to the assistant manager. The sales supervisors are all full-time, long-term employees of Flockmann's. As a general rule, the sales supervisors in each department do not actively sell, but keep the department well stocked, ensure merchandise is presentable, deal with special orders, and train sales personnel. The full-time and part-time employees do most sales work. Each assistant manager reports to the store manager, Esa Lindholm, who was a sales supervisor of a department for nine years. The store director, Karl Flockmann, has been with the family business for 30 years and will be retiring in a few years. Recently he has delegated most of the merchandising and sales responsibilities to Lindholm. All sales associates at Flockmann are paid strictly on an hourly basis. The starting wage is just above the minimum wage, and raises are given on the basis of length of employment.

Anna Poiketa is the assistant manager responsible for the basement floor, which has four departments: tools and garden equipment, furniture and small electrical appliances (such as kettles and toasters), bedding and linen, and large appliances (such as cookers and televisions). The supervisors and sales associates in Poiketa's departments seem to get along well with each other. If business is brisk in one department and slow in another, the salespeople in the slower area assist in the busy department. Anna has been with Flockmann's for four years, since graduating from a business programme. When people describe her personality, they typically use such words as meticulous, intelligent, caring, supportive, sensitive, dependable and creative. 'She likes getting her staff on board as opposed to telling them what to do,' said one full-time sales associate. Another co-employee commented, 'Anna is adept at juggling work schedules and talking things through with us.'

Esa Lindholm, Anna's supervisor, has the reputation of being a skilled merchandiser, and in the past has initiated many ideas to increase the sales volume of the store. Lindholm personifies the ambitious manager in terms of his work ethic. What drives Lindholm? In his management practices he believes in setting targets, measuring progress, and is action oriented, or what some supervisors at Flockmann's call 'the ready–fire–aim syndrome.' Beyond his hearing, people typically used such words as arrogant, egoistic, Teflon-man, selfish and obnoxious to describe Lindholm's personality. One sales associate said, off the record, 'It's his way or the highway.' What is more, some of the longer-term supervisors said that Esa Lindholm was very impatient and that he was sometimes rude to his subordinates while discussing merchandising problems with them.

The problem

Anna Poiketa consulted with her sales supervisors about the reason for the declining sales volume. The consensus reached was that the level of customer traffic had not been adequate to allow the departments to achieve a high sales volume. During a one-to-one meeting with Anna, Lindholm pointed out that some of the other departments in the store had experienced a 12 percent gain over the previous year, despite the recession. Lindholm concluded that since customer traffic could not be controlled and since the departments had been adequately stocked throughout the year, the improvement in sales must have been a result of increased effort on the part of the sales associates in each department. ▶

Later, Anna found out that Lindholm had sent a letter around to each department informing sales associates that they might be given fewer hours to work if sales did not improve.

The following week, Lindholm called Anna into his office and suggested that each sales associate be issued with a code number to record daily sales. Each sales associate would enter her or his sales along with ID number, and at the end of the day, a new computerized register would total every individual's personal daily sales. Lindholm said that by reviewing the computer printout of individual sales over a period of time, he would be able to determine who the 'slackers' were. The sales associates were to be trained to use the new computerized sales register and about the purpose of the daily tally card. They would also be told that a monthly commission would be paid on individual monthly sales, and that those associates who did not meet a minimum sales target would have their hours cut back.

Anna told Lindholm she wanted to consider this change, and also discuss it with the four department supervisors before implementing it. She told him that she would be away on vacation the next two weeks, but that when she returned to work, she would discuss this proposal with the supervisors.

On returning to the store after her vacation, Anna was taken aback to see that new computerized registers had been installed and each of her sales associates was inputting his or her ID number when completing a sales transaction. When she asked Lindholm why the new system had been adopted so hurriedly, he replied that when it came to meeting sales targets, no delay could be tolerated.

The new system changed the behaviour of the sales associates. They diligently entered all the information for each sale. Sales people became much more aggressive in their sales efforts: often customers were approached more than once by different associates in each department. The friendly conversations that had taken place among sales associates and between supervisors and customers were shortened, and sales were processed through the computerized cash registers much more quickly. When sales activity was slow in one department, associates would migrate to other departments were there were more customers. Sometimes conflicts between employees arose because associates from the small appliances and bedding departments migrated to the cookers and televisions department and competed for the 'big ticket' sales.

A month after the adoption of the new system, unloaded carts lined the aisles of the stockroom and the shelves on the sales floor were poorly stocked. Often customers asked for items that were not on display, and were told the item they desired was not in stock when in fact it was still waiting to be unpacked in the stockroom. Similar behaviour occurred in the other departments on the three main floors. When Anna reported her observations of these situations to Lindholm, she was told that it was a result of the associates' adjusting to the new system and to not worry about it. Anna pointed out, however, that sales volume had still not improved.

Three months later, at Anna Poiketa's request, Karl Flockmann, Esa Lindholm and Anna did a tour of the four departments on the basement floor. After talking with some of the supervisors and sales associates on all four floors, Flockmann sent a memo announcing that the new transaction system and sales commissions would be discontinued at the end of the month. Sales volume in the departments did not improve, and two months later Anna Poiketa resigned from Flockmann's to take up a management position at a rival store in the city.

Task

Provide a report to the director, Karl Flockmann, covering the following points:

1. How do you account for the change in the sales associates' behaviour, and what does it say about the effect of personality?
2. To what extent would you say that Esa Lindholm's personality is reflected in his approach to improving sales at Flockmann's?

3. What might our study of personality tell us about how Anna Poiketa reacted to the situation?

Sources of additional information

Barrick, M. R., Stewart, G., Neubert, M. and Mount, M. (1998) 'Relating member ability and personality to work-team processes and team effectiveness', *Journal of Applied Psychology*, June, pp. 377–91.

Lyness, K. and Thompson, D. (2000) 'Climbing the corporate ladder: do males and female follow the same route?' *Journal of Applied Psychology*, February, pp. 86–101.

Vinkenburg, C. J., Jansen, P. G. and Koopman, P. L. (2000) 'Feminine leadership – a review of gender differences in managerial behaviour and effectiveness', Chapter 9 in M. J. Davidson and R. J. Burke (eds), *Women in Management: Current research issues*, Vol. II, London: Sage.

Visit the Freud Museum in London website at www.freud.org.uk/ for a range of ideas on psychoanalysis.

Note

This study was written by John Bratton, Thompson Rivers University, Kamloops, Canada.

Web-based assignment

Form a group of three to five people, and visit the websites of any of the following organizations: Microsoft (www.microsoft.com/uk/graduates), Sainsbury's (www.sainsburys.co.uk), British Airways (www.britishairways.com), and Royal Bank of Scotland (www.royalbankscot.co.uk). What personality attributes are these organizations seeking when they recruit new employees?

Go to www.queendom.com/tests.html and www.support4learning.org.uk/ (search for psychometrics) and examine the psychometric tests. Some of these you may take yourself without applying for a job. How accurate, in your view, is your personality profile as revealed by any of the psychometric tests? Do your close friends agree with the assessment? Which kind of psychometric tests do you suppose would be more effective in revealing the more important aspects of your personality? Why? How much weight should organizations give to psychometric test results in employment selection? Explain your reasoning. Write a report detailing your findings.

OB in films

The film *The Odd Couple* (1968) centres on the lives of divorced Oscar Madison (played by Walter Matthau) and his about-to-become-divorced best friend Felix Ungar (played by Jack Lemmon). Felix moves into Oscar's New York flat, but the two men have entirely different personality characteristics. While Oscar is disorganized and untidy, Felix is tidy. This amusing film traces their many interactions as Felix moves closer to his divorce and Oscar yearns to live alone again.

Watch the first 25 minutes of the film. What personality characteristics do Oscar and Felix display? What personality types best describe the two characters? What behaviour in the film led you to your conclusions?

Notes

1 Bernstein et al. (2000: 483).
2 Townley (1994: 83).
3 See Bratton and Gold (2007), Chapter 7.
4 See for example Passer et al. (2003).
5 See for example Curtiss (1977), Davis (1940), Rymer (1994).
6 This definition of identity is based on a discussion in Mills and Tancred (1992: 240).
7 Giberson, Resick and Dickson (2005).
8 Adler and Weiss (1988).
9 Carlson et al. (2005).
10 Bernstein et al. (2000: 491).
11 Eysenck (1970).
12 Carlson et al. (2005).
13 See for example Goldberg (1990) and McCrae and Costa (1995).
14 See Dalton and Wilson (2000), McCrae and Costa (1995) and Paunonen (1996).
15 Passer et al. (2003).
16 Freud, (1933: 65), quoted in Carlson et al. (2000: 462).
17 Passer et al. (2003).
18 Rotter (1966), Bandura (1978, 1997b).
19 Jennings (1990) quoted in Passer et al. (2003: 565).
20 Frese (1982).
21 Carlson et al. (2005).
22 Maslow (1954).
23 Maslow (1964: xvi), quoted by Carlson et al. (2005).
24 Rogers (1961).
25 Bernstein et al. (2000: 503).
26 Mead (1934).
27 Ray (1999).
28 Blumer (1969: 142), quoted in Tucker (2002: 218).
29 Ray (1999: 160).
30 Mead (1934: 197), quoted in Ritzer and Goodman (2004: 400).
31 Pfuetze (1954).
32 Tucker (2002).
33 Brym et al. (2003).
34 See Lee and Klein (2002).
35 Holland (1985).
36 Brown (1987), Furnham (1997), Young and Chen (1999).
37 Thompson (2005).
38 Thompson (2005: 1015).
39 See, for example, Procter and Mueller (2000).
40 Giberson, Resick and Dickson (2005).
41 See, for example, Salgado (1997).
42 Bratton and Gold (2003: 239).
43 Passer et al. (2003).
44 Dalen et al. (2001).
45 See Bratton and Gold (2003: 240).
46 See for example Robertson et al. (2000).
47 Bratton and Gold (2007).
48 Townley (1994).
49 Hollway (1991), Townley (1994), Rose (1990).
50 Rose (1990: 72).

chapter 7
Perception

One manager's idea of creativity may be quite different from another's .... All assessments, of whatever kind and in whatever context, occur in the cognitive processing of an individual human being. As assessment occurs 'in the head', it is always, necessarily, and by definition, subjective. Now, of itself, this is neither good nor bad, it just is. The important question here is how we respond ...[1]

chapter outline

▷ Introduction
▷ The basic features and process of perception
▷ The processing limitations underlying selective attention
▷ The influence of existing knowledge in perception
▷ Perceiving causes
▷ Perception and employee relations
▷ Chapter summary
▷ Key concepts
▷ Chapter review questions
▷ Further reading
▷ Chapter case study: Why women are poor at science, by the president of Harvard
▷ Web-based assignment
▷ OB in films
▷ Notes

chapter objectives

After completing this chapter, you should be able to:

▷ understand the basic nature of human perception and its far-reaching influence on the nature of decision making, behaviour and relationships in organizations
▷ identify and define the elements of the perception process, how they relate to each other, and why the sequence in which they occur will affect how individuals view people and situations
▷ explain the influence on perception of information-processing limitations and existing knowledge and expectations, including those arising from cultural background
▷ discuss how knowledge of perception processes can generate insight into phenomena of particular significance in the workplace, such as human error, interpersonal conflict, stereotyping, performance expectations and inter-group relations

Introduction

If one manager's idea of creativity (or enthusiasm, or intelligence) is in his or her head and different from another's, how can employees know for sure that their potential and performance at work is being assessed fairly? If it happened to be another manager making the judgement, would that person have viewed things differently and given a particular employee that job, or that promotion, rather than turning her or him down? It is these types of concerns about the accuracy and consequences of individuals' perceptions that drive the use of systematic assessment procedures in many organizations.

perception: the process of selecting, organizing and interpreting information in order to make sense of the world around us

Systematic, formal procedures are used to make judgements in personnel selection and performance appraisals, and sometimes structured systems are used for assessing the strategy options and risks organizations face. In order to minimize the reliance on what is 'in the head' of one individual when important decisions are made, formal procedures usually aim to include multiple viewpoints rather than that of one person, and to use concrete definitions of the criteria by which a person or situation is to be assessed (for instance, 'creativity is defined as the number of brand new ideas generated'). But why is it necessary to employ complicated assessment procedures? Can we not just train each individual manager to be more objective so managers will all make the same judgements when faced with the same decision?

We show in this chapter how subjectivity in the way we view what we see and experience arises from the fundamental nature of human perception processes. It is not simply the result of lazy thinking, meanness or belligerence on the part of some individuals (although that is not to say that some people are not guilty of these things sometimes!). Subjectivity is the normal state of affairs in human judgement because of the particular way our senses gather information from the world, and the way our brains go about making sense of that information. So the task of ensuring fair and good-quality assessment of people and situations in organizations is not about training individuals to see things as they 'really are'. Rather the task is to understand how and why multiple realities will always exist in any given scenario, and to gain the benefits of them, or at least avoid the negative consequences of actions based on limited perspectives. In other words, the task is to understand perception.

The purpose of this chapter is to outline and discuss the psychological basis of perception: that is, what happens 'in the head' that leads us to perceive people and situations in particular ways. After introducing some examples of how individuals' perceptions can be consequential in organizational life, we explore the central features and processes of human perceptual systems that allow us to experience a seamless view of our world, through the use of cognitive efficiencies such as time and energy-saving mental short-cuts, and the packaging of information for convenient retrieval.

In order to structure our discussion, the issues that arise from the workings of perception are grouped into two main themes, those relating to selective attention and those relating to the influence of existing knowledge. The central importance of context, and the background and characteristics of perceivers in determining what is perceived, will be emphasized throughout this discussion.

The final two sections of the chapter each focus on an aspect of perception that has particular significance in the workplace. First, we shall see how perceptions formed about the causes of behaviour and events experienced have an important influence on individuals' future behaviour and motivation to pursue particular courses of action. Finally, in the last section on perception and employee relations, the broader impact of individuals' perceptions on the social climate of organizations is highlighted.

The topic of perception is at the heart of the study of human experience and behaviour, whether it occurs inside or outside work organizations, because it is through our perception that we decide what is the reality of the world. The truth is that perceptions, and therefore views of reality, are far more dependent on the perceiver than on what is actually 'out there'. The implication of this is that there is not one 'true' reality at any given moment waiting to be discovered, because what each of us believes to be the basic reality of the world around us is 'mostly convenient, internally generated fiction'.[2] Based on our goals, experience and personal qualities we each create and then act upon our own unique perceptual worlds. Crucially, this creative work is mostly automatic, so we tend to confidently act upon our perceptions while remaining blissfully unaware that there might be alternative ways of seeing things.

The topic of perception is particularly important in OB because work organizations represent a real challenge to our perceptual abilities; to use Weick's words, they are inherently 'puzzling terrain'.[3] So much of what occurs in organizations is both constantly changing and ambiguous, especially because workplaces are social settings, and interpreting other people's behaviour is rarely straightforward. Changing market conditions and competitors, diverse people with multiple roles and motivations, multiple communications in various media, organizational politics: all of these things contribute to the complexity of what people must make sense out of when they go to work each day. Because 'the way things are' in an organization is rarely indisputable, the particular perceptions formed by its members become important influences on the nature of individuals' behaviour and relations with each other, as well as on the nature and fate of the whole enterprise.

Consider, for instance, the effect of the leader's perceptions of their organization's capabilities and context. Their evaluations of these factors will determine the opportunities they see, the risks they decide to take and the type of operational strategies they put in place. Part of the reason that entrepreneurs such as Anita Roddick of the Body Shop and Stelios Haji-Ioannou of easyJet were able to create ground-breaking and successful business empires is that they perceived opportunities and ways of doing things entirely differently from the business people before them. Employees' perceptions, particularly of fairness, are also significant for the smooth running and performance of organizations, as was illustrated by the actions of British Airways (BA) ground staff at London's Heathrow Airport in August 2005.

When the BA staff perceived that workers of an allied company, the in-flight food supplier Gate Gourmet, had been sacked unfairly, they walked out on an unofficial strike in support. The workers took this action despite the potentially damaging personal consequences, including loss of earnings and maybe even their own jobs. The airline itself was forced to cancel around 700 flights at an estimated cost of £30–40 million. In fact, this particular incident was not an isolated one for BA: the company had struggled for some time to maintain good relations with its employees, which suggests that the perceptions of managers and employees about the fairness of employment terms and conditions were often at odds. This story demonstrates clearly the power of individuals' perceptions as drivers of behaviour in organizations, particularly the consequences of differences in the way 'reality' is understood.

The BA workers' collective response to perceived unfair treatment also serves to highlight the social dimension of human perception. Our perceptions do not just form in isolation and then remain in our heads. The way we view ourselves, others and the world around us will shape our behaviour, and our behaviour influences the perceptions and behaviour of others. Although this interdependence underlies many of our actions, the social dynamics of perception become more obvious in situations such as giving a presentation, conducting a negotiation or joining a new work team.

A good example of the social dynamics of perception is a lecturer giving a lecture to students. The lecturer may quickly lose confidence if he or she perceives signs from the audience that things are not going well. Now lacking confidence and feeling anxious, he or she becomes self-conscious, begins to speak far too quickly and forgets some of the key points. It is entirely possible that the lecturer misread the earlier signs from the watching students; that they were whispering to each other because they were actually very interested in the talk. But ironically, the lecturer's dive in confidence and collapse in performance may themselves have created the negative audience perceptions he or she feared had occurred earlier. The point is that our perceptions are formed in part on the basis of information or cues picked up from the environment, to which we must then attach meaning. The way we interpret the situation will then shape what we do next, which will affect our environment and the cues we pick up next, and so on and so on.

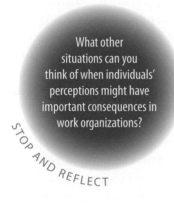

What other situations can you think of when individuals' perceptions might have important consequences in work organizations?

STOP AND REFLECT

These examples all illustrate the significance of understanding the links between individuals' perceptions and their behaviour in the work context. For one thing, different perceptions have different consequences for the performance and success of individuals and their organizations. But also, gaining an insight into how and why people form particular and differing perceptions in given circumstances means we have more chance of avoiding or preventing the escalation of conflict between people and groups of people. In order to discover why, like our poor anxious lecturer, we can be blind to our own perceptual processes, and why, like the managers and employees at BA, we can find it extremely difficult to comprehend and accept the validity of alternative viewpoints, it is necessary to consider the basic workings of human perception. The rest of the chapter will explore the nature and consequences of perception in detail.

The basic features and process of perception

The basic features of perception

Before we explore the component processes involved in perception, it may be helpful to set the scene by highlighting some inherent features of the way our brains deal with information from the world. These features seem to provide good explanations for the phenomena highlighted in the introduction. Perception is selective, subjective, and largely automatic rather than conscious.

We usually feel very certain about what we experience, and this certainty is actually helpful and adaptive because it allows us to go about our daily lives without having to think about every single thing we encounter. Have you ever needed to consciously try to match the movements of people's mouths with the sounds you can hear in order to work out whether a person is speaking? Have you had to work out from light patterns the shape and dimensions of the object in front of you before recognizing it from memory to be your desk? Under normal circumstances, the answer to both questions will be 'no'. Our surroundings make perfect sense to us without any conscious effort. We seem to need this feeling of order, but we actually have to work hard to create it, because the environment is not nicely ordered and organized. For one thing, there is just too much information available from the external environment for our senses to take it all in, and to make things more difficult, it is in the form of raw data such as light and sound waves. So the basic ingredients of our perceptions are highly ambiguous sensory stimuli, and it takes a lot of 'brain work' to sift, organize and interpret them.

It is only possible for us to deal with the continuous bombardment of sights and sounds, smells and sensations because we employ selective attention. An obvious example is being able to focus on a companion's conversation in a busy café despite a myriad of sensory distractions such as others talking and laughing, background music, clattering plates, icy draughts or uncomfortable chairs. But the target of attention is determined by factors inside the person, as well as what stands out in the immediate context or setting. Individuals' preoccupations and goals will cause them to focus attention on specific aspects of people or situations. A professional salesperson meeting a client will likely be monitoring his or her speech and body language specifically for buying signals like precise questions about the product. A manager who suspects an employee of time-wasting may start to particularly notice whenever he or she is away from his/her desk, or talking to colleagues.

So it is that two perceivers can genuinely capture different aspects of the very same situation through selective attention. We do not have unlimited capacity for taking in information, so focusing on some environmental cues necessarily means ignoring others. And because this process is automatic rather than conscious, we are usually not too aware that we have been selective. When it comes to perception, rather than acting as neutral receivers of signals, we select the part of the environment to which we attend by acting as 'motivated tacticians'.[4] The motivation at a particular time may be to prioritize speed, as when we scan information to 'get the gist of it'. We may perceive defensively, as when we 'block out' information that we do not want to receive, or we may be looking for specific types of information to support a particular theory, as when we think someone is lying to us. The point is that our intentions and goals colour our perceptions, playing a large part in determining what we draw from the environment.

Beyond selective attention, another central feature of perception is that the interpretation or meaning we attach to the external information we receive is strongly influenced by our existing knowledge: our ideas, experiences and backgrounds, including our ethnic and cultural origins. In other words, what we experience is subjective because others are unlikely to base their perceptions on exactly the same mix of motivations and prior knowledge. This principle applies to individuals who share cultural backgrounds, but culture-based assumptions will add an additional and powerful source of difference. So in the event that two individuals of different nationality, for instance, did manage to attend to exactly the same aspects of a shared situation, their cultural differences mean that they would probably still not share the same thoughts about the meaning and relevance of the information.

For instance, despite the surface similarities between their two cultures, Britons and Americans can end up with negative perceptions of each other because of cultural differences in the way communications are interpreted.[5] What the British consider to be diplomatic, Americans view as 'beating around the bush'. When Americans think they are being decisive and efficient, the British can view their actions as hasty and unconsidered. Differences in perception are not always a problem, and they can be productive and positive in some circumstances. Indeed, current ideas about the benefits of workforce and team diversity are based on the very fact that people from different backgrounds will tend to generate a broader range of ideas and solutions

selective attention: the ability of someone to focus on only some of the sensory stimuli that reach them

when they work together. This appears to be true in some cases, but the extent to which diverse groups are productive and innovative seems to depend on whether they are able to develop good social relations and maintain the necessary levels of communication to work well together.[6]

Get a copy of a paper by Dunkerley and Robinson, 'Similarities and differences in perceptions and evaluations of the communication styles of American and British managers',[7] and read about the different communication styles, perceptions and comments of the British and American managers in the study. What do you think we can do about the tendency to perceive our own cultural style as better than, rather than just different from, others?

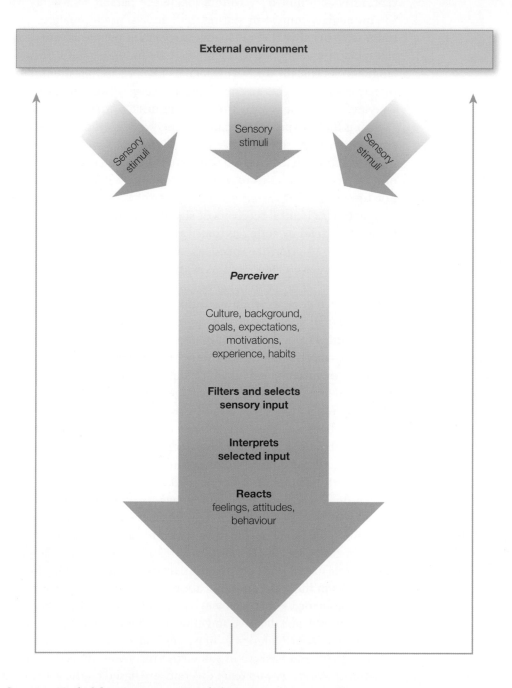

figure 7.1 The link between perception, behaviour and the environment

So existing knowledge, which includes culture, gender and age-related assumptions and expectations, as well as what we have learned and experienced in our lives, will influence how we interpret what we perceive. The key point is that existing factors specific to the perceiver will determine in good part the picture that he or she creates from the available information. So individuals' perceptions are likely to differ in the meaning attached to the information, as well as the information picked up from the environment in the first place.

The basic sequence and key factors in perception that we have discussed so far are shown in Figure 7.1. From the bombardment of sensory stimuli, the perceiver selects some of the information for attention and processing. Based on prior knowledge and current motivations, the perceiver then works out what the information means and responds accordingly. Once the person has responded in some way, her or his actions become part of the environment, and so influence her/his own and others' ongoing perceptions of what is happening.

In summary, human perception can be characterized as a process that is largely automatic, subjective and selective. Perception is not just something inside an individual; it has a social dimension because perceptions affect our behaviour, which influences others. Although highly effective in helping us easily and quickly make sense of the world around us, this amazing capability also has a downside. Our perceptions are most certainly providing only a limited perspective, because there will almost always be another point of view; and dangerously, we are often blind to this simple fact. By understanding how perception works, which means recognizing the inevitability of different world views, we become more able to understand and effectively manage our own and others' behaviour in organizations. The next section will examine the nature of perception processes in more depth.

The process of perception

Perception is, then, a topic of significance in OB because people's decision making and behaviour depend on how they interpret situations, and different interpretations are usually possible. But what exactly does the term 'perception' cover?

In truth, a definitive and comprehensive definition of human perception is not easy to find. The reason for this definitional difficulty is that perception is not really one topic or issue. Instead, the term 'perception' may be used in discussions about any one of a number of topics or issues, which can be placed at a number of different levels of analysis, from the physiological to the social. Research studies about human perception range from investigations of the inner workings of the human eye, to the impact of individuals' stereotypes on cross-cultural communication, to how others' perceptions affect people's choices about which careers to pursue. Nonetheless, it is still possible to identify a working definition to help us explore in more detail the psychological part of the perception process; the bit that happens inside our heads.

According to the cognitive psychologists Eysenck and Keane, 'At the very least, perception depends upon basic physiological systems associated with each sensory modality, together with central brain processes which integrate and interpret the output from these physiological systems.'[8] So our ability to 'perceive' depends upon three things:

1. *Receiving*: being physically able to attend to and receive signals from the environment (for instance, having sight, hearing, touch, taste and smell, and being able to control which we employ at a given moment).
2. *Organizing*: being able to mentally organize and combine those signals (which is what is happening when we see and hear speech in perfect synchronization, or see objects separate from their surroundings rather than a mass of light patterns).

3. *Interpreting*: being able to assign meaning or make sense of what we experience (for instance, attaching personal significance to particular combinations of sensory signals, like knowing when we are in a conversation and we need to talk back, a person is threatening us or a bus is approaching!).

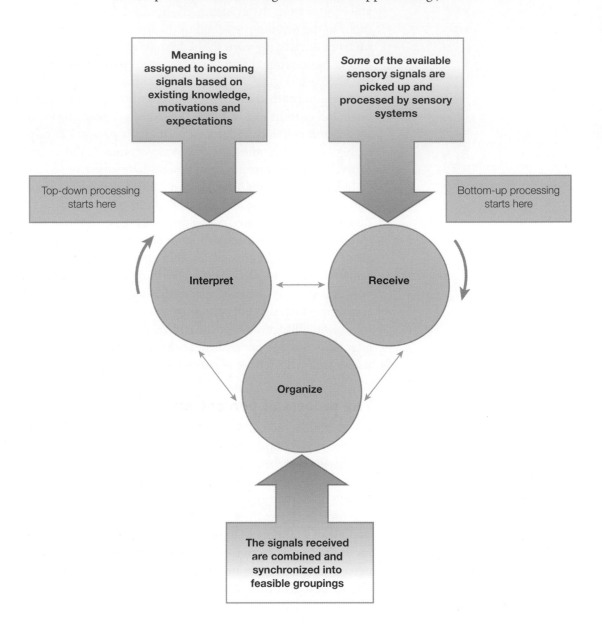

figure 7.2 The elements and process of perception

Figure 7.2 shows how these three elements are connected to each other.

To return to the features of perception already introduced, it is at the *receiving* stage that selective attention 'happens', and at the interpreting stage that subjectivity has its major influence. The *organizing* stage of perception is perhaps the most mysterious, in that our brains somehow work out those combinations of signals that are likely to go together, and those that are just not feasible. In this way, speech is attached to the face that is making the right movements even when there are other faces to choose from. This is how we know when we are looking at an image that is 'wrong' in some way, such as when the perspective is manipulated so the relative size of objects is unusual.

The sequence of perception: top-down or bottom-up?

Although it is helpful to separate the three elements of perception from one another so that we may better understand them, in reality they do not occur separately or in sequence; instead they overlap and sometimes even occur in parallel. As we have discussed, our perceptions are actually constructed in a process that combines external information with our existing ideas about the world. Rarely do we start from scratch by piecing together the external 'clues' one by one. We have already attached some meaning to what we are in the process of perceiving while we are still receiving and organizing the external information. That is how we 'know' what someone is about to do or say, and why we are frequently surprised! The weight of evidence suggests that we almost always engage these three processes simultaneously.[9] Our relative reliance on external and existing information is not fixed, however, and will depend on the specific context.

When perception is led predominantly by gathering external sensory data and then working out what it means, it is called 'bottom-up' or 'data-driven' information processing. When we think there may be consequences in getting it wrong, we are likely to rely more heavily on bottom-up processing. For instance, the requirement in most assessment centres that assessors explain and justify the ratings they award to candidates is thought to exert a 'press of accountability'.[10] The need to justify their judgements publicly leads assessors to pay extra attention to all aspects of candidate's behaviour.

According to Highhouse, rather than always ensuring accuracy, 'thinking too much' can actually hinder our attempts at sound judgement and decision making.[11] If we try too hard to take in as much information as possible, it can interfere with our ability to focus on the most important aspects of the situation. If that happens, irrelevant pieces of information end up being included in the decision-making process. But the most basic difficulty with the data-driven approach is that it is not very efficient because it takes a lot of mental effort and resources.

In contrast to the data-driven approach, when perception is led predominantly by existing knowledge and expectations it is called 'conceptually driven' or 'top-down processing'. In this case, our working theory and expectations about what is happening will shape what we look for. We may fill in the scene from memory after perceiving a tiny number of cues that we think confirm our theory.

A good example of this is an experienced student taking an exam. A common exam mistake is a student failing to read the instructions properly and answering the wrong number of questions because he or she was certain, mistakenly, about the number of answers required. This frustrating situation occurs because the student acts according to a theory or expectation, and fails to use the environmental information available (the exam paper!) to test those expectations.

Researchers have found that we tend to rely on top-down processing in circumstances that are very familiar. For instance, Roth and Woods reported that novice operators in nuclear power plants relied heavily on feedback from monitoring the environment to guide their interventions – a bottom-up strategy.[12] Experienced operators, by contrast, relied much more on their existing knowledge of the operating systems, making much less frequent checks of environmental information.

There is a danger of relying too much on existing knowledge. The danger is that changes in the environment that really require a response from us may simply go unnoticed. This can happen because we are focused on the picture of the situation that already exists in our heads, and so we fail to perceive the signals that the actual situation actually looks somewhat different from what we expected. When the cognitive task in question is making a judgement about someone or something, rather than maintaining a work system, we may never become aware of the failure

bottom-up processing: perception led predominantly by gathering external sensory data and then working out what it means

top-down processing: perception led predominantly by existing knowledge and expectations rather than by external sensory data

to consider key bits of information. Sadly there are no system alarms that go off when we judge people on their mistakes and forget about the things they did really well!

The dangers of 'thinking too little'[13] when making judgements have been well researched in the field of decision making (see Chapter 13). We have some perceptual biases, or automatic tendencies to attend to certain cues that do not necessarily support good judgements. The 'primacy effect' is the term used to describe our tendency to pay too much attention to our first perceptions about someone. Although many people are aware of the power of first impressions, and try to avoid 'judging a book by its cover', it can be surprisingly difficult to change our initial perceptions. On the other hand, if we are not careful we may be prone to the opposite bias, over-emphasizing the last things we perceived about someone, called the 'recency effect'.

perceptual bias: automatic tendencies to attend to certain cues that do not necessarily support good judgements

primacy effect: a perceptual error in which we quickly form an opinion of people based on the first information we receive about them

recency effect: a perceptual error in which the most recent information dominates one's perception of others

halo and horns effect: a perceptual error whereby our general impression of a person, usually based on one prominent characteristic, colours the perception of other characteristics of that person

Source: courtesy of London Fire Brigade

plate 19 Some people would be surprised to learn that this woman is a fire fighter. The stereotype is of men doing such hazardous work.

Another general tendency in person perception is making broad-based assumptions about a person's qualities on the basis of one or a small number of observations, the so-called 'halo and horns effect'. For instance, if an employee makes a mistake on one job task that is considered to be very important, it may bias a manager's overall perceptions, so that he or she assumes the person is incompetent in every aspect of the job. It is always useful to guard against such biases in dealing with others, but it becomes particularly significant in the context of selection and appraisal interviewing, or indeed any situation at work where we are evaluating a person in order to make a consequential decision. It is for this reason that good design is so crucial in assessment procedures.

The key point about our use of perception strategies is that there is a trade-off or balance to be struck between avoiding the risk of holding inaccurate perceptions that comes with top-down processing, but at the same time, minimizing the mental effort of perceiving everything from the bottom up.

Perceptual tricks, manipulations and illusions

The goal of human perception seems to be to make sense of the environment as quickly as possible, even if sometimes a bit of accuracy is lost along the way. As a result, it is quite easy to trick our brains by 'setting off' these tendencies to seek meaning and certainty using various common tricks and illusions. These tricks make it possible for us to get some brief glimpses of some of the usually automatic, non-conscious, workings of our perceptual systems. Indeed, history suggests that we are endlessly amused by having our senses duped! Magicians capitalize on our selective attention when they use sleight of hand in card tricks

Are you able to remember situations when you have used mostly a top-down or mostly a bottom-up perception strategy? Was this a conscious decision or did you become aware of it afterwards?

STOP AND REFLECT

and disappearing acts. Ventriloquists amuse us because we cannot stop our brains organizing, or associating the ventriloquists' voice with the dummies' mouth movements despite knowing the truth. There appears to be something pleasing for us about being perceptually confused, but paradoxically, only as long as we know it is happening!

Some 'serious' artists such as Salvador Dali and M. C. Escher also produced work that played with a feature of visual perception that means we can visually reverse the figure and the background of an image. So in a painting such as *The Great Paranoiac* by Dali, it is possible to see the image as being made up of many small scenes, or to 'phase out' the detail and see one large image of a man's head which is actually made up of the smaller images. The simplest demonstration of figure-ground reversal is the Necker cube (see Figure 7.3), which is named after Louis Albert Necker who discovered in 1832 that the perspective of the cube spontaneously changes if it is looked at continuously. So the front face becomes the back one, or if you prefer, the corner marked A 'moves' from being at the front to being at the back of the cube. This is a demonstration of what is called 'multistability' in perception.[14] When there are multiple possible interpretations of something, and they are equally good or feasible, we will sometimes choose one, sometimes another, but never two at the same time.

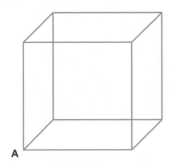

figure 7.3 The Necker cube

Using the same principles as illusionists, perception researchers manipulate sensory inputs in a controlled way in order to explore how the elements of the perception process work and how they relate to each other. A simple and now classic experimental image, the Mueller-Lyer illusion, is shown in Figure 7.4. The straight lines are actually the same length, but the placement of the arrowheads makes them appear to be different: the line on the left appears longer that the one on the right. Curiously, researchers have found that the Mueller-Lyer illusion tricks our eyes but not our hands. There was no illusory effect when the lines were made into three-dimensional figures and people were asked to reach out and grab them between their thumb and index fingers.[15] In other words, the study participants positioned their fingers at the right distance apart to grab the figures in each case. The illusory effect also seems to depend to some extent on the cultural background of the perceiver. When the illusion is depicted in the form of the rectangular corners of walls, people from cultures where the built environment does not include these angular features are less likely to perceive the lines as being of different lengths.

figure 7.4 The Mueller-Lyer illusion

In fact, the exact relationship between culture, particularly language, and thought or cognition, is the subject of much research and debate amongst psychologists. Followers of the theory of linguistic relativity argue that the language we speak has such a fundamental influence on the way that we interpret the world that we actually think differently from those who speak a different language. There is a difference, for instance, between English and Nepalese speakers in the way that the relative position of two people or objects is described.[16] In English, the positions would be described egocentrically, in relation to one's own body (for example, 'he is on my left and she is on my right'). In Nepalese, however, an environment-centred description would be given instead (such as 'he is on the west side and she is on the east side').

linguistic relativity: the theory that the language we speak has such a fundamental influence on the way we interpret the world that we think differently from those who speak a different language

The question that researchers have been trying to answer is whether such linguistic differences are linked to basic differences in the way that people raised in different cultures select and interpret environmental information. The contrasting view to linguistic relativity is that language plays a much less fundamental role in perception and cognition. From this standpoint, it is our thoughts that come first, and we use the language available to us to express those thoughts. As is often the case in the social sciences, there seems to be good evidence to support

The Exploratorium, a museum of science, art and human perception based in San Francisco, has an excellent website where you can explore a number of classic visual illusions online. Go to: www.exploratorium.edu/exhibits/

WEB LINK

plate 20 We know the fork is all in one piece, but our eyes deceive us

perceptual set: describes what happens when we get stuck in a particular mode of perceiving and responding to things based on what has gone before

both viewpoints. The 'compromise view' as explained by Bloom,[17] is that there are some universal perceptions and interpretations of the world that all people share, but that other distinctions in the meanings we attribute to what we experience are shaped by our native language.

The question of whether culture and language shapes thought and perception clearly has important implications for our understanding of cross-cultural communication in organizations. Stated simply, the notion of linguistic relativity suggests that for people attempting to live and work internationally, learning the language of the host country as an adult may not be enough to ensure that shared perceptions, understandings and ideas can be automatically developed with colleagues.

To focus on the context of OB, not all of the perceptual tricks and illusions aimed at demonstrating the fundamental principles of perception, interesting as they are, can be applied directly to organizational life. One perceptual manipulation that has been used in a work context, though, is the old sales technique of the 'agreement staircase'. The technique involves making a series of requests to a customer, to which he or she is highly likely to agree. The salesperson then immediately follows this with the main question, will he or she go ahead and buy? The idea is that the customer will instinctively say yes because he or she has fallen into the habit of doing so. Although, this technique sounds a bit naïve, executed subtly it can work, because we do develop what are known as 'perceptual sets'.

A perceptual set describes what happens when we get stuck in a particular mode of perceiving and responding to things based on what has gone before. The same effect can occur if you read a list of French words followed by an English one, for instance. You will tend to pronounce the English word as if it were French – which can be stupidly amusing if it is a particularly unromantic word like 'cabbage'! These experiments and manipulations do raise an important point which needs to be included in our exploration of perception. They demonstrate the significant effect of context on how we interpret even apparently straightforward information that we receive from the environment. When that information becomes more complex, as in social encounters, that point becomes even more significant.

The processing limitations underlying selective attention

We have already established that we attend to environmental information selectively. One central reason for selective attention is that there are actually physiological limits on how much information that we can take in at once, as well as in how much mental work or processing we can do in a given timeframe. In other words, there are capacity constraints on two of the three elements of the perception process, receiving and organizing. Perception researchers have sought to understand how much of the different kinds of sensory information we can absorb, as well as what gets priority under different conditions.

An example of research in this area is the study of what is called 'dual-task interference', or when the attentional demands of one perceptual task limit our ability to do another at the same time. Put very simply, it is easier for us to do two tasks simultaneously if they involve different kinds of information inputs and require different kinds of responses. Doing two computer screen monitoring tasks, each requiring a key stroke response, is more difficult than doing one visual and one auditory monitoring task simultaneously, for instance. As an example of the practical significance of this kind of knowledge, consider the controversy about the use of mobile phones (or cell phones if you are in the United States) while driving. This issue is of very real practical concern to the large number of people whose work involves driving, as well as their employers.

One argument against their use is that mobile phones are a cause of road accidents because holding a phone and dialling numbers distracts motorists' attention from the road ahead and interferes with their ability to operate the vehicle controls. In fact, two separate studies provide evidence that the interference with driving arises not from operating the phone, but rather from the amount of attention taken up by having a conversation. Whereas a passenger is aware of what is happening and will stop talking if the driver needs to act or concentrate, a person on the end of the phone cannot see what is happening in the car or the road, and so the conversation becomes more demanding for the driver. The findings reported in the studies included the statistic that drivers using mobile phones were four times more likely to be in an accident,[18] had slower reactions, and were two times more likely to miss traffic signals than those who were not on the phone.[19]

Other kinds of research studies concerned with the limitations of information processing have identified two perceptual phenomena called 'change blindness' and 'inattentional blindness'. In these experiments, researchers test the focus of people's attention during various 'realistic' encounters by either changing the situation in some way, or introducing something unexpected and then finding out whether the manipulation was spotted. Change blindness refers to the fact that we simply do not seem to notice even large or obvious changes to things if they are not central to our concerns. In one experiment, somewhat reminiscent of a comedy sketch, members of the public who were giving directions to a researcher failed to spot that they were talking to a different person after two men carrying a door had walked in between them![20]

Another amusing experiment in the same vein, conducted by Simons and Chabris, involved a man in a gorilla suit.[21] Study participants were asked to watch a group of people passing a basketball between them and to count the number of passes that were made in a given time period. Amazingly, around 50 per cent of participants did not even see the man in the gorilla suit that walked amongst the ball players while they were counting the passes. This phenomenon has been termed 'inattentional blindness', because it seems we do not perceive even unusual or obvious things when we have focused our attention elsewhere. We appear to be very effective in automatically filtering out information that is not needed for the current task or goal. This propensity to reduce mental workload led to the characterization of human perceivers as 'cognitive misers', using various short-cuts to deal with limited processing capacity.[22] As we shall see below, the limits of our capacity to process information have particularly serious implications for workers whose jobs make heavy demands on their perceptual capabilities.

WEB LINK

Have a look at the gorilla video and other videos too, and find out about other studies in inattentional blindness and change blindness at the researchers' websites. Gorilla video: http://viscog. beckman.uiuc.edu/djs_lab/demos.html Another website: www.nelliemuller. com/inattentional_blindness.htm

Processing limitations at work: human error in complex work systems

The inherent limitations in our capacities to process information have been a topic of studies by psychologists concerned with how people maintain, or struggle to maintain, skilled performance in difficult circumstances such as high workloads, harsh environmental conditions or when suffering from fatigue. Although individuals' performance does seem to be remarkably resilient under tough conditions, the incidence of human error takes on enormous significance in 'high-reliability' workplaces such as nuclear reactors and aircraft, where the consequences of even small mistakes can be catastrophic.

Lapses of perception, like missing crucial information such as a warning signal, are described as errors of execution, because the fault lies in carrying out the intended action, not in the intention itself.[23] Just such a lapse occurred in 1977 when the meaning of a KLM pilot's words was misunderstood by air traffic controllers and vice versa. This misunderstanding was one of a sequence of key events that led to the Tenerife air disaster in which two planes collided and over 580 people lost their lives.[24]

Of course, the consequences of perceptual errors are rarely so tragic. In fact, thankfully, critical lapses may not be very common at all, because one of the strategies that people use to maintain performance of their key tasks is actually to narrow their attention and focus on the crucial areas.[25] Protecting key tasks can exhaust a person's available mental resources, though, making the work more effortful than usual and leaving them unable to respond effectively to changes or new demands. An example of the trade-offs involved in this process is provided by Hockey, Wastell and Sauer, who studied the performance of sleep-deprived crew members in maintaining the life support system of a spacecraft cabin during a simulation.[26]

In the simulation, the spacecraft crew were able to maintain the oxygen levels and other critical aspects to the right standards despite lack of sleep. But they appeared to do this by reducing the effort they were required to exert with the use of simplified action strategies. Instead of trying to anticipate and prevent problems through monitoring the system, the crew relied more on making corrections in response to alarms generated by the system itself when levels of one of the critical parameters went out of range. This short-cut meant that they were potentially reducing their chances of avoiding system emergencies. There is quite a lot of existing knowledge from this type of simulation about how human errors can occur, which can be used to design reliable work systems that reduce the demands on operators.

WEB LINK

To find out more about research on human error and risk avoidance in complex work settings browse the project reports and case studies on these websites:
The Health and Safety Laboratory: www.hsl.gov.uk
The Industrial Psychology Research Centre at Aberdeen University: www.abdn.ac.uk/iprc

The influence of existing knowledge in perception

So far we have emphasized the idea of perceivers as 'cognitive misers', seeking the quickest,[27] most energy-efficient route to decisive perceptions with the use of a bit of external information and a lot of expectation and existing knowledge. Because existing knowledge is so influential, questions about what we store and how we store it are important in understanding perception. How we store knowledge matters as well as what knowledge we hold, because it affects how quickly and how often we are able to bring specific thoughts to mind in a particular circumstance. Our brains have the same basic architecture, so all individuals will go through the same perception process: receiving, organizing and interpreting information in some order. But similarities and differences in the content of mental models held, and when they are used as a basis for perception, will help to determine the degree to which two or more people will form overlapping views of the same experience.

The reason that we are able to bring information to mind so quickly is because our knowledge is organized in packages of related content. This means that it is only necessary to stimulate one piece of information for all the related knowledge that is held with it to come to mind. These knowledge packages are ready-made 'mental models' or simplified representations of the world, which provide the frameworks and theories against which we then 'test' and place incoming data. Cognitive psychologists call these mental models 'schemas', or 'schemata', to be accurate. A schema can be described as:

schema: a set of interrelated mental processes that enable us to make sense of something on the basis of limited information

> a set of interrelated cognitions (for example, thoughts, beliefs, attitudes) that allows us quickly to make sense of a person, situation, event, place and so forth on the basis of limited information. Certain cues activate a schema, which then fills in missing details.[28]

Source: Getty Images

plate 21 Our judgements about people are based on perceptions and interpretations. Whether someone concludes that this software designer is working or not depends on a number of perceptual factors and attributions about designers

Individuals have a large number of schemata, each of which will contain more or less information depending on how much exposure they have had to the phenomenon in question. Our schemata will include those for people (such as Elvis, your mother), for situations (such as a job interview, eating at a restaurant) and for roles (like managing director, student, bus passenger). Schemata about people, roles and places we have not experienced may contain very general, simplified information. For instance, we may hold snapshot, idealized images of exotic countries we have not yet visited, and also associate those images with particular moods, feelings and personal goals. Even without having been there or read anything about it, for someone from Northern Europe, a place like Zanzibar may conjure up images of golden beaches and sun-speckled blue seas which stimulate feelings of warmth and relaxation, along with thoughts about winning the national lottery! By contrast, self-schemata, those that contain our thoughts and feelings about ourselves, will be both numerous and complex, and will include much more detailed information.

To understand how schemata fit into perception we need to revisit the three-component model of the perception process in Figure 7.2, because what we are doing now is simply examining the perception process at a greater level of detail. In Figure 7.5 the elements of the schema activation process are shown linked to the relevant elements of the more general model. As the diagram shows, schemata fit

STOP AND REFLECT

Can you map the mental associations that you make in relation to some familiar roles, situations and people, including yourself?

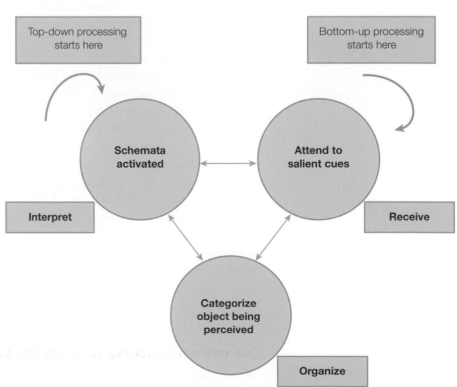

Top-down processing starts here

Bottom-up processing starts here

Schemata activated

Attend to salient cues

Interpret

Receive

Categorize object being perceived

Organize

figure 7.5 The schema activation process

into the perception process at the interpretation or making-sense stage. In top-down processing mode, when perception begins with a clear theory or expectation, relevant schemata have already been activated and drive attention selectively towards external stimuli or cues which match or confirm the mental model in use. If I expect my boss to be angry, I will be selectively looking for signs of anger. So in the event that he or she smiles welcomingly at me, I might consider the possibility that I am seeing sarcasm in action, and look for other signs of anger rather than assume my theory was wrong.

When people perceive in bottom-up mode, as the diagram indicates, it is the cues that are noticed in the environment that drive the process. If I am going to see my boss and have no idea what mood he or she is in, I will start with the smile I see and build a theory based on all the signals I am getting. We tend to use distinctive and easily detected features such as a person's physical appearance as cues for choosing schemata.[29] The stimuli that grab our attention, those that are most 'salient', are received and organized, and these salient cues activate relevant schemata. The organization element of this process includes the basic categorization of the object, person or situation in question into a class or type before any meaning is attached. As an example, some person categories might be police woman, elderly foreign man or young trendy woman. This categorization process then determines which schema will be activated, and in turn how the perceiver will evaluate and respond to the encounter.

It is quite difficult to gain any mental control over the process of schema activation because it is so automatic. The associations between environmental cues, categories and schemata are not easily broken once formed. In fact, perhaps you have had personal experience of the research finding that trying to stop yourself having a particular thought actually has the opposite effect! It appears that we suffer 'post-suppression rebound' when we try to block thoughts from our heads.[30] The effect has been found in experiments where people were asked, and failed, to suppress thoughts of white bears, sex and past romantic relationships amongst other things.

One explanation for this effect is that in order to suppress thoughts we have to first detect them and then replace them with an alternative. Whereas the 'ironic monitoring process' that scans our thoughts to check for 'forbidden' content is automatic, the replacement process is not automatic, and takes mental effort. So when we have a lot to think about and the amount of mental processing capacity available to us is diminished, the replacement process breaks down, but the monitoring process continues, making the unwanted thoughts more rather than less accessible to conscious awareness.

Like most aspects of perception, schema activation is not a neutral process. For each person, some schemata are more easily accessible than others as a result of previous experiences and stable personality characteristics (see Chapter 6). These more accessible schemata will then be brought to mind and used more often, making them even more easily retrieved as time goes on. In this way, we develop habitual tendencies to perceive the world in particular ways. When certain schemata are frequently used by an individual, they are said to be 'chronically accessible schemata'. An expatriate for instance, accustomed to living and working within different nations, may be prone to make sense of social misunderstandings in terms of cultural differences rather than the personality of the other person involved. An extrovert may interpret a wide range of situations as opportunities for social contact, as anyone cornered on a long journey with one will testify!

The use and misuse of perceptual cues

Differences in schema accessibility and use also mean that some environmental cues will be routinely more salient for some people than others. This is because schemata drive the selectivity in our attention, and lead us to notice what we expect or hope to see. In the field of interpersonal conflict, researchers have called such personal sensitivities to features of other's behaviour 'hot buttons', because specific cues may automatically stimulate responses that lead to conflict.[31]

For instance, some individuals may be particularly annoyed or frustrated by signals from managers that their effort is not appreciated, like a failure to say thank you when receiving a report. Others may not care about shows of appreciation, but become very angry if they feel their manager is constantly checking their work, or micro-managing. In each case, some aspect of another's behaviour triggers a whole set of negative thoughts, feelings and emotions, which may then lead to angry reactions, generating a heated response from the other party in return. A situation such as a performance appraisal interview between a manager and his or her employee may be particularly prone to bring to the surface these kinds of interpersonal tensions. Unless we develop an awareness of our own hot buttons, we may automatically react to these cues in a way that is sure to cause argument or conflict.

These automatic links between perceptual cues and schema activation are sometimes manipulated purposefully by marketing professionals to influence public perceptions. In fact, political marketers' tactics became the subject of debate in the UK national press during the general election of May 2005. One of the political parties, the Conservative Party, was accused of using 'dog whistle tactics' to win support from voters during its campaign. Such tactics involve making public statements that are quite ambiguous, but contain key phrases or comments likely to convey an underlying message and meaning to some people while going largely unnoticed by others. In other words, the comments act as psychologically salient cues for individuals who are sensitive to such issues, leading them to access an existing schema which then 'fills in' the unspoken parts of the speaker's message on the basis of those key phrases. In short, if the technique works, it allows a marketer to indirectly influence how people are thinking about something without directly revealing their intentions.

These tactics are considered to be somewhat underhand by some observers. This is because the 'dog whistle' is only really necessary when the message being conveyed is controversial. An open discussion of the issue runs the risk of stimulating resistance and negative reactions towards the messenger. In the example, the issues discussed publicly by the Conservative Party related to the nature of UK asylum and immigration policies. Some commentators argued that the way in which the issues were being discussed, although cleverly avoiding statements that could be considered to be racist, made an appeal to racist voters. This is because, for those who habitually evaluate people based on race and ethnicity, a 'foreigner' is likely to mean people who are racially and ethnically different to themselves rather than the more neutral meaning of someone from another place. In the case of racists, these differences will also have negative associations. Therefore, discussions about controlling the number of 'foreigners' coming into a predominantly white nation such as the United Kingdom are likely to be interpreted by this group as being about controlling the number of non-white people in the country. This somewhat controversial example serves to illustrate how the automatic nature of our perceptual processes creates opportunities for our perceptions to be easily manipulated by others.

In fact, influencing others' perceptions by managing the cues they perceive is not just the preserve of professional marketing or the politically motivated. As individuals we happen to be very good at influencing what others think of us and seek to do so much of the time. Impression management (IM) is 'the process whereby people seek to control or influence the impressions that others form'.[32] We are motivated to manage the way we are perceived in order to make real the image of ourselves we prefer, and to exert some control over how others respond to us.

hot button: personal sensitivity to a feature of another's behaviour which stimulates an automatic response

impression management: the process of trying to control or influence the impressions of oneself that other people form

Presenting the best possible picture of ourselves to others requires us to do two things: enhance our positive attributes, and minimize those that might be perceived negatively. Self-promotion techniques such as describing our actions or qualities in a selective and favourable way, as well as non-verbal behaviour like eye contact, walking and dressing in a certain style, can serve to enhance the positive in a given situation. Techniques such as providing excuses and justifications for less desirable facts about us serve to meet the goal of minimizing negative aspects. Further IM behaviours are directed towards the other people involved, such as flattery and agreement, but these still serve to create a particular image of the actor.

Relating these techniques to what we know about perception processes, we can describe IM as the way that individuals seek to actively direct others' selective attention towards the cues that will stimulate the desired interpretation. For example, by wearing a smart business suit and walking into an interview room assertively, we seek to stimulate a 'professional, confident applicant' schema in the mind of the interviewer. Actually we are not always even aware we are managing our image, but when we know we are being evaluated, as in the case of a job interview, the process becomes more of a conscious effort.

The workplace presents many evaluative situations, both formal and informal, which makes IM an important concept in OB. The significance of self-presentational techniques and their effects are perhaps most obvious in the formal setting of personnel selection and appraisal procedures. However, given that the point of paid work is to perform a specified role and set of tasks, workers' performance and behaviour will often be under a good deal of scrutiny from their peers, superiors and employees on an ongoing basis, which will motivate positive self-presentation.

One concern is that some people are just better at using IM techniques, and so will be perceived more favourably than those with equal or greater talents but who are less skilful or less motivated in their self-presentation. This is a key concern in relation to the accuracy and fairness of decisions about people at work, and the resulting opportunities made available to them. In one study, women managers were less willing than male colleagues to use IM behaviours such as networking, self-promotion and ingratiation to get ahead in their organizations, preferring instead to rely on doing an excellent job.[33] The difficulty with the women's approach is that promotion decisions are affected by seniors' perceptions of potential and promotability, as well as actual performance. Because male managers tend to be more accepting of the need to 'play politics' to secure promotion, they are more willing to actively manage their image with their seniors, and so may have advantage over the women when it comes to promotion.

This study serves to highlight the controversial and ambiguous nature of IM behaviour. The line between simply highlighting one's best points and 'false advertising' is very difficult to determine, and each of us will have a different view about how far it is acceptable to 'manage' others' perceptions.

CRITICAL INSIGHT

Get a copy of the paper 'The use of impression management tactics in structural interviews: a function of question type' by Ellis (2002)[34] and read about their study of the IM tactics used by job applicants in interviews using different types of questions. Do you think organizations should try to prevent IM? Given that the way interviews are conducted seems to make a difference, do you consider it the responsibility of interviewers, or of job applicants, to check the accuracy of what applicants say?

The stability of schemata

Schemata develop over time through learning and experience, and once formed, can be remarkably resistant to significant change. Although we add complexity to our mental models as we experience new examples of the phenomena, wholesale revision of a schema is less likely. This is because a schema acts as a lens through which relevant new information is interpreted. Data that are inconsistent with what we 'know' to be the case is just reinterpreted so that it does not challenge our existing views. As numerous recent reality television shows demonstrate, if you strongly believe yourself to be a very promising singing talent, even the most uncompromising feedback to the contrary can be easily discounted and fully explained by the nasty personality of the judge!

Some failures to take onboard feedback and change mental models, though, do have more serious consequences than publicly wounded pride. A serious fire in 1949 in the United States called the Mann Gulch disaster claimed many lives despite the fact that skilled fire fighters were in attendance.[35] A central point to come from the analysis of what happened at Mann Gulch pointed to the failure of the fire crew to acknowledge quickly enough that this was not the type of fire they thought it was. As a result, the men did not respond appropriately to the situation they were actually in, because they reinterpreted discrepant information about what they were experiencing and continued to respond according to the routine for the wrong type of fire. Tragically, some of the men could have kept their lives if they had listened seriously to one of their colleagues, who was engaging in data-driven processing and understood the need for different behaviour.

Most of what happens inside organizations is not a life-and-death matter, of course, but does nonetheless affect people's livelihoods and well-being. The consequences of senior managers failing to adjust their schemata about the organization's competition and strategy quickly enough in response to new information has been a topic of interest to researchers. For instance, Hodgkinson[36] investigated UK estate agents' (realtors') perceptions of the competitive environment in the industry just before a recession hit the property market, and again once the slump was established. The estate agents demonstrated 'cognitive inertia'. Their perceptions of the environment in which they were operating remained stable even though there was clear evidence of a downturn in the market. In other words, the estate agents were overly dependent on their schemata of the situation, failing to monitor and interpret environmental cues appropriately. As a consequence, their ability to respond effectively to the real threat to the organizations' viability posed by the downturn was seriously compromised.

Apart from demonstrating the stability of schemata, this study also illustrates that schemata are not always specific to an individual, but can be shared between groups of people. In this case, the estate agents' shared perceptions were a result of similar work roles and industry context. Broad similarities between people such as gender, ethnicity, national culture and educational background can also increase the chances that there will be some similarity in their perceptions about some things. A study found that two people randomly paired are likely to share only about 10 per cent of their chronic mental constructs, that is, their stable knowledge.[37] However, people who live or work together are not random pairings; they will share some common roles, backgrounds or experiences. Stereotypes are a class of schemata that appear to be shared between people, and are of particular consequence in organizational life because of their effects on perceptions of, and subsequent behaviour towards, individuals.

Stereotypes are a form of schemata containing generalized ideas about the qualities and characteristics of individuals within particular groups.[38] For example, people with financial worries make motivated salespeople; stock market traders

stereotyping: the process of assigning traits to people based on their membership in a social category.

are usually privately educated men in their 20s and 30s, Chinese men and women are the best mathematicians, and employees over 50 years old are too old to learn new things. These are all examples of stereotypical beliefs about groups of people because they make an assumption that the characteristics in question will be true of all or most of the individuals in the category, which most likely will not be the case. Not all stereotypes are negative or unflattering, of course. But when assumptions about certain groups are automatically applied to individuals in the work context, unfair, potentially discriminatory and probably ineffective judgements and decisions can result.

A case in point is the issue of age discrimination by employers. In the United Kingdom, the exclusion of skilled and capable older workers from the workforce based on negative stereotypes of their potential to contribute is laying to waste a sizeable portion of the nation's available labour. As well as denying opportunities and income to the older workers, this exclusion of capable individuals based on non-performance-related characteristics is making it harder for organizations to recruit enough people, leading to reduced performance and profitability.

It is also known that people do not perform as well as they are able when they feel they are being stereotyped.[39] So even when given an opportunity, a worker who is a member of a minority group in an organization may not be able to contribute fully if he or she feels the group membership is uppermost in others' minds. Gender-based stereotypes are of particular concern in organizations, because women still do not get the same rewards for paid work as their male counterparts, and some occupations appear to be 'gendered' or occupied predominantly by one or other sex (see the chapter case study).

The phrase 'think manager, think male' was coined by Virginia Schein[40] to describe the effect of sex-role stereotypes on perceptions of what it takes to be a successful manager. Many studies have shown that both men and women and people of different nationalities describe successful managers as having characteristics that they also associate more with men than women, such as competitive, decisive and ambitious.[41] As well as affecting women's motivation and expectations, such perceptions may create a bias in the evaluation of potential and existing managers by decision makers, if they are unaware or unconcerned about the effect of gender-based stereotypes on their judgements.

As we have already discussed, it is actually very difficult to intervene in the automatic processes by which we associate people or situations with particular thoughts and feelings, even if we become aware of them. Trying to suppress stereotypical thoughts will probably result in 'thought rebound', bringing them even more to the forefront of our minds. We can, though, be vigilant about questioning and exploring our perceptions, reactions and decisions about people, in order to actively counter the inevitable biases and assumptions to which we would otherwise be prone.

It is hard to imagine a person who could not be stereotyped on some dimension, so we are all potentially at risk of being judged inaccurately at some point. Why then do we form stereotypes about people? We have already discussed the marvellous efficiency of schemata for making sense of the world quickly with minimum effort. Stereotypes allow us to size up people with the same efficiency, and apparently that includes ourselves! According to self-categorization theory, which is an extension of social identity theory,[42] stereotyping people occurs from the same process we use to categorize and understand the kind of person we are in relation to others. The basis of these influential theories is that part of our self-concept is defined in terms of the series of social groups to which we belong. Such groups include demographic ones based on age, gender and socioeconomic status, as well as those we have some choice about, including student, work, sports, or more loosely defined groups such as 'clubbers' or classical music fans.

Have you ever become aware you were being stereotyped? How did you feel about it? How did it affect your behaviour?

STOP AND REFLECT

social identity theory: the theory concerned with how we categorize and understand the kind of person we are in relation to others

In order to decide whether an individual is a member of a particular group, we use as a basis what we consider to be the defining features or stereotypical attributes of members of that group. The effect of this process is to simplify the picture by maximizing the distinction between groups and minimizing any differences between individuals within groups. So we can then easily work out whether they, or we, have the key features necessary for membership. It has been suggested that one of two sources of motivation for this social comparison is to reduce uncertainty about the social world and how to behave in it, which, as we have discussed, is what our basic perceptual processes also appear to achieve.[43]

A second motivation for making these social distinctions concerns our need to maintain self-esteem, and this is crucial in relation to stereotyping. Although we categorize ourselves in the same way as others, this need to view ourselves positively means that we have an inherent tendency to evaluate the characteristics of the groups we belong to (ingroups) favourably and those of other groups and their members (outgroups) negatively. So it is possible to see how perceptions of difference and negative stereotypes can form through basic social perception processes.

The ideas of self-categorization and social identity theories can be applied to try to understand some troublesome issues in contemporary organizations.[44] For instance, the evidence from reports of mergers and acquisitions is that 'people issues' are cited as one of the most difficult aspects of integrating two previously distinct firms.[45] From the perspective of social identity theory, the hostility and culture clashes that are a feature of firm integration can be explained by the tendency to favour our own groups and view others as both distinct or different, and less desirable. It is further suggested that events such as organizational restructuring may actually stimulate people to identify even more strongly with their ingroups as they seek to reduce the uncertainty that surrounds such events.[46] On the more positive side, the comparison groups we use are dynamic and flexible. So it may be possible to intervene in situations where there is unhelpful rivalry or hostility between work groups by trying to subtly change individuals' identity perceptions. Focusing all groups' attention on external competitors rather than each other is one example.

ingroups: groups to which someone perceives he or she belongs, which he or she accordingly evaluates favourably

outgroups: groups to which someone perceives he or she does not belong, which he or she accordingly evaluates unfavourably

STOP AND REFLECT

How would you define your social identity? Think about the types of people you identify positively with (your ingroups) and the types of people you are sure you are different from (your outgroups).

Perceiving causes

As well as perceiving and judging people and situations, we are also naturally inclined to form perceptions about what has caused the behaviour and events we encounter. From the pursuit of religion to the public's fascination with getting 'into the mind' of serial killers, it is a human tendency to assume that there must be some meaning in all things, and some motive behind all people's actions. Hence, we develop ideas and expectations about causes and effects, and general ideas about how things happen and relate to each other, based on experience.

Broadly speaking, we distinguish between stable causes for things and transitory or changeable ones, and between two sources of explanation: those that are about the person (internal) and those that are about the situation (external). The explanations an individual chooses to use, 'causal attributions' as they are called, are important because they can have a significant influence on his or her expectations and behaviour. This applies to expectations about ourselves, as well as about other people.

Consider the experience of being shortlisted but then not selected for a prestigious and challenging job. The reaction of many people is to spend some time thinking about why they were not considered to be the most suitable candidate. If the rejected applicant puts the result down to lack of preparation on his or her part

causal attribution: the explanations an individual chooses to use, either internal (about the person) or external (about the situation) and either stable or transitory

– an attribution to an internal but changeable cause – he or she might well consider applying for a similar job in the future, but make changes in her/his preparation for the interview. If on the other hand, the person perceives the main cause of the rejection to be that he or she lacked the required level of intelligence – an internal, stable attribution – he or she will probably believe that such prestigious jobs are simply out of reach, and apply only for less challenging jobs in the future. Of course, the applicant might make an external attribution, deciding that the outcome was nothing to do with him or her at all, but was caused by the personal connections of the successful job-seeker. In this case, the person's perceptions create no reason to reduce his or her ambitions based on this rejection, or indeed to make changes in approach.

This example demonstrates the way in which our perceptions about what causes things to happen can shape the options for action that we consider, and our beliefs about what will result from that action. **Perceived self-efficacy** is the term used to describe 'beliefs in one's capabilities to organize and execute the courses of action required to produce given attainments'.[47] Levels of self-efficacy for a specific activity or goal will determine what goals people actually attempt, how much effort they exert to achieve those goals, and how willing they are to persevere in the face of difficulty.

By definition, in order to develop high self-efficacy in an area it is necessary to make at least some internal causal attributions for relevant outcomes, because efficacy requires us to believe in our ability to personally control what happens. The exception to this is the attribution of failures to stable, unchangeable personal qualities, which naturally will work to lower expectations of success. Of course, sometimes efficacy-lowering attributions are accurate, and in that sense they are useful. Failing to recognize appropriately when we do not have the skills or qualities required for a certain pursuit can be damaging in that it causes us to direct our effort in unproductive ways. It is when individuals' low expectations are not based on a realistic assessment of their capabilities that they constrain their ability to reach their potential.

There is solid evidence that efficacy beliefs are an important factor in determining many performance outcomes over and above actual ability.[48] An important example is in early study choices made at school, because these choices work to constrain the career options available to students later on. Sex-role stereotyping of subjects and occupations appears to affect girls and boys' interests and expectations early on, through the subtle feedback and encouragement for different pursuits children get from their social environments. From a young age girls tend to have lower perceived self-efficacy for male-typed subjects such as maths and quantitative skills, regardless of their actual capabilities. For this reason, at school girls are less likely to choose and continue to study maths, which means they are not then well equipped to enter occupations for which continued exposure is required such as science.

The case of girls and study choices shows how individuals' expectations can become **self-fulfilling prophecies**. That is, if we think it is unlikely we can achieve a particular goal, we tend not to bother even trying, and to give up easily if we do try. This means we do not actually give ourselves the opportunity to succeed, and so end up reinforcing our original expectation. Of course, this process can also work in a positive direction, where expectations of success can lead to engagement with, and increased effort to achieve, the goal in question.

The implication of this information for OB is that we cannot always assume that an individual's performance and attainment directly reflects her or his basic abilities. When setting goals and when motivating and appraising performance, it may be helpful for individuals and their managers to examine causal beliefs and self-efficacy levels in order to identify potential barriers to achievement.

perceived self-efficacy: a person's belief in his or her capacity to achieve something

self-fulfilling prophecy: an expectation about a situation which of itself causes what is anticipated to actually happen

Given its practical significance, there is a good deal of theory and research focused on the ways in which we might come to make one type of casual attribution over another, but the ideas of Kelley are particularly influential.[49] In his 'co-variation model', Kelley suggested that we use information about the co-occurrence of the person, behaviour and potential causes to work out an explanation.[50] Specifically, three aspects of the occasion are considered:

▷ *Distinctiveness*: does the person behave this way in other situations or is the behaviour uncommon for them and specific to this situation?
▷ *Consistency*: does the person always behave this way in this type of situation?
▷ *Consensus*: does everyone behave this way in this type of situation, or is this person's behaviour different?

The pattern of answers to these three questions will rule out some potential causes and suggest others. Imagine a colleague has just been very rude to you when passing on information. If this person is always rude to you (high consistency) but also rude to others (low distinctiveness), and everyone else in the organization is very friendly (low consensus), you will likely think that the person, and not you, is the cause of the problem. In the event that there is a lack of consistency in the person's behaviour in the situation – in this case, he or she is sometimes rude and sometimes friendly – we tend to discount the immediate possibilities and assume that there must be some other explanation.

One of the issues with Kelley's model is that it does not make too much sense unless we have experienced the person and situation more than once. If this is our only experience, we must use different criteria because we do not have the same information. In such cases, Kelley suggested that we use causal schemata as guiding frameworks for making attributions.

There is supporting evidence for the co-variation model, but it is not actually clear whether we always or exclusively use this particular process to attribute causation. Nonetheless, the framework has proved a useful tool for understanding the implications of these perceptions.

As with the other aspects of perception discussed in this chapter, causal attribution is not a purely rational process free of selectivity and the workings of motivation. Just as we display biases towards perceiving some environmental cues over others, we are also subject to some general tendencies in the way we attribute causes to things. One bias that has been noted in our perception of causes is the false consensus effect, which is the tendency to over-estimate the degree to which other people will think and behave in the same way as we do. We also have a tendency to favour internal attributions for the behaviour of others but external ones to explain our own behaviour. So we are likely to assume a colleague misses a deadline because she or he is unreliable or disorganized, whereas we miss deadlines because of unavoidable constraints! This is called the fundamental attribution error.

Actually, the error is not really fundamental in the sense of applying to all people. The extent to which people fall prey to this tendency appears to depend on their cultural backgrounds, because those from non-Western cultures are more likely to use external attributions.[51] It is also the case, mirroring the phenomenon of chronic accessibility of certain schemata discussed earlier, that individuals appear to adopt particular 'explanatory styles', or have a predisposition to employ some types of explanation over others.

Two familiar explanatory styles are optimism and pessimism. Most of us have met someone who is unfailingly optimistic about life regardless of circumstances, and someone for whom every silver lining has a cloud. Although we often treat such differences light-heartedly, they do have serious consequences. Optimism has been linked to achievement across life domains as well as physical health and

co-variation model: Kelley's model which uses information about the co-occurrence of a person, behaviour and potential causes to work out an explanation

false consensus effect: the tendency to over-estimate the degree to which other people will think and behave in the same way as we do

fundamental attribution error: the tendency to favour internal attributions for the behaviour of others but external ones to explain our own behaviour

psychological well-being, whereas pessimism has been linked with depression and lack of success.[52] It has been suggested that optimists are those who habitually favour external, unstable and specific (only affecting one part of their life) explanations for bad events.[53] By contrast, pessimists attribute bad results to internal, stable and global (it affects all aspects of their life) causes.

Seligman conducted research at Met Life, the US insurance company, to try to identify the practical consequences of the optimistic explanatory style. On joining the company, the explanatory style of new salespeople was measured with a questionnaire. The optimists outsold the pessimists by 21 per cent in the first year, and 57 per cent in the second year. The good news for pessimists, however, is that with concerted effort it appears to be possible to alter our attributional style and so avoid self-defeating explanations.

To find out more about learned optimism and other similar work, browse this website www.positivepsychology.org/ You will see that the researchers have made a number of questionnaires available for download, such as the Subjective Happiness Scale, which you could use for a research project of your own.

WEB LINK

Perception and employee relations

There is one final topic that needs to be included in this discussion about perception and OB, which is the role that perception plays in shaping the tone of relations that exist in the workplace. Throughout the chapter, we have discussed how it is that two people can share an experience but form altogether different perceptions about what happened and what it means. The reasons have included differences in attentional focus, in expectations and in prior knowledge. We have also seen how unalterable factors such as gender and cultural background will influence these elements of perception processes, both by shaping the nature of individuals' learning and experiences, which impacts on expectations and knowledge, and through the social categorization and stereotyping processes by which we work out where we and others fit into the social world.

In the work domain, there is another basic distinction between people that is of some importance in understanding behaviour in organizations: that between employers (and managers as the agents of employers), and employees or workers. The relations between these two groups are referred to as the employment relationship, and managing these relations is a central concern of human resource management (see Chapter 17). The relevance here is that the differences in roles, responsibilities, motivations and rewards associated with being either an employer or an employee mean that individuals in these two groups are likely to perceive what happens in the organization somewhat differently. This is significant because there is evidence that the extent of the agreement between employers' and employees' perceptions about key aspects of work will have consequences for employees' work attitudes and performance.

Perceived unfair treatment can lead to formal disputes, such as that highlighted earlier involving workers from Gate Gourmet, the in-flight meal supplier, and British Airways. More broadly, such perceptions have been found to predict employees' levels of job satisfaction and trust in managers, as well as their willingness to engage in discretionary behaviour such as staying to complete tasks beyond contracted hours and helping colleagues.[54] In fact, the notion of fairness or justice can be separated into two components: fairness of outcomes, or distributive justice, and fairness of procedures, or procedural justice. People tend to be concerned with the process by which decisions are made as well as the decision itself and in fact, may be willing to accept a personally disappointing outcome if the procedures used

distributive justice: justice based on the principle of fairness of outcomes

procedural justice: justice based on the principle of fairness of procedures employed to achieve outcomes

are perceived to have been equitable. In a complex dispute like the one at British Airways, the subject of employees' grievances may be some combination of both the decisions themselves and the way they were made by senior managers.

The importance of employees' perceptions about fairness or justice is not, however, restricted to how specific aspects of employment such as formal contract terms are viewed. The employment relationship is best seen as a series of agreements about a number of elements that are all of importance to the parties involved, such as working conditions, job security and commitment, management style, and pay and benefits. It is also an ongoing, dynamic interaction between the parties made up of a sequence of exchanges over time, each of which will influence the thoughts and perceptions of those involved. The psychological contract, a concept that has become important in OB and HRM, is a term used to capture individuals' general perceptions of the overall nature and balance of the employer-employee exchange.

A well-accepted definition of the psychological contract is provided by Rousseau, who describes it as 'individual beliefs, shaped by the organization, regarding the terms of an exchange agreement between individuals and the organization'.[55] In other words, it consists of employees' ideas about what they are expected to contribute to the organization and what they can expect to get back in return for their efforts. Two key points to note are that the psychological contract is unwritten and often unspoken, and that these are the perceptions formed by individual employees of the 'deal' promised by the employer. These expectations are formed during the recruitment process and when inside the organization, from what managers say and do, as well as the communications and culture of the company.

For all the reasons we have discussed that people's perceptions may differ, one person's ideas about what the organization has promised and expects may not be fully or even partly shared by managers or indeed other employees. Much potential exists, then, for organizations to fall short of employees' expectations and vice versa, leading to feelings that agreed promises have been broken. The results from a number of studies suggest that violations of individuals' psychological contracts are linked to outcomes such as intentions to quit, reduced job performance and lower levels of commitment.[56]

Evidence from a study of supervisors and those they managed showed significant differences in relative perceptions of the extent to which aspects of the psychological contract related to pay, advancement opportunities and a good employment relationship were fulfilled.[57] Perhaps unsurprisingly, the supervisors felt that the employer's obligations had been fulfilled more fully than did their subordinates. This study also allows us to relate the issue of psychological contract violation to the process of causal attribution discussed earlier, and particularly the phenomenon of the fundamental attribution error. Where both parties agreed some expectations were unmet, the employees were more likely to perceive the cause as intentional disregard by the employer, while the supervisors tended to see the cause as situational constraints, or events beyond the organization's control. Here then is another example of the very real and concrete organizational consequences of individuals' perceptions.

psychological contract: an individual's beliefs about the terms and conditions of a reciprocal exchange agreement between that person and another party

Chapter summary

☐ Perception is important in OB because the fundamental nature of perceptual processes means that individuals usually interpret other people and situations differently, and so routinely hold different views of reality, which in turn strongly influence their attitudes and actions. This means that avoiding conflict and ensuring important workplace decisions are based on sound judgements is not a matter of training people how to see things as they 'really are', because multiple realities always exist. More can be gained from understanding how perception works, and shaping organization activity so that the possibilities for negative outcomes are minimized.

☐ 'Perception' refers to the process by which our senses gather information from the environment and our brains make sense of that information. The perception process is characterized as inherently selective, subjective and largely automatic rather than conscious. It can be broken down into three steps or elements – receiving, organizing and interpreting – representing the path by which we mentally transform sensory stimuli from the environment into meaningful information.

☐ The three elements of the perception process do not occur separately or in sequence, but overlap and sometimes occur in parallel. When perception proceeds from the sensory data received from the environment it is called 'bottom-up' information processing. In contrast, when perception begins with existing knowledge which is used to interpret the incoming data, it is called 'top-down' processing. Whereas bottom-up processing requires a lot of mental effort, top-down processing carries the risk of assumptions and jumping to the wrong conclusions, so some balance is required between in the use of these two perception strategies.

☐ The processing limitations of our brains mean it is only because we employ selective attention that it is possible for us to experience the mass of sensory stimuli in the environment as orderly and meaningful. Our choice of what to attend to is driven by the environmental cues that are most salient, or by our own motivations, expectations and goals. This selectivity is highly resource-efficient, but the downside is that we can miss crucial bits of information and form misleading perceptions of what we are experiencing. If we then act on those perceptions we may suffer serious consequences.

☐ Existing knowledge has a powerful effect on how we perceive new experiences. We store knowledge in the form of mental models, or schemata: packages of related content (for instance thoughts, beliefs, and attitudes) about people, situations and roles. Schemata do develop over time but do not change much once formed, because they act as lenses by which we view new information. New data that is inconsistent with what we 'know' is simply reinterpreted to fit. In perception, when one bit of information related to a schema is brought to mind, everything else in the package comes to mind also, so we can very quickly make sense of something on the basis of a small bit of information. But these stable, automatic linkages between thoughts can be unhelpful, as in the case of stereotypes. Although we can choose not to act upon stereotypes, it may not be possible to stop them coming to mind in the first place.

☐ Two specific classes of perceptions were identified that hold particular significance for organizations. The causes that people perceive (or attribute) for particular outcomes will significantly affect their future expectations and behaviour. If a person sees a failure to meet a goal as the result of stable, internal causes – like intelligence – she or he is less likely to try again than if she/he perceives the cause of the failure to be more about his/her circumstances at the time. This knowledge is important for understanding individual performance and motivation. The second class of perceptions, employees' views of justice and fairness in the workplace is significant because they impact on the employment relationship. If employees perceive that they are being treated unfairly by the organization, it will negatively influence their work attitudes and motivation. The difficulty is that employees and employers are very likely to perceive things differently by virtue of their respective roles and experiences, so to ensure that employees feel fairly treated is a particular challenge for organizations.

Key concepts

causal attribution	207	perceptual errors	197
chronic accessibility	209	perceptual sets	198
cognitive inertia	205	psychological contract	211
explanatory styles	195	salient cues	202
false consensus effect	209	schemata	200
fundamental attribution error	209	selective attention	191
mental models	200	social identity theory	206
perceived self-efficacy	208	stereotypes	205
perceptual biases	196		

Chapter review questions

1. Describe the basic features of human perception processes, and why these features explain the fact that people generally perceive the same situation differently.
2. Identify and explain two consequences of selective attention that can occur in the workplace.
3. Outline the pros and cons of the mental packaging of information into schemata.
4. What is causal attribution? Outline one scenario that might occur in an organization where a person's perceptions about the causes of things affects her or his motivation to achieve a goal.
5. In what ways can individuals' perceptions affect other people, groups of people and the social climate of an organization?

Further reading

Bandura, A. (1997b) *Self-Efficacy: the exercise of control*, New York: Freeman.

Eysenck, M. W. and Keane, M. T. (2005) *Cognitive Psychology: A student's handbook* (5th edn), Hove: Lawrence Erlbaum.

Haslam, S. A. (2001) *Psychology in Organizations: The social identity approach,* London: Sage.

Hogg, M. A. and Vaughan, G. M. (2004) *Social Psychology* (4th edn), Hemel Hempstead: Prentice Hall.

Reason, J. T. (1990). *Human Error*, Cambridge, UK: Cambridge University Press.

Rosenfeld, P., Giacalone, R. and Riordan, C. A. (2002) *Impression Management: Building and enhancing reputation at work*, London: Thomson Learning.

Rousseau, D. M. (1995) *Psychological Contracts in Organisations: Understanding written and unwritten agreements*, Thousand Oaks, Calif.: Sage.

Chapter case study: *Why women are poor at science, by the president of Harvard*

'The president of Harvard University has provoked a furore by arguing that men outperform women in maths and sciences because of biological difference, and discrimination is no longer a career barrier for female academics.

'Lawrence Summers, a career economist who served as treasury secretary under President Clinton, has a reputation for outspokenness. His tenure at Harvard has been marked by clashes with African-American staff and leftwing intellectuals, and complaints about a fall in the hiring of women. He made his remarks at a private conference on the position of women and minorities in science and engineering, hosted by the National Bureau of Economic Research.

'In a lengthy address delivered without notes, Dr Summers offered three explanations for the shortage of women in senior posts in science and engineering, starting with their reluctance to work long hours because of childcare responsibilities. He went on to argue that boys outperform girls on high school science and maths scores because of genetic difference. "Research in behavioural genetics is showing that things people previously attributed to socialisation weren't due to socialisation after all," he told the *Boston Globe* yesterday.

'As an example, Dr Summers told the conference about giving his daughter two trucks. She treated them like dolls, and named them mummy and daddy trucks, he said. Dr Summers also played down the impact of sex bias in appointments to academic institutions. He said: "The real issue is the overall size of the pool, and it's less clear how much the size of the pool was held down by discrimination." At least half of his audience comprised women, several said they found the remarks offensive and one walked out. "It was really shocking to hear the president of Harvard make statements like that," said Denice Denton, who is about to become president of the University of California at Santa Cruz.

'Others said Dr Summers's comments were depressingly familiar. "I have heard men make comments like this my entire life and quite honestly if I had listened to them I would never have done anything," said Donna Nelson, a chemistry professor at the University of Oklahoma. A Harvard spokeswoman declined to comment yesterday, or to release the transcript of Dr Summers's remarks. Richard Freeman, who invited the Harvard president to speak at the conference, said Dr Summers's comments were intended to provoke debate, and some women over-reacted.

'"Some people took offence because they were very sensitive," said Dr Freeman, an economist at Harvard and the London School of Economics. "It does not seem to me insane to think that men and women have biological differences." During Dr Summers's presidency, the number of tenured jobs offered to women has fallen from 36% to 13%. In the year before he made this speech, only four of 32 tenured job openings were offered to women.
Source: Suzanne Goldenberg, *Guardian*, 18 January 2005.

Task

1. Read the transcript of President Summers' speech at Harvard University's website: http://www.president.harvard.edu/speeches/ and consider to what extent you agree with the way the newspaper journalist Suzanne Goldenberg presented his comments.

2. Consider the different views expressed by the parties involved: President Summers, the female scientists Drs Denton and Nelson, Dr Freeman and the journalist Suzanne Goldenberg. In what ways can you apply the concepts, theories and evidence about perception processes in this chapter to understand how perceptions of the same phenomenon can differ so markedly?

Note

This case study was prepared by Militza Callinan, Leeds University Business School, UK.

Web-based assignment

What attracts you to some organizations and not others?

Get a copy of the recruitment pages of a national newspaper or a professional publication, such as *People Management* or *The Grocer* in the UK. From the advertisements, identify a selection of the recruiting organizations that differ from each other and provide details of their websites. Browse each of the sites, particularly looking at the pages aimed at potential job applicants. If you are able to do this with a colleague or friend so you can have a discussion about it, that would be ideal.

Consider these questions:

- What are your perceptions of each organization as a potential employer. Are they your kind of place?
- Try to identify what perceptual cues from the advertisement and websites captured your attention, and the prior knowledge and expectations that led you to your conclusions. To what extent can you apply social categorization theory to explain your attraction or aversion to each organization?

OB in films

The award-winning film *A Beautiful Mind* (2001) tells the story of the life and mental struggles of the brilliant mathematician John Nash, who 'saw the world in ways no one could have imagined'. The film is an excellent dramatisation of the workings of human perception, and specifically, what happens to people when their views of the world become increasingly detached from those around them.

Watch the film and think about the way the producers manipulate our perceptions of the characters and events, as well as the origins and consequences of the perceptions formed by John Nash, his friends and his colleagues. You can also browse the official Universal Studios website at: www.abeautifulmind.com/.

Notes

1   Van der Heiden and Nijhof (2004: 493).
2   Ramachandran and Rogers-Ramachandran (2005: 95).
3   Weick (2001).
4   Fiske and Taylor (1991).
5   Dunkerley and Robinson (2002).
6   Jackson and Joshi (2001).
7   Dunkerley and Robinson (2002).
8   Eysenck and Keane (2005: 43).
9   Eysenck and Keane (2005).
10   Tetlock (1983).
11   Highhouse (2001).
12   Roth and Woods (1988).
13   Highhouse (2001).
14   Attneave (1971).
15   Haart, Carey and Milne (1999).
16   Mishra, Dasen and Niraula (2003).
17   Bloom (2004).
18   Redelmeier and Tibshirani (1997).
19   Strayer and Johnston (2001).
20   Simons and Levin (1998).
21   Simons and Chabris (1999).
22   Nisbett and Ross (1980).

23 Reason (1990).

24 Weick (2001).

25 Hockey (2002).

26 Hockey, Wastell and Sauer (1998).

27 Nisbett and Ross (1980).

28 Hogg and Vaughan (1995: 48).

29 Hogg and Vaughan (1995).

30 Macrae et al. (1994).

31 Capobianco, Davis and Kraus (2000).

32 Rosenfeld, Giacalone and Riordan (2002).

33 Singh, Kumra and Vinnicombe (2002).

34 Ellis et al. (2002).

35 Weick (2001).

36 Hodgkinson (1997).

37 Bargh, Lombardi and Higgins (1988).

38 Hogg and Vaughan (1995).

39 Steele, Spencer and Aronson (2003).

40 Schein (1973, 1975).

41 See for example Schein et al. (1996).

42 Tajfel and Turner (1979).

43 Hogg and Terry (2000).

44 See Haslam (2001).

45 CIPD (2000).

46 Hogg and Terry (2000).

47 Bandura (1997b: 3).

48 See Bandura (1997b).

49 See Hogg and Vaughan (1995).

50 Kelley (1973).

51 Morris and Peng (1994).

52 Peterson (2000).

53 Seligman (1991).

54 Gilliland and Chan (2001).

55 Rousseau (1995).

56 Taylor and Tekleab (2004).

57 Lester et al. (2002).

chapter 8
Learning

The whole of life is learning, therefore education can have no endings.[1]

Some firms are just more efficient at learning than others. The capacity to mine ideas for improvement and innovation from each and every incremental experience is a critical component of resource leverage .... Each new experience, each success or failure, must be seen as an opportunity to learn.[2]

chapter objectives

After completing this chapter, you should be able to:

▷ explain the importance of learning in organizations

▷ define learning and discuss the difference between formal, non-formal and informal learning

▷ discuss the contested nature of behavioural, cognitive and social learning theories

▷ articulate how adult learning theories adds to our understanding of learning processes

▷ identify the affects of social class, ethnicity and gender on learning and training opportunities in the organization

▷ discuss some practical applications of learning theories.

chapter outline

▷ Introduction
▷ The nature of workplace learning
▷ Classical learning theories
▷ Contemporary learning theories
▷ Adult learning theories
▷ Learning theories in action
▷ Chapter summary
▷ Key concepts
▷ Chapter review questions
▷ Further reading
▷ Chapter case study: Coronation Bank, a transfer of learning dilemma
▷ Web-based assignment
▷ OB in films
▷ Notes

Introduction

In traditional organizations the majority of employees had limited opportunity to engage in work-related learning. According to orthodox management texts, the factory or office was a place to work, to manufacture goods or to provide services; it was not a place to learn. Learning mainly occurred at school, college and university before people joined a work organization, as part of a formal programme of study or perhaps a hybrid system of on-the-job and off-the-job apprenticeship training.

As notions of 'knowledge work', core competencies and sustainability have entered the contemporary management discourse, there has been a growing interest in work-related learning.[3] The reliance on knowledge or intellectual capital has led to the realization that leaders need to foster 'learning-rich' contexts, and managers need to be facilitators for learning at work.[4] Some workplace learning advocates assert that there is no place for managers who do not appreciate their own vital role in fostering learning.[5]

In contemporary formulations of strategic human resource management (SHRM), work-related learning has come to represent a key 'lever' that can act as the engine for sustainable *competitive advantage*.[6] The academic interest in workplace learning can be measured by the burgeoning of books on the subject, the launch of the *Journal of Workplace Learning*, and perhaps even more noteworthy, by the three international Researching Work and Learning (RWL) conferences held in Leeds, Calgary and Sydney since 1999. Among academics and corporate leaders, the terms 'learning organization' and 'workplace learning' have become established terms for capturing formal, non-formal, informal, self-directed collective, and even tacit informal learning activities.[7] In opposition to mainstream accounts of workplace learning, in which learning tends to be disconnected from the power relations in which it is entrenched, critical theorists recognize that power relations, conflicts of interest, gender, race and ethnicity can shape the dynamics of work-related learning.[8]

organizational learning: the knowledge management process in which organizations acquire, share and use knowledge to succeed

Ever more sophisticated conceptualizations of work-related learning suggest multiple approaches for understanding the phenomenon. Central to the approach we have adopted throughout this book is an openness to expanding our understanding of learning beyond notions of individualized, psychologically driven events, to incorporate an awareness of contextual and sociocultural factors. This should enable us to build a broad understanding of how work-related learning is affected by asymmetrical power relations based on class, gender, race and ethnicity.

In this chapter, we emphasize that an inclusive understanding of learning needs to acknowledge the general nature of capitalist employment relations, the way in which organization control systems generate and express internal contradictions, and the tension between managerial control and learning. We begin by explaining the importance of work-related learning, then proceed to examine competing classical theories of learning and contemporary approaches to adult learning. The final section discusses some practical applications of adult learning theories.

The nature of workplace learning

The notion that education should serve business and the economy has been fiercely debated among adult educators. See Bruce Spencer's *The Purpose of Adult Education: A guide for students* [9] for an introduction to the debate. Look at the two opening quotes. Is it reasonable to assume that education should serve business? What are your views on this?

STOP AND REFLECT

If you have worked in a paid job, can you recall how you felt on your first day? Like many young workers, you might have been nervous, even bewildered, as an environment filled with new faces and names, new tasks and new rules replaced the familiarity of school or college. But like most young workers, you probably adjusted to this new environment within a few days or weeks. This adjustment, or adaptation, to paid work can take many forms. Some are simple, as when buzzers sound to permit morning and lunch breaks from work.

New employees acquire explicit knowledge about the organization and working conditions in orientation workshops. New information and skills needed for various aspects of the work are acquired from manuals, training workshops and co-workers. New employees also develop knowledge about which aspects of their work behaviour are likely to be punished and which are likely to be rewarded. Some behaviours are appropriate only at certain times and in certain circumstances, and those circumstances must be identified and differentiated. Critical questioning, for example, might not be as acceptable at work as at school or college, but working collaboratively and sharing information – perhaps forbidden by college academic rules – might be rewarded at work.

norms: the informal rules and expectations that groups establish to regulate the behaviour of their members

Workers also learn that there are things they can do to prevent unwanted consequences. For example, observing practices such as working at the pace set by the work team, sometimes referred to as 'norms', can prevent people from being ostracized by other members of the group. In a similar way, workers sometimes learn *not* to learn because of perceived negative outcomes. For example, an individual employee or workers collectively may be reluctant to embrace learning and self-development because the resultant changes might undermine the collective interests of the learners.[10]

learning: the processes of constructing new knowledge and its ongoing reinforcement

We can define learning as a relatively permanent change in behaviour or human capabilities resulting from processing new knowledge, practice or experience. These capabilities are related to specific learning outcomes, including cognitive skills, motor skills, attitudes and verbal information.[11] Learning plays a central role in most aspects of individual and collective behaviour in the workplace, from the knowledge and skills workers need to perform work tasks and the communication skills managers use to motivate subordinates, to clarifying the expectations, aspirations and understandings that managers and others have of each other (the psychological contract). Learning is people's primary mode of adaptation to change.[12] People learn in the organization and other different settings: in educational institutions, in families, through community activities, through recreation events, through union activities and through political campaigns and action.

In work organizations, the quality of managers' and other employees' learning experience depends upon a range of factors. The way work is designed – giving workers high or low autonomy – and the number of management levels in the organization affect work-related learning.[13] Clearly, different work regimes will affect how individuals engage, interact and construct knowledge from work situations.[14] In this context, learning can take any one of four forms: formal, non-formal, informal and incidental.

▷ *Formal learning* is associated with college and university studies or professional programmes (such as study for accountancy qualifications).

▷ *Non-formal learning* involves some form of systematic instruction, but takes place in a one-off situation (such as a workshop on workplace violence) and typically does not lead to any formal qualifications.

▷ *Informal learning* occurs when people consciously try to learn from their context and everyday life experiences. It does not involve formal instruction, but does involve individual or collective (for instance, by a work team or trade union) critical reflection on experience.

▷ *Informal and incidental learning* are interconnected, but are not necessarily the same.[15] Incidental learning occurs through an activity or as a result of trial and error, and is seen as a by-product of direct experience. Whereas people acquire explicit knowledge through formal, non-formal and informal learning processes, through incidental learning people acquire tacit knowledge.

explicit knowledge: knowledge that is ordered and can be communicated between people

tacit knowledge: knowledge embedded in our actions and ways of thinking, and transmitted only through observation and experience

intellectual capital: the sum of an organization's human capital, structural capital and relationship capital

reflexive learning: a view of adult learning that emphasizes learning through self-reflection

lifelong learning: the belief that adults should be encouraged, and given the opportunity, to learn either formally in education institutions or informally on the job or off the job

Explicit knowledge is ordered and can be communicated between people. Tacit knowledge, on the other hand, refers to information that cannot easily be captured, measured or codified and communicated from one individual to another individual or group: it is therefore more subtle.

From a managerial perspective, it is suggested that an organization's investment in training and learning acts as a powerful signal of its intentions to develop its intellectual capital. This can help develop employees' commitment to the organization rather than simply their compliance. With the wave of interest in flexible 'high-performance work systems' in the 1990s, it is not surprising that some academics and management gurus claimed that reflexive learning was a means to promote flexibility and achieve competitive advantage over rivals.[16] Those subscribing to this view on sustainable competitive advantage advised companies to gain 'mutual commitment' by investing in their workforce and encouraging lifelong learning.[17] This belief in the efficacy of continuous work-related learning is linked to a broader debate about 'progressive' HRM practices, in which it is argued that work-related learning should be encouraged in order to enhance employee performance.

Research has focused on evaluating the effectiveness of particular managerial or leadership styles in specific contexts, for achieving specific learning outcomes. The classic work of Peter Senge[18] seeks to yield understanding of how leadership practices can help bring about change and renew organizations through learning. He advocated that organizational leaders play the roles of teachers, designers and stewards in order to facilitate employee learning. Senge argued that 'leaders are responsible for building organizations where followers continually expand their capabilities to understand complexity, clarify vision, and improve shared mental models – that is, they are responsible for learning.'[19]

A case study of 'leadership activity' that promoted work-related informal learning found evidence of leaders exhibiting the three roles Senge outlined: designer, steward and teacher. The followers' perception of their leaders highlighted the role of gender and power.[20] For the most part, however, mainstream studies of leadership have given little attention to how leadership activity actually encourages individual or group learning.[21]

The emergence of critical studies of workplace learning has certainly added to the debate on the role of lifelong learning. Contributions to the debate have emphasized that 'cultural control' can be reinforced through learning.[22] Critical accounts have exposed the potential of competency training to make work more 'visible' in order to make it more manageable.[23] Others have criticized popular accounts of work-related learning for adopting a conflict-free managerialist perspective, in which it is assumed that the goals of managers and workers are shared, and inherent tensions in the employment relationship are largely ignored.[24]

Critical organizational theorists share a deep scepticism for popular prescriptive publications such as Senge's *The Fifth Discipline*,[25] which discount the influence of power and political activity on workplace learning. For critical theorists, the likely effect of new learning regimes is to reshape organizational culture and strengthen the power of managers over the managed. In fact, if learning is synonymous with change, then attempts to manage a culture of learning, through either formal or informal processes, can be regarded as a management strategy to promote a change of structures, attitudes and behaviour. It is argued that in adopting a 'learning strategy', therefore, managers hope to unfreeze traditional attitudes and work practices and foster creative thinking and new ways of doing, or innovation. Neglecting these wider socioeconomic dynamics, tensions and contested aspects of learning might mean that learning practices become a managerial tool for work intensification and control in the workplace.[26]

Despite the increasing diversity and feminization of the paid workforce in most economies of the OECD, another notable feature of the contemporary learning discourse is the tendency for the academic research to be blind to race, ethnic and gender issues. Recently, some writers have focused critically on gender issues in workplace learning. The emergence of feminist accounts of workplace learning adds depth to our understanding of how sexuality and gender relations in the paid workplace can shape learning. As these writers point out, the recent explosion of workplace learning practices still privileges men, and 'it is worth recognizing the continuities in women's unequal access to and benefit from workplace learning'.[27]

The Learning Age: A renaissance for a new Britain

'Learning is the key to prosperity – for each of us as individuals, as well as for the nation as a whole. Investment in human capital will be the foundation of success in the knowledge-based global economy of the twenty-first century. This is why the Government has put learning at the heart of its ambition. This Green Paper sets out for consultation how learning throughout life will build human capital by encouraging the acquisition of knowledge and skills and emphasising creativity and imagination. The fostering of an enquiring mind and the love of learning are essential to our future success.

'To achieve stable and sustainable growth, we will need a well-educated, well-equipped and adaptable labour force. To cope with rapid change and the challenge of the information and communication age, we must ensure that people can return to learning throughout their lives. We cannot rely on a small elite, no matter how highly educated or highly paid. Instead, we need the creativity, enterprise and scholarship of all our people. As well as securing our economic future, learning has a wider contribution. It helps make ours a civilized society, develops the spiritual side of our lives and promotes active citizenship. Learning enables people to play a full part in their community. It strengthens the family, the neighbourhood and consequently the nation.

'To realize our ambition, we must all develop and sustain a regard for learning at whatever age. For many people this will mean overcoming past experiences which have put them off learning. For other it will mean taking the opportunity, perhaps for the first time, to recognize their own talent, to discover new ways of learning and to see new opportunities opening up.

'That is why this Green Paper encourages adults to enter and re-enter learning at every point in their lives, whatever their experience at school. There are many ways in which we can all take advantage of new opportunities: [1] as parents we can play out part in encouraging, supporting and raising the expectations of our children by learning alongside them; [2] as members of the work force we can take on the challenge of learning in and out of work; and [3] as citizens we can balance the rights we can expect from the state, with the responsibilities of individuals for their own future, sharing the gains and the investment needed.

'The Learning Age will be built on a renewed commitment to self-improvement and on a recognition of the enormous contribution learning makes or our society. As President John F Kennedy once put it, "Liberty without learning is always in peril and learning without liberty is always in vain."'

David Blunkett, Secretary of State for Education and Employment

WEB LINK

Visit www.mapnp.org/library/trng_dev/
trng_dev.htm for more information on training
and development in the workplace.

It should be apparent from this introduction that as a field of study, learning can be explored and interpreted from different perspectives. Now we have examined *why* learning is important to people and organizations, we go on to address two central questions: *how* do individuals learn, and *how* is work-related individual learning interconnected to collective learning in the organization?

Classical learning theories

STOP AND REFLECT

Think about the way learning happens on your course. What pedagogical techniques do your professors use – for instance, role playing, group discussions, case analyses, question and answers, video – to help you learn? What approaches help or hinder your learning? Given that we all have different learning styles, what norms should your instructor and co-students establish on the course to ensure maximum learning?

Explicit and tacit knowledge is acquired in many different ways. The rest of this chapter gives an overview of both psychologically driven and socioculturally driven perspectives of learning. We begin by examining what can be called the 'classical' theories of learning. As in other areas of the discipline, they are considered classical partly because they represent the early contributions to our understanding of how children and adults learn, and also because some of the ideas recur in contemporary adult learning theories. It should be noted, however, that the explanations found in these different approaches are contested, and that no one theory – classic or contemporary – offers a 'correct' account of the learning process in the workplace. We would also suggest that the theories outlined here, and the organizational practices that derive from them, are not appropriate to all forms of adult learning in all situations.

The classical behavioural approach: learning through reinforcement

What factors stimulate or inhibit the learning process, and what types of learning do people engage in? Our working definition of learning – that it is a relatively permanent change in behaviour or human capabilities – emphasizes the importance of experience and reinforcement. The best-known *behaviourist* psychologists, Ivan Pavlov (1849–1936) and B. F. Skinner (1904–1990), explained learning in terms of the interaction of the human being with his or her environment. They discounted the significance of internal cognitive or mental activities – characterized by behav-

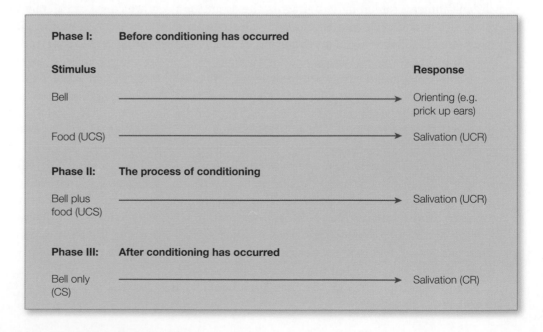

figure 8.1 Classical or Pavlovian conditioning

iourist psychologists as 'black box' activity – in the learning process. They argued that since it was impossible to measure such mental activities objectively, they had no place in the science of psychology.

The Russian Ivan Pavlov is often referred to as 'the father of behaviourism'. Pavlov and his colleagues held that all kinds of learning, human and animal, could be explained by the phenomenon of classical conditioning.[28] Working with dogs as his experimental subjects, he trained them to salivate in response to a variety of stimuli, such as the sound of a bell. This was achieved by continually pairing the sound of the bell or other stimulus, which originally produced no increase in saliva, with food. Salivation was the normal physiological response to food near or in the dog's mouth, and the repeated pairing of the bell with the food caused the dog to salivate simply upon hearing the bell, even when food was not available. Pavlov described the food as the 'unconditional stimulus' (UCS) and the sound of the bell as the 'conditional stimulus' (CS). Similarly, he described the dog's salivation when given food as the 'unconditional response' (UCR), and its salivation at the sound of the bell as a 'conditional response' (CR) (see Figure 8.1). One way to distinguish between these two types of stimuli and responses are to remember that 'unconditioned' means 'unlearned' and 'conditioned' means 'learned'.

For Pavlov, learning was nothing more than 'a long chain of conditioned reflexes'.[29] The thought of using his findings in work situations, and dangling stimuli or rewards to elicit employee salivation, may seem offensive, but there are several reasons that Pavlov's research is considered important to learning in organizations. His research illustrates how internal mental events such as learning might be measured and studied. The American John Watson (1878–1958) developed Pavlov's work to demonstrate how relationships between two variables, environment and human behaviour, could be built into an objective and testable general theory of learning.[30]

The American Burrhus Skinner is another well-known advocate of behaviourial psychology who has made an important contribution to our understanding of the learning process.[31] Skinner explained human behaviour in terms of the phenomenon of operant or instrumental conditioning, and he believed reinforcement was a necessary part of this process.[32]

An operant is a response that has some effect on the situation or environment. For example, when an animal pulls a lever and food pellets are delivered, the animal has made an operant response that influences when the food will appear. Over time, the animal acquires the lever-pulling response as a means of obtaining food. In other words, the animal learns to pull the lever. Similarly, when a child cries and is then fed, the child has made an operant response that influences when food will be served. The kind of learning is called operant learning, because the subject learns to operate on the environment to achieve certain outcomes.

---

classical conditioning: a view of 'instrumental' learning whose adherents assert that the reinforcement is noncontingent on the animal's behaviour, that is, delivered without regard to the animal's behaviour. By contrast, in instrumental conditioning the delivery of the reinforcement is contingent – dependent – on what the animal does.

WEB LINK

For more information on Pavlovian conditioning and other theories of learning go to: http://tip.psychology.org http://ccs.mit.edu/LH/

operant conditioning: a technique for associating a response or behaviour with a consequence

STOP AND REFLECT

Can there be any negative effects of learning in the workplace?

Photo: J. Bratton

plate 22 Russian Ivan Pavlov is famous for his experiments with dogs, and is often referred to as the 'father of behaviourism'. Working with dogs as his experimental subjects, Pavlov trained them to salivate in response to a variety of stimuli, such as the sound of a bell.

positive reinforcement: occurs when the introduction of a consequence increases or maintains the frequency or future probability of a behaviour

negative reinforcement: occurs when the removal or avoidance of a consequence increases or maintains the frequency or future probability of a behaviour.

A *reinforcer* increases the probability that an operant response will reoccur. Skinner believed that reinforcement operates either positively or negatively. Positive reinforcement is an event that strengthens an operant response if it is experienced after that response occurs. Positive reinforcers are therefore a form of reward. In the context of a work organization, money, recognition, praise from a manager and promotion can all act as positive reinforcers, since they all increase the likelihood of the preceding response being repeated. Negative reinforcers are unpleasant stimuli, such as a disapproving frown, a verbal reprimand or a threat, which strengthen a response if they are withdrawn after the response occurs. For example, a manager applies negative reinforcement when he or she stops criticizing an employee whose substandard job performance has improved. Reinforcements shape behaviour, and intermittent reinforcements also maintain established behaviours.[33]

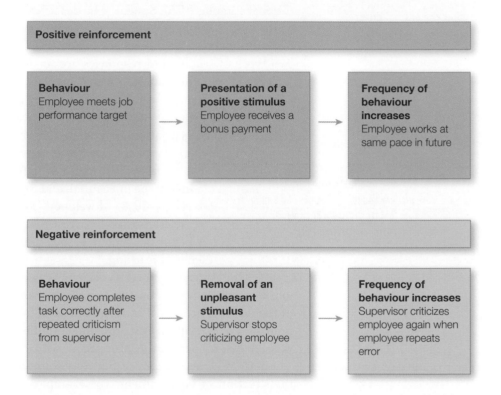

figure 8.2 Examples of positive and negative reinforcement

Figure 8.2 illustrates operant or instrumental conditioning.

Skinner also investigated the effect of punishment in shaping human behaviour, defining punishment as either the presence of unpleasant stimuli or an unpleasant outcome, or the removal of a pleasant one. Threatening an employee with disciplinary action or dismissal for verbally abusing another co-worker is an example of an unpleasant stimulus. When an employee is forced to forfeit a company car because of a poor annual appraisal, this is punishment by removing a pleasant stimulus.

Most behavioural psychologists would agree with Skinner that punishment is a less powerful means of shaping behaviour than positive reinforcement or reward. Punishment only indicates what response an individual should suppress; it cannot guide an individual towards desired behaviour. Moreover, punishment can cause anxiety and resentment, and might impact negatively on the psychological contract. Reward, on the other hand, has the virtue of indicating what desirable behaviour is required.

Skinner believed that learning in the organization was also influenced by what he called 'schedules of reinforcement'. The simplest schedule is *continuous reinforcement*: that is, every desired response behaviour is followed by a reward. A more complex schedule involves *intermittent reinforcement*, which involves applying the reinforcer after fixed or variable time intervals. For example, an employee is not rewarded each time he or she performs a desired behaviour, such as servicing a car, but the employee experiences the fixed interval reinforcement schedule when he or she receives his/her weekly pay cheque. Likewise, when a supervisor is promoted to manager for outstanding performance, he or she experiences a variable interval reinforcement schedule, because promotion only occurs at relatively long time intervals.

An American psychologist, Edward Thorndike (1874–1949), did much of the groundwork for Skinner's observations of the effects on learning of different reinforcement schedules. Thorndike developed the 'law of effect',[34] which states that if a response made in the presence of a particular stimulus is accompanied or closely followed by a satisfying state of affairs (such as a reward), that response is more likely to be made the next time the stimulus is encountered. Conversely, responses that produce unpleasant experiences are less likely to be repeated.[35]

The behaviourist theory of learning has been applied extensively in education and training institutions. For example, they often use learning objectives or outcomes framed in behavioural language, acknowledge the significance of giving immediate feedback on learners' achievements, use 'chaining' (the linking together of simpler tasks to create more complex ones), and appreciate the value for educators and trainers of positive reinforcement rather than punishment.[36]

Examples of operant conditioning pervade all formal organizations. Any manager who either explicitly or implicitly suggests that rewards (reinforcements) are dependent on some behaviour on your part is applying operant learning theory. However, the behaviourist approach to learning has been widely criticized for neglecting the individual's 'internal' mental states, for assuming that on occasion no learning occurs because others cannot 'observe' any change in behaviour, and for ignoring cognitive processes.

The cognitive approach: learning through feedback

An alternative theory of learning is the *cognitive approach*. Cognitive theorists believe that cognitive processes – how individuals perceive, evaluate feedback, represent, store and use information – play an important role in learning. Cognitive psychologists explicitly attempt to develop an understanding of the internal mental state – the 'black box' – of the learner.

The origins of the cognitive approach to learning can be traced back to research by three prominent European psychologists, Max Wertheimer (1880–1943), Wolfgang Köhler (1887–1967) and Kurt Lewin (1890–1947). At the University of Berlin's Psychological Institute, Wertheimer and Köhler became known as the Gestalt theorists, proposing that human consciousness cannot be investigated adequately by unscrambling its component parts, but only by investigating its overall shape or pattern.

There are many variants of cognitive learning theory; the aim here is to provide the reader with an introduction to the work of the Gestalt psychologist Wolfgang Köhler. His work with chimpanzees made a significant contribution to the understanding of the learning process, through his explanation of the phenomenon of *insightful learning*. In contrast to the behaviourist psychologist Edward Thorndike, who believed that animals learn gradually through the consequences of trial and error, Köhler argued that animals' problem solving does not have to develop incrementally through stimulus–response associations.[37]

Gestalt: a German word that means form or organization and Gestalt psychology emphasizes organizational processes in learning. The Gestalt slogan, 'The whole is greater than the sum of the parts,' draws attention to relationships between parts.

Köhler supported his assertion with three observations. The first observation was that once a chimpanzee solved a problem, it would immediately repeat the action in a similar situation. In other words, 'it acted as if it understood the problem.'[38] The second observation was that chimpanzees rarely tried a solution that did not work. And finally he observed that they often solved the problem quite suddenly. Through these observations, Köhler concluded that learning involves insight into the problem as a whole, occurs suddenly, is retained, and is transferred readily to new situations.

More recent interpretations, however, suggest that insight might not occur as suddenly as Köhler assumed. Insightful learning might only occur after a mental 'trial and error' process in which individuals envisage a course of action, mentally evaluate its results, compare it with logical alternatives, and choose the option that is most likely to aid decision making.[39] The notion that learning involves mentally processing feedback has led others to compare cognitive-driven learning processes to cybernetics and information-processing theories.[40]

The main differences between the behaviourialist and cognitive theories of learning are summarized in Table 8.1.

decision making: a conscious process of making choices between one or more alternatives with the intention of moving toward some desired state of affairs

feedback: any information that people received about the consequences of their behaviour

table 8.1 Approaches to learning theory

Behaviourist approach to learning	Cognitive approach to learning
Learning in terms of responses to stimuli, 'automatic' learning	Feedback must be processed
Pavlovian (respondent) conditioning	Thinking, discovering, understanding. observing practices, relationships and meaning, dialoguing
Skinnerial (operant or instrumental) conditioning. Negative or positive reinforcement	Reframing of previously learned concepts and principles
Schedules of reinforcement	Insightful learning

Source: adapted from Bratton and Gold (2003: 343)

The social-learning approach: learning through observation

This section examines a number of social-learning theories. Following the work of Albert Bandura,[41] social-learning theorists explain human development as interaction between the internal processes and the external social context. Learning is characterized as a reciprocal process that happens through indirect observation and modelling (see Figure 8.3).

Individuals learn by observing others whom they believe are credible and knowledgeable (so they can act as 'models'). What the observer acquires are symbolic representations of the model's actions. What is learned is then encoded into memory to serve as a guide for later behaviour. Observational learning involves four interrelated processes: attention, memory, motor and motivation.[42]

Before an individual can learn much from a more knowledgeable person (a model), she or he must actively attend to the other person. Attention is affected by characteristics of both the observer and the model. Memory is an important element because we may learn how to perform a behaviour, but then forget what we have learned. A motor process is another component in social learning. The observer may need to practise one or more of the motor actions required in order to perform the behaviour. Remember learning to ride a bike or snowboard? These behaviours were learned by observing others, but needed to be perfected through practice: thus the importance of hands-on experience.

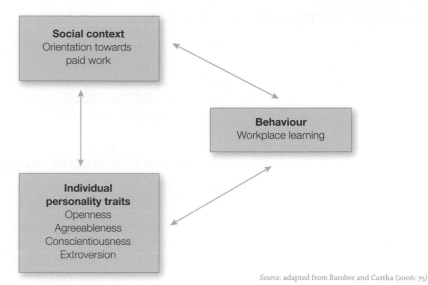

figure 8.3 Three aspects of reciprocal learning

Source: adapted from Bamber and Castka (2006: 75)

The fourth component of observational learning is motivation. Social-learning theorists believe that whether or not an individual performs a behaviour depends on whether she or he expects to be reinforced or punished for doing so. Observational learning suggests that learning new knowledge and skills comes from:

▷ actively attending to the behaviour of the relevant other (the 'expert')
▷ remembering the observed behaviour
▷ practising the observed behaviours and directly experiencing the consequences of using knowledge or skills.

Finally, social-learning theorists believe that adult learning is influenced by a person's 'self-efficacy': that is, a person's judgement about whether he or she can successfully learn new knowledge and skills, and the influence of verbal persuasion by relevant others who encourage a person to believe that she or he can accomplish a behaviour: thus the importance of expert–learner social relations.[43]

plate 23 Social learning theory suggests that individuals observe a 'model' perform a behaviour, for example a child watching her mother, which leads to an expectancy that their performance of the same behaviour will produce a favourable result

Source: Getty Images

Contemporary learning theories

The two contemporary theories that we have chosen to focus on here – cultural-historical theory and communities of practice – draw upon social-learning theory and are a reaction against the classical psychologically driven theories of learning. They have been chosen because both approaches inform much of the research and scholarly inquiry on workplace learning during the last ten years.

The cultural-historical approach: learning through social exchange

The cultural-historical activity approach to learning was first developed by the Russian social psychologist Lev Vygotsky in the 1920s and early 1930s.[44] A colleague and protégé of Vygotsky's, Alexei Leontiev, further developed the theory.[45] Vygotsky's socio-cultural theory of learning emphasized the importance of social interaction in the learning process. Learning is not just about what happens internally, but rather a product of interactions from the social to the individual.

According to Vygotsky, learning occurs through a dynamic social exchange between a mature practitioner or expert (a more capable and knowledgeable individual) and the learner (novice) in the learning community. The relationship is not passive but dynamic, and it is defined by the needs of the learner, by the forms of social practice that 'relate' the learner (novice) to the objective context, and by what that context means for the learner. Such a 'relational' view also focuses on 'semiotic mechanisms', including diagrams, cultural tools (such as language), mnemonic techniques (such as multiple-choice questions), works of art and writing, which are used to mediate the learning process and shape thinking. The acquisition of cultural tools enables knowledge to be transmitted. These semiotic mechanisms will vary across different activity contexts and cultures.

semiotics: the systematic study of signs and symbols used in communications

Another aspect of Vygotsky's theory is the importance of identifying the learner's lower and upper limits of ability. The learner's optimal performance level, called the zone of proximal development (ZPD), is achievable only with support or 'scaffolding'.[46] The concept of the ZPD exemplifies Vygotsky's concern with the role of assistance, assessment and feedback. With support, the mature practitioner bridges gaps so that the novice can act 'as if' she or he is already able to complete the given task.[47] The 'scaffold' allows learners to perform at a level beyond what they would be capable of on their own.

Vygotsky's approach to learning is, however, still a psychological model, since it focuses on the process of *internalization*. The psychological nature of his model is apparent in the clear boundary between self and social implied by Vygotsky's notion of internalization, and by the way in which sociocultural phenomena become psychological phenomena as they cross that boundary.

communities of practice: informal groups bound together by shared expertise and passion for a particular activity or interest

situated learning: an approach that views adult learning as a process of enculturation, where people consciously and subconsciously construct new knowledge from the actions, processes, behaviour and context in which they find themselves

The community of practice approach: learning through socially embedded activity

The concept of a community of practice has antecedents in the work of Vygotsky' and in social-learning theory. More recently, the approach was articulated in the work of Lave and Wenger, and Rogoff.[48] Whereas classical psychologically driven theories of learning developed primarily either in the laboratory or in classroom settings, situated learning theories have emerged out of studies of learning in workplace settings. Jean Lave,[49] for example, used the term 'situated learning' to focus attention on the development of knowledge and expertise through activity, and the context and culture in which learning occurs (that is, within which it is situated). Situated learning places greater emphasis on people learning in context, and as such has expanded key notions of the sociopsychological paradigm. Learning in context has become increasingly a matter for research and application in higher education. For example, students on professional programmes, such as nursing, increasingly spent a large proportion of their learning in a 'practicum' – actually in a hospital. A critical constituent of situated learning is social interaction and the concept of a community of practice.

Wenger further developed the notion that learning is a process of participation in a community of practice.[50] A community of practice can be defined as 'a unique combination of three fundamental elements: a domain of knowledge, which defines a set of issues; a community of people who care about this domain; and the shared practice that they are developing to be effective in their domain'.[51] The domain creates a sense of common identity for the members, the community creates the social fabric for the learning, and the practice is a set of ideas, information, stories, documents and tools that community members share. All communities of practice share this three-dimensional structure, and a set of relations among the members is central to the process. Moreover, the concept of community of practice is an intrinsic condition for learning, 'not least because it provides the interpretative support necessary for making sense of its heritage'.[52]

Examples of a community of practice include systems of apprenticeships in manual trades (such as carpentry, plumbing and mechanics). As the novice moves from the periphery of the community to its centre, he or she becomes more engaged within the culture, until he/she eventually assumes the role of 'master' or 'expert'. The apprenticeship system includes instances of formal and informal learning in various situated work activities.

Lave and Wenger's central concept in explaining the process and the path individuals take as they progress from 'apprentice' or novice to 'master' or expert is what they call legitimate peripheral participation (LPP). The authors explain the process like this:

> By this we mean to draw attention to the point that learners inevitably participate in communities of practitioners and that the mastery of knowledge and skill requires newcomers to move toward full participation in the sociocultural practices of a community. 'Legitimate peripheral participation' provides a way to speak about the relations between newcomers and old-timers, and about activities, identities, artifacts, and communities of knowledge and practice. It concerns the process by which newcomers become part of a community of practice.[53]

In developing their argument, Lave and Wenger emphasize the need for taking a holistic view of learning involving the whole person, and for activity in and with the world rather than 'receiving' a body of knowledge. Other theorists have built upon the situated learning model by the notion of 'cognitive apprenticeships', which focuses on how the learner acquires, develops and uses cognitive tools in authentic settings.[54] For example, architects, lawyers and physicians complete cognitive apprenticeships. Physicians, for instance, acquire the situated experience and knowledge on which they build their practice in their internships and residencies in hospitals.[55]

As a model for understanding how employees learn in the workplace, the community of practice approach has been the subject of some debate in the adult learning literature. An extreme position would be that there is little need for formal classroom-based learning because effective learning only occurs through the engagement of community membership. Thus, it is suggested, the learner (the new employee) is a valued member of the community, and expected to make contributions, as he or she 'learn the ropes'. The role of participants (novice and master or expert) evolves over time, as levels of mastery are achieved.

Feedback from expert members of the community (for example, managers) is formative and non-evaluative, supportive, and encourages risk taking. The 'scaffolding' provided by the expert may involve a modification of the task so that learning and success is possible. Another aspect is that the interaction between members of the community reflects the style of discourse appropriate for the context and environment. Further, the notion of movement across contexts becomes a key concept when the theory of situated learning is applied to complex work organizations.[56]

For individuals, the perspective highlights the importance of finding the dynamic set of communities they should belong to, and fashioning a meaningful pathway of experience through these communities over time.[57] Finally, situated learning assumes that the learner (novice worker) is motivated to learn, and that she or he develops and achieves the knowledge, expertise and value system that make up the community of practice.

The work of Engeström and Rogoff has built on Lave and Wenger's situated learning model.[58] Whereas Lave and Wenger downplay the importance of formal training and learning, Engeström emphasizes its necessity and value. While recognizing the central nature of social interaction in the mediation of adult learning, Engeström also emphasizes the value of structured instruction in developing knowledge and expertise. He argues that day-to-day learning consists of 'conditioning, imitation, and trial and error', but to reach a higher plane, 'investigative' and 'expansive' learning, instruction is necessary.[59] For Engeström, teacher-centred training practices complement, rather than negate, learner-centred approaches to individual development.

Barbara Rogoff's early laboratory research[60] emphasized the importance of the social milieu in which learning is embedded, arguing that 'context is an integral aspect of cognitive events, not a nuisance variable'.[61] In later work, she extended Lave and Wenger's theoretical approach by identifying two interrelated social processes, in addition to apprenticeships, that are important to learning, participatory appropriation and guided participation.

plate 24 Learning can occur, sometimes unconsciously, from the situation and everyday work experience. This is called informal learning.

Source: Getty Images

Participatory appropriation refers to the way individuals change through their involvement in apprenticeship activities. Rogoff believes that appropriation is different from Vygotsky's concept of internalization. Whereas 'internalization' implies static entities involved in the 'acquisition' of knowledge and skills, participatory appropriation treats learning as a series of active processes derived from the unfolding activity in which individuals participate. The nature of social relations required to support the apprenticeship system is captured by Rogoff's notion of guided participation, which includes direct communication about the behaviours involved, and communication, within the work setting, of organizational culture through shared language and talk (such as folktales, language, legends, myths, sagas and stories).[62]

Apprenticeship, participatory appropriation and guided participation activities all include processes such as 'scaffolding', by which is meant a novice being supported by a master in achieving goals within her or his zone of proximal development. Guided participation, however, does not only take place between the master and novice, but engages other members of the wider community of practice. In contrast to behaviourist and cognitive approaches, the social theorists reject the transmission model of instruction, in which the learner is simply a passive recipient of information, arguing that learning can never be context-free.

A recent Dutch case study uses the concept of activity theory (Vygotsky and Engeström) and the community of practice theory (Wenger) to analyse how work-related learning is interconnected between individual and group, and group and organization. In this case, the two sides of innovation, creation and exploitation, are located at different levels in the organization (see Figure 8.4). Using four key concepts – knowledge creation, an activity system, scripts and routines – the

activity theory: a view of adult learning that envisions learning as a social process whereby individual and group agency and learning occurs through interlocking human activity systems shaped by social norms and a community of practice

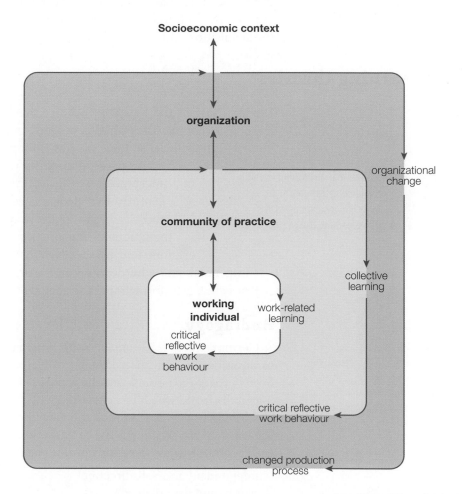

Figure 8.4 A model of work-related learning

Source: Hoeve and Nieuwenhuis (2006: 175)

community of practice arranges the connection between the individual and the organization or collective.[63]

The first concept of knowledge creation is a process whereby employees and work groups share tacit and explicit knowledge through intensive social interaction. The second concept of an activity system focuses on the dialectical relation between employees and objects. The third concept of scripts is a structure that describes appropriate sequences of events in a particular context or organization. The fourth concept used by the researchers of routines is built around the notion of recurrent or repetitive patterns of work behaviour. A domain of knowledge and the routines specific to the organization are central to the change processes. It is argued that 'Simultaneously, routines link the collective to the larger organization, as organizations are a set of interlocking routines.'[64] The evidence suggests that in innovative situations, individual, group and collective learning are a combination of cognitive, emotional and relational processes.

Detractors of situated learning and the community of practice model point to problems for learning within the organization context. Hiring practices and workplace inequalities can hamper the workplace discourse that transmits knowledge, attitudes and skills. Employees on part-time employment contracts may be removed or isolated from the community discourse, simply because they are not there as often as other employees. These part-time workers often tend to be women and minorities, and this perpetuates their marginalization. If there are language barriers, workers may struggle to participate in the community of practice. Gender and racial bias, language barriers, part-time schedules and isolating power structures create barriers to effective workplace learning. Would-be learners within the community of practice find that equal status and the opportunity to participate are withheld. Further, the 'cultural tools' of the organization are not readily accessible, and limit the acquisition and creation of knowledge.

Adult learning theories

During most of the twentieth century the behavioural approach dominated the learning discourse. The orthodox wisdom, much of it based on research conducted in artificial settings such as laboratories, assumed that learning was the objective perception of the world as it is, unmediated by personal interpretation or distortion. In the final quarter of the twentieth century, this dependence on psychologically driven learning theories began to give way to learning theories that articulated the unique characteristics of adult learning.[65] In this section we examine four perspectives that attempt to understand adult learning in general, and adult learning in a work context in particular: the andragogy, self-directed, transformational and sociocultural perspectives.

WEB LINK For more information on adult learning and lifelong learning, go to: www.lifelonglearning.co.uk www.lifelonglearning.co.uk/llp/index.htm

Andragogy

andragogy: the processes associated with the organization and practice of teaching adults; more specifically, various kinds of interactions in facilitating learning situations

A German teacher, Alexander Kapp, originally used the term 'andragogy' in 1833 to describe the educational theory of Plato.[66] But it was Malcolm Knowles[67] who over 25 years ago popularized the concept of andragogy, 'the art and science of helping adults learn', which he contrasted with pedagogy, the art and science of helping children learn.[68] Knowles took the view that knowledge is activity constructed by the learner, and learning is the construction of meaning through experience. In his early work Knowles characterized adult learners as:

▷ independent and 'self-directing'
▷ mature and experienced

▷ motivated by 'what they need to know'
▷ problem-centred
▷ internally motivated.

In his seminal book, *The Modern Practice of Adult Education: from pedagogy to andragogy,* Knowles focuses upon and portrays the two forms of education as polar opposites. The key five assumptions of andragogy are summarized in Table 8.2. As can be seen from this table, andragogy as it is conceived is an amalgam of description and prescription. It describes the motivation and assumption of adult learners in these terms: 'As a person grows and matures his [sic] self-concept moves from one of total dependency (as is the reality of the infant) to one of increasing self-directedness.'[69] It follows logically from this assumption that adult learning practitioners should embrace methodological techniques that focus on an adult's needs and life experiences, facilitation and internally driven motivation to learn.

Criticism from other adult educators caused Knowles to revise his original position that andragogy characterizes only adult learning. Many school teachers were using 'learner-centred' pedagogy that advocated problem-centred and 'discovery' learning strategies. In his later work, Knowles contended that pedagogy and andragogy represent a continuum ranging from teacher-directed to learner-directed learning, and that both approaches are appropriate with children and adults, depending on the situation.[70] It has been suggested elsewhere that self-directed learning principles became the vogue among professional adult educators because in the mid-1960s the philosophy underlying andragogy mirrored the 'Expressive Revolution' and the social and political climate of the time.[71] Since then, the methodology of self-directed learning has been has been uncritically adopted as a technology of adult instruction[72] and incorporated into mainstream formal adult education settings, from basic adult literacy through to professional development.[73]

table 8.2 A comparison of the assumptions of pedagogy and andragogy

	Pedagogy	Andragogy
The learner	The role of the learner is a dependent one. The teacher directs what, when, how a subject is learned	The learner moves from dependency toward increasing self-directedness. Teacher encourages and nurtures this movement.
The learner's experience	Of little worth. Hence learners will gain most from the teacher, textbooks, assigned readings, AV presentations.	A rich resource for learning. Hence teaching methods include discussion, problem solving and simulation exercises.
Readiness to learn	Learners learn what society expects them to, so the curriculum is standardized.	Learners learn what they 'need to know', so learning activities are designed around life application.
Orientation to learning	Learners see education as a process of acquiring subject matter organized by content.	Learners see education as a process of developing increased curriculum competence to achieve their full potential in life. Learners want to be able to apply new knowledge and skills. Hence learning activities are centred around competency-development categories.

Source: based on Jarvis (1985, 1991)

Andragogy's detractors maintain that self-directed learning as it is conceived, and deployed, in formal work organizations justifies an individualized and psychological approach to adult learning that is based exclusively on the perceived individual needs of the learner, and downplays the importance of social purpose and context. Further, it is argued, Knowles's conception of andragogy is not so much an explanatory theory about the process of adult learning as a philosophical position with regard to the relationship of the individual to society. By drawing on the work of Daniel Pratt, it is apparent that the language of andragogy is that of individual triumphalism.

Individuals are unique, they desire self-improvement, they have the power to achieve self-fulfilment in the face of social, political, cultural and historical forces, they are at the centre of adult education and their private goals dominate over collective goals, they are autonomous and capable of directing their own learning, and this self-direction and self-reliance is the true mark of mature adulthood within society. In the interests of achieving private ends, each individual must take responsibility, become self-directed, for his or her own idiosyncratic education and learning. Parallels may be drawn here with the business axiom 'the customer is always right'. In this case, the adult learner is always right. The values underpinning andragogy echo the influence of the white middle-class American belief system. The concept, it is argued, 'is saturated with the ideals of individualism and entrepreneurial democracy'.[74]

Liberatory adult educators are concerned that the social purpose and context of adult education might be relegated to the periphery.[75] Because it describes the individual in psychological terms, separate from social, political, economic, cultural and historical contexts, andragogy does not acknowledge the vast influence of these social structures on the formation of the individual's identity and ways of interpreting the world, much of which is received and accepted without conscious consideration or reflection. The learner is portrayed simply 'as an uncritical and unwitting member of institutions and structures that generate rules about meaning, dominance, and judgment in society'.[76] Nonetheless, the notion of self-directed learning continues to play an important role in adult learning in higher education and in the workplace. Education and training programmes continue to assume that adults continually learn from their experience through reflection, and that the adult learner prefers to identify her or his own learning needs, and prefers to join other learners to address real-life problems as laboratories of learning.[77]

The self-directed approach

The literature on self-directed learning has helped to define the unique characteristics of adult learning. Three main ideas are incorporated into the 'cult-like' concept of self-directed learning:

▷ a self-initiated process of learning that emphasizes the need and ability for individuals to control and manage their own learning
▷ individual empowerment as far as learning is concerned
▷ a way of organizing instruction that allows for greater learner autonomy and control over the individual's learning.[78]

The individual learner is expected to assume primary responsibility for his or her own learning, and the learning process focuses on the individual and self-development. Carl Rogers,[79] an influential writer on adult learning theory, believed empowerment through a process of 'self-directed' learning was important for personal growth. The learner's life experience is central to the learning process, which critically assumes that learning is pragmatic in nature.[80] Parallels can be drawn with the humanistic psychology of Maslow,[81] and the North American philosophical orientation of individualism (see Chapter 9).

In terms of practice, the practitioner emphasizes the importance of specifying learning objectives, facilitating as opposed to 'teaching', negotiating the content of what is learned, empowering learners, and encouraging the learner to develop plans for personal growth, often in the form of learning contracts. Others, linking adult learning to incremental social change, emphasize the need for learners to reflect

learning contract: a learning plan that links an organization's competitive strategy with an individual's key learning objectives. It enumerates the learning and/or competencies that are expected to be demonstrated at some point in the future.

on conceptions of knowledge, and question commonly held assumptions about the world in which they live and work. This internal change of consciousness occurs when process and reflection are jointed in the individual's pursuit of meaning.

This mode of adult learning represents the most complete form of self-directiveness: 'one in which critical reflection on the contingent aspects of reality, the exploration of alternative perspectives and meaning systems, and the alteration of personal and social circumstances are all present'.[82] Proponents of the 'learning organization' emphasize reflective thinking as a key part of lifelong learning in professions, including management, medicine and architecture, learning in work teams, and small-group problem-solving activity in a learning organization.[83] They assume (or hope) that reflective processes enable workers to jettison their dysfunctional and taken-for-granted assumptions, and thus enhance their work performance in an unproblematic manner.

Assuming that workers are permitted to engage in critical reflection, critics argue that learning at work is bounded by capitalist employment relations, and the voice of the architects building the learning organization nurtures only superficial critical reflection that improves the organization's financial bottom line. From a critical perspective, 'The objects for critical focus are carefully delineated to exclude the fundamental structures of capitalism ... employees' minds are expected to remain colonized and loyal to the imperial presence of their employing organization'.[84] Critical reflection does not extend to questioning the power structures and the more dysfunctional aspects of corporate governance.

The transformational approach

transformational learning: a view that adult learning involving self-reflection can lead to transformation of consciousness, new visions and courses of action

The theory of transformational learning is another perspective that attempts to articulate what is unique about learning in the workplace. Various theorists in adult education use the term 'transformational' to describe a learning process that is said to shape people by producing far-reaching changes in the learner. The individual learner is different after the experience, and the learner and others can recognize these differences. These changes have a significant impact on the learner's subsequent experiences. The transformational learning process can be sudden or incremental, and it can occur in a structured training and development situation or informally through experience in a workplace.[85]

Learning in the sense being used here is most often associated with the work of Jack Mezirow.[86] His view of transformational learning emphasizes the 'psycho-cultural' and cognitive restructuring of the self. Thus, the concept of perspective transformation is defined as:

> The emancipatory process of becoming critically aware of how and why the structure of psycho-cultural assumptions has come to constrain the way we see ourselves and our relationships, reconstituting this structure to permit a more inclusive and discriminating integration of experience and acting upon these new understandings.[87]

A set of core beliefs underscore Mezirow's conceptualization of transformational learning: philosophical assumptions about the nature of human beings, beliefs about knowledge, and ideas about the relationship between the individual and society. Each of the three core beliefs of transformational learning has its own function. At the centre of Mezirow's theory is the concept of the autonomous, responsible and rational adult. While social forces might limit individual choices, Mezirow believed that the goal of transformational learning is to gain 'a crucial sense of agency over ourselves and our lives'.[88] In the workplace, this core assumption is often associated with individuals reflecting on a dysfunctional operational system or company policy, and taking action to change it.

A second core belief of transformational learning relates to knowledge creation. Mezirow's theory of knowing is *constructivist*. In this view, reality is a subjective construction by individuals rather than an objective fact. In other words, human beings are active participants in the process of making meaning, and are the creators of knowledge. Through this process individuals in the organization engage in critical reflection, through which the underlying premises of ideas are assessed and critiqued. A number of conditions are required for critical reflection to take place, including full information, the ability to objectively evaluate arguments, and freedom from self-deception or coercion.

The third main belief of Mezirow's transformational learning has relevance to social theory, which facilitates explanations of social order, conflict and change, and the relationship between the individual and society. For Mezirow, society is made up of autonomous, responsible individuals who can act to bring about incremental change to their world. He assumes that the individual learner is free to act upon any new understanding he or she may have gained. Most of the critical attention that Mezirow has received is in this area.[89] He puts forward a vision of society in which individuals are responsible for their collective futures. Critical theorists, however, point out that class divisions and power relations in both society at large, and the work organization in particular, may severely limit the capacity of the individual learner to change his or her world. As they comment, 'the lower in the social hierarchy learners may be the more inhibiting they may find the social structures, if they seek to be socially mobile'.[90]

What contribution does this specific type of learning make to our understanding of learning in the workplace? According to Clarke,[91] the work of Mezirow expands the definition of adult learning, and emphasizes the importance of sense making, and of going beyond notions of learning as behavioural change. The approach focuses on the mechanism of internalization, highlighting the changes in consciousness within the learner, and this, it is argued, adds a new dimension to the definition of adult learning and 'carries theory to a new level'.[92] Transformational learning also makes a contribution to our understanding of learning by construing learning in terms of making sense of life experience: 'No need is more fundamentally human that our need to understand the meaning of our experience.'[93] Learning through engagement of life experience means that adult learning can be conceptualized as the vehicle of individual development.

Transformational learning also encourages a more multidimensional approach to learning. The notions of reflection and changes in consciousness mean that the learning process cannot be understood solely in behavioural terms: it challenges researchers and practitioners 'to attend to multiple psychological factors'.[94] While some theorists consider Mezirow's contribution to learning theory invaluable, others find that it is incomplete. For instance, the issue of how exactly the social context, and in particular, gender, race and ethnicity, affect the learning process would seem to require elaboration.

Class, ethnicity, gender and learning

In Chapter 1, we emphasized the importance of understanding the effect of societal factors such as social class, ethnicity and gender on human behaviour in the work organization. The same is true with learning at work. In a multicultural society like Canada or the United Kingdom, we need to understand that social class, ethnicity, culture, gender, sexual orientation and power relations affect access to learning opportunities and educational achievement. This will give us a more inclusive picture and a better understanding of the process of learning in the organization. Sociocultural perspectives of adult learning shift us from focusing on individual internal processes to an acknowledgment of the importance of social forces.[95]

Over the last half century, one focus of UK educational sociology has been on demonstrating the effects of social class on educational attainment, and explaining the conscious and unconscious mechanisms by which these effects occur, particularly in the field of secondary education, where public policy aims to promote equality of opportunity. An early significant study of secondary education found that despite educational reforms to promote equality in education, 'Middle-class pupils have retained, almost intact, their historic advantage over [the] manual working class.'[96] Studies have revealed a number of social mechanisms that serve to reproduce class differentials, including the effect of teacher expectations on student performance.

The stereotypes of the society in which teachers and trainers work influence their professional work.[97] Many teachers tend to have a preconceived idea of what constitutes the 'ideal' student, in terms of appearance, ability and conduct. Those students who fit this ideal image tend to come from 'middle' and 'upper' class groupings, and those outside this ideal image tend to come from 'lower' class groupings. They can be perceived by educators as being uninterested in learning. The under-achievement of many students from working-class or 'blue-collar' social groups may be explained by the effect of teacher expectations on student performance. The effects of social class on educational achievement, career and life experience are vividly captured in the epic television documentary series *49 Up*.

Other social mechanisms that function to promote inequality of opportunity and reproduce social class differentials include differences in the types of language – referred to as 'linguistic codes' – used by middle-class and working-class students and their teachers,[98] and differences in the patterns of socialization between middle-class and working-class families.[99] These same social mechanisms operate in the workplace. For example, managers and trainers may perceive that workers falling into the 'blue-collar' class are not trainable for certain tasks or jobs, or are less interested in developing their learning skills. In addition, those students who perform well at secondary school and experience university education enter the professional occupations, where the opportunities for career and work-related learning are greatest.

In most industrialized societies, differential access to education and workplace learning is influenced by ethnicity. Social 'exclusionary' or discriminatory mechanisms that produce differences in the learning opportunities of ethnic groups are thought to operate to a greater or lesser extent in both developed and developing societies. Research data provides evidence of variations between ethnic groups in terms of educational achievement, but the differences are not always in the same direction for students from different ethnic groups, suggesting that the social mechanisms promoting under-achievement in education and training are complex.[100] Additionally, globalization has tended to encourage researchers to focus on cultural diversity to explain differences in adult educational achievement in the workplace. Comparatively little research has been undertaken on cross-cultural differences in the meaning of learning in organizations, and in learning style.[101]

Obtain a copy of *Understanding Adult Education and Training*, edited by Griff Foley,[102] and read Chapter 1, 'A framework for understanding adult learning and education'. Also read Chapter 1, 'Understandings of workplace learning', in *Understanding Learning at Work*, edited by D. Boud and J. Garrick.[103] How do these authors characterize the adult learner, and from a leadership perspective, do you agree with the statement that learning has become too important to be left to in-house training departments? What are the implications of the different learning theories for leaders?

Much of the earlier literature examining the links between gender and under-achievement in educational settings focused on female students, and particularly working-class female students, in UK secondary schools. The basic feminist theory and feminist pedagogy is that gender differences and inequality are constructed by complex socialization processes, involving sex-role socialization in the family, gender-specific curriculum subjects which affect the trajectory of boys and girls going into science-related and arts-related careers, gender-specific occupational training, and consequent progress into gendered occupations.[104]

More recently, however, there has been a gravitation of research interest towards gender inequality in workplace learning.[105] Women have been socialized to occupy the more 'feminine' jobs, to take care of people, to be in support roles and to defer to men. Men, on the other hand, have been socialized to occupy leadership roles, and they benefit from greater privilege and power in our society. The liberatory or emancipatory model of feminist pedagogy deals with the nature of interlocking systems of oppression based on gender, and seeks to understand and deal with why women are often silenced or absent, or their contributions are discounted, in the public arenas of our society, and in the classroom at all educational levels.[106] For example, Tisdell, drawing on feminist research, argues that examples used in learning material are created by and are primarily about the white middle-class male experience, and therefore white middle-class males are more likely to be successful both in the education system and in a society that accords greater value to that cited experience.[107] While male privilege is reproduced by the system, feminist theorists suggest that the oppression of women in both paid and unpaid domestic work is reproduced by events in the educational system.

Sociocultural perspectives on learning in organizations say little about the process of learning, but provide important insights into the barriers to equality in learning. Moreover, when gender and asymmetrical power relations enter the analysis, research that seeks to investigate workplace learning strategy independently of the sociology of gender or work becomes exclusive and problematic. A growing body of research demonstrates that being born into a working-class family, or being born black, or being female, severely limits life experience, power and access to knowledge acquisition. For example, there is well-documented evidence that young men and women from working-class backgrounds have been persistently under-represented in UK and North American universities. Survey findings also suggest that those holding more routine, highly supervised manual working-class jobs are more likely to pursue community-related informal learning.[108]

Feminist learning theory calls attention to these issues, and underscores the importance of dealing directly with them. In addition, feminist pedagogical theory can offer new insights both to the field of adult learning and to those educators and trainers interested in educating for social and individual transformation. Consequently, a sociocultural perspective on adult learning encourages reflectivity among adult educators and trainers. Adult educators who are interested in challenging unequal power relations based on class, gender and race need to address the ways in which their own ideologies and practices in the learning environment either challenge or reproduce society's inequitable distribution of power.[109]

Learning theories in action

learning cycle: a view of adult learning that emphasizes learning as a continuous process

Modern approaches to learning in organizations contain elements of cognitive, behaviourist and andragogical concepts, such as self-direction, critical reflection, learning from experience and transformational learning. Kolb and his co-workers' learning cycle[110] is a popular model used by many professional trainers and adult facilitators. It synthesises the work of earlier theorists discussed in this chapter, but most importantly the model depicts learning as a circular process with no start or finish (see Figure 8.5). The conceptual model emphasized the centrality of experience in the learning process, the role of individual needs and goals in determining the type of experience sought, and the importance of completing all stages of learning before learning can occur.

The experiential learning cycle should not be viewed as an alternative to the behaviourist and cognitive perspectives, but rather as a more holistic perspective integrating behaviour, cognition, perception and authentic experience. According to the model, the process of adult learning and development is both concrete and abstract, active and passive.

Other adult educators, notably Jarvis,[111] have found problems with the learning cycle. Adopting a sociological perspective, he plausibly argues that the four phases may not be totally discrete. Experience should not be viewed in isolation, reflection contextualizes the learning, and any conclusions or actions arising from the 'testing' may be contrary to social forces, and hence learning must recognize the impact of power relations.

Although there has been a growing critique and reassessment of Kolb and his co-workers' model, it has become the orthodoxy for human resource development (HRD) specialists engaged in organization training and development.[112] The social theories of learning reviewed in this chapter are also influencing 'good practice' in the design of workplace learning in general, and apprenticeship activities in particular. The recommendations in Table 8.3 can be traced to the work of the adult educators we have reviewed in this chapter.

STOP AND REFLECT

When was the last time you felt that you had really learned something? Recall that occasion, reflect on it, and try to relate it step-by-step to the experiential learning model.

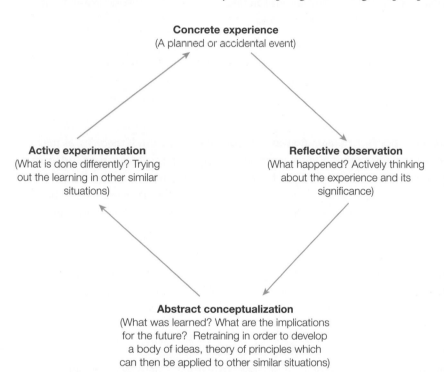

Concrete experience
(A planned or accidental event)

Active experimentation
(What is done differently? Trying out the learning in other similar situations)

Reflective observation
(What happened? Actively thinking about the experience and its significance)

Abstract conceptualization
(What was learned? What are the implications for the future? Retraining in order to develop a body of ideas, theory of principles which can then be applied to other similar situations)

figure 8.5 Kolb et al.'s experiential cycle of learning

WEB LINK

For more information on the learning organization, go to: www.ahrd.org; www.cipd.co.uk/HRD/; www.elearningnetwork.org/frameset.htm

table 8.3 Applying learning theory in the organization

Social learning and adult learning concepts	Recommendations
Zone of proximal development	Expose learners to authentic tasks
Scaffolding	Encourage learners to interact with others
Communities of practice	Design work to allow knowledge to be applied
Participatory appropriation	Provide space and time for reflectivity
Guided participation	Develop mentoring skills to managers/experts
Andragogy	Develop communities of practice through partnerships
Self-directed	Encourage learner to move towards self-directedness
Transformation	Draw on learners' life experience
	Encourage critical thinking
	Design learning activities around learners' needs

Source: based on Mezirow (1981), Knowles (1980) and Fuller and Unwin (1998)

Chapter summary

☐ There has been a growing interest in learning in organizations, as contemporary management thinking and practice emphasize notions of knowledge work, flexibility, core competencies and sustainable competitive advantage through learning.

☐ Learning can be defined as a relatively permanent change in behaviour or human capabilities resulting from processing new knowledge, practice or experience. In organizations the quality of this learning experience may depend on how the organization is structured, how work is designed, how individuals engage, interact and construct knowledge from these paid work situations, and how managers lead their subordinates. Learning in organizations can take any one of the following four forms: formal, non-formal, informal and incidental.

☐ We examined classical approaches to learning which focused on how internal mental events such as learning might be measured and studied through Pavlovian conditioning, and the importance of reinforcement in the learning process.

☐ The cognitive approach to learning was also examined. The Gestalt theorists, as they were known, proposed that human consciousness could not be investigated adequately by unscrambling its component parts, but only by investigating its overall shape or pattern. Proponents of this school of thought believe that cognitive processes – how individuals perceive, evaluate feedback, represent, store and use information – play an important role in learning.

☐ The third classical approach we examined related to social-learning theories. This suggests that individuals learn and develop through observational learning. That is, people learn by observing others – role models – whom they believe are credible and knowledgeable.

☐ We examined some contemporary approaches to learning – activity theory and community of practice – and explained that social-learning theory underpins the concept of a community of practice, which has been the subject of some debate in the adult learning literature. For example, an extreme position is that there is little need for formal classroom-based learning because effective learning only occurs through the engagement of community membership.

☐ We also discussed how psychologically driven learning theories began to give way to learning theories that articulated the unique characteristics of adult learning, and examined four perspectives that attempt to understand adult learning in general and adult learning in work: the andragogy, self-directed, transformational and sociocultural approaches.

☐ Finally, we stated that modern approaches to learning in organizations contain elements of cognitive, behaviourist and andragogical concepts, such as self-direction, critical reflection, learning from experience and transformational learning, and adult educators are increasingly aware of the importance of the sociocultural context in which adult learning takes place in the workplace and the wider community.

Key concepts

Chapter review questions

1. Why is workplace learning important for managers and workers?
2. What are the main differences between the cognitive and behaviourist perspectives on learning?
3. Why is a psychologically driven approach to workplace learning controversial?

Further reading

Billett, S. (2001) *Learning in the Workplace: Strategies for effective practice*, Crows Nest, Australia: Allen & Unwin.

Boud, D. and Garrick, J. (eds) (1999) *Understanding Learning at Work*, London: Routledge.

Bratton, J. et al. (2004) *Workplace Learning: A critical introduction*, Toronto: Garamond Press.

Livingstone, D. W. and Sawchuk, P. (2004) *Hidden Knowledge: Organized labour in the information age*, Toronto: Garamond Washington, DC: Rowman & Littlefield.

Chapter case study: Coronation Bank, a transfer of learning dilemma

Setting

In 2005, the Federal Trade Commission (FTC) in the United States received over 58,000 complaints about debt collection firms: more than from any other industry, amounting to one out of every six complaints filed. The FTC believed those who complained were just a fraction of the total number of consumers who encountered deceptive, abusive and illegal collection practices.

In the past, debt collection rules and regulations imposed by the government were very stringent but there was very little enforcement or compliance. Although it was stipulated that the collection of debts should be approached as a negotiation between the debtor and collector, this was seldom a reality. Putting collectors on the phone before they had been trained and licensed was also a violation of government regulations, but this too was widely and blatantly done by the industry.

The US government has recently announced the introduction of a new improved complaint system, whereby individuals who feel they are being harassed or abused by collection officers can file complaints against collectors and the collectors' employers using the Internet. Penalties are promised to be severe and could ultimately shut down phone-based collection efforts. In light of the US government's announcement, the industry has come under pressure to make changes in the way delinquent debts are collected.

The company

Coronation Bank is a multi-site corporation, with its main office in Seattle, Washington, providing a full range of products and services to more than 11 million individual and small business clients. It knew it had to take a new course of action. The bank had done quite well over the years, administering more than US$200 billion of assets for individuals and corporate and institutional clients.

The bank announced it wanted to maintain a good relationship with its delinquent customers during and after the debt crisis was resolved. The banking and loan business was competitive enough, it reasoned, without losing customers through abusive debt collection methods. In the past, the bank had used psychological profiles in the recruitment and selection process to help identify potential debt collection officers with extrovert and aggressive personalities. Most of the bank's debt collection supervisors had been aggressive, high-pressure collection officers themselves. Their success and rise in the organization often stemmed from their successes in ensuring debt repayment. As an incentive to encourage debt collection, supervisors were paid a salary, plus an override based on the collection performance of their subordinates.

In consideration of the desire to improve customer relations and the pressure from the government's announcement, the bank decided to turn its focus on the training of new recruits, to change the way debt collection was handled. Jason Kelly, the Debt Recovery Department's director, was given approval to hire Linda Dollimore, a new university graduate with a background in human resource development (HRD). On her first day, Linda was given the assignment to design a new five-day, phone-based collection training programme for new hires. This programme would not only promote a 'financial advisor' image for the collectors, but also change the culture surrounding the debt collection process.

Linda trusted that Jason Kelly would give her the required mandate, freedom and support necessary to ensure the success of the new training programme, so she set out quickly to begin to make the necessary changes. Linda knew the trainees would have different learning styles, and that not everyone learned at the same pace, so she endeavoured to design the course with that in mind. She arranged to have role plays filmed so that they could be viewed by the trainees, and paused at appropriate learning points for comments and suggestions from the students as well as the trainer. She brought in some examples of past complaints involving debt collection, so that trainees could suggest why the incident happened and how it could have been avoided, and she sourced an appropriate film about customer service to reinforce positive messages. To make the course fun, she implemented a competition so that teams of trainees could compete against one another in remembering the required legislation. She strove to create a training room environment where trainees were encouraged to ask questions and seek clarification of points they did not understand, and she ensured she would be available to talk with the trainees before and after each day's session and at breaks. Linda felt confident she had designed an appropriate training syllabus that would meet the requirements of the federal government and the needs of her employer.

Trainee meeting: emerging problems

Quickly the first course was delivered and ten new collectors were released into the workplace. It did not take long for one of the collectors, a new employee named Thomas Plovack, to get into trouble. A complaint was filed regarding his aggressive and threatening behaviour towards a debtor. As all debtor/collector phonecalls were regularly taped, Linda decided to listen to the relevant tape with Thomas in the room. As the conversation on the tape played out, it was obvious that Thomas had crossed the line several times by blatantly threatening the debtor.

After the tape concluded, Thomas became angry and shouted, 'You tell me one thing in the training programme and when I get out there to collect, they tell me something entirely different! What am I supposed to do?' After some encouragement by Linda to explain, Thomas told Linda that his supervisor had come over on his first day on the job and told him that he must forget everything that he had been taught in the training, and that if he did not, he would never be a good collector. Thomas also told Linda that all of his course members had been told the same thing by their supervisors, and that Mr Kelly had backed up the supervisors.

After Thomas left the room, Linda sat and pondered what to do next. What could have possibly gone wrong?

Task

Working individually or in a small group provide a written report addressing the following questions:
1.	What adult learning theories did Linda use in her course design?
2.	What are the positives aspects of Linda's course design and intended delivery methods? What did Linda not consider in her course design and delivery methods?
3.	Why did Linda not have the cooperation of the floor managers? What can be done to help facilitate the cooperation of the managers in the transfer of learning to the collection floor?

Sources of further information

Gold, J. and Smith, V. (2003) 'Advances towards a learning movement: translations at work,' Human Resource Development International.

Visit www.washingtonpost.com/wp-dyn/content/article/2005/07/27/AR2005072702473.html for information about the debt collection industry, and www.shef.ac.uk/s/sypcdu/toolkit.pdf for information on research evaluating training.

Note

This case study was written by Dr Len Hutt, assistant professor in OB and HRM, Thompson Rivers University, Canada.

Web-based assignment

There are competing views on the purpose of work-related learning. One school of thought believes creativity and innovation is more likely to be fostered in organizations where learning is valued and high quality. In this sense, workplace learning has an instrumental purpose: to 'unfreeze' employee work attitudes and practices to bring about change. Learning can also enhance an organization's performance and increase a nation's productivity. (See OB in Focus on *The Learning Age*, page 221.)

Specifically, this assignment requires you to critically evaluate these assumptions. First, enter the following websites for more information on lifelong learning: www.lifelonglearning.co.uk; www.lifelonglearning.co.uk/llp/index.htm. Second, choose two companies, enter their websites, and evaluate how each company provides for continuous work-related learning. What are the company's objectives with regard to work-related learning? How does the company's learning strategy relate, if at all, to its business strategy? Is there any evidence that work-related learning benefits both individual employees and the company? What role should work-related learning play in the workplace?

OB in films

The film *Erin Brockovich* (2000) is based on a true story. In the film, Brockovich (played by Julia Roberts), a legal assistant and a single mother of three children, investigates how a US company is illegally depositing cancer-causing chemicals in an unlined pond, causing high rates of cancer among the local community. The film raises questions about corporate crime, and also about the education and training of lawyers, and access to university education.

Watch the scenes between Brockovich and the three lawyers discussing files, and look at how Brockovich deals with the cancer victims at a personal level. Do these scenes show informal learning? How does Brockovich's work-related learning differ from the formal legal training of the lawyers? Can the lawyers learn anything from Brockovich? What does the film reveal about the opportunity for energetic and intelligent women from low-income social groups to enter higher education?

Notes

1　Lindeman (1926: 5).
2　Hamel and Prahalad (1994: 181).
3　For example, see Billett (2001b), Bratton et al. (2004), Foley (2001), Mabey et al. (1998).
4　Senge (1990), Watkins and Cervero (2000).
5　Boud and Garrick (1999).
6　See Bratton and Gold (2007).
7　Cohen and Sproull (1996), Spikes (1995).
8　Early critical accounts of the workplace learning phenomenon include Coopey (1996), Legge (2005) and Townley (1994).
9　Spencer (1998).
10　Bratton (2001).
11　Gagne and Medsker (1996).
12　Kolb (1984).
13　Bratton (1999).
14　Billett (2001b).
15　See Marsick and Watkins (1990).
16　Dixon (1992).
17　Kochan and Dyer (1995: 336).
18　Senge (1990).

19 Senge (1990: 340).

20 Agashae and Bratton (2001) and see Driver (2002a) on leaders' activities that promote follower learning.

21 Knights and Willmott (1992).

22 Legge (2005).

23 Townley (1994).

24 Coopey (1996).

25 Senge (1990).

26 Forrester (1999), Spencer (2001), Thompson and McHugh (2006).

27 Probert (1999: 112).

28 Walker (1996).

29 Pavlov (1927), quoted in Walker (1996: 20).

30 Watson and Rayner (1920).

31 Bernstein et al. (2000).

32 Skinner (1953, 1954).

33 Nye (2000: 67–9).

34 Thorndike (1913).

35 Walker (1996).

36 Tennant (1997).

37 Köhler (1925).

38 Bernstein et al. (2000: 201).

39 Bernstein et al. (2000).

40 Wiener (1954).

41 Bandura (1971, 1977a).

42 Bandura (1977a).

43 Bandura 1977a).

44 Vygotsky (1978).

45 Leontiev (1978, 1981).

46 Wood, Bruner and Ross (1976).

47 Hung (1999), Rogoff (1990).

48 Lave and Wenger (1991), Rogoff (1990).

49 Lave (1993).

50 Wenger (1998).

51 Wenger, McDermott and Snyder (2002: 27).

52 Lave and Wenger (1991: 98).

53 Lave and Wenger (1991: 29).

54 Brown, Collins and Duguid (1989).

55 Wilson (1993).

56 Østerlund (1997).

57 Billett (2001b), Wenger (2000).

58 Rogoff (1995).

59 Engeström (1994: 48).

60 Rogoff (1984, 1995).

61 Rogoff (1984: 3).

62 Beyer and Trice (1987).

63 Hoeve and Nieuwenhuis (2006).

64 Hoeve and Nieuwenhuis (2006: 184).

65 Merriam (1993).

66 Jarvis (1991).

67 Knowles (1975, 1980).

68 Knowles (1980: 43).

69 Knowles (1973: 45), quoted in Collins (1991: 22).

70 Merriam (1993).

71 Jarvis (1985).

72 Pratt (1993: 19).

73 Collins (1991).

74 See Spencer (1998).

75 Pratt (1993: 21).

76 Pratt (1993: 18).

77 See Brooks and Watkins (1994), Kolb (1984), Marsick (1988), Mezirow (1991), Knowles (1980).

78 Rogers (1983).

79 Caffarella (1993: 25).

80 Maslow (1954).

81 Caffarella (1993: 26).

82 Caffarella (1993: 26).

83 Argyris (1993), Watkins and Marsick (1993).

84 Fenwick (1998:149).

85 Clark (1993).

86 Mezirow (1981, 1990).

87 Mezirow (1981: 6).

88 Mezirow (1981: 20).

89 See, for example, Scott (1998), Spencer (1998).

90 Jarvis (1985: 103).

91 Clark (1993).

92 Clark (1993: 53).

93 Mezirow (1990: 11).

94 Clark (1993: 53).

95 Bernstein (1971), Farmer (1997), Hayes and Flannery (2000), Hofstede (1984), Probert (1999), Sharpe (1976).

96 Douglas et al. (1968), quoted by Rowe (1970: 36).

97 See Ashton and Field (1976), Becker (1971), Bernstein (1971), Becker (1984).

98 Bernstein (1971).

100 Craft and Craft (1983).

101 Martin and Nakayama (2000).

102 Foley (2000).

103 Boud and Garrick (1999).

104 Bradley (1986), Cockburn (1983, 1991), Farmer (1997), Stanworth (1981), Rowbotham (1973).

105 Probert (1999), Tisdell (1993).

106 Belenky et al. (1986), Chafetz (1988), Tisdell (1993), Wilson (1992), Gherardi (1994).

107 Tisdell (1993).

108 Livingstone and Sawchuk (2004).

109 Tisdell (1993: 102).

110 Kolb (1984).

111 Jarvis (1985).

112 Holman et al. (1997), Sawchuk (2004).

chapter 9
Motivation at work

[M]anagers and supervisors ... routinely try to make other people out of employees than the ones they are and mould them to fit preconceived notions of who they ought to be. When the mould reinforces the needs of the organization or management and ignores the needs of employees, it becomes oppressive to comply – and dangerous not to.[1]

chapter outline

▷ Introduction
▷ The nature of work motivation
▷ Theories of work motivation
▷ The sociological analysis of motivation: alienation, culture and work orientation
▷ Integrating the approaches
▷ Applying motivation theories
▷ Chapter summary
▷ Key concepts
▷ Chapter review questions
▷ Further reading
▷ Chapter case study: Motivation at Norsk Petroleum
▷ Web-based assignment
▷ OB in films
▷ Notes

chapter objectives

After completing this chapter, you should be able to:

▷ understand and explain how motivation reflects the exchange embodied in the employment relationship
▷ compare and contrast needs-based theories of motivation at work
▷ describe the expectancy and equity theories of motivation
▷ discuss the managerial implications of process-based motivation theories
▷ understand and explain sociological insights into motivation at work, including alienation, organizational culture and the orientation to work.

Introduction

The topic of motivation is of vital interest to any observer of workplace behaviour. As you move across a small section of the society of which we are part, travelling on buses and trains, entering factories, shops, offices, hospitals, schools, daycare facilities or university lecture theatres, you might observe that in any group of workers who are performing identical jobs, some do the work better than others. What is it that causes some people to exert much more effort than others in what they do in the workplace?

motivation: the forces within a person that affect his or her direction, intensity and persistence of voluntary behaviour

The observed differences in job performance among people doing identical work reflect differences in individual knowledge, skills and abilities. An individual may perform differently because he or she possesses a higher level of experience, training or intellectual endowment. Variations in work performance among workers doing identical work can also reflect differences in the extent to which individuals are prepared to direct their occupational energies. Employee performance is thus contingent upon two different kinds of variable: the ability and skill of the individual, and his or her motivation to make use of this ability and skill in the actual performance of the paid work.[2] It is the second variable – motivation – that is the focus of this chapter.

The issue of motivating workers is as old as management itself, and underscores the nature of the employment relationship. At its most basic, the employment contract represents the exchange of effort or knowledge for pay. This effort–pay contract is, however, typically indeterminate: while the contract specifies pay, benefits, hours to be worked and so on, a workers' capacity to work – in Marxist terminology, his or her labour power – is indefinable with regard to the amount of effort and commitment the employee will apply to the job. The contract implies that workers are 'free' to decide whether to accept the pay on offer, free to internalize about their work situation and develop positive or negative attitudes toward their employment, and free to seek employment elsewhere.[3] In other words, employees have, Peter Drucker once wrote, 'control over whether they work, how much and how well'.[4]

organizational commitment: the employee's emotional attachment to, identification with and involvement in a particular organization

The indeterminate nature of the typical employment contract makes motivation a central feature of the employment relationship, and the need to motivate others to 'get things done' is a running theme of management. Managers find themselves in positions of subordination as well as superordination, and as a result, they themselves have to be motivated as well as to be able to motivate others. Top managers are often mystified on a daily basis by what motivates middle managers, what motivates male and female knowledge workers, and in turn, middle managers are frequently mystified by what motivates male and female front-line employees. Why do highly paid managers and knowledge workers resign or not perform as expected? Why do low-paid manual and front-line non-manual workers baulk at resigning even when they receive better job offers? For both managers and some OB theorists, the task of discovering what motivates different categories of employees in different work settings is of the same magnitude as finding the Holy Grail.

Mainstream industrial psychologists have developed numerous theories of work motivation over the years. Some explain work motivation within cognitive-oriented frameworks that examine either the *content* of motivations or the *processes* through which they are expressed. Content theories assume that all employees have an identical set of needs.[5] Process theories assume that each employee assesses her or his own personal work situation and makes a cognitive choice about how much effort to exert in the pursuit of job fulfilment.[6] Reading mainstream management texts might lead the reader to a uncomfortable conclusion that nobody seems able to offer a magic elixir: at least, not one that managers can dispense to all the workforce, all of the time and in all situations.

needs: deficiencies that energize or trigger behaviours to satisfy those needs

In contrast to orthodox treatments of motivation, critical organizational theorists are more attentive to the contradictory nature of capitalist employment relations through which management motivation practices are expressed and reproduced.[7] In contrast to those who focus only on cognitive-oriented models, critical writers emphasize control over the labour process and the fact that workers are particularly malleable. That is, managers can get people, once employed, to do work tasks beyond what may have been specified in the original employment contract. Further, they tend to emphasize the need for a societal analysis of work motivation. For example, in this so-called 'post-industrial' age, what is the impact on employee motivation of precarious employment, corporate downsizing, continuous work-related learning, and work regimes that expect managers and non-managers to be self-motivated? How do social factors such as cultural background, social class, and gender and race impact on employee motivation?

We do not accept the 'one hat fits all' approach to work motivation, and believe it is important to include wider social factors in the analysis of work motivation. Our understanding of motivation expands beyond notions of individual needs and cognitive processes to incorporate awareness of the dynamics of employment relations, the way work organization and managerial control generate and express internal tensions and contradictions, and the effects of complex interconnecting levels of domination stemming from class, gender and race relations in society.

Our purpose in this chapter is twofold. First, it is to provide a critical evaluation of the psychological models of motivation, and second, it draws on foundational arguments of sociologists to provide a more holistic understanding of work motivation.

Before reading on, you may wish to ask yourself, what motivates you? In doing your current or planned paid work, are you motivated primarily by money, or something else? Go to our website and click on the 'Motivation questionnaire'. Consider your responses to the questions in the context of your current employment or previous work experience, and what you have read in this book so far.

STOP AND REFLECT

The nature of work motivation

In the 1950s and 1960s, Western economies expanded investment in education and people experienced relatively full employment. In this social context, workers' fear of unemployment was no longer an individual or collective motivation for work performance. If workers became dissatisfied with the effort levels expected by managers, or another aspect of the job, they could find alternative employment relatively effortlessly. As management guru Peter Drucker wrote, 'fear no longer supplies the motivation for the worker in industrial society'.[8] This post-Second World War phenomenon led to an interest in the question, 'What motivates workers to perform effectively?' 'Effectively' meant closing the gap between the workers' potential to work and their willingness to maximize effort towards the attainment of work objectives.

The indeterminacy of the employment contract is interpreted by both managers and pro-management theorists as the problem of motivation. Management concern with discovering the motivation elixir is a direct response to the constant

Source: Corporate presenter Scott Deming of Scott Deming's ESP (Extraordinary Sales Presentations)

plate 25 Finding a way of motivating workers is as old as management itself, and underscores the nature of the employment relationship

goals: the immediate or ultimate objectives that employees are trying to accomplish from their work effort

intrinsic motivator: a wide range of motivation interventions in the workplace, from inner satisfaction following some action (such as recognition by an employer or co-workers) to intrinsic pleasures derived from an activity (such as playing a musical instrument for pleasure)

extrinsic motivator: a wide range of external outcomes or rewards to motivate employees, including, bonuses or increases in pay

pressure on management to employ people even more efficiently, thoroughly and rationally.[9]

Although relatively full employment has been a feature of UK labour markets for some time, interest in theories of work motivation remains strong. In this context, the focus has shifted to the retention and productivity of the 'knowledge worker'.[10] Interest in motivation theories also stems from the current interest in differentiating managers from leaders. Leadership is about movement or change, and therefore implies the ability to motivate people.[11] There is therefore an inordinate amount of scholarship that is primarily *normative*, directed at providing prescriptions for motivating workers. The practical concern is about what it is that managers *should* do to ensure that manual and knowledge workers close the gap between potential and actual performance.

The word 'motivation' comes from the Latin *movere*, 'to move', and organizational psychologists have identified factors that move workers towards accomplishing organizational goals. We define motivation as a cognitive decision-making process that influences the effort, persistence and direction of voluntary goal-directed behaviour. The first element in our definition is '*effort*', which is a measure of intensity that maximizes workers' potential capacity to work in a way that is appropriate to the job. The second characteristic of motivation is '*persistence*', which refers to the application of effort to work-related tasks employees display over a time period. The third characteristic of motivation is '*direction*', which emphasizes that persistent high levels of work-related effort should be channelled in a way that benefits the work organization. Whereas effort and persistence refer to the *quantity* of paid manual or knowledge work, direction refers to *quality* of work done.

OB theorists distinguish between intrinsic and extrinsic motivators. An intrinsic motivator stems from a person's 'internal' desire to do something, and is therefore usually self-applied. Outside the workplace, avid participation in hobbies or sports is typically intrinsically motivated. For example, we may be willing to exert a considerable amount of effort over many months with the aim of climbing a mountain, without any thought of financial reward, because we expect it to provide personal satisfaction: that is, we are intrinsically motivated. In the workplace, pure interest in a project, or a sense of professional accomplishment or positive recognition from our peers, are examples of intrinsic motivators. Extrinsic motivators, on the other hand, stem from outside the individual, and are generally applied by others higher in the organization's hierarchy. Extrinsic motivators include such tangible rewards as pay, bonuses and promotion (see Figure 9.1).

Visit the following websites: www.ced.com for information on team-based rewards; www.dti.gov.uk/employment/useful-links/index.html for data on profit-related pay in Britain; Search '2004 employee relations survey'. This site gives a summary of the UK 2004 survey including a section on work teams www.fed.org/resrclib/articles/create-ownership-culture.html for information on the role of stock options in motivating employees.

WEB LINK

	Intrinsic	**Extrinsic**
Individual-based	Feeling of self-accomplishment	Pay increase
Organization-based	Professional pride in being a member of a 'socially responsible' company	Profit sharing

figure 9.1 Examples of intrinsic and extrinsic motivators

We should be aware that there is disagreement on these definitions and the relationship between intrinsic and extrinsic motivators, and even more disagreement on whether organizations can categorize all work motivators as precisely as these definitions suggest. For example, an employee might receive a promotion that also results in more interesting and satisfying work and additional pay. Thus, some potential motivators have both intrinsic and extrinsic qualities.[12] It should also be apparent from these examples that intrinsic and extrinsic motivators are strongly influenced by the values, ways of thinking, behaviours and social factors typical of a society. North American and European theories of motivation are embedded in human resource practices, as such practices offer the means to render workers and their behaviour predictable and measurable.[13]

Theories of work motivation

Theories of work motivation attempt to explain the nature of motivation, how employee behaviour is initiated and shaped, and the different factors that contribute to directing and sustaining that behaviour. Thus, a theory of motivation explains 'not only why goals are sought, but also the factors that influence how they are sought.'[14] Models show the relationships between variables that are thought to be involved, but as we discussed in Chapter 1, they are reconstructions of reality and a simplification of the phenomenon. Bearing in mind this caveat, there is no shortage of theorizing and modelling about how best to motivate people at work. Students of management and practising managers need to know that there are no quick solutions for releasing the motivation genie. However it is useful to know at least the main theories of motivation, and be able to judge the relevance of them in particular contexts.

Here the focus is on motivational theories that have been categorized in the literature as *content* and *process* theories of work motivation. *Content theories of motivation* assume that all workers possess a common set of basic 'needs'. *Process theories*, on the other hand, explain work motivation in terms of a cognitive process workers go through before and during their behaviour. They assume that how individuals think about their work situation will affect their behaviour. Theoretical analysis about work motivation can be grouped into two schools of thought, based around the ideas that workers have needs, and that they have choices. (This distinction is essentially a practical one, rather than a deeply philosophical one, intended to helping you navigate through a sea of theories.)

Content theories of motivation: workers with needs

Four of the better-known need theories are Maslow's hierarchy of needs, Herzberg's 'two-factor' need theory, McClelland's 'three learned needs' theory, and Alderfer's ERG theory.[15]

In what is probably the most well known of the content theories, psychologist Abraham Maslow proposed that people have a built-in set of five basic needs, which can be arranged in a hierarchy as shown in Figure 9.2. The so-called lower-level needs in the hierarchy (the physiological and safety needs) are at first predominant: people's behaviour is directed towards satisfying these needs until they are met, at which point the next higher-order need comes to dominate, and so on. For example, only once an individual's physiological needs for the basic necessities of life – food, water and shelter – are satisfied will that individual focus on the next higher need. Once lower-order needs are addressed, the theory assumes people direct their behaviours towards satisfying their needs for companionship, love and positive social regard by other people. The progression ultimately leads to behaviour change motivated principally by people's need to realize their full potential, which Maslow termed the self-actualization need.

---

needs hierarchy theory: Maslow's motivation theory of five instinctive needs arranged in a hierarchy, whereby people are motivated to fulfil a higher need as a lower one becomes gratified

self-actualization: a term associated with Maslow's theory of motivation, it refers to the desire for personal fulfillment, to become everything that one is capable of becoming

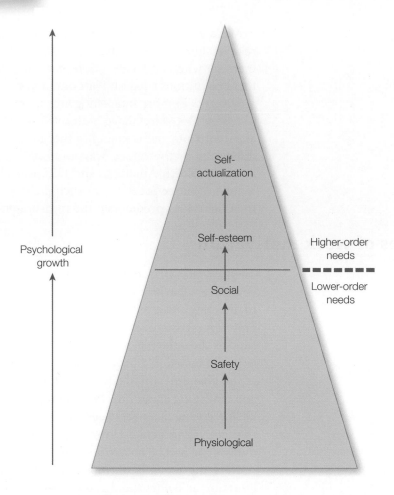

Psychological growth

Self-actualization

Self-esteem

Social

Safety

Physiological

Higher-order needs

Lower-order needs

figure 9.2 Maslow's hierarchy of needs

According to Maslow, the self-actualization need, which involves people directing their behaviour towards work learning opportunities, is the ultimate motivator, because unlike the other needs it is insatiable. The second key aspect of Maslow's theory is that a satisfied or satiated need is not a motivator of behaviour. Once a person satisfies a need at one level in the hierarchy, the need ceases to motivate him or her. Only the need at the next level up the hierarchy will motivate the person and influence her or his behaviour.

Although it was not originally intended as an explanation of employee motivation, Maslow's need hierarchy theory has been influential in mainstream management texts. It was seen as offering predictions about what directs behaviour in different contexts. In a context of relatively high unemployment, when jobs are relatively scarce and people do not automatically feel secure about meeting their basic needs, workers are motivated strongly by the need to satisfy their lower-level needs. In contrast, in a context of relatively full employment, when lower-order needs are more easily satisfied, social, self-esteem and self-actualization needs become important motivators in the workplace.

One implication of Maslow's theory is that once their social needs have been satisfied, if workers are to continue to be motivated, managers have to find ways to offer them self-actualization, which implies a focus on the intrinsic aspects of paid work. This might mean reconfiguring work structures and processes to challenge both manual and knowledge workers, and offer them a degree of autonomy. To apply Maslow's theory to the current management practices of organizational re-engineering and outsourcing, it might be feasible to motivate part-time or other 'peripheral' workers by appealing to their lower-order needs, while knowledge-based 'core' workers are motivated by satisfying their higher-order needs. The prescription offered by Maslow's theory is that managers need to know where their employees are located on the needs hierarchy, and ensure their lower-order needs are satisfied before appealing to their higher-order needs.

Maslow's need hierarchy appears to offer common-sense advice to managers, but how valid is this theory of work motivation? One of the major problems with Maslow's theory is that it is extremely difficult to identify which need is predominant at any given time. Without this information managers cannot confidently redesign the workplace or emphasize work-based learning to appeal to their employees' self-esteem or self-actualization needs, for instance: these might not in reality be their main motivators.

To take a simple example, is it really true that a person will focus on satisfying physiological needs such as hunger and thirst before he or she attends to matters which threaten his or her security or safety? Does a construction worker have a bite to eat before she checks that the scaffolding she is standing on is safe?

The significance of Maslow's work, it is suggested, might lie in its rhetorical value. Tony Watson, for example, offers a scathing critique of Maslow's theory, arguing that it has little scientific validity and its main role has been as 'a propaganda device: propaganda in a good and humanistic cause, but propaganda nonetheless'.[16]

David McClelland and Clayton Alderfer propose alternative need theories of work motivation. According to McClelland's theory of needs,[17] workers are motivated by the need to satisfy six basic human needs: achievement, power, affiliation, independence, self-esteem and security. Employees are said to accomplish the most when they have a high need for achievement. Employees with a strong need for achievement tend to set goals that are moderately difficult, to seek out feedback on their performance, and to be generally preoccupied with accomplishment.

Unlike Maslow, McClelland did not become preoccupied in specifying a hierarchical relationship among needs. Instead, he argued that employees differ in the extent to which they experience needs for achievement, affiliation and power. The work of Harrel and Strahl[18] suggests that assessing the strength of these learned needs can be helpful in identifying employees who will respond positively to different types of work contexts. The advice that follows from this alleged insight is that it might be important for managers to consider the extent to which employees possess these needs, and to design motivational strategies that permit workers to satisfy those needs that are strongest for each individual.

Clayton Alderfer developed the ERG theory, which revises Maslow's theory and makes some different assumptions about the relationship between needs and work motivation. It suggests that employee needs can be divided into three basic categories: existence (E), relatedness (R) and growth (G). Existence needs include nutritional, safety and material requirements. Relatedness needs involve an individual's relationships with family and friends, and colleagues at work. Growth needs reflect a desire for personal psychological growth and development. These three core needs are similar to the needs advocated by Maslow (see Figure 9.3).

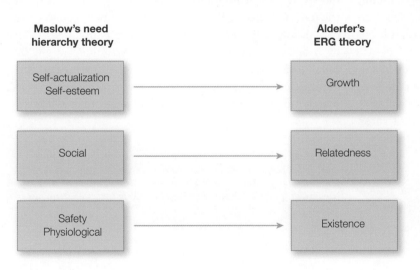

figure 9.3 Comparison of Maslow's need hierarchy and Alderfer's ERG theory

ERG theory: Alderfer's motivation theory of three instructive needs arranged in a hierarchy, in which people progress to the next higher need when a lower one is fulfilled, and regress to a lower need if unable to fulfill a higher one

growth needs: a person's needs for self-esteem through personal achievement as well as for self-actualization

Money is the key incentive to work motivation

Most OB theorists and behavioural scientists have consistently downplayed the importance of money as a motivator. They prefer to point out the value of challenging jobs, goals and participation in decision making to stir the motivation genie. We argue otherwise here: that money is the crucial incentive to work motivation. As a medium of exchange, it is the vehicle by which employees can purchase the numerous need-satisfying things they desire. Money also performs the function of a scorecard, by which employees assess the value that the organization places on their services and can compare their value with that of others.

For the vast majority of the workers, a regular pay cheque is absolutely necessary in order to meet their basic physiological and safety needs. Money has symbolic value in addition to its exchange value. People use pay as the primary outcome against which they compare their inputs to determine whether they are being treated equitably. In addition, expectancy theory attests to the value of money as a motivator. Specifically, if pay is contingent on performance, it will encourage workers to put in high levels of effort. Consistent with expectancy theory, money will motivate to the extent that it is seen as being able to satisfy an individual's personal goals, and reward is perceived as being dependent on performance criteria. The evidence demonstrates that money may not be the only motivator, but it is difficult to argue that it does not motivate!

Money doesn't stir the motivation genie!

There is no doubt that money can motivate some people under some conditions, so the issue is not really whether money can motivate. The more relevant question is, does money motivate most employees in the workforce today to higher performance? The answer, some organizational theorists argue, is 'No.' For money to motivate an employee's performance, certain conditions must be met. First, money must be important to the employee. Second, the employee must perceive the money as being a direct reward for performance. Third, the employee must consider the marginal amount of money offered for the performance to be significant. Finally, management must have the discretion to reward high performers with more money.

Since not all these conditions apply in all employment situations, money is not important to all employees. High achievers, for instance, are intrinsically motivated. Money should have little impact on these people. Money is relevant to those individuals with strong lower-order needs; but the lower-order needs of many employees are substantially satisfied. Money would motivate if employees perceived a strong link between performance and rewards in organizations. However, pay increases are far more often determined by levels of skills and experience, the national cost-of-living index, union–management pay bargaining, and the firm's overall financial prospects, than by individual performance. In theory, money might be capable of motivating employees to higher levels of performance, but most managers do not have much discretion to match individual pay with individual performance levels.

Sources: K.O. Doyle (1992), 'Introduction: money and the behavioural sciences,' *American Behavioural Scientist*, July, pp. 641–57; S. Caudron (1993) 'Motivation? Money's only no. 2,' *Industry Week*, 15 November, p. 33; B. Filipczak (1996) 'Can't buy me love,' *Training*, January, pp. 29–34.

---

exchange value: the price at which commodities (including labour) trade on the market

Go to the following websites for more information on motivation theories: http://academic.emporia.edu/smithwil/oofallmg443/eja/tuel.html for details on Maslow's hierarchy of needs; http://psychology.about.com/cs/somotiv/ for links to motivation theories.

WEB LINK

As can be seen in Figure 9.3, Alderfer's ERG theory of work motivation is not a major departure from Maslow's theory. Unlike Maslow, however, ERG theory does not assume a progression up a hierarchy. Alderfer suggests that all three levels might be important at the same time, and he believes that it is better to think in terms of a continuum, from existence needs to growth needs, with workers moving along it in either direction. Consequently, if for example growth needs are not satisfied, an inner state of frustration regression occurs, causing the person to focus on fulfilling her or his relatedness needs. For example, a supervisor unable to satisfy his or her growth needs by accepting greater responsibility might respond by demanding an increase in pay, thereby satisfying his or her existence needs. Therefore, unsatisfied needs become less rather than more important. This is the opposite of what Maslow assumed.

Further, ERG theory emphasizes the importance to employees of satisfied needs. Alderfer's work suggests that growth needs are actually more important when satisfied, whereas Maslow argued that when it is fulfilled, a need becomes less important to an individual. One implication of Alderfer's work is that work designs that satisfy workers' relatedness needs can continue to motivate workers, and that these are not necessarily superseded by growth needs. If this theory is correct, it would make it easier for managers to motivate their employees.

A recent study by Arnolds and Boshoff[19] provides data to support a key hypothesis associated with Alderfer's ERG model. Unlike many conventional studies, it incorporates personality (see Chapter 6) in the motivation conundrum, and is sensitive to potential social factors affecting motivation at work. The study investigates to what extent a personality trait (self-esteem) impacts on the relationship between need satisfactions – as modelled by Alderfer – and the performance intentions of senior managers and white-collar 'front-line' employees in the banking, legal and retail sectors (see Figure 9.4).

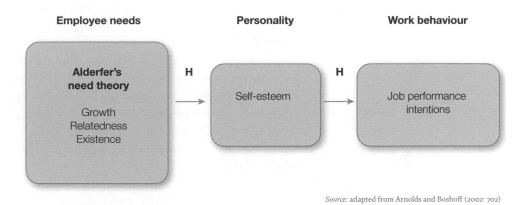

Source: adapted from Arnolds and Boshoff (2002: 702)

figure 9.4 Employee needs, personality and work behaviour

The model hypothesizes that employee need satisfaction, based upon Alderfer's theory, exerts a positive influence on self-esteem, which in turn exerts a positive influence on work behaviour in the form of job performance intentions (H). Arnolds and Boshoff argue that their data shows that self-esteem significantly influences the performance intentions of senior managers, and conclude that 'top managers are primarily motivated by growth needs, in other words, higher order needs'.[20] The empirical results suggest that front-line white-collar workers are primarily motivated by the satisfaction of relatedness needs from co-workers, existence needs and particularly monetary reward.

Interestingly, and in contrast to Maslow's belief that growth needs do not motivate lower-level workers, Arnolds and Boshoff's sophisticated study suggests that higher-order needs such as growth needs can motivate front-line workers through increasing their self-esteem, 'provided that the motivation strategies directed at these higher-order needs are correctly implemented'.[21] The importance of this study is that it provides a plausible explanation, with supporting empirical data, of the relationship between need satisfaction, an individual personality trait (self-esteem), and job performance intentions. More generally, by differentiating between different categories of employees, the analysis affirms the importance of avoiding the common tendency to generalize about managers' motivation interventions.

Although Maslow's, McClelland's and Alderfer's need theories of work motivation have been popularized in the mainstream organizational behaviour texts, detractors have identified several important limitations. It is argued that the theories are conceptually flawed; they do not provide managers with a clear, unambiguous basis for predicting specific workers' behaviour to satisfy a particular need. Recent critics have also pointed out that the need theories are strongly informed by the Anglo-American cultural paradigm of individualism. Other societal cultures might have different hierarchies of needs. Finally, there is an assumption that needs motivate regardless of the age, sex or ethnicity of those involved. As a result, it can be argued that these theories are androcentric and reflect the values of a hierarchical social order.[22]

Process theories of motivation: workers with choices

Process theories of motivation focus on how employees make conscious choices that lead to a specific work behaviour; they emphasize the role of an individual's cognitive processes in determining her or his level of work motivation. Organizational leaders using process theories to motivate employees do so by clarifying the link between effort and reward. The three process theories of work motivation examined here are equity theory, expectancy theory and goal-setting theory.

Equity theory

The basic premise of equity theory is that there is one important cognitive process that involves employees comparing what effort other employees are putting into their work and what rewards they receive, with their own experience. This 'social comparison' process results in feelings of equity or inequity, and leads employees to form judgements on the value or 'valence' of a reward or outcome. According to equity theory, employees perceive effort and reward not in absolute but in relative terms, in the form of a ratio:[23]

$$\frac{\text{Outcome (self)}}{\text{Inputs (self)}} : \frac{\text{Outcome (other)}}{\text{Inputs (other)}}$$

When employees perceive others receiving a similar ratio of inputs (such as hours worked, time studying for qualifications, relevant work experience) to outcomes (such as pay, status, promotion) as they receive themselves, they experience equity. When workers perceive an input–outcome ratio that favours other workers in the organization (underpayment) or relevant others (such as workers in a similar company) or themselves (overpayment), they experience inequity, which is assumed to be a sufficiently unpleasant experience to motivate changes in behaviour (see Figure 9.5).

equity theory: theory that explains how people develop perceptions of fairness in the distribution and exchange of resources

How helpful are Maslow's and Alderfer's theories in explaining why chief executives (CEOs) and car assembly workers might be predisposed to respond to different ways of motivating them to work?

STOP AND REFLECT

	Self	**Other**
Equity	Outcomes (100) Inputs (100)	Outcomes (100) Inputs (100)
Inequity (under-rewarded)	Outcomes (100) Inputs (100)	Outcomes (150) Inputs (100)
Inequity (over-rewarded)	Outcomes (150) Inputs (100)	Outcomes (100) Inputs (100)

figure 9.5 Adams's conditions of equity and inequity

One practical application of equity theory is in the area of *reward management.* Managers must be careful to avoid setting pay rates that cause employees to feel underpaid relative to others either in the same workplace (internal equity) or in comparison groups outside the organization (external inequity). It should be noted that the reward system is part of a diverse range of interlocking control techniques which contain internal tensions and inconsistencies. For instance, a performance-related reward system might become discredited in the eyes of employees because of perceived 'procedural injustices' caused by subjective and inconsistent appraisals by managers who do not have the skills needed to judge performance fairly. As a result, the employees experience internal inequity, and instead of the reward system motivating them, their commitment is weakened.[24] The nature of the internal inequity can generate negative feelings such as anger, which results in reduced employee commitment or even in acts of sabotage in the workplace. In addition, if the perception of external inequity is strong and is shared by a sufficient number of workers, unionization and strike action can occur.

In this context, a classic study by Baldamus of the 'wage–effort exchange'[25] is still relevant to understanding conflict behaviour in the workplace, because it links the notion of external inequity to inherent tensions and workplace conflict. A fuller understanding of this relationship between effort levels or inputs, and rewards or outcomes, is provided by the expectancy theory of motivation.

Expectancy theory

expectancy theory: a motivation theory based on the idea that work effort is directed toward behaviours that people believe will lead to desired outcomes

The role of the employee's perception of the link between levels of effort or performance and desirable reward is further reinforced in the expectancy theory of work motivation. The theory assumes a rational model of decision making whereby employees assess the costs and benefits of alternative courses of inputs and outcomes, and choose the course with the highest reward.

The first formulations of expectancy theory are found in the work of Kurt Lewin in 1935. The theory was popularized, however, by the work of Vroom, and further developed by Porter and Lawler.[26] Psychologist Victor Vroom proposed that work motivation is contingent upon the perception of a link between levels of effort and reward. Perceiving this link is a cognitive process in which employees assess:

▷ whether there is a connection between effort and their performance, labelled *expectancy*
▷ the perceived probability that the performance (such as higher productivity) will lead to those valued outcomes (such as higher pay) (labelled *instrumentality*)
▷ the expected net value of the outcomes that flow from the effort (labelled *valence*).

Expectancy theory, therefore, has three basic parts:

effort-to-performance (E→P) expectancy: the individual's perceived probability that his or her effort will result in a particular level of performance

performance-to-outcome (P→O) expectancy: the perceived probability that a specific behaviour or performance level will lead to specific outcomes

1. The effort–performance expectancy (E→P).
2. The performance–outcome expectancy (P→O).
3. The attractiveness or valence of the outcomes (V).

According to expectancy theory, work motivation can be calculated if the expectancy, instrumentality and valence values are known. The formula for the calculation is:

$$\text{Effort} = E \, \Sigma \, I \times V$$

where *effort* is the motivation of the employee to exert effort in her or his paid work, *E* is expectancy, *I* is the instrumentality of job performance, and *V* is the valence of an outcome (s). The Σ (capital sigma: the summation sign) indicates that effort is affected by a range of possible work and non-work outcomes that might result from job performance.

instrumentality: a term associated with process theories of motivation, referring to an individual's perceived probability that good performance will result in valued outcomes or rewards, measured on a scale from 0 (no chance) to 1 (certainty)

valence: the anticipated satisfaction or dissatisfaction that an individual feels toward an outcome

Expectancies are probabilities, ranging from 0 to 1, that effort will result in performance. An expectancy of 0.5 means that the person perceives only a 50 per cent probability of increased effort leading to increased performance. Instrumentalities can range from -1 to +1. An instrumentality of +1 means that performance is certain to lead to the desired outcome. For example, an insurance agent selling a home insurance policy is certain to receive a commission. The instrumentality between the two events is therefore +1. Valence is defined to vary between +10 and -10. A large anticipated satisfaction (high positive valence) and large anticipated dissatisfaction (high negative valence) when multiplied by associated instrumentalities and performance expectancy will have a large effect on work motivation.

As an example of the operation of expectancy theory, consider an employee – let's call him Joe – who perceives important work-related outcomes to be an increase in pay, promotion, longer vacation time, and job-related stress. Figure 9.6 shows his expectancy theory calculations.

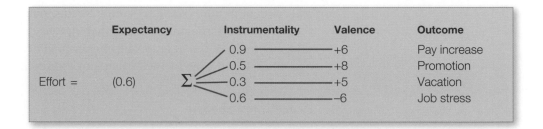

figure 9.6 Sample expectancy theory calculations

Joe has ranked four outcomes on a +10 to -10 scale, and has estimated the probability of increased effort producing each of these outcomes. He sees both positive and negative expected outcomes from increased job effort. He reckons there is only a 60 per cent chance that if he increases his effort it will lead to increased performance.

The motivational force of the job – the effort the individual is willing to expend on it – is calculated by multiplying the expectancy value (0.6) by the products of the instrumentality and valence estimates. Thus,

$$\text{Effort} = (0.6) \times [(0.9)(+6) + (0.5)(+8) + (0.3)(+5) + (0.6)(-6)] = 4.38$$

Summing the expectancy theory variables, the overall motivation to exert increased job effort is positive. Therefore, for Joe in this case, the rewards of putting in increased effort outweigh the costs.

To use expectancy theory in an attempt to increase job effort by each employee, a manager can focus on each element of the theory. For example, a manager can aim to increase the employee's perception that her or his expenditure of effort will result in completing the task successfully. The effort–performance expectancy (E→P) for Joe could increase from 60 per cent to 80 per cent, perhaps through additional training. In addition, a manager can help the employee to re-evaluate the performance–outcome expectancy (P→O). For example, the chances of promotion might be higher than is anticipated by the employee. To go back to the example of Joe, his manager might use the experiences of other employees to persuade him to increase his estimated probability of promotion if he does the job successfully from 50 per cent to 90 per cent.

Finally, a manager can attempt to increase the attractiveness of the outcome, the valence (V). Thus, in the example, Joe could perhaps be persuaded that the outcomes from exerting additional effort (a pay increase, a promotion, a longer vacation) are more important or have more value to him than he had previously thought.

Development of the expectancy theory of work behaviour is to be found in research by Porter and Lawler.[27] In their models the determinants of each element are incorporated to provide a more comprehensive explanation of both the *what* and the *how* of the work motivation process. The effort–performance expectancy (E→P) is, for example, moderated by past experiences of similar situations and communications from other people. The assumption here is that what employees learn from past experiences contributes significantly to their effort–performance expectancies. If an employee has had a series of past successes at similar work tasks, she or he will have a strengthened belief in her/his ability to perform those tasks, and to that extent her/his (E→P) expectancies will be high. The informal learning – learning that is embedded in work activities – need not only be from personal past experiences. Employees can and do learn from their observations of relevant others in similar situations, and from others communicating their past experiences to their peers. If I see Sally, for instance, succeed at a work task, and she has qualifications and work experience similar to mine, then I am more likely to calculate that I too will succeed at that task. This informal learning operates at individual and group level, and in the opposite direction as well.

The performance–outcome expectancy (P→O) link is contingent upon past experiences, communications from others, and the attractiveness of the outcomes. The past experiences determinant refers to the experience in relation to outcomes. Suppose, for example, that a manager introduces a reward system that is performance-based, and that her appraisal ratings of her staff are known to be arbitrary. With knowledge of this past experience, it is unlikely that her subordinates will believe the reward system will be truly performance-based in practice. The past experience will influence employees' (P→O) expectancies for the system. This assessment is, however, considerably affected by another determinant, communications from others, which represents an array of social interactions between employees, and between the supervised (employees) and their supervisors (managers), on a variety of outcomes, both positive and negative.

The valence of the outcomes (V) is moderated by the perceived *instrumentality* of the outcome to satisfy needs, and the perceived fairness or equity of the outcome. An outcome that is instrumental in satisfying an important need would have greater valence. Which outcome will an employee use to satisfy which need? Expectancy theorists suggest that it depends on the way the person has been socialized. Research suggests that for Anglo-American employees, at least, pay is most instrumental for satisfying physiological, security and ego-status needs, and not at all instrumental in satisfying social and self-actualization needs.[28]

The findings also explain why pay is important to both low-paid and high-paid employees. To the former, pay is instrumental in satisfying their physiological needs; to the latter, a high monthly pay cheque is instrumental in satisfying their ego-status needs.[29] The value of the outcome is also determined by the perceived equity of the reward. As we earlier discussed, employees compare their own input–reward ratio with the input–reward ratio of relevant others. If the two ratios are perceived to be equal, then equity exists and the reward's valence increases. Thus, the valence of an outcome is affected by employees' perception of its equity, considering their overall effort level relative to the effort level and reward of their co-workers.

By recognizing the importance of informal workplace learning and social comparisons, the Lawler model provides an insightful refinement of expectancy theory. The model enables managers to better understand the complexity of managing people, and in particular, how the elements of work motivation relate to one another in the motivation process.

Based on your understanding of process theories, why are some managers more effective at motivating people than others?

STOP AND REFLECT

plate 26 Expectancy theory can be used to better understand student motivation. It would predict that studying for an examination (effort) is conditioned by its resulting in answering questions in exams correctly (performance), which will produce a high mark (reward), and lead to the prestige, economic security and other benefits that accompany obtaining a desired career goal.

Source: Getty Images

Goal-setting theory

The theory of goal setting assumes that participatory goal setting and communicating accurate information on work performance can be positive motivators for employees. One version of this theory of motivation contains four major assumptions:

▷ *Challenging* goals will produce higher performance than less challenging goals.
▷ *Specific* challenging goals will produce higher performance than no goals or vague or general goals, such as 'do your best'.
▷ Goal setting with *feedback* on goal attainment will produce higher performance than goal setting alone.
▷ *Employee participation* in goal-setting will produce higher performance than no participation.[30]

goal setting: the process of motivating employees and clarifying their role perceptions by establishing performance objectives

Research conducted in several countries over the years is consistent in demonstrating that goal-setting techniques do have a positive influence on work motivation.[31] The management technique of management by objectives (MBO) is one of the best-known applications of goal-setting theory, and has been extensively used by Anglo-American management. Under MBO, a manager sets specific and challenging goals for a specified time period, periodically reviews progress towards goals that have been set previously, and provides feedback on goal accomplishment before setting goals for the next performance time period. In non-unionized workplaces, MBO also provides a mechanism for the appraisal of employee performance-pay awards.

management by objectives (MBO): a participative goal-setting process in which organizational objectives are cascaded down to work units and individual employees

Go to the following websites for more information on management by objectives:
http://www.1000ventures.com/business_guide/mgmt_mbo_main.html
www.performancesolutionstech.com/FromMBOtoPM.pdf

WEB LINK

The sociological analysis of motivation: alienation, culture and work orientation

Sociologists have developed micro-level and macro-level approaches to investigate and understand worker behaviour in the workplace. One is alienation, which refers to a feeling of powerlessness and estrangement from work and other people. The second approach is organizational culture, which is concerned with the different organizational structures in bureaucracies that compel managers and non-managers to behave similarly, and develops models of work motivation. The third approach emphasizes the orientation to work, and is concerned with the societal and group context in which work motivation occurs.

Sociological theories of work make us aware of the intricate linkage between the patterns of people's lives shaped by the societal configuration of class, gender and race that lie outside the workplace environment, and the pattern of social relations with others inside the work organization. This perspective incorporates into the analysis of work motivation issues that critical theorists call 'antagonisms', or 'contradictions' inherent in capitalist employment relations.

Alienation

The problem of alienation as a condition of modernity is found in literature. Witness Dr Robyn Penrose, a central character in David Lodge's novel *Nice Work*, condemning the mindless, repetitive work and brutalizing conditions in Vic Wilcox's factory. (The novel is set in the early 1980s.) The word 'alienation' is frequently used in everyday conversation as meaning bored or uninterested in something. It is also applied to an array of abnormal psychological states and deviant behaviours. To the sociologist, however, the term has a more precise meaning.

As we discussed in Chapter 3, the concept of alienation was developed by Karl Marx to analyse the nature of work that emerged with industrial capitalism. According to Marx, there are four aspects of alienated labour.

▷ First, workers are alienated (or separated) from the products of their labour.
▷ Second, workers are alienated from the act of production.
▷ The third aspect of alienation is self-estrangement, which develops because work simply focuses on exchange: the 'cash nexus'.
▷ The fourth aspect of alienation deals with the relationship of individuals to one another. Workers and managers are alienated from each other.

In brief, then, Marx's analysis of the social organization of work is that people express themselves through their work, and in so far as their labour is merely a commodity to be paid for with a wage, they are 'alienated'. Alienation is characteristic of a certain kind of organization of work – industrial capitalism – that is based on a set of socioeconomic conditions.

Over a hundred years later, Robert Blauner[32] asserted that there were four dimensions of alienation: powerlessness, meaninglessness, isolation and self-estrangement. Although Marx and Blauner use similar language, they have different interpretations of alienation, and Blauner's summary of the psychology of alienation illustrates the importance of perspective or standpoint, which we discussed in Chapters 1 and 3, and how theoretical concepts can be used differently depending on how academics see the world.

For Marx, it is the social conditions at work that are the determinant of alienation. For Blauner, it is the technology at work that is the most 'fateful' determinant of alienation. He also believed that over time, alienation could be lessened by certain types of technology, such as continuous production technology of the kind used in chemical or petroleum processing operations. By defining alienation in psychological terms of 'subjective feeling states', Blauner neglects the role of social structures outside the workplace in generating orientations to work.[33] For most sociologists today, alienation remains associated with Marx's notion of self-estrangement, and its source is seen as residing in the social structure rather than in personality traits. Its causes are rooted in capitalism, and are social rather than psychological.[34]

When we refer to alienation in this book, we mean a workplace phenomenon in which people have little or no control over the products or services they produce or offer, the organization of work, and the immediate work process itself. As Rinehart writes:

> [A]lienation is objective or structural in the sense that it is built into human relationships at the workplace and exists independent of how individuals perceive and evaluate this condition. Alienations can be viewed broadly as a condition of objective powerlessness.[35]

Much of the psychology-based research on work motivation appears entirely indifferent to, possibly even ignorant of, the concept of alienation.[36] For sociologists, a major source of alienated labour is division of labour. While there are a number of different types of division of labour, the most important ones are job specialization and the separation of mental and manual labour. Specialization entails a fragmentation of work, and the assignment of specific different tasks to specific individuals. Performed under such conditions, work becomes repetitive and mindless, circumscribes the development of workers' capacities, and is demotivating. Frederick Taylor's principles of scientific management involve systematically separating mental and manual labour.

As we discussed in Chapter 2, one reason that job specialization has failed to meet modern management's needs is that it disengages the worker from the immediate work process, and neglects the motivational effects of job design. Rinehart offers evidence that blue-collar and low-level white-collar workers are alienated from work, in that their low status in the organization progressively wears away their self-esteem, and consequently, their commitment to work and to the organization for which they work.[37] Consistent with need and expectancy theories of motivation, alienating work obstructs higher-level needs and valent outcomes (instrumentalities), causing low commitment and low work motivation.

What do you think of this explanation of work motivation? To what extent, if at all, can work be designed to reduce alienation in the workplace?

STOP AND REFLECT

CRITICAL INSIGHT

Few of the early content theories of motivation acknowledge personality, class, gender, race or age as factors influencing work motivation. Few of the popular theories provide empirical data to substantiate their claims. Arnolds and Boshoff state that the impact of personality traits was ignored in earlier studies of motivation, and acknowledge the need to include variables such as age, gender, cultural background and so on in motivation models.

Obtain a copy of Arnolds and Boshoff's article, 'Compensation, esteem valence and job performance: an empirical assessment of Alderfer's ERG theory'.[38] What are the strengths of this approach to investigating work motivation? Look back at research strategies in Chapter 1. What would be the advantages and disadvantages of gathering qualitative data from top managers and front-line employees on their views on what motivates them?

Organization culture

The organization culture approach to understanding work motivation identifies the unique ways of doing things in a particular organization that influence the behaviour of employees as a group. Organization culture is a pattern of shared basic assumptions, beliefs and values that are developed by members of the organization. In turn, new employees are indoctrinated into the 'correct' way to perceive, think and act in relation to events, challenges and opportunities within the organization.[39]

How does organization culture determine work motivation? We look at organization culture in more detail in Chapter 15, but here we can emphasize that it serves a number of functions. It can act as a form of managerial control, prescribing and prohibiting certain activities to shape worker behaviour in a way that is consistent with top management's expectations. It is plausibly argued, for example, that a 'strong' corporate culture is seen as the 'Holy Grail of commitment' in releasing workers' creative talents, and it is central to high-commitment HRM programmes.[40]

Similarly, the process of developing and mobilizing employee commitment is actively managed by carefully engendering 'shared values' and constructing workplace rituals and ceremonies. Activities such as 'best' employee awards, performance prizes, encouraging venom against competitors, regular statements of commitment to the firm's mission statement and so on, represent the metaphorical 'glue' that is designed to build loyalty to the organization. These things additionally bond employees together, thereby satisfying their need for social affiliation and identity.

An organization cultural analysis prompts us to see that the effort–performance relationship or 'expectancy' can be reframed by top managers.[41] However, a perceptual analysis should remind us that different individuals in the same workplace will not necessarily perceive its culture in the same way, and a 'strong' culture that motivates one employee will not necessarily work with another employee.[42]

STOP AND REFLECT

Look at the photo on page 264. What motivates non-Christian women employees?

WEB LINK

Go to the following website for more information on organization culture: www.managementhelp. org/org_thry/culture/culture.htm

Work orientation

work orientation: an attitude towards work that constitutes a broad disposition towards certain kinds of paid work

Work orientation refers to the meaning that individuals give to paid work, and the relative importance and function they assign to work within their lives as a whole. This perspective to understanding workplace behaviour encourages greater awareness of the connections between work attitudes, values and behaviour patterns, and the structure and culture of society. People's working and non-working lives are shaped by the societal configuration of class, gender and race that lies outside the workplace, as well as the behaviour of managers and non-managers inside the organization. Interest in individual differences in to work orientation has led some researchers to investigate the connection between work motivation and social factors. These social factors include age, class, gender, education, marital status and race.[43]

An early US study found that individuals living in communities with white middle-class Protestant norms of occupational achievement and responsibility appeared to choose paid work with fewer than average opportunities for personal advancement and responsibility.[44] The researchers argued that it was misguided to try to motivate workers who 'trade off' the satisfaction they might gain through their work for relatively high monetary reward, and who find intrinsic motivation from work performed in the community.

A classic study by Goldthorpe and his colleagues[45] focused on the relationship between work orientation and social class. The investigation attempted to explain the varying patterns of work motivation among British car workers in the 1960s. The British researchers argued that, before it was assumed that the particular patterns of occupational behaviour found on car assembly lines (such as high absenteeism, high turnover of workers, and strikes) meant that the workers are short of higher-level needs to motivate them, it was necessary to inquire what the workers were looking for when they entered that particular occupation.

The researchers argued that if individuals enter an impoverished work situation in the full knowledge that intrinsic rewards are not available, their work motivation is not likely to be significantly influenced by the absence of such rewards. In essence, they suggested that for a majority of workers in their study, extrinsic rewards from their work – such as pay, benefits and security – or what they called the 'cash nexus', were much more important than intrinsic rewards. They explained that a majority of workers choose to do this job:

> [A]s the result of some more or less calculated decision; that they have in effect chosen to abandon employments which could offer them some greater degree of intrinsic reward in favour of work which enables them to achieve a higher level of economic return. In more technical terms it could be said that a decision has been made to give more weight to the instrumental at the expense of the expressive aspects of work.[46]

Numerous studies have investigated possible gender-related differences of work orientation, and the determinants of work satisfaction.[47] For example, data from a variety of manual and non-manual occupations suggest a number of similarities as well as differences in the orientations to work of men and women. Testing the hypothesis that men and women have different expectations from paid work, it has been found that although women are more likely to enter an impoverished work situation than men, they have lower expectations and hence are as satisfied with their paid employment as men are.

Sociological studies tend to offer us a more nuanced approach to understanding gender differences in work-related values. When men and women in management positions are compared, it has been found that both have very similar orientations to work. However in lower-level, non-managerial occupations, a much different picture emerges: 'Men tend to assign greater importance to intrinsic rewards than women, while the latter are more concerned with the social aspects of work.'[48]

One possible explanation for this gender-related work orientation is that it reflects basic differences in sex-role socialization. In support of this argument, there is well-documented evidence that women are socialized to pursue occupations reflecting their stereotyped sex-roles, regardless of individual abilities and talent.

plate 27 The task of discovering what motivates different categories of employee in different work settings is of the same magnitude as finding the Holy Grail. For example, what factors motivate this woman at work?

Source: Getty Images

Fiona Wilson, for example, in a review of the literature, suggests that women's employment aspirations and choices are frequently far lower than the aspirations of men with comparable ability.[49] The data are insufficient to substantiate this argument, but it seems intuitively plausible that 'women workers in lower-level occupations may adjust their work values somewhat in terms of what the situation has to offer.'[50]

Although this type of research provides additional insight into the nature of gender-related differences in work orientation, a limitation is that it does not address the gendered nature of organizations, or men's power within them, where white male privilege is a major factor.[51] An insightful investigation by Wajcman[52] convincingly demonstrates that the symbolism of manual shop-floor work is dominated by masculine images and values. Consequently, 'Women have by and large been frozen out of the shop-floor culture of working-class men, which is based on mechanical skills and toughness.'[53]

The work orientation approach was seen as an alternative to need theories of work motivation. According to John Goldthorpe and his colleagues,[54] researchers and practitioners should make a distinction between different types of work orientation. Some workers might have an 'instrumental orientation' whereby their important work motivation is a tangible monetary reward, while other workers might have a 'bureaucratic orientation', whereby the primary meaning of, and motivation for, work is a career with advancement through the management hierarchy, and the associated privileges.

The work orientation approach adds support to expectancy theory, in that it emphasizes the need to focus on the expectations that individuals bring to the workplace in order to understand work motivation. As Goldthorpe and his colleagues insisted, the question of how to motivate workers cannot usefully be considered until we know what people are looking for in work, their orientation towards work: 'Until one knows something of the way in which workers order their wants and expectations relative to their employment.'[55] The theoretical roots of this approach lie in the *symbolic interactionist* tradition developed by the German sociologist Max Weber and the American George Herbert Mead (see Chapter 3). Applied to work motivation, this approach looks for an explanation beyond individual cognition and the workplace, by suggesting that the welter of workers' social experience and socialization processes strongly influence and shape individual expectations and the subjective meaning of work, and that this affects behaviour in a particular direction.

Although the orientation to work thesis is a useful corrective to the psychological universalism of need and process motivation theories, there is a problem in interpreting work orientation studies. What do these findings actually mean? The survey results, for example, could be describing 'levels of resignation'.[56] It is also important not to be drawn into a pessimistic determinism about the possibilities for work motivation.[57] Orientations to work are ever-changing, and can alter with the particular circumstances in which they become relevant to shaping behaviour. Individual work orientation may change as individual or organization circumstances change or even transform. Examples of change include attitudes to work–life balance – from both managers' and other employees' perspectives – job insecurity arising from non-standard or precarious employment relationships, and employer disempowerment and coercion of employees.[58]

So for example, some types of individual, at a specific period of time, may be acting to improve their pay (an extrinsic motivator) rather than focusing on a desire to get a sense of accomplishment or achievement from performing their job (an intrinsic motivator). However, other individuals, or even these same individuals at different points in their lives, will have other priorities. A primary income earner who has always worked mostly 'for the money', but has now managed to pay off the mortgage and has cash to spare, might find the level of pay is less important, and begin to look at his or her job differently. This could be the time to take an interest in the job itself – or to look for another job if it provides none.

The orientations of individuals or even entire workforces can be modified if they perceive a growing level of job insecurity, experience downsizing through corporate restructuring, and identify a 'no guarantees' attitude by senior management. For example, in 1983 union leader Ron Todd summed up the effect of unemployment and redundancy on the work orientations of the British workers when he declared, 'we've got 3 million on the dole, and another 23 million scared to death.'[59]

Not just pay, but other reward issues such as pension provision and health care provision, can affect people's attitudes to their work. For example, in 1998 a stock market collapse led to the scaling-back of health care provision in North America. Research in 2003 suggested that the 'baby-boomers' affected by this had modified their retirement plans and work–leisure choices. They were giving greater priority to job security than to job interest or satisfaction.[60]

All these examples suggest there is nothing fixed about the orientation to work of individuals or whole workforces. It can be modified by changes in the dynamic context of employment relations, within the workplace and/or in the wider economy, which are in turn affected by management strategies, trade union bargaining, government policies and other issues.

The notion of 'dynamic orientations' suggests that an individual's orientation to work at any particular time, and as a result the factors that will motivate the individual, can be seen to be embedded in the individual's psychological contract with the employing organization.[61] Further, gender, social class and race will influence how individuals or groups interpret the messages they receive, and this too will affect the way this information influences their work orientation.

Integrating the approaches

The phenomenon of organizational culture and the work orientation approach complement the psychologically driven expectancy theory of work motivation. What employees actually get out of their work is subject to modification by management. Managers achieve this either through cultivating a strong organization culture or through influencing the psychological contract directly or indirectly. The integrated motivation model (Figure 9.7) goes beyond notions of individual motivational drive, and takes into account the cultural and orientation approaches.

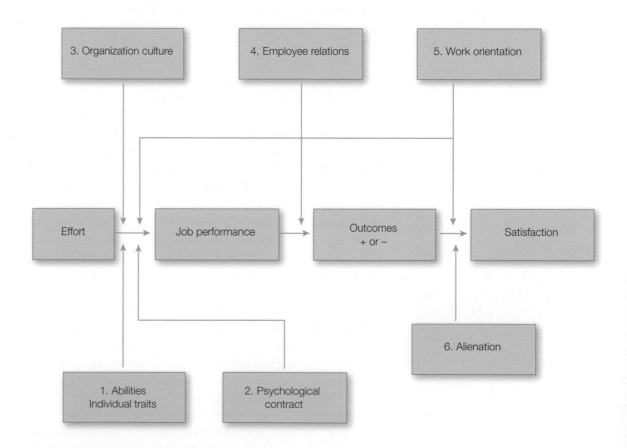

figure 9.7 Integrating psychological and sociological approaches to work motivation

This model suggests that the individual work motivation that is based on the three expectancies – effort-to-performance, instrumentalities and valence – is also influenced by individual abilities and personality traits (such as self-esteem) (Box 1), by the psychological contract (Box 2), by organizational culture (Box 3), by employee relations (Box 4), by work orientation (Box 5) and by the alienating aspects of work (Box 6). We believe that these variables and social relations offer a more complex and integrated view of individual and group work motivation, which is based on psychology, sociology and anthropology. The variables and social forces are subject to the pressures arising from the inherent conflicts of interest in the capitalist employment relation.

Applying motivation theories

Implementing motivational theory successfully in the workplace is challenging, and managers cannot simply transplant one of the theories discussed in this chapter and apply it in its 'pure' form. For this reason, managers' motivation interventions must be based on an assessment of employee needs. This must take into account the occupation (such as managers, knowledge workers, first-level employees) and the employees' age, gender, race, ethnicity and disabilities (if any). This is only possible when managers know their employees. The research findings reviewed in this chapter affirm the importance of employee relations styles (see Chapters 4 and 5) and HR practices (Chapter 17). The research indicates that when motivation strategies are planned, it is necessary to consider carefully the most appropriate rewards, job design and leadership style.

Every individual is unique and will respond differently to attempts to motivate him or her. What factors motivate a 56-year-old computer engineer? What factors motivate working mothers with young children? What factors motivate Muslin women at work? Managers need to be sensitive to the differences in individual needs and values among the people they manage. They need to avoid viewing their 'employees' as a homogeneous group. People are different in what they need and what they value, and in how they perceive and judge their work situation.

People engage in paid work for many reasons besides the weekly or monthly pay cheque. They work so that they can be with others, gain respect, form an identity and realize their human potential. Needs vary from individual to individual, and for the same individual at different life stages. What are needed are an understanding of what motivates particular employees, and more managerially adroit handling of the motivation interventions in the organization. Managers also need to be aware that rewarding one employee necessarily changes the motivation of other employees.

As an illustration, consider possible motivation interventions for knowledge workers. When we examined the changing nature of work in Chapter 2, we said that knowledge work is 'ambiguity intensive' and that knowledge workers are defined in terms of the requirement to share and apply their professional knowledge with others in the organization. Drawing on a study by Horwitz and his colleagues,[62] Table 9.1 shows the most popular, highly effective, and least effective motivation interventions for managing knowledge workers.

As column 2 indicates, the most highly effective motivation interventions for knowledge workers included employment practices which allow them the freedom to plan work independently (in another word, autonomy). Although an important limitation of the research data is that it is based on employer perceptions of effectiveness rather than on knowledge workers' views on what motivates them, the results are consistent with other studies surveying knowledge workers themselves.[63]

table 9.1 Most popular, highly effective, and least effective motivation strategies for knowledge workers

Most popular		Highly effective		Least effective	
Strategy type	**Rank**	**Strategy type**	**Rank**	**Strategy type**	**Rank**
Freedom to plan and work independently	1	Freedom to plan work	1	Flexible work practices	1
Regular contact with senior executives	2	Challenging work	2	Large cluster of knowledge workers	2
Incentive bonuses	3	Access to state-of-art technology and products	3	Generous funding for conferences	3
Challenging work	4	Top management support	4	Cash awards for innovations	4
Top management support	5	Ensure fulfilling work	5	Recruit people who fit organization culture	5

Source: adapted from Horwitz et al. (2003: 31–2)

These rankings are based on the number of responses that were marked as the five most frequently used motivation interventions, and the five most highly effective and ineffective in motivating knowledge workers.

Reward design

In line with content theories of motivation, top managers need to design a reward package that gives employees rewards they value. In the case of knowledge workers, Horwitz and his colleagues' study revealed some interesting contradictions. While the use of incentive pay was a popular HR practice, it was not considered a highly effective motivation strategy. Arguably, incentive bonuses were not effective for already highly paid knowledge workers because these individuals considered additional extrinsic rewards less important than intrinsic motivators, such as work designed to be fulfilling.

In line with the expectancy theory of motivation, managers need to increase employees' expectations that their effort will result in effective performance. (In other words, they need to increase E→P or efficacy expectancies.) Low E→P expectancies guarantee low levels of motivation. In order to ensure that these expectancies are high, managers must ascertain that employees have the ability to do their jobs effectively, and that they possess sufficient self-confidence to believe that their effort will result in effective performance. Obvious key elements in this process are recruitment practices, and the effective use of employee learning and development to overcome any ability deficiencies.

Managers must ensure that employees correctly understand the basis upon which rewards are administered, and that they believe they will get the promised rewards if they reach the stated standards of performance. This is supported by recent research emphasizing that first-level employees want to receive 'a fair and equitable pay for a fair day's work'.[64] In other words, they want to share the rewards from any gains in productivity they achieve.

Job design

Work is a social activity, and for many people it is not regarded simply as a means to an end. Jobs are central to the lives of most people, in that they provide identity, status and experienced meaningfulness. In line with alienation avoidance techniques, recent literature suggests that managers need to design jobs so their

skill variety: the extent to which employees must use different skills and talents to perform tasks in their job

task identity: the degree to which a job requires completion of a whole or an identifiable piece of work

task significance: the degree to which the job has a substantial impact on the organization and/or larger society

core characteristics (skill variety, task identity, task significance, autonomy and feedback), which are believed to be key influences on employee motivation, provide a good fit with the abilities, goals, knowledge, values and skills of each employee. For knowledge workers, autonomy and challenging work through appropriate job design is the most effective motivation strategy (see Table 9.1).

Contrary to conventional management thinking, higher-level growth needs have been shown to have a significant influence on the self-esteem of first-level employees as well as of higher-level employees (see Figure 9.4). As Arnolds and Boshoff put it, 'frontline employees … also like to make one or more important decisions every day, use a wide range of their abilities and have the opportunity to do challenging things at work'.[65] However, although the job design motivation strategy focuses on notions of self-fulfilment, identity, and employee perceptions of task characteristics, the way two employees view a particular job and perceive an identical task may be quite different depending on such factors as their age, personality and orientation to work, so achieving this is not straightforward.

Gender, for example, influences identity formation among women. Josselson, in her work on identity, found that 'in comparison to men, women orient themselves in more complicated ways, balancing many involvements and aspirations, with connections to others paramount; their identities are thus compounded and more difficult to articulate'.[66] Following from this, and the requirement for differentiation between occupational groups, it is insufficient to make objective changes in skill variety, autonomy or other job dimensions. Managers need to also appreciate and monitor how those objective changes influence the perceptions of different employees (see Chapter 7).

Leadership style

We looked in Chapter 5 at how leadership is shaped by work organization, organization culture, and HRM practices and policies, and also affected by the interplay between organization imperatives and external variables, which include the interconnected levels of power embedded in society. And since leadership is almost always about change or even transformation, communication is paramount. So is behaviour that encourages dialogue, creativity and informal learning among other employees.

creativity: the capacity to develop an original product, service or idea that makes a socially recognized contribution

Recent studies suggest that managers need to develop a leadership style that creates a work culture permitting relative autonomy, particularly for knowledge workers: as it is said these days, they need to 'let go'. In line with the motivational technique of MBO, conventional wisdom suggests that top managers need to encourage employees to set performance goals that are specific, measurable, attainable, realistic and timed (SMART). Goals should not be dictated to employees. Rather, they need to be generated in a fashion that creates a sense of personal ownership and acceptance of those goals by the individuals responsible for achieving them.

Equity theories of motivation have important implications for managing people and behaviour in the workplace. Managers need to ensure that employees feel management is treating them equitably. This places three sets of demands on managers. First, managers need to treat workers fairly and equitably in comparison to one another. Second, the policies and practices in the workplace must compare favourably with those in other organizations of a similar type. Finally, employees need be provided with accurate and complete information on the organization's policies and practices, in order to ensure that they perceive and understand them accurately. In a sense, the recent empirical data underscores the complex nature of work motivation and the importance of understanding the whole interplay between individual cognition and the social, the historical, and the connection between different theories of motivation and HR practices.

Chapter summary

☐ This chapter has emphasized the centrality of motivation in the employment relationship. Motivation refers to the driving force within individuals that affects the direction, intensity and persistence of their work behaviour in the interest of achieving organizational goals.

☐ We examined two broad competing approaches to understanding motivation, need-based and process theories. According to Maslow's needs hierarchy, employee behaviour is directed toward satisfying lower-level needs before seeking to satisfy higher-order needs. It is based on the principle that when a drive or need is met, its value as a motivator is reduced. Maslow's theory helps to explain the dynamic nature of work motivation. It recognizes that needs and drives change continuously in everyday life. Behavioural theorists adopting the needs or content model of work motivation assume that when a person's need is not satisfied, the person experiences internal tension or states of deficiency, and this motivates the person to change behaviour to satisfy that need.[67] All the need theories tend to be heavily prescriptive in nature, since as well as assuming workers share a common set of basic needs, they also attempt to identify what needs prompt their behaviour.

☐ The practical implications of needs-based motivation theories are that managers need to recognize that different employees have different needs at different times, to avoid relying on pay as a sole source of work motivation, and to balance the demands and influences of the different innate drives.

☐ We explained how process theories of work motivation place emphasis on the actual psychological process of motivation. According to the equity theory, perceptions of equity or inequity lead employees to form judgements on the value (or valence) of a reward or outcome. When an employee or group of employees perceives a reward item to be inequitable, the individual or group will not be satisfied by that reward. This dissatisfaction will result in the individuals or work groups not finding the outcome attractive, and to that extent the reward or outcome will not be effective in motivating the employees.

☐ Expectancy theory is based on the idea that work motivation results from deliberate choices to engage in certain behaviours in order to achieve worthwhile outcomes. The three most important elements of expectancy theory are the perception that effort will result in a particular level of performance (E→P), the perception that a specific behaviour or action will lead to specific outcomes (P→O), and the perceived value of those outcomes, the valences. The attractiveness of work activities (their valence) depends on an employee's individual differences, cultural factors and orientation to work.

☐ This chapter had two principal objectives. Our first objective was to provide a critical evaluation of the psychologically oriented motivation models. Our second principal objective was to provide a sociological treatment of the subject. We have suggested that if we are to understand what motivates people in the workplace, we must go beyond psychological notions of individual needs and cognitive processes. We need to incorporate into any analysis the dynamics of employment relations, the way work organizations and managerial control of work activities generate and express internal tensions and contradictions, and the effects of complex interconnecting levels of domination, which stem from the class, gender and race relations in society.

Key concepts

Chapter review questions

1. To what extent is motivating workers increasingly more or less challenging for managers in the early twenty-first century? Explain your answer.
2. Compare and contrast Maslow's needs hierarchy theory and Alderfer's ERG theory. How are they similar? How are they different? What do both theories imply for managerial practice?
3. Identify two different types of expectancies referred to in the expectancy theory of work motivation. What can a manager do to influence these expectations?
4. What are the limitations of expectancy theory in predicting an employee's work behaviour and performance?
5. How can a strong corporate culture affect an individual's work effort?
6. How can the orientation to work of an individual influence valence and work effort in the workplace?

Further reading

Belasco, J. and Stayer, R. (1993) *Flight of the Buffalo*, New York: Warner Books.

Horwitz, F. M., Chan Teng Heng and Quazi, H. A. (2003) 'Finders, keepers? Attracting, motivating and retaining knowledge workers', *Human Resource Management Journal*, **13** (4), pp. 23–44 (see p. 33).

Lawler, E. E., Mohrman, S. and Ledford, G. (1998) *Strategies for High Performance Organizations*, San Francisco: Jossey-Bass.

Pfeffer, J. (1998a) *The Human Equation: Building profits by putting people first*, Boston, Mass.: Harvard Business School Press.

Zaleznik, A. (1990) *Executive's Guide to Motivating People*, Chicago: Bonus Books.

Chapter case study: *Motivation at Norsk Petroleum*

Norsk Petroleum is a leading gas and oil exploration company based in Oslo, Norway. It employs 2564 people, and its business operations comprise the exploration, production and marketing of crude oil, natural gas and natural gas liquids. In 2007 most of its business was conducted in Norway and Canada, although its interests included ventures in West Africa, Australia, the Gulf of Mexico and Venezuela.

When Lisa Bohm, the human resources director for Norsk Petroleum, read an email message from Elizabeth Pedersen she knew she had another urgent issue to deal with that week. Elizabeth Pedersen was a petroleum engineer who had the task of deciding how to extract the oil once it had been found by geologists, and extraction had been estimated to be viable by the company's team of geophysicists. Elizabeth had requested a meeting with Lisa for the next day, but she did not say what the purpose was. Lisa suspected that Elizabeth was intending to tender her resignation.

Lisa's problem was not new, or unique to Norsk Petroleum. In the previous five years, the major oil companies such as Amoco, BP, Exxon and Shell had accelerated their oil exploration and extraction operations. With the expansion of exploration and extraction in Iraq, following the US and British military intervention, many small independent gas and oil companies had also entered the market or stepped up their operations.

After graduating from university, the 'knowledge workers' of the industry – geologists, geophysicists and petroleum engineers – need at least three years' field experience before they become fully qualified and valued professionals. There was a shortage of, and an urgent need for, qualified professionals. Many small companies had resorted to using executive recruitment agencies or 'head hunters'. In the previous 12 months, 18 (15 per cent) of the Norsk Petroleum scientists had resigned after receiving offers from rival companies.

As Lisa was pondering what she would do about the loss of petroleum engineers, and specifically what she would say to Elizabeth Pedersen, there was a knock on her office door. Gottfred Eng, manager of computer services, walked into the office and asked her to sign an 'Advertising request form', for an ad for a replacement for Ola Rennemo, a computer technician.

'Why is he leaving?' Lisa asked.

'His new company is closer to home and it will reduce his travel to work time,' Gottfred replied.

'Ask him to come and see me on Friday before he leaves. I would like to conduct an exit interview with him.'

The meeting with Elizabeth Pedersen took place the next day. It began with comments on the weather, her daughter who had recently married, and brief discussion about the progress on the latest drilling project. Then Elizabeth made a flawless statement: 'Lisa, I'm really grateful for all the support the company has given; the work has been challenging but I'm leaving Norsk to take up a new position at Petrowest.' Anticipating the next question, she continued, 'It's a small, independent company which has won a major contract to explore off the Newfoundland Coast in Canada. I'm excited by the job. And I'll have greater responsibility for managing two three-person teams of petroleum engineers, and negotiating contracts with the suppliers.'

Lisa mulled over on the words 'small, independent company'. Unlike large companies such as Norsk Petroleum, where petroleum engineers focused on specialized tasks related to their knowledge, the small exploration companies required their engineers to take on wider projects and managerial responsibilities, negotiate with customers and suppliers, and work on capital projects.

Lisa knew from labour market surveys that Elizabeth was already well paid, but she offered a 5 per cent increase in her salary, additional stock options and a company car. She also pointed out that the company's share values had been steadily increasing despite a sluggish stock market. Elizabeth said she would consider the new pay package, saying she needed 'to sleep on it'.

'Let me ask you this, Elizabeth,' Lisa added. 'Are you unhappy with your supervisor, or are you having problems with your team members?' Elizabeth replied that her team leader and other team members were fine. The meeting ended with Elizabeth promising to consider the improved compensation package.

On Friday morning that week Lisa conducted an exit interview with the technician Ola Rennemo. After enquiring about his wife, who was expecting a baby, and their new home, she asked, 'Why are you leaving the company? Your performance appraisal has been consistently excellent and I believe you would have a bright future if you chose to stay with Norsk Petroleum.'

'To be closer to my family,' Rennemo responded.

Lisa was aware that thousands of large, medium and small technology businesses across the country were trying to recruit and keep high-tech talent such as Ola. She was also aware that in line with the company's stated policy on being a 'learning organization', she had agreed to pay for his technical upgrade courses, and a team leadership course held at the local college. She knew she had to stop, or at least slow down, the haemorrhage of talent from the company. She also knew from reading Ola's latest appraisal report that he was ambitious, so she tried what she considered an innovative approach to the problem: professional development.

'If the company paid the tuition for a diploma in management, would you stay?'

'Thanks, but it's too late. I'm committed to the new job,' Ola replied.

At 4 o'clock that afternoon, Lisa received Elizabeth Pedersen's letter of resignation. On Monday morning, she would be calling a meeting of departmental managers to garner ideas for recruiting and keeping their petroleum engineers and their high-tech support staff.

Task

1. Use your understanding of motivation theories to explain both Elizabeth Pedersen's and Ola Rennemo's motivation toward their jobs at the time of their resignation.
2. If you were Lisa Bohm, what would you do to handle this situation? Be specific in your recommendations.
3. What are the practical implications of this case to you as (a) a future employee and/or (b) a future manager?

Sources of additional information

Arnolds, C. A. and Boshoff, C. (2002) 'Compensation, esteem valence and job performance: an empirical assessment of Alderfer's ERG theory,' *International Journal of Human Resource Management*, **13** (4), pp. 679–719.

Pfeffer, J. (1998b) 'Six dangerous myths about pay,' *Harvard Business Review*, May–June, pp. 9–13.

Websites:

Gainsharing: www.gainshare.com/profile.html

www.forskningsradet.no Search for: 'science and technology indicators' to access the 2005 Science and Technology Indicators in Norway. (The report is available in English or Norwegian.)

Notes

This case study was written by John Bratton, Thompson Rivers University. Norsk Petroleum is a fictitious company, but the background material for the case is derived from Agashae and Bratton (2001).

Web-based assignment

Form a study group of three to five people, and go to the website of any of the following organizations, or a similar one that interests members of the group:

Compaq Computers (www.compaq.com)
Airbus Industrie (www.airbus.com)
Wal-Mart (www.walmart.com)
General Electric (www.ge.com (select the 'Job Seekers' link))
Virgin Airlines (www.virgin.com)

When there, go to the 'Company overview' and the HRM section of the site, and look at the language, assumptions and espoused values. Evaluate the organization's dominant culture in the light of our discussion in this chapter. Write a report that draws out the common features.

Alternatively, go to the websites of a number of universities, and compare and contrast your own university with others in the United Kingdom or abroad. As a guide to your search, ask the following questions. What artefacts are displayed that expresses the institution's culture? (Hint: do departments display the publications of the teaching faculty?) In the advertising material, does the institution emphasize teaching excellence, research, or both? What are the President's espoused values? What rituals and ceremonies dramatize the institution's culture? What practices shape the university's culture? (Hint: Ask your lecturer what is the most important criterion for promotion, excellence in teaching or the number of articles/books published?) Do the visible artefacts and processes provide a guideline for behaviour at the university? If so, why?

OB in films

The film *Dangerous Minds* (1995) centres on a former US Marine turned teacher, LouAnne Johnson (played by Michelle Pfeiffer). Ms Johnson accepts a teaching position at a inner-city high school and tries to motivate her students. The school principal, however, does not approve of her unorthodox motivation methods.

Watch the scene, starting with a shot of the school hallway, after the principal has reprimanded Johnson for taking students to an amusement park without signed permission. The film raises cognitive and behaviour motivation issues. Ask yourself, what methods does Ms Johnson use to motivate her students? Do the students change their behaviour as a result of her teaching approach? What lessons can be drawn from the film for motivating young workers in the workplace?

Notes

1   K. Cloke and J. Goldsmith (2003) 'It's time to wake up: employees share obligation with bosses to change corporate culture to better suit needs of workers and business,' *Globe and Mail*, 13 August: C1.
2   Vroom and Deci (1970: 10).
3   Legge (2005).
4   Drucker (1954: 14).
5   See for example Maslow (1954), Herzberg et al. (1959), McClelland (1961) and Alderfer (1972).
6   See for example Vroom (1964), Adams (1965), Porter and Lawler (1968).
7   See for example Fox (1974), Friedman (1977), Salaman (1979), Clegg and Dunkerley (1980) and Thompson (1989).
8   Drucker (1954: 303).
9   Salaman (1981).
10   Drucker (1999).
11   Bratton, Grint and Nelson (2005).
12   Vallerand (1997).
13   Townley (1994).

14 Lawler (1971: 80).
15 Maslow (1954), Herzberg et al. (1959), McClelland (1961), and Alderfer (1972).
16 Watson (1986: 110).
17 McClelland (1961).
18 Harrel and Strahl (1981).
19 Arnolds and Boshoff (2002).
20 Arnolds and Boshoff (2002: 712).
21 Arnolds and Boshoff (2002: 713).
22 See for example Cullen (1994), Gordon and Whelan (1998), Wajcman (1998).
23 Adams (1965).
24 Bratton and Gold (2007).
25 Baldamus (1961).
26 Lewin (1935), Vroom (1964), Porter and Lawler (1968), and Lawler (1973).
27 Porter and Lawler (1968), Lawler (1971, 1973).
28 Lawler (1971).
29 Kanungo and Mendonca (1992).
30 Locke (1968).
31 See for example Tubbs (1986), Latham and Locke (1990).
32 Blauner (1964).
33 Early post-Marx work includes Mills (1959) and Salaman (1981).
34 Mandel and Novack (1970), Rinehart (2006).
35 Rinehart (2006: 14).
36 Salaman (1981).
37 Rinehart (2006).
38 Arnolds and Boshoff (2002).
39 Schein (1991).
40 Thompson and McHugh (2006), Bratton and Gold (2003), Legge (2005).
41 See for example Roddick (1991), Tichy and Sherman (1993).
42 Hofstede (1998a/b).
43 Mottaz (1985).
44 Hulin and Blood (1968).
45 Goldthorpe et al. (1968).
46 Goldthorpe et al. (1968: 33).
47 Mottaz (1986), Murry and Atkinson (1981), Metcalfe (1989), Cullen (1994), Hodson (1999).
48 Mottaz (1986: 372).
49 Wilson (2003).
50 Mottaz (1986: 373).
51 Andersen and Collins (2004), Wajcman (1998).
52 Wajcman (1998).
53 Wajcman (1998: 49).
54 Goldthorpe et al. (1968).
55 Goldthorpe et al. (1968: 36).
56 Salaman (1981: 84).
57 Watson (1986).
58 Daniel (1973), Rousseau (1995), Watson (1986), Kelly (2005), Kersley et al. (2005), Vosko (2000), Charles and James (2003).
59 Quoted in Bratton (1992: 70).
60 See for instance Heath-Rawlings (2003).
61 Rousseau (1995).
62 Horwitz, Chan Teng Heng and Quazi (2003).
63 Horwitz, Chan Teng Heng and Quazi (2003: 33).
64 Arnolds and Boshoff (2002: 713).
65 Arnolds and Boshoff (2002: 715).
66 Josselson (1987: 8) quoted in Mills and Tancred (1992: 240).
67 Kanter (1990).

chapter 10
Equity in organizations: issues of gender, race, disability and class

'Injustice anywhere is a threat to justic everywhere.'[1]

chapter outline

▷ Introduction
▷ Equity and justice in work organizations
▷ Gender
▷ Race and ethnicity
▷ Disability and work: an emerging focus for research?
▷ Social class
▷ Chapter summary
▷ Key concepts
▷ Chapter review questions
▷ Further reading
▷ Chapter case study: The Glass Ceiling Commission
▷ Web-based assignment
▷ OB in films
▷ Notes

chapter objectives

After completing this chapter, you should be able to:

▷ understand and explain how equity affects organizations
▷ describe some of the principal means by which equity issues are handled in organizational practices
▷ compare and contrast the current status of gender, race/ethnicity, disability and class policy in organizational life in major English-speaking countries
▷ outline relevant areas where further investigation is needed in the many areas relating to equity in the workplace.

Introduction

Understanding issues of equity across the major social divisions of society as it relates to work is vital for a deep understanding of organizational behaviour. The institution of paid work brings together people of all kinds. Indeed, with increased global migration, the workplace is becoming ever more diverse. Over the last 50 years remarkable changes have occurred, beginning with the movement of women into paid work in greater and greater numbers. Civil rights movements around the world have affected how all people think about visible minority status. And more recently people with disabilities are more effectively demanding the full rights of citizenship, which involve among other things the freedom to participate in paid employment, as is signalled by the increased efforts of the United Nations, for example, to help them achieve this.

employment equity: a strategy to eliminate the effects of discrimination and to make employment opportunities available to groups who have been excluded

These broad social changes help set the stage for our discussion, but interwoven with them all is a particularly broad concern that is not often addressed in textbooks on OB. This concern is for the role of 'social class'. The fact that work is implicated in the production and reproduction of class divisions has been understood for at least 150 years. Indeed, this connection between work and social class may have become so taken for granted that it has slipped off the radar screens of many organizational analysts. In addition, we might say that if class divisions are a necessary component of paid work, how can we problematize these divisions if we do not at the same time problematize the way work itself is organized and understood?

Ironically, outside OB literature, up until the 1970s a large proportion of literature on work and inequities focused exclusively on issues of social class. Over the last 30 years, however, there has emerged a great deal of practical concern, policy and research about issues of gender, race and ethnicity. This, of course, should not be understood as making a case for the irrelevance of social class: clearly social class is a major factor that shapes the work experience. Rather, it means that people's general understanding, as well as academic analyses, of work must become more sophisticated and nuanced to bring to light the relationships between race, gender, disability and social class.

In general terms, this chapter provides a systematic exploration of several of the key areas of equitable/inequitable practice in OB, as well as more broadly in the institution of work, including labour markets. We begin with a general section on the sub-field of 'organizational justice', which has been developing for almost a quarter of a century.

Before getting started, take a moment to ask yourself, how do I understand the term 'equity' now? After you have considered this, take a moment to explore the web for sites devoted to equity across different countries. Two sites you might like to compare and contrast are:
www.mtholyoke.edu/offices/comm/csj/040700/gender.html
www.publicservice.co.uk/pdf/dfid/winter2003/DfID1 per cent20MMS per cent20Mdladlana per cent20ATL.pdf

STOP AND REFLECT

Equity and justice in work organizations

organizational justice: In OB literature, the perceived fairness of outcomes, procedures and treatment of individuals.

Take a moment to come up with a list of key factors that could be used to compare different jobs for their relative 'value'. Now, using your set of factors, analyse some occupations. How did your system of comparison measure up? Do you think it produced a fair outcome?

STOP AND REFLECT

human rights: Conditions/treatment expected for all human beings.

The concept of 'organizational justice' will serve as the starting point for this chapter because, although we explore a variety of other forms of research literature, it is the topic that most firmly connects us to the field of OB, organizational psychology and the like. In other words, this discussion is essential, though not sufficient, for the full development of a broad and useful theory of equity in the context of OB. But first it is perhaps relevant to briefly look at the general issues of pay and employment equity, a sub-field of legal and social studies of work that is well established but that stands quite separate from the literature on organizational justice.

Pay and employment equity legislation is defined as laws intended to eliminate established inequalities in the pay received by women and (often specifically identified) members of minority groups working for a given employer.[2] Different forms of this type of legislation exist across many countries. In social democratic countries such as those of northern Europe, it is linked with general work environment legislation. In countries without these types of centralized legislative framework, such as the United States, Canada and the United Kingdom, it appears in stand-alone legal frameworks where litigation (as opposed to collective bargaining) is central. In these types of countries, pay and employment equity laws do not, as such, focus on the broader experiences of workers and inequity, even though employers found to be in violation of the legislation are often required to identify and eliminate many of the factors that have produced the violation. Rather, the focus is on comparisons based on the principle of equal pay for work of equal value. Establishing this value is not easy, of course, and, it reveals the many presumptions that infuse the world of work, which most of us take for granted.

A broader set of concerns, both in the work-based literature and in practice, revolves around human rights legislation. Here the concern is again discrimination, but the focus is much broader than that seen in pay and employment equity legislation. First, more personal characteristics are taken into account (that is, more than just gender and visible minority status), including disability, sexual orientation, age and even political or religious beliefs. Any analysis of human rights violation necessarily explores the full range of forms of discrimination and the factors involved, including those examined in the context of pay and employment equity. Here we might look at issues of the conditions of employment, harassment, mental duress, legal expenses (as well as pay) and so on. Employers found to be in violation of the legislation are often required by law to make employees 'whole' by restoring them to the circumstance they would have been in had discrimination not occurred.

This brief introduction to the legal dimensions of equity law provides a lead-in for a broad and introductory exploration of the issue of equity, and specifically organizational justice, in the research literature on OB. Indeed, as we shall see, the two basic legal frameworks outlined above (as well as case research on collective bargaining) offer examples of the many different forms of organizational justice. First, however, we must ask, what is known about how the issue of justice and the perceptions which surround it affect the actual behaviour of and within organizations?

Valuable work has recently been completed on these issues, in the form of general reviews of research and theory.[3] This research comes in a variety of forms: field research, experimental research and 'action' (or 'proactive') research. Each form and method has made important claims about the relations between different types of justice and variables such as job satisfaction, employee commitment and evaluation of authority.

We can identify three basic lines of inquiry in the area of organizational justice: the distributive, procedural and interactional approaches. (Some researchers identify four or more approaches, for instance distributive, procedural, interpersonal and informational, but here we use a three-type model.) Briefly, the types can be roughly defined as follows:

▷ *Distributive justice* refers to outcomes and allocations emerging from processes.
▷ *Procedural justice* refers to the procedures set in place to produce the perception of fairness.
▷ *Interactional justice* refers to the interpersonal treatment of people using these procedures.

In general, it is important to note that 'justice', in this field of research, is understood to be socially constructed. It concerns practices and organizational structures, and the policies and procedures that shape them. Note too that typically, justice is understood to be subjective, in the sense that 'fairness' is what the majority perceives it to be.[4] However, justice can also be understood in more objective terms – involving proportional shares of resources, outputs and so on – and we use this understanding in this discussion. We feel it is necessary to include both the subjective and objective dimensions of justice at work, because when the focus is on subjective formulations of justice – what people think to be just – it is easy to sidestep many contentious issues regarding rights, responsibilities and social justice in a broader, more politicized sense.

CRITICAL INSIGHT

The writings of G. S. Leventhal are important original attempts to define 'organizational justice'. Early on, Leventhal and his colleagues generated six criteria for procedures to be perceived as 'fair'. How many criteria can you come up with? After your attempt, read Leventhal, Karuza and Fry's article, 'Beyond fairness: a theory of allocation preferences'.[5]

plate 28 Women continue to be over-represented in the care-giving professions

Source: Getty Images

Some of the research that has been carried out certainly sheds light on behaviour in work organizations. As in most sciences, the researchers tend to be preoccupied with how powerful the effects they identify are, and which specific theories are the most powerful predictors. Interested readers can look at the primary sources, but, for our purposes we can say that organizational justice (or at least perceptions of it) correlates highly with positive outcomes and experiences of work as follows. Not only do we see that certain dimensions of personality shape organizational justice,[6] but we also see that increased organizational justice is found to be correlated with higher job satisfaction,[7] higher organizational commitment,[8] higher levels of trust,[9] more positive evaluations of managers,[10] enhanced organizational citizenship behaviour (OCB),[11] lower turnover and absenteeism,[12] as well as lower levels of workplace sabotage and revenge.[13] The literature on work performance is mixed, but overall it shows a positive correlation between forms of justice and better work outputs.[14]

For our purposes, perhaps the most important point to be taken from all this is that the concept of 'justice', and with it 'equity', emerges and takes on personal relevance only in the context of the existence of systematic injustices and inequities. That is, it occurs in a system of tension and conflict. Work, in other words, is contentious; and it is this fact that makes it reasonable for any of us to notice or care about justice and equity in this context. What makes work contentious is, of course, the subject of whole bodies of literature across a wide range of disciplines from political economy to industrial relations, including women's studies, sociology and so on. For this chapter, however, we can say that this system of conflict and tension can be understood in two major dimensions, horizontal and vertical, which bear directly and distinctly on each of the social variables of gender, race and ethnicity, disability and class we examine later in the chapter.

The tension in the employer–employee relationship should not be confused with tension in the relationships between groups and individuals. Although in reality they coexist with each other, analytically they represent two relatively distinct sets of dynamics, structures and determinants. This distinction is essential if we are to understand the different dynamics of justice and equity across different social groups which feature a mix of characteristics. Tensions that emerge from individual participation in group, team or organizational contexts are related to human individuality, the burdens of negotiating scarce resources, and conflicts arising from interdependency within work structures and processes. Organization theorists call these *horizontal* tensions. They tend to emerge from the relationship between the individual and the group or organization, where individual agency meets forms of collective need and social structure. Strictly speaking, these tensions can emerge in any form of collective activity, both in and beyond the workplace (such as in social movements, community groups, families, non-profit work and trade unions).

The tensions that arise in the context of employer/employee (or capital/labour) relationships necessarily involve these tensions which are inherent in individual and group/organizational relationships, but there is a distinct set of further tensions that are more or less unique to economic life under capitalism. These tensions revolve around a specific class-based form of what could be called *vertical* tensions, which appear both within specific work organizations and in society generally. This set of relationships and tensions is rooted in the processes of appropriation. By this is meant the process by which the capital accumulation that defines the success of a business firm requires control to be placed in private hands, in ways that are shaped by market exchanges, technological development and inter-capitalist competition, in the last instance.

It is true that the vast majority of decisions by firms in capitalist economies revolve around the satisfaction of projected, rather than direct, huma needs. This may or may not be a problem, depending on your viewpoint, but what is generally not

horizontal tension: Tensions and contradictions that emerge in terms of people's participation in group endeavours irrespective of hierarchical institutional relationships.

vertical tension: Tensions and contradictions that emerge in terms of hierarchical institutional relationships.

appropriation: The process through which, in capitalist workplaces, a proportion of the value produced in work activities – above investment in raw materials, equipment, health benefits, facilities and so on – is retained under the private control of owners, ownership groups and/or investors. A more critical perception of this process sees it as 'exploitation' of collective activities of the organization for private use.

OB IN FOCUS

Two recent articles on discrimination in the workplace, one by Brief and colleagues, 'Just doing business: modern racism and obedience to authority as explanations for employment discrimination',[15] and another by Yoder and Berendsen, '"Outsider within" the firehouse: African American and white women firefighters',[16] add depth and subtlety to our understanding of how and why these practices per-sist. Each article outlines detailed research on the issues involved, including racial prejudice, tokenism, justice and power relationships. At the same time, these articles do not identify the core problems and barriers in quite the same way. Compare and contrast these two articles (and one or more others you find most relevant). Then see how each speaks to the general models of organizational justice discussed in this section.

disputed is that the employer/employee relationship that emerges is full of vertical tensions and contradictions. These and other distinctions draw our attention to the essence of the central contradiction and lines of tension that define the employer and employee relationship under capitalism. The distinction between vertical and horizontal tensions also provides a foundation for understanding some of the more specific discussions about equity across different social groups. We present these below, beginning with the issue of gender.

Gender

gender bias: behaviour that shows favouritism toward one gender over the other

gender identity: a person's perception of the self as female or male

gender role: attitudes, behaviour and activities that are socially defined as appropriate for each sex and are learned through the socialization process

gender socialization: the aspect of socialization that contains specific messages and practices concerning the nature of being female or male in a specific group or society

glass ceiling: The pattern of employment opportunities that disproportionately limits achievement of top administrative posts by certain social groups.

sticky floor: The pattern of employment opportunities that disproportionately concentrates certain social groups at lower-level jobs.

sex: a term used to describe the biological and anatomical differences between females and males

sexual harassment: unwelcome conduct of a sexual nature that detrimentally affects the work environment or leads to adverse job-related consequences for its victims

To understand organizational behaviour and gender, we must take time to understand the aggregated results of organizational behaviours from the specific standpoint of women. Over the last 30 years, women have come to account for approximately half the labour force in most core capitalist countries (such as the G10 countries). At the same time, however, the wage gaps between men and women have hardly narrowed. Indeed, in the 1990s the gap may even have widened.[17] It is clear when we look at the available statistics that differential wages as well as differential occupational distributions persist.

Two phrases seem to best describe the status of women in the workplace. One is the 'glass ceiling', the concept that despite their equal or greater educational training and performance, women remain systematically excluded from top corporate jobs. The other is the idea of 'sticky floors' on which women workers appear to be disproportionately glued. In other words, while women participate in paid work in numbers equal to men, they appear to be excluded from the top jobs, while vast numbers are clustered in low-paying, low-prestige jobs with little or no opportunity for advancement.[18] This appears to happen through a combination of outright discrimination as well as educational and occupational segregation.

To take a specific example, in the United States the median wage for women continues to be only three-quarters that of men.[19] Studies of hiring practices in the United States have found that women are more likely to be found working in firms that are owned or managed by other women.[20] Finally, gender-based harassment at workplaces both persists and has recently been shown to be much more broad than had originally been thought. This harassment undermines efforts to develop career progression and decent working conditions for women.[21]

A significant amount of research over the last decade has looked at the dynamics of gender and management. 'Good news' stories are occasionally seen in the media about the burgeoning numbers of business and governmental leaders who are women. However, these are not necessarily representative of the contemporary reality. For example, in 1999 there were only two female chief executive officers (CEOs) of Fortune 500 companies (the largest 500 companies in the United States), and a mere 4 per cent of all senior corporate officers in the United States were women. Similar statistics show that in the United Kingdom, less than 4 per cent of corporate leaders were women.[22] Yet another sobering comparison: in the United States, at the current rate of change it will take approximately 300 years for women to reach the representative 50 per cent mark in corporate leadership, and a remarkable 500 years for them to provide 50 per cent of political leaders.[23]

It is not just a matter of fairness. Gender inequities in the workplace have recently been shown to have important, and under-examined, effects on the health of women. One researcher who has examined this issue explicitly shows that, at both the macro (large-scale) and micro (individual) levels, there is a close correlation between gender inequality at work, itself shaped by organizational practices, legal infrastructures and cultures of specific countries, and the overall mental and physical health of women.[24]

Some studies have effectively conceptualized gender effects in small-group behaviour,[25] and a variety of key researchers have linked general changes in work to a critical discussion of the emergence of new managerial styles which, on the surface, might seem to favour women.[26] Of course, as Wajcman points out, we need to consider to what degree these claims are based on gender stereotypes that may or may not be warranted:

> Traditionally, men have been seen as better suited than women to executive positions. The qualities usually associated with being a successful manager are 'masculine' traits such as drive, objectivity and an authoritative manner. Women have been seen as different from men, as lacking the necessary personal characteristics and skills to make good managers. The entry of women into senior levels within organizations over the last decade or so has brought such stereotypes into question.[27]

At the same time, of course, denying the essential validity of stereotypes does not prevent stereotypes from having real material effects in people's lives.[28] In the majority of workplaces these stereotypes flourish, and through this and other factors, major barriers to female advancement are constructed.

Is there a really a 'male' and 'female' style of management? According to Wajcman's careful studies, the answer is no. Perceptions of difference persist, for example in the area of 'risk preferences',[29] and certainly some variation is to be expected,[30] but assessments of managerial practices show that there are far more similarities between female and male managers than there are differences, particularly in the areas that are seen as the most definitive of managerial work.

Wajcman's conclusions are not particularly hopeful, but there are some positive proposals in Meyerson and Fletcher's 'A modest manifesto for shattering the glass ceiling'.[31] While Meyerson and Fletcher do not question the basic principles of the capitalist model, which may very well be an important source of this and many other forms of inequity, they nevertheless build on the type of argument Wajcman provides by seriously questioning both the efficacy of the current legislative structures and the reality behind the apparently increased 'sensitivity' of corporations.[32]

Meyerson and Fletcher are particularly harsh critics of attempts merely to change attitudes. They prefer to change the very way work organizations operate, while arguing for an incremental approach of what they call 'small wins' within firms.[33]

In Canada, authors like Falkenberg and Boland offer a slightly different prescription.[34] Their careful research of employment equity programmes in workplaces reveals that negative stereotypes are strongly persistent. They go on to show that employment equity programmes have probably created a significant backlash, which is led by males targeting, in particular, those women who have successfully overcome the barriers. For Falkenberg and Boland the solution is to be found not in regulation of the workplace, but rather through government-led education programmes. A variety of other research calls these conclusions seriously into question, however.[35]

There is also a very clear business case against gender inequity, and this makes the reasons for the persistence of discrimination even more complex. Several researchers highlight the tendency for team decision-making processes to be male dominated, and argue that it is highly ineffective for men to dominate team-based work.[36] Others outline the negative effects of gender stereotypes on mixed-gender negotiations at the bargaining table. They draw on fascinating experimental work which builds on the general 'stereotype threat' theories.[37]

An article by Ngo, Foley, Wong and Loi reports, among other things, on the way that such inequity leads to a decline in morale and performance levels, which

patriarchy: a hierarchical system of social organization in which cultural, political and economic structures are controlled by men

feminist perspective: the sociological approach that focuses on the significance of gender in understanding and explaining inequalities that exist between men and women in the household, in the paid labour force, and in the realms of politics, law and culture

STOP AND REFLECT

Does success for women in corporate leadership mean becoming 'more like a man'? Should it? Does feminist critiques such as Wajcman's offer a threat to 'male identity' which undermines reforms? Why, or why not? And, is this a significant barrier to equitable changes to the workplace?

ultimately erodes the capacity of firms to retain top women (and in some cases, top men too).[38] On the surface, this would seem to be an issue in which the very principles of 'market competition' would bear progressive fruit, but this is not the case; that is, the market does not seem to be very effective at 'weeding out' weak firms on this basis. Ngo and colleagues provide a review of the literature, and also a case study which suggests that changes to organizational structures, not individual attitudes, are most important for addressing perceived inequities.

Although the glass-ceiling issue is clearly important, in many ways the greater problem of gender inequity – at least in terms of the pure number of workers affected – is experienced by women who are stuck to the 'sticky floor'. They range from Chinese garment workers in Canada and the United States[39] to women across the world who labour in sweatshops.[40] Few surfaces are stickier than those to which domestic workers are fixed. A recent study by Parrenas sheds light on just why this is. Her focus is on Filipinas, labouring across more than 130 countries, who represent one of the largest and widest flows of female migrant labourers on the contemporary scene.[41] She shows the incredible difficulties these particular women face. They appear to be unable to take advantage of what legislation there is to prevent discrimination.

In many ways, Parrenas's study highlights the difficulties in separating out different types of discrimination. Gender, race, disability and class issues are generally highly interwoven in an interactive complex of effects. How, we might ask, can we approach the issue of gender inequities and work in such as way as to encompass the fantastically diverse experiences of both those on the floor *and* those pushing against the ceiling?

Race and ethnicity

In autumn 1998, a fascinating article in the *Guardian* newspaper in the United Kingdom reported a pronounced pessimism about the future of race relations.[42] It outlined how most young people in the United Kingdom (in this context, those aged 18 to 24) felt that race relations would worsen rather than improve over the coming years. Excellent historical texts add depth to our understanding of the landscape of ethno-racial inequities and work.[43] Since there seems to be an incredible persistence in a wide range of ethno-racial injustices in the context of work, it is appropriate to ask ourselves several important questions to begin with. What are we to make of this suggestion that young people in the United Kingdom see a growing, not narrowing, schism between ethno-racial groups? Is this pessimism well-founded? And, how does it involve the workplace?

General research over the last three decades has confirmed that while some progress has been made in achieving greater equity for ethno-racial minority groups, it is relatively minor and the results are mixed internationally. In 2002, for example, Blacks and Hispanics in the United States held just 13 per cent of all managerial and professional positions.[44] In a parallel with women's experience, studies of hiring practices in the United States have found that Blacks are more likely to be employed in firms that are owned or managed by other Blacks.[45]

In the United Kingdom, Labour Force Surveys show that during the 1980s and 1990s there was some upward mobility among ethno-racial minorities.[46] Figure 10.1 compares the levels of income enjoyed by different ethno-racial groups in the United Kingdom, again in the 1990s.

Source: Fotosearch

plate 29 Gender inequality is in many ways felt most strongly by women workers who are stuck to the 'sticky floor', from Chinese garment workers in Canada and the United States to women across the world who labour in sweatshops

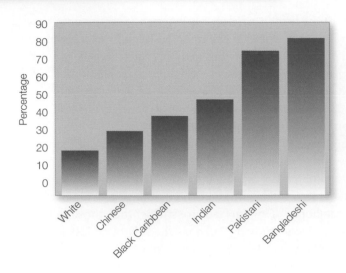

figure 10.1 Proportion of people living in households in the UK with less than half the national average income, 1994

Source: Modood et al. (1997)

According to some researchers, in the workplaces of the United Kingdom ethno-racial minorities are greatly under-represented in the highest positions and over-represented in the lowest ones.[47] Modood notes how there are also significant differences between minority ethno-racial groups. For example, in the United Kingdom the earnings of Chinese men are on par with those of white men, while Caribbean and South-East Asian immigrants are the worst off. According to the most recent UK Labour Force Survey, in 2001 the unemployment rate for people of Bangladeshi origin was 24.6 per cent and for Pakistanis it was 16 per cent, compared with 5.4 per cent for white people. Since these latter groups have been in the UK in significant numbers for generations now, this too suggests that if conditions *are* changing, they are changing very slowly indeed.

As we have begun to suggest, there are differences in the experiences of different non-white groups, and there are also systematic distinctions between groups with the same skin colour. Phillips and Lloyd, for example, have shown how there is not always a clear match between race and ethnicity, and attitudes, opinion and values. They go on to show that diversity in general seems to promote more effective decision making, and in particular encourages the voicing of dissent in organizations.[48]

In general, any exploration of different ethno-racial work experiences needs to bear in mind the cultural background. This includes both the history and culture of a group's country of origin, and the relationship between that country and the country where the group is now resident. We need to consider the effects of colonialism and imperialism, and how these continue to impact migrants from formerly colonized countries. Different groups have different varieties of diaspora (patterns of dispersion of émigré communities), and different cultural and material resources available to them. These same issues help to illuminate the processes by which stereotypes are produced, for example of African-Americans, Caribbean-Canadians and South Asian British.

Another leading researcher on these types of question, Robinson, brings into play a range of other possible factors with the potential to deeply inform the types of inequities that occur in and through specific forms of organizational behaviour.[49] For example, we can look at the degree of general social integration or marginalization of specific ethno-racial minority communities, and at their 'desire for social mobility'. We need to consider whether these groups are excluded generally from all forms of mobility, or whether they are 'segmented' into and isolated in specific industries, where they may experience some partial upward mobility. Often, the difference pivots on groups' differential success in schooling and their English language skills, but economic isolation is a factor not explained completely by these factors alone.

Modood goes beyond the concepts of exclusion and segmentation to explore how ethno-racial groups experience work differently.[50] He looks at aspects of communities such as how 'tightly knit' they are, the degree of hierarchy in communities and between families, and the strength of connections to the country of origin, which have grown immensely with advanced telecommunications. All this makes it clear that we cannot ignore the background of home and community life when we try to assess equity in the context of work.

Much empirical research provides us with details of practices within organizations. There are obvious inequities associated with segmentation, exclusion, promotion and earnings, but there is also recent evidence explaining the processes that reproduce inequity across virtually every element of the workplace experience, from hiring practices to the labour process. There are some fascinating and highly instructive case studies that look at ethno-racial dimensions of the experience of work processes.[51] In searching for an organizational perspective on issues of inequity, we can begin with the research of Brief, Dietz, Cohen, Pugh and Vaslow, which looks at Black applicants for jobs.[52] Drawing on an interesting experimental methodology, they highlight the complex web of relationships between managerial justifications, ethno-racial prejudice and decisions to employ individuals. They show convincingly that the concentration of authority in firms is a key factor in inequitable hiring.

Other researchers have provided a solid analysis of how African-Americans are systematically excluded and 'tokenized' in public services such as fire fighting, and some of them focus specifically on women ethnic minority workers.[53] Participation in training programmes is obviously key for workers who want to obtain promotion and greater earnings. Some researchers have shown how non-English speaking immigrants typically experience great difficulties in getting access to this kind of training.[54]

WEB LINK

Throughout the world there are many ethno-racial organizations, advocacy groups and so on doing important and interesting work. www.irr.org.uk/employment/ gives a sense of the activity in the United Kingdom. To further expand our ability to understand the linkages between racism and economic life explore this lecture available on the web which provides an historical and international overview: http://mp3.lpi.org.uk/resistancemp3/marxism-and-race.mp3 Explore these and other relevant sites, and report back to your class on what you find.

Disability and work: an emerging focus for research?

It is vital to assess gender and ethno-racial issues in the workplace in order to generate a broad and critical view of organizational behaviour and its context in contemporary society. Later we look at one of the major sources of difficulty that is so pervasive as to have become invisible (social class), but first we explore an important, under-studied, though perhaps emerging area of equity studies in the workplace: disability.

The category of disability is broad and diverse. By convention it is divided into five sub-groupings: sensory disability (such as blindness), physical disability, mental and psychiatric problems (such as depression), intellectual and developmental problems (like those experienced by individuals with Down's syndrome), and learning difficulties (such as dyslexia). Beyond these categories, in a recent committee session of the United Nations on disability, Kevin McLaughlin put forth this definition for consideration:

Impairment + Disenabling factor = Disability

Disability is defined differently across countries, but available statistics confirm that in general terms, a large number of people experience some form of disability, and that many of these people experience difficulty in obtaining and retaining paid work. In the United States, for example (where the American Disability Act (ADA) is a key piece of legislation), according to some researchers an estimated 31 per cent of non-institutionalized citizens (aged between 18 and 64) who are considered to have a disability are employed. In other words, there is a 60–69 per cent unemployment rate amongst people with disabilities.[55] In the United Kingdom (where the Disability Discrimination Act (DDA) is in force), according to the Labour Force Survey longitudinal database in 2003, the unemployment rate amongst disabled people was 58 per cent. There were more than 2.4 million people in the UK who were disabled, out of work, and wanting to work.

STOP AND REFLECT

The World Health Organization's International Classification of Functioning, Disability and Health website (www3.who.int/icf/photo_gallery/index.htm) features a photo contest entitled 'Images of health and disability'. Go to the website and examine the images you find there. There are several entries that deal with work. What kinds of questions do they raise for you? How does this relate to issues of equity? Now consider the disability attitudes quiz at www.equalopportunity.on.ca, as well as an important paper by one of the leaders in the field of disability studies, Mike Oliver, found at http://www.independentliving.org/docs4/oliver.html.

Recent research suggests that people who are disabled have difficulty finding work in which they can effectively apply their skills and talents. They also find difficulty in keeping paid employment. Research suggests that this is largely because of stereotyping and discrimination.[56] Once employed, workers with disabilities report a range of other difficulties, including issues of getting to and from work, movement within the workplace, lack of adaptations of work stations, flexibility in work arrangements, lack of job coaches, and lack of Braille or other forms of text translation assistance. Bruyere has done further research into employer work practices, and reports that the most important challenges disabled workers faced involved the attitudes of supervisors and employees in the firms sampled (see Table 10.1).[57]

table 10.1 Employer-reported difficulties in integrating workers with disabilities in the United States

Difficulty in making workplace change	Private sector %	Public sector%
Changing co-workers'/supervisors' attitudes	32	33
Modifying return to work policy	17	11
Creating flexibility in performance management system	17	15
Change in leave policy	10	8
Adjusting medical policies	7	9
Ensuring equal pay and benefits	2	4

Source: Bruyere (2000)

Importantly, these statistics point toward a view of disability that moves away from the (unfortunately still prevalent) view that 'disability' is a problem an individual *has* (that is, he or she is a 'disabled person'), and towards the view that disability is a problem that individuals face *in society*. In other words, it is a problem of how we organize society, including workplaces. This is exemplified by a statement by the Society for Disability Studies in 1993, that its field 'examines the policies and practices of all societies to understand the social, rather than the physical or psychological, determinants of the experience of disability'. This is a crucial shift in how people, including academic researchers, can best understand the phenomenon of disability.

There are various overviews available of international disability policies, including comparative employment policies.[58] The journal *Disability and Society* is perhaps the most accessible English-language source of information on research in this area. However, its discussions of work and employment tend to focus on policy issues.[59] The issue that is of greatest interest in an OB context is the dynamics of behaviour towards those with disabilities, but there is comparatively little literature on this.

MacGillivray, Fineman and Goden provide a look at managerial perspectives and practice on discrimination claims, including a comparative look at the United States and the United Kingdom, although they do not focus on disability alone.[60] An article by Premeau published in 2001 provides a provocative discussion of the hiring process for applicants with disabilities (in particular, mental disabilities).[61] An important determinant of equitable access to jobs and promotion is access to training, and Tharenou's 1997 article on organizational development reported significant barriers in this context.[62]

How much do you know about disability and employment? To test your knowledge why not check out the following website:
www.wage.eu.com/glasgow/quiz.html
WEB LINK

An interesting case that raises complex questions for organizations can be found in the recent work of Reed,[63] who looks at litigation under the ADA over the last 30 years in the United States, and notes that the consideration of personal risk through employment is something that can now legitimately be taken into account. However well intentioned this legislation, in effect it provides grounds for discrimination. The duty to provide a safe work environment opens the door for important questions for human resources departments. Reed asks, should employer 'paternalism' take precedence over the rights of a person with disability, as established under the ADA? A related question is how the kind of social definition of disability offered by the Society for Disability Studies relates to these legal structures, but Reed does not specifically consider this.

Social class

Should issues of social class be included in a discussion of equity and organizational behaviour? Should we bother to resuscitate the term 'class society' from the apparently bygone industrial era? And (even if our answer is 'yes' and 'yes'), what is the relationship of social class to other dimensions of equity, and why would we position it at the end of a chapter?

We would suggest that class is indeed highly relevant. In fact, we position this section at the end of the chapter to emphasize that while each of the dimensions we discuss above involve substantial proportions of the population, relationships of social class underpin the most damaging effects of each of them.

Class can be defined in a variety of ways. It can be understood in terms of culture (such as a bourgeois or working-class culture), status (seeing people as a 'wage earner' or 'owner/manager', for example), or through highly segmented classifications based on occupational and socioeconomic status (with categories such as professional, unskilled, upper-middle class and underclass). These definitions emerge respectively from cultural studies theory, from Marxist theory and from theories of class inspired by the sociologist Max Weber and others. There is an excellent, concise and accessible discussion in Milner's *Class*.[64] In all cases, however, class involves hierarchy, the means of generation of this hierarchy, and

STOP AND REFLECT

Do you think that disability is more about a disabling environment than physical impairment? Why have employers largely ignored the legislation aimed at securing equal employment rights for disabled people? A leading activist in Canada (David Lepofsky) frames these issues in terms of challenging our ideas about the meaning of legitimate workplace 'accommodation': (as a lawyer who is blind) he remarks, 'lights are an accommodation for people who see.' (see also http://atwestern.typepad.com/convocation_addresses/2006/10/october_19_pm_d.html).

plate 30 In male (main) stream OB, the interests and ideas of women, racial minorities and people with disability are largely neglected or marginalized.

Source: Getty Images

the resulting different experiences, different levels of power, control, resources, sensibilities, behaviours and forms of practices.

Differences in class are generated by the full range of activities in the world (such as consumption, politics and education), but they are typically thought to be rooted in economic and employment experiences. In this chapter our focus is on those who find themselves at a disadvantage (such as women in our discussions of gender, minorities in our discussions of race and ethnicity), so here we deal primarily with those who are subordinated by class processes – that is, the working classes. It should be emphasized that class issues interrelate with other issues of discrimination, so those at a disadvantage because of their gender, disability, race or ethnic origin find themselves doubly (triply, quadruply) so if they are waged workers.

We can introduce our discussion of how class hierarchies work under a capitalist system by looking at the pay rates of corporate CEOs and the average workers in the same firms. According to the *New York Times*, in 2002 the average CEO of a major corporation in the United States received US$10.8 million in total compensation. That was 400 times as much as the average worker in those corporations: a proportion that has grown from a relatively modest 42 times in 1980. The available statistics suggest that the ratio is tighter in most other countries, but this is still evidence of considerable and growing differentials rooted in the world of work (see Table 10.2).

table 10.2 International earnings ratios

Country	Ratio of average CEO earnings to earnings of manual workers
Japan	7.8 to 1
Germany	10.2 to 1
United Kingdom	15.5 to 1
United States	25.8 to 1

Source: Streek (1996)

If we look at the major international journals on organizational behaviour, human resource development and organizational studies, or at most major textbooks in each of these fields, we discover something interesting, as we mentioned in Chapter 1: there is little mention in them of social class as such. Why is this? As we suggested earlier, perhaps it is because class relationships are so fundamental to the institution of work under capitalism that they have effectively become invisible. However, class is discussed in a wide range of indirect ways – perhaps most prevalently, in discussing the role of trade unions. Why should *this* be the case?

trade unions: An organization whose purpose is to represent the collective interest of workers.

Trade unions can be seen as an institutional expression of the class interests of subordinate groups. They operate on the principle that workers need to act collectively to balance the playing field of negotiation with employers. They are certainly not perfect. It is hardly controversial to acknowledge that trade unions, like society more broadly, show fairly consistent patterns of inequity and hierarchy, in relation to gender, race and ethnicity, and disability although these organizations have in the recent past shown an enormous capacity to face up to these challenges.[65] It can be said, then, that unions pursue generalized class interests, but until recently they have not been very effective vehicles for supporting the interests of specific disadvantaged groups. In this sense (to return to a theme introduced at the start of the chapter), we might say that unions pursue the problem of 'vertical' tensions and conflicts, but tend to leave issues related to more 'horizontal' tensions and conflicts to fester. For all their inadequacies, however, for the average worker unions remain perhaps the only consistent vehicles for bettering conditions and increasing their say, or 'democracy', in the realm of work. As such, they are valuable institutions for addressing inequities in the context of organizational life.

In the 1960s, 1970s and 1980s many women, ethno-racial minorities and progressives held out great hopes that equity and anti-discrimination legislation would improve equity in the workplace. (This was similar to the struggle that has moved on to advocates for those with disabilities today.) As the statistics bear out, their hopes have only been marginally satisfied, however. Although small shifts have taken place, minorities continue to experience widespread and multiple forms of discrimination, and the fortunes of women are not much different. For both groups, it has become increasingly clear that labour unions are an important means of helping the majority of women and people of colour overcome barriers in the workplace.[66] Indeed, perhaps soon disability advocates will realize this too.

While racism and sexism are seen in labour unions, increasingly unions have actively addressed these issues, for both the sake of social justice and their own survival. Some have done so with considerable success. In general, we believe that unions are vital for alleviating some of the major difficulties that it seems neither legislation nor corporate anti-discrimination programmes can adequately address. According to the US Bureau of Labor Statistics, for example, unions continue to play the most significant role in closing the gender wage gap. Unionized women earn an average of 31 per cent more than non-unionized women. Wage inequality in Canada is much lower than in the United States, but in Canada, according to the national statistics service, in 2002 unionized women earned 38 per cent more than non-unionized women. When race and ethnicity are factored in, the 'union advantage' drops only marginally, to 34 per cent.

In general terms, in the United States, the United Kingdom and Canada, where there is greater working-class representation (through unions) there is a less ethno-racial and gender pay inequity. According to an OECD report in 1996, in the social democratic countries of Scandinavia, in countries with related 'social market' policies such as Germany and the Netherlands, and in France and Italy, where union coverage is very high (50–90 per cent), the same basic correlation holds true. However, we can usefully ask how exactly class representation, equity in the workplace and economic activity are related in broader terms.

Most mainstream economists see unions as almost exclusively concerned with raising the wages of their members. This, we are told, is a bad thing which 'distorts' the 'proper' functioning of labour markets and the economy. In this mainstream approach, the gains of unionized workers come at the expense of other workers, and perhaps even of society as a whole. In fact, however, this mainstream view does not hold water. While there are any number of ways of alleviating class inequities, the most developed economic literature recognizes that unions may in fact increase overall wage levels (across all workers, unionized and non-unionized) without detrimental effects on the economy. At the same time unions provide a host of other mechanisms for challenging ethno-racial and gender inequities, giving a greater democratic say to employees, and providing a portion of human dignity at work.

It is sometimes claimed that unionization is detrimental to economic success, but this too is not borne out by the facts. For example, a large-scale study by the World Bank (itself no union partisan) showed no relationship between levels of unionization and the economic or employment performance of a country.[67] Likewise, in 1996 the OECD (looking at the 1980s and 1990s) found no valid statistical proof that unionization is related to the greater or poorer economic/employment performance of industrialized countries. The International Labour Organization similarly demonstrated in 2001 that high unionization is quite compatible with good economic and employment performance.

Equity is as compatible with a flourishing economy as it is for a fair and just society, and this is true in class terms as well as for ethno-racial minorities, women and the disabled.

Chapter summary

☐ We began this chapter with the claim that understanding issues of equity across the major social divisions of society is vital for a full understanding of organizational behaviour. We explored the general and specific tensions in organizations that make the issues of equity, inequity and justice a relevant topic for learning and research. Vertical and horizontal conflicts were shown to help us understand the complex forms of power that play out across organizations.

☐ Some suggest that the institution of work, including practices in work organizations, divisions in pay, and related issues such as access to training and employment, has become fundamentally more equitable over the years. We argue that this is only partially correct. There is still lots to be done.

☐ Women, people from ethno-racial minorities, people who are disabled, and the working class (and all the combinations of these categories) continue to face major difficulties in gaining just and equitable treatment in relation to paid work. Students and scholars of organizational behaviour will benefit from a broader appreciation of these dynamics to inform the direction of future learning and research. Taken together, the vast majority of people in our society are subject to some form of discrimination. This begs the question, if the vast majority of people experience systematic inequities in relation to work, why is it so difficult to realize significant, positive change? Some of the answers to this question lie within the realm of existing OB research, but, many others have not yet been addressed. To address these questions of equity it is necessary to take a fundamental look at how work and society is organized. Through some of the inter-disciplinary dimensions of this chapter, we hope readers will start on that journey of further exploration.

Key concepts

Disability	285	institutional racism	289	sexual division of labour	281–3
ethnicity	283–5	labour market segmentation	280	sexuality	281
femininities/masculinities	281–3	patriarchy	282	social class	287
gender	281–3	race	283–5	social exclusion	284

Chapter review questions

1. What are the meaning and value of 'equitable practices' in organizations?
2. What is the relationship between the different dimensions of organizational justice and the specific social differences we explored in this chapter?
3. What do the terms 'sticky floors' and 'glass ceiling' have to do with gender, as well as other forms of social difference?
4. How do these forms of social difference relate to one another to intensify or reduce inequities in organizations?

Further reading

Brief, A., Dietz, J., Cohen, R., Pugh, S. D. and Vaslow, J. (2000) 'Just doing business: modern racism and obedience to authority as explanations for employment discrimination', *Organizational Behavior and Human Decision Processes*, 81 (1), pp. 72–97.

Folger, R. and Cropanzano, R. (1998) *Organizational Justice and Human Resource Management*, Thousand Oaks, Calif.: Sage.

Jackson, A. (2000) *The Myth of the Equity–Efficiency Trade-Off*, Ottawa: Canadian Council on Social Development.

Loprest, P. and Maag, E. (2001) *Barriers and Supports for Work among Adults with Disabilities: Results from the NHIS-D*, Washington, D.C.: Urban Institute.

Chapter case study: *The Glass Ceiling Commission*

In 1991, the US Department of Labor created a 'Federal Glass Ceiling Commission' (FGCC) to identify obstacles to the advancement of visible minorities and women in business. The FGCC defined the glass ceiling as 'those artificial barriers based on attitudinal or organizational bias that prevent qualified individuals from advancing upward in their organization into management-level positions'. Its mandate was to study the barriers to the advancement of minorities and women in corporate hierarchies, to issue a report on its findings and conclusions, and to make recommendations on ways to dismantle the glass ceiling. We will look at the issues defined in and through the terms of reference of the commission, but we also focus here on the notions of equality versus equity in terms of opportunities as well as outcomes.

As part of the background to the case it is important to recognize that despite civil rights movements and advances in civil rights, there is still plenty of evidence of a glass ceiling preventing women and members of minorities from achieving business leadership at senior management levels. In the United States, at the new millennium African-Americans comprised 12.9 per cent of the population, but only 2.5 per cent of senior managers in the private sector. The FGCC obtained information from white and non-white business leaders, as well as human resource professionals whom it considered to be leading voices in the area of equity and career development.

Search for the report of the FGCC at: (http://digitalcommons.ilr.cornell.edu/). Take a look at it, then read the comments below (published in *CIO* magazine, http://www.cio.com/resources):

'My biggest challenge has been overcoming initial impressions because I have worked in traditional industries that have had few African Americans,' says George Williams, a senior sales executive in the supply chain solutions group at TRW Inc. in Cleveland and former president of Black Data Processing Associates (BDPA). In a previous job, Williams sold software in the materials handling industry. 'I used to feel that being an African American played against me as a sales rep, so when it came down to a comparison, it was not a competitive edge for me. I think it was more of a discomfort on my part knowing I was in a competitive situation and had to be better – much better – than my [white] competition.'

And as much as white executives might be reluctant to admit it, stereotypes often come into play. 'An African American male of large stature with a deep voice might be viewed negatively by a white person,' explains Carl Williams, senior vice president and CIO of Principal Financial Group in Des Moines, Iowa. 'The [white] person might be intimidated – people are threatened [by that sort of thing].'

'All people have perceptions of what people should look like, be like, to fill senior-level roles,' says R. Steve Edmonson, CIO and vice president of pharmaceutical manufacturer R.P. Scherer Corp. in Basking Ridge, N.J. Carl Williams adds, 'It's very simple: Some people are comfortable only when they are bringing people into the environment that look like them, think like them, act like them. A lot of the perception is that "I'm going to have a very difficult time dealing with that individual because I'm not comfortable with the person." Some people can't get past that.'

Task

It is important to think about the implications of equality and equity principles applied to treatment and outcomes. That is, typically *equality* refers to treatment of people and outcomes which are the same, whereas *equity* refers to either similar or differential treatment of people in order to produce equality of outcomes. Then consider these questions:

1. How do the recommendations of the FGCC relate to this distinctions?
2. In light of the difficulty in removing the glass ceiling, how might an OB professional respond to this ongoing issue?

▶

Sources of additional information

Meyerson, D. E. and Fletcher, J. K. (2000). 'A modest manifesto for shattering the glass ceiling', *Harvard Business Review*, **78** (1), pp.127–37.

Wajcman, J. (1998) *Managing Like a Man: Women and men in corporate management*, Cambridge: Polity Press.

www.un.org/womenwatch/ UN website offers a variety of different weblinks and documents related to the current situation of women in the world.

Note

This case study was written by Peter Sawchuck, University of Toronto, Canada.

Web-based assignment

Web-based assignment

This chapter covered many areas of inequity in organizations, but it certainly did not cover them all! Issues of ageism (discrimination based on age) and discrimination based on sexual orientation are two of the key ones that were not explored. The latter forms the basis of this case study. With over 75,000 employees worldwide and 16 billion in revenue, one of the leading corporations in the area of support for employees who are lesbian, gay, bisexual and transgender (LGBT) is Raytheon.

First, take some time to think of some of the issues faced by LGBT employees. Then go to the following website and see Raytheon's perspective www.raytheon.com/feature/equal0606/

OB in films

In *Dirty Pretty Things* (2002) we get a glimpse into the intersection of race, ethnicity, immigration, gender and class, as characters Okwe and Senay, who have both recently emigrated to England, must cope with various inequities, injustice and violence. While the examples represented in the film are extreme, nevertheless we see a modern portrayal of multiple forms of inequity and social difference in relation to the 'lower-tier' service economy that is growing in all G8 countries.

Notes

1   Martin Luther King Jr., letter from Birmingham Jail, USA, 16 April 1963.
2   Godard (2005).
3   See for example Greenberg and McCarty (1987), Cropanzano and Greenberg (1997), Cohen-Charash and Spector (2001), Colquitt et al. (2001), Sawyer, Houlette and Yeagley (2006) and Johnson, Selenta and Lord (2006).
4   Colquitt et al. (2001).
5   Leventhal, Karuza and Fry (1980).
6   Colquitt et al. (2006) and Roberson (2006).
7   See for example McFarlin and Sweeney (1992).
8   See for example Tyler (1990).
9   See for example Folger and Cropanzano (1998).
10 See for example Ball, Trevino and Sims (1993).
11 See for example Organ (1990).
12 See for example, Masterson et al. (2000)
13 See for example Ambrose, Seabright and Schminke (2002) and Aquino and Douglas (2003).
14 See for example Masterson et al. (2000).
15 Brief et al. (2000).
16 Yoder and Berendsen (2001).

18 Kim (2002), Hirsch and MacPherson (2003).

19 Hartmann (2003).

20 See for example Carrington and Troske (1998).

21 Glomb et al. (1997).

22 Wajcman (1998).

23 Rubenstein (2003).

24 Moss (2002).

25 Colarelli, Spranger and Hechanova (2006).

26 See for example Wajcman (1998), Meyerson and Fletcher (2000), Rubenstein (2003).

27 Wajcman (1998: 55).

28 See for example Yoder (2002) on 'gender tokenism'.

29 Siegrist, Cvetkovich and Gutscher (2002).

30 Walters, Stuhlmacher and Meyer (1998).

31 Meyerson and Fletcher (2000).

32 Wajcman (1998).

33 Meyerson and Fletcher (2000).

34 Falkenberg and Boland (1997)

35 See for example Wajcman (1998) and Meyerson and Fletcher (2000).

36 See for example LePine et al. (2002).

37 Kray, Galinsky and Thompson (2002).

38 Ngo et al. (2003)

39 See for example Bao (1991), Hanson (2003).

40 See for example Brooks (2002).

41 Parrenas (2001).

42 Ward (1998).

43 See for example Linden (1995), or in Canada Galabuzi (2006).

44 US Bureau of Labor Statistics (2002).

45 Bates (1994), Raphael, Stoll and Holzer (2000).

46 Jones (1993).

47 Modood et al. (1997).

48 Phillips and Lloyd (2006).

49 Robinson (1990).

50 Modood et al. (1997).

51 See for example Dombrowski (2002) on aboriginal workers in the lumber industry of Alaska; Davis (2002) and Nelson (2001) on Black longshoremen; Bao (2002) on Chinese garment work.

52 Brief et al. (2000).

53 Yoder and Berendsen (2001).

54 VandenHeuvel and Wooden (1997).

55 See for example Houtenville (2003).

56 Loprest and Maag (2001).

57 Bruyere (2000).

58 Thornton and Lunt (1997).

59 See for example Shang (2000) on recent changes in China; Kitchin, Shirlow and Shuttleworth (1998) on the experience of workers with disabilities in Ireland.

60 MacGillivray, Fineman and Golden (2003).

61 Premeaux (2001).

62 Tharenou (1997).

63 Reed (2003).

64 Milner (1999).

65 Burke et al. (2003).

66 Bronfenbrenner (2003).

67 Aidt and Tzannatos (2003).

GROUPS AND SOCIAL INTERACTION

In this part of the book, we examine some of the important social processes that take place in the context of work groups, communications, decision making and power.

In Chapter 11 we explore the development, nature and behavioural implications of work groups and work teams. The nature of work groups is analysed through the concepts of size, norms, cohesiveness and group learning. We go beyond the popular rhetoric, and present arguments and evidence to suggest that self-managed teams shift the focus away from hierarchical, bureaucratic control structures and processes, to flatter organizational structures with a culture of self-control.

In Chapter 12 we explain how the communication process in the workplace reflects management style, the degree of employee involvement in decision making and organizational culture. We emphasize that people engage with their world through symbols (verbal, non-verbal and written language). Language creates the organizational concepts that define the culture of an organization and give form to notions of control, delegation and rationality.

In Chapter 13 we examine different models of decision making. Here we are careful to explain that in reality, decision makers must suffer from bounded rationality. We go on to discuss the advantages of group decision making, but point out that through the social phenomenon of groupthink, work groups might make decisions that are more risky or conservative than those of individuals.

Finally, in Chapter 14 we explore the abstract concept of power and, drawing on the work of Gramsci and Foucault, examine the deep social roots of power systems.

Work groups and teams

Communications

Decision making

Power, politics and conflict

chapter 11

Work groups and teams

The team concept is one of the most important organizational developments to hit business since the industrial revolution.[1]

chapter outline

▷ Introduction
▷ Work groups and work teams
▷ Group dynamics
▷ Work teams and management theory
▷ Paradox in team-based work
▷ Chapter summary
▷ Key concepts
▷ Chapter review questions
▷ Further reading
▷ Chapter case study: Teams at Land Rock Alliance Insurance
▷ Web-based assignment
▷ OB in films
▷ Notes

chapter objectives

After completing this chapter, you should be able to:

▷ distinguish between informal and formal work groups
▷ explain the current popularity of teams in work organizations
▷ articulate how group norms and cohesiveness exert influence on individual and group behaviour
▷ describe and critically evaluate the theories of team development
▷ identify the different theoretical perspectives and paradoxes related to work teams.

Introduction

Without doubt, everyone will find him or herself at some point in life to be a member of a group. You have probably already experienced group membership through participating in a sports team, climbing or caving club, jury service, church, political party or study group. In many organizations people are called upon to work in groups. Work groups influence the behaviour of their members, often promoting conformity. Avoiding dissent in an attempt to achieve group consensus over an issue or decision might provide a feeling of belonging, but at the extreme group pressure might be unpleasant, result in ineffective decision making, and it can even be harmful. This chapter introduces the complex phenomenon of work groups and work teams in organizations.

Before reading on, consider your own experience of group membership. Do people behave differently in groups? You might have experienced working in a study group at college or university. Reflect on your experience, and consider what specific behaviours exhibited during the group sessions were helpful to the group. What specific behaviours exhibited were detrimental to the group? How did the group deal with a member who was constantly late or did not complete his or her assigned work for a group assignment?

STOP AND REFLECT

Work groups are not something invented by management consultants. History shows that they have been part of human social development since ancient times. For thousands of years men and women lived in small hunting and gathering groups, and later they lived in small farming or fishing groups. It is only in the last 200 years, with the advent of industrial capitalism and the development of the factory system, that small groups became the exception rather than the rule.[2] Prior to the introduction of the factory system in Europe, work processes centred around the 'cottage', with workers using their own tools, organizing their own work, and relying on cooperation from other workers to make goods. With little division of labour and machine technology, and the necessity for cooperation and social interaction, work groups were ubiquitous in the pre-factory system. The factory system facilitated the minute division of labour and supervision, and thereby offered a more efficient means of controlling, and if necessary disciplining, a recalcitrant work force in order to increase labour productivity and profits. By the late twentieth century, management orthodoxy identified large bureaucratic organizations, with managers and workers specializing in specified task(s), as a 'problem' to be solved by top managers (see Chapter 2).

In managerialist theory, it is argued that large bureaucratic organizations with centralized control undermine innovation, flexibility, and threaten to make organizations uncompetitive.[3] Work teams are intended to transcend the alleged problems of inflexibility, poor quality, low employee commitment and motivation associated with the early work structures of the hierarchical factory. Clearly work teams are not new, but what is new is the recognition by top managers that work teams are a vital aspect of competitiveness. Their increased prevalence in European and North American organizations is partly a recognition that employers need to utilize their human capital more effectively. Work teams as a management concept have a history, and the enthusiasm for teams is linked to strategic goals.[4] Thus, the apparent increased diffusion of team working should be understood in the context of the contemporary management analysis of alleged problems of traditional work arrangements, competitiveness in globalized markets, and the alleged advantages of using teams to transform moribund labour productivity in order to facilitate capital accumulation. In the critical literature, work team initiatives are a means of increasing work intensification, obtaining higher productivity and controlling workers indirectly through a culture of self-control.[5]

If you paused and thought about the questions we asked in the 'Stop and reflect' box above, you should appreciate that understanding groups and teams in organizations is important for several reasons. Working in groups and teams has become a significant feature of organizational life. Individuals behave differently when in a work group than they do when they work independently. Team synergy, rather than individual employees, can potentially improve organizational performance. Finally, understanding the nature and dynamics of groups is seen to be an important aspect of managing (controlling) people more effectively.

This chapter begins by examining the background, nature and behavioural implications of work groups. We also explore the nature of work groups through the concepts of group norms, cohesiveness and learning. Finally we go beyond management rhetoric, and present arguments and evidence to suggest that self-managed teams shift the focus away from the hierarchy, and direct and bureaucratic control processes, to a culture of self-control.

Work groups and work teams

What are work groups?

The term 'group' can be used to describe a cluster of individuals watching a hockey game or queuing for a bank teller. When studying the behaviour of groups it is important to distinguish between a mere cluster of individuals, and what organizational theorists call a 'psychological group'. This term is used to describe individuals who perceive themselves to be in a group, who have a shared sense of collective identity, and who relate to each other in a meaningful way. We can define a work group as two or more people who are in face-to-face interaction, each aware of their membership in the group, and striving to accomplish assigned work tasks.

work group: two or more employees in face-to-face interaction, and each aware of positive interdependence as they endeavour to achieve mutual work-related goals

The first part of this definition suggests that there must be an opportunity for people to interact socially with each other: that is, communicate with each other, behave in each other's presence, and be affected by the other's behaviour. Over time, group members who regularly interact socially become aware of each other's values, feelings and goals, which then influence their behaviour. Although theoretically a work group can range from two members to an unspecified upper limit, the need to interact limits the size of the group.

The second part of the definition refers to group members' perception of the group itself. Members of the group are able to distinguish who is and who is not in the group, and are aware that an action affecting one member is likely to affect all. This part of the definition helps us to exclude mere clusters of people who are simply individuals who happen to be assembled at the same location at a particular time (such as soccer fans, bank customers or airline travellers). These individuals do not consider themselves a part of any identifiable unit, nor do they relate to one another in any meaningful fashion, despite their close proximity.

On the other hand, a soccer team, an airline crew or a project team at the Bank of Scotland would fulfil the criteria for a work group. In a situation of extreme danger – such as the hijacking of an airline – an aggregate of passengers could be transformed into a group. For example, several passengers on US United Airlines Flight

93, which crashed on 11 September 2001, apparently formed a group which stormed the cockpit to prevent the hijackers from carrying out any further terrorist acts.

The third part of the definition implies that group members have common goals, which they work collectively to accomplish. Six individuals drinking coffee in the company rest area at the same time would not necessarily be considered a group. They do not have common goals, nor are they dependent on the outcome of each other's actions. However, six union shop stewards drinking coffee together regularly to discuss health and safety issues or grievances would be considered a work group.

formal work group: two or more employees in face-to-face interaction, and each aware of positive interdependence as they endeavour to achieve mutual work-related goals

job design: the process of assigning tasks to a job, including the interdependency of those tasks with other jobs

Groups in organizations can be formal or informal. Organizational decision makers create formal work groups to permit collective action on assigned task(s). In this sense the rationale for creating work groups can be linked to an organization's competitive strategy. A manufacturing strategy that emphasizes flexibility can result in tasks and responsibilities being reassigned from individual employees and supervisors to a group of employees. This process of dividing up the tasks, assigning responsibility and so on, is called job design, and it is through the restructuring of work that formal work groups are created and consciously designed. Managers are interested in ensuring that the behaviour of the formal group is directed toward organizational goals. Not surprisingly therefore, much of mainstream OB research focuses on the dynamics of formal work groups.

informal group: two or more people who form a unifying relationship around personal rather than organizational goals

In addition to formal work groups, organizations also contain informal work groups. Managers do not specifically establish these work-based groups. They emerge from the social interaction of workers. Although an organization employs people for their intellectual capital, unlike with other forms of capital, it gets the whole person. People bring their personal needs to the workplace. Organizational behaviour theorists suggest that informal work groups are formed as an outcome of psychological processes: the perception of a shared social identity and to fulfil social needs for affiliation and supportive relationships. A cluster of employees can become an informal work group when members influence other's behaviour and contribute to needs satisfaction. Informal work groups are important in that they can help shape communication flows in the organization.

What are work teams?

teams: groups of two or more people who interact and influence each other, are mutually accountable for achieving common objectives and perceive themselves as a social entity within an organization.

The words 'group' and 'team' are often used as substitutes. In the management literature the word 'team' is more likely to be used in a normative sense as a special type of group with positive traits.[6] Like a soccer team, it has connotations of collaboration, mutual support and shared skill and decision making.[7] The observation and implied criticism that 'S/he is not a team player' or 'This group is not a team' expresses the difference in meaning between 'group' and 'team' in the management lexicon. A mainstream text defines a team as 'a set of interpersonal interactions structured to achieve established goals',[8] and two popular writers define a team as 'a small number of people with complementary skills who are committed to a common purpose, performance goals, and approach for which they hold themselves mutually accountable'.[9]

self-managed work teams (SMWTs): cross-functional work groups organized around work processes, that complete an entire piece of work requiring several interdependent tasks, and that have substantial autonomy over the execution of those tasks

Another variant of 'teams' has become part of current managerial rhetoric: the words 'self-managed work team' (SMWT). The SMWT, which suggests a new way of organizing work, is not the same as a 'work group': a SMWT is 'a group of employees who are responsible for managing and performing technical tasks that result in a product or service being delivered to an internal or external customer'.[10] The difference between work groups and SMWTs is explained in terms of the degree of interdependency and accountability. The interdependence among SMWT members is typically high, and the accountability for the work focuses primarily on the team as a whole rather than the individual group member. Another distinguishing

Source: Getty Images

plate 31 A self-managed work team allows employees in the core work unit to have sufficient autonomy to manage the work process

feature of SMWTs is their longevity: SMWTs are typically an integral part of a redesigned organizational structure, brought together for long-term performance goals.

Work teams can be classified according to their position in the organization's hierarchy and their assigned tasks. Figure 11.1 shows three types of work teams most commonly found in organizations. Teams that plan and run things are positioned in the top echelon (senior level) of the organization, teams that monitor things occupy the middle levels, and teams that make things occupy the lower levels of the organization. It is important to emphasize, however, that the nature of teams varies considerably among organizations, depending on whether they are engaged in value-added activities in small batches or large batches, or whether they provide financial or other services.

The formal definitions of work teams are not so different from the definition of a formal work group, which might explain why both words are used interchangeably in the OB literature. However, the conscious use of the word 'team' is not simply a question of semantics. As we discuss in Chapter 12, mainstream management rhetoric is awash with what Bendix called 'a vocabulary of motivation'.[11] In this instance, communication emphasizes the 'team' (with phrases like 'we must all pull together') and the 'family' (suggesting that employees are brothers and sisters and customers are family guests), using these metaphors to obfuscate the power differentials and conflicting interests between management and workers. Whether employees are organized into a 'work group' or a 'work team', the effectiveness of the work configuration will be the outcome of complex group behaviours and processes, which is the focus of the next section.

WEB LINK

www.managementhelp.org/grp_skll/ slf_drct/slf_drct.htm is an online library devoted to self-managed teams. At http://groups.yahoo.com/ people form their own social groups to exchange ideas. Visit the site and see how 'virtual groups' work.

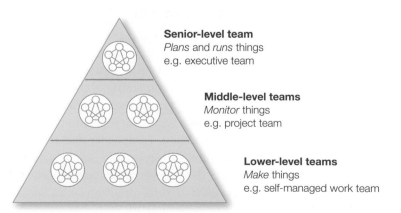

Senior-level team
Plans and *runs* things
e.g. executive team

Middle-level teams
Monitor things
e.g. project team

Lower-level teams
Make things
e.g. self-managed work team

figure 11.1 Classification of work teams

Group dynamics

group dynamics: the systematic study of the human behaviour in groups including, the nature of groups, group development, and the interrelations between individuals and groups, other groups, and other elements of formal organizations

Group dynamics is the study of human behaviour in groups.[12] The field studies the nature of groups, group development, and the interrelations between individuals and groups. Group dynamics or processes emphasize changes in the pattern of activities, the subjective perceptions of individual group members and their active involvement in group life. Studies on group dynamics by mainstream researchers draw attention to two sets of processes that underlie group processes: task-oriented activities and maintenance-oriented activities. Task-oriented activities undertaken by the group are aimed at accomplishing goals or 'getting the job done'. Maintenance-oriented activities, on the other hand, point to the subjective perceptions of group members and their active involvement in keeping acceptable standards of behaviour and a general state of well-being within the group. Conventional wisdom argues that the two processes constantly seek to coexist, and over-emphasis of one realm at the expense of the other leads to discontent and withdrawal. An effective group or team is one that creates a reasonable compromise between both realms.[13]

Some of the major factors influencing group dynamics are shown in Figure 11.2. The framework does not attempt to offer a theory of group dynamics, nor does it necessarily follow that all elements of the model must, or can, be applied to every work group. We offer it here as a useful heuristic for understanding the complexities of group dynamics. Four major elements are graphically depicted in the model: a context, team structure and processes, a series of outcomes, and a feedback loop which links the outcomes back to the other main components. We look at each of the first three elements over the next few pages.

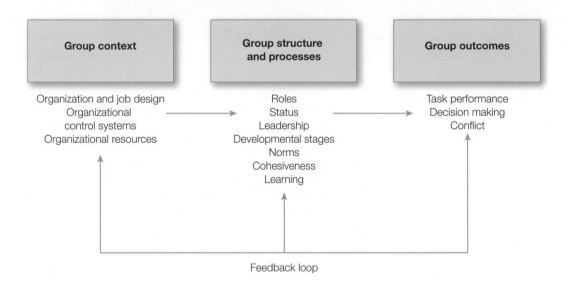

figure 11.2 A model of group dynamics

Group context

group context: refers to anything from the specific task a work group is engaged in to the broad environmental forces that are present in the minds of group members and may influence them

Although the work group or team is a structure in itself, it is also a subset of a larger structure, the organization. Thus the work group is constrained to operate within the structure of the organization, and **group context** refers to organizational and job design, organizational control systems, and resources.

The implementation of team-based working requires organizational restructuring. By restructuring we mean changing the core dimensions of the organization: its centralization, complexity and formality (see Chapter 15). Tasks and responsibilities must be designated within and between teams. Task interdependence, which refers to the level of relationship among members in the work activities, can affect group structure, processes and outcomes. Alternative work configurations are typically followed by alternative control systems. For example, when work groups are introduced, direct supervisory control of employees is typically replaced by computer-based control of group performance. The adoption of team work is normally contingent on management installing a system to control the redesigned work process.[14]

Resources are another contextual factor affecting group structure and processes. The amount of resources management is willing to commit to teams is directly related to the organizational context. Specifically, the policies and procedures of the organization must provide for sufficient physical (such as computer software), financial and human resources to enable the team to function and complete the task. Inadequate resources, it is argued, will delay group development and have a negative impact on group outcomes.[15]

Group structure and processes

Work groups and teams have a structure which influences the way members relate and interact with one another, and makes it possible to explain individual behaviour within the group. Have you ever noticed that when people come together in a new group, some listen while others talk? Such differences between group members serve as a basis for the formation of group structure. As differentiation takes place, social relations are formed between members. The stable pattern of relationships among the differentiated elements in the group is called group structure.

The group can be differentiated by a number of variables including size, roles, status and leadership. The size of the group plays a critical role in how group members interact with one another. Simmel pointed out that increasing the size alters the group's dynamics, since the increased number of relationships results in different interactions.[16] Figure 11.3 shows the incremental impact of group size on relationships. Two individuals form a single relationship; adding a third person results in three relations; a group of seven however has 21 relationships. According to Simmel, as groups grow beyond three people, the personal attachments between individuals become looser, and coalitions emerge in which some group members align themselves against other group members. Thus, the more impersonal relationships need additional formal rules and regulations. At the same time, the group's growth allows it to become more stable, because the intensity of the interactions is reduced, and because it becomes better able to withstand the loss of some members.

group structure: a stable pattern of social interaction among work group members created by a role structure and group norms

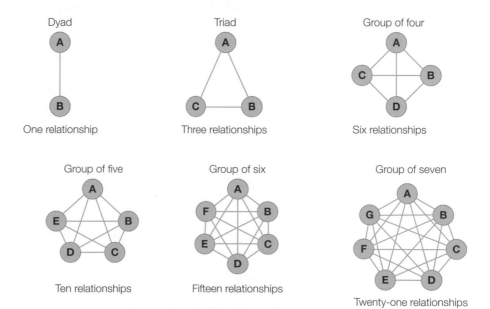

figure 11.3 The incremental effects of group size on relationships

role: a set of behaviours that people are expected to perform because they hold certain positions in a team and organization

role ambiguity: uncertainty about job duties, performance expectations, level of authority and other job conditions

role conflict: conflict that occurs when people face competing demands

role perceptions: a person's beliefs about what behaviours are appropriate or necessary in a particular situation, including the specific tasks that make up the job, their relative importance, and the preferred behaviours to accomplish those tasks

status: the social ranking of people, the position an individual occupies in society or a social group or a work organization

All group members are expected to carry out certain functions when they interact with one another. The set of expected behaviour patterns associated with a position within the group constitutes the role of the occupant of that position. The concept of role helps us understand how a member's behaviour is structured by the prescriptive dictates of the group. Role definition is often used as a diagnostic tool by management consultants to determine causes of poor team performance. Problems of role ambiguity – uncertainty on the group member's part about what exactly s/he is supposed to do – and role conflict – conflicting requests from more than one source – allegedly have far-reaching negative outcomes on group performance.[17]

Status is the relative ranking that a member holds, and indicates the value of that member as perceived by the group. Status is important because it motivates individuals and has consequences for their behaviour. Almost every work group has either a formal or informal leader, who can influence communications, decision making, learning and similar processes, thereby playing an important part in group's outcomes.

It is necessary, but not sufficient for team efficacy, to have an organization design strategy that incorporates adequate resources, effective control systems, role clarity and leadership. To be effective, managers and group members must learn to work in the new work structure. The group processes responsible for group development, norms, cohesiveness and learning are extremely important.

> For more information on team learning
> and team leadership, go to:
> http://web.mit.edu/ist/competency/summary.html
> www.managementandleadershipcouncil.org

WEB LINK

Group processes

group processes: refers to group member actions, communications and decision making

The term group processes refers to the manner in which group behaviour is constructed on a continuing basis. Orthodox OB theorists typically highlight the importance of developmental stages that a group must pass through: groups are born, they mature and they die. It is suggested that a group must reach the mature stage before it achieves maximum performance. Of course, it is also acknowledged that not all groups pass through all these stages, and some groups can become fixed in the early stage and remain ineffective and inefficient. A good example of the lifecycle metaphor is Tuckman and Jensen's five-stage cycle of group development model: forming, storming, norming, performing and adjourning.[18]

In the *forming* stage, individuals are brought together and there tends to be ambiguity about roles and tasks. Group members are polite as they learn about each other and attempt to establish 'ground rules' for accomplishing the assigned task(s). Dependency on the group leader is said to be high at this stage.

In the *storming* stage individual members become more proactive by taking on specific roles and responsibilities. Frequently members compete for positions in the group, and conflict occurs between individuals, and/or alliances are formed between members. The group leader must be able to facilitate dialogue and handle conflict at this stage.

When group members begin to accept differences of opinion, conform to their roles, and cooperate (for instance, sharing information), the group has reached what is called the *norming* stage. As a consensus forms around the group's goals and means of attainment, group cohesion grows.

High productivity is typically achieved at the *performing* stage of group development. A high level of trust in each group member is prevalent at this phase, and there is 'consensual validation' in the sense that members are positively valued for their specific attributes and qualities.

A work group does not exist infinitely. The *adjournment* stage refers to individuals leaving the group and being replaced by others, or to the group's disbandment. Social rituals, such as having a party, often accompany group disbandment.

Tuckman and Jensen's model is predicated on the premise that a group must go through each stage before being able to move on to the next, and every transition holds the potential risk of regression to an earlier stage. OB theorists taking a managerialist perspective have tended to interpret the five-stage model in terms of levels of performance, with group productivity being higher after the second stage. While this assumption may be correct, what makes a work group effective is more complex than this model acknowledges. Although the model has become entrenched in mainstream OB texts and in management training, more recently it has been shown 'to be of little or no assistance in getting teams to perform better'.[19]

An earlier critique of Tuckman and Jensen's five-stage model found the phenomenon of 'punctuated equilibrium' a more useful concept to explain group development.[20] Specifically, a team does not accomplish a great deal up to about the halfway point to completion (this midpoint occurs regardless of the time frame involved). At the midpoint, there is an acceleration of activity by members to accomplish their assigned work. In essence, the 'punctuated equilibrium' model characterizes work groups as exhibiting long periods of inertia interspersed with shorter bursts of activity, initiated primarily by their members' awareness of the impending completion deadline. This would suggest, therefore, that not all groups develop in a universal linear fashion.

The research on group development has drawn criticism because much of it has tended to be laboratory-based rather than workplace-based research. For example, old favourites like Tuckman and Jensen's model were developed from work with therapy, laboratory or training groups, not 'real teams in real contexts'. Group development models that predict linear sequential phases have particularly been criticized. As Kline graphically points out:

> Imagine the following situation. The cockpit crew of a 747 boards the plane twenty minutes before take-off. You are seated in seat 117B, and as the airplane rushes down runway nine you hope like hell that this team is past the storming stage of group development.[21]

She argues that there is something, personalities aside, about the aircrew that enables them to fly the aircraft safely, even when they have just met each one another. These 'contextual variables', she asserts, are powerful tools for understanding group dynamics and group performance.

Although alternative research suggests that every group does not go through all development stages, Tuckman and Jensen's model can be a useful heuristic for understanding group dynamics and why some groups fail to perform. A group might be ineffective and inefficient because individuals are pulling in different directions, since the goals of the group have not been agreed. Alternatively, individuals might have the tendency to dismiss or ridicule other's thoughts, ideas and feelings, which leads to low trust among the group. For all these reasons, effective group functioning and learning might be hindered. The main conclusion drawn from the group development models presented here is that a team-based organizational structure does not imply an effective and efficient organization. Top managers introducing team-based work structures need to attend to the development of group interactions.

Have you ever noticed that professors do not normally criticize other professors? Why? The answer is 'norms'! Groups significantly influence their members' behaviour through the operation of norms. Social norms are a set of expected

Source: Getty Images

plate 32 Organizations send their employees to outdoor corporate training centres where they learn to work as teams

patterns of behaviour that are established and shared by the group's members. Norms inform members what they ought and ought not to do under certain situations. A group's norms do not occur in a vacuum: they represent the interaction of historical, social and psychological processes. In the workplace, for example, a new employee joining a group will assess the norms for work effort from how most individuals in the group behave. In turn, members of the group observe the extent to which the new member's behaviour matches the group's norms. Norms develop in work groups around work activities (the means and speed), around attitudes and opinions that should be held by group members regarding the workplace, and around communications, concerning appropriate language.

group norms: the unwritten rules and expectations that specify or shape appropriate human behaviour in a work group or team

The Hawthorne studies[22] highlighted the importance of **group norms** to management theorists. The researchers identified three important norms: no 'rate-busting' (working too hard), no 'chiseling' (working too little), and no 'squealing' (telling the supervisor anything that could undermine the group). Group members who significantly deviated from these norms were subjected to either ridicule or physical punishment. Groups typically enforce norms that:

▷ facilitate the group's survival
▷ allow members to express the central values of the group
▷ reduce embarrassing interpersonal problems for group members – for instance, a ban on discussing religion or politics at work.[23]

Norms are communicated to new employees through a process called 'group socialization', whereby the new member learns the group's principal values and how these values are articulated through norms.

cohesiveness: refers to all the positive and negative forces or social pressures that cause individuals to maintain their membership in specific groups

The term **cohesiveness** refers to the complex forces that give rise to the perceptions by members of group identity and the attractiveness of group membership. The cohesiveness of a group has a major effect on the behaviour of its members, because higher cohesion amplifies the potency of group norms. A series of experiments conducted by Solomon Asch in 1952 and Stanley Milgram in 1963 suggested that group membership can engender conformity, and also that members are likely to follow the directions of group authority figures, even when it means inflicting pain on another individual.

A cohesive group can develop norms that can be a great asset to the organization: for example, a norm that prescribes voluntary overtime working when required. Equally, a cohesive group can undermine organizational goals: for example, by

WEB LINK

For more information on the experiments undertaken by Asch and Milgram, visit:
www.qeliz.ac.uk/psychology/Asch.htm
www.new-life.net/milgram.htm

enforcing conformity to a work effort below what is considered acceptable by managers. Not surprisingly, therefore, sources of group cohesiveness are of considerable interest to mainstream OB theorists and managers.

The attractiveness of a group is partly determined by its composition. Members of the group need to get along with each other, which might be difficult if members have very different values, attitudes towards work or interests. Research suggests that behaviour in work groups is shaped by a sex difference in aggressiveness, with male members engaging in more dominating behaviour than female members. Studies have found that in groups men talk more frequently, interrupt others and express anger more than women.[24] As a result, more men than women are chosen as group leaders. In institutions of learning, the experiences of work groups by women and faculty members from racial and ethnic minorities tend to differ significantly from the experiences of white male group members.[25]

Ensuring diversity in a work group or team is not only an equity matter; a lack of diversity might inhibit some of the benefits of group working. An early study suggests that moderate heterogeneity in a work group balances the requirements of cohesion and productivity.[26]

groupthink: the tendency of highly cohesive groups to value consensus at the price of decision quality

One notable disadvantage of groups that are *too* cohesive is that their decision-making ability can be impaired by what Janis termed 'groupthink'.[27] He defined this group phenomenon as a psychological drive for consensus at any cost, which suppresses dissent and the evaluation of alternatives in cohesive decision-making groups. Interestingly, to illustrate the concept of groupthink, Janis analysed the ill-fated attempt by President Kennedy's administrative team to invade Cuba in 1961. He argues that the executive group advising the US President displayed all the symptoms of groupthink: they were convinced of their invulnerability, and 'self-censorship' prevented members from expressing alternative views even when intelligence information did not align with the group's beliefs. There was, according to Janis, an illusion of unanimity, with silence being interpreted as consent. In other words, the pressures for conformity that can arise in a highly cohesive group can cloud members' judgement and the decision-making process.

Another example of groupthink occurred before the invasion of Iraq in 2003. The US Senate, investigating the intelligence leading up to the war, reported that President George W. Bush made declarative statements about Iraq's possession of weapons of mass destruction to build the case for war. However, among the scathing findings of the Senate's 2004 report on the build-up to the war was that the Central Intelligence Agency (CIA) ignored input from other US intelligence agencies, and that 'the intelligence community was suffering from a collective "group think", which led analysts and collectors and managers to presume that Iraq had active and growing WMD programmes'.[28]

WEB LINK

For more information on how 'groupthink' can influence decision making, visit:
www.afirstlook.com
www.abacon.com
Search for 'groupthink'.

We turn now to another aspect of interaction within groups and teams: work-based learning. It will be apparent from this review of team theory and practice that expanding workers' skill sets and empowering workers to make prescribed decisions has significant implications for learning in the workplace. Rather than learning a narrow set of skills, the need for flexibility and interchangeability necessitates that workers acquire new knowledge and technical skills to perform the new repertoire of tasks. In addition, the experience of 'lived reality' – decision making, trial and error experimentation – and the social relations associated with teams create their own dynamic environment for enhancing informal work-based learning.

empowerment: a psychological concept in which people experience more self-determination, meaning, competence, and impact regarding their role in the organization

If the group or team is going to make its own decisions, control quality, and control its own behaviour, members must engage in learning. Adult educators and

HRD theorists have suggested that in order for a group or team to learn, individual members of the unit must be able to learn: that is, to experiment, reflect on previous action, engage in dialogue, and share and build on their individual knowledge.[29] As we pointed out in Chapter 8, adopting a culture of learning in the workplace impacts on work organization, employment relations and leadership style.

Group outcomes

Most group theory examines group outcomes in terms of group performance or effectiveness. And since the diffusion of team-based working, much recent research on teams has been occupied with investigating the link between teams and performance. Three aspects of group outcomes are examined briefly in this section: task performance, decision making and conflict.

Work groups with a high level of cohesion and norms consistent with organizational objectives will, it is argued, have a high level of task performance.[30] Figure 11.4 illustrates the relationship between group cohesiveness and task performance.

> Sociologists maintain that relationships formed in groups shape members' behaviour. Think about your own experience of working in a group. What norms and values did the group exhibit? Did any particular members challenge a particular group norm? If so, how did the other group members respond to the challenge? If they did not, why not?
>
> STOP AND REFLECT

Work groups appear to support employees' need for relatedness, which might explain the improved job performance of employees in SMWTs.[31] One advantage of a cohesive group is that their decision-making ability can be significantly superior to the total of all individual capabilities. In mathematical logic, this phenomenon of groups, called synergy, suggests that 2+2 is greater than 4. The concept is used extensively in mainstream texts to understand group processes and to justify the implementation of work teams. The general assumption is that moderately cohesive work teams (sufficiently diverse to avoid groupthink), together with 'enlightened' leadership, are best able to encourage the group processes – in particular the sharing of information and group learning – that result in superior group performance.

In organizations, work groups do not exist in isolation; they are linked by a network of relationships with other groups. Although it is not inevitable, inter-group conflict can be another outcome of group-based work structures. There are many definitions for the term *conflict*. A broad definition describes conflict as 'that behaviour by organization members which is expended in opposition to other members'.[32] Two main explanations of inter-group conflict exist. The first explanation is known as *social identity theory*, which argues that individuals use group membership as a source of pride and self-worth. In order to feel such pride individuals assume that their group is superior to others. When a group is successful, members' self-esteem increases, and conversely when group members' self-esteem is threatened, they are more prone to disparage members of other groups. As a consequence inter-group bias and conflict occur.[33] The second explanation is referred to as functional theory, and assumes that groups form for functional reasons.[34] Functional theorists argue that conflict is the result of one group's perceiving another group as a threat to its goal attainment.[35]

functional theory: a sociological perspective that emphasizes that human action is governed by relatively stable structures

The traditional managerial perspective tends to hold that conflicts between individuals and groups, and between workers and management, are a bad thing. An alternative perspective, the interactionist view, is that conflicts in work groups are productive and can increase rather than decrease job performance.[36] The interactionists suggest that group leaders should encourage an ongoing 'optimum' level of conflict, which allows the group to be self-critical, creative and viable. But notions of 'win–lose' scenarios complicate estimates of what constitutes an 'optimal level' of conflict. It has been suggested, for instance, that the more the inter-group conflict is defined as a 'win–lose' situation, the more predictable are the effects of the conflict on the social relationships within the group and on relations between work groups.[37]

interactionism: what people do when they are in one another's presence, for example, in a work group or team

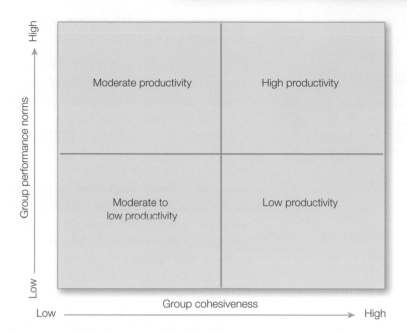

figure 11.4 Cohesiveness, norms and group performance

For examples of team working in European and North American companies, visit:
www.honda.com www.sony.com
http://ptcpartners.com/Team/home.htm
www.dti.gov.uk/employment/useful-links/index.html
Search for '2004 employee relations survey'.
This site gives a summary of the UK 2004 survey, including a section on work teams

WEB LINK

Clearly, group processes are complex and contentious, and are strongly influenced by the individual characteristics of team members and by dominant gender, race and power patterns. The wealth of research and interest in work teams over the last decade is related to the changing fashion in US and European management theory on how to compete against Japanese companies.

Work teams and management theory

The theoretical interest in work groups or teams draws upon human relations, sociotechnical and Japanese perspectives on organizational design.[38] Pioneering work on human relations by Roethlisberger and Dickson, Mayo, Maslow and McGregor focused top managers' attention on the importance of social relations within work groups.[39]

The collaborative research by Roethlisberger, an industrial psychologist from Harvard University, and Dickson, a manager at the Western Electric plant, involved studying the job performance of two groups of front-line workers doing identical work but in separate rooms. Each work group's productivity was carefully monitored. One work group – the study group – experienced ergonomic changes including increasing the intensity of the lighting in the workshop. The study group's productivity increased. The other work group – the control group – experienced no changes in lighting. However, to the astonishment of the researchers, its productivity increased also. Even more mystifying to the researchers, when the level of light intensity was lowered for the study group, the results showed that output continued to go up. After repeated experiments over many years, the researchers began to make connections between social interaction and job performance. In 1939, Roethlisberger and Dickson wrote:

> The study of the bank wiremen showed that their behaviour at work could not be understood without considering the informal organization of the group and the relation of this informal organization to the total social organization of the company. The work activities of the group, together with their satisfactions and

dissatisfactions, had to be viewed as manifestations of a complex pattern of interrelations.[40]

After the Second World War, the work of Maslow and McGregor helped US human relations advocates to clarify their perspective, with its focus on the interrelations between workers and the quality of the employment relationship.

In Europe, much of the early research on work teams was conducted within the framework of sociotechnical systems theory. This theory developed from work in 1951 on autonomous work teams in the British coal mining industry under the supervision of Trist and Bamforth. These researchers proposed that 'responsible autonomy' should be granted to primary work groups, and that group members should learn more than one role, so that interchangeability of tasks would be possible within the group. The flexibility would permit the completion of sub-whole units. The studies showed that the labour process in mining could be better understood in terms of two systems: the technical system – including machinery and equipment – and the social system, including the social relations and interactions among the miners.

Later advocates of the sociotechnical systems approach to organizational design argued that work teams provide a work regime for achieving the 'best match' between technical and social considerations or 'systems'. The term 'best match' is used to describe the relationship between the social and technological systems of the organization, where each is sensitive to the demands of the other.[41]

Attempts to implement the sociotechnical systems approach have included work redesign to 'enrich' jobs. The concept of job enrichment refers to a number of different processes of rotating, enlarging and aggregating tasks. It increases the range of tasks, skills and control workers have over the way they work, either individually or in teams. Job enrichment theory, also known as job characteristics theory, was given theoretical prominence by the work of Turner and Lawrence, and Hackman and Oldham.[42] As a counter to the thinking underlying Taylorism and Fordism, the job enrichment model has been influential in the design of work teams. It suggests a casual relationship between five core job characteristics and the worker's psychological state. If this relationship is positive, it leads in turn to positive outcomes. The five core job characteristics contained in the model are defined as:

▷ *Skill variety*: the degree to which the job requires a variety of different activities in carrying out the work, requiring the use of a number of the worker's skills and talents.
▷ *Task identity*: the degree to which the job requires completion of a whole and identifiable piece of work.
▷ *Task significance*: the degree to which the job has a substantial impact on the lives or work of other people.
▷ *Autonomy*: the degree to which the job provides substantial freedom, independence and discretion to the worker in scheduling the work and in determining the procedures to be used in carrying it out.
  ▷ *Feedback*: the degree to which the worker possesses information on the actual results of her or his performance.

The more that a job possesses the five core job characteristics, the greater the motivating potential of the job (see Figure 11.5).

The model also recognizes the importance of learning to achieve motivation and outcome goals. Workers' work-related learning is implicitly linked to the existence of the 'moderators' – knowledge and skills, growth need strength, and context satisfaction – contained in the model. The presence of moderators is used to explain why jobs that are theoretically high in motivating potential will not automatically generate high levels of motivation and satisfaction for all workers.

STOP AND REFLECT

Think about your experience of working in a group. Do the Roethlisberger and Dickson findings resonate with any aspect of your own view on group working? Why?

systems theory: a set of theories based on the assumption that social entities, such as work organizations, can be viewed as if they were self-regulating bodies exploiting resources from their environment (inputs), transforming the resources (exchanging and processing) to provide goods and services (outputs) in order to survive

job enrichment: employees are given more responsibility for scheduling, coordinating and planning their own work

job characteristics model: a job design model that relates the motivational properties of jobs to specific personal and organizational consequences of those properties

job enlargement: increasing the number of tasks employees perform in their job

job rotation: the practice of moving employees form one job to another

job satisfaction: a person's attitude regarding his or her job and work content

STOP AND REFLECT

What do you think of this job characteristics model? Think about any jobs you have had. Can you use this model to assess the 'quality' of the work you were paid for? What is missing from the model?

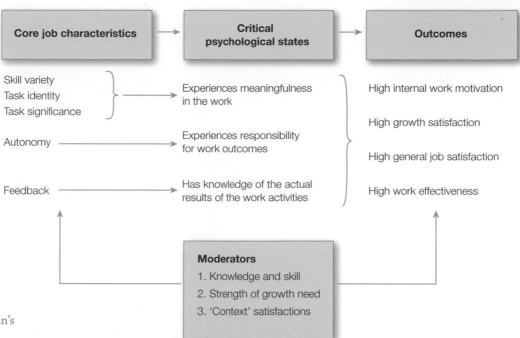

figure 11.5 Oldham and Hackman's job characteristics model

The argument goes that an employee with a low 'growth need' is less likely to experience a positive outcome when her or his work is 'enriched'. Thus, the neo-human relations approach to job design in general, and the job characteristic model in particular, emphasized the fulfilment of social or relatedness needs by recomposing fragmented jobs. Under certain circumstances, self-managed teams could provide an alternative to individual job enrichment.

The quality of work and work-related learning in small SMWTs rests on five principles of 'good' job design.

▷ The first principle is wholeness: the scope of the job is such that it includes all the tasks to complete a product or process.

▷ The second principle involves individual and group learning and development. Opportunities exist to engage in a variety of fulfilling and meaningful tasks, allowing team members to learn a range of skills within a community of practice, and facilitating job flexibility.[43]

▷ The third principle relates to governance and self-regulation. With the focus on product differentiation and the rise of knowledge-based economies, the imperatives of work do not permit managers to master all the challenges. As a result, they must allow team and project members to assume responsibility for the pace of work, problem solving and quality control.

▷ The fourth principle involves occupational wellness and safety. Work is designed to maintain the safety and wellness of team members and to support a good work–life balance.[44]

▷ Finally, the fifth principle is social interaction. The job design permits interaction, cooperation and reflexivity among team members.

Drawing upon the work of Klein and McKinlay et al.,[45] the principles of 'good' job design are achieved by management interventions in the technical, governance and sociocultural dimensions of work (see Figure 11.6).

The horizontal axis represents the functional or technical tasks that are required to produce the product or service. Group working involves combining a number of tasks on the horizontal axis to increase the cycle times and create more complete and hence more meaningful jobs. The technical dimension is then regarded as the

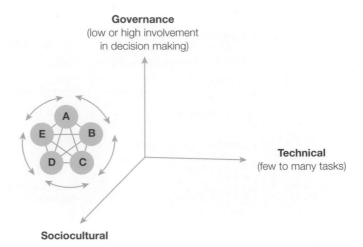

figure 11.6 The three dimensions of group work: technical, governance and social

central purpose of work teams, and is concerned with the range of tasks undertaken by members, multi-skilling and functional flexibility. The vertical axis represents the governance aspects of the labour process, and shows the extent of workers' autonomy on the job. The third axis, the diagonal, represents the sociocultural aspects of work, one of which is the social interaction that takes place in work groups. The sociocultural dimension is perhaps the most interesting as far as OB is concerned, since it represents the behaviour or 'normative' considerations – what ought to happen – to secure effective team performance. This dimension of group work recognizes that employees' compliance and cooperation depend upon the complex interplay of social interactions in the group. It should be noted that in a five-member team, there are ten relationships (see Figure 11.3).

The SMWT represents an *ideal-type* work regime because it restores the craft paradigm by enlarging tasks on the horizontal axis and by giving members greater autonomy over how the work is accomplished on the vertical axis. The movement along the diagonal axis represents the implications of group working in terms of group norms, group cohesion and organizational culture. The three dimensions of work organization in Figure 11.6 help to illustrate the point that top managers make strategic choices regarding how work is designed, and alternative work structures have an impact on social behaviour and organizational culture.

Both managerial and critical observers agree there is evidence that a growing number of organizations have been successful in devolving decision making to work groups, and getting members to think and act like managers. Who are the prime beneficiaries of team-based working? Visit www.workteams.org and read Chapter 11, 'New economy, new organizations', in Thompson and McHugh's *Work Organizations*.[46] When work teams are introduced, how do organizations shape employee attitudes in spheres such as cooperation and self-discipline?

Work teams: ending bureaucracy and extending employee empowerment?

Whereas groups as social entities go back thousands of years, management interest in work teams is much more recent. From early experiments in sociotechnical job design techniques in the 1970s, teams became the hallmark of postmodern work organizations in the 1990s. Teamworking has been popularized by mainstream OB theorists and management consultants as a panacea for curing inflexible work systems and alleged inefficient bureaucratic structures, and enhancing employee higher-order 'growth' and 'relatedness' needs by job enrichment and empowerment.

Motivated by the prospect of connecting the synergy of work teams with corporate goals, managers have focused on teams to help improve organizational performance. In Sweden, the most celebrated example of work teams was introduced at the new Volvo car plant in Uddevalla in 1987. It was reported that the new assembly line avoided the classic problems associated with Fordism.[47] However, in 1992 Volvo closed its Uddevalla factory. For many OB researchers, the Swedish plant had become an icon for a European, human-centred and productive organization, and its closure suggested that Taylorist and neo-Taylorist solutions still dominate management thinking in the automobile industry.[48]

In critical accounts of work teams, in which group practices are connected to the class power relations in which they are embedded, there is considerable debate over whether or not Japanese-style work teams constitute a significant departure from Western-style 'high-autonomy' work teams.[49] Some argue that the difference lies in the fact that Japanese-style work teams utilize a control orientation that depends upon 'self-control'. Others persuasively argue that self-managed teams create a work culture that enhances management control via self-regulation. This insight into group dynamics focuses on the socialization and organization culture, and on behaviour deemed necessary to make teams work effectively.[50]

The discussion on different group and team concepts highlights the array of definitions, and the need for commentators to define work groups carefully if comparisons are to be made. As mentioned earlier, the reason that so many organizations have 're-engineered' work processes around teams is that managers are looking for improvements in productivity resulting from the positive synergy associated with teams. Thus, the perceived connections between the way work is designed and organizational performance need to be appreciated to understand the current wave of corporate interest in teams.

In standard accounts of teamworking, team-based work regimes do not necessarily lead to improved organizational performance. People must learn to work in team-based structures: clearly a lesson from the sociotechnical theory, which acknowledges the importance of the dialectic relationship between the technical and social aspects of work. In critical accounts of teams there is deep scepticism. Work teams do not eradicate three chronic capitalist antagonisms that centre on issues of managerial control: producing goods and services for a global market, which creates uncertainty and pressure to control costs; designing work structures and employee relations systems that maximize shareholder interests; and managerial top-down control over employee behaviour in contrast to employee autonomy.

Contrary to the management rhetoric, work teams involve elaborate computer information systems developed to support a control-oriented management philosophy.[51] This observation illustrates the work of critical scholars who tend to be interested in understanding the power relations in team design. For example, one study found that while team members had increased autonomy in performing their work and additional responsibilities, managers had actually increased their control over value-added activities through a computerized production system. This control-oriented approach can be given the name 'computer-controlled-autonomy'.[52] Another study offered a scathing account of teamworking in white-collar work, arguing 'that workers experience forms of team organization as being no less coercive than classically understood Taylorism'.[53]

Paradox in team-based work

How are we to interpret the effects of group membership on employee behaviour? As with other aspects of organizational behaviour we cover in this text, it depends on the author's approach to the subject. For some, team synergy can be a panacea to bureaucratic ills: 'Teams foster a sense of dignity, self-worth, and a greater commitment to achieving the performance that makes an organization competitive.'[54] For others, teamworking, far from being 'empowering', actually intensifies management control over workers by cultivating a form of self-management through constant peer and self-monitoring.[55] This critical perspective focuses, among other things, on the effect of team ideology and behaviour on the working lives of workers. Whereas the managerialist approach found in most standard OB texts focuses on the technical and the empowering dimensions of teams and team efficacy, a feature of a critical approach is a focus on the normative dimension of groups and teams, the 'tyranny' arising from teamwork and paradoxes in team-based work structures.

A paradox involves ambiguity and inconsistency, and both are evident in work group design. A central pillar of teamwork involves combining a number of tasks on the horizontal axis. This has led many traditional scholars to argue that SMWTs reverse Tayloristic deskilling tendencies by enhancing workers' skills. It is suggested that SMWTs exemplify the re-emergence of the craft model.[56] Critical OB theorists, however, have challenged the popular logic that SMWTs lead to a more highly skilled workforce. Detractors argue that although they apparently give limited empowerment to workers, they do not necessarily reverse the general 'deskilling' trend, but generate new forms of control which assist management in extracting higher productivity from workers via work intensification as the range of horizontal and vertical tasks expands.[57]

Those subscribing to this critique almost invariably draw parallels with Taylorism and Fordism. A number of accounts stress that with the assistance of micro-technology, re-engineering work into teams is an 'up-dating of Taylor's crusade against custom and practice in which the silicon chip plays an equivalent role in [re-engineering] to that performed by the stop watch in Scientific Management'.[58] In other words, it provides a disguised form of intensified managerial control. Others offer more optimistic analyses, in which the outcomes of teamworking are less deterministic. Whether work teams result in the 'upskilling' or 'deskilling' of workers depends, amongst other things, on factors such as batch size, managerial choice and negotiation.[59]

Critical organizational theorists have illustrated paradox in another way. The behavioural dimension of the teamwork model emphasizes how SMWTs empower workers while simultaneously increasing management's control over the labour process. This is achieved using both 'hard' technology (such as computers) and 'social' technology (such as group norms). When decision making is devolved to the team, members begin to think and act like managers, and they internalize company values. In this way, small SMWTs influence the attitude and behaviour of their members by creating a work culture that reproduces the conditions of employees' own subordination. In other words, team members perceive a moral obligation to increase their level of effort on the job, and 'put in a full day' because of peer group pressure, or 'clan control', thereby unwittingly creating a control culture system.[60] Critical studies have found team members' discipline to be more punitive than that of the managers: 'Team members are tougher on fellow workers than management is.'[61] A 50-year-old male explained how peer-group surveillance influenced the behaviour of the team's members like this:

> I think it's a matter of conscience. A person who under the old system might go away for an hour, now he will think twice: Are they [co-workers] going to

think they are carrying me because I've been away? … Because you are a close-knit community in the [team] system. You get niggly remarks: 'Where have you been all morning?' That sort of thing, and it gradually works its way in psychologically.[62]

Few employees have a 'good' job

Despite the hype about improved quality of work arising from the growth of teamworking, it is reported that 'only 39 per cent of workers think that their job is "good", according to new research from the Chartered Institute of Personnel and Development (CIPD)'. 'Good' roles are defined as 'exciting but not too stressful', according to a new report from the UK institute, *Reflections on Employee Well-Being and the Psychological Contract*.

The research explored how employees felt about their job and their relationships with managers and colleagues. It concluded that employers should make jobs more appealing and interesting to improve commitment from employees. 'Most jobs can be made interesting or even exciting if they are well managed,' Mike Emmott, CIPD

employee relations adviser, said. An interesting and exciting job was one with variety and security, and where the role of the employee was clear. Many workers did not believe that their job had these qualities. A fifth of respondents thought that the demands of their job were unrealistic, and the same proportion found their jobs either very or extremely stressful.

Nic Marks, head of well-being research at the New Economics Foundation and co-author of the report, said that interest and excitement were key elements in the psychological contract between employers and employees. 'If employees don't feel their role is exciting, this will be reflected in underperformance and their lack of commitment and satisfaction,' he said.

Source: adapted from Julie Griffiths, Personnel Management Online, 9 August 2005

In their account of team learning processes, Kasl and colleagues unwittingly provide further evidence of the control culture generated by work teams.[63] When one particular work team 'failed', some team members left the company, while others worked on 'disheartened'. Moreover:

> The team became the laughing stock of the whole company and the people who weren't involved in it at all, the people who worked on a different floor would walk right in and say, 'How's logistics, ha ha ha?' They heard about it, it was like this big disaster.[64]

The discourse on work teams illustrates competing interpretations. On the one hand, the thinking and prescriptions in mainstream accounts tend to focus on the technical and the 'growth need' dimension of team-based work configurations, as well as the links between group processes and group performance. On the other hand, critical evaluations of teamworking focus on paradoxes and the effect of team ideology and behaviour on workers. Thus, arguably teamworking resembles Morgan's 'psychic prison', in the sense that peer pressure and self-surveillance are the norm, and this more accurately resembles reality than the optimistic notion of the learning-empowering self-managed work team.[65]

Chapter summary

- ❏ In this chapter we have examined the background, nature and behavioural implications of work groups. We have suggested that the current wave of interest in team-based work structures is linked to business strategy and the perceived shortcomings of large bureaucratic organizational structures.

- ❏ The nature of work groups was explored through the concepts of size, norms, cohesiveness and group learning. Management try to persuade workers of the need for working beyond contract for the 'common' good and to engage in self-regulatory norms. The self-managed work team is said to be upskilling and empowering workers.

- ❏ However we have also gone beyond management rhetoric, and presented arguments and evidence to suggest that self-managed teams shift the focus away from the hierarchy, directive and bureaucratic control processes, to a culture of self-control mechanisms.

- ❏ The discussion has emphasized that orthodox and critical accounts of teamworking provide very different views of this form of work organization and employment relations. Both perspectives however conceptualize teamworking as influencing individual behaviour and contributing to improved organizational performance. While both approaches make employee autonomy central to their analyses, each conceptualizes team membership as having a different influence. Additionally, autonomy is theorized as leading to different outcomes (such as growth need versus self-regulation) in each perspective.

Key concepts

group dynamics	302	peer pressure	314–15
group processes	304	psychic prison	315
group structure	303	work group	299
job characteristic model	310	work team	300

Chapter review questions

1. How useful are group development models for understanding group or team behaviour?
2. What effect, if any, do you expect workforce diversity to have on group processes and outcomes?
3. 'Self-managed work teams are simply attempts by managers to control individuals at work by mobilizing group processes.' Do you agree or disagree? Discuss.
4. Students often complain about doing group projects. Why? Relate your answer to group processes and the critique of self-managed work teams.

Further reading

Kasl, E., Marsick, V. and Dechant, K. (1997) 'Teams as learners', *Journal of Applied Behavioral Sciences*, **33** (2), pp. 227–46.

Proctor, S. and Mueller, F. (eds) (2000). *Teamworking*, Basingstoke: Macmillan Business.

Sewell, G. (1998) 'The discipline of teams: the control of team-based industrial work through electronic and peer surveillance', *Administrative Science Quarterly*, **43**, pp. 406–69.

Chapter case study: *Teams at Land Rock Alliance Insurance*

Background

Since the 1940s, the use of asbestos in building materials and other products has led to many claims for damages as a result of personal injury or wrongful death. The procedure for those making claims is complicated and time-consuming. Insurance companies employ groups of employees trained to process the claims from each particular industry. The employees are given information on the history, use and current medical research results on the product. The processing of each individual claim application form is tedious but very important: any mistakes may affect the total amount paid to the claimant.

Land Rock Alliance Insurance has successfully bid for the contract to process the claims for over 213,000 asbestosis-related chest impaired cases (ACD) and vibration white finger (VWF) victims, their partners or descendants.

The company

Land Rock Alliance Insurance's main office is based in Sheffield, England. The company has decided to open a branch office in Edinburgh to manage the new contract. It will be dedicated to processing the asbestosis and VWF claims. The plan is to hire 60 new employees including supervisors and line managers. Senior managers at head office, however, disagree on how the work should be organized at the new office.

Planning meeting

At the meeting to review how the work will be organized at the Edinburgh office, Eleanor Brennan, the HR director, suggested it would be more effective and efficient to create four teams of around 15 employees, with each team processing the claims according to geographical area: Scotland, Wales, northern England and southern England. She explained that each application form would be processed by team members, to enable each member to complete the whole processing task and to contribute to the recommendation of the final settlement. Presenting some of the advantages of teamworking, Eleanor commented, 'The synergy generated by teamworking and communication will enhance efficiency and motivate employees to actively participate in reaching a decision in optimum time.' She argued that there was a direct link between job enrichment and high performance.

However, the director of facilities, Thomas Campion, strongly disagreed. He informed the assembled management team that in his opinion, 'self-regulated teams were b*** s***!' Besides, work teams required a much longer training period for employees. Moreover, it was his belief that 'increased communication impeded decision making rather than enhanced it'. Campion, continuing to dominate the meeting, outlined an alternative work arrangement for the processing of claimants' forms. The work, he said, was to be divided into three major steps:

Step 1: Scrutinize and verify biographical details, DOB, gender.
Step 2: Scrutinize and verify employment details, start/end/job description.
Step 3: Scrutinize and verify medical history including lifestyle (such as smoker or non-smoker, or whether there was evidence of exposure to second-hand smoke).

Of the 60 new employees, 20 would be trained to complete task one, 20 to complete task two, and 20 to complete task three. Each major step in the claim process would also have a supervisor, a technical advisor and section manager. Organizing the work this way, Campion insisted, would optimize training time, and enable the easy replacement of any employee resigning from the company. Individual employees would be assigned a target to achieve each month, which would determine an annual bonus payment. Every six months, their section manager would appraise each employee based on how quickly he or she successfully processed the application forms.

Task

Workings individually or in teams, provide a written recommendation for or against teamworking at the Edinburgh office.

Sources of additional information

Francis, H. (2003) 'Teamworking and change: managing the contradictions', *Human Resource Management Journal*, **13** (3), pp. 71–89.

Kuipers, B. S. and de Witte, M. C. (2005) 'Teamwork: a case study on development and performance', *International Journal of Human Resource Management*, 16 (2), pp. 185–201.

Websites: Centre for the Study of work groups: www.workteams.unt.edu; Studies of social loafing: www.theabc.org/work.htm

Note

This case study was written by Carolyn Forshaw, Thompson Rivers University, Kamloops, Canada.

Web-based assignment

Work groups and teams is one of the most important topics of organizational behaviour, and given that many students have experienced group working and will be called upon to work in groups in organizations, it is important to reflect on how groups influence human behaviour.

For this assignment we would like you to gain more information on work teams by visiting www.workteams.org; www.dti.gov.uk/er/emar/2004wers.htm. In addition, you are asked to explore examples of team working in European and North American companies by visiting the following websites: www.honda.com
www.sony.com
http://ptcpartners.com/Team/home.htm
www.dti.gov.uk/er/emar/2004wers.htm

What main principles can be identified as 'good' job design when applied to work teams? Looking at the companies that have introduced teams, what behaviours or 'norms' are expected of employees? How does the team-based model impact on other aspects of management such as HRM? Discuss your findings with other students on your course.

OB in films

The film *Twelve Angry Men* (1957) examines the behaviour of 12 members of a jury who have to decide on the innocence or guilt of a young man from a working-class background. At the beginning, 11 jurors are convinced of the youth's guilt and wish to declare him guilty without further discussion. One member of the jury (played by Henry Fonda) has reservations and persuades the other members to review the evidence. After reviewing the evidence the jury acquits the defendant.

A modern version of this film can be seen in a 2005 episode of the television series *Judge John Deed*, in which Judge Deed (played by Martin Shaw) serves as a member of a jury and persuades the other members to review the evidence in a sexual assault case.

What group concepts do the film or the *Judge John Deed* episode illustrate? What types of power are possessed by the characters played by Henry Fonda and Martin Shaw? What pattern of influencing behaviour is followed by Henry Fonda and Martin Shaw?

Notes

1   Manz and Sims (1993: vii).

2   Johnson and Johnson (2000).

3   For example, Katzenbach and Smith (1994), Kline (1999), Orsburn and Moran (2000).

4   Procter and Mueller (2000).

5   See Bratton (1992), Proctor and Mueller (2000), Thompson and Ackroyd (1995), Sewell (1998), Wells (1993).

6   Hertog and Tolner (1998).

7   Buchanan (2000: 33–4).

8   Johnson and Johnson (2000: 539).

9   Katzenbach and Smith (1994: 45).

10 Yeatts and Hyten (1998: xiiii).

11 Bendix (1956).

12 Johnson and Johnson (2000).

13 Crawley (1978), Hertog and Tolner (1998), Gil et al. (2005).

14 Bratton (1992).

15 Kline (1999).

16 Simmel (1908/1950).

17 Kline (1999).

18 Tuckman and Jensen (1977).

19 Kline (1999: 34).

20 Gersick (1988).

21 Kline (1999: 5).

22 Mayo (1946).

23 Feldman (1984).

24 See Wilson (2003), especially pp. 181–3.

25 Smith and Calasanti (2005).

26 Hackman and Oldham (1980).

27 Janis (1972).

28 Quoted by Paul Koring, 'Iraq war based on "flawed" reports', *Globe and Mail,* 10 July 2004, p. A11.

29 For example, see Senge (1990) and O'Brien and Buono (1996).

30 Banker et al. (1996), Cohen and Bailey (1997), Steiner (1972).

31 See Horwitz et al. (2003).

32 Thompson (1960: 389), cited by Robbins (1990: 411).

33 Tajfel (1978, 1981), Turner (1987), Miller and Brewer (1984).

34 Sherif and Sherif (1982).

35 Johnson and Johnson (2000), Kline (1999), Sherif et al. (1961).

36 De Dreu and Van de Vliert (1997).

37 Johnson and Johnson (2000).

38 Bratton (1992), Yeatts and Hyten (1998), Benders and van Hootegem (1999), Procter and Mueller (2000).

39 Roethlisberger and Dickson (1939), Mayo (1946), Maslow (1954), McGregor (1960).

40 Roethlisberger and Dickson (1939: 551–2), quoted by Heatts and Hyten (1998: 6).

41 Yeatts and Hyten (1998).

42 Turner and Lawrence (1965), Hackman and Oldham (1980).

43 Hoeve and Nieuwenhuis (2006).

44 Lowe (2000).

45 Klein (1994).

46 Thompson and McHugh (2006).

47 In *Business Week*, August 1989.

48 Cressey (1993).

49 See for example Elger and Smith (1994), Procter and Mueller (2000).

50   Thompson and Wallace (1996).

51   Heatts and Hyten (1998).

52   Bratton (1992).

53   Baldry et al. (1998: 168–9).

54   Manz and Sims (1993: 10).

55   See for example Thompson and McHugh (2006).

56   Piore and Sabel (1984).

57   Turnbull (1986), Sayer (1986), Tomaney (1990), Clarke (1997), Malloch (1997), Willmott (1995).

58   Thompson (1989: 96).

59   Bratton (1992).

60   Burawoy (1979, 2002), Sewell (1998), Shalla (1997), Wells (1993), Wood (1986).

61   Wells (1993: 75).

62   Quoted in Bratton (1992: 186).

63   Kasl, Marsick and Dechant (1997).

64   Kasl, Marsick and Dechant (1997: 238).

65   In his book *Images of Organizations* (1997: 199), Morgan explains that the notion of organizations as psychic prisons is a metaphor which connects the idea that organizations are a psychic phenomena, in the sense that they are ultimately constructed and sustained by conscious and unconscious processes, with the belief that people can actually become imprisoned or confined by the ideas, thoughts, and actions to which these processes give rise.

chapter 12

Communications

Homo sapiens should really be called *homo fabulans* – the teller of stories – because storytelling is central to our understanding of our place in the world, our very identity.[1]

Language is the site of the power struggle.[2]

Ancient rhetoricians were well aware that language is a powerful force for moving people to action.[3]

chapter outline

▷ Introduction
▷ Perspectives on communication
▷ Communication and management
▷ Channels of communication
▷ Leadership, persuasion and communication
▷ Communication and cultural diversity
▷ Gender and communication: 'She said, he said'
▷ Communication and paradox
▷ Chapter summary
▷ Chapter review questions
▷ Further reading
▷ Chapter case study: Edenvale Hospital
▷ Web-based assignment
▷ OB in films
▷ Notes

chapter objectives

After reading this chapter, you should be able to:

▷ discuss the importance of communication in the workplace
▷ discuss alternative perspectives on managing diversity in the organization
▷ explain the communication process, including non-verbal communication
▷ understand the use of communication in the leadership process
▷ understand the relationships between culture, gender and communication
▷ appreciate the existence of paradox in communication processes in the workplace.

Introduction

The quotes that open this chapter address the core themes of power, the relationship between the self and the social, and gender. The orthodox view of language is that it is a means of communicating ideas. People express themselves to each other in symbolic form. Language is a powerful force for moving people to action, which emphasizes its persuasive force. It is used by those in charge of organizations as a means of shaping and controlling members' behaviour. In the modern organization, where it is claimed that flexibility, learning and innovation are key issues, the processes of dialogue and communication have become critical core skills for managers and non-managers alike.[4]

dialogue: a process of conversation among team members in which they learn about each other's mental models and assumptions, and eventually form a common model for thinking within the team

The exchange of information and the transmission of meaning are the very essence of formal work organizations. Information about the organization's products, services, its external competitors and its people is essential to management, workers, shareholders and customers. The string of accounting scandals that rocked the US business community in the summer of 2002 illustrate how information that is communicated (or not communicated) helps to define a certain type of behaviour we expect from the organizations we deal with. Communication in formal organizations, however, is a more complex process than simply information disclosure.

communication: the process by which information is transmitted and understood between two or more people

According to the behaviourial perspective on communication, it is a symbolic process in which individuals act to exchange perceptions and ultimately to build a knowledge bank for themselves and for others, for the purpose of shaping future actions.[5] Language allows for the possibility of meaningful social interaction, and shapes the self – that part of an individual's identity composed of self-image and self-awareness. Language is also closely connected to power, and it shapes gender relations in organizations and the wider society. According to the symbolic interactionism thesis, identity is created through interaction with others. Language – broadly understood as a system of signification – is the most important source of symbolic meaning in human social life. Symbolic interactionism, which originates from the work of the American philosopher George Herbert Mead (1863–1931), is concerned with how language enables individuals to become self-conscious beings, aware of their own individuality.

symbolic interactionism: the sociological approach that views society as the sum of the interactions of individuals and groups.

language: a system of symbols that express ideas and enable people to think and communicate with one another

The key element in this process is the symbol, something that represents something else. For example, the words that people use to refer to objects are in fact symbols which represent what we mean. The word 'cup' is the symbol we use to describe a receptacle that we use in Western society to drink coffee or tea. Non-verbal messages or forms of communication – such as hand signs, nods of the head or eye contact with others – can substitute for words. The use of symbols in social encounters both outside and inside the organization necessarily involves other people interpreting what they mean. However, language is ambiguous and changes over time, and non-verbal symbols too can signify a multiplicity of meanings and ideas at any point in time. The phrases 'fat chance' and 'slim chance' might seem to be opposites, but they have the same meaning in English-speaking North America. Non-verbal symbols can signify different things depending on where they are used. For example, a thumbs-up sign is a gesture of approval in Britain, but in Ghana it is an insult. An open palm is an insulting gesture in Greece, while in West Africa it means you have five fathers, an insult akin to calling someone a bastard.[6]

Language has become important for the sociological exploration of contemporary societies. It is associated, for example, with power and gender relations. In this context it is argued that writing is an ideological act in the process of gender redefinition.[7] The interplay of power and language comes through clearly in how people use masculine words to signify greater force, significance or value. For instance, the positive word 'seminal', meaning ground-breaking, is derived from the word 'semen' or 'male seed'. The positive adjective 'virtuous', meaning morally worthy, is derived from the Latin word *vir*, meaning man. By contrast, the disparaging adjective 'hysterical' comes from the Greek word *hyster*, meaning uterus or womb.[8]

Language plays a crucial role in establishing the status and power of a profession, particularly for high-status, knowledge-based occupations such as the law and medicine.[9] A monopoly of esoteric knowledge is the essence or 'hallmark' of a profession: it marks out its members as 'privilege-knowing subjects' (and often seems to imply white male experience and a white male standpoint). The work of Erving Goffman demonstrates the importance of language and power in physician–patient relations, particularly when a patient is obliged to enter hospital for medical treatment.[10] Through the work of the historian and philosopher Michel Foucault, the relationship between language and knowledge has been turned 180 degrees. Far from language symbolizing original creative thought, Foucault argued that language as a social construct actually dictates the thoughts individuals have: 'Languages do not represent our meaning so much as construct them for us.'[11]

From a managerialist standpoint, 'effective' communications is one means of how managers 'get things done', for example by articulating a vision, informing workers of organizational rules, and giving feedback in face-to-face interviews. In this sense, it should be self-evident that the process of management, as shown diagrammatically in Figure 4.3 (page 108), depends critically on communication between managers and non-managers. Not surprisingly therefore, management texts emphasize the importance of open, clear and precise communication. They also emphasize that managers cannot afford to underestimate the complex interconnections that can result in unanticipated face-to-face encounters. When managers fail to 'think in circles' they get into trouble.[12] The nature of the communication process established in the organization reflects the management style, degree of employee participation, culture and efficiency in the workplace. It is suggested that 'improving the communication of senior executives, especially the CEO, may be the most cost-effective way to improve employees' satisfaction with communication in their organizations'.[13]

Theorists have implied that the two constructs of 'communication' and 'organization' are equivalent.[14] Thus, all organization models contain implicit notions about communication theories, and all communication theories, in turn, provide important insights about managing the employment relationship.[15] From a critical standpoint, organizational communication is an important tool for shaping and controlling various aspects of workers' behaviour in the workplace. It is a means of gaining commitment to the organization's goals, a means of conveying the organization's disciplinary practices, and ultimately of making workers more governable.[16]

This chapter examines different approaches to studying communication: functionalist, interpretivist and critical. It describes the functions and directions of communications in the workplace. It also explores the communication implications of culture, gender and diversity in the workplace, as well as the importance of persuasion in the communication process.

STOP AND REFLECT

Do you see language as a reflection of power in society?

Look again at Figure 4.3 which shows the management process. Why is communication so important to the management process and leadership?

STOP AND REFLECT

Perspectives on communication

When reading about organizational communication it is important to be alert to the different perspectives that authors and researchers select. We shall consider three major perspectives for understanding organizational communications, the functionalist, interpretivist and critical approaches.

Functionalist approach

functionalist perspective: the sociological approach that views society as a stable, orderly system

The functionalist or mechanistic approach is the dominant perspective in management studies, and sees communication as intended or unintended action. The work organization is viewed as an entity, and different communication acts are variables that shape and determine the operations of that entity.[17] Communication occurs as a chain, the weakest link of which determines the effectiveness of the communication as a whole. Messages are concrete 'things' with properties that can be measured. Communication can be broken down into smaller and smaller units (known as message bits). The functionalist approach views communication as a metaphorical pipeline through which information is transmitted between a sender and receiver. Organizational members have three basic methods of transmitting information, as shown in Figure 12.1.

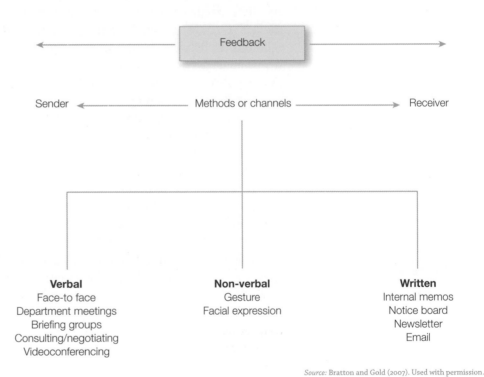

figure 12.1 Organizational communication as action

Source: Bratton and Gold (2007). Used with permission.

Looking at Figure 12.1, consider what barriers to communication exist in organizations.

STOP AND REFLECT

Verbal communication ranges from a casual conversation between two employees to a formal speech by the managing director. In face-to-face meetings the meaning of the information being conveyed by the sender can be reinforced through gesture or facial expressions: what is referred to as non-verbal communication. Written communication ranges from a casual note to a co-worker to an annual report. Electronic mail systems, video machines and webcams have revolutionized written and verbal communication in organizations. Functionalists categorize behaviours or messages in terms of accomplishing goals and objectives.[18]

Mainstream authors suggest that aspects of organizational communications include mechanistic, interpretive symbolic, and systems-interaction perceptual and psychological processes.[19] Another approach recognizes that the function of communication is to control, motivate and inform workers, and enable them to release emotional expression.[20] Thus, it is argued, the life-blood of the organization is communication: information is carried to all parts of the organization so that decisions and actions may be taken.

More critical authors (such as Putnam and his colleagues) identify seven clusters of metaphors or perspectives used in organizational communication theories – conduit, lens, linkage, performance, symbol, voice and discourse – which correspond to the theoretical approaches used in this chapter.[21] They look at how the organizational context affects communication, and how communication shapes the organizational context. By privileging communication as the producer of organizations, and examining the metaphors used in organizational communication literature, they show that 'metaphors reveal alternative ways of thinking about the origin and nature of organizing, its processes, and the constructs that form its ontological roots'.[22]

Early organizational communication theories include classical or scientific management, and bureaucracy. The predominant metaphor applied to these organizations was the machine. Organizations were viewed as the primary vehicle through which lives were rationalized, 'planned, articulated, scientized, made more efficient and orderly, and managed by experts'.[23] The pipeline or chain images were absorbed into the conduit and lens metaphor clusters identified by Putnam and his co-workers. Communication was seen as the linear transmission of information. It was treated as a variable that influenced individual and organizational performance. The dominant interest was in the skills that make individuals more effective communicators, or factors that characterize system-wide communication effectiveness. Workers were viewed as a passive audience incapable of responding, interpreting, arguing or countering this form of control. Mainstream literature uses the words 'conduit', 'channel' and 'media' in descriptions of organizational communication.[24] The lens metaphor provides a different slant on the transmission of information. The assumption is that information is incomplete.

When a message is transmitted, if the senders and receivers have different cultural backgrounds and goals it increases the likelihood that the information will be converted, simplified, reduced or summarized. The inevitability of misconception challenges traditional notions of accuracy, clarity and communication effectiveness by introducing meaning and interpretation into message transmission. One research domain that adopts a lens metaphor is media richness. Media richness theorists contend that managers will be more effective if they choose a communication medium that matches the ambiguity of their task.[25] Lean and rich media diagrams are found in mainstream texts. Grint characterizes the functionalist approach, or the transmission model, in concrete terms: the 'language, technologies' are simply channels for telling somebody something. The manager chooses the most appropriate channel of communication to convey the information, accomplish goals and improve efficiency.[26]

Interpretivist approach

The interpretivist approach is a reaction against the functionalist perspective.[27] It attempts to understand human communication as something *in* the work organization, rather than something that *manages* the organization. Interpretivists argue that human beings do not behave as predictably as is suggested by the functionalist school. Thus, we may be able to predict that most people, or some people in the workplace, will react to a certain message in a certain way, but we cannot make the prediction for all workers. Some employees will do one thing and some another when presented with identical information. Interpretivist scholars argue that because people are so

media richness: refers to the number of channels of contact afforded by a communication medium, so for example face-to-face interaction would be at the high end of media richness and a memorandum would fall at the low end of media richness

interpretivism: the view held in many qualitative studies that reality comes from shared meaning among people in that environment

complex in their behaviours and exhibit choice in responding to stimuli, functionalist explanations of organizational behaviour are inappropriate. The organism metaphor is associated with this approach. It is applied to a system of mutually connected and dependent parts constituted to share a common life.[28]

Communication is the transference and understanding of meaning. Most communication models convey this as a linear process (although they assume that both sender and receiver have an active role), but we need to be aware that the construction of meaning is affected by the skill, attitude and knowledge of the participants, and also by the sociocultural context in which the communication takes place. The creation of shared meanings is the basis of the interpretive-symbolic perspective. These shared meanings create the organization's culture, and can also serve to create and shape social reality. An organization's culture is partially created by the shared talk of its members. Organizational members capture complex experiences which are combinations of sense, emotion, reason and imagination, using narration and storytelling to impart meaning.

Cultural factors are strong influences on the interpretive process. The definition and meaning of culture has been contested more than any other concept in the social sciences. Raymond Williams, the father of 'cultural studies', suggests that it has three core meanings:

▷ a general process of intellectual, spiritual and aesthetic development
▷ a meaning that relates to the works and practices of intellectual and artistic activity
▷ a meaning that refers to a particular way of life, whether of people, a period or a group.[29]

The prominent sociologist Anthony Giddens claims the last of these is the definition used by sociologists. He claims the way of life is composed of 'the values the members of a given group hold, the norms they follow and the material goods they create', which may describe a work culture.[30] An important part of work culture is the social interaction involved in the interpretation of narratives, rites and rituals. These symbolic 'shared meanings' serve to socialize newcomers, solve problems, and impart organizational values and beliefs. Rites such as award ceremonies, retirement dinners and new member orientations are elaborate dramatic activities that consolidate cultural expressions into one event. Rituals such as handshakes, coffee breaks, gift giving and staff meetings are the norms and behaviours that embody the rites. The interpretive approach to organizational communication seeks to make sense of organization members' actions as part of the social constructions of individuals that have become shared. These symbols are more than manifestations of an organization's culture: they are the means through which organizing is accomplished.

Metaphors have been used in OB studies to understand the workplace. A metaphor is a particular linguistic expression that can link abstract social constructs to concrete things, and metaphors can be used to legitimize managers' actions, set goals, and guide managers and non-managers' behaviour in the workplace.[31] Metaphors help theory building by enabling us to examine images at different levels of analysis. A theory is metaphorical if it suggests, through language, enlightening comparisons between organizational communication and other processes. For example, scientific management theory compares organizations to machines. The predominant metaphor used during the Summit of Americas in Quebec was the family of nations. Images of family and teams, the latter utilizing the language of sports, recur frequently in mainstream management texts on organizational design (see Chapter 15). In the Western tradition metaphor has the privilege of revealing unexpected truth. As Aristotle put it, 'Midway between the unintelligible and the

culture: the knowledge, language, values, customs and material objects that are passed from person to person and from one generation to the next in a human group or society

STOP AND REFLECT

To what extent do social factors such as status differences, social conformity and cultural differences act as barriers to communication? Can you think of examples?

commonplace, it is metaphor which most produces knowledge.'[32] Similarly, others believe that metaphors inform action and shape organizational practices.[33]

Many workplaces are pervaded by game and military metaphors, and metaphors of friends, family and home.[34] Accordingly, 'A metaphor works through invoking a concept originating from another field or level than the one that is being understood. The former modifies the latter and forms a specific image or gestalt'.[35] The knowledge of theories about organizational communications enables us to participate in a particular <mark>discourse community</mark>, which in this case is made up of individuals who share an interest in organizations and communication. To join in this ongoing conversation, as communication theorist Kenneth Burke describes it, we need to be aware of the previous and present conversations. Theories enhance our ability to understand and explain a variety of practical issues, such as where the idea of organization originated and what motivates people to work. Theories can show how communication and efficiency are linked. Because organizational communication theories are dynamic, we should view each theory as a participant in a larger, ongoing discourse. One theory should not be given prominence over another; rather we should recognize its origins, bias and relationship to other theories.

Critical approach

The critical approach derives from the critical theory school, which seeks to expose the often hidden but pervasive power that post-industrial organizations have over individuals, while also challenging the assumed superiority of unfettered market capitalism. While the functionalist approach is concerned with making the organization more efficient, the critical theorist is more concerned with examining organizational communication, such as myths, metaphors and stories, as a source of power. Critical theorists also try to understand why organizational practices that maintain strong controls over workers are considered legitimate, and so are not resisted.[36]

Organizational communication is thus studied in terms of hidden exercises of power and managerial influence. The metaphors of voice and discourse enable us to analyse the questions of who can speak, when and in what way. We need to consider communication as the expression or suppression of organization members' voices. Morgan identifies a number of metaphors used to convey the perspectives of critical theorists.[37] We shall consider the metaphors of culture, political system, language game and text/discourse in the next few pages.

Discourse analysis, inspired by Gramsci and Foucault, is a useful way of theorizing culture. Rather than seeing culture as something static and real which is common to all members of a nation or ethnic group, it sees it as 'social processes operating in contested terrains in which different voices become more or less hegemonic in their offered interpretations of the world'.[38] Organizational culture is a set of meanings, ideas and symbols that are shared by members of a collective and have evolved over time. Talking about culture then means 'talking about the importance for people of symbolism – rituals, myths, stories, and legends – and about the interpretation of events, ideas, and experiences that are influenced and shaped by the groups within which they live'.[39]

Two critical theorists, Alvesson and Due Billing, argue that culture facilitates social life but also includes elements of constraint and conservatism.[40] It tends to freeze social reality in order to subordinate people to dominating ideas, beliefs and assumptions which are taken for granted. Wittgenstein's metaphor of a language game suggests that organizational activity is a game of words, thoughts and actions.[41] As individuals engage with their worlds, through specific codes and practices (using both verbal and non-verbal language), organizational realities arise as rule-governed symbolic structures. Language creates the organizational

discourse community: a way of talking about and conceptualizing an issue, presented through ideas and concepts, spoken or written, within a social group or community (such as lawyers or physicians).

concepts that define the culture of an organization and give form to notions of control, delegation and rationality. Meetings, or 'technologies of power', are an example of the social reality created and controlled by management, which endorse and encourage certain understandings and feelings that reflect managerial interests and perspectives.[42]

Alvesson's empirical research[43] suggests that the meeting is one element of the ongoing creation and recreation of the organization. Management of meaning is part of everyday leadership. Attention is placed on some things and not on others. Language is carefully chosen. One example of simple, but powerful, word choice is the familiar 'them and us' concept being superseded by the use of 'we' and 'you'. During meetings the phrase 'We did as you said', is used frequently. 'We' in this context is top management and 'you' the collective workforce. This counteracts the idea that power is directed from the top downwards. It suggests that decisions are anchored in the workforce, and that top management is carrying out the wishes of the collective. 'We' is used to suggest a common identity among those present at the meeting; they are encouraged to consider themselves as part of the same unit, with common interests and objectives. As Frost puts it, 'Communication structures, channels, networks, and rules are avenues of power .... Thus the communication medium is never neutral.'[44]

> empirical approach: research that attempts to answer questions through a systematic collection and analysis of data

Critical theory draws attention to the political and exploitative aspects of organizational life. This perspective seeks to expose the 'order' that interpretive theory seeks to understand, and functionalist theory to enhance, as superficial. Critical theorists suggest that like other aspects of organizational life, the organizational communication process is complicated by organizational characteristics such as hierarchy and power relations, and by the fact that individual managers and non-managers have idiosyncrasies, abilities and biases. They argue that organizational communication is central to the other processes of power, leadership and decision making. Organizational communication involves more than providing employees with information about their employment and wider issues relating to the organization in which they work. It is as complex as human behaviour itself.

According to this perspective, every human act, both conscious and unconscious, contains information that is then interpreted by a receiver. The three notions associated with communications – behaviour, meaning and context – are synthesized in this definition of organizational communication: 'Both behaviours and symbols, generated either intentionally or unintentionally, occurring between and among people who assign meaning to them, within an organizational setting.'[45]

In modern organizations symbolic power is particularly noticeable compared with technical and bureaucratic means of control. The management of meaning is regarded as symbolic action. The creation of a managerially biased social reality reduces the number of available variations in the way things can be perceived, when the possibilities of describing, understanding and evaluating workplace conditions and objectives are being negotiated:

> Generally dominance is manifested not in significant political acts but rather in the day-to-day, taken for granted nature of organizational life. As such, the exercise of power and domination exists at a routine level, further protecting certain interests and allowing the order or organizational life to go largely unquestioned by its members.[46]

Consequently, dominance is exercised chiefly by ensuring that the current reality in the organization is regarded as natural, rational, self-evident, problem-free, sensible and so on. Therefore the power aspect is of crucial importance in organizational communication. Communication provides the means through which power can be exercised, developed, maintained and enhanced.

Communication and management

Now we have seen something of the different *perspectives* for studying organizational communications, it should not surprise us to find that the *function* of organizational communications is contested. Traditional approaches to organizational communication identify at least two functions of communication: to exchange information and to bring about change. Figure 12.1 illustrated the first function of communication, the process by which information is exchanged between a sender and a receiver. This function of organizational communication can be seen in studies of managers and their work. One classic study found that managers spend 80 per cent of their contact time on activities devoted exclusively to the transmission of information.[47] The second function of communication is to help those who manage the organization to bring about change, by persuading others to adopt a different work regime and/or behaviour.

Channels of communication

formal channels: a communication process that follows an organization's chain of command

informal channels: a communication process that follows unofficial means of communication, sometimes called 'the grapevine', usually based on social relations in which employees talk about work.

genre: a term to describe the different kinds of writing and reading in the workplace including, reports, letters and memoranda

Communication theorists refer to formal and informal channels of communication in a work organization. The three basic communication media – written, verbal and non-verbal – can be used in either of these types of channel. Formal channels are established by the organization, and transmit messages relevant to job-related activities, using for example memos, voicemail, email and meetings. Informal channels, such as personal or social messages, contribute to the culture and social reality of an organization. Among those who have studied and researched these differences is Mikhail Bakhtin, a Russian literary and cultural critic. He is interested in language in actual use, the 'utterance', or primary speech genres. From these, the more complex 'secondary' genres of writing are derived.

In the workplace (as elsewhere), genre is the word used to indicate the different kinds of writing required to complete the communication loop, and ensure efficient action is taken. Empirical studies of workplace writing reveal the complex social, cultural and institutional factors at play in the production of specific trends of writing.[48] Two researchers, Freedman and Medway, point to the interaction and interpersonal dynamics that are part of creating texts in an organization. The features of the text are often 'conventionalized by tacit agreement – the lore of the tribe'.[49] They can function as the social glue which helps an organization to establish its own culture. The interpersonal dynamics that surround and support the creation of texts in an organization reflect the levels of relative power, influence and access to information.[50]

Verbal and non-verbal aspects of communication are inextricably linked. Even a verbal message on a computer-generated voice telephone voicemail system has a 'gender' and 'ethnicity', and so has a non-verbal aspect. Verbal communication ranges from a casual conversation between employees to the company president's speech transmitted to branch offices throughout the country. Face-to-face interaction is the most effective form of verbal communication when the sender wants to persuade or motivate the receiver. Research has found that face-to-face talk is preferred because it provides for the maximum amount of information to be transmitted during a communication episode. That is, it offers multiple information cues (through words, postures, facial expression and gestures), and the personal touch of 'being there'. Non-verbal cues may be organized into seven categories: the environment, proxemics, postures, gestures, facial expressions, eye behaviour and vocalics.[51]

The £1 million comma

It could be the most costly piece of punctuation in Canada. A grammatical blunder may force Rogers Communications Inc. to pay an extra $2.13 million [about £1 million] to use utility poles in the Maritimes after the placement of a comma in a contract permitted the deal's cancellation. The controversial comma sent lawyers and telecommunications regulators scrambling for their English text books in a bitter 18-month dispute that serves as an expensive reminder of the importance of punctuation.

The disputed sentence: 'This agreement shall be effective from the date it is made and shall continue in force for a period of five (5) years from the date it is made, and thereafter for successive five (5) year terms, unless and until terminated by one year prior notice in writing by either party.'

Rogers thought it had a five-year deal with Aliant Inc. to string Rogers' cable lines across thousands of utility poles in the Maritimes for an annual fee of $9.60 per pole. But early last year, Rogers was informed that the contract was being cancelled and the rates were going up. Impossible Rogers thought, since its contract was ironclad until the spring of 2007 and would automatically be renewed for successive five-year terms.

Armed with the rules of grammar and punctuation, Aliant Inc. disagreed. The contract can be cancelled at any time provided one year's notice is given. The construction of a single sentence in the contract allowed the entire deal to be scrapped with only one year's notice, the company argued.

When regulators with the Canadian Radio-television and Telecommunications Commission (CRTC) parsed the wording, they reached another conclusion. The presence of the second comma means the conditions of cancelling the contract apply to both the initial five-year term and subsequent five-year terms. The validity of the contract and the millions of dollars at stake all came down to one point – the second comma in the sentence. Had it not been there, the right to cancel would not have applied to the first five years of the contract and Rogers would be protected from the higher rates it now faces. 'Based on the rules of punctuation,' the comma in question 'allows for the termination of the [contact] at any time, without cause, upon one year's written notice,' the regulator said. 'This is the classic case of where the placement of a comma has great importance,' Aliant said.

Source: Grant Robertson, *Globe and Mail*, 8 August 2006, pp.B1–2

Face-to-face interaction is considered the richest medium on the communication channel continuum. It is most suitable for non-routine messages, whereas routine messages use the poorest media: flyers, bulletins or general reports. Marshall McLuhan's popular phrase 'The medium is the message' refers to the idea that the sender's choice of communication channel transmits meaning beyond the message content. The symbolic meaning of choosing one medium over another may vary from one manager to another. For example, some people might see the use of email as a sign of professionalism and/or efficiency, while others might view it as impersonal and inappropriate.

One example of managerial insensitivity is the announcement on television that Canadian Airlines was shutting down. Employees learned of their fate by listening to the national news. We must be sensitive to the meta-message, the larger message within which the smaller message is contained. The symbolic meaning of the selected communication medium should clarify rather than contradict the meaning found in the message content. Another example of a poor choice of medium is a memo sent to workers at the Women's Television Channel by their new employers. The first paragraph welcomed them to the company; the final paragraph informed them they would receive dismissal notices shortly.

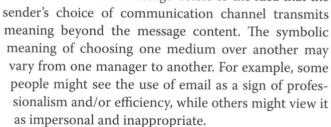

plate 33 Face-to-face communication might be more effective than sending an email

Source: Getty Images

The direction of communication

Communication flows downwards, upwards and horizontally in formal organizations (see Figure 12.2). Vertical communications are the formal mechanisms established to disseminate information that involves the coordination of subordinates' work activities.

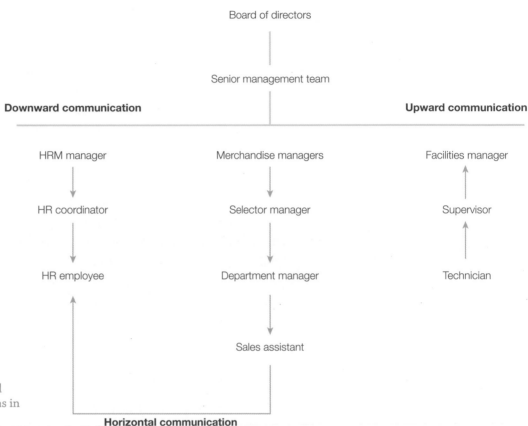

figure 12.2 Downward, upward and horizontal communications in a retail store

Downward communication includes management directives, electronic newsletters, emails, telephone hotlines and corporate video programmes. In 1997, a North American survey of 2039 respondents in six industrial and service categories explored the state of communication in Canadian businesses. The discrepancy between senior managers' perception of how well they communicated with employees (61 per cent thought they did well) and the non-managerial employees' opinion of effective communication in the workplace (22 per cent thought the managers did well) highlights the difference between OB prescriptions and reality.[52]

Upward communication in the workplace is underdeveloped in most forms, but employee surveys, reports from self-managed teams and various employee involvement arrangements are forms of upward communication.

Lateral communications among people at the same level in the organization are useful for increasing coordination between individuals and departments.

The informal communication network, known as the grapevine, is formed and maintained by social relationships. Communication can flow across all levels and boundaries, and can use any or all of the channels available. The grapevine operates outside the usual bounds of the organization, and is also the main source of organizational narratives and other symbols of the organization's culture.

WEB LINK

For further details on how managers communicate with other employees, go to the website of WERS 2004: www.dti.gov.uk/employment/useful-links/index.html and search for '2004 employee relations survey'. This site gives a summary of the survey. See also www.data-archive.ac.uk

grapevine: an unstructured and informal communication network founded on social relationships rather than organizational charts or job descriptions

Leadership, persuasion and communication

The second major function of communication is to bring about change, and hence communication is said to be one of the most critical skills for organizational leaders.[53] Leadership is defined as a process that brings about movement or change, and involves persuasion. Persuasive communication changes followers' behaviour when they accept the information, the information becomes part of their structure of beliefs about the workplace, and as a result it changes their opinions about reality. This is an integral element in the leadership process, and in turn in the creation of the culture of an organization, which serves to create a homogenous group who share ways of knowing, and interpret a range of symbolic activities in the same way. The manager, or leader, as a persuader should be aware of the elements that can influence acceptance. Leadership theorists have emphasized the role of communication in developing an appropriate corporate culture and encouraging the acceptance of change among organizational members:

> Corporate culture stands for ideas, meanings and norms bringing about homogeneity and predictability in understanding, thinking and valuing among people. This is vital for the efficient functioning of complex large-scale organizations. The need for smooth communication and the reduction of uncertainty and, relatedly, the importance attached to knowing the rules of the game, means a strong pressure towards conformity.[54]

rhetoric: the management of symbols (such as a language) in order to encourage and coordinate social action. 'Rhetorical sensitivity' is the tendency for a speaker to adapt her or his messages to audiences to allow for the level knowledge, ability level, mood or beliefs of the listener

Exercising leadership depends on the use of verbal and non-verbal language, both words and behaviour, and communication style is linked to the notion of rhetoric.[55] Rhetoric, from the Greek word *rhator* (speaker in the assembly), is the art of using speech to persuade. This involves the ability to motivate colleagues to take action rather than just accept arguments. Recent interest in the study of rhetoric by managers indicates an awareness of the importance of communication to leadership.[56] Since almost 75 per cent of a manager's time is ostensibly involved in conversation, we may assume that most management is secured through talk, and therefore most leadership is too.[57] What kinds of conversation do managers have? It has been suggested that social order at any level (from family life through hospital discipline to international relations) is unthinkable without negotiations. In other words, order itself is better conceptualized as 'negotiated order', in so far as some form of negotiation is always critical to organizations.

negotiation: occurs whenever two or more conflicting parties attempt to resolve their divergent goals by redefining the terms of their interdependence

Research into emotional intelligence in organizations concluded that effective leaders possess this quality to a high degree.[58] Empathy is the most easily recognized dimension of emotional intelligence, and is an important component of leadership for at least three reasons: the increasing use of teams, the rapid pace of globalization, and the growing need to retain talent. The social skill of managing leader–follower relationships is also closely linked to the powers of persuasion. Persuasiveness can be viewed as a social skill that is a component of emotional intelligence. Black contends that effective managerial communication involves taking responsibility for and ownership of the content (the message), ensuring recipients' understanding of the message, and knowing the organization's position on difficult issues and its rationale for decisions. To be competent the leader-manager needs to create the right impact on her or his audience.[59]

Keith Grint, a prominent researcher in leadership, adopts classical rhetoric as his model to describe persuasive communication.[60] People's ethos – which includes their perceived expertise on the topic, their credentials and experience – contributes to their ability to persuade. Their expertise in how they speak also greatly influences listeners. This concerns issues such as speaking confidently and relatively quickly, using some technical language, and avoiding pauses ('um' or 'uh') and hedges ('you

plate 34 Organizations send employees to indoor climbing centres where they learn to solve communication problems and work as a team

Source: Nicholas P. Tutton

know' and 'I guess'). Establishing trustworthiness and respect enables a communicator to be more effective. If listeners perceive that the communicator will not benefit personally from the proposal he or she is putting forward, and the communicator acknowledges that the opposing position has one or two positive elements, this helps to convince listeners of the reasonableness of the argument.

The message content is of course a critical feature of persuasive communication. If the speaker expects the audience to be resistant to the message, he or she must first present viewpoints that validate the audience's viewpoint, before presenting his or her own position. If the issue is highly emotive, a good alternative is the Rogerian structure of presenting arguments.[61] This is appropriate if the leader wants to avoid threatening those who hold opposing views, since 'Rogerian persuasion basically aims at achieving consensus around a correct position. The objective is truth, not victory.'[62] Both classical and Rogerian rhetoric rely on emotional and logical appeals, which form Aristotle's three criteria of persuasiveness, as shown in Figure 12.3.

In organizational communications it is often difficult to separate personal character and emotional appeal. Logical proof is seldom as effective as Aristotle maintains. This does not mean that appeals to rationality – to the 'truth' and to the 'facts' – are irrelevant. Far from it, they are crucial elements of persuasion, but they are not in and of themselves sufficient to persuade others on each and every occasion. This is blatantly clear when scientific 'experts' disagree on the 'facts', such as in the case of genetically modified foods or global warming. Effective communication involves a combination of speech (content), speaker, situation (context) and spectators (audience), and also the active roles of individuals and groups who socially shape the contents and contexts, rather than merely responding to them.[63] We must consider the rhetorical context of the communication process as including the social and collective forms of organization (that is, the culture) which generate persuasive interpretations of the message (see Figure 12.4).

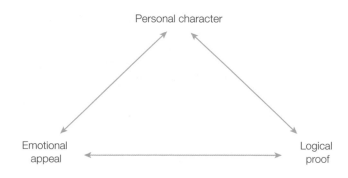

figure 12.3 Aristotle's model of rhetoric

Source: Grint (2001). Used with permission.

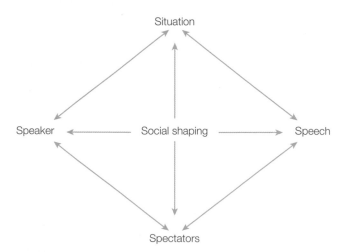

figure 12.4 The immutable four Ss model of speech making

The rhetorical context of meetings designed to convey information, which was studied by Alvesson,[64] reveals the techniques of power and discipline that are used in effective managerial communication. The seemingly neutral conveying of information and use of language can reinforce asymmetric power relations and contribute to the disciplinary function, which is so central to management and to many other manifestations of organizational culture. Symbolically charged activities, events and words condense important ideas and assumptions, and convey them forcefully to the audience. Using 'we' and 'you' in this specific situation may have considerable rhetorical appeal. Managers are therefore agents of power, creating or reproducing shared meanings, ideas and values through acts of communication, which suspend social reality, or, at least counteract an open, questioning approach to how it should be negotiated.

Communication and cultural diversity

With the globalization of markets, and an increase in mergers and acquisitions, the workplace is seeing greater interaction and communication among peoples of different cultures and experiences.[65] The multicultural communication environment of organizations is an indisputable thriving reality. It can be argued that the way in which businesses manage cross-cultural communication between colleagues will determine their economic survival and competitiveness in the global marketplace. Managers who have a systematic understanding of the cultural and organizational dynamics of cross-cultural communication will enhance organizational effectiveness and performance. Managers and researchers need to guard against ethnocentrism, a tendency to judge other cultures by the standards of one's own.

Diversity in organizations

Narrow definitions of diversity emphasize race, ethnicity and gender. Broader definitions of diversity tend to focus on issues of 'racism, sexism, heterosexism, classism, ableism, and other forms of discrimination at the individual, identity group, and system levels'.[66] Broad definitions contend that everyone is different, and comply with the individualistic concept that structures thinking about organizations. Essentially scholars are referring to 'diversity in identities' based on social and demographic groups: 'A mixture of people with different group identities within the same social system.'[67] So the concept of identity is at the core of understanding diversity in organizations. This has implications for effective communication in the workplace. Studies of work teams reveal that people's identification with subgroups (*micro identities* in the organizational context) takes precedence over their identification with the organization as a whole (their *macro identity*). The ability of people to work together in teams composed of members from different group identities may be hampered by the consequences of group identification.[68]

The interpersonal communications model discussed earlier in this chapter (Figure 12.1) ignores different cultures and how culture impacts on the communication process.[69] Critics of this linear communication model argue that people communicate differently because of their culture, their gender, and how they have learned to perceive the world. Cultures differ in both their verbal and non-verbal communications. A culturally diverse workforce has the potential to improve organizational effectiveness. It can provide improved decision making, creativity and innovation, and marketing knowledge to different types of consumers, all of which benefits the global organization. Employees must overcome their reluctance to communicate with co-workers from other cultural groups.

A Canadian study of cultural diversity in Toronto's major hotels found that 'language barriers made it difficult for managers to give non-English employees meaningful feedback to help them improve their jobs'.[70] Even when people speak the same language, interpreting voice intonation can be problematic. In some cultures, the tone changes depending on the context, such as home, a social situation or work. Using a personal, informal style in a situation where a more formal style is expected affects the meta-meaning behind the message.

There was considerable research on racio-ethnicity and gender following the passing of equal opportunities and anti-discrimination legislation in the United States and Britain in the late 1960s and early 1970s. Taken as a whole, these studies suggest that Blacks and women face both access and treatment discrimination in organizations. However, it is important to note that assimilation theory underlies the questions studied and the solutions that are proposed. The successful integration of racial minorities and white women into organizations requires their loss of identity: they must adapt to the norms and behaviours of the dominant group.

The theory and research is dominated by dichotomous thinking about identity: that is, thinking that divides people into two opposed groups, such as Black versus white, Anglo versus Latino, or male versus female. Oppositional thinking implies not only that there is a difference but also that there is a hierarchy, where one group is superior to the other. The dominant group obtains its privilege by suppressing the other group. In much of the research on diversity in organizations, the legitimacy and basic values of the organization are not questioned. Organizations are regarded as fundamentally sound and neutral sites. However, we argue that it is essential for attention to be paid to what sustains and maintains the pattern of power relations in organizations. Communication plays an essential role in the establishment and maintenance of these power relations.

Discourse theory and analysis, referred to above, also covers the study of all types of written texts and spoken interaction (both formal and informal), with particular attention to the functions served by language. It asks how certain sorts of talk and writing can accomplish particular goals, such as exclusions, blamings or justifications. It is important to study the language we use to talk about diversity in identities because as one researcher points out, 'Language is so structured to mirror power relations that often we can see no other way of being, and it structures ideology so that it is difficult to speak both in and against it.'[71]

In the globalized marketplace, international communication across political or national borders is an integral part of business negotiations. Success can depend on the implicit and explicit nature of the communication process (both verbal and non-verbal). The informational context and the degree of background data that has to be transmitted varies from culture to culture.

The anthropologist E. T. Hall developed a useful system for understanding the communication implications of culture.[72] He classified cultures on a scale that ranges from 'high context' to 'low context'. (These are also sometimes described as individualistic (low context) and collectivist (high context) cultures.) In low-context societies, people are less able to agree or solve disputes without resorting to written contracts or litigation than they are in high-context ones. Explicit written and verbal messages are the norm in, for example, the United States, Canada, Scandinavia, Germany and Switzerland. High-context cultures emphasize collaboration and personal relationships as important aspects of doing business. Informal and unwritten contracts are the norm, together with the non-verbal language that surrounds the explicit message. This happens for example in Korea, China, Japan and Arab countries.

These two types of culture also differ in their patterns of time usage. Low-context cultures are characterized by monochronic time patterns. This is a linear and compartmentalized view of time. These cultures value quick responses and a direct approach to the issue, without the use of much background information. High-

high-context culture: a culturally sanctioned style of communication that assumes high levels of shared knowledge and so uses very concise sometimes obscure speech

low-context culture: a culturally sanctioned style of communication that assumes low levels of shared knowledge and so uses verbally explicit speech

context cultures tend to work with polychronic time, which is more contextually based and flexible. Oral and written communication is less direct and more circular in nature. Discussion in business meetings may go off at tangents; the direct approach, to refocus on the agenda, can be considered rude. In resolving conflicts in cross-cultural communications, all parties involved must not only know about their own culture but also demonstrate a willingness to accept differences in other cultures.

A variety of gestures are only used in certain cultures, or their meaning changes between cultures. In Canada and the United Kingdom, for example, nodding the head up and down signals 'yes' and shaking it back and forth means 'no'. In Bulgaria, parts of Greece, Turkey, Iran and Bengal it is the reverse. The gesture where the thumb and forefinger form a simple circle means 'OK' or 'everything is fine' in Canada, the United Kingdom and the United States, but in France it means zero or worthless, and in Japan it is the signal for money. In many other countries it is considered a sexually rude gesture.[73] Canadians are taught to maintain eye contact with the speaker to show interest and respect, yet this is considered rude to some Asian and Middle Eastern people, who are taught to show respect by looking down when a supervisor or older person is talking to them.

Gender and communication: 'She said, he said'

Just as culture affects interpretation, research has demonstrated that gender plays a role in influencing what is considered to be the appropriate communication medium. There appear to be important differences between the conversational styles of men and women, which can be summarized in terms of 'report' and 'rapport' respectively.[74] A plausible explanation of why genders can create communication barriers is that men tend to see conversation as a tool: they use it to exchange information, accomplish a task, offer advice or advance their status. For many men, conversations are primarily a means to preserve independence. On the other hand, it is suggested that women talk in order to nurture, support and empathize. Women speak and hear a language of cooperation, connection and intimacy.

Studies have also indicated that female managers use an open communication style when dealing with personnel problems, which centres on cooperation and request. However, male managers use their position in the organization's chain of command to resolve the problem. Interestingly they tend to use their position of power when dealing with female employees, whereas when dealing with male employees they use communication strategies.

From a managerial perspective, gender issues play a part in the better utilization of human resources. An awareness of sex discrimination and conservative gender patterns enables recruiting, keeping, placing, training and promoting labour to be carried out in a more rational way. Embracing and welcoming diversity, and validating the viewpoints of women and men, may facilitate organizational learning and creativity. It is argued that managers need to address organizational cultures, structures and practices in terms of gender. We have used the term 'diverse' to convey cultural and gender differences between colleagues in a company, and cognitive and relational differences between Eastern and Western cultures. However, diversity is itself a contested term.

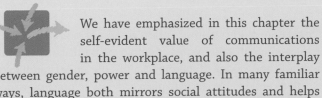

We have emphasized in this chapter the self-evident value of communications in the workplace, and also the interplay between gender, power and language. In many familiar ways, language both mirrors social attitudes and helps to perpetuate them. It also confers different value on the two sexes. An introduction to the issue of language and its importance for sociological research of contemporary societies is presented in *Introductory Sociology* by Bilton et al.[75] Obtain a copy and read Chapters 18 and 19. Explain the role of language in the construction of self. How does language define women and men differently?

Deborah Tannen has done extensive research on how language defines men and women differently, usually to the advantage of men. Obtain a copy of Tannen's book, *You Just Don't Understand: Women and men in conversation.*[76] In what ways do men define life experiences differently to women? What implications does Tannen's work have for organizational communication? How important is the social context in explaining the success or failure of particular forms and styles of communication?

Communication and paradox

plate 35 Non-verbal messages can be a very powerful mode of conveying meaning

Source: Getty Images

Contradictions and paradoxes are found everywhere in the organizational communication literature. The case studies on employee involvement arrangements in worksites reveal tensions in communication and employee empowerment practices. The term 'paradox' comes from the Greek words *para* and *dokein*, and means to reconcile two apparently conflicting views.[77] Four main types of paradoxes are apparent in management practices to improve organizational performance: structure, agency, identity and power.[78]

Although teams are intended to enhance productivity by empowering workers to make decisions, senior management make the 'really important decisions', for example, on investment in new technology. In other words workers can participate in learning, innovating and voicing their opinions only using the channels established by the organization.

The idea of agency refers to an individual's sense of being, and a feeling that she or he can or does make a difference.[79] A conflict may arise if self-managed work teams rely on the active subordination of team members to the will of the team. Members must retain their creative individuality while accepting 'our way'. Consequently, workers may become ambivalent and hesitant about participating in such a regime.

The paradox of identity addresses issues of boundaries, space, and the divide between the in-group and the out-group. The paradox involves commitment to the group, embracing learning, discussion, diversity and difference. However, 'commitment is expected to equal agreement'.[80] Voicing an alternative view is seen as lack of commitment. The workers must comply with organizational priorities.

The paradox of power centres on issues of leadership, access to resources, opportunities for voice and the shaping of employee behaviour. It is argued that managers must meet the challenge of nurturing creativity and innovation in an atmosphere of 'Be an independent thinker, just as I have commanded you.'

The area of organizational communications is part of the broader field of OB studies. In this chapter we have explored a body of literature that many standard OB texts have previously neglected. The nature of communication and the links between communication, power and decision making suggest that metaphors, cultural diversity, gender and rhetorical adroitness deserve greater attention in management theory and practice.

Chapter summary

☐ We have explained that the nature of the communication process established in the organization reflects the management style, degree of employee participation, culture and efficiency in the workplace. Knowledge of theories clarifies our understanding of organizational communications and enables us to explain a variety of practical issues, such as where the idea of the organization originated and what motivates people to work.

☐ It is important not to give one theory prominence over another. The three major perspectives for understanding organizational communications – functionalist, interpretivist and critical – allow us to comprehend the central role communications has in the management process. The metaphors used to describe the perspectives – for example machine, organism and psychic prison – enhance our ability to view communications as not just about the transmission and exchange of information in the context of organizational efficiency, but rather as central to the other processes of power, leadership and decision making.

☐ We have emphasized that individuals engage with their world through specific codes and practices (verbal, non-verbal and written language). Language creates the organizational concepts that define the culture of an organization and give form to notions of control, delegation and rationality. Meetings are an example of the management of meaning. The choice of media, interaction and personal dynamics are part of the creation of texts within an organization, which in turn contribute to the establishment of its culture.

☐ We went on to explain how an understanding of the cultural and organizational dynamics of cross-cultural communications will enhance organizational effectiveness and business performance. E. T. Hall provides a useful system for understanding the communication implications of culture, both verbal and non-verbal.

☐ Research has revealed differences between the conversational styles of men and women. As managers women try to develop *rapport* with colleagues, whereas men often *report* information or problems. It is important to embrace and welcome diversity in the organization to facilitate creativity and encourage the learning community. However, there are paradoxes tied up with the concepts of individual, micro and macro identities, and these might inhibit full participation in the organization. Although workers might apparently be encouraged to be creative, the organization typically places limitations on where, how and when they can speak.

☐ The material reviewed in this chapter illustrates that managers are aware of the importance of persuasive communication in their role as negotiators. The growth of teams, globalization and the need to retain employees require managers to acquire expertise as accomplished presenters of rational arguments. Knowledge of the rhetorical context of the communication process enables the manager to create a managerially biased social reality.

Key concepts

4Ss model of speech making	333	exchange model of communication	325–6
Aristotle's model of rhetoric	333	non-verbal communication	329
channels of communication	329–31	transmission model of communication	324–5

Chapter review questions

1. Explain the difference between a transmission model of communication and an exchange model.
2. If communication is so central to the management process, why do managers often fail to communicate effectively to others in the organization?
3. To what extent does electronic transmission affect communications?
4. What kind of communication skills should managers concentrate on?
5. How important is the context in explaining the success or failure of particular forms and styles of communication?

Further reading

Eisenberg, E. M. and Goodall, H. L. (2004) *Organizational Communication: Balancing creativity and constraint* (4th edn), New York: St Martin's Press.

Martin, J. and Nakayama, T. (2000) *Intercultural Communication in Contexts* (2nd edn), Mountain View, Calif/Toronto: Mayfield.

Morgan, G. (1980) 'Paradigms, metaphors, and puzzle solving in organization theory', *Administrative Science Quarterly*, **25**, pp. 605–22.

Chapter case study: *Edenvale Hospital*

Background

Edenvale Hospital, located in Auckland, New Zealand, is a public facility employing 523 full and part-time employees from diverse ethnic and social origins. The New Zealand Nurses Organization (NZNO), a major health and public employee union, represents the majority of workers, excluding doctors. The HR Department is non-unionized.

In the last year the hospital experienced a change in senior administration and also appointed a new human resources director. Because of budget requirements, a flexibility initiative was undertaken to try to find ways to improve productivity. One proposal that came out of this was to outsource the catering services. If implemented, the plan would result in a loss of 28 positions.

Below is the email Human Resources sent to the 28 employees targeted for redundancy. Anita Hill, a cook, showed it to her local union representative, Sophia Himelstein.

TO: **Anita Hill**
FROM: **Jennifer Chen, HR manager**
DATE: **September 17, 2007**
C.C.
SUBJECT: **DEPARTMENT REVIEW**

To be sure of obtaining optimal efficiency steps will be undertaken immediately to investigate the number of workers required in the catering department.

At this point in time, in view of the fact that budget projections indicate a shortfall for the current year, it is necessary to create a reduction in staff. This is to inform you that 28 positions will be eliminated from various hospital departments.

Jennifer

Sophia discussed this at a meeting of the Shop Stewards Committee, and afterwards a meeting was arranged between management and NZNO representatives.

The meeting between the parties

At the meeting with management, Sophia spoke on behalf of the union members. She said they were particularly concerned about the process of the labour review, the lack of explanation of the rationale behind the number of layoffs, and the effect on the morale of her members.

Troy Venables, the HR director, told her that the hospital could not maintain current staffing levels because there had been a decrease in the number of patients admitted over the past two years, and this trend was expected to continue as more money was put into community nursing.

Sophia responded that if the hospital was experiencing budget deficits, she would like to know why the HR Department had recently created seven new administrative positions, including Venables' own new post. She also pointed out that the email contained a paradox. It indicated that an investigation 'will be undertaken', but it also stated that there would be 28 job losses, and this suggested the decision had been made before the investigation process had been completed. More importantly Sophia accused the HR director and manager of being disingenuous by mentioning 'various hospital departments' in the email, when clearly the Catering Department has been targeted for the layoffs. 'Firing people by email is inappropriate: I thought people matter here', she said.

Jennifer explained that other departments were also to be investigated. She agreed the email to Anita Hill had been badly worded, but it was not intended to suggest the Catering Department was the only target.

The managers admitted they did not have a three-year strategic plan for the hospital to support the projected loss of patient numbers, and neither were they able to explain the criteria for targeting catering. In response, the union representatives accused the senior hospital administration of arbitrariness, and of following an ideologically driven agenda to privatize the hospital services.

The meeting ended without an agreement or a date for a follow-up meeting.

Task

Acting in the role of a mediator, and working either alone or in a small group, prepare a report drawing on the material from this chapter. Address the following:

1. What suggestions would you give to the HR Department to improve its written communication strategies?
2. Suggest more appropriate ways the HR Department could have communicated management's strategic plan to the parties involved.

Sources of additional information:

Visit www.stiffsentences.com and view documents written for a range of corporate, private and public audiences. www.nzno.org.nz/ is the website of the New Zealand Nurses Organization, and www.hrinz.org.nz is the website for the country's professional association, the Human Resources Institute.

Canavor, N. and Meirowitz, C. (2005) 'Good corporate writing: why it matters and what to do', *Communication World*, 22, July, p. 4.

Gray, R. and Robertson, L. (2005) 'Effective communication starts at the top', *Communication World*, 22, July, p. 4.

Weiss, E., H. (2005) 'The elements of international English style: A guide to writing correspondence, reports, technical documents and internet pages for a global audience', Armonk, NY: M.E. Sharpe.

Notes

This case study is based on real organization(s) and real organizational experiences. The names, facts and other details have been changed to protect the privacy of individuals and organizations.

The case study was written by Carolyn Forshaw, Thompson Rivers University, Kamloops, Canada.

Web-based assignment

We have explained that the nature of the communication process established in the organization reflects the management style, degree of employee participation, culture and efficiency in the workplace. Communication is essential for effective decision making. Ineffective communication is linked to a 'command and control' vision of management.

This web-based assignment requires you to investigate the extent of communication processes in workplaces in Britain. Visit the website for the Findings from the 2004 Workplace Survey: www.dti.gov.uk/er/emar/2004wers.htm and review the survey findings. What arrangements for direct communications with employees are most popular in (a) the private sector and (b) the public sector? Based on your understanding of this chapter, what 'downward' communications arrangements do you believe are most effective? Explain your answer.

OB in films

My Cousin Vinnie (1992) is about a former car mechanic, Vincent Gambini, played by Joe Pesci, getting his first legal case after passing his law examination. His cousin Bill Gambini, played by Ralph Macchio, retains him as his defence lawyer in his trial for allegedly murdering a grocery store employee. In the first 10 minutes of the film, there is a scene in which Bill Gambini and a friend drive up to the store. It ends with the two men sitting on a bench in handcuffs. What is the basis of the miscommunication shown in the scene?

Notes

1   Grint (2005b: 309).
2   Howells (1987: 186).
3   Crowley and Hawhee (1999: 14).
4   Bratton et al. (2005), Dean and Sharfman (1996).
5   Byers (1997), Stacks et al. (1991).
6   Guffey, Rhodes and Rogin (2005).
7   Calás and Smircich (1996), Howells (1987).
8   Macionis, Jansson and Benoit (2005: 93).
9   Hodson and Sullivan (2002).
10 Goffman (1967).
11 Bilton et al. (2002: 509).
12 Weick (1979).
13 Gray and Robertson (2005: 26).
14 Smith (1993), Taylor (1995) in Putnam, Philips and Chapman (1999).
15 Putnam et al., in Clegg, Hardy and Nord (1999: 146).
16 Townley (1994).
17 Neher (1997).
18 Neher (1997).
19 Field and House (1995).
20 Robbins (1990).
21 Putnam et al., in Clegg et al. (1999: 126).
22 Putnam et al., in Clegg et al. (1999: 126).
23 Scott, as quoted in Eisenberg and Goodall (1997: 57).
24 Robbins and Langton (2001), McShane (2006).
25 Daft and Huber (1987).
26 Grint (2000).
27 Neher (1997).
28 Morgan (1980).
29 Yuval-Davis (1997).
30 As quoted in Yuval-Davis (1997: 40).
31 Putnam et al., in Clegg, Hardy and Nord (1999).
32 Ashcroft et al. (1989: 151).
33 See for example Riley (1983), Morgan (1980, 1986), Alvesson and Due Billing (1997).
34 Riley (1983), Filipczak (1996).
35 Alvesson and Due Billing (1997: 112).
36 Eisenberg and Goodall (1997).
37 Morgan (1980).
38 Yuval-Davis (1997: 40).
39 Frost et al., quoted in Alvesson and Due Billing (1997: 104).
40 Alvesson and Due Billing (1997).
41 Morgan (1980).
42 Alvesson (1996).

43 Alvesson (1996).

44 Quoted in Alvesson (1997: 68).

45 Byers (1997: 4).

46 Deetz and Mumby (1986), quoted in Alvesson and Due Billing (1996: 66).

47 Mintzberg (1973).

48 Freedman and Medway (1994a).

49 Freedman and Medway (1994b: 148).

50 Freedman and Medway (1994b: 149).

51 Field and House (1995).

52 Robbins and Langton (2001).

53 Bratton, Grint and Nelson (2005).

54 Kanter (1977), quoted in Alvesson and Due Billing (1997: 107).

55 Witherspoon (1997).

56 Grint (2001).

57 Stewart (1967).

58 Goleman (1998).

59 Black (1996).

60 Grint (2001).

61 Coe (1990).

62 Coe (1990: 397).

63 Grint (2001).

64 Alvesson (1996).

65 Kidd et al. (2001).

66 Nkomo and Cox (1999: 88).

67 Clegg et al. (1999: 88).

68 Ashforth and Mael, in Nkomo and Cox (1999).

69 Tan (1998).

70 McShane (2006: 187).

71 Parker (1992: 100).

72 Hall (1976).

73 Field and House (1995).

74 Robbins and Langton (2001).

75 Bilton et al. (2002).

76 Tannen (1990).

77 Krippendorff (1985).

78 Stohl and Cheney (2001).

79 Giddens (1984).

80 Stohl and Cheney (2001: 380).

chapter 13

Decision making

> It is … important to study how it is that those who make decisions well arrive at such decisions and how they differ from those who habitually make judgments less well.[1]
>
> The organization stops dead in its tracks, not on the substance of an issue but on how a decision will be made.[2]

chapter outline

- ▷ The nature of decision making
- ▷ The rhetorics of decision making
- ▷ The realities of decision making
- ▷ Employee involvement in decision making
- ▷ Ethics and decision making
- ▷ Developing decision-making skills
- ▷ Chapter summary
- ▷ Key concepts
- ▷ Chapter review questions
- ▷ Further reading
- ▷ Chapter case study: A new venture for Echo Generation Publishing
- ▷ Web-based assignment
- ▷ OB in films
- ▷ Notes

chapter objectives

After completing this chapter, you should be able to:

- ▷ define organizational decision making
- ▷ explain the rational model of decision process
- ▷ compare and contrast the rational model with how managers actually make decisions
- ▷ describe the benefits of employee involvement in decision making
- ▷ summarize the pros and cons of using groups to make decisions
- ▷ discuss techniques for improving organizational decision making.

Introduction

In technical terms, it was a piece of foam about the size of a laptop computer that caused the disintegration on re-entry into Earth's atmosphere of the space shuttle *Columbia* in February 2003. However, a scathing US government report concluded that the root cause of the fatal crash was managerial myopia and the culture of the US National Aeronautics and Space Administration (NASA). Individuals in NASA made decisions affecting *Columbia*. Senior managers determined NASA's goals, mission schedules and budget. Middle-level managers also made decisions impacting on *Columbia*'s mission. They determined production schedules, space shuttle design and safety, and decided to reduce its workforce and rely increasingly on outside contractors. NASA's engineers 'found themselves in the unusual position of having to prove that the situation was *unsafe* – a reversal of the usual requirement to prove that a situation *is safe*,' the report states.[3]

Of course, making decisions is not the sole prerogative of managers. Non-managerial employees at NASA also made decisions that affected their work and *Columbia*. The more obvious of these decisions might include whether to comply with a request made by a manager, knowing that safety standards are being compromised. Individual decision making, therefore, is an important part of organizational behaviour.

The work conducted at NASA is frequently used to illustrate the highest levels of cognitive ability, reflected in the popular comment, 'This isn't rocket science.' So how could so many smart people who do engage in rocket science make a series of such bad decisions? We shall find out in this chapter. First, we define decision making and present a model of decision making that characterizes the process as a rational act. As we work through this model, we shall be especially concerned with exploring the neoclassical economic assumption that managers act rationally towards a common purpose, and the practical limitations of managerial rationality. We investigate whether work groups make better decisions than individuals, and can improve creative thinking in the workplace. Then through political theory we explore decision making as an enactment of power, which will provide further insight into the limits of managerial rationality. Finally, the chapter closes with a consideration of ethics in decision making and a description of some techniques to improve decision making. The purpose of the chapter is not only to give an overview of 'best practice' but also to situate decision making in the context of managerial rationales, opportunities, constraints and power.

The nature of decision making

decision making: a conscious process of making choices between one or more alternatives with the intention of moving toward some desired state of affairs

Decision making is the conscious process of making choices from among several alternatives with the intention of moving towards some desired course of action.[4] Three things are noteworthy about this definition. First, decision making involves making a *choice* among several action alternatives: for instance, NASA's engineers can choose to have a spacecraft carry more or less inventory, and can decide to use different materials or rely on external contractors to make and assemble space components. Second, decision making is a *process* that involves more than simply the final choice among alternatives – if a NASA manager decides to outsource work, we want to know how this decision was reached. Finally, the 'action' mentioned in the definition typically involves some commitment of *resources*, such as money, personnel or time. The *Columbia* shuttle project required a substantial resource commitment.

Decision making is possibly the most important management function. Ever since Fayol's seminal work,[5] which identified management as a series of rational activities related to planning, organizing, directing and controlling, it has been appreciated that managerial behaviour involves decision making. This perspective of management assumes that managers act rationally as they continually strive to enhance the efficiency and competitive position of the organization. The control perspective of management also proceeds from the general assumption that managers act rationally, which, according to this school, involves making decisions designed to maximize control of the labour process and the level of 'surplus' extracted from workers.

Table 13.1 show that organizational decision making can be studied at different levels: the individual, group and organizational. Each level centres on its own set of assumptions and theoretical approach, and its own key issues. However, the levels are interconnected, with each one influencing and being affected by the other two levels.

STOP AND REFLECT

Before reading on, think about your own work experience, or your knowledge of work organizations. Can you think of a group or an individual decision that has led to success or failure?

table 13.1 Levels of organizational decision-making behaviour

Level of analysis	Theoretical approaches	Key issues
Organizational	Theories of organization power, politics, conflict and decision making	Effects of power, politics and conflict
Group	Group conformity, group dynamics, group size and networks	Effects of group dynamics, individuals' perceptions and behaviours
Individual	Information-processing theory Cognitive psychology	Information overload Personal biases

The rhetorics of decision making

The rhetoric and debate about organizational decision making draws heavily on what is referred to as the 'rational' economic model of decision making. The model has its roots in neoclassical economic theory. Managers continually strive to find the right mix of factor inputs (such as raw materials, machinery and labour) to enable them to minimize per unit production costs and maximize profits. The rational economic model underscores the importance of managerial decision making on the issues of resource allocation, efficiency and labour productivity. The model is primarily normative, providing a guide on how managerial decision making ought to be done. It is shown in Figure 13.1.

The first step in the rational decision model is to identify a problem or recognize an opportunity. A *problem* is the deviation between the current and desired situation – the gap between 'what is' and 'what ought to be'. An *opportunity* is a deviation between current expectations and a potentially better situation, which had not previously been expected. In other words, decision makers realize that alternative decisions may produce outcomes beyond current expectations or goals.

The second step is to gather all relevant information related to the problem or opportunity, and the third step is to generate a list of possible solutions. This typically involves searching for off-the-shelf or ready-made solutions, such as practices that have been effective elsewhere in similar situations. Step four is to evaluate each alternative solution. In a purely rational process, this involves decision makers identifying all factors against which the alternatives are judged, assigning weights reflecting the importance of those factors, rating each alternative on those factors, and then calculating each alternative's total value from the ratings and factor weights.

Step five involves choosing the best solution based on the systematic rating exercise, and in step six, the chosen solution is implemented. The final step in the rational decision-making model involves evaluating the decision to see whether the solution has narrowed the gap between 'what is' and 'what ought to be'. Ideally, these seven steps are informed by relevant and objective feedback in the form of a feedback loop.

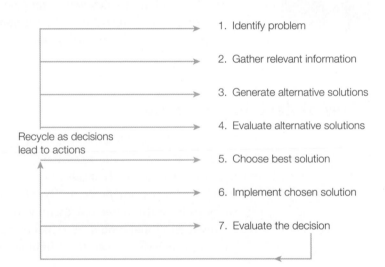

1. Identify problem

2. Gather relevant information

3. Generate alternative solutions

4. Evaluate alternative solutions

Recycle as decisions
lead to actions

5. Choose best solution

6. Implement chosen solution

7. Evaluate the decision

figure 13.1 A rational decision-making model

Assumptions of the rational economic decision-making model

Assumptions inevitably enter analyses of decision making. Take for example problem identification: this first step in the decision-making process makes assumptions on rationality. In the case of NASA managerial decisions, one might ask, why outsource work in the first place? Perhaps in order to ensure safety standards are not compromised, NASA engineers could manufacture and assembly the shuttle's components on-site under rigorous supervision. Or why assume that outside contractors can meet safety standards and remain within budget? Perhaps the criterion for the decision is not simply to choose the low-cost option.

Multiple criteria might be to balance the cost of the component, demonstrable safety results, and the time taken to deliver the component. In order to be rational, NASA decision makers must assign weights to each of these three criteria. The weights indicate how important each is compared with the others. Given these weights a new optimal production operation can be chosen. While the decision to rely on outside contractors, for example, appears to fit the rational model, assumptions have been built into the solution.

Criterion weights are assumptions because they are based on the values and preferences of the decision maker. The point we are making here is that even decisions made with the rational model have assumptions built in. These assumptions deal with the way the problem is identified and the way objectives are defined. The designers of the rational decision-making model hold a cluster of assumptions about human tendencies when it comes to decision making in the workplace. Let us briefly review some of those assumptions.

▷ *Problem clarity.* The problem is clear and unambiguous. The decision maker is assumed to have complete information regarding the decision situation.

▷ *Known options.* It is assumed the decision maker can identify all the relevant criteria and can list all the viable alternatives. Additionally, the decision maker is aware of all the possible consequences of each alternative.

▷ *Clear preferences.* Rationality assumes that the criteria and alternatives can be ranked and weighted to reflect their importance.

▷ *Constant preferences.* It is assumed that the specific decision criteria are constant and that the weights assigned to them are stable over time.

▷ *Maximum payoff.* The rational decision maker will choose the alternative that yields the highest efficiency or return on factor inputs.

▷ *No time or cost constraints.* The rational decision maker can obtain full information about criteria and alternatives because it is assumed that there are no time or cost constraints.

STOP AND REFLECT

Examine your own choice of which college or university to attend. To what extent did your decision follow the rational decision-making approach?

The realities of decision making

The rational model is a rhetoric used by managers at the very top of an organization bureaucracy, and it reinforces managers' claim to knowledge and competence. There is evidence, however, that this normative model of decision making is rarely realized fully or extensively in practice. Over the last three decades, numerous organizational theories have attempted to explain why individuals, groups and organizations fail to follow the rational model. We shall discuss major impediments to rational decision making which operate at the individual, group, and organizational level.

At the individual level

Individual rationality is constrained by at least four factors: information processing failure, perceptual biases, intuition and emotion, and escalation of commitment.

Information processing failures

Individual managers do not make wholly rational decisions because they may not acquire sufficient information to make a 'perfect' decision, or they have too much information, and this prevents them from making a good decision. Individuals may make bad or non-rational decisions because of incomplete information. Herbert Simon called this bounded rationality.[6] The bounds of rationality often force managers to make decisions based on intuition, or what is commonly called their 'gut feeling'. While intuitive decisions may be seen as non-rational because they do not follow the model, it can be argued that hunches or guesses can be an effective way to decide, in which the subconscious brain provides the conscious brain with information.[7]

bounded rationality: processing limited and imperfect information and satisficing rather than maximizing when choosing among alternatives

intuition: the ability to know when a problem or opportunity exists and select the best course of action without conscious reasoning information overload: a situation when the receiver becomes overwhelmed by the information that needs to be processed. It may be caused the *quantity* of the information to be processed, the *speed* at which the information presents itself, and the *complexity* of the information to be processed.

While incomplete or imperfect information can be a barrier to rational decision making, too much information can also prevent optimal decisions. Information overload is the reception of more information than is necessary to make effective decisions. Rather than improving decision making, information overload can lead to errors, omissions, delays and cutting corners. Managers facing information overload often attempt to use all the information at hand, then get confused and permit irrelevant or low-quality information to influence their decisions.

For example, you may have experienced information overload when writing an essay. To impress your instructor you attempt to incorporate too many viewpoints and too many references into the paper, and this results in a disjointed, confusing and low-quality essay. So more information does not necessarily lead to optimal decisions.

Managers may also choose the first alternative that does the job, or meets the requirements of the problem to a satisfactory degree, rather than the 'best' alternative. Simon called this behaviour satisficing – selecting an alternative that is satisfactory rather than optimal. Satisficing occurs because of information overload. It is not possible to identify all the feasible alternatives, and information about the alternatives is imperfect.

satisficing: selecting a solution that is satisfactory, or 'good enough' rather than optimal or 'the best'

Even if individuals have all the relevant information, they cannot possibly think through all the alternatives and the outcomes of those alternatives as prescribed by the rational model because they lack the cognitive capacity.[8] This is not because they are dim-witted, but rather because managers typically have limited time in which to make decisions, and some decisions simply to do not lend themselves to purely rational 'scientific' calculation. Complex managerial decisions usually involve both measurable and non-measurable, or qualitative, considerations. Consequently, managers normally look at only a few alternatives, and only some of the main outcomes of those alternatives.

Students of decision process theory essentially argue that decisions are made and actions taken depending on the individuals who happen to be involved and the alternatives they happen to identify. For example, there are scores of MBA programmes to choose from and dozens of modules to consider, yet people typically evaluate only a few MBA offerings and the main features of each programme of studies. In summary, although relevant and timely information improves decisions, managers often obtain less or more information that is necessary for adequate decision making.

Perceptual biases

Along with processing information and evaluating quantitative and qualitative considerations, individuals make imperfect decisions because of flawed perceptions. As we learned in Chapter 7, selective interest mechanisms cause relevant information to be unconsciously filtered out. Moreover, managers, workers and others with vested interests try to influence people's perceptions so that it is more or less likely that a situation is perceived as an opportunity or challenge.

Another perceptual problem, also noted in Chapter 7, is that people see opportunities or challenges through their mental models. These working models of reality help individuals make sense of their world, but they also perpetuate assumptions that obscure new realities. Table 13.2 presents a list of these individual biases in decision making. For example, people judge actions that are more vivid in their memory, they fail to pay sufficient attention to the skewed effects of sample size when evaluating the importance of data, and they tend to be overconfident about the accuracy of their judgement when addressing moderately to extremely difficult problems.

table 13.2 Individual biases in decision making

Perceptual bias	Description
Ease of recall	Individuals judge events that are more easily recalled from memory to be more numerous than events of equal frequency whose instances are less easily recalled
Insensitivity to sample size	Individuals frequently fail to appreciate the role of sample size in evaluating the accuracy of sample information
Over-confidence	Individuals tend to be over-confident about the accuracy of their judgement when they answer moderately to extremely difficult questions
Method of memory search	Individuals are biased in their assessment of the frequency of events based upon the way their memory structure affects the search process
Illusory correlation	Individuals tend to overestimate the probability of two events co-occurring when their memory recall finds that the two events have occurred together in the past
Hindsight	After finding out whether or not an event occurred, individuals tend to overestimate the degree to which they would have predicted the event without the benefit of hindsight
Regression to the mean	Individuals fail to note the statistical fact that extreme events tend to regress to the mean on subsequent trials

Intuition and emotion

Individuals in the workplace can make decisions based on their intuition. This is usually called making a decision by 'gut instinct'. Many managers will tell you they pay attention to their intuition or hunches when making decisions. Intuition is the ability to know when an opportunity or problem exists and to select the best course of action without conscious reasoning. These intuitions however, are rarely the sole factor in the decision-making process. Individuals quite often analyse the available information, and then turn to their intuition to complete the process.

Intuitive decisions may be seen as non-rational because they do not follow the rational model, but research evidence suggests that intuition can play a role in strategic decision making.[9] More than 80 per cent of organizational knowledge – information that has been edited, put into context, and analysed in a way that makes it meaningful to decision makers – is implicit and is difficult to quantify or even describe accurately.[10] It is suggested that intuition is the channel through which individuals use their implicit or tacit knowledge. Tacit knowledge is the wisdom learned from life experience, observation and insight, which is not clearly understood and therefore is impossible to transfer to others.

To grasp the significance of tacit knowledge in decision making, try to describe the physical characteristics of a good friend who buys antiques for a living. Now try to describe the methods your friend would use to make purchase decisions at an auction. The former involves explicit knowledge, while the latter involves your tacit knowledge of your friend. At an auction, your friend's behaviour appears to be instinctual, but it is based on her or his past experience, what she or he has heard and read, and the state of the market for a particular antique. Thus, intuition allows individuals to draw on a vast reservoir of knowledge, experience and process discoveries.

The neoclassical rational model neglects to factor into the process the effects of emotions on individual decision making.[11] While we know the rational dimension of the brain processes information about the various alternatives (imperfectly, because of cognitive capacity and time limits, as we just learned), the emotional dimension more rapidly creates emotional markers that attract individuals to some alternatives and cause them to be repelled by others. For example, some research suggests that people's general disposition or mood can support or obstruct the decision-making process. Specifically, individuals tend to evaluate alternatives more accurately when in a negative or neutral mood, whereas they tend to engage in more perceptual biases when they are in a positive mood. This suggests that we need to be aware that decision making and logical analysis are affected by human emotion.

The rational model disregards the effects of gender on the decision-making process, which suggests that its underlying character is a male-related phenomenon and not applicable to all employees. Social factors, such as how collective social norms and expectations frame 'sense-making' or problem definition, tend to be neglected in orthodox treatments of decision making.[12] As we saw in Chapter 12, there are important differences between the conversational styles of men and women. It seems plausible that gender can create communication barriers in the decision-making process when, as some academics have argued, women have a 'different voice'.

The difference thesis contends that men see conversation as a tool – to exchange information, accomplish a task or preserve power – while women see conversation as a way to nurture, support and empathize, and that female managers use a more open communication style when dealing with people issues than typical male managers. Radical feminists might argue that the collective and systematic oppression of women by men results in different moral values. Women construct and value knowledge in ways that are relational, and oriented more towards sustaining relationships than achieving autonomy and power. Adopting this view of women – the notion that they have a different voice and a more holistic view of reality – suggests that the decision-making process will be strongly influenced by the gender balance of the decision makers.[13]

Escalation of commitment

escalation of commitment: the tendency to allocate more resources to a failing course of action or to repeat an apparently bad decision

The fourth factor that limits individual rationality in decision making is escalation of commitment to a losing course of action. While it is clear why an individual would become more committed to a decision whose outcomes are positive, why does commitment sometimes increase when outcomes are negative? For example, a project manager reviewing lack of progress and a financial planner examining declining share prices might increase their commitment to their initial decision.

The objective characteristics of a project will be important in determining continued commitment to a decision.[14] For example, large early losses or major setbacks can cause a project to be abandoned, while small losses or minor setbacks can be tolerated. However, as small losses become larger, the total loss accumulates, until so much is committed that an individual will tolerate future risk to try to avoid the certain loss. If the individual decision maker determines that early losses are the result of a temporary problem and that further investment is likely to ensure a good return, then project commitment is likely to increase.

Psychological and political factors can also cause an individual to escalate commitment to a decision. Despite large losses, individuals can tend to become more committed to a course of action when their decision is explicit and unambiguous, irrevocable, made publicly, made repeatedly, and/or is personally important.

Can you think of examples in which a CEO, politician or military commander showed escalated commitment to a bad decision?

STOP AND REFLECT

Source: Getty Images

plate 36   Group decision making might allow individual members to escape responsibility, and encourage 'groupthink'

At the group level

While research comparing the performance of individuals and groups on decision making indicates that groups are more effective then individuals, the by-products of group dynamics have received a considerable amount of attention from researchers. As we discussed when we examined work groups, the phenomenon of group conformity or 'groupthink' has the potential to undermine a group's ability to make effective decisions.

For people to change their behaviour or choose an alternative to fit the norms of a social group is called conformity. It may make sense to follow others' behaviour or judgement when you are inexperienced or when the situation is ambiguous, but just how strongly do group norms influence individual behaviour and decision making when the situation is unmistakable? Research by Solomon Asch and Stanley Milgram provided the answer to this question.[15] Asch recruited several groups of students, allegedly to study visual perception. Before the experiment began, he explained to all the students, apart from one student in each small group, that the real purpose was to put pressure on the selected one student. Each group of students was asked to estimate the lengths of lines presented on a card. A sample line was shown at the left, and the group was to choose which of the three lines on the right matched it (see Figure 13.2). Group members were seated so that the subject answered last. Group pressure did not affect the subjects' perception, but it did affect their behaviour. Initially, as planned, group members made the correct matches (B on Card 2). When, however, Asch's accomplices made incorrect responses, the uninformed subject became uncomfortable, and 76 per cent of the subjects chose to

Card A1   Card 2

figure 13.2   An example of the cards used in Asch's experiment in group conformity

conform by answering incorrectly on at least one trial. The study shows how strong the tendency to conform can be, even when the pressure comes from people we do not know.

In Milgram's controversial study, a researcher explained to male recruits that they would be participating in an experiment on how physical punishment affects adult learning. The learner, actually an accomplice of Milgram's, was seated in a fake electric chair, with electrodes fastened to the wrist and secured by leather straps. In an adjoining room the subject, playing the role of educator, was seated in front of a replica 'shock generator' with the capacity to administer an electric 'shock' of between 15 to 315 'volts' to the learner. The educator was directed to read aloud pairs of words, and the learner was asked to recall the second word. Whenever the adult learner failed to answer correctly, the educator was instructed to apply an electric shock. Although the educator heard moans and then screams as the level of volts increased, none of the subjects questioned the experiment. Milgram's research suggests that people are likely to follow the directions of 'legitimate authority figures', even when it means inflicting pain on another individual.

Another well-known study by Irving Janis illustrates how 'experts' can succumb to group pressure.[16] Janis coined the term 'groupthink' to describe how highly cohesive groups can overestimate the strengths of the group. This can result in an illusion of the invulnerability of the group, and a belief in the inherent morality of the group. The group becomes closed-minded about the decision under consideration, and pressures in the group create group conformity. Table 13.3 outlines some symptoms of groupthink.

For more information on the experiments undertaken by Asch and Milgram visit:
www.qeliz.ac.uk/psychology/Asch.htm
and www.new-life.net/milgram.htm

WEB LINK

table 13.3 Symptoms of groupthink

Symptom	Description
Illusion of invulnerability	Group members are arrogant and ignore obvious danger signals
Illusion of morality	Groups decision(s) are not only perceived as sensible, they are also perceived as morally correct
Rationalization	Counter-arguments are rationalized away
Stereotypes of outsiders	Members construct unfavourable stereotypes of those outside the group who are the targets of their decisions
Self-censorship	Members perceive that unanimous support exists for their decisions and action
Mindguard	Individual(s) within the group shield the group from information that goes against its decisions

Obviously, groupthink results in low-quality decisions. More seriously, it has been implicated in the decision processes that led to NASA's fatal launch of *Challenger* in 2003, and the US and UK invasion of Iraq in 2003. Prior to the invasion, the US official position was that Iraq illegally possessed weapons of mass destruction in violation of UN Security Council Resolution 1441 and had to be disarmed by force. The decision to embark on the Iraq invasion, termed 'Operation Iraqi Freedom', was made by President George W. Bush and a small group of military and intelligence advisers. After investigating the events, which continue to shape the course of twenty-first century history as we write, a US Senate Committee found that the

Central Intelligence Agency (CIA) had dismissed alternative reports, and that the intelligence community as a whole suffered from 'collective group think'.[17]

The research by Asch, Milgram and Janis tells us that social groups influence the behaviour of their members, altering perceptions of reality and often promoting conformity, which can lead to imperfect and even catastrophic decisions.

At the organization level

Individuals and groups in work organizations do not make decisions in a vacuum. Individual and group decision making is polycontextual: that is, it involves multiple ongoing tasks, and changing interlocking constraints and opportunities. Each individual and group decision invokes its own micro-world, informed by a stream of information and alternatives that shape perception and talk, the decision and ways of acting. The neoclassical rational model of decision making has been insightfully likened to a garbage can:

> To understand processes within organizations we view a choice opportunity as a garbage can into which various kinds of problems and solutions are dumped by participants as they are generated. The mix of garbage in a single can depends upon the mix of cans available, on the labels attached to alternative cans, on what garbage is currently being produced and on the speed with which garbage is collected and removed from the situation.[18]

Rather than viewing managerial decision making as linear and mechanistic, 'decision process' theorists view decision making as a cyclical process of acting and reacting to various problems, necessities and opportunities. To better comprehend decision making in such a 'garbage can' organization, consider organizational decision making as a reflective learning process involving some thinking ahead, reflection on action, as well as some adjustment en route. Others have pointed out that strategic decisions, typically taught as an example of senior-level managerial rationality, are rarely 'purely deliberate, just as few are purely emergent. One means no learning, the other means no control.'[19]

plate 37 Encouraging controversy in small groups can generate new ideas and challenge old ways of doing things

Source: Getty Images

The organization itself constrains decision makers. Historical precedents, the organization's human resource systems, and imposed time constraints shape organizational decision making. Decisions on the future evolve from reflection on past experience. Decisions made in the past are ghosts that continually haunt current choices. For instance, past commitments may constrain current options. In the 1970s, for example, when consumers demanded more energy-efficient small cars because of soaring petrol prices, North American car manufacturers' choices were constrained by past decisions to invest in machinery to produce gas-inefficient large cars.

The organization's human resource management system influences decision makers. Managers are strongly influenced in their decision making by the criteria by which they are evaluated and rewarded. For example, if a manager believes that the section or division under her or his control is operating most efficiently when there are 'zero defects', we should not be surprised to find the manager avoiding risks and making decisions that discourage other workers from experimenting and trying new ways of doing their tasks.

Time not only disciplines workers, it imposes deadlines on decision makers. A multitude of decisions must be made quickly to satisfy the requirements of production or customers. For example, managers need to complete budgets by an organizationally imposed deadline. These self-imposed time constraints put pressure on decision makers and often make it difficult, if not impossible, to gather all the information they might like to have before making a final choice. For example, a manager might need to purchase a piece of equipment before the end of the budget year, since the rule is 'spend it or lose it'. Thus, past decisions and established routines, and HR assumptions and practices, become embedded in managerial practices over time, and together with time constraints, they influence how decision makers define and perceive problems, which shapes organizational decision making.

An alternative approach to explaining the nature of organizational decision making is the political theory model. The proponents of this model characterize the workplace as a purposive miniature society, with politics pervading all managerial decision making. By 'politics' we mean the power relationships between managers and relevant others, and the capacity of an individual manager to influence in turn others who are in a state of dependence. This perspective to studying decision making offers an approach that examines individual managers as 'knowledgeable human agents' functioning within a dynamic arena where they compete for resources, power and status.

Thus, managers may attach great importance to forming alliances and building networks of cooperative relationships with other important decision makers in their organization. For example, a college president may decide to break up a department of continuing education and 'decentralize' the provision of lifelong learning programmes to other divisions in the college, to sustain his or her power and to 'warn' other recalcitrant administrators to 'watch out'.

Organizations need a governance structure that encourages multiple voices and stimulates change. Such a political environment is often required because of the ambiguity and uncertainty identified under the decision process model, which compels decision makers to rely on more subjective criteria. Politics also encourages multiple voices to be heard on an issue. And political manoeuvring may dislodge the 'vested interest' of an organization and stimulate necessary change: 'It is politics that is able to work as a kind of "invisible hand" – "invisible underhand" would be a better term – to promote necessary change.'[20] The political perspective, however, has been criticized for failing to give sufficient attention to 'power struggles' in the workplace.[21]

The decision process and political theories offer alternative insights into the nature of managerial decision making on a day-to-day basis. Rather than viewing

political theory model: an approach to understanding decision-making whose adherents assert that formal organizations comprise of groups that have separate interests, goals and values, and in which power and influence are needed in order to reach decisions.

decisions as a series of linear and rational steps, these schools of thought see managerial decision making as a cycle involving enactment, reflection on experience, reframing of meaning, and reenactment under conditions of competition, ambiguity and uncertainty, and subject often to the 'invisible hand' of internal politicking. Not surprisingly, organizational decision making may appear complex, variable, inconsistent and often contradictory. However, it would be a mistake to believe that managerial decision making really is chaotic and irrational. Underneath the surface, it might be more rational in substance than it is in form.[22] Senior managers are generally able to use their power to impose rationality. It is also true that the management process takes place in an environment of capitalist employment relations, where it is overarched by powerful organizational and market imperatives. These permit few substantial irrational decisions that would threaten the organization's standing or competitive position.

Employee involvement in decision making

The nature of employee involvement

employee involvement: the degree to which employees influence how their work is organized and carried out

Employee involvement (EI) is entrenched in contemporary management theory. It is most often associated with theories of post-bureaucratic organizational structures, work teams and 'diffuse' or 'empowered' styles of managerial leadership. EI refers to the degree to which subordinates influence how their work is organized and performed. Meaningful decision making requires that workers are able to exert some influence over their work and the conditions under which they work.

EI initiatives suggests a commonality of interest between workers and management. Managerially driven EI initiatives can only be understood in their historical and sociological context. Employers tend to pursue EI practices to improve employee cooperation, enhance productivity and for their rhetorical appeal for change. The emergence and take-up of EI practices is clearly linked to changes in work organization, and tends to be faddish in character.[23]

Ethics in decision making

Is 'business ethics' a contradiction in terms? Should ethics play a part in everyday managerial decision making in organizations? In an influential essay, the American economist Milton Friedman argued that the role of ethics in business management is rather limited: 'there is one and only one social responsibility of business – to use its resources and engage in activities designed to increase its profits'.[24] Others have countered that business managers can pursue a socially responsible course without the objectionable results claimed by Friedman.[25] Those who manage organizations have to work out their own code of conduct, but the ethical framework in which decision making takes place is embedded in society.[26]

Barring legal interventions, others have noted that the major incentive for organizations to engage in ethical activities is customer power. Shell's behaviour over the Brent Spar incident is an example of how customer boycotts can change corporate behaviour. There is evidence, however, that ethical HR practices are more likely to be offered to permanent knowledge workers employed within an organization's legal boundaries, than to routine production or in-service workers on non-standard employment contracts.[27]

Read a chapter on 'The ethical context of HRM' by Karen Legge.[28] What business does ethics have in business organizations? In an era defined by increasing economic globalization and virtual organizations, can organizations manage people at work and engage in value-added activities in an ethical way?

There are two types of EI, direct and indirect. *Direct involvement* refers to those forms of participation where individual workers are involved in the decision-making processes that affect their everyday work routines, albeit often in a very limited way. Examples of direct EI include briefing groups, quality circles, problem-solving teams, and self-managed teams (see Chapter 11 for a discussion on work groups). At the lowest level, involvement involves asking workers for information. They might not even know what the problem is about and do not make recommendations. At a moderate level of direct involvement, workers are told about the problem and asked to provide recommendations to the decision maker. At the highest level of direct involvement, the decision-making process is handed over to workers. They identify the problem, chose the best alternative, and implement their choice.

Indirect involvement refers to those forms of worker participation where representatives or delegates of the main body of workers participate in the strategic decision-making process. Examples of indirect participation include joint consultation committees (JCC), European Works Councils (EWC) and 'worker directors'. All these forms are associated with the broader notion of industrial democracy. Some EU countries require worker involvement at both the work site and corporate levels through a process of codetermination. In Sweden and Germany, for instance, employee representatives sit on supervisory boards, making decisions about executive salaries and recommendations about the company's strategic goals. At the same time, employers must consult with employee representation committees regarding matters of new technology, employment staffing, and work and HR processes. Survey data indicates that indirect EI became less extensive in the period between 1980 and 2004.[29]

industrial democracy: a broad term used to describe a range of programmes, processes, and social institutions designed to provide greater employee involvement and influence in the decision-making process, and to exchange ideas on how to improve working conditions and product and service quality in the workplace

Advantages of employee involvement

The current enthusiasm for EI needs to be viewed within the context of changing business and associated human resource (HR) strategies, where the purpose of the latter is to secure employee involvement, support and commitment to high-performance work systems.[30] EI supports management's goals, either directly through potentially improving the quality of decision making by ensuring that problems are recognized faster and defined more accurately, or indirectly through organizational commitment. Workers are, in many respects, the barometers of the workplace's environment. When work activities, systems or machines fail to meet performance standards, workers are usually the first to know. EI ensures that problems are quickly identified and corrected.

For general information on EI schemes, go to: www.acas.org.uk
www.dti.gov.uk/er/emar/2004wers.htm (Britain)
www.fdmmag.com/articles/03aco.htm
http://hrdc-drhc.gc.ca
www.eia.com
www.clc-ctc.ca (Canada)
www.workindex.com/ (USA)

WEB LINK

EI also supports management's goals indirectly through commitment.[31] The general premise is that increasing workers' involvement in decision making will strengthen organization citizenship. That is, involving people in decision making potentially increases their commitment to the organization's goals, and that in turn will result in enhanced individual and organizational performance. Surveys of managers have shown that EI is typically initiated by management, with the objective of enhancing worker commitment to organizational goals.[32] The involvement–commitment cycle is shown in Figure 13.3, and is the reverse of the vicious circle of control first discussed by Clegg and Dunkerley.[33]

Management theorists have put forward three main reasons for senior management to introduce EI schemes: moral, economic and behavioural.[34]

What do you think of the assumptions underpinning the involvement–commitment cycle? Can the growth of EI be explained by employer 'needs' or are there other forces determining this employee relations practice?

STOP AND REFLECT

▷ First, EI is derived from an ethical, political and moral base. The argument is that in a democratic society, workers should be involved in the decision-making process when the outcomes of those decisions impact on their lives. EI therefore presents a socially acceptable management style. Development of EI and communications will be encouraged because generally companies desire to project 'a socially responsible stance on such issues'.[35]

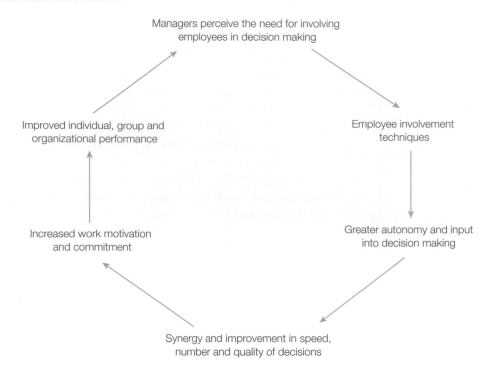

figure 13.3 The involvement–commitment cycle

> Second, employee involvement, according to the 'model of excellence' school in North America, improves the quality of decision making and productivity. For example, work groups, teams or communities of practice generate more complete information and knowledge. By collecting the information and expertise of several individuals, groups or communities of practice bring more input into the decision process. In addition to more input, groups or communities of practice can bring increased diversity of views to the decision process, which offers the opportunity to consider more alternatives. The evidence indicates that a group, team or communities of practice will generally generate higher-quality decisions.

For more examples of companies introducing EI practices, go to the websites of the following companies: General Electric (www.ge.com), Wal-Mart (www.walmart.com), IBM (www.ibm.com), ICI (www.ici.com), or another company you are studying. Once there, go to 'employee participation' or/and 'communications' and follow the prompts.

WEB LINK

> Decisions made collectively in a group, team or community of practice tend to lead to increased acceptance of a solution. Members who participated in making a decision are likely to enthusiastically support the decision and encourage others to accept it. EI potentially also improves the quality of a decision and its chances of successful implementation on the factory floor. Similarly, it is asserted that EI improves productivity and energizes workers, as well as increasing employees' trust in management and reducing workplace stress. Research on the link between EI and firm performance suggests that giving employees a 'voice' on a range of organizational decisions yields benefits to both the organization and the workforce.[36]

> Further, employee involvement potentially reduces dysfunctional behaviour: resistance to change, absenteeism or other forms of conflict. By accepting EI interventions, 'Employers hope that participative mechanisms will create a greater coincidence of interests between employers and employees, thereby increasing trust, reducing the potential for conflict, and increasing the potential for an effective mutual influence process.'[37] As critics point out, by promoting a direct relationship between the worker and management, EI practices can be used to 'educate' and 'reconstitute' the individual as a more malleable and productive employee.[38]

As we mentioned earlier, groupthink is one phenomenon that has the potential to undermine the group's ability to appraise alternative choices and make quality decisions. Another phenomenon that has the potential to adversely affect group decision making is group polarization. This refers to the tendency of work groups to make more extreme decisions than managers and employees working alone. For example, suppose that a board of governors of a college meets to make a decision on the future of a new sports complex for the college. Individual board members might come to the meeting with various degrees of support or opposition to the project. However, by the end of the board meeting, it is highly possible that the board of governors will agree on a more ambitious (that is, a higher financial cost) plan than the average individual had when the board meeting began.

One reason for the more ambitious preference is that individual board members feel less personally responsible for the decision consequences because the entire board of governors makes the decision. Another reason is that board members become comfortable with more extreme positions when they realize that co-members also support the same position. Persuasive arguments favouring the dominant position convince doubtful members and help form a consensus around the most ambitious or extreme option. So persuasion, group support and shifting responsibility explain why groups make more extreme decisions.

OB IN FOCUS

Teams make better decisions than individuals

Teams clearly outperform individuals in economic decision making. That is the key result of a recent laboratory study by Professor Kocher and Professor Sutter. The two researchers show that the type of the decision maker – an individual or a team – makes a significant difference in an interactive economic environment, whether it's the investment and marketing strategies of companies and fund managers or the budget and monetary policy making of governments and central banks.

Small teams are smarter decision makers than individuals because they are better at processing information and better at predicting other decision makers' choices. The growing importance of teams in organizations and decision making in general renders these findings highly relevant. Decision-making teams are everywhere, including families, boards of directors, legislatures and committees. Households and firms, the main players in the economy, are typically not individuals but teams of people with a joint stake in their decisions. Similarly, political and military decisions as well as decisions on monetary policy are frequently taken by teams rather than by individuals.

In the laboratory setting that the researchers used to study the differences in decision making between small teams and individuals, there are four decision makers. Each of them can choose a number between (and including) zero and 100. The winner of the game is the decision maker with the number that is closest to two-thirds of the average of the four chosen numbers. The game is repeated four times. Despite its simplicity, this so-called 'beauty-contest' or 'guessing' game captures important features of investment decisions in financial markets. Kocher and Sutter find that teams (consisting of three people) are much better at guessing what other decision makers do in this game. In their experiment, teams win the game about 80 per cent more often than individuals in cases where small teams compete against individuals.

Source: an article by M. Kocher and M. Sutter in the *Economic Journal*[39]

For further information: visit www.res.org.uk/society/mediabriefings/pdfs/2005/jan05/kocher-sutter.pdf

Ethics and decision making

So far, we have considered individual, group and organization decision making, but given little consideration to whether that decision making is ethical or unethical. Ethics, according to the *Oxford Dictionary*, is 'a set of moral principles'. In 2003 and 2004 cases of corporate leaders engaging in criminal and fraudulent accounting practicing focused greater consideration on ethical and unethical practices in corporate governance and decision making. As a member of the Toronto Stock Exchange's Committee on Corporate Governance, stated:

> It is important, both to the corporate community and to society in general, that business achieve a higher degree of credibility. To do this, business must put its own house in order, starting with fundamental ethics and corporate governance issues and flowing on to responding more actively and publicly to the concerns of our society.[40]

These emergent norms emphasize efficiency, shareholder value and profitability affecting decision-making behaviour, but they also signal a concern beyond profit making: a concern for transparency in accounting practices, the democratic rights of shareholders, and 'a program of moral reform'.[41] Of course, decision makers should internalize a fundamental set of ethics or moral values. How can we explain unethical decision-making behaviour in work organizations? Do immoral individuals such as Kenneth Lay and David Duncan of Enron, Bernard Ebbers and Scott Sullivan of WorldCom, Martha Stewart, and Fausta Tonna at Parmalat promote unethical behaviour? Is it the work context that promotes unethical activity?

Research evidence suggests that moral or immoral behaviour is a function of *both* the individual's traits and the context in which the decision-making process occurs. Figure 13.4 offers a model to account for ethical or unethical decision-making behaviour.[42]

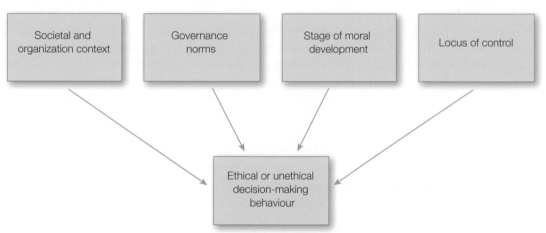

figure 13.4 Determinants of ethical behaviour in work organizations

The *societal and organizational context* refers to an individual's perception of societal and organizational expectations. Does society or the organization encourage and support ethical behaviour by rewarding it, or discourage unethical behaviour by punishing it? Guidelines, public policy statements, codes of ethics, high moral behaviour by senior politicians, corporate leaders, financial performance expectations, appraisal methods that evaluate means as well as ends, visible recognition and promotions for managers and non-managers who display high ethical behaviour, and visible punishment for those who act unethically, are examples of societal and organizational context that is likely to promote high ethical decision making. Commenting on the public backlash against US corporate leaders accused and convicted of engaging in fraudulent accounting practices, one of us elsewhere noted:

> Simply focusing on [individual] traits such as honesty and integrity inappropriately separates the leader from the followers and the context. Those

corporate leaders … who engaged in criminal or highly unethical practices … did so largely because of profound changes in the context. In the late 1990s, shareholder-value-driven capitalism emphasized stock appreciation, the use of stock options to compensate leaders, and the attainment of short-term financial targets, which produced a culture of avarice.[43]

Governance norms focus on democratic decision making that is intended to encourage free and full discussion in order to stimulate the mutual informal learning that can occur under conditions of social symmetry rather than hierarchy.[44] Stages of moral development estimate an individual's capacity to judge what is the 'morally right thing to do'. The higher a person's moral development, the less dependent she or he is on external influences, and hence the more she or he will be predisposed to behave ethically. Leadership theorists have emphasized the importance and centrality of the moral dimension of managerial leadership. Leaders who do not act ethically do not demonstrate true leadership, and this stresses that leaders ultimately must be judged on the basis of a system of values, not just in terms of the instrumental value of profit.[45]

Employees with an internal locus of control (that is, those who believe they are responsible for what takes place, or the outcomes of their decisions and actions) are more likely to rely on their own internal standards of right or wrong to guide their actions. Those with an external locus of control (who believe what happens to them in life is due to chance or luck) are less likely to take responsibility for the consequences of their actions, and are more likely to rely on external influences.

To sum up, corporate leaders and decision makers who lack a strong moral commitment are much less likely to behave unethically and make unethical decisions if they are constrained by a societal and organizational context that disapproves of such behaviours. Conversely, very honourable employees can be corrupted by an organizational context that 'turns a blind eye', permits or encourages unethical behaviour. Sociologists use the term socialization to refer to the lifelong social experience by which individuals develop their human potential and learn moral standards. Stages of moral development and loci of control can change as we interact with different agents of socialization: family, school, our peer group and the mass media.

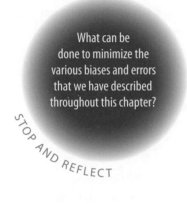

What can be done to minimize the various biases and errors that we have described throughout this chapter?

STOP AND REFLECT

socialization: the lifelong process of social interaction through which individuals acquire a self-identity and the physical, mental and social skills needed for survival in society.

Developing decision-making skills

We have learned that the neoclassical rational model of decision making neglects to factor into the process the effects of culture, gender and race, and tends to give little consideration to social factors, such as how social norms and expectations frame problem definition, and the decision-making process. We have also learned that groups potentially make higher-quality decisions than individuals in certain situations, but group dynamics can also lead to conformity and poor decisions. What can be done to improve the decision-making process and its outcomes?

Researchers have identified various tactics and specific group structures to minimize the biases and errors that we have identified in this chapter. Tactics that can improve decision making include the setting of objectives, maintaining an optimal group size, and not permitting one individual in the group to dominate the process. These tactics help the group to remain focused on outcomes in a timely manner, and encourage individuals to become engaged in critical and creative thinking rather than be restricted by 'groupthink'. Four group structures help to minimize the biases and errors and potentially improve decision making: brainstorming, nominal group technique, computer-mediated-brainstorming and the Delphi technique.

Brainstorming

brainstorming: a freewheeling, face-to-face meeting where team members generate as many ideas as possible, piggyback on the ideas of others, and avoid evaluating anyone's ideas during the idea-generation stage

divergent thinking: involves reframing a problem in a unique way and generating different approaches to the issue

Brainstorming is a group technique to encourage creative thinking and alternatives to problems. It focuses on the generation of ideas and options rather than the evaluation of them. If a group engages in brainstorming it is assumed that group members can feed off each other's ideas and be stimulated to offer more **divergent** and creative ideas.

To be effective, brainstorming requires group members to abide by four rules:

▷ *Speak freely.* Individuals are encouraged to suggest 'off-the-wall' or wacky ideas. Group members should believe that no idea is considered too unusual or extreme to be voiced.

▷ *Multiple ideas.* It is assumed that groups generate better ideas and solutions when they generate multiple ideas. Brainstorming is based on the belief that creative thinking occurs after orthodox ideas have been examined and rejected.

▷ *No criticism.* Group members are more likely to break out of traditional practices and thinking and voice their crazy ideas if other group members are not permitted to ridicule or criticize them.

▷ *Build on the new ideas.* Group members are encouraged to synthesize, combine or 'piggy-back' on the new ideas presented. It is assumed that building on new ideas encourages the synergy of group processes.

The face-to-face brainstorming process might generate fewer ideas than individuals working alone, and thereby not fulfil its full creative potential, if the group is dominated by an outspoken member or if members suffer from inhibition.[46]

Nominal group technique

The nominal group technique is a variation of the traditional brainstorming method that attempts to unite individual creative thinking with group dynamics. The technique curbs discussion during the decision-making process, hence the term nominal. Group members are all physically present, as in a traditional face-to-face brainstorming session, but they operate independently. In theory, this is how it works:

1. A problem or question is presented to the group.
2. Each member independently writes down her or his ideas to solve the problem.
3. Each member in turn describes one idea to the group. This process is repeated until all ideas have been presented and recorded.
4. Members discuss and evaluate each idea.
5. Each member independently ranks the ideas presented. The idea or solution with the highest ranking determines the final decision.

The advantage of the nominal group technique is that it allows the group to meet formally but does not restrict individual input, as the traditional face-to-face brainstorming meeting potentially does.

Computer-mediated-brainstorming

Computer-mediated-brainstorming (CMB) permits group members to share ideas while minimizing many of the problems in group dynamics described earlier. An online facilitator begins the CMB process by posting a problem or question. Members then post their answers or ideas on their computer terminal. All the group's ideas are posted anonymously and randomly on the computer screens. Members individually rank or vote electronically on the ideas or solutions presented. Typically, face-to-face discussion follows the CMB process.

Research suggests that CMB generates more ideas than traditional face-to-face brainstorming, and that participants are more confident and motivated to participate in the decision-making process than in other group structures.[47] CMB groups tend to be more egalitarian than face-to-face groups: that is, gender and status barriers tend to be broken down, and participation is more evenly distributed among men and women members than in face-to-face meetings.

The Delphi technique

Delphi technique: a structured team decision-making process of systematically pooling the collective knowledge of experts on a particular subject to make decisions, predict the future or identify opposing views

The Delphi technique methodically collates the collective knowledge of experts on a particular subject to scan the environment, predict the future, make decisions or identify opposing views. Its name derives from the future-telling ability of the famous Greek Delphic oracle. Delphi groups do not meet face to face, and participants are often located in different parts of the country or world and may not know each other's identity. As with the CMB process, group members do not know who 'owns' the ideas or possible solutions. The Delphi method relies solely on a nominal group and participants – usually experts in a relevant field – do not engage in face-to-face interaction.

Typically, Delphi group members submit ideas or possible solutions to the facilitator in response to a series of questionnaires. The respondents' replies are compiled and returned to the group for a second round of comments. This process may be repeated a couple more times until consensus or dis-consensus emerges. It should be emphasized that the 'experts' taking part do not actually make a final decision: they provide expert advice and information for organizational decision makers.

The advantage of the Delphi technique is that the process pools a large number of expert judgements while avoiding the problems of conformity and polarization that can occur in interacting groups. A disadvantage of the method is the rather lengthy time frame involved, and its effectiveness depends on the respondents' interest in the problem and commitment to the organization.

As we can see, decision making is a complex phenomenon because it involves dealing with technical matters and power struggles. The four group processes reviewed can help managers and other employees deal with the technical challenges and minimize human biases and errors. But decision making is central to managers' ability to alter work organizations and employment relations in the workplace. In this sense, it is at the heart of relationships of class and gender domination. The neoclassical rational model of decision making is associated with a bureaucratic 'command and control' vision of management, as well as a vision of managers as omnipresent and omnipotent. The extent to which organizations can be designed with decentralized decision-making processes is examined in Chapter 15.

Chapter summary

☐ When in July 2006 the owners of the TV company CHUM Ltd decided to sell their company to Bell Globemedia of Canada, 281 people became redundant. Peter Murdoch, media vice-president of the Communications Energy and Paperworks Union, which represents employees in CHUM newsrooms said, 'It's absolutely a sense of betrayal. It's a sense of bewilderment.' From a different angle, CHUM chief executive Jay Switzer commenting on the sale said, 'This is a challenged sector and we have some work to do.'[48] Such decisions by top managers impact on people almost on a daily basis in the corporate world.

☐ Decision making, the conscious process of making choices from among several alternatives to achieve a desired course of action, is said to be perhaps the most important management function. We have explained that decision making is central to managers' ability to alter the activities of the organization, influence the behaviour of employees, and is at the heart of relationships of class and gender domination. Decision making is a complex phenomenon because it involves technical problems and power struggles. We have addressed a number of questions in this chapter, including how managers make decisions, how groups influence decision making, and how decision making can be improved.

☐ We have explained that the dynamics of organizations create a need for decision making. Decision can be viewed as being primarily concerned with the allocation of resources and exercise of power. The neoclassical rational model of decision making has eight steps: identify the problem, define the objectives to be met, make a decision of who to involve in the solution and how to make the decision, generate alternatives, evaluate those alternatives, make a choice from among the alternatives, implement the choice, and follow up on the results of the decision. As decisions lead to actions and the discovery of new problems, another cycle of the rational model is begun.

☐ In reality, decision makers must suffer from bounded rationality. They do not have free and easy access to information, and the human mind has limited information-processing capacity and is susceptible to a variety of cognitive biases. Time constraints and political considerations can outweigh anticipated economic gain.

☐ The neoclassical rational model neglects to factor into the process the effects of gender on individual and group decision making. Nor does it consider social factors, such as how social norms and expectations frame sense-making or problem definition, and the decision-making process. We have reviewed some of the literature that suggests that women construct and value knowledge in ways that are relational and oriented more towards sustaining relationships than achieving autonomy and power. The notion that women have a different voice and take a more holistic view of reality suggests that decision-making processes are influenced by the gender balance of the decision makers.

☐ Groups can often make higher-quality decisions than individuals can because of their vigilance and their potential capacity to generate and evaluate more ideas. Also, group members might accept more readily a decision in which they have been involved. However, groups might experience groupthink and also make decisions that are more risky or conservative than those of individuals.

☐ Organizations are increasingly concerned about their members making ethical decisions. One response has been to develop codes of conduct so that individual decision makers with different moral standards and bases of moral judgment will have a consistent basis for their decisions.

❑ Finally, traditionally decision making remains associated with a 'command and control' vision of management, as well as a vision of managers as omnipresent and omnipotent. Decision making in the organization can be improved by using four group structures which help to minimize the biases and errors: brainstorming, nominal group technique, computer-mediated-brainstorming, and the Delphi technique.

Key concepts

bounded rationality	348	employee involvement	356–9
brainstorming	362	escalation of commitment	351
computer-mediated brainstorming	362	ethics in decision making	359–61
decision making	346	groupthink	352–3
Delphi technique	363	nominal group technique	362

Chapter review questions

1. 'For the most part, individual decision making in organizations is an irrational process.' Do you agree or disagree? Discuss.
2. What factors do you think differentiate good decision makers from poor ones? Relate your answer to the eight-step rational decision making model.
3. If group decisions consistently achieve better-quality outcomes than those achieved by individuals, how did the phrase 'a camel is a horse designed by a committee' become so popular and ingrained in our culture?
4. Are unethical decisions more a function of the individual decision maker or the decision maker's work environment? Explain.

Further reading

Dennis, A.R. and Valacich, J. S. (1999) 'Electronic brainstorming: illusions and patterns of productivity', *Information Systems Research*, **10** (2), pp. 375–7.

Harley, B., Hyman, J. and Thompson, P. (2005) *Participation and Democracy at Work*, Basingstoke: Palgrave.

Marx, R., Stubbart, C., Traub, V. and Cavanaugh, M. (1987) 'The NASA space shuttle disaster: a case study', *Journal of Management Case Studies*, **3**, pp. 300–18.

Miller, S. J., Hickson, D. and Wilson, S. D. (1999) 'Decision making in organizations', pp. 43–62 in S. R. Clegg, C. Hardy and W. Nord (eds), *Managing Organizations: Current issues*, London: Sage.

Munby, D. K. and Putnam, L.L. (1992) 'The politics of emotion: a feminist reading of bounded rationality', *Academy of Management Review*, **17**, pp. 465–86.

Chapter case study: A new venture for Echo Generation Publishing

Background

Recent trends reveal an increase in the growth of magazine readership. The quarterly figures of Echo Generation Publishing (EGP) show an increase in the circulation numbers of its lifestyle publications. EGP currently publishes six magazines targeting the 18–29 age group, catering to readers interested in sports, fashion, current affairs, the arts and new trends in healthy living.

The company

Echo Generation Publishing is a privately owned enterprise located in downtown Sydney, Australia. The owners, Peter and Laura Griffith, are chief executive officer (CEO) and chief financial officer (CFO) respectively, and play a leadership role in all aspects of the company. This 'power couple' have a successful reputation based on willpower and force of personality. They take turns in chairing executive meetings made up of the six magazine editors. Each magazine has a team of 12 people: the editor, assistant editor, features editor, news editor, marketing manager, assistant marketing manager, four marketing assistants, product manager and assistant product manager.

The executive meeting, April

At the meeting, chaired by Peter, Laura presented her proposal for a new magazine. Her PowerPoint slides conveyed a well-researched, financially viable expansion of the company's market figures. As she spoke, the editors began to look at each other with amazement. Laura was proposing a radical departure for the company: two new magazines aimed at the gay and lesbian communities. At the end of this totally unexpected proposal, Laura asked, 'Any questions?'

Peter was the only one not surprised by the proposal. He could see a lot of possibilities in the venture, even though he knew it would be dismissed as impulsive by a number of the editors. Laura's research included information on a gay and lesbian speciality television channel currently available to 50 million households in North America. Peter wanted to access the potential market in Australia and promote his reputation as a progressive publisher.

Now he turned to Leo Oldham, editor of *Up Front* magazine, whose recent appointment was largely due to Laura's support. 'Well, Leo, it's an interesting proposal we have in front of us,' he said. 'What do you think?'

'I think it's a splendid idea. And I'm sure the market is ready for this type of magazine.'

Several other editors protested strongly against the proposal. The most vociferous of these was Richard Johnson, the longest-serving editor, who was highly regarded in the journalist fraternity. The argument presented by Laura, Peter and Leo managed to quiet these objections, however, at least to the point where a vote was taken to examine the marketing and financial implications of the proposal at the next meeting.

The executive meeting, May

When the executive met again, a month later, members had made up their minds. Richard Johnson spoke first. 'I move that we dismiss the proposal for two new magazines,' he said. 'This publishing company produces informative, mainstream, entertaining magazines that appeal to a particular demographic. Let's keep to the formula that we know is successful.'

Laura Griffith, however, was ready with an answer. 'I know how you feel,' she said. 'But I'd like you to consider the results of our survey. As I see it we have been ignoring the 10 per cent of the population that statistics tell us make up our communities. Our marketing department conducted a straw poll. Results indicate that gays and lesbians are doctors, lawyers, teachers, and athletes, parents at home, who have the same interests and kind of problems as heterosexuals, and would welcome a magazine written by sympathetic and sensitive journalists.'

Leo Oldham addressed the meeting by saying he saw this as an opportunity to validate and normalize the reality of gay and lesbian life. A heated debate followed. While some previously uncommitted members now leaned toward acceptance of the proposal, others, led by Richard Johnson, opposed it. It was decided to meet again the following month to resolve the crisis, if possible.

Before the next meeting, Laura Griffith invited Richard Johnson for lunch. After some polite discussion on editorial matters, she brought up the proposal. 'Look, Richard,' she said, 'it's unfortunate you don't support the proposal for the new magazines.'

'Why's that?' he replied.

'Well,' explained Laura, 'it's just that Peter and I both agree that this proposal requires a person with sensitivity and renowned editing skills to enable it to be successful. And we both came up with your name, Richard.'

'I'm glad that you both recognize my contribution to the success of this company,' said Richard.

'I hope we can move forward when the Board next meets,' Laura added as she paid the bill and stood to leave.

'I'm not sure,' Richard uttered.

The executive meeting, June

At the board meeting, Richard announced that after careful consideration, he had changed his mind and would now support the proposal. Several weeks later the Human Resources Department sent a circular to all employees announcing that Richard Johnson would be executive editor for two new magazines the company was launching in December, *Adonis* and *Ceres*.

Task

Working individually or in groups, provide a written report addressing the following questions.
1. To what extent did the executive board comply with or deviate from the rational decision-making model?
2. Referring to Table 13.3, is there any evidence in the case of groupthink?
3. Can you suggest any improvements that could have been made to the decision process?

Sources of additional information

Drazin, R. Gylnn, M. A. and Kazanjian, R. (1999) 'Multilevel theorizing about creativity in organizations: a sensemaking perspective', *Academy of Management Review*, April, pp. 286–307.

Guzzo, R. and Salas, E. (1995) *Team Effectiveness and Decision Making in Organizations*, San Francisco, Calif.: Jossey-Bass.

Websites: www.thinksmart.com for information on problem solving; www.epsincor.com/nomgrtec.htm for nominal group technique; www.groupthink.ca for web links on groupthink; www..epfnet.org/polei.htm for information on the connection between employee involvement and productivity.

Note

This case study was written by Carolyn Forshaw, Thompson Rivers University, Kamloops, Canada.

Web-based assignment

Decision making has been acknowledged as the fundamental element in the manager's job. Yet it is a complex phenomenon because it involves not only technical considerations but also power struggles. It remains associated to a 'command and control' vision of management, as well as to a vision of managers as omnipresent and omnipotent. Decision making can be improved by using group processes which help to minimize the biases and errors.

This web-based assignment requires you to investigate the extent of decentralized decision making processes. We would like you visit the websites for the Findings from the 2004 Workplace Survey: www.workteams.org; www.dti.gov.uk/er/emar/2004wers.htm.

What type of manager–employee decision-making processes are you likely to find in the workplace? What issues is discussed at these decentralized committees? What appears to be excluded from discussion? Do committees make 'good' decisions? Explain your answer.

OB in films

Apollo 13 (1995) has some excellent scenes that show decision making. The film tells the story of the effort of US astronaut Jim Lovell, his crew and NASA to return their damaged spacecraft back to Earth. One scene shows NASA's Mission Control flight director Gene Kranz (played by Ed Harris) writing on a chalkboard and saying, 'So you are telling me you can only give our guys 45 hours.' The scene ends when he leaves the room insisting, 'Failure is not an option.' What do the scenes tell us about the decision-making process? Are the decisions made primarily by an individual or a group?

Notes

1   Williams (1981: 1), quoted in Katz (1999: 25).
2   Gadiesh and Olivet (1997: 59).
3   *Globe and Mail*, 'Managerial myopia attacked' 27 August 2003, p. A10.
4   March (1997), Miller, Hickson and Wilson (1999), Mintzberg (1979), Shull et al. (1970).
5   Fayol (1949).
6   Simon (1957).
7   See Solomon (1990).
8   Cohen, March and Olsen (1972).
9   Brockmann and Anthony (1998), Leonard and Sensiper (1998), Lieberman (2000).
10 Stamps (1999).
11 See Ashkanasy et al. (2002) on how emotion might influence decision making.
12 See Martin (2000) for an analysis of how gender has been neglected in studies of decision making.
13 Gilligan (1982), Smith (1987), Wilson (2003), Millett (1985).
14 Staw and Ross (1989), Ross and Staw (1993).
15 Asch (1951), Milgram (1973).
16 Janis (1972).
17 See P. Koring, 'Iraq war based on "flawed" reports', *Globe and Mail*, p. A11.
18 Cohen, March and Olsen (1972: 2).
19 Mintzberg et al. (1998: 11).
20 Mintzberg (1989: 250).
21 See for example Salaman (1979), Willmott (1989).
22 Godard (2005).
23 Ramsay (1991); Chapter 1, 'The paradox of participation,' in Harley, Hyman and Thompson (2005).
24 Friedman (1970).

25 Mulligan (1986).

26 Cadbury (1987)

27 Legge (2000).

28 Legge (2000).

29 See Cully et al. (1999), Kersley et al. (2006), Millward et al. (2000).

30 Bratton and Gold (2007).

31 Marchington (2001).

32 See Delbridge and Whitfield (2001), Marchington et al. (1992), Marchington (2001), Benders (2005).

33 Clegg and Dunkerley (1980).

34 Verma and Taras (2005).

35 Marchington and Wilding (1983: 32).

36 Mackie et al. (2001), Mabey, Skinner and Clark (1998), Verma and Taras (2001), Heller et al. (1998).

37 Beer et al. (1984: 53).

38 See Ramsay (1991), Townley (1994), Legge (2005).

39 Kocher and Sutter (2005).

40 Brown (1994), quoted in Carroll (2004: 34–5).

41 Carroll (2004: 35).

42 Figure 13.7 draws upon the work of Trevino (1986), Carroll (2004) and Bratton, Grint and Nelson (2005).

43 Bratton et al. (2005: 323).

44 Carroll (2004).

45 See Burns (1978), Gardner (1990).

46 See for example Madsen and Finger (1978).

47 Dennis and Valacich (1999).

48 Quoted by Grant Robertson (2006) 'Layoffs come as a deal is unveiled,' *Globe and Mail*, 13 July, p. A6.

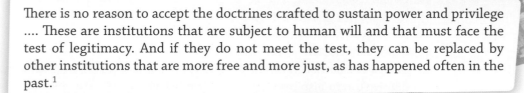

chapter 14
Power, politics and conflict

There is no reason to accept the doctrines crafted to sustain power and privilege .... These are institutions that are subject to human will and that must face the test of legitimacy. And if they do not meet the test, they can be replaced by other institutions that are more free and more just, as has happened often in the past.[1]

chapter outline

▷ Introduction
▷ Power: a matter of definitions
▷ Power: evidence from the workplace
▷ Chapter summary
▷ Key concepts
▷ Chapter review questions
▷ Further reading
▷ Chapter case study: Las Vegas general strike
▷ Web-based assignment
▷ OB in films
▷ Notes

chapter objectives

After completing this chapter, you should be able to:

▷ recognize and explain key debates concerning the concept of power in the context of the organizational behaviour (OB) field
▷ understand and explain the following key concepts: systems of power, authority, influence, hegemony
▷ compare and contrast major macro-theoretical approaches to the concept of power in the writings of Mann, Foucault, Lukes, Weber and Gramsci
▷ discuss possible implications of theories and research for workplace practice.

Introduction

In the field of physics, 'power' is defined as a quantity expressing the rate at which energy is transformed into work. In fact, thermodynamic laws see energy as flowing in one direction only. In addition, power is active. The concept that slows it down, 'resistance', is passive. We begin with these points for a reason. Simply put, some of these basic principles appear remarkably persistent in many common-sense views about the notion of 'power' in its more general forms, what it is and how it works.

This chapter takes up the issue of power and behaviour in work organizations. It provides an introduction to a range of thinking and research. Throughout, it explicitly rejects the common-sense view of power expressed above. We argue that power is not simply something the powerful have and the powerless lack. Power, to borrow from Michel Foucault, is not possessed – it is exercised. In addition, power does not simply limit what people do (that is, it does not simply 'say no'), but rather is productive too (it also says 'yes' to certain behaviour). Across the work of the many intellectuals we discuss in this chapter, some looking at macro phenomena, some looking at micro phenomena and others focusing on the many elements in between, the most astute understandings of power see it as being, at its heart, relational or interactive in nature.

Although it is most often a charge levelled at the work of others, it has been fairly common in recent OB writing to note that 'power', as a concept, is underdeveloped in this literature. In fact, it has been noted in the editorial introduction to a special journal issue devoted to the concept of power that very little has been written by behavioural analysts on the topic.[2] It runs like a thread throughout the chapter that building on what has just been established, power is not an individual phenomenon. Despite the fact that there appears in all our lives the figure of the 'powerful person', in fact there is no individual who creates, constitutes or sustains 'power' as such.

Imagine, for example, the power of a police officer, a judge, a professor or a chief executive officer (CEO). What are all the 'things' – the history, the traditions, the institutions, the distribution of resources, the socially granted authority and so on – that are necessarily in place to create this seemingly individual embodiment of 'power'? Take away the vastly networked, social, material, historical, cultural and ideological dimensions of the phenomenon, and what we find is that the person's 'power' virtually disappears. While individuals may embody a variety of traits that seem to constitute and legitimize their 'power', we must not confuse individual traits with power as such, because where changes occur across the many dimensions of power, the meaning of these traits can be radically transformed.

Before proceeding with your reading of the chapter, take a moment to think about your definition of the term 'power'. Do you hold any of the 'common-sense' views on power discussed above? As you make your way through the reading be sure to keep in mind that a good definition of power should offer you the capacity to see the areas through which it might be questioned, challenged or altered where warranted.

STOP AND REFLECT

plate 38 City of Toronto (Canada) employees (garbage workers) picked an ideal moment to leverage their power by going on strike in the heat of the summer of 2002

Source: Toronto Star Newspapers Ltd

In this sense we begin, as we usually must, with the matter of definitions and related but distinct terms. Indeed, a sizeable proportion of this chapter must grapple directly with these matters of definition.

Power: a matter of definitions

power: a term defined in multiple ways, involving cultural values, authority, influence and coercion as well as control over the distribution of symbolic and material resources. At its broadest power is defined as a social system which imparts patterned meaning.

A reasonable starting point for many discussions of power is some version of the sociologist Robert Dahl's much-quoted phrase, 'A has power over B to the extent that he can get B to do something that B would not otherwise do'.[3] Closely related is a definition by French and Raven which likewise focuses on the potential ability of one individual to influence another within a certain social system.[4] In fact, French and Raven went on to develop five bases of power, the most important of which, first suggested by Warren,[5] are those related to systemic reward and coercion.

Our goal in this chapter is to incorporate such statements into a more comprehensive understanding of power, then test the current analyses of power in work organizations in relation to this new understanding. In doing this we might add to Dahl's basic definition to relate it directly to the paid workplace: power is the ability to say no to certain behaviours, yes to others, and to shape how something should be done.

This, of course, is inseparable from many of the other issues addressed in the text including equity and diversity, the organization of labour processes, the selection of technologies, the technical and social divisions of labour, and the accountability and reporting structures and pacing that shape, or rather influence, 'power' in organizations.

It is vital that we recognize that to further complicate matters, the concept of 'power' is often confused with the relatively distinct questions of 'influence' and 'authority'. We see this in the definitions of both Dahl and French and Raven, in fact.

authority: the power granted by some form of either active or passive consent which bestows legitimacy

The goal of our definition here is to recognize that authority is closely related to, but analytically distinct from, the concept of power. 'Authority' as it is defined in social science literature also tends to have a complex relational dimension, but can be said to involve power granted by some form of active or passive consent – whether the consent is linked to specific individuals, groups or institutions – which bestows on it some level of legitimacy.[6]

Some theorists use these words in ways that overlap a good deal. For example, the German sociologist Max Weber's work deals with issues of power but mostly elaborates on types of authority.

legitimacy: a term describing agreement with the rights and responsibilities associated with a position, social values, system and so on

The issue of legitimacy opens up a range of important questions, which we discuss more directly below. Legitimacy depends on one's perspective in communities, organizations, institutions and the world (as a world-view). What is legitimate for some may not be legitimate for others, and this can and does change over time.

Even here, in these conceptually humble beginnings, we see that our rejection of individual models of power in favour of relational ones holds firm. In order to move further beyond conventional discussions of power, we can look beyond organizational-based literatures to some of the most general, macro approaches.

Traditionally sociology has understood the concept of power in broad macro terms. Indeed, there is a noticeable preoccupation with how the state, the church, the military, and sometimes corporations and economic systems, may or may not be involved in systems of power. One of the key writers of this type is Michael Mann. His *Sources of Social Power* is considered a key text in these theoretical discussions, and builds from detailed study of ancient Rome and world religions.[7] The 'sources of social power' are determined to be ideological, military, political and economic. Indeed, he goes on to say that the object of this type of social power approach should be the development of an analysis of 'multiple overlapping and intersecting socio-spatial networks of power'.[8]

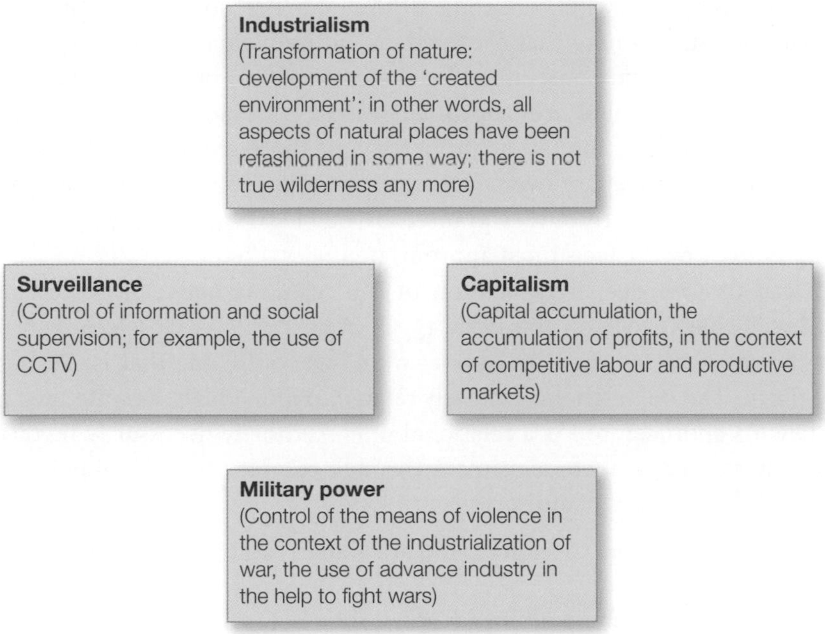

Industrialism
(Transformation of nature: development of the 'created environment'; in other words, all aspects of natural places have been refashioned in some way; there is not true wilderness any more)

Surveillance
(Control of information and social supervision; for example, the use of CCTV)

Capitalism
(Capital accumulation, the accumulation of profits, in the context of competitive labour and productive markets)

Military power
(Control of the means of violence in the context of the industrialization of war, the use of advance industry in the help to fight wars)

figure 14.1 Giddens' model of power

Power, under this approach, is diffuse and what we might call 'infra-structural'. It can be understood, according to Mann, by taking into account a specific set of universal relations or dynamics: universalism–particularism, equality–hierarchy, cosmopolitanism–uniformity, decentralization–centralization and civilization–militarism. Each is concerned with the dynamic between control and diffuse freedoms, and when applied to his four sources of social power, produces a way of thinking about power that has been influential in social theory as well as history.

Mann's type of approach more or less rejects the explanation of power as simply a form of 'institutionalization' (which we discuss in relation to Weber below), but another key example that is influential in the mainstream sociological tradition is the work of Anthony Giddens.[9] His work on the 'central problems of social theory' seeks to provide an overarching theory while avoiding what he sees as the pitfalls of many broad social theories of power (from schools of social theory such as Marxism, phenomenology and structural-functionalism). His theory of 'structuration' is intended to demonstrate the complex interrelations of human freedom (or agency) and determination (or structure), and emphasizes that in the modern world there has been a fundamental shift based on the enormous growth in the resources (what he refers to as 'containers') of power. Central to Giddens' thesis are societal surveillance, capitalist enterprise, industrial production and centralized control over the 'means of violence' by the state (see Figure 14.1).[10]

structuration: a concept focusing on balancing the dichotomies of agency, or human freedom, and social organization, or structures where individual choices are seen as partially constrained, but they remain choices nonetheless

It is important to the theory of structuration that these sources of power are not 'out there' but rather the result of specific forms of human interaction mixed with 'authority' and a distribution of 'resources', which together shape and control time and space. This is important, in part, because of its lack of what we would

ideology: multiple uses but in particular refers to perceptions of reality distorted by class interests and the ideas, legal arrangements and culture that arise from class relations

call 'closure'. That is, power is always an open, historical question; things can and do change. Although we do not review it here, it is worth noting the meta-theory of German social theorist Jürgen Habermas. He describes ideology as structure of communication (in his theory of communicative action) that has been systematically distorted by power in such a way as to mostly exclude the realm of daily human activity (what Habermas calls the 'lifeworld') when its activity does not align with dominant institutions and their unique interests and needs.

Such domination comes to penetrate individuals' life-world, personal identity and inner mental experience – on the same level of analysis as Giddens' approach to human interaction deals with – leading to their further domination by social systems. Finally, we should note that for Giddens, all individuals 'have power', but this power is influenced and constrained by the distribution of different types of resources. In this model, there are 'allocative resources', which refers to control over physical things such as money or property, and there are also 'authoritative resources', which involve control over people's practices. For example, a business owner has the authoritative resources granted by our legal institutions to set her workplace up in the way she feels most appropriate.

This can lead us to a deeper discussion of the relations between power and authority. Max Weber's work on the basic types of authority is closely linked to, though not the same as, the theories of power we have outlined. That is, Weber's theory of authority can be much more closely related to individuals, despite the fact that ultimately his approach too is a relational one. Authority necessarily involves others who grant this authority or legitimacy through complex systems of power.

Weber outlines three types of authority:

▷ *Charismatic authority* refers to leaders who are able to exercise power based on their personal traits.
▷ *Traditional authority* is dependent on a historical trajectory of past authority.
▷ *Rational authority*. Weber is most widely known for his analysis of this in his writing on bureaucracy. Here authority rests on a specific system of laws or rules which establish a hierarchy in, for example, a public or private-sector work organization.

Weber's perspective on authority is echoed in the work of Wrong, who lays out a basic model of the relations between influence and power (see Figure 14.2).[11]

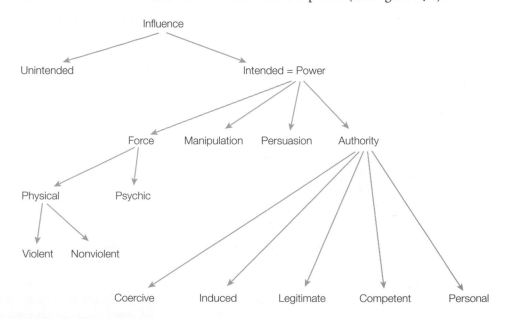

figure 14.2 Wrong on influence and power

Source: Wrong (1979)

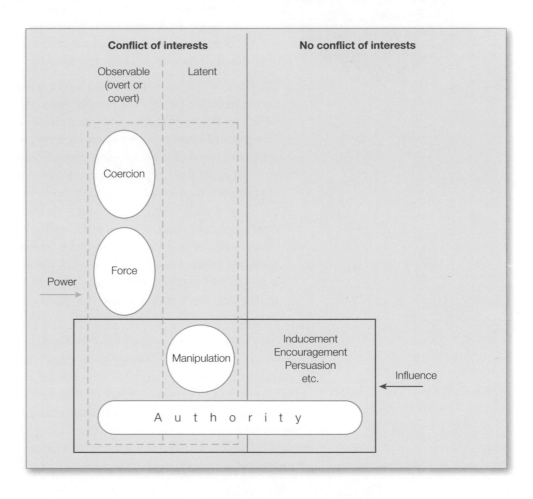

plate 39 There are many deep social roots or sources of power, including the influence of wealth and politics

Another key body of writing on the concept of power is Steven Lukes' *Power: A radical view.*[12] Lukes' theory is partially summarized in Figure 14.3. Lukes understands power and authority with the notion of 'bringing about consequences', not unlike, for instance, the way a teacher might seek to encourage students to

figure 14.3 Steven Lukes' vision of power

complete their reading assignments prior to lectures. Part of this type of analysis is the recognition that obtaining compliance can require a multi-faceted effort. It can be secured by the use of force or by people choosing to surrender to others. In fact, usually both are involved, as we shall see in our discussion of Gramsci later on. When people choose to accept the will of others as legitimate, according to Lukes we can describe the relationship as one of authority. Some of the studies of behaviour in organizations that we discuss in the following section of this chapter appear to draw on this type of approach.

conflict of interest: a condition in which the needs of one party (such as an individual or group) run counter to the needs of another

Equally important to Lukes's explanation are the conditions of a conflict of interest. The identification of structural and idiosyncratic conflicts of interest is a key challenge for OB literature. Where, for example, is conflict just a matter of fine-tuning existing organizational structures, and where might conflict be so deeply rooted in a structure that to challenge it is to simultaneously challenge the very nature of the organization itself? As Figure 14.3 shows, where such structural conflicts of interest do not exist Lukes uses the word 'influence'. Where such conditions do exist he uses the word 'power'. Both planned decision making (overt or covert varieties) and latent (or unintended) uses of power play a role in Lukes' model, while issues of authority, not unlike those outlined by Weber, operate in both non-conflict and conflict of interest contexts.

Take a moment to think back to your own employment experiences (or those of friends or family members, if you have none as yet). How can you distinguish between the Weber's concept of 'authority' and broader systems of power as discussed in Lukes or Giddens? How has the social infrastructure of power systems supported the 'authority' of those in charge?

STOP AND REFLECT

Michel Foucault is another key thinker in this field. His work in, among many other texts, *Discipline and Punish* and *Power/Knowledge*,[13] though oriented by a stated interest in the 'micro-politics' of power and preoccupied with individual identity or 'subjectivity', is in the end a very broad macro theory as well. In this way Foucault, like Giddens, is interested in breaking down the distinction between individuals and society, or 'agency' and 'structure'. Unlike Lukes, however, Foucault's definitions of power make it particularly clear that there is a double edge to power. It prevents some behaviours while at the same time positively encouraging others, both at the broadest political and historical levels and at the deepest level of individual identity:

[I]t seems to me now that the notion of repression is quite inadequate for capturing what is precisely the productive aspect of power. In defining the effects of power as repression, one adopts a purely juridical conception of such power, one identifies power with a law which says no, power is taken above all as carrying the force of a prohibition. Now I believe that this is a wholly negative, narrow, skeletal conception of power, one which has been curiously widespread. If power were never anything but repressive, if it never did anything but to say no, do you really think one would be brought to obey it? What makes power hold good, what makes it accepted, is simply the fact that it doesn't only weigh on us as a force that says 'no', but that it traverses and produces things, it induces pleasure, forms knowledge, produces discourse. It needs to be considered as a productive network which runs through the whole social body, much more than a negative instance whose function is repression.[14]

For Foucault, power is all-pervasive. Indeed power constitutes what we know as a society, including, of course, how we think about work organizations. Power is everywhere: 'there are no "margins" for those who break with the system'.[15] Thus, in his analysis power is discussed in terms of the many ways through which it is exercised – 'economies of power', 'regimes of power', 'networks of power', 'technologies of power' – as well as using a concept that perhaps requires some further discussion, 'hegemonies'.

hegemony: a conception of power that includes both conflict as well as consent and leadership by generating a particular world-view or 'common sense' on relevant and appropriate action.

Hegemony is an important term in critical social theory which involves the complexity and mixture of consensus and conflict, and hence power relations in a broad sense. It derives from the Greek, where it originally referred to a leader or ruler (*egemon*), but was taken up in the English language in the nineteenth century, and has come to describe a very nuanced form of sociopolitical predominance. It describes control that is both direct and indirect, and rests on the notion of a whole way of seeing the world, a 'normal reality' or 'common sense'.

Specifically, the term 'hegemony' can express two types of power relations. The first describes a group's *domination* over other groups, and the second describes a group's *leadership*. The concept represents a whole body of practices as well as expectations, assignment of energies, and ordinary understandings of the world in terms of meanings and values. In essence, the concept expresses the relationships of leadership and domination that produce a general sense of coordinated reality for most people. However, it is a concept that lends itself to wider discussion than Foucault's thesis encourages. Power is seen as all-pervasive in the sense that there can also be something called 'counter-hegemony'. Counter-hegemony is composed of and expresses competing ways of seeing the world and behaving, although this behaviour can at times be clandestine and underdeveloped.

The term 'hegemony' is now most closely associated with the writings of a early twentieth-century Italian Marxist, Antonio Gramsci. Gramsci used a historical analysis of specific periods of French and Italian society in order to refer to a system of alliances within a 'hegemonic bloc' of interests. A bloc necessarily contains significant competing interests but it is unified on some core principles. This bloc was dependent on what Gramsci referred to as the 'powerful system of fortresses and earthworks' of civil society, including the multitude of social, economic, cultural organizational, group and corresponding ideologies amongst which there is significant room for compromise (although only on non-hegemonic terrain).[16] As the English cultural studies theorist Raymond Williams notes, however, much influential work on counter-hegemonic practices has ignored contemporary scenes of consensus and conflict, including work organization. This is not without problems.[17]

CRITICAL INSIGHT

Based on your own current or past employment experiences, try to apply Gramsci's notion of a 'hegemonic bloc' by tracing the key groups that hold sway in an organization. Look at how they differ and what principles they share a commitment to. Finally, consider any 'counter-hegemonic' groups in the organization. How unified are they? How is their degree of unity related to how they challenge the hegemonic bloc?

An important contribution to our general understanding of power, and in turn of power as it relates to work organizations and behaviour, comes from the notion of emergent forms of practice that lie in some form of opposition to a dominant or hegemonic bloc in the sense that Gramsci and Williams described. First, the notion provides a basic framework for understanding the character of alternative (resistant) practices in opposition to a complex of dominant presumptions. An entire subschool of industrial sociology/organizational studies literature has specifically addressed the issue of resistance.[18] Building from this notion, we can see that OB emerging from non-dominant (that is, workers' rather than managers') standpoints need not strictly reproduce a particular hegemonic order. It can at times run tangentially to it, and possibly even in direct opposition to it. In both cases it represents an active, living process in which alternatives struggle against incorporation.

In less abstract terms, we are talking about people's behaviour that is rooted in processes that align with the basic assumptions and structures of the organization, have little to do with these dominant assumptions, or in some cases actively resist the major premises upon which the organization is based. To put this in the language of social class, we are talking about OB that can be easily incorporated into capitalism, is somehow outside this logic, or opposes capitalism in some way (and everything in between).

These macro theories of power in studies of society set the context. We can now turn to a consideration of theories of power in local, everyday interaction or behaviour. Analyses of micro-interaction form another distinct set of theories on power. For example, we can ask what Nietzsche's 'will to power' (a term that defines social interaction as an ongoing contest between people striving to exercise power over others) might mean in terms of behaviour in organizations. Is the will to power a generalized (overt or covert) phenomenon, as Nietzsche's work suggests, or are there other central motivations in people's lives?

will to power: the notion that people are inherently driven to develop and expand power and control in their environments

The work of another famous micro-sociologist, Erving Goffman, is also relevant in this context. His analysis of 'contests' as a major frame of social interaction offers a fascinating exploration of how people think and negotiate order in their daily interactions. Another concept that has similarities, although it is not the same as Goffman's notion of 'contests', comes from the school of sociology called game theory. This is a subset of the rational choice tradition,[19] and is popular among economists and economic sociologists for its apparent pragmatism.

game theory: a social theory premised on the notion that people do what is best for themselves given their resources and circumstances, as in some form of a competitive game

This school of thought invites us to understand individual actors as acting in a way that they believe will provide the best outcome for them, given their objectives, resources, and circumstances as they see them. Its focus is on voluntary actions and inter-actor exchange, and it encompasses both conflictual and cooperative games. It begins from the rather traditional economic assumption that individuals act to maximize their utility (that is, to do as well as is possible in the circumstances).

We can also consider micro-interactions through the work of discourse analyst Robin Tolmach Lakoff, which is discussed by Krippendorf.[20] How might 'power' be evident in this simple, everyday exchange?

> Man: Wanna go to the movies?
> Woman: Oh, I don't know. Do you?

Krippendorf correctly points out that this is one example of a very common, gendered 'language game' that allows us to explore a host of possibilities. The male makes a proposal. The female has several options in response, including ignoring, accepting, counter-proposing and clarifying (and in fact a vast array of others). Her different options (including the response she gives above) allow us to consider the system of power in operation at the micro-level. For example, a counter-proposal might signal some sort of equal power relation; a stern rejection might signal an unequal power relation; a deferral (as in her response above) might signal another form of unequal power relation; and of course any and all of the possibilities might be part of a clever, expanded set of negotiations which defy simplistic categorization.

In this exchange, of course, the word 'power' is never used. The point here is that we can quite easily, even in this smallest of examples, draw into our analysis the concept of power. We can also see how it can include a whole infrastructure of, for example, gender relations.

Finally, returning to the work of Erving Goffman for a moment, micro-power can also be understood as part of people's 'presentation of self in everyday life'.[21] It is echoed in the work of range of others such as Finkelstein,[22] who writes extensively on how people's physical appearance or self-presentation

STOP AND REFLECT

The example of going to the movies can readily be extended to a work context. How might you go about a micro-analysis of the following exchange?

Woman: Tell me how to fix this Xerox machine.
Male: Oh, don't you worry about this, honey. Leave it to me.

Now take a next step and continue the exchange, taking account of the distinct backdrops of power and/or gender relations.

involves a whole range of broader 'macro-forces' or systems of power. In a particularly striking section of her 1995 book, she gives an example of a Jewish prisoner in a Nazi concentration camp. His memoirs show him taking incredible pains to keep himself 'respectable' in appearance. As the prisoner notes, his captors' general beliefs about his 'respectability' could in fact hold the balance between life and death: 'He needed no more than his spruce suit and his emaciated and shaven face in the midst of the flock of his sordid and slovenly colleagues to stand out and thereby receive benefits from his captors.'[23] This is an extreme example, but the point is that the micro-management of appearances has been understood for some time to be a vital component of how 'power' operates. It provides a mechanism of sorting, in Finkelstein's terms of 'social passport and credential', for how people can participate in the systems of power they are presented with.

STOP AND REFLECT

Can the management of appearances hold the balance between success and failure in organizations? What instances of this have you seen in your own experiences? How are appearances given meanings in relation to broader 'systems of power' within and beyond a specific work organization?

Explore company dress codes as best you can over the web. While some dress-code demands are related to health and safety, others are not. How does power in organizations work in terms of a dress code? What ideological values are represented in such codes?

A recent book by Ruth Rubenstein discusses *Dress Codes: Meaning and messages in American culture*.[24] What further details does it give you about the relationship between appearance and power?

Power: evidence from the workplace

Through the 1990s and into the new millennium, the number of strikes by employees in industrialized countries around the world has tended to decline.[25] What are we to make of this? Should we conclude that the power struggles in organizations have been reduced, giving way to greater consensus? Not according to some researchers.[26] Collinson's work is worth looking at in detail for its discussion of power in organizations. It represents an important type of research that has linked past discussions from industrial sociology and labour process theory (a stream in the field of sociology of work) to more contemporary concerns about individuals, identity and meaning under what are sometimes referred to as 'postmodern' conditions of globalization and the (apparently) 'new' knowledge or information economy.

Collinson argues that despite the decline of formal workplace disputes, the power struggle continues to rage on in diffuse and pervasive forms. Power is exemplified not simply by either domination *or* resistance in organizations, but rather domination *and* resistance. In this context, power is to be found in situations of apparent consent and domination as well as where there is resistance. Collinson maintains that labour process theory has made a distinctive contribution to the analysis of work by highlighting the 'irreducible interrelationship between employee resistance and managerial control ... [e]mphasizing the extensive power asymmetries in contemporary organizations.'[27] He goes on to claim that the founding preoccupations of traditional labour process theory with scientific management and Taylorism are still relevant, and so is the classic critique offered in the work of Harry Braverman.[28]

Collinson's specific contribution, however, emerges from his assessment that knowledge and information are key aspects of power. He draws on the work of Foucault, on writers who make use of Mann's work on power[29] and the 'game metaphor',[30] but he goes on to say that despite the seemingly uneven distribution of access to organizational knowledge and information, other forms of knowledge are available to workers (that is, technical and production-based knowledge). These alternative resources can be mobilized through a wide variety of strategies, and this variety in turn accounts for the very uneven and variegated results of power struggles in organizations.

The first of the two main strategies he outlines is 'resistance by distance', in which workers restrict information from management. This is referred to as a type of 'escape attempt' and a denial of involvement or interest in work processes. The second strategy, 'resistance through persistence', involves efforts to extract information from management. In a sense, this involves voluntarily increasing involvement and interest in work processes. Of course, management in this framework tries to use the opposite strategies of extracting and restricting information respectively, and this results in a complex spiral of control resistance, greater efforts at control and so on, or rather a series of strategies and counter-strategies.

Finally, Collinson emphasizes the role played by both management and workers' personal identities, or we might say social background, which significantly shapes which strategy is used. He qualifies his conclusions, which depend heavily on the exact context, but in general concludes that 'resistance through persistence' turns out to be a more effective strategy. However, as he notes, neither strategy constitutes a deep challenge to the structure of power (that is, management rights) in organizations.

The key point for this chapter is that although power is often revealed in overt forms of conflict and resistance (such as strikes or sabotage), both subtle and alternative forms of resistance can also be identified. You should be able to understand that better in the light of the various conceptual frameworks we explored earlier in the chapter.

Even the existence of consensus can be used to support the claim that work organizations are in many ways constituted by power relations. Drawing on Collinson as well as Kondo,[31] we can note that effective resistance requires elements of conformity to a rival power source. Collinson sees this as discursive and knowledge-based, but we would suggest that this concept can easily be extended to include well-functioning communities of workers: bargaining units, neighbourhoods, social movements or occupational groupings. This brings us back in a sense to Giddens' claim that 'everyone has power' but it is expressed in different ways depending on their (allocative and authoritative) resources. There is the power of enforcing democracies, forcing people to learn, and ultimately there is the power to remake existing power relations into something better.

Although there is not exactly a flood of interest in power issues in most of the recent empirical research outlined in the main OB journals, they nevertheless reveal significant consideration of issues of power. Studies in this area deal with a variety of topics, such as practical governance and managerial practices in work organizations. Often, though not exclusively, there is a particular interest in organizational change initiatives. Below we explore some key findings of the most recent studies that touch on important issues in the field. The aim is to balance our earlier conceptual discussion with some more concrete findings.

In a provocative study of relations between supervisors and their subordinates, Elangovan and Xie[32] explore the results and perceptions of supervisory 'power'. Even this brief introductory line reveals that they conceive power in a way that is partially, though not absolutely, at odds with the relational perspective we have developed here. The focus is on employees and supervisors, which is obviously a relational issue, but Elangovan and Xie tend to see power largely as something a supervisor has, rather than as a dimension of the social system (on the macro or micro level) which is put into effect by all individuals subjected to the system. Nevertheless they offer some important findings on how power is *experienced* by the individuals subject to it.

Among the important issues in workplaces today are motivation, on the one hand, and stress and people's individual and collective responses to it, on the other. These authors find that people's backgrounds play an important role in their behaviour. For example, they focus on the issue of 'self-esteem'. This is seen as a product of nurture as opposed to nature: that is, it is inextricably linked to people's lives inside the workplace, but also to their lives outside work, and indeed developmentally before they ever began to work. Broader theories of power also see these expansive connections as important. Elangovan and Xie conclude that those with low self-esteem show signs of higher motivation and lower stress as their perceptions of supervisory power increase. Importantly, those with high self-esteem actually show lower motivation and increased stress when they give a higher score to the perceived power of their supervisor.

This has important implications for the types of worker that the typical work organization appears to favour. Elangovan and Xie go on to explore the concept of 'locus of control' which we discussed earlier, looking at workers with internal or external orientations. Those with an internal orientation were seen to respond to different types of power, authority and influence (the authors tend to see these as equivalent). Their motivation levels drop in relation to the perceived rewards and the levels of coercive power that they associate with supervisors. Those with a predominantly external locus of control had lower stress levels when they gave higher assessments of expert power to their supervisors.

Broadly similar dynamics to those analysed by Elangovan and Xie are seen in two other important recent studies. Overbeck and Park, and Raghubir and Valenzuela, explore the relationship between positional power and the strategic use of 'social in/attention' in different work team contexts.[33] Like Elangovan and Xie, these researchers make some important observations, particularly about how managerial decision making takes place, but the way in which they frame 'power' in organizational behaviour as involving individual/positional use of resources tends to downplay the broader systemic nature of power as something that is exercised.

Collinson's approach to resistance can be applied to these findings. For example, the changing levels of motivation and stress can be interpreted as representing a form of resistance. This might be turned inwards in the form of stress or loss of psychological commitment to the organization, but it is still apparent. Both motivation and stress are, of course, also the roots of more outward resistance, which could lead to expression in the form of political action (say, becoming more active in an employee association or union), industrial action or at its most individualist level sabotage, or simply resigning from the organization.

Self-esteem is seen to be an important variable, but how does it come to be established? Mann's goal of identifying 'overlapping socio-spatial networks of power' might offer us some help in this context. Likewise the work of Richard Sennett provides an accessible exploration of how deep wounds to self-esteem are inflicted in the form of 'hidden injuries'[34] and a 'corrosion of character'.[35] These writers help to show how visible symptoms have ideological roots. To what degree could Giddens' interest in exploring the power of 'surveillance' be brought to play in looking at how stress develops in relation to perceived power issues? Might increased surveillance in the workplace actually force conflict inward to produce these effects?

exit and voice: 'exit and voice': a concept referring to the basic choice that defines an important part of employees' experience at work: they can either exit (leave) or exercise 'voice' (have a say) in how the workplace is run

The issue of 'exit and voice', has long been a subject of debate in industrial sociology. We touch on it above, and it is dealt with in the OB tradition by the researchers Mayes and Ganster.[36] In a rich and detailed look at the responses of public service workers to questions posed in questionnaires and interviews, they detail the relationship between 'voice' (or 'political action') and 'exit' behaviours on the one hand, and job stress on the other. Importantly, this analysis builds from observations which can be roughly aligned with Collinson's model of alternative, countervailing sources of power.

In Mayes and Ganster's terms, the countervailing source lies outside the bounds of the employee's formal, legitimate role in the organization. For these authors, what is at the heart of the matter is the fit between the employee and the environment. They note that when employees sense 'ambiguity' in their role in the organization, this is a immobilizing factor: it prevents their achieving 'voice' via political action in the workplace. This sense of ambiguity is found, they add, despite high levels of organizational commitment.

How can we understand variables such as worker–organizational 'fit' and 'commitment' in relation to our opening set of theoretical discussions? Certainly Foucault's and Gramsci's discussion of domination and consent as two sides of the same 'power coin' is useful here. Commitment, for example, is the side of power that Foucault speaks of when he describes 'induce[ing] pleasure, form[ing] knowledge, produce[ing] discourse. It needs to be considered as a productive network.'[37] That is, commitment is what comes out when power works in a positive and productive way. We could also tentatively link this to Lukes's distinction between power in the context of 'conflicts of interest' which may or may not be apparent. When conflicts of interest are evident, power is reflected as coercion, force and manipulation, while when they are not, it is expressed as inducement and encouragement. It is not hard to see that stress, resistance, exit and voice flow from the former a good deal more often than from the latter.

One of the most fascinating and recent sets of exchanges on the matter of 'power' in the organizational behaviour tradition is to be found in a special issue of the *Journal of Organizational Behavior Management*.[38] At the centre of the debate is the work of Sonia Goltz and Amy Hietapelto, and the question of resistance to organizational change.[39] Goltz and Hietapelto's operant and strategic contingency models of power are based on the behavioural approach, as the concept of 'operant' might suggest. They are linked to the founder of this psychological tradition (B. F. Skinner), to the management of stimulus response, and in some sense to punishment and reward. Despite its classical behaviourialist stance, this model includes some form of relational analysis. To extend this, we might say it focuses on the relations of the distribution of authority over the application of consequences. Built on well-established operant principles their model states that 'the power an individual has' is based on:

▷ how many reinforcing and aversive stimuli the power holder controls
▷ which important dimensions of these stimuli, such as magnitude, delay and frequency, the power holder controls
▷ which particular combinations and dimensions of the reinforcing and aversive stimuli the power holder controls
▷ for how many people the power holder controls these stimuli.

If we set aside the obvious major shortcoming of this model (the suggestion that people 'have' power: see our discussion of Foucault above), we can see that it marshals a range of valuable evidence, including that power is subject to both intentional and unintentional results. We might compare this with, for example, Wrong's model outlined above. One very interesting component of the model, which fits into the broad perspective on power introduced here, is that both those who lead and those who follow are subject to this leadership experience, and behave in ways consistent with notions of 'resistance' in organizations. The authors also insist that a central unit of analysis for power and resistance is the change to pre-existing relationships of action and consequence.

The special issue of the journal also includes a range of articles that provide critiques of Goltz and Hietapelto, and constructively extend or challenge their thinking. Quite separate from each author's critique of Goltz and Hietapelto, we can also apply many of the basic conceptual observations we have developed over the course of this chapter. In Boyce's contribution, for example, we might note that there is a need for conceptual clarity.[40] Boyce's work raises some questions when seen in the light of Collinson's observations, for example. How is 'resistance' related to power, and from whose perspective is power and resistance defined?

plate 40 Michel Foucault conceived power as a universal, inescapable feature of all human relationships, because it constitutes the very way we talk and think about ourselves.

Source: Bruce Jackson

Another contributor, Malott, takes Goltz and Hietapelto to task for their presumptuous leaps from laboratory findings to real-world applications,[41] while Geller extends the discussions further.[42] The consequences someone controls and/or is subject to in any organizational structure are shown to be an expression of organizational power. In support of the Goltz and Hietapelto model, Geller goes on to show that power can, in fact, be measured in terms of quality and quantity of control over consequences.

To conclude this section we can briefly look back at the work of Mann and others in posing the question, 'How on earth can students of OB see the linkages between practice in workplaces and such broad ideological, military and political-economic sources?' To accomplish this intellectual jump, you first need, as we have seen, to move from individual to relational perspectives on power. It is not difficult to understand how broader national ideologies or local ideological cultures surrounding particular workplaces are implicated in 'power'. Of course, it should be obvious that political economic factors, such as market dynamics, industrial relations and employment law, and trade policy, all deeply affect the phenomenon of power. However, even in highly developed capitalist countries, the military (including the police) provide an important foundation to the industrial relations legal regime. In many cases in history in North America and Europe, the police and even the army have been called out to intervene in workplace-based conflicts. They do this whenever worker–managerial conflict reaches levels, or is concerned with issues, that those in power judge to be unacceptable to the principles of the economic system. These principles include challenges to private ownership of economic resources (such as factories or even forests).

WEB LINK

Visit the following websites: www.colostate.edu/Depts/Speech/rcc/theory54.htm for Foucault on power/knowledge; http://www.educationforum.co.uk/sociology_2/power2.htm www.mngt.waikato.ac.nz/depts/sml/journal/vol3/kate.htm for a review of power models in organizational analysis

Chapter summary

◻ In this chapter we began with broad theory, to provide a basis for a better appreciation of grounded research at the work organization level. Commonsense views of power were outlined to explore the half-truths in them. Power appears to us to be 'embodied' in individuals, as something they possess and exert. However, macro theories of power show that there are many deep social roots or 'sources' of power systems, including the influences of ideology, military, politics and economics. Gramsci and Foucault outlined perhaps the most extensive theories of power, noting that it is anywhere and everywhere, because it constitutes the very way we talk and think about ourselves, let alone our organizational surroundings. Importantly, these two authors argue that power is a coin with two sides: on the one, consent, accommodation and domination; on the other, lack of commitment, stress, resistance, political action and 'voice'.

◻ This knowledge was then applied to a critical look at key examples of work organization research. Collinson is a representative example of the new social analysis of organization, which links old industrial sociology with labour process theory and contemporary analysis of meaning and identity in the workplace. We then explored some key examples of OB research that deal directly with the concept of 'power'. The OB field has hardly seen a flood of research on the topic of 'power', and when it does consider this, it usually adds the prefix 'perceived', further limiting the strength of its analysis. Nevertheless, some fascinating and provocative findings and debates were detailed.

❑ Clearly not all power, authority and influence is bad. Good parenting, teaching, policing, political advocacy, and in a certain sense management, can be understood as positive influences. The question of legitimacy, which in turn evokes questions of larger political and economic systems, comes into play as we recognize that there are two main justifications for disobedience to authority. One is when a subject is commanded to do something outside the legitimate range of the commanding authority, and the other is when the history of acquiring the commanding authority is no longer considered legitimate or acceptable (which includes being an unjust burden).

❑ These types of challenge to authority, building from the Gramscian and possibly the Foucauldian models above, start with recognizing people's complicity in the taken-for-granted nature of systems of power, or rather hegemonic blocs of assumptions. Challengers dare to articulate these taken-for-granted assumptions in order to engage in rational analysis of legitimacy. What some refer to as a crisis in organizational commitment or loyalty may be the thin edge of this kind of wedge. That is, it represents the removal of blind obedience, an erosion of the 'other side' of the power coin, consent and complicity. Managers as well as workers (and students of OB!) have a right to think through and question the sources of legitimacy. Mahatma Gandhi, Martin Luther King and others operated on the principle of removal of consent, which for our purposes relates directly to a broad, social perspective on power.

Key concepts

authority	372	power/motivation/stress relations	380–1
hegemony	376	relational perspective on power	378
influence	374	sources of countervailing power	377
micropolitics of power	378	sources of social power	373

Chapter review questions

1. What is the substance of the different social theoretic models of Mann, Giddens, Foucault, Weber, Lukes and Gramsci?
2. What is the difference between power and authority?
3. What is the relationship between power and resistance?
4. What is meant by the phrases 'power is relational' and 'power is not possessed, it is exercised'?
5. What are the strengths and weaknesses in current conceptualizations of 'power' in OB research?

Further reading

Clegg, S. (1989) *Frameworks of Power*, London: Sage.

Foucault, M. (1980) *Power/Knowledge*, ed. C. Gordon, New York: Pantheon.

Lukes, S. (1974) *Power: A radical view*, Basingstoke: Macmillan.

French, J. R. P. and Raven, B. H. (1959). 'The bases of social power', pp. 150–67 in D. Cartwright (ed.), *Studies of Social Power*, AnnArbor, Mich.: Institute for Social Research.

Sennett, R. (1980) *Authority*, London: Faber and Faber.

Chapter case study: *Las Vegas general strike*

This is an imaginary 'historical case study', drawing on experiences in key industrial disputes around the world.

In 1972, the dismissal of a gaming worker for taking unauthorized toilet breaks galvanized co-workers across the casinos of Las Vegas in efforts to seek legal union recognition. After additional dismissals of what the Las Vegas Casino Management Association (LVCMA) spokesperson Chuck Stoddart called 'recently hired agitators' (that is, workers who were trying to organize the unions), an organized walk-out occurred, leaving the casino floors virtually empty. Workers vowed to stay away from work for as long as it took to achieve their goals.

A series of complex events tumbled forward. A protest outside the famous Star Dust Hotel was met with rubber bullets, resulting in the death of two blackjack dealers from complications from the wounds they sustained. Following this the entire city was polarized across class lines, and a range of various workers from across the city joined in the industrial action. The Las Vegas police department proved unwilling to challenge the workers, many of whom were their spouses, friends, parents or children.

In a dramatic evening broadcast, the television channels carried press conference comments from the US President denouncing the work stoppages as an attack on the American way of life, an attack on hard-working consumers who just wanted to enjoy themselves, and an attack on the rights of business owners who had a legal right to run their operations without the interference of a union.

Following the shootings of the blackjack workers, an unusual clandestine meeting took place between union organizers and various middle management and pit supervisors for several hotels.

'What can we do to help put this horrible situation behind us?' began Michelle Watkins, the outspoken, informal leader of the management contingent who helped arrange the meeting. 'We know there need to be changes to how we run day-to-day operations. We know there is plenty of room for employees to have more voice in how we do things, and solve the types of problems that arise here and there.'

Janice Wilkins, one of the lead organizers, who had been a close friend of one of the dead workers and had also been denounced as an 'agitator' by the LVCMA, looked around and said, 'You're right. It is about having a voice. It's about sharing power. That's all.'

Task

Either alone or in a group, analyse the relational perspectives on power in this conflict, and develop some recommendations that address power in its many guises. Draw on the concepts reviewed in this chapter.

First, complete the conversation above between Watkins and Wilkins in whatever way you feel is appropriate.

Ask yourself these questions:

1. How is power in this conflict perceived differently from the perspectives of the President of the United States, the casino owners, the pit supervisor, the gaming workers and the consumer?
2. Is the conflict 'idiosyncratic' or 'structural', and would the changes your group recommends fundamentally challenge the way casino organizations are run?
3. How do concepts such as authority, influence and legitimacy relate to the power of the President, the casino owners, pit bosses and workers?

Additional information

A similar event occurred in Winnipeg, Canada, in 1919. You might check out the website for clues as to how such events might unfold: www.geocities.com/CapitolHill/5202/win1919.htm

▶

Note

This case study was written by Peter Sawchuk, University of Toronto, Canada.

Web-based assignment

The discussion in this chapter provided the basis for a comparison of different theories of power. Take some time to obtain and read the discussion of power in the special 2002 issue of *Journal of Organizational Behavior Management*.[43] Also visit the following websites:

http://www.colostate.edu/Depts/Speech/rccs/theory54.htm for Foucault on power/knowledge.

After reviewing the material, do as we began to do in the last section of this chapter: test the assumptions of the conceptualizations of power in this issue against the broader social theories of power we outlined in the first half of the chapter.

OB in film

The 1994 film *Oleanna,* written and directed by David Mamet, is an ideal study of power as a highly complex phenomenon, in this case in the context of working and studying at a university.

In first half of the film you will notice a display of a variety of subtle and not-so-subtle forms and processes of power, authority and coercion. In the second half there is a reversal of power relationships. Watch carefully and try to note the myriad processes at play. See whether you can identify many of the concepts discussed in this chapter.

Notes

1 Noam Chomsky as quoted in Albert (2003, Part 2).
2 Austin (2002)
3 Dahl (1957: 202–3).
4 French and Raven (1960).
5 Warren (1968).
6 A fascinating treatment of this notion of coercion, consent and legitimacy can be read in the analysis of the American system of slavery as documented in Genovese (1972).
7 Mann (1986).
8 Mann (1986: 1).
9 See for example Giddens (1985).
10 Giddens (1985: 5).
11 Wrong (1988).
12 Lukes (1974).
13 Foucault (1977) and (1980) respectively.
14 Foucault (1980: 119).
15 Foucault (1980: 141).
16 Gramsci (1971: 161).
17 Williams (1977).
18 Roscigno and Hodson (2004).
19 See for example Coleman and Fararo (1991).
20 Krippendorf (1995).
21 Goffman (1959).
22 Finkelstein (1995).
23 Finkelstein (1995: 136).

24 Rubenstein (2001).

25 Krahn and Lowe (2002).

26 See for example Collinson (1994), Aligisakis (1997).

27 Collinson (1994: 25).

28 Braverman (1974).

29 See for example Clegg (1989).

30 See for example Burawoy (1979).

31 Kondo (1990).

32 Elangovan and Xie (1999).

33 Overbeck and Park (2006), Raghubir and Valenzuela (2006).

34 Sennett and Cobb (1972).

35 Sennett (1998).

36 Mayes and Ganster (1988).

37 Foucault (1980: 119).

38 Volume 22, Issue 3.

39 Goltz and Hietapelto (2002).

40 Boyce (2002).

41 Malott (2002).

42 Geller (2002)

43 Volume 22, Issue 3.

ORGANIZATIONAL CHANGE AND PERFORMANCE

In this final part of the book, we shift our focus once again, this time to explore how organization design and culture, technology and human resource management (HRM) practices influence the behaviour of people in organizations.

In Chapter 15 we explain that organization structure refers to the formal division of labour and the formal pattern of relationships that coordinate and control organizational activities. Several theoretical frameworks are examined around the notions of the bureaucratic and post-bureaucratic. We also explore the nature of organizational culture, which we define as a pattern of shared basic assumptions, beliefs, values, artefacts, stories and behaviours, and discuss how the concept has become closely associated with the notion of postmodern organizations and contemporary management theory.

In Chapter 16 we suggest that students need to think of technology as a social phenomenon by recognizing both consent and conflict within processes of adoption. We aim to stimulate a variety of questions, but perhaps more importantly, after reading this chapter students should be better able to understand, evaluate and affect the current landscape and trajectory of new technology.

In Chapter 17 we examine the developments in HRM practices, how these influence the behaviour of people in organizations, and the growth in interest in international HRM as a spin-off from globalization. We discuss how contemporary HRM practices are a product of our times, the ascendancy of a new political and economic ideology. Paradox is an ongoing part of the employment relationship, and we expose some internal paradoxes in HRM.

The Epilogue reviews the key contents of the book, draws some general conclusions about organizational behaviour, and sets the scene for future developments in organizational behaviour against the backcloth of global capitalism, organization restructuring and governance.

Chapter 15

Organizational design and culture

'New' organizations and economies seem to have been around for quite a long time.[1]

The corporation is an institute – a unique structure and set of imperatives that direct the actions of people within it.[2]

The concept of culture is one of the key areas of strategic HRM thinking and associated approaches to organizational restructuring.[3]

chapter outline

- ▷ Introduction
- ▷ Organizational structure and design
- ▷ Dimensions of structure
- ▷ Typologies of organization structure
- ▷ Organizational restructuring: a conceptual framework
- ▷ Traditional designs of organization structure: bureaucracy
- ▷ Contemporary organizational designs: horizontal and network
- ▷ Determinants of organization structure: making strategic choices
- ▷ Organizational culture
- ▷ Gender, sexuality and organizational design
- ▷ Chapter summary
- ▷ Key concepts
- ▷ Chapter review questions
- ▷ Further reading
- ▷ Chapter case study: ABC's just-in-time supply chain
- ▷ Web-based assignment
- ▷ OB in films
- ▷ Notes

chapter objectives

After studying this chapter, you should be able to:

- ▷ identify and define the foundation concepts of organization structure and design
- ▷ understand the meaning and significance of complexity, formalization and centralization
- ▷ describe the features of bureaucratic and contemporary organization designs
- ▷ assess the nature of the relationships between strategy, size, technology and capitalist development, and the structure of an organization
- ▷ understand that organization designs shape and are shaped by gender and sexuality
- ▷ explain the nature of organizational culture and its importance in understanding organizational behaviour.

Introduction

In his influential book *Beyond Reengineering*,[4] Michael Hammer cited the Ford Motor Company as an exemplar of how a few American corporations had restructured and transformed 'beyond recognition' their old ways of doing things in order to meet the challenges of global competition. A decade later, in July 2006 as we were writing this book, Ford chairman and chief executive officer (CEO) Bill Ford publicly announced that the company would accelerate or deepen its restructuring plan. This plan had originally been scheduled to close 14 plants and eliminate as many as 30,000 hourly paid jobs by 2012 (see OB in focus, page 394).

In the same month the business press reported on the frantic pace and complexity of corporate deal making and restructuring. This included Lego Systems AS, the Danish iconic plastic building blocks manufacturer, deciding to transfer its manufacturing operation to Mexico, laying off 1200 people in the United States and Denmark, and Bombardier Inc., the Canadian-based aircraft manufacturer, deciding to transfer 'significant sections' of its Q400 turboprop's fuselage production to one of its parts suppliers in China. Further, faced with competition from Toyota Motor Corporation and declining sales of fuel-inefficient cars, General Motors Corporation, Renault SA and Nissan began negotiating a possible 'alliance' between the three auto giants.[5]

These restructuring initiatives are not unique to the North American corporate world. In the last decade Chrysler, Daimler Motors, General Motors, Volvo, Apple, Hewlett-Packard, British Midland, Royal Bank of Scotland and Rover Motor Group are just a few companies that have restructured their organization. Managers, front-line employees, local communities, national governments and customers face major challenges arising from the way in which organizations and conglomerates structure and restructure their companies. Arguably, the way organizations are structured and restructured fundamentally changes work and reshapes employment relations. Moreover, asymmetrical power relations means that top managers decide on the alternative structural configurations. A knowledge of organizational design is essential for a deeper understanding of organizational behaviour.

What exactly are Ford's senior managers 'restructuring'? What determines organization design? What is organizational culture? What is the link between organizational structure and culture? What is the relationship between structure and organization performance? And how does organizational design and culture influence organizational behaviour? The answer to these questions has occupied observers of industrial capitalism for well over 200 years.

The systematic study of how work is organized first developed from Karl Marx's writings on the British factory system in the nineteenth century; and from the work of Max Weber on bureaucracies at the turn of the twentieth century. It was Weber, a German sociologist, who was most responsible for drawing attention to the rela-

formal organization: a highly structured group formed for the purpose of completing certain tasks or achieving specific goals

tionship between large-scale formal organizations and the techniques for creating orderly structure and standardizing people's behaviour.

At this stage into your OB studies it will come as no surprise to you that there are multiple schools of thought and approaches to studying organizational structure and culture. In keeping with the approach throughout this book, we can distinguish between two broad schools of thought, managerialist and critical. The managerialists are interested in structures and 'strong' organizational cultures from a particular standpoint: how to design and manage them more effectively. The critics are invariably attracted to investigating how a particular structural arrangement enhances managerial control, and exploring the paradoxes it creates.

We begin this chapter by explaining the meaning and nature of organizational structure and design. This is followed by an examination of the basic elements of organizational structure: span of control, complexity, formalization and centralization. To help with our analysis of distinct organizational forms, we offer a conceptual framework of the various types of organizational reconfiguring. We then move on to examine some traditional formal organizational designs: functional, product/service, divisional and matrix. New organizational structures that have allegedly supplanted the traditional forms, such as business process reengineering and virtual organizations, are also examined.

The latter part of this chapter examines some issues that shape organizational design, including strategy, size, technology and the external environment. The interplay between organizational structuring and restructuring, culture and work, technology and human behaviour in the workplace is complex (see Figure 1.2). We conclude this chapter with a discussion on the links between structure and organizational behaviour, and between gender, sexuality and organizational design.

STOP AND REFLECT

Think about an organization where you have worked or studied. Can you identify a set of characteristics that help describe its structure?

Organizational structure and design

organization structure: the formal reporting relationships, groups, departments and systems of the organization

As we discussed in Chapter 1, formal work organizations are created to produce goods or services and to pursue dominant goals that individuals acting alone cannot achieve. According to Peter Drucker, the purpose of the work organization 'is to get the work done.'[6] However, organizational structure is not easy to define because it is not a physical reality, but rather a conceptual one. Let us begin to explain the concept in this way. To accomplish its strategic goals an organization typically has to do two things: divide the work to be done among its members, and then coordinate the work. Organization structure refers to the formal division of work or labour, and the formal pattern of relationships that coordinate and control organizational activities.

The work is divided horizontally into distinct tasks that need to be done, either into jobs, sub-units or departments. Horizontal division of labour is associated with specialization on the part of the workforce. The vertical division of labour is concerned with apportioning authority for planning, decision making, monitoring and controlling: who will tell whom what to do? For example, in a small restaurant the horizontal divisions might be divided into three main work activities: preparing the food, service and running the bar. A vertical division of labour would describe the coordinating and directing work of the head chef, the restaurant supervisor and the head bartender, all of whom report to the restaurant manager.

This small business has a simple structure. However, the structure could become more complex as more people are hired and as coordination and control becomes more difficult. As business expands and management becomes more complicated, the manager might not have enough time to deal with the accounts and hiring and training of new staff. To solve these problems the restaurant manager might hire

OB IN FOCUS

Restructuring Ford Motor Company

Ford Motor Company will close five assembly plants, cut more than 12,000 jobs and kill off one of its historic car nameplates in a sweeping restructuring plan unveiled this morning, sources say. The five plants are the Ontario Truck Plant in Oakville, Ont., and assembly plants in St. Louis, Edison, N.J., Avon Lake, Ohio, and Cuautitlan Mexico, sources familiar with the announcement said. Among the vehicles to be yanked from Ford's roster are the Lincoln Continental – a name that once exemplified luxury – and the Mercury Villager minivan. 'This has to be a huge, huge restructuring,' said one source, who pegged the number of job cuts at more than 12,000. Buzz Hargrove, president of CAW [Canadian Auto Workers, a trade union], said Ford plans to cut one million units of production capacity as part of the plan. 'We're frustrated, we're angry,' he said.

Dag Svihus straggled out of Ford's truck assembly plant in Oakville, Ont., at precisely 3.18 yesterday afternoon when his shift ended, a ritual for him for the past seven months. This morning, Mr. Svihus will find out whether he is one of 12,000 Ford Motor Co. employees worldwide who will lose their jobs. The mood was grim outside the chain-linked fence at the entrance to the plant as workers finished their shift, even among those with enough seniority to bump their less-experienced colleagues. 'Some people are kind of panicking,' said John Betts, a 16-year veteran of Ford's assembly lines and a single father with two daughters.

Ann Mulvale, Mayor of Oakville, said Ford's operations account for 5 per cent of the area's industrial and commercial tax base. Although Ford's plans are well beyond the City's control, she said her office will move quickly in an effort to make the best of a bad situation by looking at such things as other uses for the site. 'We'll have a very anxious night,' she said. 'It's not the outcome we wanted.'

Source: Karen Howlett, *Globe and Mail*, 11 January 2002, pp. B1–B4

---

an accountant and a human resource manager, which would increase the vertical division of labour. As an organization grows, therefore, it might lead to a greater degree of specialization of its workforce.

Alternatively, the restaurant manager might create work teams and allow the team members to coordinate their work activities, hire and train their members. This limited 'empowerment' of the workers would then free up time for the head chef, the restaurant supervisor and the head bartender to handle the accounts for their departments.

specialization: the allocation of work tasks to categories of employees or groups. Also known as division of labour

Specialization occurs when people focus their effort on a particular skill, task, or customer or territorial area. This simple example illustrates two important points. Managers have choices over how to divide labour, and different organizational configurations impact on people's work experience. (For instance, if teams are introduced, additional tasks have to be learnt and the pace of work might intensify.)

organization chart: a diagram showing the grouping of activities and people within a formal organization to achieve the goals of the organization efficiently

organization design: the process of creating and modifying organizational structures

An organization chart graphically shows the various parts as boxes, and the coordination and control by lines that connect the boxes. This system is used in Figure 15.1 to demonstrate the simple structure of the restaurant just described, and is used in the sample organization charts that follow. Organization design refers to the process of creating a structure that best fits a strategy, technology and environment. For example, Ford Motor Company has created a structure on a product basis, with separate divisions for specific models. Why do managers redesign structures? Management designs new structures in order to reduce costs, to respond to changing customer buying patterns or business boundaries, to reset priorities, to shift people and align capabilities, to shift perceptions of service among users, or to 'shake things up'.[7]

Why is organizational structure important? From a managerial perspective, structure may make the task of managing employees more complex, bringing into play questions of efficiency and consistency that are likely to arise more often when different groups report directly to departmental managers, rather than to a single owner or manager in an organization employing relatively few people. Structure

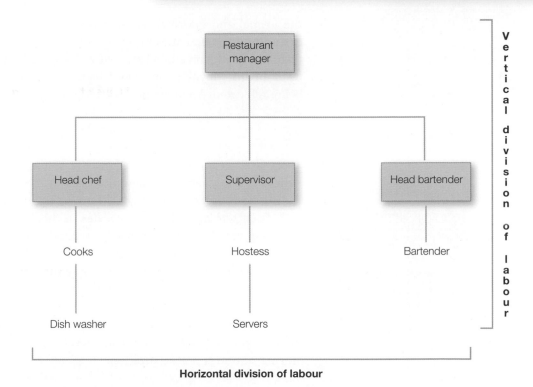

figure 15.1 An example of a simple organizational structure

therefore defines lines of responsibility and authority. In terms of organizational performance, a 'good' structure is not a panacea, but it is very important, argues management guru Peter Drucker: 'Good organizational structure does not by itself produce good performance .... But a poor organization structure makes good performance impossible, no matter how good the individual managers may be.'[8] The structure of an organization also affects the ability of workers to learn, to be creative, to innovate, and to participate in decision making.[9]

From a worker's perspective, different structural configurations affect not only productivity and economic results, defined by the marketplace, but also job satisfaction, commitment, motivation, and perceptions about expectations and obligations. Redesigning organization structure will therefore affect the intangible 'psychological contract' of each individual worker (see Chapters 2 and 7).

The concept of the psychological contract has an important implication for those redesigning organization structures. Each individual employee will have different perceptions of his or her psychological contract, even when the structure within which he or she works is identical. Therefore there will be no universal notion of mutual expectations and obligations.[10] Changes in the organization's structure also affect employee relations and organizational governance. All this serves to remind us that organizational success and failure depend on the behaviour of people, who work within the formal structure and who mould and imprint their personality into their work activities.

So far, we have given what could be described as the orthodox or mainstream position, in which organizational structure is rationally designed by managers to meet dominant organizational goals in as efficient a way as possible within the constraints they perceive. However, a critical approach to studying organizational behaviour examines the informal aspects of structure: which consist in part of unofficial working arrangements, social networks, cabals, and the internal politicking of people. Conceptually, it is argued that these two aspects of organizational structure,

informal structure: a term used to describe the aspect of organizational life in which participants' day-to-day activities and interactions ignore, bypass or do not correspond with the official rules and procedures of the bureaucracy

networking: cultivating social relationships with others to accomplish one's goals

organizational politics: behaviours that others perceive as self-serving tactics for personal gain at the expense of other people and possibly the organization

the formal and informal, are dialectically related, in that they are influenced by each other, and activities in one encourage activities in the other.[11] For example, a team-based organizational structure designed by senior management to increase flexibility may invite unofficial strategies among line managers who choose to resist being relocated. An organizational structure reflects internal power relationships.[12]

Dimensions of structure

STOP AND REFLECT

Think about an organization where you have (or someone you know well has) worked. Can you identify a management practice that was designed to encourage one behaviour but also resulted in another behaviour that impacted on the activity?

There are a variety of dimensions for conceptualizing organizational structure. There is disagreement among theorists over what makes up the term 'structure', but a relatively recent way of thinking about organizations and structure is as 'discursive metaphors'. Advocates of this approach suggest that organizations are 'texts', created through discourses, which have symbolic meaning for managers and workers. These meanings are open to multiple readings even when particular meanings become sufficiently privileged and concrete. Here we take a more orthodox approach to examine how researchers have analysed structure, before discussing how it affects organizational behaviour.[13]

While we acknowledge the elastic definitions and various labels attached to organizational phenomena, here we examine three aspects: complexity, formalization and centralization.

Complexity

complexity: the intricate departmental and interpersonal relationships that exist within an work organization

Complexity is the degree of differentiation in the organization. Complexity measures the degree of division of tasks, levels of hierarchy, and geographical locations of work units in the organization. The more tasks are divided among individuals, the more the organization is *horizontally complex.* The most visible evidence in the organization of horizontal complexity is specialization and departmentalization.

Specialization refers to the particular grouping of activities performed by an employee. Division of labour – for example, accounting activities – creates groups of specialists (in this case, accountants). The way these specialists are grouped is referred to as departmentalization. As the vertical chain of command lengthens, more formal authority layers are inserted between top management and front-line workers. In such circumstances, the organization becomes more *vertically complex.* Therefore vertical complexity refers to the depth of the organization's hierarchy: the number of levels between senior management and the workers. Organizations with the same number of workers need not have the same degree of vertical complexity. Organizations can be 'flat', with few layers of hierarchy, or 'tall', with many levels of management between the top CEO and front-line employees (see Figure 15.2).

WEB LINK

Go to www.shell.ca for an example of team-based organization design.

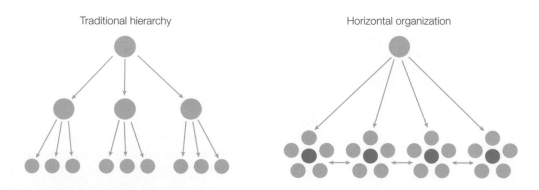

figure 15. 2 A tall organization structure versus a flat (team-based) structure

span of control: the number of people directly reporting to the next level in the organizational hierarchy

During the last decade organizations have moved towards flatter configurations by eliminating whole levels of middle managers and generally 'doing more with less'. This form of restructuring, commonly called 'downsizing', increases the span of control for the managers who remain. The span of control defines the number of subordinates that a single manager or administrator can supervise effectively. If this span is narrow, managers have few subordinates reporting to them. If it is wide, managers are responsible for many subordinates. The larger the span, the less potential there is for control by direct supervision. When work tasks are routine, control of subordinates through technology and output performance substitutes for direct supervision. At lower operational levels, it is not unusual to have spans of control up to 20. In the managerial ranks, work is less routine and spans of control tend to be smaller. Thus the complexity of the task often dictates spans of control.

The vertical complexity can also affect managerial behaviour by impacting on other factors such as communication networks and manager–worker dynamics. For example, a wide span of control makes it more difficult for a manager to hold face-to-face meetings.

An organization can perform the same work activities in geographically separate locations, a fact emphasized by globalization. The existence of multiple workplaces increases complexity. *Spatial complexity* refers to the degree to which the organization's operations and core workforce are geographically dispersed. As spatial complexity increases, managers face coordination, control and communication challenges with their subordinates.[14]

Formalization

formalization: the degree to which organizations standardize behaviour through rules, procedures, formal training and related mechanisms

Formalization is the second core dimension of organization structure, and describes the degree of standardization of work and jobs in the organization. It refers to the extent to which work is defined and controlled by rules. The more rules there are about what is to be done, when it is to be done, and how it should be done, the more an organization is formalized. Where formalization is low, employees are given freedom to exercise discretion in their work. The degree of formalization can vary widely within and among organizations.

The extent of formalization typically varies with the nature of the work performed and the size of the organization.[15] The most complex and creative paid work is amenable to low degrees of formalization. Formalization also tends to be inversely related to the hierarchical level in the organization. Individuals lower in the organization are engaged in activities that are relatively simple and repetitive, and therefore these people are most likely to work in a highly formalized environment. While formalization regulates workers' behaviour, it can also impose constraints on managers and subordinates. In an unionized workplace, for instance, contract rules negotiated by union and management can constrain managers' ability to mobilize the skills, creativity, commitment and values of their subordinates.[16]

Centralization

centralization: the degree to which formal decision authority is held by a small group of people, typically those at the top of the organizational hierarchy

Centralization, the third core dimension of organizational structure, refers to the degree to which decision making is concentrated at a single point in the organization. In essence it addresses the question, who makes the decisions in the organization? A decentralized organization is one in which senior managers solicit input from members when making key decisions. The more input members provide or the more autonomy they are given to make decisions, the more decentralized the organization.

The degree of centralization affects workers' ability to make decisions, levels of motivation and the manager–subordinate interface. An ongoing challenge for managers is to balance the degree of centralization necessary to achieve control on the one hand, and to gain commitment through participation and work-related learning, on the other.

Typologies of organization structure

mechanistic organization: an organizational structure with a narrow span of control and high degrees of formalization and centralization

organic organization: an organizational structure with a wide span of control, little formalization and decentralized decision making

STOP AND REFLECT

Can you identify organizations that have organic features and organizations that display mechanistic features?

The three core dimensions of formal organizational structure – complexity, formalization and centralization – can be combined into a number of different types or models. Two popular descriptive models have received much attention: the mechanistic model and the organic model.[17]

The mechanistic organization has been characterized as a machine. It has high complexity, high formalization and high centralization. A mechanistic organization resembles a bureaucracy. It is characterized by highly specialized tasks which tend to be rigidly defined, a hierarchical authority and control structure, and communications that primarily take the form of edicts and decisions issued by managers to subordinates. Communication typically flows vertically from the top down.

Organic organizations are the antithesis of mechanistic organizations. They are characterized by being low in complexity, formality and centralization. An organic organization is said to be flexible, informally coordinated, and managers use participative decision-making behaviours. Communication is both horizontal (across different departments) and vertical (down and up the hierarchy), depending on where the information resides.

The underlying rationale for mechanistic and organic organizations is, according to conventional organizational theory, explained by the choice of competitive strategy. The mechanistic organization strives for competitive advantage by maximizing efficiency and productivity, whereas an organic organization's competitive strategy is based on maximum adaptability and flexibility. Thus, structural characteristics concern contextual factors within the organization and affect the management process.

Organizational restructuring: a conceptual framework

Much discussion on organizational structure in standard OB textbooks tends to be historically blind, economically shallow, culturally illiterate and politically naïve. Although organizational structure and redesign are widely assumed to influence behaviour in the workplace, most treatment of the subject gives scant attention to the complex interplay of organizational structure, management strategies and the changes in global capitalist development. To help the analysis of the interplay of different dimensions that appear to have been critical in recent organizational restructuring, we have drawn upon the work of Mabey and his colleagues[18] and constructed a conceptual framework using four interconnected dimensions. Each of these is shown in Figure 15.3.

On the bottom horizontal axis is the dimension of capitalist global development over the last century, from national economies to a global scale. On the right vertical axis is the dimension of competitive strategy, covering the spectrum from low cost to differentiation. On the left vertical axis is the dimension of formalization, showing the contrast between high/directive and low/autonomous, and on the horizontal axis at the top of the figure is the dimension relating to decision making, which contrasts centralized and decentralized modes.

At the risk of over-simplification, some alternative structural designs are shown for illustrative purposes. In the first half of the twentieth century, at the lower left of Figure 15.3, the bureaucratic form is located to suggest a low-cost, mass-production

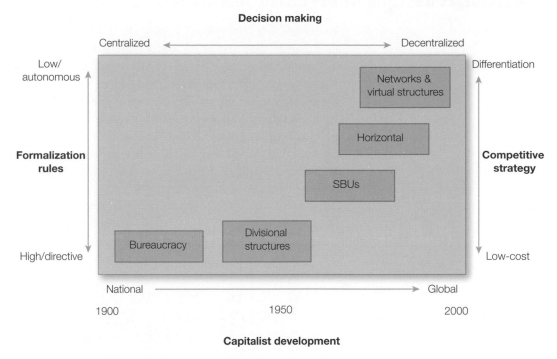

Source: adapted from Mabey, Salaman and Storey (1998: 235)

figure 15.3 Types of organizational restructuring

competitive strategy, a high degree of formalization and direction, and a centralized decision-making mode. Ascending and moving to the right in the figure, from about the 1960s, we see the development of divisionalized configurations, to the development of strategic business units (SBUs) and then networks and virtual organizations.

In addition to the changes in conventional structural boundaries, organizations have recently undertaken other types of restructuring involving new commercial relationships. Manufacturing companies have outsourced production of some parts – note the influence of just-in-time systems – and services (such as payroll, training and benefits handling), and in the public sector so-called non-core activities (such as laundry, catering and cleaning) have been privatized.

This framework is useful in illustrating the different organizational forms and design options facing top managers, when considered in relation to the core dimensions of formal organizational structure and in relation to each other. The argument of this book is that if we are to understand contemporary workplaces and explain what is happening in them, we need to locate restructuring initiatives in a multidimensional framework which includes capitalist global development. While we believe that the actions of transnational corporations and international division of labour are intimately interconnected with organizational design and restructuring, the inclusion in the framework of capitalist global development does not suggest any inevitable linear progression.[19] We must remember that millions of people still work in 'sweatshops' and bureaucratic organizations in core and newly industrialized economies, and these traditional modes of organizing work exist alongside 'new' horizontal and process-based forms and 'frame-breaking' network-based organizations.

The next two sections review the traditional and contemporary types of organizational structures shown in Figure 15.3.

Traditional designs of organization structure: bureaucracy

In Henry Mintzberg's *Structure in Fives: Designing effective organizations*,[20] he suggests that any work organization has five core parts, which vary in size and importance (see Figure 15.4). Three line roles include senior management (the strategic apex), middle management (the middle line), and the production (operating) core. The production core consists of those who do the work of the organization, making its products or servicing its customers. Two staff roles include technical support (techno structure) and clerical support (support staff). The model suggests that given these five different parts, organizations can adopt a wide variety of structural configurations, depending on which part is in control.

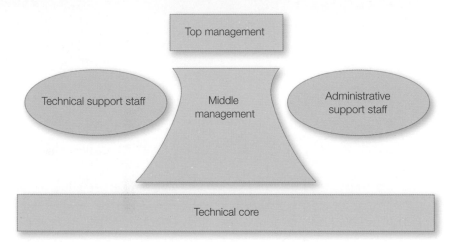

figure 15.4 Five basic elements of an organizational structure

At its simplest, work organizations must perform four essential functions to survive and grow in a capitalist economy:

1. A product or a service must be developed which has value.
2. The product must be manufactured or the service rendered by employees who rely on paid work as their only or major source of income.

plate 41 Government organizations are typically bureaucratic. They have numerous rules and procedures that white-collar workers must follow, and concentrate decision making with high-ranking bureaucrats.

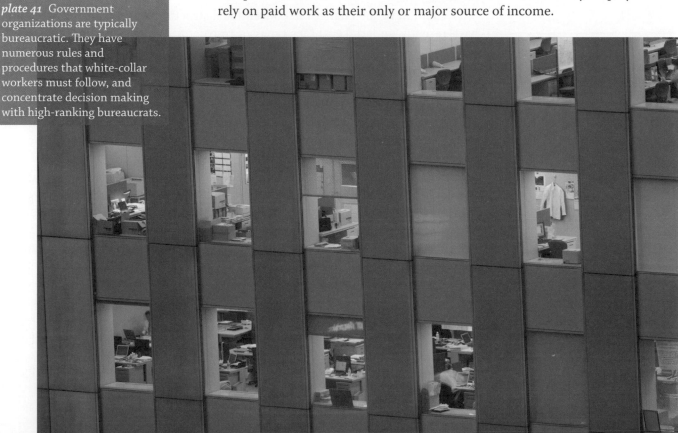

3. The product or service must be marketed and made available to those who are to use it.

4. Financial resources are needed in order to develop, create and distribute the product or service provided.

These 'task' functions are the basic activities of the organization, and are undertaken within each of Mintzberg's five basic elements: developing (support), manufacturing the product or providing the service (technostructure and operating core), marketing the product and service (support), and financing the organization (strategic apex and support).

The process of developing, manufacturing the product or providing the service, and marketing it in a capitalist economy also results in a number of organizational imperatives (an imperative is something that dictates something) that centre on issues of control. For those who sit at the strategic apex and middle-line managers, producing for a market creates pressures to control costs and control uncertainties. Organizations that compete in the marketplace typically face two types of competitive pressure: pressures for cost reductions and pressures to be responsive to changing customer tastes.

Responding to pressures for cost reductions means that managers must try to minimize unit costs by, for example, producing a standardized product and achieving economies of scale. On the other hand, responding to pressures to be responsive to customers requires that managers differentiate the firm's product offering in an effort to accommodate differences in consumers' tastes and preferences. These two types of competitive pressures are even more intense in the global marketplace.[21]

Additionally, the indeterminacy of employees' job performance creates pressures to render individual behaviour predictable and manageable. The control imperatives inherent in capitalist production and employee relations create a need for other managerial behaviour that is supportive of the operating functions of the organization, including HRM, industrial relations and public relations. Together, the pressures arising from 'task' functions and 'control' functions shape formal organizational structure as a hierarchy, where decision making is top-down, with sub-units or departments, and with managers hired to control employee behaviour.

In the industrial technology era, the organizational dynamics just described caused managers to adopt one of four common structural configurations. They could structure the organization by:

▷ function
▷ product/service
▷ division
▷ function and product, a matrix.

No formulas exist to guide the choices for organizational structure. Each structure has advantages and disadvantages. The guiding principle is that while there is no one right organizational structure, for top managers the right structure is the one that offers the most advantages and the fewest limitations, or to put it another way, the one that 'make their profits'.

Several newer contemporary forms of organizational design have evolved over the last two decades, and are well established in the organizational discourse. These new designs, which are examined in the next section, focus on processes or work teams, or the electronic connection of widely dispersed locations and people to form an extended 'virtual' organization. Understanding the strengths and limitations of each structural design helps us to understand what informs design choices, as well as the interplay between different structural configurations and organizational behaviour.

A **functional configuration** is one in which managers and subordinates are grouped around certain important and continuing functions. For example, in an

functional configuration:
an organizational structure that organizes employees around specific knowledge or other resources

engineering company all design engineers and planners might be grouped together in one department, and all marketing specialists grouped together in another department (see Figure 15.5). In a functionally designed organization, the functional department managers hold most of the authority and power. Key advantages of functional organizations include the development of technical expertise and economies of scale: it is the classic bureaucratic structure. Disadvantages can include the encouragement of narrow perspectives in functional groups, alienation and demotivation, and poor coordination of interdepartmental activities.

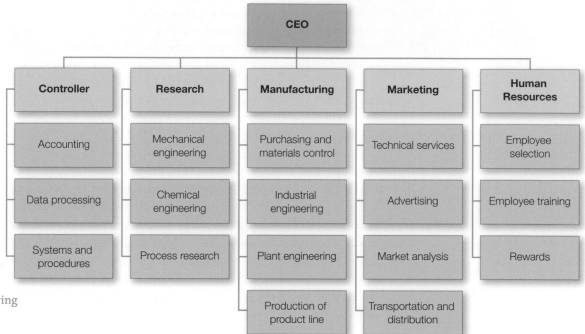

figure 15.5 Engineering company with a functional design

A *product or service design* arrangement is one in which managers and subordinates are grouped together by the product or service they deliver to the customer. For example, at Volvo Motors there is a car division, a truck division and so on. Another example is a hospital where a medical team and support workers are grouped together in different departments or units dealing with particular treatments, such as maternity, orthopaedic surgery and emergencies (see Figure 15.6).

The advantages of product or service structures include increased coordination of functional departments, improvements in decision making, and the location of accountability for production and profit. Disadvantages of product or service structures can include a loss of economies of scale, the duplication of scarce resources, and the discouragement of cooperation between divisions.

A divisional structural arrangement uses decentralization as its basic approach. The decentralized divisions can group employees together in one of three ways: by the products or services on which they work, by the sets of customers they serve, or by the geographical locations in which they operate. In the 1980s, these divisional structures developed into strategic business units (SBUs), often with 20 levels of management between the corporate CEO and front-line employees in the business units.

The Body Shop uses a divisional structure based on its major operating regions around the world. The company's products are sold in different markets in different parts of the globe. This is based on the premise that marketing the Body Shop's products in Canada is different from marketing skin and hair products in England or the Asian region.

divisional structure: an organizational structure that groups employees around geographic areas, clients or outputs

strategic business unit (SBU): a term to describe corporate development that divides the corporation's operations into strategic business units, which allows comparisons between each SBU. According to advocates corporate managers are better able to determine whether they need to change the mix of businesses in their portfolio.

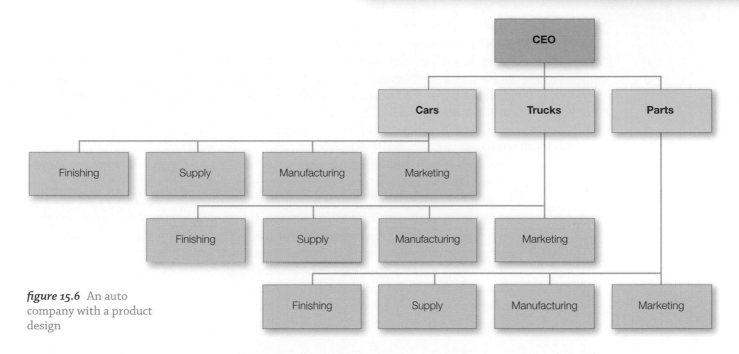

figure 15.6 An auto company with a product design

Figure 15.7 shows one possible conception of a multi-divisional corporation with strategic business units, built around core products and core competencies. Organizations often evolve from a functional design to a divisional arrangement. As the external environment changes and becomes more complex and uncertain, management might find that it must diversify its operations to remain competitive.[22] Divisional organizational design emphasizes autonomy in divisional managers' decision making.

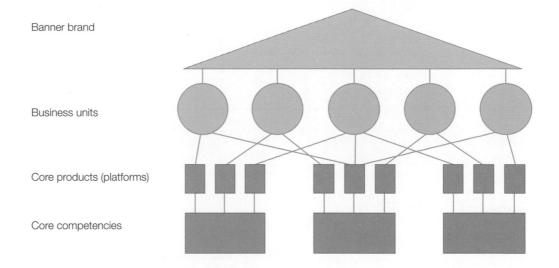

figure 15.7 Divisional organizational structure based on strategic business units

Source: Hamel and Prahalad (1994: 279)

There are several advantages associated with a divisional configuration. It improves decision making by allowing many decisions to be delegated to division managers, who are generally more knowledgeable about the local markets. Divisional managers are more accountable for their decisions. In many divisional organizations, units are 'profit centres' and divisional managers are evaluated on the overall performance of their unit.

The disadvantages of a divisional structure come partly from its decentralized activities. Economies of scale are lost because many task functions of the organization, such as marketing, and control functions, such as accounting and HRM, are duplicated in each division. Specialists in one division may not be able or willing to share information with similar specialists in other divisions. Thus, the autonomy given to each division to pursue its own performance goals becomes an obstacle to achieving overall corporate goals. As a consequence, warn Hamel and Prahalad in *Competing for the Future*, 'corporate' strategy is little more than 'an amalgamation of individual business unit plans' and managerial strategic behaviour tends to be parochial focusing only on existing business units.[23] From a worker's perspective the outcome can be catastrophic: relocating to another geographical location means job loss as the firm's products or services are relocated to typically low-wage economies or outsourced, and in the case of public corporations, privatized.

matrix structure: a type of departmentalization that overlays a divisionalized structure (typically a project team) with a functional structure

In the matrix structure both functional specialities and product or service orientation are maintained, and there are functional managers and product managers. Functional managers are responsible for the selection, training and development of technically competent workers in their functional area. Product managers, on the other hand, are responsible for coordinating the activities of workers from different functional areas who are working on the same product or service to customers. In a matrix design employees report to two managers rather than to one manager (see Figure 15.8).

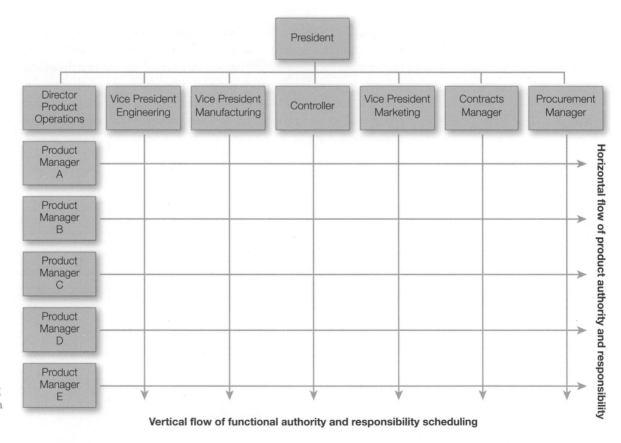

figure 15.8
An engineering company with a matrix design

Vertical flow of functional authority and responsibility scheduling

Contemporary organizational designs: horizontal and network

Since the 1980s, faced with accelerated changes in global capitalism and the limitations of bureaucracy, the notion of post-bureaucratic organizational designs has emerged as a central theme in organizational theory. At the heart of the post-bureaucratic organization is a more flexible work regime which empowers workers and facilitates continuous work-related learning, integrated with a strategic set of employment practices. A central plank of the employment relations in the post-bureaucratic organization is a performance-based reward system.[24] Two leading-edge post-bureaucratic configurations are shown in Figure 15.3: horizontal and network or virtual organizations.

horizontal or 'lean' structure: an integrated system of manufacturing, developed originally by Toyota in Japan. The emphasis is on flexibility and team work.

The horizontal or 'lean' structure is the division of work into teams or 'cells' that are responsible for completing a whole process. A team-based organization uses decentralization to move decisions to the work teams, and gives limited autonomy to those teams to decide about product and service design, process design, quality and customer service (see Chapter 11, 'Groups and teams'). Typically, work-based regimes are accompanied by other management techniques such as just-in-time and total quality management.

Business process re-engineering

One design methodology with a process emphasis in a horizontal structure is business process re-engineering (BPR). According to the re-engineering guru James Champy, BPR is 'about changing our managerial work, the way we think about, organize, inspire, deploy, enable, measure, and reward the value-adding operational work. It is about changing management itself.'[25]

business process re-engineering (BPR): a radical change of business processes by applying information technology to integrate operations, and maximizing their value-added content

Structurally, the typical pyramid-shaped industrial model is stood on its head, management structures are leaner or 'delayered', and decision making is pushed down to the 'front line' to meet the contemporary demands for quality, flexibility, low cost and entrepreneurial autonomy. Some writers have described these anti-hierarchical characteristics in organization design as a shift from 'modernist' to 'post-modernist' organizational forms and employee relations practices.[26]

Visit www.wbs.ac.uk/faculty/research, the website at the University of Warwick for information on publications on BPR. Alternatively, visit www.accenture.com and search for 'business process engineering'.

WEB LINK

table 15.1 The re-engineered and virtual organization

Characteristic	Bureaucratic model	Re-engineered model
Market	Domestic	Global
Competitive advantage	Cost	Speed and quality
Resources	Capital	Information
Quality	What is affordable	No compromise
Focal point	Profit	Customer
Structural design	Hierarchical	Flattened
Control	Centralized	Decentralized
Leadership	Autocratic	Shared
Labour	Homogeneous	Culturally diverse
Organization of work	Specialized and individual	Flexible and in teams
Communications	Vertical	Horizontal

The re-engineered organization has allegedly a number of common characteristics (see Table 15.1). Central to these organizational forms is the 'reconceptualization' of core employees, from being considered a variable cost to being represented as a valuable asset; capable of serving the customer without the need for a directive style of organizational leadership.[27] With the ascendancy of 'customer democracy', employees are encouraged not only to exercise initiative but also to display

plate 42 Global organizations have developed their own networks to facilitate communication between the parent company and its subsidiaries abroad

emotional labour: the effort, planning and control needed to express organizationally desired emotions during interpersonal transactions

network structure: a set of strategic alliances that an organization creates with suppliers, distributors, and manufacturers to produce and market a product. Members of the network work together on a long-term basis to find new ways to improve efficiency and increase the quality of their products.

'virtual' organization: an organization composed of people who are connected by video-teleconferences, the Internet and computer-aided design systems, and who may rarely, if ever, meet face to face

core competency: underlying core characteristics of an organization's workforce which result in effective performance and give a competitive advantage to the firm

emotional labour in creating value for customers. According to BPR proponent Hammer, 'Loyalty and hard work are by themselves quaint relics … organizations must now urge employees to put loyalty to the customer … because that is the only way the company will survive.'[28] Unlike earlier movements in organization design, re-engineering is market driven – the 'dictatorship of the customariat' – and by focusing on the social interaction between buyer and seller of services, rather than the relationship between employer and employee, BPR emphasizes emotional labour as a key aspect of competitiveness.

Re-engineering has been criticized largely by academics.[29] It is argued, for example, that the 'leaner' organization actually gives more power to a few: 'Removing some of the middle layers of organizations is not the same as altering the basic power structure …. By cutting out intermediary levels [of management] … the power resources of those at the top can be increased.'[30]

Networks and virtual structures

The network structure – sometimes called the 'virtual' organization – is a temporary or permanent arrangement of otherwise independent companies or individuals to produce a product or service by sharing costs and core competencies. Several factors have driven organizations to adopt network-based modes of organizing: an increased requirement for flexibility and global learning, reducing market uncertainty, managing joint production, a high-tech base and the perceived need to manage cultural diversity.[31] A core competency is a knowledge and expertise base that resides in the organization.[32] The Internet, the World Wide Web and information technology connect members of the network wherever they are in the world.

A pure network structure would have neither a corporate head office nor an organizational chart. Hierarchy would be sacrificed to speed decision making, advocates argue, and vertical integration would be supplanted by horizontal integration across organizational boundaries. Each business unit in the network focuses on a set of competencies. This structure enables the unit to be flexible and responsive to fast environmental changes.[33]

Figure 15.9 gives a schematic representation of a possible spatial distribution of a British corporate network (line A); the potential interconnections between British and German corporations (as in line C), as part of a European network (lines A, B and C), within a developing global corporate network that reaches well beyond the European Union (line D).

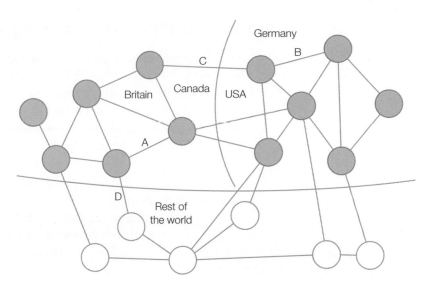

figure 15.9 A network of UK and global corporate interconnections

Source: adapted from Carroll (2004: 89)

Corporate global connections have forerunners in the eighteenth and nineteenth centuries, but they have figured as a pervasive, major aspect of organizational life mainly since the second half of the twentieth century.[34] Examples of contemporary network structures exist at Cisco Systems, Dell Computers and Nortel Networks, but perhaps the best-known company using a network structure is Amazon.com, a virtual bookstore with no inventory, online ordering and electronic links to its customers.

In their influential text *Managing Across Borders: The transnational solution*,[35] Bartlett and Ghoshal (1989) describe how a world-scale production plant in France may depend on world-scale component plants in Australia, Mexico and Indonesia; major sales subsidiaries worldwide may in turn depend on China for their finished products. Thus, the transnational corporation's (TNC's) resources and capabilities are represented as an integrated network, a concept emphasizing the shift from inflexible to permeable organizational structures and processes, accompanied by significant flows of components, products, resources, information and people. Unilever is an example of a TNC that has pursued a transnational strategy, with 17 different and largely decentralized detergent plants in Europe alone.

The network structure allegedly offers employers access to wider markets, lower production costs, and the potential to respond fast to new product and service developments and markets. The weakness of the network arrangement is that associates have little direct control over the functions done by other members of the network. The number of independent members in the network creates a high-dependency relationship between each company within the network. This requires new behaviours and high trust in network members.

Countering the academic hype around 'post-bureaucratic' organizations is a recent study by Pulignano and Stewart. Analysing primarily qualitative data from global automotive companies between 2000 and 2001, they persuasively argue that new employment arrangements have, paradoxically, revitalized Weber's typology of bureaucracy. According to the researchers, new employee performance-related incentives have generated behavioural rules that reinforce bureaucratic control at Fiat, VW and Renault: 'Thus, intriguingly, the use of bureaucratic control emerges as the main element of labour control in this type of workplace.'[36] Arguably the binary bureaucratic/post-bureaucratic view of organizational design is a somewhat misleading analytical device.

Determinants of organization structure: making strategic choices

So far, although we have examined a number of basic principles and considerations that underscore the design of formal organization structures, and given examples of several organization forms, we have not provided much insight into why organizational structures vary so much, and the forces behind corporate restructuring. The purpose of this section is to discuss theories of organizational design in terms of their relevance for understanding recent restructuring attempts.

Early management theorists put forward universalistic organization structure theories: that is, design principles that could be applied in all work organizations. Over the last 30 years, conventional management literature emphasizes that there are a number of factors that affect management choice on organizational structural design. Contingency theorists have modified the classical prescriptive approach by suggesting that organizational structure is contingent (or depends) on a variety of variables or contextual factors. The contingency approach to organizational design takes the view that there is no 'one best' universal structure, and emphasizes the need for flexibility. The significant contingency variables are strategy, size, technology and environment.

WEB LINK

Visit http://jmis.bentley.edu/keywords/k_533/ for more information on contingency theory.

Strategy and structure

As we discussed in Chapter 4, strategy can be viewed as a pattern of activity over time to achieve performance goals. The dominant approach to studying strategy emphasizes that strategic formulation involves top managers evaluating the interaction of strategic factors and making strategic choices that guide the organization to meet its goal(s). The classical position that 'structure follows strategy' assumes that managers choose the structure they have: 'A new strategy required a new or at least refashioned structure.'[37] This hypothesis is represented in Figure 15.10.

For example, if top management chooses to compete through product and service innovation and high quality – a differentiation strategy – then managers need to adopt an organic or horizontal organizational structure. A cost leadership strategy, on the other hand, requires products or services to be standardized with minimum costs. A mechanistic, functional structure with more formalization and centralization is most appropriate with this strategy, so that managers can closely control quality and costs.

figure 15.10 The strategy–structure thesis

A counter-thesis sees strategy related less directly to organizational design. In this, 'strategy follows structure'.[38] The design of the organization is the context in which top managers form the business strategy. Thus, the existing organizational configuration affects top managers' perceptions of internal strengths and weaknesses, and threats and opportunities outside the organization, and helps shape a strategy.

Empirical research offers support for both views of strategy affecting the design of an organization; this is illustrated in Figure 15.10 by a two-headed arrow between structure and strategy. This recognizes that the link between strategy and structure is affected by other contingency factors, such as size, technology and environment.

In her book *No Logo*, globalization critic Naomi Klein provides a more controversial account of the link between corporate strategy – a focus on 'branding' and the relocation of manufacturing capacity from the core capitalist economy to the periphery where wage levels are low – and multifaceted structures spanning national frontiers:

> The astronomical growth in the wealth and cultural influence of multinational corporations over the last fifteen years can arguably be traced back to a single, seemingly innocuous idea developed by management theorists in the mid-1980s, that successful corporations must primarily produce brands, as opposed to products ... by the eighties [a] consensus emerged that corporations were bloated, oversized; they owned too much, employed too many people, and were weighted down with too many things. The very process of producing – running one's own factories, being responsible for the tens of thousands of full-time, permanent employees – began to look less like the route to success and more like a clunky liability.
>
> At around this time a new kind of corporation began to rival the traditional all-American manufacturers for market share; these were the Nikes and Microsoft, and later, the Tommy Hilfigers and Intels. These pioneers made the bold claim that producing goods was only an incidental part of their operations, and thanks to recent victories in trade liberalization and labour-law reform, they were able to have their products made for them by contractors, many of them overseas. What these companies produced primarily were not things, they said, but images of their brands. Their real work lay not in manufacturing but in marketing. This formula, needless to say, has proved enormously profitable, and its success has companies competing in a race towards weightlessness: whoever owns the least, has the fewest employees on the payroll and produces the most powerful images, as opposed to products, wins the race.[39]

Of course, as globalization theorists have observed, the notion of 'weightlessness' is only feasible because of the developments in transportation, namely containerization and computer-based satellite communication technology: for example, the Internet.

Visit www.corpwatch.org, a US-based organization that monitors and critiques global capitalism through education and social action.

WEB LINK

Size and structure

Most studies define organizational size as the total number of employees. Researchers suggest that larger organizations have different structures from smaller organizations. As organizations increase in size, they tend to develop more written rules and procedures, and division of labour becomes more specialized. A number of theorists have argued that size is an important factor affecting organizational design.[40] It seems credible that there is a positive relationship between size and the degree of formalization, specialization and centralization.

Critics of the size imperative have countered that neither formalization nor complexity can be inferred from organizational size. An equally valid alternative interpretation of early empirical data is that size is the result, not the cause, of structure.[41] The key point here is that there are obvious structural differences between large and small organizations, but a statistically significant relationship between size and structural dimensions does not imply causation. For example, technology influences structure, which in turn determines size.

Technology and structure

Technological change is quintessentially a defining feature of the 'knowledge economy', and is also another important contingency variable explaining organizational structure. Researchers have adopted either a restrictive or an expansive definition of technology, and the early research on technology suggests a positive relationship between types of technology and organizational structure.[42]

The 'technology–structure' thesis has sought to analyse technology as an independent explanatory variable. The British academic Joan Woodward, for example, classified production technology into three main categories for analysis: unit production (as in a tailor's shop), mass production (as in an auto plant), and continuous-process production (like that of a pulp mill). Perrow classified four types of technology: routine, engineering, craft and non-routine. Routine technologies have few exceptions and easy-to-analyse problems (for example, pulp and paper mills or chemical plants belong to this category). Engineering technologies have a large number of exceptions, but can be managed in a systematic manner (as with the construction of bridges). Craft technologies deal with relatively difficult problems with a limited set of exceptions (such as in hand-crafted furniture making). Non-routine technologies are characterized by many exceptions and difficult-to-analyse problems (as with research and development).

The research found evidence of different types of technology being associated with different organizational designs. Non-routine technology, for instance, is positively associated with high complexity. So as the work becomes more customized, the span of control narrows. Studies also suggest that routine technology is positively related to formalization. Routine technologies allow leaders to implement rules and regulations because the work is well understood by followers. It has been proposed that routine technology might lead to centralized decision making and control systems if formalization is low. Within this theoretical framework, it is suggested that advanced technological change leads to mechanical and integrated forms of management control, which are incorporated into the technology itself. This relieves managers of the need to direct and personally supervise employees, whose performance is subject to control by machinery.

The structure of an organization and technology are both multidimensional concepts, and it is not realistic to relate technology to structure in any simple manner. All the technological paradigms have their strengths and weaknesses. Conceptualizing technology by degrees of 'routineness' leads to a generalizable conclusion that technology will shape structure in terms of size, complexity and formalization. The strategic choice discourse also suggests that it is managerial behaviour at critical points in the process of organizational change – possibly in negotiation with trade unions – that is critical in reshaping managerial processes and outcomes, including organizational structure.

Environment and structure

environment: refers to the broad economic, political, legal and social forces that are present in the minds of organization members and may influence decision-making and constrain strategic choices, such as the national business system

The **environment** is everything outside the organization's boundary. The case for the environmental imperative argues that organizations are embedded in society, and therefore a multitude of economic, political, social and legal factors will affect organizational design decisions. For example, following the attack on the World Trade Center on 11 September 2001, airline traffic plummeted around the world, resulting in the major restructuring of many airlines, including the collapse of Canada's second-largest airline, Canada 3000 Inc. This is a clear instance of an occurrence outside the organization bringing about change within it.

An early study by Burns and Stalker in 1966[43] proposed an environment–structure thesis. In essence, their study of UK firms distinguished five different kinds of environments, ranging from 'stable' to 'least predictable', and two divergent patterns of managerial behaviour and organizational structure, the organic and the mechanistic configurations. They suggested that both types of structural regimes represented a 'rational' form of organization that could be created and sustained according to the external conditions facing the organization. For instance, uncertainty in the environment might cause top managers to restructure in order to be more responsive to the changing marketplace.

An organization's environment can also range from *munificent* to *hostile*. Organizations located in a hostile environment face more competition, an adversarial union–management relationship, and resource scarcity.

These four distinct dimensions of environments shape structure. The more dynamic the environment, the more 'organic' the structure, and the more complex the environment, the more 'decentralized' the structure.[44] The explosive growth of e-commerce, for example, has created a dynamic complex environment for much of the retail book and clothing industry, and is therefore spawning highly flexible network structures. Despite the criticisms of contingency theory, it has provided insights into understanding complex situational variables that help shape organizational structure.

Global capitalism and organizational restructuring

Our aim in this chapter has been to offer a multidimensional understanding of organizational structure and restructuring. Existing OB texts tend to be more narrowly focused, and give limited, if any, coverage of the causation and consequences of global capitalism.

As a field of study, the term globalization is controversial, as are its alleged effects. Clearly, a detailed study of globalization is beyond the scope of this chapter, but to ground the arguments on organizational structure and culture we need to at least acknowledge the interplay of continuity, restructuring and the diversity of experiences of globalization.

For some, globalization involves the spread of transplanetary connections between people.[45] For others, globalization primarily resolves around two main phenomena. The first is the emergence of a capitalist global economy based on a sophisticated system of production, finance, transportation, communication and consumption driven by globalizing transnational corporations (TNC). The second is the notion of global culture, which focuses on the spread of particular patterns of consumption and the ideology of consumerism at the global level.[46]

The more radical globalization literature helps us to locate the main driver of organizational design and restructuring in the dialectical development of global capitalism. This argument is based on the theory that organizational restructuring occurs because of systematic contradictions.[47] This approach, which has occupied an immense space in Marxist literature, searches for inherent tendencies in the global capitalist system that create tension and bring about their own conflicts, until such a system can no longer maintain itself without far-reaching structural adjustments. Thus, every phase of capitalist expansion is characterized by the particular model

Can you think of any developments in the UK or Europe that have changed organization design?

STOP AND REFLECT

globalization: when an organization extends its activities to other parts of the world, actively participates in other markets, and competes against organizations located in other countries through which business organizations 'make their profits'. In Marxist literature this is referred to as 'accumulation'.

To apply accumulation theory to the various restructuring initiatives shown in Figure 15.3, in the first half of the twentieth century profit maximization was achieved through the use of bureaucracies modelled on Fordist-style production and employment relations. The whole point about bureaucratic Fordism as a profitable undertaking is that it achieves economies of scale: the system produces standardized products at relatively low unit costs.

However, as we explained in Chapter 2, the downside to Taylorism and Fordism is that the success of the operation depends on an expanding market for the same standard product, and mass production cannot adjust readily to changing consumer tastes. The offer to consumers of 'Any colour of car provided it is black' is less compelling when the market is saturated with black cars and competitors are offering a choice of colours. It is perhaps not surprising that an early response of employers to the catalogue of problems associated with bureaucratic Fordism, in order to maintain profitability, was to decentralize and transplant assembly-line systems from core capitalist countries (such as Germany) to the periphery where wage levels were very low (for example, to Mexico). The systematic contradiction of Fordism and corporate imperatives created divisionalized structures, including SBUs, as manufacturing was relocated to the newly industrialized economies of South-East Asia, Brazil and Mexico.

In recent years, market changes compelled further restructuring and 'downsizing' towards 'horizontal' or 'lean' organizations. As two US management theorists write, 'American companies were weighted down with cumbersome organizational charts and many layers of management'.[48] Critical accounts of organizational restructuring also describe the associated changes in social relations: non-standard or precarious employment, and a new 'international division of labour' in which a small number of newly industrialized economies (NIEs) participate in the global dispersal of manufacturing by TNCs.

Feminist scholars have highlighted the exploitative and patriarchal nature of the new international division of labour. The critics of global capitalism argue that as the dominance of the capitalist global system spreads and deepens, it simultaneously sows the seeds of organizational restructuring by providing resources, forms of organizational capacity and the ideological rationale.[49]

Figure 15.11 is an adaptation of Figure 1.2, and offers a synthesis of current thinking. It suggests that organization structure is influenced by business strategy,

WEB LINK
Visit https://www.cia.gov/cia/publications/factbook/index.html, for more information on the relative size, by revenue, of transnational corporations.

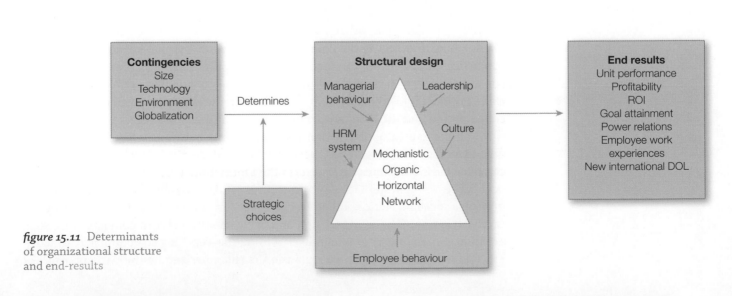

figure 15.11 Determinants of organizational structure and end-results

size, technology, environment and the economics of global capitalism. It is also influenced by internal situational variables, such as culture, managerial and worker behaviour, and the strategic choices available to dominant organizational decision makers. The end-results include increased profits for TNCs and a new international division of labour.

Implications for organizational behaviour

The dismantling of large bureaucratic Fordist organizational structures and restructuring to a horizontal or process-based model requires fundamental changes in the behaviour of managers and non-managers. Restructuring initiatives are designed to increase flexibility and reduce operating costs. Employees are therefore usually correct in predicting job losses, extensive changes in the way they perform their work, skill changes and changes in employee relations (see Figure 2.3). Of course, relocating operations to an NIE or outsourcing and privatizing a service in a public-sector organization can have major employment implications. For the survivors it can be detrimental to motivation and commitment-building, as well as fundamentally redefining the contours of employment relations.[50]

Network organizations require managers and knowledge workers to change their behaviours. Strategic planning is no longer an independent activity, but a process needing coordination, information sharing and global learning.[51] Well-documented empirical research reveals that organizational restructuring, particularly when it involves significant downsizing, is a 'destroyer of work groups and thus goodwill, loyalty and morale'.[52] The effects of downsizing and layoffs also include negative perceptions about top managers and a drop in trust in management on part of the survivors.[53]

Organizational culture

Organizational culture has become a pivotal concept in management theories of organizational redesign and employee relations over the last two decades. In complex horizontal and process-based organizations, culture has shifted from the periphery – something that attracted people to an organization – to the core, where it has become something that sustains them. Increasingly, the concept of organizational culture has been linked to management theory around strategic HRM.[54] Among entrepreneurial academics and practitioners there is much controversy over the desirability of a 'strong' corporate culture, and over whether culture can be 'managed'.

The word 'culture' originates from the Latin *cultura*, meaning cult or worship. Cult members believe in specific ways of doing things, and thus develop a culture that safeguard those beliefs.[55] The works of Durkheim and Weber are representative of the early literature on understanding work organizations as a cultural phenomenon.[56]

The more recent notable studies of organizations as cultures essentially divide into what should by now be two familiar schools. For the managerially oriented, organizational culture is treated as a *variable*: it is something that an organization *has*.[57] The alternative critically oriented school sees organizations through the lens of anthropologists *as if* they were cultures: a metaphor which emphasizes the symbolic, consciousness and subjective aspects of the formal workplace.[58]

Organizational culture is a pattern of shared basic assumptions, beliefs, values, myths, stories and rituals that are created by organizational members, as they learn to cope with the labour process. For managerialists, culture is something that is transmitted to new employees as the correct way to perceive, think and act in relation to challenges and opportunities facing the organization.[59]

Visit www.culturalleadership.org.uk for an article on culture and leadership, and www.accenture.com. Search for 'organizational culture'.

WEB LINK

organizational culture: the basic pattern of shared assumptions, values and beliefs governing the way employees in an organization think about and act on problems and opportunities

For critics, organizational culture is socially constructed and reconstructed over time, and contains implicit notions of communication and ideologies. Cultural values are hierarchically defined (that is, defined by management), and in turn provide a means of reconstituting employee beliefs, which are designed to remove the need for direct supervision. Thus, culture management assumes that culture can be controlled: top managers mould middle managers, and in turn managers attempt to mould their subordinates to organizational ends.[60]

Standard OB texts tend to present a too uniform view of organizational culture, which, it is argued, reflects an over-developed sense of the omnipotence of managerial rationality in the workplace.[61] Critics point out that subcultures – collective interests that are different from the formal culture – emerge in work groups through beliefs and norms which shape and reinforce behaviour. The culture of the society in which the organization is embedded will also affect how people perceive their work reality, space and time, and the assumptions they make about human activity.[62]

To help us understand organizational culture we need to examine its parts, even though any organizational culture is greater than the sum of its parts. To draw on the work of Schein, Limerick and Hofstede,[63] organizational culture is manifested through physical structures and artefacts, through language and through collective behaviour: see Figure 15.12. The uppermost sub-triangle might be viewed as the tip of an iceberg, representing the visible parts of culture, which are embedded in collective human values, assumptions and beliefs that are invisible to the human eye.

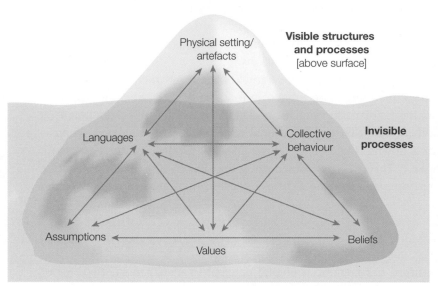

figure 15.12 The parts of organization culture

artefacts: the observable symbols and signs of an organization's culture

The organization's physical setting – its structure and physical space – expresses its culture. For example, if senior managers have their own private car-parking and dining areas and are in opulent offices on the top floor of the office block, the cultural message is that traditional control and power structures are valued by the organization. Artefacts are observable material objects such as technology and art that the organization uses to express its culture. For example, when a high-tech company only uses email for internal communication, the cultural message is that information technology is a highly valued resource. Displaying art on the walls of offices sends a cultural message to employees and visitors that creating a stimulating cultural context in which employees can explore ideas and aesthetics is highly valued.[64] The adoption of a dress code, flags and statutes belong to this category.

Language shapes organizational reality for its members, and different kinds of shared language describe manifestations of the organizational culture. How managers address others, greet customers and describe employees are all ways in which members of the organization use verbal symbols and written signs to convey meaning to each other. For example, Wal-Mart retail stores refers to its employees as 'associates', and at Disneyland they are known as 'cast members'. Management use metaphors and stories to create, change or to sustain a particular culture. James Champy, in *Reeningeering Management: The mandate for new leadership*, contends that ultimately new leaders should aim through 'inspirational rhetoric or catchy metaphors', to 'mobilize the talent and energies of people'.[65] Organizational metaphors may 'reflect' leaders' espoused values (what they want their subordinates to believe in) rather than exacted values (what they truly believe in).

Source: Getty Images

plate 43 Organizational culture refers to dynamic layers of assumptions, values, artefacts and behaviour which are held by individuals or groups in the organization. Annual award ceremonies are an example of a behaviour that aims to reinforce organizational values.

rituals: the programmed routines of daily organizational life that dramatize the organization's culture

Collective behaviour in the workplace shapes an organization's culture. These behaviours serve to define the organization's purpose and what it values. These collective actions include rituals and ceremonies. Rituals are collective routines of the workplace that 'dramatize' the organization's culture. Rituals include methods of integrating new members (through, perhaps, the office social), of enhancement or celebration (such as presenting a best lecturer award), of conflict resolution (for example grievance procedures), and of admonishment (such as disciplining a manager to emphasize the importance of a corporate goal).

Ceremonies are planned, and represent more formal social artefacts than rituals: for example, the 'call to the bar' ceremony for graduating lawyers. Some symbols and rituals together can be called 'practices' because they are visible and members interpret their cultural meaning in a definable way. For example, they cover how people are promoted or rewarded for superior performance. Ritualistic behaviour may also be used to deter change, and to intimidate employees. An example of an intimidating ritual is defaming a potential reformer or 'whistle blower'.

The role of culture in organizational behaviour

The physical setting and artefacts, language and behaviours shown in Figure 15.12 are embedded in an invisible yet very powerful set of assumptions, values and beliefs. Edgar Schein, who is probably the most frequently cited author on organizational culture, largely focuses his analysis on entrenched values and beliefs: the shared mental models that guide people's perceptions and behaviours. Accordingly, for him culture is 'a pattern of shared basic assumptions that have been invented, discovered, and/or developed by a group as it learns to cope with problems of external adaptation and internal integration'.[66] The core of organizational culture is formed by beliefs. *Beliefs* reflect a person's perception of reality, and *values* are broad stable tendencies to promote certain states of affairs. Values deal with, for instance, evil versus good, unnatural versus natural, and irrational versus rational.[67]

Can organizational culture be managed?

Much mainstream management theory identifies a 'strong culture' as an important factor in promoting work motivation. The prescription for competitive advantage requires management to abandon 'command and control' mechanisms for a 'strong' corporate culture to win the commitment of their workers.[68] Specifically, organizational culture functions as a form of social control, prescribing and prohibiting certain activities that shape worker behaviour in a way that is consistent with management expectations. Thus, a 'strong' corporate culture is seen as the 'Holy Grail of commitment' in releasing worker's creative capacity,[69] and is considered central to high-commitment HRM programmes.[70] The belief is that 'properly implemented, the use of culture as a managerial strategy is seen to be potentially very effective in promoting loyalty, enthusiasm, diligence and even devotion to the enterprise.'[71]

competitive advantage: the ability of a work organization to add more value for its customers and shareholders than its rivals, and thus gain a position of advantage in the marketplace

Given that employees' values enter the workplace through the selection process, it is suggested that a particular organizational culture can be created by employees learning the practices of the organization, its symbols, stories and rituals: 'The fact that organizational cultures are composed of practices rather than values makes them somewhat manageable: they can be *managed* [our emphasis] by changing the practices.'[72] The basis of this argument is that through the use of 'shared values' embodied in stories, rituals and ceremonies, a strong culture helps workers identify and 'bond' with their work organization. This metaphorical 'glue' bonds people and encourages employees to internalize the organization's culture because it fulfils their need for social affiliation and identity.

For instance, the dominant culture of the Body Shop's promotion of animal rights shapes what employees should think, believe or value in this social discourse. A strong organizational culture can also help to activate latent values, which workers possess but which have laid dormant or been discouraged.[73] For example, lecturers in a teaching-centred institution can be encouraged to engage in research activities through displaying published work by other lecturers (artefacts), giving annual awards for scholarly achievements (rituals), and regularly placing research as an item of discussion on the department's agenda (language). Finally, art artefacts and artists embedded in the workplace may serve as a form of informal 'pedagogy' to help the sense-making process and to encourage creative thinking and innovation.[74]

An organizational cultural analysis suggests that the effort–performance relationship or 'expectancy' can be reframed by corporate leaders. It must be kept in mind, though, that individuals in the same workplace will not necessarily perceive the culture of their workplace in the same way, and a 'strong culture' motivating one employee will not necessarily work with all employees.

While popular management literature presents organizational culture as a variable that can be manipulated and changed to 'fit' a new organizational form, the counter-argument is that organizational culture *as a whole* is something that an organization 'is', not 'has': it cannot be 'created, discovered or destroyed by the whims of management.'[75]

First, measuring culture changes is problematic. Simply citing what CEOs proclaim that they value – referred to as espoused values – does not necessarily express an organization's culture. When senior managers project an image of the organization by proclaiming their values to the outside world, the image and the values may be inconsistent with what they truly value – referred to as enacted values – and internal stakeholders' experience. Put another way, a leader's feet (action reflecting created values) may not follow his or her lips (espoused values). In this respect, given the dynamics between employees, insiders and community outsiders, incongruence between the corporate culture (or image) projected outwards and what is fed back into the organization is likely to breed cynicism.[76] Thus, culture is partly a result of processes involving how employees perceive, enact and *respond* to management interventions to create an organizational identity.[77]

Second, inherent contradictions may make the management of culture difficult. For example, an organization may seek to create a culture of 'high trust and commitment', and emphasize the importance of emotional labour: smiling and maintaining eye contact with clients. If at the same time it installs surveillance technology to monitor employees' job performance, and the number of irate customers increases, this would clearly contradict the cultural objectives.[78]

Third, organizational culture can never be wholly managed, because it emerges from complex processes involving how employees construct their sense of identity in ways that are beyond management's control. For example, workers' values are shaped by outside variables such as class, gender, race, and profession or trade. At the very best, interventions to manage culture are only successful at the observable behavioural level rather than the subconscious level.[79] Feminist social inquiry and scholarship also remind us that by and large the culture of work organizations is predominantly male, and its dominant symbolism is suffused with masculine images of aggressiveness, competitiveness and the capacity for violence.[80] Finally, adding to the complexity of managing culture is the omnipresent Internet. It has, for example, been recently argued that the Internet adds both new operational capacities and a 'space dimension' which affects organizational culture in new ways.[81]

Visit www.asanet.org the site of the American Sociological Association. Here you will find more links on current research and publications on culture.

WEB LINK

CRITICAL INSIGHT

Culture: the missing concept in OB

For many OB theorists, organizational culture is crucial to work motivation. In essence, it is argued that individuals and small groups perform best where employees' and organizations' beliefs and values are mutually compatible. Edgar Schein suggests, however, that OB theorists have failed to take culture seriously when analysing workplace behaviour.

Obtain a copies of Schein's article, 'Culture: the missing concept in organizational studies'[82] and V. L. Meek's article, 'Organizational culture: origins and weaknesses'.[83] Why have OB theorists failed to take culture seriously when studying workplace behaviour? Is organizational culture something that can be managed?

Gender, sexuality and organizational design

Alongside management debates on organization structures, there is a body of critical literature that focuses on relationships between gender, sexuality and organization design. The term 'sexuality' refers to sexual characters and sexual behaviour in the workplace. Sexuality pervades organizations through pornographic pin-ups, innuendo, gossip and sexist joking. While it serves to affirm men's sense of shared masculinity, in a male-dominated workplace sexuality can serve to make women feel uncomfortable. Leaving the organization is often seen as the only alternative.[84]

Studies of the gendering of organizations emphasize that gender and sexuality make an overwhelming difference to organizational reality.[85] Gender analysis questions research findings and analysis that segregate studies of organizational behaviour from those of gender divisions in the labour market, patriarchal power, issues of workplace inequality and 'dual-role' work–family issues.[86] More importantly, however, including the 'gender and sexuality paradigm' in the study of the organizational structure and restructuring has pushed the boundaries of organizational behaviour by examining the people who are deemed to be the 'recipients' of organizational design.

As sociologist Judy Wajcman observes in her insightful study, the individual and the modern bureaucracy are not gender-neutral. Indeed, more controversially perhaps, she presents a powerful argument for gender-inclusive organizational theories if we accept her main premise that 'gender is woven into the very fabric of bureaucratic hierarchy and authority relations.'[87]

Chapter summary

☐ We have attempted to cover a wide range of complex issues in this chapter. Organizational structure refers to the formal division of work or labour, and the formal pattern of relationships that coordinate and control organizational activities, whereas organizational design refers to the process of creating a structure that best fits a strategy, technology and environment.

☐ The three core dimensions of formal organizational structure – complexity, formalization and centralization – can be combined into different types or models. Three descriptive models were examined: mechanistic, bureaucratic and organic. The mechanistic organization has been characterized as a machine. It is characterized by highly specialized tasks that tend to be rigidly defined, a hierarchical authority and control structure, and communications that primarily take the form of edicts and decisions issued by managers to subordinates. Communication typically flows vertically from the top down. Thus it has high complexity, high formalization and high centralization. A mechanistic organization resembles a bureaucracy. A bureaucratic organization is a rational and systematic division of work. Within it, rules and techniques of control are precisely defined. A bureaucratic design allows for large-scale accomplishments. The disadvantages associated with bureaucracy include suppression of initiative through over control.

☐ Organic organizations are the antithesis of mechanistic organizations. They are characterized by being low in complexity, formality and centralization. A post-bureaucratic organizational structure, such as team-based structures and those produced by business process reengineering, is organic and highly adaptable. However, the binary bureaucratic/post-bureaucratic view of organizational design may be a somewhat misleading analytical device.

☐ The contingency view of formal organizational design focuses on strategy, size, technology and environment. A change in business strategy may require changing the manufacturing process and the organizational design: for example, moving from a functional to a team-based organizational structure. Large organizations will tend to be more centralized and have more rules and techniques of control. Organizations with complex non-routine technologies will tend to have more complex organizational arrangements. Organizations with routine technologies will tend to use written rules and procedures to control people's behaviour, and decision making will be more centralized than in establishments using non-routine technologies.

☐ An organization's external environment can range from 'stable' to 'dynamic' and from 'hostile' to 'munificent'. Distinct external environments help explain divergent patterns of managerial behaviour and organizational structure. For example, organic configurations are better suited to dynamic and hostile environments so that organizational members can adapt faster to changes.

☐ The external context has a significant impact on managerial and employee behaviour. The external domain influences the formal structure and functioning of a work organization, and in turn organization leaders influence the wider society. The linkage between external contexts and the search for competitive advantage through employee performance and managerial activities is complex. We have therefore emphasized that OB studies must be able to deal with the new complexities and nuances. Today, caught up as we are in the drama of globalization, there is a need for a multi-dimensional approach to the study of OB.

☐ We explored the nature of organizational culture – a pattern of shared basic assumptions, beliefs, values, myths, stories and rituals – which has become closely associated with organizational redesign and management theory around strategic HRM. Two approaches to the study of culture were examined. For the managerially oriented, organizational culture is treated as a variable: it is something that an organization has, and it can be managed. For critically oriented scholars, organizations are seen as if they were cultures, a metaphor which emphasizes the symbolic, consciousness and subjective aspects of the formal workplace.

☐ The analysis offered here provides a guide to how formal organizational structure helps shape the behaviour of managers and employees. The contingency elements identified – strategy, size, technology, environment, culture and HRM systems – are not separate, but integrated and linked in complex ways. It is within this integrated framework that interpretations of competing resources, conversations and interests take place, and influence people's behaviour in many ways.

Key concepts

bureaucracy	400	organic	398
horizontal	405	organization culture	413
mechanistic	398	technological change	410
network structure	395	virtual organization	406

Chapter review questions

1. Compare and contrast a 'mechanistic' and a 'reengineered' organization. What is it like to be a manager making decisions in these two types of organization? What employees' behaviours are likely to be rewarded? What type of competitive strategy is each best suited to?
2. Why is there no 'one best way' to design an organization's structure?
3. What are the major contingency factors of organizational design? How do developments in global capitalism relate to organizational restructuring?
4. How does organizational culture affect (a) structure and (b) behaviour?
5. Review the 'new' forms of organizational design described in this chapter. Discuss the designs that you and other students finding appealing and challenging. Explain your reasons.

Further reading

Bakan, J. (2004) *The Corporation*, London: Penguin.

Grey, C. (2005) *A Very Short, Fairly Interesting and Reasonably Cheap Book About Studying Organizations*, London: Sage.

Grint, K. (1995) 'The culture of management and the management of culture', in *Management: A sociological introduction,* Cambridge: Polity.

Hambrick, D. C. (1989) 'Putting top managers back into the picture,' *Strategic Management Journal*, Special issue, **10**, pp. 5–15.

Hammer, M. (1997) *Beyond Reengineering*, New York: HarperBusiness.

Ogbonna, E. and Harris, L. (2006) 'Organizational culture in an age of the Internet: an exploratory case study,' *New Technology, Work and Employment*, **21** (2), pp. 162–75.

Pulignano, V. and Stewart, P. (2006) 'Bureaucracy transcended? New patterns of employment regulation and labour control in the international automotive industry,' *New Technology, Work and Employment*, **21** (2), pp. 90–106.

Chapter case study: ABC's just-in-time supply chain

Background

AB Components (ABC) is a small/medium-sized enterprise (SME) operating as a components supplier in the automotive sector. In line with contemporary supply-chain best practice, ABC supplies its customer, Z Systems, on a just-in-time (JIT) basis, and Z supplies the final customer – CarCo – on the same basis. CarCo and Z Systems were both set up as 'greenfield' operations, allowing the possibility of establishing ideal-type processes and structures for inter-firm relations and for the internal recruitment and selection of staff.

Z Systems' relationship with CarCo is based around a high-trust, single-source partnership arrangement, whereby Z Systems gains an exclusive contract with CarCo in exchange for some loss of independence. Z Systems expects a high degree of intervention from CarCo in its internal processes that affect the cost, quality and design of products supplied to CarCo.

The logic of JIT

The relationship between Z Systems and ABC is designed to operate on the same principle. ABC has an exclusive contract to supply Z Systems, in exchange for Z Systems being granted full access to ABC's pricing and quality processes. ABC is also expected to ensure high-quality, frequent deliveries to Z Systems at agreed prices. Z Systems gives it some assistance in developing the core systems and skills required to do this.

All of this follows 'the logic of JIT' as proposed by Oliver.[87] Traditionally, a number of suppliers were given contracts to supply each part, and this continuing competition was reckoned to keep each supplier in check. Under JIT, though, a single, highly trusted supplier is used. This saves on duplication costs and provides economies of scale. In this scenario, however, the final customer organization (in this case, CarCo) is highly dependent on its supplier (Z Systems) to deliver products exactly on time and without defects. As a consequence, the supplier is also made to be completely dependent on the single customer. This two-way buyer–supplier dependency is then, in theory, pushed down the supply chain.

However, ABC finds it very difficult to pass the demands from CarCo that come to it via Z Systems down to its own suppliers. We can see why if we look at the companies' relative dependency on their customers. Z Systems constitutes 100 per cent of ABC's business, yet ABC supplies only constitute 30 per cent of the sales value of Z Systems, so ABC is more dependent on Z Systems than the other way around. ABC's own main suppliers are large-scale stockists or multinational producers, and ABC accounts for a tiny proportion of their sales.

On other comparisons, ABC's capitalization is a few hundred thousand pounds, while Z Systems' capitalization is tens of millions of pounds. Z Systems is research and capital-intensive, and its market positioning is based on high value added. ABC's market position is based on its geographical location (near to Z Systems), price and flexibility. It is therefore labour-intensive: that is, its efficiency is determined by labour costs and practices.

All this tends to mean that the buck stops at ABC. ABC has to absorb the demands of Z Systems, passed down from CarCo, and it cannot pass these demands down further to its suppliers with anything like the same kind of responsiveness.

All of these external factors have knock-on effects on the internal dynamics in ABC, and there are some internal characteristics to consider too. The internal culture of ABC is determined by the leadership style of the owner, who is entrepreneurial and charismatic. He is hostile to the idea of trade unions as a means of communicating with his staff, and prefers a direct approach: one-to-one meetings supplemented by ad-hoc briefings made to the entire workforce.

Z Systems requires six deliveries per day. This is not negotiable. ABC should, in theory, be able to adjust its methods to produce at a rate capable of ensuring that raw materials arrive on site, are processed and sent out to Z Systems according to JIT methods. However it does not have technology or the knowledge to make this system work on its own. In addition, it cannot get its suppliers to move away from sending their deliveries on a large batch basis (rather than a high-frequency, small-batch basis as required in JIT). As a result of all of this, ABC is operating in a very traditional way, holding large amounts of stock, and producing on a large-batch basis with old machinery.

So ABC is constantly struggling to meet Z Systems' delivery demands. Sometimes quality is sacrificed in order to meet tight delivery demands, and sometimes deliveries are late. To ensure that Z Systems are unaffected by the quality problems, the ABC quality manager goes to Z Systems to hand-sort parts on the Z Systems production line. The failure to deliver on time cannot be resolved as easily.

The combination of internal and external factors has led to a series of consequences in ABC. Let us look at the key jobs. Over time, it seems that the quality manager has gained status compared with the production control manager, although they are formally on the same hierarchical level in the organization. The quality department has grown steadily in size over the last two years, from one manager to one manager plus three assistants. Meanwhile there has been considerable volatility in the establishment, and high staff turnover, in the production control function. Table 15.2 shows what has happened there.

table 15.2 Production control staff turnover at AB Components

Position affected	Event
Production manager	Resigned
Production controller	Appointed
Production planner	Dismissed
Production manager	Appointed
Buyer	Dismissed, job reallocated
Production manager	Dismissed
Production planner	Dismissed
Works supervisor	Appointed, promoted from team leader
Production planner	Appointed, promoted from team leader

Task

Write a report, either individually or in a group, addressing the following questions:

1. How can the managing director/owner of ABC's source of authority be defined?

2. The difficult situation that ABC finds itself in when it comes to meeting the needs of Z Systems is because it must be fully responsive to the wishes of Z Systems, yet cannot force its own suppliers to meet its needs. Explain this difference in terms of power resources.

3. It would seem that the effect of ABC's vulnerable position in the supply chain has had knock-on effects for individuals within ABC. However, despite quality and delivery both being problems, the problems seem to have affected the quality and production control departments differently. Explain why.

▶

Sources of additional information

Oliver, N. (1991) 'The dynamics of JIT', *New Technology, Work and Employment,* September, pp. 19–27.

Roper, I., Prabhu, V. and Van Zwanenberg, N. (1997) '(Only) just-in-time: Japanization and the "non learning" firm', *Work, Employment and Society*, 11 (1), pp. 27–46.

Websites: centres for research on work teams:

www.workteams.unt.edu/

www.cwrn_rcmt.org/

for a trade union view of work teams: www.caw.ca/whoweare

Note

This case study was written by Dr Ian Roper, Senior Lecturer at University of Middlesex Business School, London, UK.

Web-based assignment

This chapter discusses the different types of organizational designs, and the interconnectedness between structure and restructuring, and organizational behaviour. Organizations can adopt a large number of structures to match their strategy, size, technology and profit-making imperative. Restructuring affects job design and individual workers' perception of the employer, and work motivation.

This web-based assignment requires you to explore the web to find a site that displays an organizational chart, or that discusses a method of managing its structure. For example, enter the website of Dell Computers: www.dellcomputers.ca or Canadian TV and media company Globalmedia: www.globalmedia.ca or a car manufacturer www.saturnbp.com for an example of a 'flatter' organizational structure.

Consider these questions:

1. What kind of organizational structure does the company have (for example, in terms of decision making is it centralized or decentralized)?
2. In what ways is the organizational structure appropriate for the company?

OB in films

The documentary film *The Corporation* (2003) offers an excellent collection of case studies, anecdotes and true confessions from corporate elites, which reveal structural contradictions and behind-the-scenes tensions. The documentary also features many critical perspectives, including interviews with Noam Chomsky, Michael Moore, Maude Barlow and Naomi Klein.

What examples are given to substantiate the claim that corporations, if left unregulated, behave much like individuals with 'a psychopathic personality', creating destruction? What examples of corporate crime does the film illustrate?

Notes

1   Thompson and McHugh (2006).

2   Bakan (2004: 1).

3   Mabey, Salaman and Storey (1998: 453–4).

4   Hammer (1997).

5   *Globe and Mail*, 18 July 2006, pp. B10, B11; 21 July 2006, p. B4.

6   Drucker (1997: 4).

7   Gadiesh and Olivet (1997).

8   Drucker (1954/1993: 225–6).

9   Galbraith (1996), Bratton (1999).

10 Herriot (1998).

11 See Watson (1995), Thompson and McHugh (2006).

12 Clegg and Dunkerley (1980), Hardy and Clegg (1999).

13 Clegg, Hardy and Nord (1999).

14 Hamel and Prahalad (1994).

15 Daft (2001).

16 Champy (1996).

17 Burns and Stalker (1961).

18 Mabey, Salaman and Storey (1998).

19 Mabey, Salaman and Storey (1998). See also Scholte (2005).

20 Mintzberg (1983).

21 Hill and Jones (2004).

22 Jacoby (2005), Hill and Jones (2004), Hamel and Pralahad (1994).

23 Hamel and Prahalad (1994: 309).

24 Pulignano and Stewart (2006).

25 Champy (1996: 3).

26 Hammer and Champy (1993).

27 Willmott (1995).

28 Hammer (1997: 158–9).

29 See Reed (1993), Thompson (1993), Craig and Yetton (1993), Oliver (1993), Willmott (1995), Grint and Willcocks (1995).

30 Thompson (1993: 192).

31 Ferlie and Pettigrew (1998).

32 See Hamel and Prahalad (1994).

33 Davidow and Malone (1992).

34 Scholte (2005).

35 Bartlett and Ghoshal (1989).

36 Pulignano and Stewart (2006: 104).

37 Chandler (1962: 15).

38 Keats and Hitt (1988).

39 Klein (2000: 4).

40 See Blau and Schoenherr (1971), Pugh et al. (1969), Child (1972).

41 Aldrich (1972).

42 Woodward (1965) and Thompson, J. D. (1967).

43 Burns and Stalker (1961).

44 Mintzberg (1993: 137–8).

45 Scholte (2005: 59).

46 Sklair (2002).

47 See Hoogvelt (2001: 16).

48 Orsburn and Moran (2000: xiii).

49 Sklair (2002).

50 Mabey et al. (1998: 260).

51 Bartlett and Ghoshal (1989).

52 Arnolds and Boshoff (2002: 714).

53 Clarke and Koonce (1995).

54 Mabey et al. (1998).

55 Punnett (1998).

56 Durkheim (1893/1997), Weber (1947).

57 Smircich (1983), Ogbonna (1992). Examples of managerialist-oriented approaches are Deal and Kennedy (1982, 2000), Peters and Waterman (1982).

58 See for example Alvesson (1993), Alvesson and Berg (1992), Frost et al. (1985), Handy (1978), Morgan (1997), Schein (1985, 1991), Smircich (1983), Trice and Beyer (1992) and Willmott (1993).

59 Cray (1998), Geertz (1973), Schein (1991).

60 Hodson (1999), Grey (2005: 71).

61 Noon and Blyton (2002: 336).

62 Hofstede (1993).

63 Schein (1992), Limerick (1990), Hofstede (1998a).

64 Harding (2003).

65 Champy (1996: 57).

66 Schein (1994: 247).

67 Hofstede (1998a).

68 See for example Lincoln and Kalleberg (1990).

69 Thompson and McHugh (2006).

70 Legge (2005).

71 Hofstede (1998a: 240).

72 Hofstede (1998a).

73 Bratton and Garrett-Petts (2005).

74 Meek (1992: 209).

75 Herrbach and Mignonac (2004)

76 See Alvesson and Willmott (2002), Meijs (2002).

77 Ogbonna (1992: 91).

78 Ogbonna (1992).

79 Wajcman (1998).

80 Ogbonna and Harris (2006).

81 Schein (1996).

82 Meek (1992).

83 Brewis and Linstead (2000).

84 See for example Mills and Tancred (1992), Hearn et al. (1989).

85 See Dex (1988), Witz (1986), Knights and Willmott (1986), Philips and Philips (1993), Wilson (2003).

86 Wajcman (1998: 47).

87 Oliver (1991).

chapter 16

Technology in work organizations

Governments everywhere try to formulate productivity-enhancing policies ... [E]conomists have found that technological change is a principal source of economic growth and rising per capitum income. Students of business identify it as basic cause of the growth of the corporation. Its effects on employment, the distribution of income and regional differences in growth are carefully scrutinized.[1]

The call centre can be seen as an emblematic creation of a neo-liberalist age, in which labour has been intensified and the rate of exploitation increased. For some in this brave new world, the prospect was bleak.[2]

chapter outline

▷ Introduction
▷ Defining technology: a critical look at trends
▷ Historical and philosophical contexts of ICT and work
▷ Applications of ICT legislation, policy and programmes
▷ Skills and practices related to technology and workplace adoption
▷ Chapter summary
▷ Key concepts
▷ Chapter review questions
▷ Further reading
▷ Chapter case study: Technological change at the *Observer-Herald* newspaper
▷ Web-based assignment
▷ OB in films
▷ Notes

chapter objectives

After completing this chapter, you should be able to:

▷ outline current trends in the relationship between technology and work organizations
▷ understand and explain the following key concepts: participatory design, configurations, technology agreement, four key forms of technological thought, Luddite revolt
▷ compare and contrast major theoretical approaches to technology and work organizations including the post-industrialism thesis and the deskilling/enskilling debates
▷ discuss possible implications of theories and research for workplace practice.

Introduction

A recent report from the Society for Human Resource Management[3] tells us that technology, and specifically computers and the Internet, will become embedded in previously unheard-of numbers of work organizations. While it took 74 years for telephones to reach the lives of 50 million people, and 13 years for television, the Internet has achieved this and much, much more in only four years. National based expenditures on information and communication technology (ICT) have approached double digits as a percentage of GDP, with the United States, Japan and the European Union countries breaking the 7.5 per cent mark: these expenditures represent over US$1.5 trillion per year.

At the same time, Organization for Economic Cooperation and Development (OECD) policy analysts and an enormous array of others suggest this is not enough.[4] For them, it is clear that economic success is dependent on ICT: investment in the technology, its application and its diffusion. This thinking represents a type of orthodoxy that is rarely challenged. In this chapter we shall look at it closely, alongside the many different, competing theories which are often left out of most work-based and government policy-based discussions.

The challenge of this chapter is to explore the relevance of this orthodoxy to a critical understanding of organizational behaviour (OB). We can, and should, begin this in a simple way by asking: How is 'technology' itself defined and understood? What are the presumptions made about the relationship between ICT development, OB and ICT use?

In this chapter, we include discussion not often seen in OB textbooks which points to broad work-based policy and practice surrounding ICT. National and international policy and programmes are examined with reference to the United States, Canada, the European Union, and finally Sweden and Norway. We look at important types of policy and practice at the level of the firm, with a focus on first, technology agreements, and second, scholarship on the practice of ICT innovation and its use in the labour process. There is an emphasis on what is known in the sociology of work field as the deskilling/enskilling debate for what it can teach us about OB.

We begin, however, with a brief discussion of the key concepts, main literatures and central ideologies of technological thought. Together, this review sets the stage for critical and creative thinking about the relationship between technology, work and OB.

STOP AND REFLECT

Before reading on, you may wish to think carefully about how you define 'technology' now, based on how you have seen it applied in the workplaces you are familiar with. Is this definition narrow or broad, do you feel? When are either types of definitions useful? Important to the chapter generally will be the notions of conflict and consensus. From your experiences, is technological change at work associated with conflict, consensus or both?

plate 44 New technology can eliminate jobs. For instance workers can be replaced by industrial robots welding car bodies on a mass-production assembly line.

Source: Getty Images

Defining technology: a critical look at trends

technology: the means by which organizations transform inputs into outputs, or rather the mediation of human action. This includes mediation by tools and machines as well as rules, social convention, ideologies or discourses.

In the context of workplace organizations, technology is conventionally defined as 'the means by which an organization transforms inputs into outputs … includ[ing] the techniques and process used to transform labour, knowledge, capital and raw materials into finished goods and services'.[5] Classic post-Second World War researchers developed a research programme that looked carefully at the relationship between technology and work. For example, Woodward studied the relationship between production technology and the organizational structure of firms, testing also for the possible roles of authority, control, division of labour and intra-firm communications.[6] She found that the type of organization corresponds to the (product or service) production technologies it uses.

This perspective has been criticized by a range of authors for the amount of influence granted to the technology, or rather its 'technological determinism'. Other 'classic' researchers of this period added additional insights into the relationship between technology and organizational forms, stressing not simply the correlation between the two, but causative relationships: that is, the 'why' and 'how' of the relationship.[7]

post-industrial economy:
an economy that is based
on the provision of services
rather than goals

knowledge worker: knowledge
workers: a worker who
depends on her or his skills,
knowledge and judgement
established through additional
training and/or schooling.

Around the same time there emerged an influential series of arguments (which are, nevertheless, contestable) that organizational structures, OB and technology were combining to form 'post-industrial', 'knowledge' and/or 'information' economies, which were significantly different from the styles and structure of work to that point. Promoted by a variety of influential researchers,[8] this school of thought is still with us today, trumpeting the collapse of workplace drudgery, low-skill jobs to be replaced by 'knowledge workers', 'information workers' or 'symbolic analysts', all with an emphasis on the use of computerized technology. Even more recently, others have taken up the torch to perpetuate the tradition.[9]

The current argument of these gurus of the 'perpetually coming but never arriving good times' is, in brief, that technology with informating properties – that is, the capacity to provide relevant information and generate analytically based knowledge – encourages the development of computer, social and analytical skills, and hence contributes to both the emergence of new occupations (such as software developers) and worker empowerment. ICT alters management–employee relations by encouraging decentralized activities and new forms of 'panoptic' (that is, all-embracing) managerial control.

Decentralized work activities can foster more collaborative work teams, even allowing them to function over the barriers of time and space, so it is viewed as a key enabler of new forms of work organization. There is an assumption that ICT and new forms of technology will lead to new firms, new products and new jobs. Some writers on the topic are particularly fascinated by the prospect of greater 'outsourcing', which is made easier since ICT reduces the transaction costs associated with contracting. This places downward pressure on wages and employee control, but it is said to encourage innovation.

These accounts, however, tend to ignore the messy work through which real technological or economic change emerges in society. In sum, they tend to downplay the conflictual dimensions of change, and overplay the consensual or rather mechanistic dimension: the view that change is simply an anonymous, faceless force of nature.

Economic history teaches us that the claims of links between technology, productivity and the emergence of apparently 'new' phases in the economy are not as straightforward as they may seem. The key technologies of modernism that are said to have defined the first, second and third industrial revolutions – that is, steam, electricity and ICT – have seen fascinating and complex pathways to application in the workplace.[10] Amongst these 'general-purpose technologies' (GPT), electricity[11] and ICT,[12] and in particular steam,[13] clearly emerged, not out of some inventor's mind, as much as from the push and pull of the forces of political and economic struggle. The details of the emergence and diffusion or transfer of GPTs provide important clues about the actual nature of technology as a phenomenon. Is technology a 'thing' or is it a social process? Lazonick seems to suggest the latter in his discussion of the meaning of 'technological transfer':

> Insofar as the utilization of technology requires complementary human inputs with specific cognitive capabilities and behavioural responses, the transferred technology will have to be developed in the new national environment before it can be utilized there. As a result, when 'transferred' technology is ultimately developed so that it can be productively utilized in a new national environment, it is in effect a new technology.[14]

configurations: defining
technology as the combination
of social and technical factors.
Configurations are a complex
mix of standardized and locally
customized elements which are
highly specific to an organization.

The type of description that Lazonick provides is aligned with Fleck's notion of 'configurations' (as opposed to 'technologies' as such).[15] Configurations are defined as complex mixes of standardized and locally customized elements which are highly specific to an organization. In fact, those who have been most insightful in considering the very nature of technology have defined the term quite broadly to reflect this broad set of considerations. These scholars tend to produce statements which are at first glance simple, but at a second glance can be seen to be deeply informed. Technology is not this or that tool, artefact or machine, and neither is it a GPT such as steam, electricity or ICT. Rather, it is 'the way we do things around here',[16] the 'organization of resources',[17] 'society made durable'[18] and so on.

Students of work, technology and society gain the potential for valuable leadership when they break the bonds of conventional wisdom to explore its terms critically. In this chapter, we suggest that we must approach technology and organizational behaviour as a thoroughly social phenomenon.

However, the question remains: what kind of social phenomenon are we talking about? We have mentioned already that steam, electricity and ICT all emerged from the push and pull of economic and political power. It is a contested terrain, or as Feenberg says, 'technology is a scene of struggle … a parliament of things'.[19] Historically, as now, the intersection of work, learning and technological change has occasioned conflict: from the Luddite revolts of early nineteenth century to the countless more recent industrial conflicts caused by the imposition of technological change. More recently, this has involved the transformation of occupations including engineering,[20] textile work,[21] postal work,[22] computer programming[23] and, one of the more frequently documented occupations, printing.[24] Wallace and Kalleberg, working in the US context, summarize it like this:

> We have argued that while technology is the proximate cause of this transformation, the underlying and fundamental sources for these changes are found in historically developed social relations of production .... The stated goal of automation in printing, as in other industries, is the rationalization of the labor process: the streamlining of production and elimination of costly sources of human error .... However, efficiency is not a value-neutral goal in capitalist economies.[25]

Thus it is the core point of departure in this chapter that our conceptions of ICT and work must be conditioned by an impulse to 'de-reify', to move beyond mere appearances. ICT as an isolated device, tool or machine is an abstraction; in reality it is an elaborate historical process. It is both a social and highly conflictual phenomenon.

WEB LINK

Check out www.Informationweek.com for the most interesting and latest business stories on the relationship between technology and work. Test your knowledge of this chapter by picking an article that interests you, then try to apply a critical, social approach to the technology issue.

Historical and philosophical contexts of ICT and work

According to Theodore Roszak,[26] the word 'computer' entered the North American public vocabulary in the 1950s, at a time when the most advanced models were still room-sized beasts that burned enough electricity to present a serious cooling problem. Building on the principle of ICT, work and OB as a conflictual social phenomenon, it is important to note that, as with the emergence of steam and electricity, historical scholarship has demonstrated that computers were not simply 'discovered' in the conventional sense of the term. Rather, ICT was brought into being by specific historical and political economic processes: by politics, policy and practice.

Noble provides the definitive analysis,[27] noting that contemporary ICT emerged through a series of concerted and contested activities through which companies like General Electric, Westinghouse, RCA, AT&T and IBM, relying upon private control over public funds for what could be called the 'university-industrial-military' complex of the post-Second World War era in the United States, developed specific forms of computer technology. These included numerical control, computerized numerical control (CNC), automated robotics and now advanced ICT including the Internet. Importantly, Noble makes it clear that in fact alternatives to CNC could have just as efficiently been developed, and that strategic choices revolved around issues of power and control over the organization of production.

Luddites: A group of textile workers, led by General Ned Ludd in early nineteenth-century England, who systematically smashed new workplace technologies because they directly undermined their working knowledge and economic interests as workers

Just as the Luddites of nineteenth-century Britain were in favour of technologies that supplemented rather than displaced human skills,[28] the key alternative during the early history of computers was 'record/playback' (R/P) technology. This system was actively ignored largely because, as Noble puts it, 'to the software engineer, this places far too many cards in the hands of the lowly machinist'.[29]

While this historical background is important, if we are to understand the intersection of ICT, work and OB as a contested as well as a consensual social phenomenon, it is equally important to have a basic understanding of the competing ideologies or philosophical approaches that inform ICT development and use. As Williams and Edge remark, 'these debates are not merely "academic": they relate to policy claims and objectives'.[30] We can categorize the different approaches into four basic categories: instrumental/technocratic, substantive, constructivist, and what Feenberg refers to as a 'critical theory' of technology.[31]

instrumentalist or technocratic approach: approaches to technology that are uncritical of its broader social, political and economic significance viewing technologies as autonomous and positive

Instrumentalist or technocratic approaches tend to be the source of either the positive or neutral characterizations of ICT in the workplace. This is the dominant approach in government, business and mainstream policy sciences. Here the transfer of technology is inhibited only by cost, what works in one context can be expected to work equally well in another, and 'the only rational stance is an unreserved commitment to its employment'.[32] More discussions of the origins of this approach can be found in the work of a variety of leading sociologists of the immediate and later post-Second World War era, who wrote at length on the issues of technology and industrial progression.[33] More often than not under this approach technology comes to take on a kind of autonomous, creative and deterministic role (and thus it makes sense that *Time* magazine can designate a computer 'person of the year'). This autonomous casting, in turn, gives rise to exaggerated tales of the emergence of 'knowledge workers' and 'symbolic analysts'.[34]

substantive approach: approaches that tend to see technologies as producing negative social and political effects.

A contrasting approach to technocratic thought is said to be the substantive approach, represented best in the writings of Jacques Ellul or Martin Heidegger.[35] In a type of mirror image, however, this approach also attributes an autonomous force to technology, although it sees it as a 'cultural system' that orients the world as an 'object of control'. This approach tends to see the future as dark (for instance, 'Only God can save us now' – Heidegger), and argues that a return to simplicity or primitivism offers the only viable alternative.

constructivist approach: approaches to technology that tend not to focus on social or political influences but rather see technologies as defined strictly in how they are put to use

Standing in many ways separate from either of these approaches is the constructivist approach.[36] These works emphasize how technology is rooted in human interaction, and the local activation or use of technologies by human beings. The meaning and effects of technology are determined in their use by actors, and not necessarily in any prior way by designers. Among all the approaches to ICT, it is the constructivist approach that most clearly articulates how users implement and appropriate ICT, sometimes in keeping with the intentions of the designers and those who contracted them, sometimes not. Others have echoed the importance of this approach for technological development, emphasizing how design, implementation, use (and re-design) are interrelated, and opening up new ground in conventional understandings of 'choice' in the course of technological development.[37]

critical approach: approaches to technology that tend to focus on how the social and political effects are produced through contestation and negotiation

Finally there is the critical approach. Its roots are largely in the Frankfurt School of critical social theory,[38] although a variety of work such as that of Lewis Mumford has relevant connections to this approach as well.[39] In general, the approach rejects the presumptions of both the technocratic and the substantive approach, charting a course, as Feenberg says, between the resignation and utopian visions of efficiency.

To the degree that the approach is defined by its reference to issues of power, it might overlap with certain elements of the constructivist approach. Some constructivist researchers[40] overtly declare that there are inherent political dimensions to technological development (for instance Latour's comment, 'Technologies are politics pursued by other means'). However, central to the critical approach is what Feenberg calls the 'democratic advance': that is, the democratic participation of citizens in the establishment of both the goals and means of technological development, implementation and diffusion.

Echoing this concern in terms of policy analysis, Gärtner and Wagner[41] have carried out careful case studies in Europe, and drawn attention to the difficulties faced by design efforts situated in 'fragmented political cultures'. Mumford's pan-historic discussions also emphasize what he calls 'authoritarian and democratic technics'.[42] By 'authoritarian tecnics' he means a development that is 'system-centred, immensely powerful and yet unstable due to its centralization of control'. Indeed, he goes on to say that 'if democracy did not exist, we would have to invent it'[43] if we are to deal effectively with the technologies of the modern era.

We suggest that these four basic approaches to technological thought will be useful for analysing policy and practice, providing us with as a type of philosophical compass. In other words, they orient us to the more general directions and purposes that all too often remain hidden beneath the surface of legislation, policy, programmes and practice that expresses them.

Applications of ICT legislation, policy and programmes

If we commit to understanding the intersection of ICT, work and OB as a broad, conflictual social phenomenon, then we are in essence seeking to understand a process of change. Both personal and organizational change can perhaps most usefully be studied as a process of 'learning', either individual, group or organizational. We benefit greatly by looking at work-based learning, whether it is organized as a training programme or undertaken informally in everyday participation in the labour process, as a phenomenon that sits above, gives meaning to, reacts upon and in turn affects legislation, policy and programmes regarding ICT.

CRITICAL INSIGHT

The purpose and outcomes of the introduction of new technology in organizations have been assessed and reassessed many times in the literature over the years. Earlier in the chapter we mentioned classic readings in this area, and now let us take a careful look at some of them.

Read Joan Woodward's *Industrial Organizations: Theory and practice* and J. D. Thompson's *Organizations in Action*.[44] Compare and contrast their assessments. Be sure to note the research on which each set of arguments is based.

Research and development (R&D) is central to the efforts of leading firms, as well as being carried out on a national scale by the core countries of global capitalism,[45] although there is considerable variation in the degree and focus that countries bring to it.[46] When it comes to the relationship between direct and indirect involvement in technology development and industrial relations, we see that Northern European governments are often the most directly involved, with other European governments such as France and Germany (as well as non-European countries such as Japan) being moderately involved, and the governments of countries such as the UK, the

United States, Southern Europe, Australia and Canada least directly involved on a regulatory basis.

The most 'interventionist' government responses are to be found in countries like Norway and Sweden, where issues from ICT research and application, as well as industrial relations more broadly, are shaped by a commitment to 'co-determination'. However, in general, the power of national or international governmental bodies to use regulation to influence the introduction and application of ICT in actual work processes and workplaces is quite limited. In the United States, for example, while Carnoy, Pollack and Wong have noted that labour relations structures, policies and practices are coming to the centre of the debate on the design and adaptation of new technologies,[47] the most common model of employer/employee negotiation and ICT adoption is adversarial and antagonistic.

> ### The zen of workplace participation
>
> A major challenge for business leadership today is to find ways to engage employees' full capacities to learn, be creative and so on. Livingstone and Sawchuk's *Hidden Knowledge: Organized labour in the information age*[48] documents enormous unused capacities of this kind. They argue that management must overcome its traditional biases that keep it from trusting the capacities of workers.
>
> Special agreements are sometimes drawn up to form the legal basis of ongoing discussions about how the firm should use technology in its development. These are typically called 'technology agreements' or 'co-determination policy'. Try to imagine the pros and cons of this type of approach to organizational behaviour, planning and change. What would it take to develop the zen of workplace participation among business leaders: that is, a more holistic, trusting and 'social' approach to technological innovation?

STOP AND REFLECT

However, we can briefly note that a parallel system of private-sector policy and (corporate-based) governance has blossomed. For example, there have been a growing number of international agreements between large corporations about various forms of ICT development and application. According to Archibugi and Coco,[49] between the periods of 1981–86 and 1993–98 international firm-to-firm technological development agreements doubled. In particular, strategic technology partnerships (for R&D) between Europe and the United States rocketed in the ten years to 2006. These partnerships may also involve collaborations with public research institutions and universities, which play an increasingly important role in the international dissemination of knowledge and ICT development.

While this layer of ICT and work policy is important, a solid grasp of the range of governmental legislation, policy and programmes in the area remains the most relevant for our discussion here. To review these, we look at several selected examples involving different countries as well as different political levels of enactment.

The US system

The US system of training, ICT development and implementation is often set up as an ideal in the policy world, in terms of leading-edge practices of ICT-based innovation. However, closer examination reveals a complex, sometimes chaotic, mix of federal, state and regional efforts.

At the level of the firm and sector, the US system of industrial relations places decisions on technological change and work organization firmly under the 'management rights clause' of any company–union collective agreement.[50] In the context of a corporate culture that is hostile to unions, and of comparatively high levels of involvement in 'inter-firm' technological development agreements, there is not a great deal of likelihood of genuine 'co-determination' of organizations' technological direction in the United States.

In slightly broader terms, but directly bearing on the translation of technological policy and actual organizational behaviour and change, we can look at the vocational and work-based training policy in the United States. This too has come to be recognized to be a patchwork of state and federal programmes. Legislation began in 1962 with the Manpower Development Training Act, which was followed by the Comprehensive Employment and Training Act of 1973, the Job Training Partnership Act (1983) and the School-to-Work Opportunities Act (1994–2001).[51]

A host of authors have lamented the general historical lack of industrial policy in the United States, and this is reflected in the arena of ICT R&D policy.[52] At the same time, however, Herman has documented some important examples of multilateral partnership agreements over ICT implementation and training.[53] These appear to hold a good deal of promise for the future. Based on 14 case studies of 'high-road' partnerships between employers, government, unions and local communities, Herman concludes that in the United States, the most successful ICT/work/learning policy tends to be found at the sectoral rather than the state or federal level.

Canada

Canada provides an alternative to the type of decentralized, largely corporate-controlled policy models seen in the United States. Here there has been innovative experimentation with government policy. 'Sector skills councils' in Canada generally focus on technological change, and offer a unique model not seen elsewhere in the world. At the federal level, these councils have their roots in the industrial adjustment services established in 1963. Following the establishment of the Sectoral Partnership Initiative by the federal government in the early 1990s, they reached the level of 22 councils in the mid-1990s, 17 of which involved union participation. Related initiatives also emerged at the provincial level in Canada.

In general, the Skills Council built on pioneering examples such as the Canadian Steel Trade and Employment Congress.[54] Both federally and provincially, sectoral skills council had their origins in the inability of the private sector to develop workable options for high levels of training and adjustment on their own, where a chief concern of corporate leaders was the 'free-rider' problem: the fear that firms that trained workers well would simply lose the worker to other firms offering higher wages.

'free-rider' problem: the fear that firms have that if they invest in training for workers, these workers might eventually leave the firm for one offering higher wages/benefits thus losing the firm its investment

Mechanized high-tech workers?

It is often assumed that those with the greatest technical skills and education are most ideally situated on the labour market. Certainly most people wouldn't expect 'computer programmers' to have a difficult time, but business analysts are now saying otherwise. Charles Simonyi, former programmer with Microsoft and founder of Intentional Software Corp., claims on www.informationweek.com that the:

outsourcing trend indicates that an ever-larger part of IT work has become routine, repetitive and low-bandwidth – one might even say unexciting or boring .... Outsourcing has been historically a prelude to mechanization, and mechanization is a high-value domestic opportunity ... in the long run these jobs will be 90% mechanized, with the help of senior domestic talent.

Strangely, there are ever-increasing numbers of highly skilled programmers available from all over the world, and yet there does not seem to be enough 'skilled work' for them to do. Why can't employers create enough jobs that allow skilled workers to apply their talents? Does it have anything to do with the wage level they would have to pay them at? How does 'outsourcing' play a role?

An important example at the provincial level was established in Canada's most industrialized province, Ontario. It followed a mixed governmental/firm/corporate model which, as in the United States, seems most effective at the sectoral level. The Technology Adjustment Research Programme (TARP) was first envisaged by the first Premier's Council of Ontario in the late 1980s, and was later funded by the Ontario Federation of Labour and the provincial government's Ministry of Economic Development and Trade.[55] It involves the participation of 16 specific unions.

In connection with this programme, the government established sectoral strategic initiatives in areas including aerospace, steel, biotechnology, plastics and automotive parts. Sectoral skills councils emerged, a variety of sectoral initiatives were established, and a variety of innovative multilateral research efforts were undertaken. However, the results were mixed at the level of the workplace, ICT implementation and learning. After the withdrawal of the government, only remnants of the programme persist today.

These efforts made it clear that without both broader legislative support as well as ongoing resources for developing the multilateral model (inclusive of a genuinely multilateral industrial policy), even the best efforts would be hampered. Frequently, those at the centre of policy implementation and programme research lamented a lack of a broader 'European' approach (and funds to match).

Western Europe

One of the most comprehensive sets of studies of ICT, work and organizational change was conducted in Western Europe in the early 1990s. It was entitled 'Participation in Technological Change' and was undertaken by the European Foundation for the Improvement of Living and Working Conditions. Based on 64 case studies and a large (n = 7,326) survey, the study showed that technological change was dependent on national industrial relations regimes as well as, in broader terms, the 'historical and cultural factors' associated with particular nations and sectors. In keeping with our discussion, two key factors for success were unionization and the skill level of workers.

The European Union is a key example of how international policy and programmes are created and carried out, and provides important information on the current status of the intersection of ICT, work and OB in advanced capitalism. In general terms, this model of policy development contrasts starkly with the decentralized model in the United States. EU policies in the area of technology and training revolve around the principle that the circulation of knowledge is as important as a common currency. To put it more starkly, 'economic growth, employment and welfare in the old continent are strictly associated with its capability to generate and diffuse new technologies'.[56]

As a student of OB, you should explore the outputs of such bodies to gain a sense of where practice, research and policy are headed. Perhaps as important as the centralized organization of ICT-related policy, however, is the willingness and ability of the European Union to carry out combined R&D, training and implementation research programmes which link corporations, research institutions and governmental resources.

The most relevant example in this regard is the European Commission's information technology program entitled 'European Strategic Programme of Research on Information Technology' (ESPRIT, 1994–98).[57] ESPRIT represents an international example of an attempt at the policy/programme level to organize R&D and ICT-based innovation, as well as work and learning outcomes, to respond to the needs of the workplace. Its outcomes, however, have remained partially ambiguous from a critical viewpoint. This is in part because of the phenomenon that Gärtner and Wagner describe as narrow forms of 'agenda setting':

> What is politically and ethically legitimate and desirable cannot be simply solved by establishing participatory structures. The kind of close partnership between designers and users at which, e.g. situated design, aspires is not a

sufficient answer to the core question of what makes a 'good system'. Our case analysis points at the importance of understanding agenda setting. Each arena has its own set of legitimate agenda, from questions of user interface design to qualify of working life and privacy issues.[58]

The ESPRIT programme and the associated European Commission policies on which it was built were largely democratic, but at the same time its agenda was largely predefined along technocratic lines. At the point of learning and ICT use, for example, its motive was tied, mostly though not exclusively, to serving markets and relatively narrow interests of profitability, rather than to more broad issues of quality of working life, sustainability, equity and so forth.

Scandinavia

In Northern Europe, however, there is a different tradition at the intersection between ICT, work and OB. Again, Gärtner and Wagner's work is instructive.[59] Their work looked closely at the role of formal national legislative frameworks, such as the Norwegian Work Environment Act (NWEA), which detail the relations between the various industrial partners and the norms of work, technological development and ICT use. The NWEA defines participation in work-related areas related to ICT systems (among other things), and suggests a much deeper form of participation in policy formation.

Specifically, the 1970s was a watershed decade for progressive policy and legislation around ICT design, implementation and work in Northern Europe. The Norwegians put the NWEA into place in 1977, giving workers formal participation in 'company assemblies' and the right to appoint trade union representatives in the area of technological change. Co-determination procedures were established and a system of penalties was set in place.

Similarly, in the late 1970s Sweden enacted a series of 'work democracy' regulations including establishing a legal framework for labour representatives on company boards, disclosure acts, and other items under the Work Environment Act of 1978. This set of acts, described by some as the most important reform in Swedish society since the universal right to vote, also included the Joint Regulation Act of 1977 which guaranteed co-determination specifically around issues of the design and use of new technology. While management did retain certain rights of ownership, articles in these acts stipulated that employers must negotiate with local unions before making any major changes to work processes, that the workers can initiate such negotiations as well, and that all parties have the rights to relevant documentation (financial and technical).

Significantly, in Sweden these legislative and policy frameworks were complemented by specific ICT development research programmes, namely DEMOS and UTOPIA,[60] which had as their central goal to investigate how technical design could respond to this radical new legislative environment. Also complementing these legislative frameworks were innovative experiments in user-based design: Scandinavia's UTOPIA programme[61] as well as the Effective Technical and Human Implementation of Computer-based Systems (ETHICS) programme.[62] As a result the network of policies, programmes and legislation was particularly thick with ideas and potential.

The conclusions from this exciting period in Northern Europe were that local participants must be deeply involved in the process, but also that participatory design is necessary but not sufficient for genuinely progressive socioeconomic outcomes surrounding technology design, implementation, learning and use.[63] It also became

One critical scholar of technology puts forth the argument that today machines take precedence over people in the workplace.[64] He goes further, adding that such environments 'seriously upset the habits of mind applied to the work world', and that '[w]hether one conceives work in the capitalist model of costs of production or the Marxist one of the organic composition of labor, information machines disrupt the models of comprehending work'. Do you think this is true? Why or why not? Reading the original article might help you to consider the issues.

STOP AND REFLECT

participatory design: an approach to design and implementation of technologies that is premised on user participation

apparent that often trade unions were not prepared to adequately take advantage of their new powers and responsibilities. They lacked the resources and organizational structure to produce levels of expertise comparable to business.

Skills and practices related to technology and workplace adoption

We have explored the conceptual, historical and philosophical context of ICT, and reviewed key legislative, policy and programmatic initiatives. We have also emphasized that policy takes on its meaning within the cycle of social processes that includes OB and learning. With this in mind, in this section we review existing literature on workplace ICT, skill and learning to fill in an important gap in our discussion thus far. This section also completes our discussion on different theoretical approaches to ICT and OB, by exploring different sociological and organizational theory approaches to work.

Technology agreements

technology agreements: agreements with legal standing that set in place rules for negotiation over technological selection, adoption and implementation.

Clearly one of the ways that policy and practice intersect in the workplace is through what are known as 'technology agreements'. These agreements, often though not exclusively seen in unionized firms, establish a form of co-determination (jointly between management and workers) over issues of ICT adoption and use. In some ways, these agreements mirror on a smaller scale the kinds of national legislative frameworks seen in Norway and Sweden. However, they have appeared in a much wider range of countries.

Although technology agreements are not quite as common now as when they were first introduced in the 1970s and 1980s, the basic technology agreement remains an important form of workplace-based policy concerning ICT adoption and effective use. In the early days of their emergence, according to some writers,[65] these agreements typically included two basic components. First, there were 'procedural' elements which included broad statements on the need for new technologies, and arguably more importantly, agreements on timely disclosure of information by employers. These were to include the likely effects of the changes and to set out options. The options often included procedures for the development of joint union/management committees and change monitoring practices, the establishment of worker technology representatives, and arrangements for union and management to draw on outside experts or consultants. Occasionally unions were given veto powers if management clearly violated the agreed procedures.

A second component to technology agreements was what are called 'substantive' elements: specific statements on how various issues should be handled. The aspects covered included job security, retraining and adjustments, methods of sharing economic benefits, health and safety, and surveillance issues.

Small and Yasin[66] have noted the varied effects that technology agreements have on practice in the workplace, and also note the importance of the related industrial relations infrastructure in a firm. (Basically, they emphasize the importance of unionization.) Although many factors affect the overall success of technology agreements, evidence suggests that they tend to lead to better firm performance, a broader and more productive labour process, and a collective learning feedback loop which leads to better choice and implementation of new technologies.

plate 45 Technology has the capacity to either deskill or enskill

Source: Getty Images

ICT and workplace skills

To complete the picture, we need to look carefully at specific discussions of ICT and workplace skills. For this we turn to writings on adult education, industrial relations and the sociology of work to expand our understanding of OB.

Skill and knowledge development in the workplace has regularly been associated with the introduction of new technology. In different historical phases of the labour process this has been seen under the paradigms of craft production, Taylorism, Fordism, neo-Fordism, flexible specialization and virtual organizational design. Approaches to work, learning and policy – for example, those associated with the technocratic approach – largely presume that ICT requires advanced skills.[67] However, many of those who have looked closely at skill and learning practice associated with workplace technological change have questioned this assumption.[68]

Poster,[69] for example, suggests that levels of learning may be reduced in some ways by the introduction of ICT, and that either way, accurate assessments of performance and skill change remain elusive. Important empirical analyses in North America seem to support Poster's claim, with some suggesting there may in fact be a surplus in computer literacy: that is, there are inadequate real opportunities for workers to apply their skills at work.[70] For example, Lowe studied computer literacy in Canada, and specifically states that typically 'job structures deprive workers of opportunities to use their education and talents'.[71]

In research from both North American countries, the most powerful analysis shows that, despite calls from the corporate and government sectors to increase computer literacy, 'empirical evidence certainly suggests that there are now more people with basic computer literacy than there are jobs which need it'.[72] By all estimates, North American workplaces are not alone in this paradoxical situation, of on the one hand the relatively widespread availability of ICT, and on the other, apparent barriers to effective diffusion, implementation, learning and use.

Kelley provides a useful review of sociological literature on the issue of work-based skills, as well as empirical analysis of her own, which focuses on practice at the level of the firm.[73] She concludes that translating a firm's adoption of ICT into skilful application of the new technology is dependent on a host of organizational as well as broader industrial relations policy and practice issues. In this, she builds on and broadens the observations of the 'classical' post-Second World War scholarship that we explored earlier in the chapter. According to Kelley, the 'least complex' firms are most effective at successful adoption. That is, open participation of workers in all facets of production, including management operations, appears to be vital.

In some sense, the conditions that Kelley describes represent the spirit of the 'co-determination' legislation, policy and programmes we discussed earlier. Nevertheless, how any organization achieves this type of open participation remains an open question. Small firms seem to offer hope for translating ICT adoption into effective production outcomes, but typically lack the levels of capital for significant ICT investment. Large firms have the capital but may not have an industrial relations infrastructure (in the sense of recognized unions) to generate accountable, genuine, shared decision making across all levels of the organization. Unionized firms offer an infrastructure for shared decision making, but, given that in most countries workers must actively fight to obtain union representation, these firms can experience bitter management/labour relations. However, for some time it has been a demonstrated fact that union representation often provides the best chance for achieving effective technological adoption and skill-enhancing outcomes.[74]

Deskilling and enskilling

Research related to what is known as the 'deskilling/enskilling' debate provides a key conceptual approach for understanding questions surrounding the successful application of technology in the workplace. This debate was initiated in the work of Harry Braverman.[75] His ground-breaking research was based on an elaboration of Marxist theory through a critique of Taylor's scientific management (or Taylorism).

Braverman and other advocates of the deskilling thesis note that the goal of the labour process under capitalism is to generate managerial control for maximization of efficiency and profitability.[76] In seeking control, managers often dispense with the very employee capacities that are claimed to be so vital by today's managerial theories:

> The focus on the labour process points also to the irremediable necessity of a coercive system of control and surveillance, leading to a critical perspective towards the role of 'management'. Of crucial importance, such a focus also helps deflate the ideology of 'technology' as a neutral, autonomous and irresistible force.[77]

deskilling: a reduction in the proficiency needed to perform a specific job, which leads to a corresponding reduction in the wages paid for that job

In Taylorist, Fordist and neo-Fordist models of production, the deskilling argument focuses on the stark division of mental and manual labour, and the breaking up of complex tasks into smaller, more discrete ones. Often, though not exclusively, this is achieved with the aid of new technologies. As Hyman suggests,[78] there is often a significant growth in surveillance of workers as well.[79] The classic assembly line, and the myriad of similar work design principles we see today across manufacturing as well as in many service-sector workplaces, attempted to generate profit and managerial control by breaking up knowledge and skill that was 'owned' (for lack of a better word) by individual or groups of workers. It converted these skills into a feature of the work system itself, so they became 'owned' by the business owners/shareholders, and under the control of managers.

This classic form of deskilling still occurs widely, as you will know if you or your friends have worked in, for example, fast food or retail outlets, but the introduction of new forms of advanced ICT has redefined the deskilling process for a small number of occupational groups.[80] The classic separation of mental and manual has evolved into something more complex, although it remains difficult to argue that it is fundamentally distinct from the classic deskilling dynamics.

In other words, in some firms and amongst certain occupational groups, we now see a more nuanced form of the division between mental and manual labour, which is associated with the struggle over macro-design (or 'agenda setting') and the creative micro, or local, design and use of ICT. Hosts of workers are now being asked to use the tools provided for them in creative and responsive ways, but in contexts and with goals that are preestablished and beyond their control. We can of course see this predicted by commentators such as Marx: more than a century ago, he noted that the capitalist labour process can (although it does not necessarily have to seek to) eliminate the mental capacities of labour in order to appropriate and control work outcomes.

enskilling: changes in work, often involving technology, that result in an increase in the skill level of workers. The issue of control is often implicated.

The so-called 'enskilling' thesis claims the contrary: that increased technology leads to more, not less, worker skill. Its advocates point to niches in the economy (often involving small firms) where stark divisions between mental and manual labour are less often seen. A range of other researchers discussed earlier in the chapter are in this sense the forefathers of the enskilling thesis,[81] collectively suggesting that unskilled jobs will be simply be 'automated away', while Reich and a host of technocratic analysts can be viewed as more contemporary advocates.

Between these two camps are other researchers, including types of what are known as 'contingency' and 'institutionalist' theorists, who emphasize a range of organizational, institutional and market factors that shape the deskilling/enskilling outcomes of the introduction of new technology.[82] Burris sums things up nicely by noting that a commonly held corollary of technocratic restructuring is:

> 'skill restructuring' (Cockburn, 1983), 'skill disruption' (Hodson, 1988) and new types of alienation, stress and occupational hazards (see Hirschhorn, 1984).

Source: Fotosearch

plate 46 It has been suggested that call centres are a typical creation of a neo-liberal age, in which labour has been intensified and the rate of exploitation increased. They are sometimes described as 'electronic sweatshops'.

Both de-skilling and re-skilling occur, and the balance between the two depends upon both the design of the technology and the way in which it is implemented.[83]

Adoption practices and outcomes

Invaluable as the deskilling/enskilling debates is for our understanding, it cannot help but gloss over the actual behavioural processes that surround technological change and organizational development. The 'how' of successful ICT adoption remains obscure.

Lam provides a good comparative international analysis of how institutions, legislation and policy in different countries (he looks at Japan, the UK, the United States and Denmark) support or inhibit ICT innovation and adoption.[84] At the centre of this analysis is the concept of 'tacit knowledge', rooted in the relationships of discretionary communities of practice (which can be established either within an organization, or more widely across a specific occupational group).

In the United States, anthropologist Charles Darrah has exhaustively described this type of knowledge production process, with some specific attention to advanced ICT.[85] A host of detailed empirical studies of exactly how ICT and learning practice relate is provided by Luff, Hindmarsh and Heath.[86] Each of these studies shows that ICT is not merely 'adopted' by a workplace, but rather is *activated*, and in some sense *reconfigured*, by users in the course of (learning) practice.

A particularly relevant piece of work in this area was carried out by Livingstone and Sawchuk.[87] Their collection of case studies provides an important complement to OB scholarship, as well as the sociology of work and deskilling/enskilling debates. It is based on a comparative examination of workplaces across five sectors in the Canadian economy (auto assembly, garments, light manufacturing, chemicals and public service), and draws on in-depth 'learning life-history' interviews. These case studies demonstrate, among other things, how ICT adoption is shaped by the industrial relations climate and the dynamics of a specific sector, as well as the struggle by workers for greater participation in the labour process. The analysis also makes it clear that issues of race, gender and age (see Chapter 10), as well as occupational type, are significant indicators of skill and knowledge development.

Some related work on computer literacy development among manufacturing workers in Canada[88] delves even more deeply into the types of linkages (cultural, economic, and political) between ICT and skill at work. Providing a critical but complementary partner to the work of Darrah, it shows how learning as a dimension of OB is rooted in collective, informal groupings of workers, and operates interactively across the workplace, home and community spheres. This learning is carried out in order to cooperate with the needs of industry and labour markets as well as in order to satisfy individual needs that may diverge from the interests of business.

Overall in the work of Livingstone and Sawchuk, we see computer literacy skills among workers that far outstrip the actual needs of their workplace. Thus, as we saw in the context of previous sections, important assumptions informing mainstream, technocratic approaches to policy surrounding ICT, work and learning are questioned.

Chapter summary

☐ Comparative international analyses of concepts and theoretical debates, as well as policies and programmes, provide an important basis for understanding how technology is related to work and OB. We suggest a broad, multi-levelled approach that suggests technology should be thought of as a social phenomenon, recognizing both consent and conflict in processes of adoption. In reviewing these areas, we are aided by a general understanding of the ideologies of technological thought, which we summarized early on. How do specific technologies and attempts at technological adoption relate to the technocratic, substantive, constructivist or critical approaches? For example, how do the substantive critiques of Heidegger or Ellul colour the messages offered by the likes of Negroponte, Castells and Reich?[89] What can the constructivist approach of Suchman, Latour or Callon add to the deskilling/enskilling debates surrounding ICT, work and OB, and so on?

☐ After reading this chapter, a variety of answers to these and other questions should begin to emerge, but perhaps more importantly you should be in a better position to understand, evaluate and perhaps even affect the current landscape and direction of ICT, work and related issues. These are all important matters in our society today.

Key concepts

co-determination	432	ICT and enskilling	438
configurations	428	Luddite revolt	430
four key forms of technological thought	430–1	post-industrialism	428
ICT and deskilling	438	technology agreement	436

Chapter review questions

1. What is the substance of the claims by authors since the Second World War, such as Woodward, Bell, Blauner and others, regarding technology and changes to society?
2. What are the four key modes of technological thought?
3. Explain the deskilling and enskilling debate in the context of technological change.
4. How do different nations compare in their approach to technological development and work-based adoption?
5. How can OB research benefit from broad understandings of international policy regarding technological development and workplace change?

Further reading

Beirne, M. and Ramsay, H. (eds) (1992) *Information Technology and Workplace Democracy*, London: Routledge & Kegan Paul.

Bell, D. (1973) *The Coming of the Post-Industrial Society*, New York: Basic Books.

Ellis, V. and Taylor, P. (2006) '"You don't know what you've got till it's gone": recontextualising the origins, development and impact of the call centre', *New Technology, Work and Employment*, **21** (2), pp. 107–22.

Gee, J., Hull, G. and Lankshear, C. (1996) *The New Work Order: Behind the language of the new capitalism*, Boulder, Colo.: Westview.

Noble, D. (1984) *The Forces of Production: A social history of industrial automation*, New York: Knopf.

Thomson, R. (ed.) (1993) *Learning and Technological Change*, New York: St Martin's Press.

Zersan, J. and Carnes, A. (eds) (1991) *Questioning Technology: Tool, toy or tyrant?* Philadelphia, Penn.: New Society.

Chapter case study: *Technological change at the* Observer-Herald *newspaper*

The setting for this case study is London, England in 1980. The *Observer-Herald* newspaper has been around for over a half a century, and printing workers there, as elsewhere, have been regarded as master craftworkers, building their skill, knowledge and judgement through distinctive apprenticeships. Over the years they have earned high wages, exercised considerable control over their work environments, and by and large been indispensable to the production process. Relations between the printers and management at the newspaper are good. Each respects the other, and each views the product (one of the leading daily newspapers in the country) with a good deal of pride.

But the 1970s had seen growing unemployment. Industry all over Britain had seen the introduction on the shopfloor of new automated computer technologies. Computers were being touted in manufacturing and even in office work as the way of the future. Workers all over feared for their jobs and their future. Printing industry trade journals had for several years been talking about technological change too. New 'computerized' presses were said to be able to save companies thousands of hours of labour.

James Armstrong, a master printer at the *Observer-Herald*, had decades of experience in the detailed work of typesetting the text of the newspaper. However, on a cool spring evening James arrived at work to face a new challenge. Along with the other printers, he had been called to a meeting, at which he learned that the newspaper would be introducing a new computer-based typesetting technology. He felt a stone in his stomach. His ideas about his work were transformed.

'Together we've got over a hundred and fifty of years of knowledge,' James said to the manager. 'Do you really think a machine can replace that!'

Craig Withnall, the production manager, had known James and the rest of the print workers for a long time. He looked sympathetically toward them, then turned to James. 'I know what you're saying, Jim. But if the company didn't think it would work they wouldn't be doing this. You'll all have a job here, rest assured. It will just be different. You'll have to learn some new things, that's all.'

Task

1. After reviewing the suggested readings below along with this chapter, what do you think will change in terms of skill level, control and sense of the job for James and his fellow printers?
2. What is gained and lost in technological change initiatives of this kind? Are there ways in which you can see the company building on the years of knowledge and experience of workers like James, or is replacement of such skills and knowledge simply inevitable?

Sources of additional information

Gordon, D. (1976) 'Capitalist efficiency and socialist efficiency', *Monthly Review*, **28**, pp.19–39.

Wallace, M. and Kalleberg, A. (1982) 'Industrial transformation and the decline of craft: the decomposition of skill in the printing industry, 1931–1978', *American Sociological Review*, **47**, pp. 307–24.

Websites: www.iacd.oas.org/La%20Educa%20123-125/edw.htm on deskilling; http://atschool.eduweb.co.uk/trinity/t_and_g.html for information on technology and gender.

Note

This case study was written by Peter Sawchuk, University of Toronto, Canada.

Web-based assignment

There are competing views on the purpose of work-related learning. One school of thought believes creativity and innovation is more likely to be fostered in organizations where learning is valued and high. In this sense, workplace learning has an instrumental purpose: that is, to 'unfreeze' employee work attitudes and practices to bring about change. Learning can also enhance an organization's performance and increase a nation's productivity. (See OB in focus, page 433.)

Specifically, this assignment requires you to critically evaluate these assumptions. First, enter the following websites for more information on lifelong learning: www. lifelonglearning.co.uk; www.lifelonglearning.co.uk/llp/index.htm. Second, enter the websites of two companies and evaluate how each company provides for continuous work-related learning. What are the company's objectives with regard to work-related learning? How does the company's learning strategy relate, if at all, to its business strategy? Is there any evidence that work-related learning benefits both individual employees and the company? What role should work-related learning play in the workplace?

OB in films

The film *Enemy of the State* (1998) features a successful labour lawyer, Robert Clayton Dean (played by Will Smith) who without his knowledge is given a video that ties a top official of the US National Security Agency (NSA) to a political murder. NSA agents use sophisticated technology to target Dean and disrupt every aspect of his private life. Dean and his colleague (played by Gene Hackman) use their wits and computing skills to survive.

What does the film illustrate about the abuse of communication and surveillance technology in society? How is the Internet affecting our lives in the home and the workplace?

Notes

1   Thomson (1993: 1).
2   Ellis and Taylor (2006: 120).
3   Patel (2002).
4   OECD 1999; see also for example Reich (1991), Thomson (1993), Castells (1996), Archibugi and Lundvall (2001), Patel (2002).
5   Anderson and Kyprianou (1994: 178).
6   Woodward (1965).
7   See for example Thompson (1967) and Perrow (1970).
8   See for example Bell (1973) in the United States, Porter (1971) in Canada, Touraine (1971) in France, Richta (1969) in Eastern Europe.
9   Reich (1991), Castells (1996), Kumar (1978).
10 See Von Tunzelmann (1978), Devine (1983), Gospel (1991), Thomson (1993), Lipsey, Bekar and Carlaw (1998).
11 Hughes (1983).
12 Noble (1979, 1984).
13 Devine (1983).
14 Lazonick (1993: 194).
15 Fleck (1993).
16 Franklin (1990).
17 Hacker (1991), Mumford (1964).
18 Latour (2000).
19 Feenberg (1991).
20 Jones (1988).
21 Lazonick (1979).

22 Louli and Bickerton (1995).

23 Kraft (1977).

24 See Zimbalist (1979), Wallace and Kalleberg (1982), Cockburn (1985), Smith (1988).

25 Wallace and Kalleberg (1982: 321–2).

26 Roszak (1994).

27 Noble (1984).

28 Sale (1995).

29 Noble (1984: 190).

30 Williams and Edge (1996: 2).

31 Feenberg (1991).

32 Feenberg (1991: 6).

33 Dahrendorf (1959), Kerr (1962), Bell (1973).

34 Bell (1973), Naisbitt (1982), Reich (1991).

35 Ellul (1964), Heidegger (1977).

36 Exemplified (differently) by the likes of Latour (2000), Callon (1992), Suchman (1987).

37 See for example Rip, Misa and Schot (1995), Suchman (2002).

38 Feenberg (1991).

39 See for example Mumford (1964).

40 Latour (2000), Callon (1992).

41 Gärtner and Wagner (1996).

42 Mumford (1964).

43 Mumford (1964: 21).

44 Woodward (1965), Thompson (1967).

45 Archibugi and Lundvall (2001).

46 See Mani (2002) for how developed and developing countries compare.

47 Carnoy, Pollack and Wong (1993).

48 Livingstone and Sawchuk (2003).

49 Archibugi and Coco (2000).

50 Kelley (1990).

51 Grubb (1996).

52 See *Industrial Policy: Investing in America* (Volume 5, Number 1).

53 Herman (2001).

54 Sharpe (1997).

55 Schenk and Anderson (1995).

56 Archibugi and Coco (2000: 1).

57 Cressey and Di Martino (1991).

58 Gärtner and Wagner (1996: 203).

59 Gärtner and Wagner (1996).

60 Ehn (1988).

61 Bjerknes, Ehn and Kyng (1987).

62 Beirne and Ramsay (1992).

63 Poster (2002).

64 Gärtner and Wagner (1996).

65 Evans (1983), Small and Yasin (2000).

66 Small and Yasin (2000).

67 See for example Reich (1991), Archibugi and Lundvall (2001).

68 Hyman (1991), Gee, Hull and Lankshear (1996).

69 Poster (2002).

70 Berg (1970), Livingstone (1999), Sawchuk (2003), Livingstone and Sawchuk (2004).

71 Lowe (2000: 170).

72 Livingstone (1999: 50).

73 Kelley (1990).

74 Doeringer and Piore (1971), Mishel and Voos (1992), Livingstone and Sawchuk (2004).

75 Braverman (1974), Penn and Scattergood (1985).

76 Glenn and Feldberg (1979), Zimbalist (1979), Noble (1979), Shaiken, Herzenberg and Kuhn (1986).

77 Hyman (1982: 93).

78 Hyman (1982).

80 Burris (1999), Rothman (2000).

81 Friedmann (1961), Blauner (1964), Bell (1973).

82 Kelley (1990), Piore and Sabel (1984), Sorge and Streeck (1988), Form et al. (1988).

83 Burris (1999: 40–1).

84 Lam (2002).

85 Darrah (1994, 1996, 1999).

86 Luff, Hindmarsh and Heath (2000); see also selected contributors to Engeström and Middleton (1992).

87 Livingstone and Sawchuk (2004) ; see also Sawchuk (2006).

88 Sawchuk (2003).

89 Negroponte (1995), Castells (1996), Reich (1991).

chapter 17
Human resource management

The role of human resources is becoming as important if not more than any other executive leadership function.[1]

Definitions of success now transcend national boundaries. In fact, the very concept of domestic business may have become anachronistic.[2]

chapter objectives

After studying this chapter, you should be able to:

▷ explain the nature of human resource management
▷ summarize the key HRM functions
▷ explain the theoretical issues surrounding the HRM debate
▷ explain the meaning of strategic HRM and give an overview of its conceptual framework
▷ explain how developments in global capitalism affect corporate and HR strategies in multinational corporations (MNCs).

Introduction

This book has covered a wide range of theories and research on management, individuals, work groups, organizational design and technology in an attempt to provide an understanding of work and behaviour in workplaces. We have highlighted how organizational behaviour is a result of complex processes involving how work and organization is designed and redesigned, how technology is introduced and used in the labour process, and how employees perceive, act in and respond to the external environment, the distribution of power, technological change and other interventions by management. However, while we have made direct reference to employment relations, there has been little discussion on employment relations practices developed by management.

human resource management (HRM): an approach to managing employment relations that emphasizes that leveraging people's capabilities is important to achieving competitive advantage

strategic human resource management (SHRM): the process of linking the human resource function with the strategic objectives of the organization in order to improve performance

In recent years, the practices used to manage people in the workplace have assumed new prominence as concerns persist about global competition. It is argued that market imperatives require managers to change the way they manage the employment relationship to allow for the most effective utilization of people in the organization.

The 1980s and 1990s were characterized by the increasing ascendancy and influence of the human resources function. During this period, a debate emerged on the concept of human resource management (HRM), which had its theoretical roots in US business schools. A seminal book edited by John Storey in 1989, *New Perspectives on Human Resource Management*,[3] generated the 'first wave' of debate on the nature and ideological significance of 'progressive' HRM. A 'second wave' of debate emerged with four distinct themes: the significance of the economic and social context in shaping and reshaping the HRM arena; the links between HRM and performance, new organizational forms and relationships, and the importance of 'knowledge' management and learning in the workplace in the late 1990s. This debate, mostly among academics, produced normative models, evidence of a direct connection between 'bundles' of best HRM practices and organizational performance, and exposed familiar conflicts in the social world of work.

A 'third wave' of HRM debate explored an approach to HRM labelled strategic human resource management or SHRM. Both terms, HRM and SHRM, have been contested. For some HRM is simply a grander term for 'personnel management', representing 'old wine in new bottles'. Others argue that HRM is quite distinct in theory and practice, and reflects something like a paradigm shift in the management of the employment relationship.

In the managerial models, HRM is associated with a distinctive organizational culture and set of 'best' HR practices, which aim to recruit, develop, reward and manage people in ways that create a sustainable commitment to 'high-commitment management' (HCM). Apart from the traditional personnel-related practices, HRM identified new roles for HR specialists: strategic planner and change agent.[4] The

high-commitment management (HCM): a term that gained currency in the 19990s, describing efforts to manage employment relations and work operations using a set of distinctive 'better' HR practices. These are intended to improve outcomes such as employee commitment, flexibility and cooperation which in turn enhances the organization's competitive advantage.

change agent: a generic term for an individual championing or facilitating change in the organization

debate has been particularly fierce among British academics, and several conceptual models have been developed to explain the HRM phenomenon.[5]

More critical accounts emphasize that the ascendancy of HRM, with its Protestant Anglo-Saxon individualist-oriented philosophy, coincided with a significant decrease of trade union membership and power, and more collective approaches to managing employment relations. As such, HRM is characterized as an integral component of the 'soft' control processes in organizations.[6] The ideological significance of HRM can be linked to the broader economic and political context of the 1980s, a context defined by 'Thatcherism'.[7] The central elements of Margaret Thatcher's social reengineering were the curbing of trade union influence, the reordering of the balance of power between different factions of capital in Britain, and the restructuring of the role of government in the economy. Most of the HRM literature examines a wide range of management practices – recruitment and selection, rewards, training, appraisal, employee relations – which endeavour to make employees' behaviour more predictable and manageable.

Just how important each of these HR practices is in helping us to understand organizational behaviour and employment relations is illustrated throughout the remainder of this chapter. We address a number of questions, some of which are essential to our understanding of how people behave in the workplace in the early twenty-first century, and the role of HRM therein. How do HRM techniques shape work behaviour? Do organizations adopting different business strategies adopt different HR strategies? Does HRM make a difference to the 'bottom line'? The debate on different theoretical perspectives brings out an important point: there are fundamental structural constraints that emphasize the complexity of implementing different HRM models.

The nature of HRM

human capital: the view that people are worth investing in as a form of capital: that people's performance and the results achieved can be considered as a return on investment and assessed in terms of cost and benefits

To grasp the nature and significance of HRM it is necessary to remind ourselves why managing people is different from managing other resources. It is people in organizations who set overall strategies and goals, design work systems, produce goods and services, monitor quality, allocate financial resources, and market the products and services. People become 'human capital' by virtue of the roles they assume in the organization. In organizational behaviour (OB) theory, human capital refers to the traits individuals bring to the workplace – intelligence, aptitudes, commitment, tacit knowledge and skills, and the ability to learn. But as we have discussed earlier, the contribution this human 'resource' makes to the organization is typically variable and unpredictable. It is this indeterminacy of an employee's job performance which, according to one management guru, makes the human resource the 'most vexatious of assets to manage'.[8]

The theory and practice of HRM continues to draw on psychologically driven research in OB, and is still viewed as a possible solution to such perennial problems as low worker commitment, low worker productivity and worker resistance (see Table 17.1). One set of perspectives, drawing on psychology, suggests that human behaviour in the workplace is a function of at least four variables: ability, motivation, role perception and situational contingencies. Another set of perspectives, drawing on sociology, emphasizes the problematic nature of employment relations: contradictions and tension, and the interrelated problems of control and commitment.

As we have discussed in the preceding chapters of this book, human capital differs from other resources, partly because individuals are endowed with varying levels of ability (including aptitudes, skills and knowledge), with personality traits, gender, role perceptions and differences in experience, and partly as a result of differences in motivation and commitment. In other words, people differ from other resources because of their ability to evaluate and to question management's actions, and their commitment and cooperation always has to be won. In addition, employees have the capacity to form groups and organize into trade unions to defend or further their economic interest.[9]

table 17.1 OB theories and HRM practices

OB theories	HRM functions	HRM practices
Personality analysis Individual perception Race and ethnicity	Selection	Structured interviews and personality tests to 'match' the right person into right job
Adult learning Organizational design Technological change Leadership styles	Training	Designing orientation and training workshops for new employees, job redesign and leadership to encourage informal learning and change
Motivation Alienation	Rewards management	Pay systems, bonuses and benefit packages to maximize individual performance
Motivation Communication Psychological contract Group dynamics	Appraisal	Interview appraisal; pay policy, training policy, disciplinary policy
Conflict Workplace resistance Groupthink	Employment relations	Handling individual and group grievances, communication of policies, negotiating with unions

The importance of the HRM function results from the dynamic nature of the relationship between the employee and the employer. First and foremost, the employment relationship embraces an *economic* relationship: the 'exchange of pay for work'. The contract permits the employer to buy a potential level of physical or intellectual labour. The function of HRM is to narrow the gap between employees' potential and actual job performance: '[HRM] practices ... offer a technology which aims to render individuals and their behaviour predictable and calculable ... to bridge the gap between promise and performance, between labour power and labour.'[10]

In Britain (and elsewhere), the employment relationship involves a *legal* relationship: a network of common law and statutory rights and obligations affecting both parties to the contract. A responsibility of all managers, and especially HR specialists, is to keep abreast of and implement a complex network of UK and European Union statutory 'floor of rights' affecting the employment relationship.

Much of the analysis on perception affirms that the employment relationship is also a dynamic two-way exchange of perceived promises and obligations between employees and their organization: the *psychological* relationship. The 'psychological contract' is a metaphor that captures a wide variety of largely unwritten expectations and understandings of the two parties about their mutual obligations: 'individual beliefs, shaped by the organization, regarding terms of an exchange agreement between individuals and their organization.'[11] At the heart of the concept of the psychological contract are levers for individual commitment, motivation and task performance beyond 'expected outcomes'. The concept of the psychological contract has become a fashionable framework within which to study and manage people at work.

The term 'human resource management' has been subject to considerable debate, but given the nature of the employment relationship and the shift in HRM towards a macro-strategic perspective we define it as:

> A strategic approach to managing employment relations which emphasizes that leveraging people's capabilities is critical to achieving sustainable competitive advantage, and this is achieved through a distinctive integrated set of individual and collective employment policies, programmes and practices.

This definition underscores a belief that people really make the difference: only people have the capacity to generate value. It follows from this premise that human knowledge and skills are a strategic resource that needs to be adroitly managed, and in the process, HRM plays a pivotal role in a sophisticated organization.

Another distinguishing feature of our definition relates to the notion of *integration*. A set of individual and collective employment policies, programmes and practices needs to be coherent and integrated with organizational strategy. It follows, therefore, that if the workforce is so critical for organizational success, then the responsibility for HR activities rests with all line managers and should not be left to HR specialists.

A third aspect is the inclusion of the word 'collective', which refers to a feature of the employment relationship already mentioned: it involves an *exchange*, meaning that the relationship is partly cooperative – employee and employer have a shared interest in the success of the organization – but also entails an inherent conflict of interest between the parties, which cannot be designed out of the management process by better HR practices.[12] The necessarily exchange, hierarchical and imbalanced power character of the employment relationship constitutes the distinctive attributes of an inclusive analysis of HRM: managing people involves aligning internal human resources with strategic business plans and at the same time, managing the unavoidable conflict between the parties.

plate 47 A diversified workforce requires more sophisticated and inclusive HR practices

Source: Getty Images

HRM functions

HRM policies and practices shape the nature of work and regulate the behaviour between the employer and employee, the employment relationship. Drawing on employment relations surveys, we can identify eight key HRM functions.[13] These are policies and practices designed in response to organizational goals and contingencies, and managed to achieve those goals. Each function contains alternatives from which managers can choose. The eight functions are outlined below.

Strategic planning

This involves analysing an organization's HR needs and preparing forecasts of future requirements in the light of an organization's current human resources, the nature of the labour market, the environment, the organization's mission and objectives, business strategy, and internal strengths and weaknesses including its structure, culture, technology and leadership.

Staffing

This is concerned with obtaining people with appropriate skills, abilities, knowledge and experience to fill jobs in the work organization. The first step usually involves a detailed job analysis, followed by choosing the most appropriate method of recruitment (such as advertising in national or local newspapers or the use of professional agencies, education institutions, government job centres or websites). The recruitment process aims to attract a pool of qualified candidates.

Selection of candidates is done using a variety of techniques including application forms, face-to-face interviews, psychometric testing and assessment centres. The selection technique needs to be consistent in what it is measuring over repeated use: this is the *reliability* criterion. In addition, the selection technique must actually measure what it sets out to measure: the *validity* criterion. Key practices are HR planning, job analysis, recruitment and selection testing.

Training and development

This calls for analysing the type of training required to ensure that employees possess the knowledge and skills to perform satisfactorily in their jobs or to advance in the organization. This can range from informal on-the-job learning to sending people on an MBA programme. In many large organizations the training and development of managers is seen as part of a strategy involving long-term planning and individual professional development. Although performance appraisal is a contentious issue and sometimes resisted by trade unions, it can help to identify employee key skills and 'competencies' and plan for individual career development.

Motivation

Central here is the design and administration of reward systems. This is a complex set of HR practices involving decisions about pay or salary levels, often determined by negotiating with trade union representatives; and judging the effectiveness of different types of performance-related rewards, including payment by results, bonuses, commissions, profit-sharing and a range of benefits such as a company pension, additional health coverage, company car, mortgage assistance and the like. Specific techniques used include job evaluation, pay surveys and performance appraisal.

Maintenance

This refers to the administration and monitoring of workplace safety, health and wellness policies to retain a competent workforce and comply with statutory standards and regulations. While workplace health and safety have long been legitimate areas for regulation, as evidenced by health and safety legislation, typically occupational safety has been given precedence over more general workplace health concerns.

The concept of workplace wellness goes beyond the management of work-related health and safety to focus on influencing employees' entire lifestyle and well-being. Rising costs associated with work-induced injuries and ill health, 'psychological contract' issues, and new laws are important reasons why workplace health, safety and wellness are of growing importance to HRM. This area is also important because, if strategic HRM means anything, it must encompass the development and promotion of a set of health and wellness policies to protect the organization's most valued asset, its employees.

workplace wellness: all HR and health and safety programmes and interventions that can assist an employee to live at her or his highest possible level as a whole person, including physical, social, emotional and spiritual, and expand an employee's potential to live and work more effectively

Managing relationships

Under this heading may be a range of employee involvement/participation schemes in non-union or unionized workplaces. In workplaces where a trade union is recognized for collective bargaining purposes, it includes negotiating the substantive (pay and hours) and procedural (such as grievances, sabbatical leaves, redundancy) issues of employment contracts, and administrating collective agreements at industrial, organizational and workplace levels. Once collective agreements have been made, any disagreement over the administration and interpretation of the collective agreement may involve third-party intervention in the form of a mediator or arbitrator. With the developments in UK and EU employment law, many HR managers are seen as a source of knowledge in employment law matters, and act as guides to line managers.

Visit the following websites: www.tuc.org.uk for details of trade unions in Britain www.ilo.org, for comparative information on trade unions and http://europa.eu/index_en.htm (search for 'collective bargaining') for information on collective bargaining developments in the European Union.

WEB LINK

table 17.2 Work responsibilities of human resource managers

	All workplaces (%)	Type of manager	
		Generalist %	Specialist %
Handling disciplinary matters	96	96	95
Handling grievances	95	95	95
Recruitment	94	94	93
Staffing plans	90	93	82
Employee consultation	90	91	89
Training	89	90	86
Performance appraisal	88	90	85
Health and safety	88	93	76
Equal opportunities	84	86	83
Working hours	80	80	80
Rates of pay	68	69	63
Holiday entitlements	62	60	65
Pension entitlements	37	37	37
Responsible for all areas	27	29	22
Average number of areas of responsibility	10.6	10.8	10.4

Source: adapted from Kersley et al. (2006: 48)

Managing change

This involves helping others to envisage the future, communicating this vision, setting clear expectations for performance, and developing the capability to reorganize people and reallocate other resources. The HR specialist is often given responsibility for communicating general information to the workforce on strategic changes, as well as communicating any 'new' corporate values and identity.

Evaluation

This is concerned with designing the procedures that measure, evaluate and communicate the value-added component of HR practices and interventions to the rest of the management team.

As is the case with general management (see for example Figure 4.7), it is important to recognize that the role of HR managers is shaped by the internal and external contexts, including employment law and the presence of trade unions. A recent major study of workplaces found that handling disciplinary matters, grievance procedures, and recruitment and selection of employees were the most common job responsibilities of managers who were primarily responsible for HRM matters (see Table 17.2).

OB IN FOCUS

Raising the profile of the HR agenda

HR professionals need to be more questioning of the function's fundamental values if they are to raise the profile of the HR agenda with top management. Before engaging in any kind of family debate, my father used to say: 'State your terms'. So here they are: I'm an ex-HR director from the SME sector who cares deeply about people strategy, and I want to get critical about the HR function. In my role I routinely ask managers: 'Who believes that their HR function adds strategic value?' On average, only 15 per cent stand up for their hard-working HR colleagues, and that figure hasn't changed in eight years. So the good news is that there are effective strategic HR leaders among us – but what about the other 85 per cent? Research by Guest and King, published last year, highlights what little progress has been made over a 25-year period in raising the priority of the HR agenda with top management, and in the business generally. This kind of assessment should be of great concern to the profession and suggests that it needs to be more questioning of the fundamental values behind the HR mission.

The HR function needs to address three crucial issues urgently. The first is the profession's relentless drive for consistency and alignment. The business context is now too messy and individualized for corporate neatness. Second, allied to the drive for consistency is the mantra of best practice. Research at Cranfield reveals a wide disjuncture between HR best-practice priorities and the real needs of the business. Best practice provides safety and reassurance for HR, but can't really enable an organization to gain strategic advantage. Third, much research about HR raises concerns about the business acumen of HR professionals. This is not about professional qualifications but about the willingness of HR staff to develop themselves beyond an HR mindset.

To redress this, HR specialists need to consider whether the starting point for HR is their own values and practices or those of the business. Managing is full of ambiguity, so HR needs to embrace rather than reduce the complexity of the role. This means devolving power to line managers. Construct your people strategy from a mindset that seeks to create the least number of uniform policies, rather than pursue a level of consistency usually unwanted by your internal customers. Be critical about your department: where does it really add value? Finally, acknowledge that businesses will always be a sea of competing interests. Embrace these different agendas in order to build processes relevant to your stakeholders. Let go of the illusion of alignment. In other words, get critical before HR 'goes critical'.

Martin Clarke, Director of the Cranfield general management programme (source: *People Management*, 1 September 2005).

Think back to the Fayolian management cycle (page 103). Are these HRM tasks different or similar?

STOP AND REFLECT

Surveys have shown some difference in the number of tasks performed by generalists and specialists responsible for HRM matters, and some variation in the tasks performed by managers depending on whether they are employed in the private or public sector. Managers in public-sector workplaces are less likely to be responsible for rates of pay, working hours, holiday and pension entitlements, and equally responsible for the remaining tasks. Overall, generalists are more likely to have responsibility for all issues than specialists. In smaller organizations, HRM managers are more likely to do all the tasks listed than their counterparts in larger organizations.

The eight key HRM functions discussed above and the main work responsibilities of HR managers listed in Table 17.2 give little indication of how power struggles inside the organization dictate the relative importance of HRM compared with other management functions, and what makes HRM particularly different from traditional 'personnel management'. Within most organizations there are power struggles over which management functional area – finance, marketing, production, HRM – will dominate and fashion executive decisions. These disputes are partly the result of individual self-interest and power contests inside the management team, but they also represent differences on how best to

Visit the website of the 2004 Workplace Employee Relations Survey: www.dti.gov.uk/er/emar/2004WERS.htm for data on job responsibilities of HR specialists. What changes in the functions performed by HR managers have occurred in recent years? Are HR specialists involved in all the eight areas of activity discussed above?

WEB LINK

Source: Getty Images

plate 48 Research suggests that employees on standard employment contracts have more opportunities than they once did to balance their work and family commitments

compete in the marketplace, whether to emphasize market share and product price or high-quality 'branding' and employee skill. The role of HRM, how it is organized and how much power it has relative to other management functions is affected both by internal factors unique to the organization (such as product or service range, and organizational culture) and by external contexts (such as labour shortages and national employment legal regimes).[14]

What makes HRM different from personnel management? Over the past 20 or so years, academics have given us something resembling Weberian ideal-type models that emphasize the alleged unique features of HRM, the integrated nature of HR activities and HRM's strategic importance to the organization. It is to these theoretical models that we now turn.

Theoretical models of HRM

So far we have focused on the meaning of HRM and the contribution it makes to the functioning of the work organization. We now turn to an important part of the HRM discourse, the search for its defining features, which allegedly demonstrate analytically the qualitative differences between traditional personnel management and HRM.

Theoretical models fulfil at least four important intellectual functions for those studying the links between HRM and OB. First, they provide both an analytical framework for studying HRM (for example, situational factors, stakeholders, strategic choice levels and notions of individual commitment and competence). Second, they legitimize certain OB theories that underpin HRM practices. Third, they provide a characterization of HRM that establishes variables and relationships between dependent and independent variables to be researched. Fourth, they serve as a heuristic device for explaining the nature and significance of key HR practices.

Academics in the United States and the UK have offered several different HRM models. The early US models developed by Fombrun, Tichy and Devanna and by Beer et al.[15] have proven controversial among both managerialists and critics. From a European perspective, these models prescribing how work and the employment relationship should be managed are American imports and, as such, reflect a more individualistic-oriented culture, different management styles and a general absence of trade union organization in the workplace. The widely cited UK model developed by Hendry and Pettigrew[16] is a complex model that gives explicit attention to the wider 'outer' and 'inner' contexts in which HR practices are designed and executed. In the following section, we examine the models and some of the strengths and weaknesses of these perspectives.

The Fombrun, Tichy and Devanna model of HRM

HRM cycle: an analytical framework that diagrammatically connects HR selection, appraisal, development and rewards to organization performance

The early HRM model developed by Fombrun, Tichy and Devanna emphasizes the interrelatedness and the coherence of HRM activities. The HRM 'cycle' in their model consists of four key constituent components: selection, appraisal, development and rewards (see Figure 17.1). These four HR activities aim to increase organizational performance. The strength of the model is that it expresses the coherence of internal HR policies and the importance of 'matching' internal HR policies and practices to the organization's external business strategy.

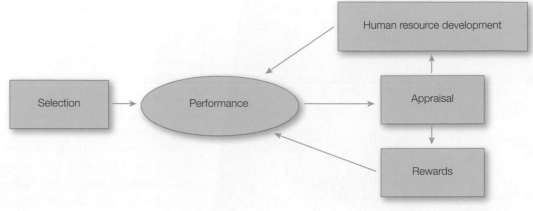

figure 17.1 The Fombrun, Tichy and Devanna model of HRM

Source: Fombrun, Tichy and Devanna (1984)

STOP AND REFLECT

For some Muslim women, wearing a niqab is a symbol of emancipation and a commitment to their faith; for others it represents patriarchal pressure. What issues does the wearing of a niqab raise for organizational behaviour and HR practices in the workplace?

The HRM cycle is a simple model that serves as a heuristic framework for explaining the nature and significance of key HR practices, and the interactions among the factors making up the complex fields of HRM. The weakness of the Fombrun et al. model, however, is its apparent prescriptive nature, with its focus on four HR practices. It also ignores different stakeholder interests, situational factors and the notion of management's strategic choice.

The Harvard model of HRM

The analytical framework of the 'Harvard model' offered by Beer and his colleagues consists of six complex components:

▷ situational factors
▷ stakeholder interests
▷ HRM policy choices
▷ HR outcomes
▷ long-term consequences
▷ a feedback loop through which the outputs flow directly into the organization and to the stakeholders.

The Harvard model for HRM is shown in Figure 17.2.

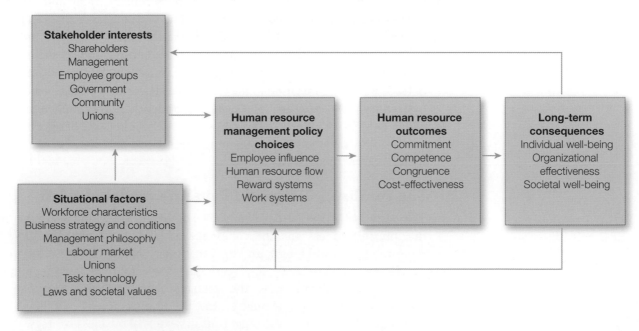

figure 17.2 The Harvard model of HRM

Source: Beer et al. (1984)

The situational factors influence management's choice of HR strategy. This normative model incorporates workforce characteristics, management philosophy, labour market regulations, societal values and patterns of unionization, and suggests a meshing of both 'product market' and sociocultural logics.[17] Analytically, both HRM scholars and practitioners are more comfortable with the contextual variables included in the model because it conforms to the reality of the employment relationship: an amalgamation of business and societal expectations.[18] The stakeholder interests recognize the importance of 'trade-offs', either explicitly or implicitly, between the interests of owners and those of employees and their organizations, the unions. Although the model is still vulnerable to the charge of 'unitarism', it is a much more pluralist frame of reference than is found in some other models.

HRM policy choices emphasize that management's decisions and actions in HR management can be appreciated fully only if it is recognized that they result from an interaction between constraints and choices. The model sees management as a real actor, capable of making at least some degree of unique contribution within environmental and organizational parameters, and of influencing those parameters themselves over time.[19] The human resource outcomes are high employee commitment to organizational goals and high individual performance, leading to cost-effective products or services. The underlying assumptions here are that employees have talents that are rarely fully utilized at work, and they show a desire to experience growth through work. Thus, the Harvard HRM model takes the view that employment relations should be managed on the basis of the assumptions inherent in McGregor's approach to people-related issues, which he labelled 'Theory Y'.[20]

The long-term outcomes distinguish between three levels: individual, organizational and societal. At the individual employee level, the long-term outputs comprise the psychological rewards workers receive in exchange for effort. At the organizational level increased effectiveness ensures the survival of the organization. In turn, at the societal level, as a result of fully utilizing people at work, some of society's goals (for example, employment and growth) are attained.

A feedback loop is the sixth component of the Harvard model. As we have discussed, the situational factors influence HRM policy and choices. Conversely, however, long-term outcomes might influence the situational factors, stakeholder interests and HR policies. The feedback loop in Figure 17.2 reflects this two-way relationship.

An advantage of the Harvard model is that it serves as a heuristic device for explaining the nature and significance of key HR practices. The model was developed as a teaching aid for the university's MBA syllabus in HRM in the early 1980s.[21] It also contains elements that are analytical (that is, situational factors, stakeholders, strategic choice levels) and prescriptive (that is, notions of commitment, competence and so on).[22] Another advantage of the Harvard model is the classification of inputs and outcomes at both organizational and societal level, creating the basis for a critique of comparative HRM.[23] A weakness is the absence of a coherent theoretical basis for measuring the relationship between HR inputs, outcomes and performance.[24]

The Warwick model of HRM

This model comes from the Centre for Corporate Strategy and Change at the University of Warwick, England, where it was developed by two researchers, Hendry and Pettigrew.[25] The Warwick model extends the Harvard framework by drawing on its analytical aspects. The model takes account of business strategy and HR practices, the external and internal context in which these activities take place, and the processes by which change takes place, including interactions between changes in both context and content.

The strength of the model is that it identifies and classifies important environmental influences on HRM. It maps the connections between the outer (wider environment) and inner (organizational) contexts, and explores how HRM adapts to changes in the context. The implication is that those organizations achieving an alignment between the external and internal contexts will experience superior performance. A weakness of the model is that the process whereby internal HR practices are linked to business output or performance is not developed.

The five elements of the model are:

▷ outer context
▷ inner context
▷ business strategy content
▷ HRM context
▷ HRM content.

They are shown in Figure 17.3.

Reviewing the three models, what beliefs and assumptions do you find implied in them? For example, look at the direction of the arrows in the Fombrun et al. model. What is the message for managers? What OB theories do you see in each model? What is missing?

STOP AND REFLECT

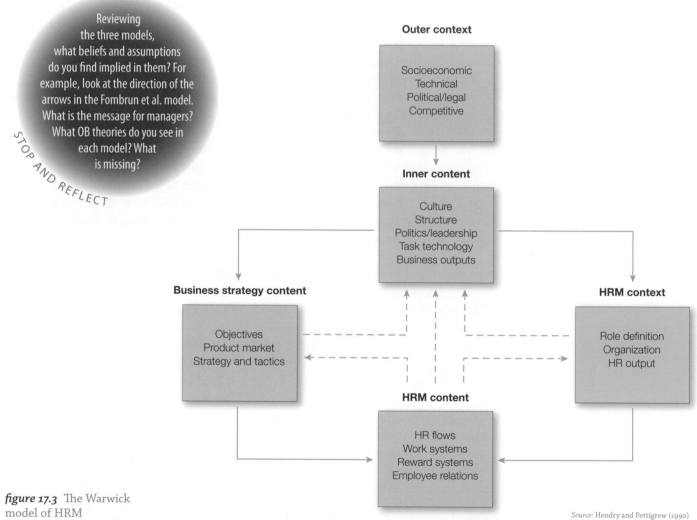

figure 17.3 The Warwick model of HRM

Source: Hendry and Pettigrew (1990)

Strategic HRM

By the mid-1980s, an increasing number of HRM academics were emphasizing the need for HRM to focus on aligning the organization's human resource function with its competitive strategy: in other words for HRM to have a 'strategic' role.[26] This approach, not surprisingly, saw a new labelling: strategic human resource management (SHRM). Just as the term HRM has been contested, so too has the notion of SHRM.

The SHRM literature is rooted in 'manpower' [sic] planning. But it is the work of influential management gurus, affirming the importance of the effective management of people as a source of competitive advantage, which encouraged academics to develop frameworks emphasizing the strategic role of the HR function.

The precise meaning of SHRM is problematic. It is unclear, for example, whether the term refers to an outcome or a process.[27] For some, SHRM is an outcome: 'as organizational systems designed to achieve sustainable competitive advantage through people'.[28] For others, its viewed as a process: 'the process by which organizations seek to link the human, social, and intellectual capital of their members to the strategic needs of the firm'.[29]

John Purcell made a significant contribution to research on business HRM strategy by identifying what he labels 'upstream' and 'downstream' types of strategic decisions.[30] The upstream or 'first-order' strategic decisions are concerned with the long-term direction of the corporation. If a first-order decision is made to take over another company, for example a Germany company acquiring a software company in Ireland, a second set of considerations apply concerning the extent to which the new operation is to be integrated with or separate from existing operations. These are classified as downstream or 'second-order' strategic decisions. Different strategies, for example HRM, are called 'third-order' strategic decisions because they establish the basic parameters for managing people in the workplace. In theory at least, 'strategy in human resources management is determined in the context of first-order, long-run decisions on the direction and scope of the firm's activities and purpose ... and second-order decisions on the structure of the firm,' wrote Purcell.[31]

Another part of the strategic HRM debate has focused on the integration or 'fit' of business strategy with the HR strategy. This shift in managerial thought calls for the HR function to be 'strategically integrated', and is shown in Beer and his colleagues' model of HRM. The authors saw a need to establish a close two-way relationship or 'fit' between the external business strategy and the elements of the internal HR strategy: 'An organization's HRM policies and practices must fit with its strategy in its competitive environment and with the immediate business conditions that it faces.'[32]

The concept of integration has three aspects:

▷ the linking of HR policies and practices with the strategic management process of the organization
▷ the internalization of the importance of HR on the part of line managers
▷ the integration of the workforce into the organization to foster commitment or an 'identity of interest' with the strategic goals.

'matching' model: an HR strategy that seeks to 'fit' or align the organization's internal HR strategy with its external competitive strategy

Not surprisingly, this approach to SHRM has been referred to as the **'matching' model**. Early interest in the 'matching' model is evident in a model by Devanna and associates. HRM and strategy-structure follow and feed upon one another and are influenced by environmental forces (see Figure 17.4).

resource-based model: an HR strategy that views employees as an asset as opposed to a cost and assumes that the sum of people's knowledge and distinctive competences has the potential to serve as a source of competitive advantage

An alternative formulation of SHRM is grounded in the belief that each employee is an asset as opposed to a variable cost. This approach to SHRM is called the **resource-based model**. The essence of the argument is that superior organizational performance through exploiting unique skills and human intellectual capital is underscored when advanced technology and other inanimate resources are readily available to competing organizations. The sum of people's knowledge and intellectual capital, and social relationships, has the potential to provide non-substitutable capabilities that serve as a source of competitive advantage.[33]

This approach has raised questions about the inextricable connection between work-related learning, the mobilization of employee consent through learning strategies, and competitive advantage. Given the upsurge of interest in resource-

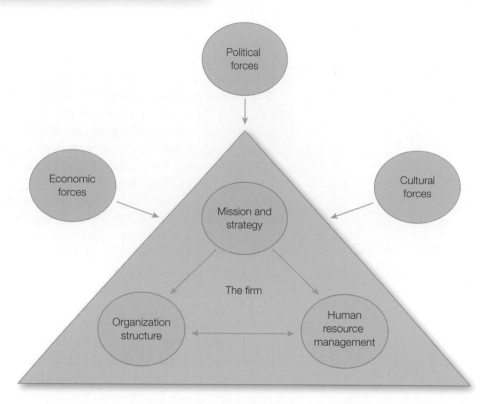

figure 17.4 A matching model of strategic HRM

Source: Fombrun, Tichy and Devanna (1984)

based models, and in particular the new 'workplace learning' discourse, we need to take a closer look at this conceptual model.

The origins of the resource-based model can be traced back to Selznick,[34] who suggested that work organizations each possess a 'distinctive competence' that enables them to outperform their competitors, and to Penrose,[35] who challenged the view (which had largely been taken for granted by economists) that a firm's resources are homogeneous, and instead conceptualized the firm as a 'collection' of 'heterogeneous' resources. Over three decades later, organizational theorists argued that *sustained* competitive advantage is not achieved through an analysis of an organization's external market position, but through a careful analysis of the skills and capabilities possessed by people in the organization: characteristics which competitors find themselves unable to imitate. Putting it in terms of a simple SWOT analysis; the resource-based perspective emphasizes the strategic importance of exploiting internal 'strengths' and neutralizing internal 'weaknesses'.[36]

Figure 17.5 summarizes the relationships between resources and capabilities, strategies and sustained competitive advantage. Four characteristics are important in sustaining competitive advantage: value, rarity, inimitability and non-substitutability. From this perspective, the collective learning in the workplace by managers and non-managers, especially on how to coordinate workers' diverse knowledge and skills and integrate diverse information technology, is a strategic asset that rivals find difficult to replicate. In other words, management capabilities are critical to harnessing the organization's human assets.

Others emphasize the strategic importance of managers identifying (or at least predicting) and marshalling 'a set of complementary and specialized resources and capabilities which are scarce, durable, not easily traded, and difficult to imitate' to enable the company to earn 'economic rent' (that is, profits).[37]

The resource-based approach to competitive advantage gives high standing to the HR function. Survey findings, however, suggest that only a minority of workplaces

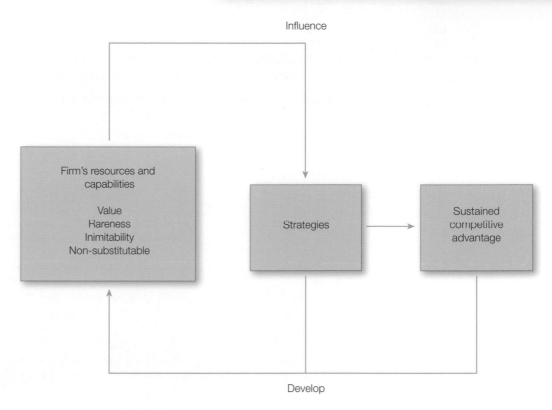

Influence

Firm's resources and capabilities

Value
Rareness
Inimitability
Non-substitutable

Strategies

Sustained competitive advantage

Develop

Sources: based on Barney (1991) and Hill and Jones (2004)

***figure* 17.5** The relationship among resource endowments, strategies and sustained competitive advantage

Based on your own work experience, or on your studies of organizations, do you think continuous learning at the workplace is more or less important for some organizations than others? If so, why?

STOP AND REFLECT

have followed the approaches advocated by proponents of SHRM (either the matching model or the resource-based model). There is little evidence of a clear connection between SHRM and product market strategies (matching model), and recent survey data from the United States and the UK reveals hardly any change in the proportion of organizations incorporating employees' intellectual capital and development in their strategic business plans (resource-based model).[38]

SHRM: does it work?

In addition to focusing on the validity of the matching SHRM model, in recent years HRM theorists have tried to measure the connection between HRM and performance. The question 'does HRM work?' is more than a debating point. Evidence that better HR practices can indeed contribute to the organization's performance or 'the bottom line' has fundamental implications for whether or not an organization should invest in HR interventions.

It has not been lost on both HRM academics and practitioners that evidence on the effectiveness of HR interventions, and HR professionals' related involvement in strategic planning, enhances the status of the academic discipline, and the authority and self-importance of HR specialists in the workplace. All the SHRM models tend to make three assumptions:

▷ Management is a 'strategic player' capable of making choices which can fundamentally alter the nature of the employment relationship.

▷ These choices extend to fashioning a business strategy and aligning HR strategy to it.
▷ This alignment between business strategy and HR strategy will enhance competitiveness and organizational performance.[39]

During the last decade, demonstrating that there is indeed a positive link between particular clusters or 'bundles' of HR practices and business performance has become 'the dominant research issue'.[40]

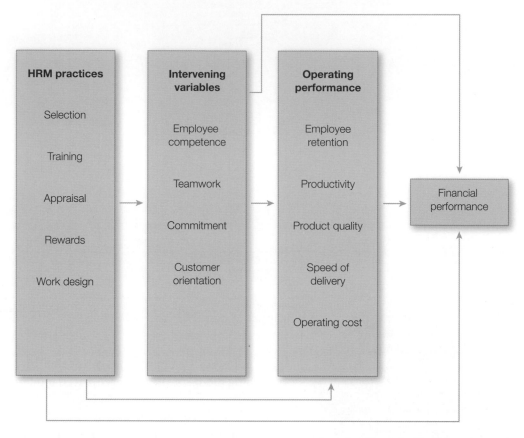

figure 17.6 A model of the HRM–performance linkage

Source: adapted from Paul and Anantharaman (2003: 1249)

A number of recent empirical studies have found that bundles of HR practices such as selection, training, work design and performance appraisal are positively associated with superior organization performance.[41] The suggested causal linkage process between HRM practices and the financial performance of the organization is presented in Figure 17.6. In this genre, a recent study found support for the HRM–performance linkage. The researchers concluded that although no single HR practice affects financial performance, 'every HRM practice influences financial outcomes indirectly through one or more intervening variables (for example, employee competence, teamwork, employee commitment to the employer, stronger customer orientation) and operational performance dimensions'.[42] Such claims of a positive linkage between sets of HR practices and performance are particularly associated with the redesign of work to produce what is commonly referred to as a high-performance working environment, which is realized through 'high-commitment' HRM practices.

Some doubts remain, however. First, if there has been a 'breakthrough' in that researchers have provided evidence of this, any knowledge of the HRM–commitment/performance link seems to have fallen on the deaf ears of managers, as indicated by the surveys. Particularly galling was the finding of little evidence of

high-performance working environment: describes efforts to manage employment relations and work operations using a set of distinctive 'better' HR practices. These are intended to improve outcomes such as employee commitment, flexibility and cooperation which in turn enhance the organization's competitive advantage.

a 'coherent' HRM agenda, and the 2004 WERS findings indicating a mixed take-up of high-commitment HRM practices, especially among smaller organizations.[43] It would appear that high-performance organizations can work with practices that negatively affect employees and unions.[44] Thus, it would seem that in the UK, there is still some way to go before HRM professionals are able to voice claims that have a persuasive appeal equal to that of marketing and finance.

There are problems with measuring performance at work when worker outcomes need to be included, and many argue that there is a need for multiple measures of performance to match the variety of goals and interests.[45] It would also seem that depending on which measures are used, even in larger samples, the results of a HRM–performance connection could be positive, neutral or even negative.[46] So a number of academics continue to express doubts about the claims for a link, and even when a positive link is established between HRM activities and outcomes, there can be no certainty of the direction of causality.[47] A cluster of HRM practices, for example, might be introduced as the *result* of favourable profits or overall organizational performance.

The complexity of the task to establish the HRM–performance connection is complicated by experiences and processes in each organization. Each organization has, for example, its own history, culture and ways of doing things, all of which influence in a unique way the choices and decisions that are made. The accounting scandals in some prominent US corporations in 2002 further illustrate the difficulty of using valid and reliable organizational performance measurements. In arguing for the HRM–performance linkage, there is a need to understand how the link actually works: what others refer to as the 'strength' of the HRM system.[48] Crucial here are the role of national business systems, local culture and organizational culture, and the meanings made in everyday interactions.

WEB LINK

Visit http://leadertoleader.org and search for Jeffrey Pfeffer for an article discussing the links between a 'high-commitment' HR strategy and an organization's financial performance.

International HRM

leverage: the use and exploitation by an employer of his or her resources, particularly human resources, to their full extend. The term is often linked to the resource-based HRM model.

A central concern of contemporary literature on HRM is with examining the consequences of intensified global competition, and the transferability of 'better' HRM policies and practices to countries outside the United States and the European Union. The proliferation of interest in international HRM springs directly from the globalization of market competition, globally integrated modes of production, and creating new boundaryless (sometimes virtual) organizations.

As organizations increasingly seek to **leverage** human resources to compete in global markets, academics and practitioners alike have progressively begun to explore the impact of these changes on national patterns of employment relations and the international potential of SHRM. In so doing, they have generally addressed HR practices relating to global and local recruitment and selection, international training, international reward management, and performance appraisal of expatriates. It is these issues that define international HRM (IHRM). The fact that these four core HRM activities need to be culturally sensitive and to be effective in a cross-cultural multi-national environment distinguishes IHRM from domestic HRM.[49]

In this section we explore the explicit connection between developments in global capitalism and HRM in multinational companies. It seems credible that as the world of business is becoming more globalized, the employment relationship will be influenced by national systems of employment legislation and the cultural contexts in which big business operates. Different national regulatory systems, labour markets, institutional and cultural contexts might, for example, constrain or shape a tendency

Source: Nicholas P. Tutton

plate 49 Can western HRM practices be transplanted to Asia and other countries, like Starbucks and other Western phenomena?

to converge on a universal model of 'best' HR practices. Supporters of an integrated approach to globalization and national patterns of employment relations suggest that both global economic trends and nationally based institutions are important in structuring national patterns of employment relations. Nonetheless, because different kinds of market economies are integrated into the global economy in different ways, global economic pressures are likely to be divergent. The integrated approach focuses our attention on the effects of global economic developments on the 'interests of different groups of employers, workers and policy-makers within different institutional settings'.[50]

International HRM and strategic international HRM

international human resource management (IHRM): refers to all HRM policies and practices used to manage people in companies operating in more than one country

Academics have debated the difference between international human resource management (IHRM) and strategic international human resource management (SIHRM). For example, IHRM has been defined as 'HRM issues and problems arising from the internationalization of business, and the HRM strategies, policies and practices which firms pursue in response to the internationalization process'.[51] It has been argued that IHRM tends to celebrate a dominant Western type of culture, one that emphasizes the subordination of domestic culture and domestic employment practices to corporate culture and corporate HRM practices.[52] As a result, many contemporary IHRM studies tend to be seen as a managerial tool unashamedly connected to the neo-liberal corporate agenda.

As we discussed above, SHRM is the process of explicitly linking the HRM function with the strategic management goals of the organization. Thus, SIHRM is described in terms of connecting IHRM with the business strategy of a global organization: a multinational or transnational company (MNC or TNC). In defining SIHRM we follow others and define it here as the HR policies and processes that result from the global competitive activities of MNCs, and that explicitly connect international HR practices and processes with the worldwide strategic goals of those companies.

The SIHRM literature acknowledges the need to address the tension between the global and local. This tension concerns balancing global competitiveness strategies (rationalization and integration) and local responsiveness (flexibility) strategies pursued by MNCs alongside leveraging global learning within and across the MNC. Thus, strategic IHRM links 'IHRM explicitly with the strategy and with the MNC'.[53]

Critics, not surprisingly, have questioned both the effects and the wisdom of transplanting Western HR policies and practices into culturally diverse domestic environments. Global companies share with their domestic counterparts the intractable problem of managing the employment relationship to reduce the indeterminacy resulting from the unspecified nature of the employment contract. To apply this perspective to IHRM, it would seem that the role of knowledge to make people in the workplace more manageable is further problematized by the intertwining of highly complex local, regional, national and global cultures.[54]

WEB LINK

For further information on cultural diversity go to www.ciber.bus.msu.edu; www.shrm.org/diversity and www.shrm.org/trends

The internationalization of the HRM cycle

The global business strategies examined above, and in particular the supposed ascendancy of TNCs with global communication networks, have far-reaching implications for the IHRM function and practices. In leveraging the core HR activities, MNCs must achieve a dynamic balance between the pressures for central control and the pressures for local responsiveness across diverse national locations and intercultural contexts.[55] Here we extent the HRM cycle (Figure 17.1) to briefly explore the international aspects of recruitment and selection, rewards, training and development, and performance appraisal. Each part of the international HRM 'cycle' contributes to the international job performance of individual employees and the strategic goals of the global organization.

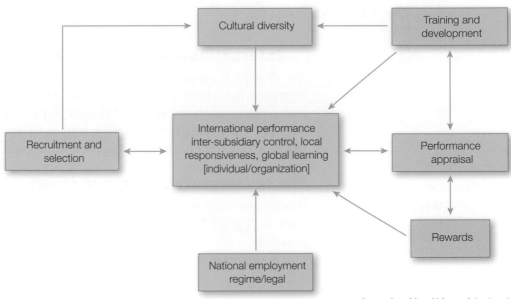

figure 17.7 The international HRM cycle

Source: adapted from Mabey et al. (1998: 210)

This conceptual framework (Figure 17.7) adds the dimensions of cultural diversity and national employment regimes. Others have noted that cultural diversity poses a number of new challenges for managing these four HR practices. The MNC typically has a multicultural workforce made up of employees from a variety of ethnic, racial and religious backgrounds, with very different cultural values and customs.

Indeed, it has been suggested that the central operating method for the global company is the creation and effective management of multicultural work teams that represent diversity in competencies, levels of experience, cultural and language backgrounds.[56]

International recruitment and selection

A transnational company transmits management 'know-how', and in most IHRM publications, recruitment and selection is seen primarily as an issue of expatriate selection. Problems seem to occur because the focus of decision making is embedded in the local culture and norms where the MNCs corporate office is located, and therefore expatriate staff at the company's head office may have little idea what culturally derived expectations would be needed to 'fit' the local context where the person recruited is to work.[57] Informal selection decisions are also often affected by illogical elements like ethnocentrism, ignorance, stereotyping and sometimes discrimination.[58]

ethnocentrism: the tendency to regard one's own culture and group as the standard, and thus superior, whereas all other groups are seen as inferior

International rewards

Managing international rewards requires that managers responsible for implementing HR policies and practices are familiar with a range of other issues, including, the foreign country employment law, national labour relations, the availability of particular allowances or benefits, and currency fluctuations in particular host countries. Studies suggest that effective performance management requires that expatriates should know whether and how their performance in their overseas assignment is linked to pay and the next step in their career.[59]

International training and development

The notion of strategic alignment suggests that MNCs will tend to provide managers, knowledge workers and key technical personnel with the competencies for the successful transfer of the distinctive competencies and culture of the organization from the parent-headquarters to the subsidiaries.

International performance appraisal

The desire to control and predict an employee's current and potential job performance has resulted in both national and global firms developing integrated performance appraisal systems. Studies show that performance appraisal is the favoured way to ensure that strategic employee competences, employee behaviour and motivation are performed effectively in the host country.[60]

The convergence/divergence debate

convergence thesis: the hypothesis that industrialized societies become increasingly alike in their political, social, cultural and employment characteristics

A common question in the international HRM literature is whether there is a trend towards convergence of HR practices resulting from globalization, reflecting the dominant influence of US capitalism. Does globalization bring into being a convergence of HR practices? To address this conundrum, we have drawn on various studies to examine the convergence/divergence debate, which is expressed diagrammatically in Figure 17.8.[61]

Of course, this is an extreme simplification, but the general understanding in the diagram is that Western capitalism works on a left-to-right order of domination, with line 'A' representing various theories of how Western capitalist globalization exploits resources and markets through direct economic

The term 'glass border' describes the irrational assumption held by some parent-country top managers that female managers are less suitable than men for overseas appointments. What can be done to promote equal opportunity for female managers to undertake international assignments?

STOP AND REFLECT

For further information on cultural diversity go to www.ciber.bus.msu.edu; www.shrm.org/diversity and www.shrm.org/trends and for information on comparative HRM, go to http://findarticles.com for 'comparative HRM'; www.workindex.com/ (USA); and www.clc-ctc.ca (Canada)

WEB LINK

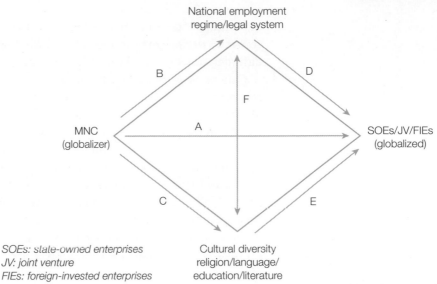

figure 17.8 Diagram representing the convergence/divergence debate on IHRM

SOEs: state-owned enterprises
JV: joint venture
FIEs: foreign-invested enterprises

Cultural diversity
religion/language/
education/literature

Source: adapted from Tiffin and Lawson (1994: 18)

and political control. Lines 'BD' and 'CE' represent differing concepts of the ideological regulation of people employed in organizations – of different kinds such as state-owned enterprises (SOEs), joint ventures (JV) and foreign-invested enterprises (FIEs) – in developing (globalized) countries. This regulation includes subordination through legal and trade institutions (such as the World Trade Organization (WTO), the World Bank, the International Monetary Fund (IMF), the International Labour Organization (ILO) and the European Union (EU)) and the manufacture of consent (for instance, through the spread of Western popular culture in films and literature).

Theories that recognize a tendency to converge that proceeds only along line 'A' are in essence rationale theories of management: that is, they reject the basic thesis that national employment regimes, cultural diversity, norms and social contradictions are countervailing forces against the convergence of HR practices. However, theories that explore the path of capitalist global economic power primarily along line 'BD' focus on the effects of national government employment laws, local business systems and the influence of professional fields of knowledge in different countries on shaping 'Western' HR practices. Theories that focus primarily on line 'CE' in this diagram examine the ways in which a standard global culture tends to develop through the strategic use and spread of Western consumerism, advertising, popular culture and literature and so on.

If we combine these forces, and look at the totality of the interplay stemming from a different national institutional set-up and different ethnic or national cultures (that is, lines 'BD' and 'CE'), we see a tendency to challenge the dominance of Anglo-Saxon HR practices. This would undermine the HR–performance linkage and force a divergence of HR practices worldwide.

This pattern of globalized relations is further complicated through the complex intertwining relationships between national institutional and legal regimes – at the top of line 'F' – and cultural and political backgrounds – at the bottom of line 'F'. These, it is argued, help to regulate globalized capitalist relations.[62]

Although global and national relations are complex, Figure 17.8 clearly suggests a plausible challenge to a universal vision of order and convergence on Western HR practices. These countervailing forces stem from local rationalities, local realities, local political ideologies and local culture.[63] Evidence of continued diversity in local or national patterns of economic activity and employment relations has contributed to the notion of 'varieties of capitalism'. Although the global economy continues to be more interconnected, 'societies with different institutional arrangements will continue to develop and reproduce varied systems of economic organization with different economic and social capabilities in particular industries and sectors'.[64]

Others have persuasively argued that with the existence of distinct national contexts and cross-cultural differences, the notion of a 'European' or 'Asian' HRM model is problematic, and the 'universalist' assumption that Protestant Anglo-Saxon HRM philosophy and HR individual-oriented practices are directly transferable is wrong.[65] To illustrate the point, any comparative analysis of European HR practices begs the question, 'What really constitutes Europe?' The whole of Europe, excluding Russia and Turkey, comprises a landmass not much more than half the size of China or the United States. However, in the intensity of its internal differences and contrasts, Europe is said to be unique.[66] At the last count it comprised 46 countries: 25 of these were members of the European Union in 2006, and two new member states – Bulgaria and Romania – will join in 2007. All have their distinct and overlapping histories, politics, cultures, memories and languages. Within the European Union there are 21 official languages.

Similarly, any grand claim of an 'Asian' HRM model is even more problematic. Asia comprises a wide range of countries, national institutional systems and complex diverse cultures. As we discussed in an earlier chapter, competitive advantage in most Asian countries is based on cheap manual and intellectual labour, yet some Asian countries use highly skilled paid workers. Some Asian countries are marked by cultural homogeneity, while others are marked by cultural diversity. Within the Asian-Pacific region 2200 languages are spoken,[67] and people believe in widely different religions and philosophies, ranging from Buddhism, Confucianism and Hinduism to Islam and Christianity.

Despite economic pressures towards convergence, strikingly resilient differences in cultural and institutional contexts produce divergent employment relationships.[68] Following on the notion of diversity in national business systems, more reflective observers are increasingly acknowledging that the issue of convergence and divergence in European HRM 'needs more careful nuance than has been the case hitherto', and European national institutional patterns are so variable that 'no common model is likely to emerge in the foreseeable future'.[69] Thus, cross-national research suggests that national conceptions of better HR practices remain dominant.[70]

Similarly, studies suggest that there is considerable divergence of HR practices in Asian economies. Contrary to the convergence hypothesis underpinning globalization, the idea that 'best' HR practices have 'universal' application does not hold water when they have to be applied in the context of a different national institutional profile, culture and variety of capitalism. In Japan, for example, employment practices are embedded in national social relations and shared social values, rather than modelled on those in the United States.[71] In the Republic of China there have been noteworthy shifts away from the 'iron rice bowl' system to a more 'market-responsive' system of employment relations, but this is still some way from the HRM ideal-type Western model.[72]

Contemporary HR practices in Asia partially reflect identifiable enduring continuities which stretch back to either a colonial or post-revolutionary era. A central aspect of practice in former colonies is 'patriarchal authoritarianism' rather than the rational-bureaucratic style dominant in North America.

The persistence of national HR practices will endure because managers know how these work in practice and the likely outcomes.[73] At best, it is argued,

STOP AND REFLECT

As you read this section, consider to what extent Western 'best HR practices' can be applied to the Asian business environment, culture and values.

WEB LINK

For further information on HRM in Asia–Pacific countries, go to www.wfpma.com/apfhrm.html. The site includes newsletters, publications and contact information for HR professionals.

globalization may be causing an increasing degree of 'relative convergence' across 'regional clusters' such as China, South Korea and Japan, resulting from globally driven market forces.[74] Thus, the theory of a universal model of HRM (which often is interpreted to mean a Protestant Anglo-American model of HRM) is challenged by national rationalities, national institutional settings, and national, regional and local cultures. We would therefore expect to find that HR practices differ between countries, by sector, by size and by ownership of the work organization.

HRM best practices: chimera or cul-de-sac?

HRM theorists have cautioned against an over-emphasis on a model of 'best' practice in HRM and on the notion of 'best fit' between HRM strategy and business strategy. John Purcell, for example, argues that a body of US and UK HRM literature has led to extravagant claims on the universal applicability of the best practice model, which suggests 'one hat fits all' for successful HR activity.

Obtain a copy of Purcell's article, 'Best practice and best fit: chimera or cul-de-sac?'[75] Why is the notion that a bundle of best HR practices is universally applicable problematic for (a) UK-based organizations and (b) MNCs operating outside the EU?

Paradoxes in HRM

The more critical evaluations of HRM models expose internal paradoxes. Paradox involves ambiguity and inconsistency, two or more positions that each sound reasonable, yet conflict or even contradict each other. Paradox is inherent in HRM. It results when, in pursuit of a specific organizational goal or goals, managers call for or carry out actions that are in opposition to the very goal(s) the organization is attempting to accomplish.

Critics of the HRM model have drawn upon the Weberian notion of a 'paradox of consequences' arising from HRM policies and practices.[76] For example, new organizational designs have been introduced to improve productivity and employee autonomy. On the other hand, the productivity benefits arising from the new organizational forms are accompanied by a number of negative effects on the 'psychological contract', which have the effect of undermining other goals such as retaining employee loyalty and commitment. More broadly, there is ambiguity over whether the main role of the HRM function is a 'caring' or a 'controlling' one.

An incisive critique of the HRM phenomenon identifies further ambiguities in the 'soft' and 'hard' schools of HRM.[77] There is a huge difference between the 'rhetoric' and 'reality' of HRM. Whereas, for example, the rhetoric asserts that 'we are all managers now' as a result of 'empowerment', it conceals the legitimate question of whether a social group holding privileges (senior management) and material returns can hold on to power. Similarly, the inclusion of the HR director onto the strategic management team, the act of 'giving away HR management' to line managers, and the outsourcing of more specialized HR activities might ultimately lead to the end of the HR professional: the 'Big hat, no cattle' syndrome.[78] The tendency in UK companies to be ruled by short-term accounting controls might well undermine the long-term HR employee-development oriented goals.[79]

One notable feature of much of the HRM literature is the tendency for the research and debate on the HRM model to be gender blind. More recently, however, there has been more interest in the gender implications of HRM models.[80] The HRM model 'might be at odds with the promotion of equal opportunities' and pronouncements on the value of diversity and individual learning are part of the rhetoric rather than the reality.

Chapter summary

☐ In this chapter we examined the development of HRM, and emphasized that it is a product of its times, linked to the ascendancy of a new political and economic ideology and the changed conditions of national and global capitalism.

☐ We examined three widely cited HRM models. The US models include Fomberg et al. and Beer et al. One European HRM model developed by British academics, Hendry and Pettigrew, extends Beer's Harvard framework by drawing on its analytical aspects, connecting the outer (wider environment) and inner (organizational) contexts, and exploring how HRM adapts to changes in the context.

☐ We discussed a core assumption underlying much of the SHRM research and literature, that each of the main types of generic competitive strategies used by organizations (such as a cost leadership or differentiation strategy) is associated with a different approach to managing people: that is, with a different HR strategy.

☐ We examined the so-called 'matching model' and the 'resource-based' SHRM model. The former focuses on the notion of 'fit', while the latter places emphasis on an organization's human endowments as a strategy for sustained competitive advantage. Paradox is an ongoing part of the employment relationship. The more critical evaluations of HRM expose internal paradoxes.

☐ The driving force behind the growth of interest in strategic IHRM and IHRM is the resurgence of neoliberalism and the unprecedented growth in global markets. Critics argue that unfettered markets have created a new international division of labour, causing the transfer of manufacturing jobs from high-wage old industrialized regions to low-wage developing economies. They also argue that international HRM tends to emphasize the subordination of national culture and national employment practices to corporate culture and HR practices.

☐ The cross-national transfer of Anglo-Saxon HR practices for recruitment and selection, rewards, training and development, and performance appraisal will require some degree of cultural sensitivity, as well as consultation with host-country nationals about local suitability.

☐ Despite the economic and political pressures from globalization, a divergence of HR practices continues to remain. This is influenced and shaped by national and organizational cultures in the developed and the developing world. Variations in national regulatory systems, labour markets, business-related institutions, and cultural and polyethnic contexts are likely to constrain or shape any tendency towards 'convergence' or a 'universal' model of 'better' HR practice. The sheer variation of economies, national institutional profiles and cultures makes claims for convergence simplistic and problematic.

Key concepts

collective bargaining	451	resource-based model	457–9
human resource management	446	strategic HRM	446
international HRM	463	trade unions	447

Chapter review questions

1. What role does HRM play in organizations?
2. What does a 'resource-based' SHRM model of competitive advantage mean? What are the implications for HRM of this competitive strategy?
3. What are meant by strategic international HRM and international HRM?
4. Discuss how differences in national institutional systems influence a corporation's decision to locate its profit-making operations.

Further reading

Bratton, J. and Gold, J. (2007) *Human Resource Management: Theory and practice* (4th edn), Basingstoke: Palgrave.

Geppert, M. and Williams, K. (2006) 'Global, national and local practices in multinational corporations: towards a sociopolitical framework', *International Journal of Human Resource Management*, **17** (1), pp. 49–69.

Legge, K. (2005) *Human Resource Management: Rhetorics and realities*, Basingstoke: Palgrave.

Scullion, H. and Linehan, M. (2005) *International Human Resource Management*, Basingstoke: Palgrave.

Chapter case study: *ServiceTech's HRM strategy*

Background

Not many companies would turn away from the opportunity to hire highly educated, enthusiastic employees at a fraction of the cost it would take to obtain workers with same level of skill in their own country. India, with its 229 universities, 8000 colleges and 6.4 million students, has the second largest higher education system in the world, and is a magnet for companies looking to lower costs without sacrificing quality in their human resources. These organizations, usually based in the high-tech sector, are also viewed as attractive employers for India's workforce. In fact, the number of people employed by call centres in India tripled between 2000 and 2001.

The challenges facing these companies are not limited to defending their outsourcing practices in the political and social arenas back in their home countries. Developing and utilizing human resources in a foreign setting requires sensitivity to cultural factors and the awareness of the limitations of the transferability of management concepts and training activities. Proven Eurocentric management practices and training methods may not translate into managerial or organizational effectiveness in the global arena.

The Company: ServiceTech Inc.

ServiceTech Inc. is a privately owned enterprise, providing customer care, software support and billing services for many of North America's top banking and telecom firms through its call centre operations located in Dublin, Ireland. While business has been expanding since the early 1990s, high turnover and absenteeism rates in its call centres have been troubling. The turnover rate had increased from 5 per cent to 25 per cent in the last two years, and absenteeism rates were now approaching historical highs. The centres had advertised their vacancies extensively without success.

Board of directors meeting

The review of the labour issue was the focus of the quarterly board of directors meeting. Marketing director Sue Escobar suggested using voice recognition software to automate some of the more routine interactions.

'There is a limit on how much we can automate,' remarked Paul McRae, the director in charge of technology.

Human resources Director Kevin Sayers shook his head, adding, 'It won't be enough to solve our labour problem.'

CEO Karen Manning decided it was a good time to discuss a new global sourcing strategy, with the possibility of transferring staff positions abroad. 'I'm thinking we could start with 10 per cent of our 2500 staff positions moving to new offices in India.' As she said this, Karen noticed Kevin had a concerned look on his face. 'Is there a problem with this approach?' she asked.

Kevin put down his pen and leaned forward. 'We need to do this the right way,' he said. 'There are a number of issues to consider before moving your human resources to another country and culture.'

Karen asked Kevin to provide a report to the board by the next quarterly meeting on what they needed to know before proceeding with the new strategy.

Task

On your own, or in a group, provide a written report answering the following questions:

1. What are the first steps the company should take before making a decision?
2. In terms of HRM functions, what should be considered in the plan to move operations to India?
3. Is there an alternative to moving the staff positions overseas?

Sources of additional information

For details on India's higher education system, see www.gse.buffalo.edu/ and search for 'India'.

For information and links to research on employment issues in Ireland, go to: www.tcd.ie/ERC/

Chew Keng Howe, I. et al. (1990) 'The role of culture in training in a multinational context', *Journal of Management Development*, **15** (2).

Diekmeyer, P. (2006) 'Canadian companies find skilled workers in India', *Vancouver Sun*, 15 July.

Thompson, P. (forthcoming) 'Technological innovation and the office: call centres and the reorganization of clerical and service work', draft chapter in P. Boreham et al. (eds), *New Technology @ Work*; or at www.hrm.strath.ac.uk/teaching/ugrad/classes/41314-core/2005-6/Clerical%20Work,%20chapter%20by%20Paul%20Thompson.pdf

Note

This case study was written by Lori Rilkoff, MSc, CHRP, Senior Human Resources Manager at the City of Kamloops, and part-time lecturer in HRM at Thompson Rivers University, BC, Canada

Web-based assignment

This chapter has discussed the importance of strategic HRM and the links between SHRM and organizational performance. This web-based assignment requires you to explore the research findings from the 2004 Workplace Employment Relations Survey.

Visit: www.dti.gov.uk/er/emar/2004WERS.htm, and use its information to consider these questions:

1. In UK workplaces, who is 'strategic' about employment relations?
2. In recent years have workplaces become more strategic in their people management? Try to explain the findings.

OB in films

The film *Norma Rae* (1979) is about trade union organization in the face of management opposition in a US textile mill. One of the textile workers, Norma Rae (played by Sally Field) organizes her co-workers into a union, assisted by a full-time union organizer (played by Ron Leibman). The mill management attempts to divide the workforce by pinning up a notice that claims black workers are instigating trouble and seeking to control the union. This leads to acts of violence between white and black workers.

In one scene, Norma Rae writes the words 'UNION' on a piece of cardboard and then holds the notice above her head for all the shopfloor workers to see. In response, the machine operators switch off their machines, one by one. What does the film illustrate about employment relations in the workplace? What were the major problems that led to unionization? Could 'better' HR practices avoided the conflict? If so, how?

(This example was originally suggested by Mills and Simmons (1995).)

Notes

1   Maureen Shaw, COE quoted in the *Globe and Mail*, 16 January 2002, p. M2.

2   N. Adler, 'Preface', p. vii in Lane and DiStefano (1992).

3   Storey (1989).

4   Fombrun et al. (1984), Beer et al. (1984), Ulrich (1997).

5   Guest (1997), Hendry and Pettigrew (1990), Storey (1992).

6   Blyton and Turnbull (1998), Townley (1994), Legge (2005), Godard (1991).

7   Jessop et al. (1988).

8   Fitz-enz (2000: xii).

9   Bratton and Gold (2007).

10   Townley (1994: 14).

11   Rousseau (1995: 9).

12   For further analysis, see Kelly (2005).

13   Millward et al. (1992, 2000), Kersley et al. (2006), Ulrich (1997).

14   Jacoby (2005).

15   Fombrun et al. (1984), Beer et al. (1984).

16   Hendry and Pettigrew (1990).

17   Evans and Lorange (1989).

18   Boxall (1992: 72).

19   Beer et al. (1984).

20   According to David McGregor (1960), 'people work because they want to work', not because they have to work. Thus, the Theory Y view of people assumed that when workers are given challenging assignments and autonomy over work assignments, they will respond with high motivation, high commitment, and high performance.

21   Noon (1992).

22   Boxall (1992).

23   Boxall (1992).

24   Hendry and Pettigrew (1990).

25   Guest (1997).

26   Tyson (1987).

27   Bamberger and Meshoulam (2000).

28   Snell et al. (1996: 1996).

29   Bamberger and Meshoulam (2000: 6).

30   Purcell (1989).

31   Purcell (1989: 71).

32   Beer et al. (1984: 25).

33   Cappelli and Singh (1992).

34   Selznick (1957).

35   Penrose (1959).

36   Barney (1991).

37   Amit and Shoemaker (1993: 37).

38   Kersley et al. (2006), Jacoby (2005).

39   Buyens and De Vos (2001), Sisson and Marginson (2003).

40   Guest (1997, 2000).

41   See Baker (1999), Guest (1997), Hutchinson et al. (2000), Ichniowski et al. (1996), Paauwe (2004), Paul and Anantharaman (2003), Pfeffer (1998a).

42   Paul and Anantharaman (2003: 1261).

43   Taylor (2002), Guest (2000), Kersley et al. (2006).

44   Godard (2005).

45   Paauwe and Boselie (2005).

46   Guest et al (2003).

47   For example, Legge (2005), Thompson and McHugh (2006).

48   Bowen and Ostroff (2004).

49 Scullion and Linehan (2005).

50 Bamber et al. (2004: 1483).

51 Scullion (2001: 288).

52 Boxall (1995).

53 Scullion and Linehan (2005: 23).

54 Crane (1994).

55 Adler (2002).

56 Rhinesmith (1993), quoted by Mabey, Salaman and Storey (1998a: 210).

57 Gamble (2003).

58 Torbiörn (2005), Linehan (2005).

59 Tahvanainen and Suutari (2005).

60 Sparrow et al. (2004).

61 The conceptual framework draws on the work of Rowley and Bae (2002) and Tiffin and Lawson (1994).

62 Said (1979).

63 Clegg et al. (1999), Whitley (1999).

64 Whitley (1999: 3).

65 Elenkov (1998).

66 Judt (2005).

67 I am grateful to Professor W. Foley, University of Sydney, Australia, for this information: Pfeffer (1998a: 5).

68 Clark and Pugh (2000).

69 Brewster (2001: 268).

70 Sparrow et al. (2005).

71 Jacoby (2005).

72 Hassard et al. (2004).

73 Webster, Wood and Brookes (2006).

74 Rowley et al. (2004).

75 Purcell (1999).

76 Weber (1968).

77 Legge (2005).

78 Caldwell (2001), Fernie et al. (1994).

79 Armstrong (1989).

80 Dickens (1994, 1998), Healy, Hansen and Ledwith (2006).

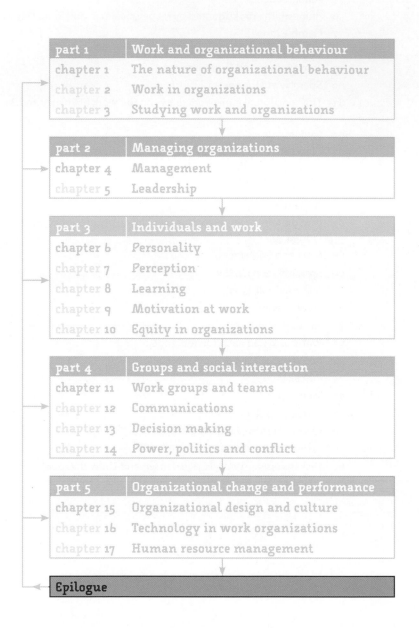

Epilogue

Debates on work cannot be divorced from their organizational context.[1]

Between 1998 and 2004 ... few workplaces systematically monitored or reviewed their policies across gender, ethnicity, disability and age.[2]

The purpose of this epilogue is to review the main points of the book, attempt to draw general conclusions about organizational behaviour, and to set the scene for the future against the background of developments in global capitalism and organization restructuring and governance. As in the film *Back to the Future* (1985), directed by Robert Zemeckis, the present and the future are both dependent on the route taken in the past, and the same goes for organizations and organizational behaviour. In each case where we are going in the future depends upon our past and how we have travelled from the past to the present.

Work experiences and work behaviour are not just about organizational leaders setting the strategic goal and then leaving managers to motivate others to get the organization to some point in the future. People acquire identities and roles in organizations as they interact with their co-workers. The behaviour of people in organizations is best understood as a series of complex active 'processes' in which often they interact and participate formally and informally at different levels in the organization, and recreate social differences of all types, shaped by institutional roles and power.

The nature of organizational behaviour

In Part One of this book we examined the nature of OB, gave a summary of the historical dimensions of paid work, and presented concepts and theories to provide a basis for evaluating the competing perspectives on OB. Chapter 1 explained that organizational behaviour is a multidisciplinary field of study with no agreed boundaries, and draws from a variety of disciplines including psychology, sociology, anthropology, economics and political science. We emphasized that external contexts have a significant impact on the way individuals and groups work and behave. The external environment influences the structure of and behaviour in a work organization, and in turn, organizations influence the wider society. Globalization means that there is a need for a multidimensional approach to the study of behaviour in organizations.

We also focused on diversity and equity because we consider that the social dynamics of class, gender, disability, race and ethnicity underpins contemporary organizational behaviour, and because understanding the significance of class, gender, disability, race and ethnicity puts the behaviour of individuals and groups in the organization into a wider social context.

Finally, we noted that there are multiple schools of thought with which organizational behaviour theorists identify and which they defend with passion. We discussed four competing ideological camps into which many, or most, fall: the managerialist, conflict, symbolic-interactionist and feminist perspectives. These perspectives serve as points of reference for understanding competing views and organizational practices discussed throughout this book. For example, managerialist OB analysis assumes that work behaviour takes place in rationally designed organizations and is inseparable from the notion of efficiency. The critical and feminist perspectives on OB set out to discover the ways in which power, control, conflict, class, disability, race, ethnicity and gender affect the dynamics of manager and non-manager relations.

One of the major themes running through this book has been the continuities as well as the discontinuities across time. Changes occur all the time, but these must be contextualized adequately if we are to appreciate their relevance. Thus, we can only really appreciate the debate on the gendering of work if we know what existed previously.

We have endeavoured to highlight diversity/equity issues in the workplace to balance out the conventional preference for male history. What can be salvaged from the past is a conclusion that paid work or employment is inherently and irreducibly constructed, interpreted and organized through social actions and social discourse, as we detailed in Chapter 2.

We explained how the three founders of the sociology of work – Marx, Durkheim and Weber – all continue to have their contemporary adherents and detractors. Marx's fascination with class, conflict and the labour process has formed the basis for much research in the sociology of work for the last 30 years. Durkheim's moral concerns also continue to pervade the market economy, making predictions about human actions based on amoral, economically rational behaviour less than convincing. Weber's theories of rationalization and bureaucracy have never been far from the minds of those analysing the trend towards larger and larger organizations, or indeed from the apparent movement towards more flexible work organization patterns today.

Organizational theorists have used different theoretical approaches or conversations to explore work organizations, including the technical, human relations, neo-human relations, systems thinking, contingency, cultures, learning, control, feminist, social action, political and postmodernism approaches, as we illustrated in Chapter 3.

Part Two explored the context of organizational behaviour, and emphasized just how difficult it is to separate managerial and other employee behaviour in the workplace from internal organizational requirements and the external context. Management and organizational leadership have an enormous influence on how people are managed in the workplace, how they experience their work, and how successful their organization is in terms of its performance goals. If work behaviour is essentially connected to the totality of the organization, then it is also important to examine the role of management and the drama of globalization.

In Chapter 4 we explored the issue of management through a three-dimensional management model which, for analytical purposes, separates management activities and behaviours from contingencies, which are grouped into three broad categories: the external context, business strategy and organizational design. This encourages us to go beyond simply describing managerial behaviour, to provide an understanding of the contingencies that explain why managerial policies and behaviour vary in time and space.

We demonstrated that managers' behaviour does not follow the famous Fayolian management cycle. Managers are engaged in an assortment of frenetic, habitual, reactive, fragmented activities. The model we used to conceptualize management suggests that it is a multi-dimensional integrating and controlling activity, which permeates every facet of workplace experience and strongly fashions the employment relationship.

At one time many courses in OB separated the material rather differently into individual, groups and organization, but we suggest here that these divisions are no longer helpful since they imply a degree of separation between the elements that really does not exist. That is why we said above that our integrated model divides the world up into apparently discrete units only 'for analytic purposes'. Of course, the world is much more confused and overlapping than such models imply, but the problem remains: how can we talk about everything affecting everything simultaneously? The paradox, then, is that we have to 'analyse' the world – to split it into elements – simply to try to make sense of the individual elements, while at the same time we need to remember that the world is actually only understandable as a systemic whole. This integrated model therefore acts as a heuristic device – something to help us understand the world – but it should not be taken as a model of the world itself. The importance for OB here is to understand that managers and workers are not discrete units; they are not isolated from the rest of society but are deeply embedded in it.

Chapter 5 explained that leadership in organizations is a dialectical process, in which an individual persuades others to do things they would not otherwise do. This is a result of the interaction of the leader and followers within some context, and is equated with power. It was explained that leadership is not the same as management. Management is associated with functions such as planning, organizing, controlling and efficiency, whereas leadership is associated with vision making and significant change. Management processes produce a degree of order and consistency in work behaviour. Leadership processes produce significant change or movement.

We reviewed the major perspectives on leadership, including the trait, behaviour, contingency, power and gender-influence approaches. We noted too that the systematic research on leadership has evolved from a narrow focus on the leader's traits to a multidimensional model of leadership which looks at the exercise of leadership as a complex reciprocal process. It is affected by the interaction between the leader, the followers, and the opportunities and constraints afforded by the external and internal contexts in which they find themselves.

In Part Three, we turned our attention to how various individual differences affect individual behaviour in the workplace. Individuals have different personalities, perceptions and learning styles. We also emphasized that the work experiences of women, visible minorities and the disabled may be different from those of white male employees.

Chapter 6 examined personality, which we stated is the distinctive and relatively enduring pattern of thinking, feeling, and acting that characterizes a person's response to her or his environment. Trait theorists try to identify and measure personality variables. However, they disagree concerning the number of traits needed to adequately describe personality, and we noted that traits have not proved to be highly consistent across situations, and they also vary in consistency over time. We went on to examine sociocultural theorists who emphasize the social context, the subjective experiences of the individual, and deal with perceptual and cognitive processes. A key concept is reciprocal determinism, relating to two-way causal relations between personal characteristics, behaviour and the environment.

In Chapter 7 we learned that perception, like personality, is interdependent with our socialization and impacts on people's behaviour in the workplace in complex ways. Understanding perception is important because the fundamental nature of perceptual processes means different individuals usually interpret other people and situations differently, and so routinely hold different views of reality. These in turn strongly influence their attitudes and actions. We explained that as a consequence, avoiding conflict and ensuring that important workplace decisions are based on sound judgments is not a matter of training employees how to see things as they 'really are', because multiple realities always exist. More can be gained from understanding how perception works, and shaping organizational activity so that the possibilities for negative outcomes are minimized.

Chapter 8 explored learning in the workplace. We discussed the growing interest in learning, as contemporary management thinking and practice have emphasized notions of knowledge work, flexibility, core competencies and sustainable competitive advantage through learning. We defined learning as a relatively permanent change in behaviour or human capabilities resulting from processing new knowledge, practice or experience. The quality of this learning experience may depend upon how the organization is structured, how work is designed, how individuals engage, interact and construct knowledge from these paid work situations, and how managers lead their subordinates.

In Chapter 9 we stated that motivation refers to the driving force within individuals that affects the direction, intensity and persistence of work behaviour in the interest of achieving organizational goals. Two broad competing approaches to understanding motivation were explored – need-based theories and process theories. According to Maslow's needs hierarchy, employee behaviour is directed to satisfying lower-level needs before seeking to satisfy higher order-needs. It is based on the principle that when a drive or need is met, its value as a motivator is reduced. Maslow's theory helps to explain the dynamic nature of work motivation. We noted that all need theories tend to be heavily prescriptive in nature.

We went on to explain how process theories place emphasis on the actual psychological process of motivation. According to equity theory of work motivation, for example, perceptions of equity or inequity lead employees to form judgements on the value (or valence) of a reward or outcome. When individual employees or groups of employees perceive the reward item to be inequitable, they will not experience satisfaction with that reward item.

Expectancy theory is based on the idea that motivation to work results from deliberate choices to engage in certain behaviours in order to achieve worthwhile outcomes. The three most important elements of expectancy theory are the perception that effort will result in a particular level of performance, the perception that a specific behaviour or action will lead to specific outcomes, and the perceived value of those outcomes, the valences. We emphasized that the attractiveness of work activities (valence) depends on employees' individual differences, cultural factors and their orientation to work. We also noted that there might be differences between men and women, and Christian and non-Christian employees in terms of work motivation.

We began Chapter 10 with the claim that understanding issues of equity across the major social divisions of society is vital for a full understanding of organizational behaviour. In mainstream (or male-stream) OB textbooks, issues of gender and male power, class, race, and ethnicity and disability are either ignored or marginalized. We explored the general and specific tensions in organizations that make the issue of equity, inequity and justice a relevant topic for learning and research. Vertical and horizontal conflicts were shown to help us understand the complex forms of power that play out across organizations. We further explored how women, ethno-racial minorities, and people who are disabled as well as the working class continue to face major difficulties in gaining just and equitable treatment in relation to paid employment.

Taken together, the number of people who are subject to forms of discrimination amount to the vast majority in our society. We asked, if the vast majority of people in our society experience systematic inequities in relation to work, why on earth is it so difficult to realize significant, positive change? Some of the answers to this question lie in the realm of existing OB research, but many others have not yet been addressed. Addressing these questions of equity means taking stock of the very heart of the way work and society is organized. It is our hope that through some of the inter-disciplinary dimensions of this book, you, the reader, will begin a journey of further exploration.

In Part Four of this book, we examined some of the important social processes that take place in the context of work groups, communications, decision making and power. Chapter 11 explored the background, the nature and the behavioural implications of work groups and teams. The nature of work groups was explored through the concepts of size, norms, cohesiveness and group learning. We went beyond management rhetoric and presented argument and evidence to suggest that self-managed teams shift the focus away from the hierarchy, direct and bureaucratic control processes, to a culture of self-control mechanisms.

Chapter 12 explained how the communication process established in the workplace reflects management style, degree of employee involvement in decision making and organizational culture. Three major perspectives for understanding organizational communications were presented – functionalist, interpretivist and critical – to allow us to comprehend the central role communications has in the management process. The metaphors used to describe the perspectives enhance our ability to view communications not just as the transmission and exchange of information in the context of organizational efficiency, but rather as central to the other processes of power, leadership and decision making.

We emphasized that human beings engage with their world through symbols (verbal, non-verbal and written language). Language creates the organizational concepts that define the culture of an organization and give form to notions of control, delegation and rationality. Finally, we provided evidence which revealed the differences between the conversational styles of men and women. As managers, women try to develop 'rapport' with colleagues, whereas men often 'report' information or problems. Although individuals are encouraged to be creative, the organization places limitations on them in the form of where, how and when they can speak.

plate 50 At the heart of notions of post-bureaucratic organizations is a flexible, empowered and cooperative workforce. The Internet adds a 'space dimension' to organizational culture, and research suggests that it might require us to re-evaluate existing conceptions of organizational culture.

Source: Getty Images

Chapter 13 examined different models of decision making. We were careful to explain that in reality, decision makers must suffer from bounded rationality. They do not have free and easy access to information, and the human mind has limited information processing capacity and is susceptible to a variety of cognitive biases. Furthermore, time constraints and political considerations can outweigh the anticipated economic gain of obtaining better information.

Research suggests that work groups and teams can often make higher-quality decisions than individuals because of their vigilance and their potential capacity to generate and evaluate more ideas. However, we pointed out that through the social phenomenon of groupthink, groups might make decisions that are more risky or conservative than those of individuals. It was noted that organizations are increasingly concerned about their members making ethical decisions. We explained that decision making in the organization can be improved by using four techniques: brainstorming, nominal group technique, computer-mediated brainstorming, and the Delphi technique.

Chapter 14 explored the abstract concept of power. Power appears to be 'embodied' in individuals, something they possess and exert. In reviewing the macro theories of power, we explored the many deep social roots or 'sources' of power systems, including the influences of ideology, the military, politics and economics. We said that Gramsci and Foucault outlined perhaps the most extensive theories of power, noting that power is everywhere because it constitutes the very way we talk and think about ourselves, let alone our organizational surroundings. Importantly, these two authors are clear in their argument that power is a coin with two sides: on the one, consent, accommodation and domination; on the other, lack of commitment, stress, resistance, political action and 'voice'.

We then moved on to explore some key examples of OB research that deal directly with the concept of power. We argued that managers as well as workers (and students of OB!) have a right to think through and question the legitimacy of our current social and work arrangements. Mahatma Gandhi, Martin Luther King and others operated on the principle of removal of consent, which for our purposes relates directly to a broad, social perspective on power.

Finally, Part Five shifted the focus once again, this time to explore how organization design and culture, technology and HR practices fashion the behaviour of people in organizations. Chapter 15 explained that organization structure refers to the formal division of work or labour, and the formal pattern of relationships that coordinate and control organizational activities, whereas organizational design refers to the process of creating a structure that best fits a strategy, technology and environment. Several theoretical frameworks were examined, centred around the notion of the bureaucratic and post-bureaucratic organization.

We explained that the contingency view of formal organizational design suggests that a change in business strategy may require a change in the organizational design: for example, moving from a functional to a team-based organizational structure. It was explained how the external environment influences the formal structure and functioning of a work organization, and in turn, organization leaders influence the wider society.

We also explored the nature of organizational culture, which we defined as a pattern of shared basic assumptions, beliefs, values, artefacts, stories and behaviours, and discussed how the concept has become closely associated with the notion of postmodern organizations and management theory around strategic HRM. Two approaches to the study of culture were examined. First was the managerialist-oriented approach which treats organizational culture as a variable: it is something that an organization has, and can be managed. Second was the critically oriented approach, which conceptualizes organizations as if they were cultures: a metaphor which emphasizes the symbolic, consciousness and subjective aspects of the formal workplace. Finally, we emphasized that OB studies must be able to deal with the new complexities and nuances.

In Chapter 16, we emphasized how comparative international analyses of concepts and theoretical debates, as well as policies and programmes, provide an important basis for understanding how technology is related to work and organizational behaviour. We suggested a broad, multi-levelled approach that suggests OB students need to think of technology as a social phenomenon, by recognizing both consent and conflict in processes of adoption. Through our review of the literature, we hoped to stimulate a variety of questions, but perhaps more importantly students should be in a better position to understand, evaluate and perhaps even affect the current landscape and future direction of new technology, work and related issues in our society.

OB IN FOCUS

A culture of overwork exacts an extreme price

At China's biggest telecoms maker, every new employee is issued with a mattress. The reason? So they can grab a nap beneath their desks, day or night, when they succumb to exhaustion from their endless working hours. The frenetic work habits of the 40,000 employees of Huawei Technologies have become known as the 'mattress culture' – and it's a prime example of the intense pressures that kill up to one million Chinese workers every year. Until recently, China was proud of its mattress culture.

Many worked for months without a day off, sleeping in their offices at night so they could keep working as soon as they awoke. But there is mounting concern about the toll of death and illness from overwork. Experts estimate that 600,000 to one million Chinese workers are dying from it every year. Huawei, previously seen as a model company, is now a symbol of the overwork phenomenon. One of its star employees, 25-year-old software engineer Hu Xinyu, died suddenly May 28 after nearly a month of overtime work. He was a former athlete and sports enthusiast, yet he became so exhausted at the company that he often slept at his office instead of going home. His death has helped ignite a national debate about the culture of excessive work.

Almost all sectors of Chinese society, from manual labourers to intellectuals, are prone to overwork. In the past five years, for example, 135 professors and other scholars in Beijing have died prematurely as result of overwork, according to media reports. Their average age was just 53. And a survey of 2600 high-tech workers in Beijing found that 84 percent were unhappy with their excessive workload and nearly 90 percent were worried about the impact on their health. 'People are starting to look at the human cost of China's phenomenal growth rate,' said Robin Munro, research director at China Labour Bulletin, a labour rights organization based in Hong Kong. 'It's an awful indictment of the work culture in China and the pressure on ordinary people.'

Under Chinese law, he noted, workers are prohibited from working more than 36 hours of overtime a month. Yet this limit is routinely exceeded in most export-oriented manufacturing industries. 'It's the mentality of a slave labour camp,' Mr. Munro said. Even the state-owned propaganda newspaper, *People's Daily*, has criticized the amount of overwork, which it blames partly on the rising unemployment rate and the 14 million jobless people in the country. 'With the growing numbers of people ready to take their places, few workers are willing to turn down overtime,' the newspaper said in an editorial last month.

One of the most poignant cases was the story of Gan Hongying, a 35-year-old worker in a garment factory in southern China. Desperate to raise money for her husband and two children, she worked 22 hours of overtime in a four-day period this spring. She began to complain of dizziness and headaches, and she talked constantly of how she needed to sleep. On May 30, after more than 54 hours of work over four days, she died suddenly. Her last words to her sister were: 'I am so tired. Give me the key to your home, I want to have a rest.' After her death, a local newspaper investigated and found that the garment factory had routinely forced its employees to work overtime. If the workers failed to finish their orders, the factory gate was sometimes locked to keep them inside, and they were threatened with a loss of pay.

Geoffrey York, *Globe and Mail*, 21 August 2006, p. A2.

Chapter 17 examined the developments in human resource management (HRM) practices, how these fashion the behaviour of people in organizations, and the growth in interest in international HRM (IHRM) as a spin-off from increased glo-balization. We explored how contemporary HRM practices are a product of their times, the ascendancy of a new political and economic ideology. After examining three widely cited HRM models, we explored a core assumption underlying much of the strategic HRM (SHRM) discourse: that each of the main types of generic competitive strategies used by organizations (a cost leadership or differentiation strategy) is associated with a different approach to managing people: that is, with a different HR strategy.

To this end, we examined the so-called 'matching model' and the 'resource-based' SHRM model. The former, we stated, focuses on the notion of 'fit', while the latter places its emphasis on an organization's human endowments as a strategy for sustained competitive advantage. Paradox is an ongoing part of the employment relationship, and we exposed some internal paradoxes in HRM.

The future of work and OB

The interdependencies and particularities of organizational needs and the multi-dimensional nature of workplace change or even transformation make the task of predicting the future pattern of work and organizational behaviour a heroic, some may say foolhardy, challenge. Without wishing to take any particular perspective, this section considers several OB themes that we have addressed in this book. Using the integrated model (Figure 1.2) used in the preceding chapters and drawing heav-ily from WERS survey findings,[3] we indicate some possible future directions for OB-related matters and discourse.

In the early twenty-first century, much of the debate in OB has been about the growth of non-standard or precarious employment, the quality of work, balancing responsibilities inside and outside of work, the search for performance-enhancing employment practices, the process of organizational transformation and the alleged shift to post-bureaucratic organizations. The research evidence affirms that the employer is an 'active agent'[4] in transforming work patterns, redrawing the boundaries between standard 'core' and non-standard 'precarious' employment. Evidence points to the continuing growth of precarious employment arrangements in Canada, the European Union, the United States and many parts of Asia.[5]

The new employment relationships have profound implications for OB theorists and practitioners. Most of the existing OB theories and frameworks are implicitly grounded in the assumption of standard employment conditions,[6] and therefore more inclusive models of precarious employment need to be developed. One basic question to be addressed is how workers' motivation and commitment are affected by factors associated with non-standard employment contracts in the new organizational context. As precarious and low-security employment policies and practices become increasingly prevalent, the 'standard employment' paradigm is fast becoming an anachronism to future OB researchers.

Survey data also shows that between 1998 and 2004, new forms of work resulted in an intensification of work: 'Employees' perceptions of work intensity have not changed ... their jobs required them to work very hard and that they never seemed to have enough time to get their work done.'[7]

In the UK, encouraged by the government's promotion of a work–life balance, since 1998 there has been an increase in the provision of flexible working arrange-ments for workers employed on standard employment contracts. While there is some evidence of employer flexibility, it is, however, reported that 'The majority of managers still believe that it was up to the individual to balance their work and family commitments.'[8]

plate 51 Non-heterosexual families highlight questions of work–life balance, organizational commitment and equity in the workplace

Source: Getty Images

The WERS 2004 findings did not, for the most part, find a demonstrable connection between 'better' HR practices and organizational performance. Neither did the influential study find evidence that HRM has become more 'strategic' in UK workplaces. The pursuit of a competitive strategy of low costs and developing human capital may well be confined to 'leading-edge' organizations, therefore, where competitive advantage depends more on leveraging the skills of knowledge workers.

New work configurations and employment arrangements cannot be uncoupled from their organizational and national contexts.[9] As we explained in an earlier chapter, in recent years the notion of post-bureaucratic organizations, often characterized as 'lean' or 'networks' or 'virtual', has become an important theme in OB studies. It has been notably associated with the accelerating growth of global capitalism, information technology, and with developments in corporate governance and new flexible employment practices.

At the heart of notions of the post-bureaucratic organization is the idea of a more flexible, empowered and cooperative workforce, together with a strategically integrated set of employment relations. A central aspect of work in post-bureaucratic organizations involves individuals being rewarded on the basis of individual or/and organizational performance. Pulignano and Stewart's study[10] persuasively argues that new employment arrangements have, paradoxically, revitalized Weber's typology of bureaucracy. Analysing primarily qualitative data from global automotive companies between 2000 and 2001, the authors contend that new performance-related incentives have generated behavioural rules that reinforce bureaucratic control in the workplace: 'Bureaucratic forms of control have been refined rather than supplanted,' they state.[11] Arguably, the binary bureaucratic/post-bureaucratic view of organizational design may be a somewhat misleading analytical device.

Both mainstream and critical OB literature bear witness to an increasing and accelerating interest in analysing OB within its societal fabric. We have departed from most mainstream OB texts by recognizing the need of an analytic readjustment in OB analysis, which values the insights of sociological and feminist theories. The uneven effects of global capitalism have created disparities both between and within organizations. Not only this, but dominant OB ideology and research has ignored one of the central insights of classical sociological theory: that the behaviours of people in organizations and management practices are embedded in wider institutional, cultural and social relations.[12] As a result, any management intervention is demonstrably adapted and applied in ways which simultaneously change or transform existing employment relations. At the same time these interventions are necessarily collectively internalized with existing recurring patterns of social behaviour and complex reciprocal interdependent relations in society.[13] This makes the 'effects' of any management intervention in the workplace unpredictable if it is analysed only within a sanitized organizational context rather than a societal context.

The importance of embeddedness can also be illustrated at a macro level. At the time of writing – August 2006 – the problem of global warming has entered mainstream popular culture, as is witnessed by Al Gore's film and book *An Inconvenient Truth*. There appears to be a seismic shift in public opinion, which recognizes that organizations and governments need to use resources and engage in activities that provide for a sustainable lifestyle.

Another example of the importance of embeddedness relates to organizational governance. As some US corporate executives start jail sentences and others end their term of imprisonment (including the iconic Martha Stewart), there is a growing backlash against corporate chief executive officers who have been accused, and in some cases convicted, of fraudulent accounting practices. President George W. Bush's rhetoric in 2002 promised harsh punishment for corporate executives who 'cook the books' and violate the public trust. The implication here is that removing a few 'bad apples' could solve corporate white-collar crime. However, the notion of the embedded organization suggests that if we simply focus on traits – for instance honesty and integrity – we are making the error of separating top organization leaders from their context.

Those corporate leaders who engaged in criminal or highly unethical practices did so largely because of profound ideological changes in society. In the final decade of the twentieth century, shareholder-value-driven capitalism emphasized stock appreciation, the use of stock options to compensate senior executives, and the attainment of short-term financial targets. All this produced a culture of avarice. According to the US Federal Reserve Board chairman, Alan Greenspan, the late 1990s produced 'an outsized increase in opportunities for avarice. [And] an infectious greed seemed to grip much of our business community.'[14] Thus, we are reminded that managers operate within a wider institutional, cultural and social context, and changing the way managers behave requires a fundamental change in organization context and culture.

It means changing the way organizations are regulated by government, changing the way managers are compensated, and changing the values that ultimately prevail in society. Western governments are coming under increasing pressure to create a system of regulations and corporate governance to prevent organization managers from behaving in illegal or highly unethical ways, and to make Western capitalism more efficient and socially acceptable.

The notion of embeddedness is also relevant when studying OB. With a few notable exceptions,[15] most OB textbooks and research are embedded in a dominant managerialist perspective, which serves the interests of big business, as well as being largely blind to race, ethnic and gender issues. The vast majority of OB textbooks present the managerialist approach, with its primary focus on organizational efficiency, effectiveness and performance, as the logical approach. Workers are typically represented as a 'problem': they need to be 'controlled' or 'motivated'. Managers on the other hand are portrayed as primarily engaged in rational activities designed to increase profits for shareholders, for the most part without exercising wider social responsibilities. In the dominant managerialist paradigm, there is generally malign neglect of the interests and ideas of women workers, of racial minorities, of non-Christians and the disabled. Yet women's work experiences, for example, may be quite different from those of white male workers. Similarly, black women's work experiences may be quite different from those of their white sisters.

The powerful arguments presented by feminist writers to redefine employment relations can equally be applied to the interdisciplinary field of OB.[16] We would suggest that orthodox OB has presented an under-theorized and sanitized analysis of the workplace. Most of the mainstream OB theories and frameworks are implicitly grounded in the dominant Protestant Anglo-Saxon paradigm, based around 'individualism', 'managerialism', 'standard work' and male dominance. Similar to research in other areas of social studies, more inclusive frameworks of OB must be developed. The literature on workplace diversity and equity issues has shown that this became a particularly important field in the final quarter of the twentieth century, with globalization and immigration creating ever more diverse societies and organizational settings. Diversity and equity analyses will continue to be one of the core research issues in the twenty-first century.

Finally, we believe that the dominant perspective of OB, which mainly ignores or denies the importance of class, gender, race, ethnicity, disability and the wider social fabric in which paid work is embedded, helps to preserve the status quo. In our view, OB will be more relevant to students if it takes account of the notion of social embeddedness and the interests and ideas of women, racial minorities, non-Christians and the disabled. This book has tried to address the imbalance. We hope it stimulates a variety of serious work-related questions. Perhaps it will even help students to forge a more equitable workplace in the future.

Reflecting on the journey

Our journey through OB studies is now drawing to a close. The time has come for you to reflect on what you have learned from this journey. Adult education scholars emphasize the need for reflectivity as a critical component of the learning process. Reflection is like using a mirror to help us to look back on our actions and thought processes. Reflective learning occurs where we have experiences and then step back from them to evaluate the learning we have experienced.

There are several ways of carrying out reflection. One approach is to read your learning journal, which we set as a web-based assignment in Chapter 1. Questions you might ask include, how well did the OB material connect to your other management courses? What assumptions were made? Were the examples that are supposed to be common to all students consistent with your own life or work experience?

Alternatively, systematically go back through the additional reading listed at the end of each chapter in this book. Other sources of information, particularly material that tends to differ with the approach in this book, provides mirrors for us and allows us to look at topics from another perspective. Other people – friends, relatives and co-workers – also provide mirrors for us, allowing us to understand leadership from another perspective. Talk to other people about the topics covered in *Work and Organizational Behaviour*.

Your own experience of the workplace is also excellent material for reflection, and can provide insight into many of the topics explored in this book. To help you start the reflection process, go back to the beginning of each chapter and consider whether you have personally achieved the major learning objectives. Finally, we hope our guided tour through OB studies has proved worthwhile, and we hope you remain positive yet sceptical rather than negative and cynical.

Notes

1 Morris (2004: 273).
2 Kersley et al. (2006: 307–8).
3 Kersley et al. (2006).
4 Rubery (1998: 251).
5 Connelly and Gallagher (2004).
6 Pfeffer and Baron (1988).
7 Pfeffer and Baron (1988: 317).
8 Kersley et al. (2006: 311).
9 Morris (2004), Maurice and Sorge (2000), Jacoby (2005).
10 Pulignano and Stewart (2006).
11 Pulignano and Stewart (2006).
12 Smart (2003).
13 Maurice and Sorge (2000).
14 Quoted in Bratton, Grint and Nelson (2005: 323).
15 Such as Mills, Simmons and Helm Mills (2005), Wilson (2003).
16 Wajcman (2000), Hansen (2002), Healy, Hansen and Ledwith (2006).

Bibliography

Aart Scholte, J. (2005) *Globalization: A critical introduction* (2nd edn), Basingstoke: Palgrave.

Adams, J. S. (1965) 'Inequality in social exchange', pp. 267–99 in L. Berkowitz (ed.), *Advances in Experimental Social Psychology*, New York: Academic Press.

Adler, L. (2002) *Hire With Your Head*, Chichester: Wiley.

Adler, N. J. (1997) *International Dimensions of Organizational Behaviour* (3rd edn), Cincinnati, Oh.: South-Western.

Adler, S. and Weiss, H. (1988) 'Recent developments in the study of personality and organizational behavior', in C. Cooper and I. Robertson (eds), *International Review of Industrial and Organizational Psychology*, New York: Wiley.

Agashae, Z. and Bratton, J. (2001) 'Leader–follower dynamics: developing a learning organization', *Journal of Workplace Learning*, **13** (3), pp. 89–102.

Aidt, T. and Tzannatos, Z (2003) *Unions and Collective Bargaining: Economic effects in a global environment*, Washington, D.C.: World Bank.

Aktouf, O. (1996) *Traditional Management and Beyond*, Montreal: Morin.

Alban Metcalfe, B. (1989) 'What motivates managers: an investigation by gender and sector employment', *Public Administration*, Spring, pp. 95–108.

Albert, M. (2003) *Parecon: Life after Capitalism*. London: Verso.

Aldrich, H. (1972) 'Technology and organizational structure: a re-examination of the findings of the Aston Group', *Administrative Science Quarterly*, **17** (1), pp. 26–43.

Alderfer, C. P. (1972) *Existence, Relatedness and Growth*, New York: Free Press.

Aligisakis, M. (1997) 'Labour disputes in Western Europe: typology and tendencies', *International Labour Review*, **136** (1), pp. 73–94.

Alvesson, M. (1987) *Organization Theory: Technocratic consciousness*, Berlin: De Gruyter.

Alvesson, M. (1993) *Cultural Perspectives on Organizations*, Cambridge: CUP.

Alvesson, M. (1996) *Communication, Power and Organization,* New York: Walter de Gruyter.

Alvesson, M. and Berg, P. O. (1992) *Corporate Culture and Organizational Symbolism*, Berlin: De Gruyter.

Alvesson, M. and Due Billing, Y. (1997) *Understanding Gender in Organizations,* London: Sage.

Alvesson, M. and Willmott, H. (eds) (1992) *Critical Management Studies*, London: Sage.

Alvesson, M. and Willmott, H. (1996) *Making Sense of Management: A critical introduction,* London: Sage.

Alvesson, M. and Willmott, H. (2002) 'Identity regulation as organizational control: producing the appropriate individual', *Journal of Management Studies*, **39** (5), pp. 619–44.

Ambrose, M., Seabright, M. and Schminke, M. (2002) 'Sabotage in the workplace: the role of organizational injustice', *Organizational Behaviour and Human Decision Processes*, **89** (1), pp. 947–65.

Amit, R. and Shoemaker, P. J. H. (1993) 'Strategic assets and organizational rent', *Strategic Management Journal*, **14,** pp. 33–46.

Anderson, A. H. and Kyprianou, A. (1994) *Effective Organizational Behavior: A skills and activity-based approach*, Oxford: Blackwell.

Anderson, M. and Collins , P. (2004) *Race, Class and Gender* (5th edn), Thomson.

Apps, J. (1994) *Leadership for the Emerging Age*, San Francisco, Calif.: Jossey-Bass.

Aquino, K. and Douglas, S. (2003) 'Identity threat and antisocial behavior in organizations: the moderating effects of individual differences, aggressive modeling, and hierarchical status', *Organizational Behavior and Human Decision Processes*, **90** (1), pp. 195–208.

Arblaster, A. (1970) 'Education and ideology', pp. 49–55 in D. Rubinstein and C. Stoneman (eds), *Education for Democracy*, London: Penguin.

Archibugi, D. and Coco, A. (2000) *The Globalisation of Technology and the European Innovation System*, Rome: Italian National Research Council.

Archibugi, D. and Lundvall, B. (eds) (2001) *The Globalising Learning Economy*, Oxford: Oxford University Press.

Argyris, C. (1957) *Personality and Organizations: The conflict between system and the individual*, New York: Harper.

Argyris, C. (1993) *Knowledge for Action: A guide to overcoming barriers to organizational change*, San Francisco: Jossey-Bass.

Argyris, C. and Schön, D. (eds) (1978) *Organizational Learning*, Reading, Mass.: Addison-Wesley.

Armstrong, P. (1989) 'Limits and possibilities for HRM in an age of management accountancy', pp. 154–66 in J. Storey (ed.), *New Perspectives on Human Resource Management*, London: Routledge.

Arnolds, C. and Boshoff, C. (2002) 'Compensation, esteem valence and job performance: an empirical assessment of Alderfer's ERG theory', *International Journal of Human Resource Management*, **13** (4), pp. 697–719.

Arthur, W., Woehr, D. J. and Graziano, W. (2001) 'Personality testing in employment settings.' *Personnel Review*, **30** (6), pp. 657–76.

Asaro, P. (1996) 'Transforming society by transforming technology: the science and politics of participatory design', *CMS Conference Stream: Information Technology and Critical Theory*, Urbana, Ill.: University of Illinois at Urbana-Champaign.

Asch, S. E. (1951) 'Effects of group pressure upon modification and distortion of judgements,' in H. Guetzkow (ed.), *Groups, Leadership and Men*, New York: Carnegie Press.

Ashcroft, B., Griffiths, G. and Tiffin, H. (1989) *The Empire Writes Back,* London: Routledge.

Ashforth, B. and Mael, F. (1989) 'Social identity theory and the organization', *Academy of Management Review*, **14**, pp. 20–39.

Ashkanasy, N. M., Zerbe, C. E. and Hartel, J. (2002) 'Introduction: managing emotions in a changing workplace', pp. 3–18 in N. Ashkanasy, C. Zerbe and J Hartel (eds), *Managing Emotions in the Workplace*, New York: Sharpe.

Ashton, D. and Field, D. (1976) *Young Workers*, London: Hutchinson.

Attneave, F. (1971) 'Multistability in perception', in R. Held and W. Richards (eds), *Recent Progress in Perception*, San Francisco: W. H. Freeman.

Austin, J. (2002) 'Editorial', *Journal of Organizational Behavior Management*, **22** (3), pp. 1–2.

Avolio, B. J. (1999) *Full Leadership Development*, Thousand Oaks, Calif.: Sage.

Bakan, J. (2004) *The Corporation*, London: Penguin.

Baker, T. (1999) *Doing Well by Doing Good.*, Washington: Economic Policy Institute.

Baldamus, W. (1961) *Efficiency and Effort*, London: Tavistock.

Baldry, C., Bain, P. and Taylor, P. (1998) '"Bright satanic offices": intensification, control and team Taylorism', pp. 163–83 in P. Thompson and C. Warhurst (eds), *Workplaces of the Future*, Basingstoke: Macmillan.

Ball, G., Trevino, L. and Sims, H. (1993) 'Justice and organizational punishment: attitudinal outcomes of disciplinary events', *Social Justice Research*, **6**, pp. 39–67.

Bamber, D. and Castka, P. (2006) 'Personality, organizational orientations and self-reported learning outcomes', *Journal of Workplace Learning*, **18** (1 & 2), pp. 73–92.

Bamber, G., Ryan, S. and Wailes, N. (2004) 'Globalization, employment relations and human indicators in ten developed market economies: international data sets', *International Journal of Human Resource Management*, **15** (8), pp. 1481-1516.

Bamberger, P. and Meshoulam, I. (2000) *Human Resource Management Strategy*, Thousand Oaks, Calif.: Sage.

Bandura, A. (1971) 'Psychotherapy based upon modeling principles', pp. 173–83 in A. E. and S. L. Garfield (eds), *Handbook of Psychotherapy and Behaviour,* New York: Wiley.

Bandura, A. (1977a) *Social Learning Theory*, Englewood Cliffs, NJ: Prentice-Hall.

Bandura, A. (1997b) *Self-Efficacy: The exercise of control*, New York: Freeman.

Bandura, A. (1978) 'The self system in reciprocal determinism', *American Psychologist*, **33**, pp. 344–58.

Banker, R. D., Field, J. M., Schroeder, R. G. and Sinha, K. (1996) 'Impact of work teams on manufacturing performance: a longitudinal study', *Academy of Management Journal*, **39** (2), pp. 867–90.

Bao, X. (1991) *Holding up More Than Half the Sky: Chinese women garment workers in New York City, 1948–1992*, Urbana and Chicago: University of Illinois Press.

Bao, X. (2002) 'Sweatshops in Sunset Park: a variation of the late 20th century Chinese garment shops in New York City', *International Labor and Working-Class History*, **61**, pp. 69–90.

Bargh, J. A., Lombardi, W. J. and Higgins, E. T. (1988) 'Automaticity of chronically accessible constructs in person x situation effects on person perception: it's just a matter of time', *Journal of Personality and Social Psychology*, **55**, pp. 599–605.

Barnes, C. (1996) 'What next? Disability, the 1995 Disability Discrimination Act and the campaign for disabled peoples' rights', National Bureau for Disabled Students Annual Conference, 2 March , Leeds.

Barney, J. B. (1991) 'Firm resources and sustained competitive advantage', *Journal of Management*, 17 (1), pp. 99–120.

Bartlett C. A. and Ghoshal, S. (1989) *Managing across Borders: The transnational solution*, London: Random House.

Barrick, M. R., Stewart, G., Neubert, M. and Mount, M. (1998) 'Relating member ability and personality to work-team processes and team effectiveness', *Journal of Applied Psychology*, June, pp. 377–91.

Bates, T. (1994) 'Utilization of minority employees in small business: a comparison of nonminority and black-owned enterprises', *Review of Black Political Economy*, **23**, pp. 113–21.

Bazerman, M. H. (1994) *Judgement in Managerial Decision Making* (3rd edn), New York: Wiley.

Becker, H. S. (1971) 'Social change variations in the teacher–pupil relationship', in B. Cosin et al. (eds), *School and Society*, London: Routledge & Kegan Page.

Becker, H.S. (1984) 'Social class variations in the teacher-pupil ratio', in A. Hargreaves and P. Woods (eds), *Classrooms and Staff Rooms: The sociology of teachers and teaching*, Milton Keynes: Open University Press.

Beer, M., Spector, B., Lawrence, P. R., Quin Mills, D. and Walton, R. E. (1984) *Managing Human Assets*, New York: Free Press.

Beirne, M. and Ramsay, H. (eds) (1992) *Information Technology and Workplace Democracy*, London: Routledge & Kegan Paul.

Belasco, J. and Stayer, R. (1993) *Flight of the Buffalo*, New York: Warner.

Belenky, M. F., Clinchy, B. M., Goldberger, N. R. and Tarule, J. (1986) *Women's Ways of Knowing: The development of self, voice, and mind*, New York: Basic Books.

Bell, D. (1948) '"Screening" leaders in a democracy', *Commentary*, 5, pp. 368–75.

Bell, D. (1973) *The Coming of the Post-Industrial Society*, New York: Basic Books.

Benders, J. (2005) 'Team working: a tale of partial participation', pp. 55–74 in D. Knights, P. Thompson, C. Smith and H. Willmott (eds), *Participation and Democracy at Work*, Basingstoke: Palgrave.

Benders, J. and Van Hootegem, G. (1999) 'Teams and their context: moving team discussion beyond existing dichotomies', *Journal of Management Studies*, **36** (5), pp. 609–28.

Bendix, R. (1956) *Work and Authority in Industry*, New York: Wiley.

Bennis, W. and Nanus, B. (1997) *Leaders: Strategies for taking charge* (2nd edn), New York: Harper Business.

Berg, I. (1970) *Education and Jobs: The great training robbery*, New York: Praeger.

Berg, M. (1988) 'Women's work, mechanization and early industrialization', in R. E. Pahl (ed.), *On Work*, Oxford: Blackwell.

Bernstein, B. (1971) *Class Codes and Control,* Vol. 1, London: Routledge & Kegan Page.

Bernstein, D. A., Clarke-Stewart, A., Penner, L. Roy, E. and Wickens, C. (2000) *Psychology* (5th edn), New York: Houghton Mifflin.

Beyer, J. and Trice, M. (1987) 'How an organization's rites reveal its culture', *Organization Dynamics*, **15** (4), pp. 4–24.

Beynon, H. (1984) *Working for Ford*, Harmondsworth: Penguin.

Bhaskar, R. (1989) *Reclaiming Reality*, London: Verso.

Bijker, W. and Law, J. (eds) (1992) *Shaping Technology/Building Society: Studies in socio-technical change,* Cambridge, Mass.: MIT Press.

Billett, S. (2001a) 'Co-participation: affordance and engagement at work', *New Directions for Adult and Continuing Education*, **92**, pp. 63–72.

Billett, S. (2001b) *Learning in the Workplace: Strategies for effective practice*, Crows Nest, Australia: Allen & Unwin.

Bilton, T., Bonnett, K., Jones, P. and Lawson, T. (2002) *Introductory Sociology,* London: Palgrave Macmillan.

Bjerknes, G., Ehn, P. and Kyng M. (eds) (1987) *Computers and Democracy: A Scandinavian challenge*, Aldershot: Avebury.

Black, O. (1996) 'Addressing the issue of good communication', *People Management* (online) http://proquest.umi.com

Blanchard, P.N. et al. (2000) 'Training evaluation: perspectives and evidence from Canada', *International Journal of Training and Development*, **4** (4), pp. 1253–63.

Blank, W., Weitzel, J. R. and Green, S. G. (1990) 'A test of situational leadership theory', *Personnel Psychology*, **43**, pp. 579–97.

Blau, P. M. and Schoenherr, R. A. (1971) *The Structure of Organizations,* New York: Basic Books.

Blauner, R. (1964) *Alienation and Freedom: The factory worker and his industry*, Chicago: University of Chicago Press.

Bloom, P.(2004) 'Children think before they speak', *Nature*, **430**, pp. 410–11.

Blyton, P. and Turnbull, P. (1998) *The Dynamic of Employee Relations* (2nd edn), Basingstoke: Macmillan.

Bolden, R. and Gosling, J. (2006) 'Leadership competencies: time to change the tune?' *Leadership*, **2** (2), p. 160.

Bolman, L. G. and Deal, T. E. (1997) *Reframing Organizations*, San Francisco, Calif.: Jossey-Bass.

Bolton, S. and Boyd, C. (2003) 'Trolley dolly or skilled emotion manager? Moving on from Hochschild's managed heart.' *Work, Employment and Society* 17 (2), pp. 289–308.

Boud, D. and Garrick, J. (eds) (1999) *Understanding Learning at Work*. London: Routledge.

Bowen, D. E. and Ostroff, C. (2004) 'Understanding HRM–firm performance linkages: the role of the "strength" of the HRM system', *Academy of Management Review*, **29** (2), pp. 203–21.

Boxall, P. F. (1992) 'Strategic human resource management: beginnings of a new theoretical sophistication?' *Human Resource Management Journal*, **2** (3), pp. 60–79.

Boxall, P. F. (1995) 'Building the theory of comparative HRM', *Human Resource Management Journal*, **5** (5), pp. 5–17.

Boyce, T. (2002) 'The power is in parsimony: commentary on Goltz's operant analysis of power interpretation of resistance to change', *Journal of Organizational Behavior Management*, **22** (3), pp. 23–7.

Bradley, H. (1986) 'Technological change, management strategies, and the development of gender-based job segregation in the labour process', pp. 54–73 in D. Knights and H. Willmott (eds), *Gender and the Labour Process*, Aldershot: Gower.

Bratton, J. (1992) *Japanization at Work*, Basingstoke: Macmillan.

Bratton, J. (1999) 'Gaps in the workplace learning paradigm: labour flexibility and job design', in C*onference Proceeding of Researching Work and Learning*, First International Conference, University of Leeds: UK.

Bratton, J. (2001) 'International strategic human resource management: integrating human intelligence and strategic management', pp. 18–43 in J. Kidd, Xue Li and F. J. Richter (eds), *Maximizing Human Intelligence Deployment in Asian Business,* Basingstoke, Palgrave Macmillan.

Bratton, J. and Garrett-Petts, W. (2003) 'Learning together: culture-based lifelong learning and the economic development of Canadian small cities', pp. 78–86 in *Proceedings of the Third International Conference on Researching Work and Learning*, University of Tampere, Finland.

Bratton, J. and Garrett-Petts, W. (2005) 'Art at work: culture-based learning and the economic development of Canadian small cities', pp.111–27 in W. F. Garrett-Petts (ed.), *The Small Cities Book*, Vancouver: New Star Books.

Bratton, J. and Gold, J. (2003) *Human Resource Management: Theory and practice* (3rd edn), Basingstoke: Palgrave.

Bratton, J. and Gold, J. (2007) *Human Resource Management: Theory and practice* (4th edn), Basingstoke: Palgrave.

Bratton, J., Grint, K. and Nelson, D. (2005) *Organizational Leadership*, Mason, Oh.: Thomson-South-Western.

Bratton, J., Helms Mills, J. and Sawchuk, P. (2003) *Workplace Learning: A critical introduction*. Toronto: Garamond.

Bratton, J., Helms Mills, J., Pyrch, T. and Sawchuk, P. (2004) *Workplace Learning: A critical introduction*, Toronto: Garamond Press.

Braverman, H. (1974) *Labor and Monopoly Capitalism: The degradation of work in the twentieth century*, New York: Monthly Review Press.

Brewis, J. and Linstead, S. (2000) *Sex, Work and Sex Work: Erotizing oganization*, London: Routledge.

Brewster, C. (2001) 'HRM: the comparative dimension', pp. 255–71 in J. Storey (ed.), *Human Resource Management: A critical text*, London: Thompson Learning.

Brief, A., Dietz, J., Cohen, R., Pugh, S. D. and Vaslow, J. (2000) 'Just doing business: modern racism and obedience to authority as explanations for employment discrimination', *Organizational Behavior and Human Decision Processes*, **81** (1), pp. 72–97.

Broadbeck, F. C., Frese, M. and Akerblom, S. (2000) 'Culture variation of leadership prototypes across 22 European countries,' *Journal of Occupational and Organizational Psychology*, **73** (1), pp. 1–29.

Brockmann, E. N. and Anthony, W. P. (1998) 'The influence of tacit knowledge and collective mind on strategic planning', *Journal of Managerial Issues*, 10 (Spring), pp. 204–22.

Bronfenbrenner, K. (2003) 'Organizing women: the nature and process of union organizing efforts among US women workers since the mid-1990s', paper presented at the Cornell ILR Conference on Women and Unions, Ithaca, NY (November).

Brookfield, S. (1986) *Understanding and Facilitating Adult Learning: A comprehensive analysis of principles and effective practices*, San Francisco, Calif.: Jossey-Bass.

Brooks, A. and Watkins, K. E. (1994) 'The emerging power of action inquiry technologies', *New Directions for Adult and Continuing Education*, 63, pp. 131–43.

Brooks, E. (2002) 'The ideal sweatshop? Gender and transnational protest', *International Labor and Working-Class History*, **61**, pp. 91–111.

Brown, D. (1987) 'The status of Holland's theory of career choice', *Career Development Journal*, September, pp. 13–23.

Brown, J. S., Collins, A. and Duguid, S. (1989) 'Situated cognition and the culture of learning', *Educational Researcher*, **18** (1), pp. 32–42.

Brown, R. K. (1992) *Understanding Industrial Organizations*, London: Routledge.

Bruyere, S. (2000) *Disability Employment Policies and Practices in Private and Federal Sector Organizations* (March), Ithaca, N.Y.: Cornell University, Program on Employment and Disability, School of Industrial and Labor Relations.

Brym, R., Lie, J., Nelson, A., Guppy, N. and McCormick, C. (2003) *Sociology: Your compass for a new world*, Scarborough, ON: Thomson Wadsworth.

Bryman, A. (1996) 'Leadership in organizations', pp. 276–92 in S. R. Clegg, C. Hardy and W. R. Nord (eds) *Handbook of Organizational Studies*, London: Sage.

Bryman, A. and Teevan, J. (2005), *Social Research Methods*, Oxford: Oxford University Press.

Bryson, V. (2003) *Feminist Political Theory* (2nd edn), Basingstoke: Palgrave.

Buchanan, D. (2000) 'An eager and enduring embrace: the ongoing rediscovery of teamworking as a management idea', in S. Procter and F. Mueller (eds), *Teamworking*, London: Macmillan.

Burawoy, M. (1979) *Manufacturing Consent*, Chicago: University of Chicago Press.

Burke, B., Geronimo, J., Martin, D., Thomas, B. and Wall, C. (2003) *Education for Changing Unions*, Toronto: Between the Lines Press.

Burke, W., Richley, E. A. and DeAngelis, L. (1985) 'Changing leadership and planning processes at the Lewis Research Center, National Aeronautics and Space Administration', *Human Resource Management*, **24** (1), pp. 81–90.

Burns, J. M. (1978) *Leadership*, New York: Harper and Row.

Burns, T. and Stalker, G. M. (1961) *The Management of Innovation*, London: Tavistock.

Burrell, G. and Morgan, G. (1979) *Sociological Paradigms and Organizational Analysis*, London: Heinemann.

Burris, B. (1999) 'Braverman, Taylorism and technocracy', in M. Wardell, T. Steiger and P. Meiksins (eds), *Rethinking the Labor Process*, New York: SUNY.

Buyens, D. and De Vos, A. (2001) 'Perceptions of the value of the HR function', *Human Resource Management Journal*, **11** (3), pp. 70–89.

Byers, P. Y. (ed.) (1997) *Organizational Communication: Theory and behaviour*, Boston: Allyn & Bacon.

Cadbury, A. (1987) 'Ethical managers make their own rules', *Harvard Business Review*, September/October, pp. 69–73.

Caffarella, R. (1993) 'Self-directed learning', *New Directions for Adult and Continuing Education*, **57**, pp. 25–35.

Calás, M. B. and Smircich, L. (1996) 'From the woman's point of view: feminist approaches to organization studies', pp. 212–51 in S. Clegg and C. Hardy (eds), *Studying Organization: Theory and method*, Thousand Oaks, Calif.: Sage.

Caldwell, R. (2001) 'Champions, adaptors, consultants and synergists: the new change agents in HRM', *Human Resource Management Journal*, **11** (3), pp. 39–52.

Callaghan, G. and Thompson, P. (2001) 'Edwards revisited: technical control and worker agency in call centres', *Economic and Industrial Democracy*, **22**, pp. 13–37.

Callon, M. (1992) 'The dynamics of techno-economic networks', pp.72–102 in R.

Camilleri, J. M. (1999) 'Disability: a personal odyssey', *Disability and Society*, **14** (4), pp. 79–93.

Canavor, N. and Meirowitz, C. (2005) 'Good corporate writing: why it matters and what to do', *Communication World*, **22**, July, p. 4.

Capobianco, S., Davis, M. H. and Kraus, L. A. (2000) *Conflict Dynamics Profile Technical Guide*, St Petersburg, Fl.: Management Development Institute.

Cappelli, P. and Singh, H. (1992) 'Integrating strategic human resources and strategic management', pp. 165–92 in D. Lewin, O. S. Mitchell and P. Sherer (eds), *Research Frontiers in Industrial Relations and Human Resources*, Madison, Wisc.: Industrial Relations Research Association.

Carlson, N., Buskist, W., Enzle, M. and Heth, C. (2005) *Psychology* (3rd edn), Toronto: Pearson Education.

Carlson, S. (1951) *Executive Behaviour: A study of the workload and working methods of managing directors*, Stockholm: Stromberg.

Carnoy, M., Pollack, S. and Wong, P. L. (1993) *Labour Institutions and Technological Change: A framework for analysis and a review of the literature*, Stanford University/International Labour Organization.

Carr, E. H. (1961) *What is History?* Basingstoke: Macmillan.

Carrington, W. and Troske, K. (1998) 'Sex segregation in U.S. manufacturing', *Industrial and Labor Relations Review*, **51** (3), pp. 445–65.

Carroll, W. K. (2004) *Corporate Power in a Globalizing World: A study of elite social organization*, Don Mills: Oxford University Press.

Castells, M. (1996) *The Rise of the Network Society, Vol.1*, Oxford: Blackwell.

Castells, M. (2000) 'Information technology and global capitalism', pp. 52–74 in W. Hutton and A. Giddons (eds), *On the Edge: Living with global capitalism*, London: Cape.

Chafetz, J. (1988) *Feminist Sociology: An overview of contemporary theories*, Itasca, Ill.: Peacock.

Champy, J. (1996) *Reengineering Management*, New York: HarperCollins.

Chandler, A. (1962) *Strategy and Structure*. Cambridge, Mass.: MIT Press.

Charles, N. and James, E. (2003) 'The gender dimensions of job insecurity in the local labour market', *Work, Employment and Society*, **17** (3), pp. 531–52.

Charmaz, K. (2005) 'Grounded theory: objectivist and constructivist methods', pp. 509–35 in N. Denzin and Y. Lincoln (eds), *Handbook of Qualitative Research* (2nd edn), Thousand Oaks, Calif.: Sage.

Chartered Institute of Personnel and Development (CIPD) (2000) *People Implications of Mergers and Acquisitions, Joint Ventures and Divestments: Survey report*, London: CIPD.

Chew Keng Howe, I. et al. (1990) 'The role of culture in training in a multinational context', *Journal of Management Development*, **15** (2).

Child, J. (1972) 'Organizational structure, environment and performance: the role of strategic choice', *Sociology*, **6** (1), pp. 331–50.

Child, J. (1984) *Organization* (2nd edn), London: Harper & Row.

Chomsky, N. (1999) *Profit Over People*, New York: Seven Stories Press.

Christiansen, C. H. and Townsend, E. A. (2004) *Introduction to Occupation: The art and science of living*, Upper Saddle River, N.J.: Prentice Hall.

Clark, T. and Pugh, D. (2000) 'Similarities and differences in European conceptions of human resource management', *International Studies of Management and Organizations*, **29** (4), pp. 84–100.

Clarke, J. and Koonce, R. (1995) 'Engaging organizational survivors', *Training and Development*, **49** (8), pp. 22–30.

Clarke, L. (1997) 'Changing work systems, changing social relations? A Canadian General Motors Plant', *Relations Industrielle/Industrial Relations*, **52** (4), pp. 839–65.

Clarke, M. C. (1993) 'Transformational learning', pp. 47–56 in S. Merriam (ed.), *An Update on Adult Learning Theory*, San Francisco, Calif.: Jossey-Bass.

Clarke, P. (2005) 'The supervision of learning projects in British Columbia: the New Panopticon', *Our Schools*, **14** (3), p. 52.

Clarke, T. and Clements, L. (1977) *Trade Unions under Capitalism*, London: Fontana.

Clarkson, L.A. (1971) *The Pre-Industrial Economy of England, 1500–1750*, London: Batsford.

Clegg, S. (1989) *Frameworks of Power*, London: Sage.

Clegg, S. and Dunkerley, D. (1980) *Organization, Class and Control*, London: Routledge & Kegan Paul.

Clegg, S. and Hardy, C. (1999) *Studying Organization: Theory and method*, Thousand Oaks, Calif.: Sage.

Clegg, S., Hardy, C. and Nord, W. (eds) (1999) *Managing Organizations: Current issues*, Thousand Oaks, Calif.: Sage.

Cockburn, C. (1983) *Brothers: Male domination and technological change*, London: Pluto.

Cockburn, C. (1985) *Machinery of Dominance: Men, women and technical know-how,* London: Pluto.

Cockburn, C. (1991) *In the Way of Women: Men's resistance to sex equality in organizations*, Basingstoke: Macmillan.

Coe, R. M. (1990) *Process, Form, and Substance: A rhetoric for advanced writers* (2nd edn), N.J.: Prentice Hall.

Cohen, M. D., March, J. G. and Olsen, P. (1972) 'A garage can model of organizational choice', *Administrative Science Quarterly*, **17**, pp. 1–25.

Cohen, M. and Sproull, L. (eds) (1996) *Organizational Learning*, Thousand Oaks, Calif.: Sage.

Cohen, P. S. (1968) *Modern Social Theory*, London: Heinemann.

Cohen, S. G. and Bailey, D. E. (1997) 'What makes team work: group effectiveness research from the shopfloor to the executive suite', *Journal of Management*, **23** (3), pp. 239–90.

Cohen-Charash, Y. and Spector, P. (2001) 'The role of justice in organizations: a meta-analysis', *Organizational Behavior and Human Decision Processes*, **86** (2), pp. 278–321.

Colarelli, S., Spranger, J. and Hechanova, M. (2006) 'Women, power, and sex composition in small groups: an evolutionary perspective', *Journal of Organizational Behaviour*, **27** (2), pp. 163–84.

Coleman, A. and Fararo, T. (eds) (1991) *Rational Choice Theory*, Berkeley, Calif.: University of California Press.

Collins, J. (2002) 'Level 5 leadership' (online) www.jcollins.com/lab/level5/p3.html

Collins, M. (1991) *Adult Education as a Vocation: A critical role for the adult educator*, London: Routledge.

Collinson, D. (1994) 'Strategies of resistance: power, knowledge and subjectivity in the workplace', pp. 25–68 in J. Jermier, D. Knights and W. Nord (eds), *Resistance and Power in Organizations*, New York: Routledge.

Colquitt, J., Scott, B., Judge, T. and Shaw, J. (2006) 'Justice and personality: using integrative theories to derive moderators of justice effects', *Organizational Behaviour and Human Decision Processes*, **100** (1), pp. 110–27.

Colquitt, J. A., Conlon, D. E., Wesson, M. J., Porter, C. O. L. H. and Ng, K. Y. (2001) 'Justice at the millennium: a meta-analytic review of 25 years of organizational justice research', *Journal of Applied Psychology*, **86** (3), pp. 425–45.

Conger, J. A. (1988) *The Charismatic Leader: Behind the mystique of exceptional leadership*, San Francisco: Jossey-Bass.

Connelly, C. and Gallagher, D. (2004) 'Emerging trends in contingent work research', *Journal of Management*, **30** (6), pp. 959–83.

Conti, R. F. and Warner, M. (1994) 'Taylorism, teams and technology in "reengineering" work-organization', *New Technology, Work and Employment*, **9** (2), pp. 93–102.

Coopey, J. (1996) 'Crucial gaps in the 'learning organization', in K. Starkey (ed.), *How Organizations Learn*, London: International Thomson Business Press.

Coyle-Shapiro, J. A.-M., Shore, L., Taylor, M. S. and Tetrick, L. (2005) *The Employment Relationship*, Oxford: Oxford University Press.

Craft, M. and Craft, A. (1983) 'The participation of ethnic minorities in further and higher education', *Educational Researcher*, **259** (1), pp. 45–51.

Craib, I. (1997) *Classical Social Theory*, Oxford: Oxford University Press.

Craig, J. and Yetton, P. (1993) 'Business process redesign: a critique of *Process Innovation* by Thomas Davenport as a case study in the literature', *Australian Journal of Management*, **17** (2), pp. 285–306.

Crane D (ed.) (1994) *The Sociology of Culture*, Cambridge, Mass.: Blackwell.

Crawley, J. (1978). 'The lifestyles of the group', *Small Groups Newsletter*, **2** (1), pp. 26–39.

Cray, D. (1998) 'Culture', pp. 3–8 in M. Poole and M. Warner (eds), *The IEBM Handbook of Human Resource Management*, London: Thomson Business Press.

Cressey, P. (1993) 'Kalmar and Uddevalla: the demise of Volvo as a European icon', *New Technology, Work and Employment* (8), pp. 88–96.

Cressey, P. and Di Martino, V. (1991) *Agreement and Innovation: The international dimension of technological change*, New York: Prentice Hall.

Cropanzano, R. and Greenberg, J. (1997) 'Progress in organizational justice: tunneling through the maze' pp. 317–72 in C. L. Cooper and I. T. Robertson (eds), *International Review of Industrial and Organizational Psychology*, New York: Wiley.

Crow, G. (2005) *The Art of Sociological Argument*, Basingstoke: Palgrave.

Crowley S. and Hawhee, D. (1999) *Ancient Rhetorics for Contemporary Students*, Needham Heights, Mass.: Allyn & Bacon.

Cullen, D. (1994) 'Feminism, management and self-actualization', *Gender, Work and Organization*, **1** (3), pp. 127–37.

Cullen, D. (1997) 'Maslow, monkeys and motivation theory', *Organization*, **4** (30), pp. 355–73.

Cully, M., Woodland, S., O'Reilly, A. and Dix, G. (1999) *Britain at Work*, London: Routledge.

Cunliffe, A. L. (2001) 'Managers as practical authors: reconstructing our understanding of management practice', *Journal of Management Studies*, **38** (3), pp. 351–72.

Curtiss, S. (1977) *Genie: A psycholinguistic study of a modern-day 'wild child'*, New York: Academic Press.

Cyert, R. M. and March, J. G. (1963) 'A behaviour theory of organizational objectives', in M. Haire (ed.), *Modern Organizational Theory*, New York: Wiley.

Daft, R. (2001) *Organization Theory and Design* (7th edn), Cincinnati, Oh.: South-Western.

Daft, R. L. and Huber, G. P. (1987) 'How organizations learn: a communication framework', *Research in the Sociology of Organizations*, **5**, pp. 1–36.

Dahl, R. A. (1957) 'On the concept of power', *Behavioral Science*, **2**, pp. 201–15.

Dahrendorf, R. (1959) *Class and Class Conflict in an Industrial Society,* London: Routledge & Kegan Paul.

Dalen, L. H., Stanton, N. A. and Roberts, A. D. (2001) 'Faking personality questionnaires in personal selection', *Journal of Management Development*, **20** (8), pp. 729–41.

Dalton, M. (1959) *Men Who Manage*, New York: McGraw-Hill.

Dalton, M. and Wilson, M. (2000) 'The relationship of the five-factor model of personality to job performance for a group of Middle Eastern expatriate managers', *Journal of Cross-Culture Psychology*, March, pp. 250–58.

Daniel, W. W. (1973) 'Understanding employee behaviour in its context', in J. Child (ed.), *Man and Organization*, London: Allen & Unwin.

Darrah, C. (1994) 'Skill requirements at work: rhetoric versus reality', *Work and Occupations*, **21** (1), pp. 64–84.

Darrah, C. (1996) *Learning and Work: An exploration in industrial ethnography,* New York: Garland.

Darrah, C. (1999) *Learning Tools Within a Context: History and scope*, Washington, D.C.: U.S. Department of Education, National Institute on Postsecondary Education, Libraries, and Lifelong Learning (PLLI) of the U.S. Department of Education.

Davidow, W. H. and Malone, M. S. (1992) *The Virtual Corporation: Structuring and revitalizing the corporation for the 21st century*, New York: Harper Business.

Davis, C. (2002) "Shape or fight?': New York's black longshoremen, 1945–1961', *International Labor and Working-Class History*, **62**, pp. 143–63.

Davis, K. (1940) 'Extreme social isolation of a child', *American Journal of Sociology*, **45** (4), pp. 554–65.

De Dreu, C. and Van de Vliert, E. (eds) (1997) *Using Conflict in Organizations*, London: Sage.

Deal, T. E. and Kennedy, A. A. (1982) *Organization Cultures: The rites and rituals of organizational life*, Reading, Mass.: Addison-Wesley.

Deal, T. E. and Kennedy, A. A. (2000) *The New Corporate Cultures, New York: Texere.*

Dean, J. W. Jr. and Sharfman, M. P. (1996). 'Does decision process matter? A study of strategic decision making effectiveness', *Academy of Management Journal*, **39** (2), pp. 368–96.

Delaney, T. (2004) *Classical Social Theory: Investigation and application*, Upper Saddle River, NJ: Pearson/Prentice-Hall.

Delbridge, R. and Whitfield, K. (2001) 'Employee perceptions of job influence and organizational participation', *Industrial Relations*, **40** (3), pp. 472–89.

Den Hartog, D. N. and Verburg, R. M. (2004) 'High performance work systems, organizational culture and firm effectiveness', *Human Resource Management Journal*, **14** (1), pp. 55–78.

Dennis, A. R. and Valacich, J. S. (1999) 'Electronic brainstorming: illusions and patterns of productivity', *Information Systems Research*, **10** (2), pp. 375–7.

Despres, C. and Hiltrop, J-M. (1995) 'Human resource management in the knowledge age: current practice and perspectives on the future', *Employee Relations,* **17** (1), pp. 9–23.

Devine, W. (1983) 'From shafts to wires: historical perspective on electrification', *Journal of Economic History,* **43**, pp. 347–72.

Dex, S. (1988) 'Gender and the labour market', pp. 281–309 in D. Gallie (ed.), *Employment in Britain*, Oxford: Blackwell.

Dickens, L. (1994) 'Wasted resources? Equal opportunities in employment', in K. Sisson (ed.), *Personnel Management: A comprehensive guide to theory and practice in Britain,* Oxford: Blackwell.

Dickens, L. (1998) 'What HRM means for gender equality', *Human Resource Management Journal,* **8** (1), pp. 23–45.

Dixon, N. (1992) 'Organizational learning: a review of the literature with implications for HRD professionals', *Human Resource Development Quarterly*, **3**, pp. 29–49.

Dobb, M. (1963) *Studies in the Development of Capitalism*, London: Routledge.

Dobbin, F. (2005) 'Is globalization making us all the same?', *British Journal of Industrial Relations,* **43** (4) pp. 569–76.

Doeringer, P. B. and Piore, M. (1971) *Internal Labor Markets and Manpower Analysis*, Lexington, Mass.: C. Heath.

Dombrowski, K. (2002) 'Bill Budd, choker-setter: native culture and Indian work in the Southeast Alaska timber industry', *International Labor and Working-Class History,* **62**, pp. 121–42.

Dougherty, D. (1999) 'Organizing for innovation', in S. Clegg, C. Hardy and W. Nord (eds), *Managing Organizations: Current issues*, Thousand Oaks, Calif.: Sage.

Douglas, J., Ross, J. and Simpson, H. (1968) *All Our Future*, London: Peter Davies.

Drazin, R. Gylnn, M. A. and Kazanjian, R. (1999) 'Multilevel theorizing about creativity in organizations: a sensemaking perspective', *Academy of Management Review*, April, pp. 286–307.

Driver, M. (2002a) 'Learning and leadership in organizations', *Management Learning*, **33** (1), pp. 99–126.

Driver, M. (2002b) 'The learning organization: Foucaldian gloom or utopian sunshine?' *Human Relations*, **55** (1), pp. 33–53.

Drucker, P. (1954/1993) *The Practice of Management*, New York: HarperCollins.

Drucker, P. F. (1997) 'Toward the new organization', pp. 1–5 in F. Hesselbein, M. Goldsmith and R. Beckhard (eds), *The Organization of the Future*, San Francisco, Calif.: Jossey-Bass.

Drucker, P. (1999) *Management Challenges for the 21st Century*, New York: Harper Business.

Du Gay, P. (1996) *Consumption and Identity at Work*, London: Sage

Dunkerley, K. J. and Robinson, P. (2002) 'Similarities and differences in perceptions and evaluations of the communication styles of American and British managers', *Journal of Language and Social Psychology*, **21**, pp. 393–409.

Dunlop, J. T. (1958) *Industrial Relations System*, New York: Holt.

Durkheim, E. (1893/1997) *The Division of Labor in Society*, New York: Free Press.

Dyck, R. (2000) *Canadian Politics* (3rd edn), Scarborough, ON: Nelson.

Easterby-Smith, M., Thorpe, R. and Lowe, A. (1991) *Management Research: An introduction*, London: Sage.

Edwards, P. K., Geary, J. and Sisson, K. (2001) 'Employee involvement in the workplace: transformative, exploitative or limited and controlled? in J. Bélanger, G. Murray and P.-A. Lapointe (eds), *Work and Employment Relations in the High Performance Workplace*, London: Cassell/Mansell.

Ehn, P. (1988) *Work-Oriented Design of Computer Artifacts*, Stockholm: Arbetslivscentrum.

Eisenberg, E. M. and Goodall, H. L. (2004) *Organizational Communication: Balancing creativity and constraint* (4th edn), New York: St Martin's Press.

Elangovan, A. R. and Xie, J. L. (1999) 'Effects of perceived power of supervisor on subordinate stress and motivation: the moderating role of subordinate characteristics', *Journal of Organizational Behavior*, **20** (3), pp. 359–74.

Elenkov, D. (1998) 'Can American management concepts work in Russia? A cross-cultural comparative study', *California Management Review*, **40** (4), pp. 133–56.

Elger, T. and Smith, C. (eds) (1994) *Global Japanization?* London: Routledge.

Ellis, A. P. J., West, B. J., Ryan, A. M. and DeShon, R. P. (2002) 'The use of impression management tactics in structured interviews: a function of question type?' *Journal of Applied Psychology*, **87**, pp. 1200–08.

Ellis, V. and Taylor, P. (2006) '"You don't know what you've got till it's gone": recontextualising the origins, development and impact of the call centre', *New Technology, Work and Employment*, **21** (2), pp. 107–22.

Ellul, J. (1964) *The Technological Society*, New York: Vintage.

Engeström, Y. (1987) *Learning by Expanding: An activity-theoretical approach to developmental research*. Helsinki: Orienta-Konsultit.

Engeström, Y. (1994) *Training for Change: New approaches to instruction and learning*, Geneva: International Labour Office.

Engeström, Y. (2001) 'Expansive learning at work: toward an activity theoretical reconceptualization', *Journal of Education and Work*, **14** (1), pp. 133–56.

Engeström, Y. and Middleton, D. (1992) *Cognition and Communication at Work*, New York: Cambridge University Press.

Esland, G. and Salaman, G. (1980) *The Politics of Work and Occupations*, Milton Keynes: Open University Press.

Etzioni, A. (1988) *The Moral Dimension*, New York: Free Press.

Evans, A. L. and Lorange, P. (1989) 'The two logics behind human resource management', in P. Evans, Y. Doz and A. Laurent (eds), *Human Resource Management in International Firms*, Basingstoke: Macmillan.

Evans, J. (1983) 'Negotiating technological change', pp. 152–68 in H. J. Otway and M. Pletu (eds), *New Office Technology: Human and organizational aspects*, London: Frances Pinter.

Eysenck, H. (1953) *Uses and Abuses of Psychology*, Harmondsworth: Penguin.

Eysenck, H. J. (1970) *The Structure of Human Personality* (3rd edn), London: Methuen.

Eysenck, H. (1973) *The Inequality of Man*, London: Temple Smith.

Eysenck, M. W. and Keane, M. T. (2005) *Cognitive Psychology: A student's handbook* (5th edn), Hove: Lawrence Erlbaum.

Falkenberg, L. and Boland, L. (1997) 'Eliminating the barriers to employment equity in the Canadian workplace', *Journal of Business Ethics*, **16** (9), pp. 963–75.

Farmer, H. S. (1997) *Diversity and Women's Career Development: From adolescence to adulthood*, Thousand Oaks, Calif.: Sage.

Fayol, H. (1949) *General and Industrial Management*, London: Pitman.

Feenberg, A. (1991) *Critical Theory of Technology*, New York: Oxford University Press.

Feldman, D. C. (1984) 'The development and enforcement of group norms', *Academy of Management Review*, **1**, pp. 47–53.

Felstead, A. and Ashton, D. (2000) 'Tracing the links: organizational structures and skill demands', *Human Resource Management Journal*, **10** (3), pp. 5–20.

Felstead, A. and Jewson, N. (2000) *In Work, At Home*, London: Routledge.

Fenwick, T. (1998) 'Questioning the concept of the learning organization', pp. 140–52 in S. Scott, B. Spencer and A. Thomas (eds), *Learning for Life*, Toronto: Thompson Educational.

Ferlie, E. and Pettigrew, A. (1998) 'Managing through networks', pp. 200–22 in C. Mabey, G. Salaman and J. Storey (eds), *Strategic Human Resource Management: A reader*, London: Sage.

Fernie, S., Metcalfe, D. and Woodland, S. (1994) 'Does human resource management boost employee management relations?' London School of Economics CEP Working Paper 546, London: LSE.

Fiedler, F. E. (1964) *A Theory of Leader Effectiveness*, New York: McGraw-Hill.

Fiedler, F. E. (1965) 'Engineering the job to fit the manager,' *Harvard Business Review*, **43**, pp. 115–22.

Fiedler, F. E. (1967) *A Theory of Leadership Effectiveness*, New York: McGraw-Hill.

Fiedler, F. E. (1970) 'Leadership experience and leader performance: another hypothesis shot to hell', *Organizational Behaviour and Human Performance*, **5**, pp. 1–14.

Field, R. and House, R. (1995) *Human Behaviour in Organizations: A Canadian perspective*, Ontario: Prentice Hall.

Filipczak, P. (1996) 'The soul of the hog', *Training*, February (online) http:/proquest.umi.com

Fincham, R. and Rhodes, P. (2005) *Principles of Organizational Behaviour* (4th edn), Oxford: Oxford University Press.

Findlay, P., McKinlay, A., Marks, A. and Thompson, P. (2000) 'Flexible when it suits them: the use and abuse of teamwork skills', pp. 222–43 in S. Procter and F. Mueller (eds), *Teamworking*, London: Macmillan.

Finkelstein, J. (1995) *The Fashioned Self*, Cambridge: Polity.

Fischer, F. (1990) *Technocracy and the Politics of Expertise*, Newbury Park, Calif.: Sage.

Fiske, S. T. and Taylor, S. E. (1991) *Social Cognition* (2nd edn), New York: McGraw Hill.

Fitz-enz, J. (2000) *The ROI of Human Capital*, New York: AMACOM.

Fleck, J. (1993) 'Configurations: crystallizing contingency', *International Journal of Human Factors in Manufacturing*, **3** (1), pp. 15–36.

Fleishman, E. A. (1953) 'The description of supervisory behaviour', *Journal of Applied Psychology*, **37**, pp. 1–6.

Foley, G. (1998) *Learning in Social Action: A contribution to understanding informal education*, London: Zed.

Foley, G. (ed.) (2000) *Understanding Adult Education and Training* (2nd edn), London: Allen & Unwin.

Foley, G. (2001) *Strategic Learning: Understanding and facilitating organizational change*, Sydney: Centre for Popular Education.

Folger, R. and Cropanzano, R. (1998) *Organizational Justice and Human Resource Management*, Thousand Oaks, Calif.: Sage.

Fombrun, C. J., Tichy, N. M. and Devanna, M. A. (eds) (1984) *Strategic Human Resource Management*, New York and Chichester: Wiley.

Form, W., Kaufman, R., Parcel, T. and Wallace, M. (1988) 'The impact of technology on work organization and work outcomes', pp. 303–28 in G. Farkas and P. England (eds), *Industries, Firms and Jobs: Sociology and economic approaches*, New York: Plenum.

Forrester, K. (1999) 'Work-related learning and the struggle for subjectivity', in K. Forrester, N. Frost, D. Taylor and K. Ward (eds), *Proceedings of First International Conference: Researching Work and Learning*, Leeds, England: University of Leeds.

Foucault, M. (1977) *Discipline and Punish: The birth of the prison*, New York: Pantheon.

Foucault, M. (1979) *The History of Sexuality*, Harmondsworth: Penguin.

Foucault, M. (1980) *Power/Knowledge*, ed. C. Gordon, New York: Pantheon.

Foucault, M. (1986) *The Foucault Reader*, ed. P. Rabinow, Harmondsworth: Penguin.

Fox, A. (1971) *The Sociology of Work in Industry*, London: Collier Macmillan.

Fox, A. (1974) *Beyond Contract, Power, and Trust Relations*, London: Faber and Faber.

Francis, H. (2003) 'Teamworking and change: managing the contradictions', *Human Resource Management Journal*, **13** (3), pp. 71–89.

Franklin, U. (1990) *The Real World of Technology*, Toronto: CBC Enterprises.

Freedman, A. and Medway, P. (eds) (1994a) *Genre and the New Rhetoric*, London: Taylor & Francis.

Freedman, A. and Medway, P. (eds) (1994b) *Learning and Teaching Genre,* Portsmouth, N.H.: Heinemamn.

French, J. P. R. Jr. and Raven, B. (1960) 'The bases of social power', pp. 607–23 in D. Cartwright and A. Zander (eds), *Group Dynamics*, New York: Harper and Row.

Frese, M. (1982) 'Occupational socialization and psychological development: an underemphasized research perspective in industrial psychology', *Journal of Occupational Psychology*, **55**, pp. 209–24.

Friedman, A. (1977) *Industry and Labour: Class struggle at work and monopoly capitalism*, London: Macmillan.

Friedman, M. (1970) 'The social responsibility of business is to increase its profits', *New York Times Magazine*, 13 September, p. 32.

Friedmann, G. (1961) *The Anatomy of Work*, Glencoe, Ill.: Free Press.

Frost, P. J., Moore, L., Louis, M., Lundberg, C. and Martin, J. (1985) *Organizational Culture*, Beverly Hills, Calif.: Sage.

Fuller, A. and Unwin, L. (1998) 'Reconceptualising Apprenticeship: exploring the relationship between work and learning', *Journal of Vocational Education and Training,* **50** (2).

Furnham, A. F. (1997) 'Vocational preference and P–O fit', in J. Arnold (ed.), 'The psychology of careers in organizations,' *International Review of Industrial and Organizational Psychology*, **12**, pp. 1–37.

Gadiesh, O. and Olivet, S. (1997) 'Designing for implementability', pp. 53–78 in F. Hesselbein, M. Goldsmith and R. Beckhard (eds), *The Organization of the Future*, San Francisco: Jossey-Bass.

Gaertner, G. H. and Ramnarayan, S. (1983) 'Organizational effectiveness: an alternative perspective', *Academy of Management Review*, **8**, pp. 97–107.

Gagne, R. M. and Medsker, K. L. (1996) *The Conditions of Learning,* Fort Worth, Texas: Harcourt Brace.

Galabuzi, G-E. (2006) *Canada's Economic Apartheid: The social exclusion of racialized groups in the new century,* Toronto: Canadian Scholars' Press.

Galbraith, J. R. (1996) 'Designing the innovative organization', pp. 156–81 in K. Starkey (ed.), *How Organizations Learn*, London: International Thomson Business Press.

Gallie, D., Felstead, A. and Green, F. (2004) 'Changing patterns of task discretion in Britain', *Work, Employment and Society*, **18** (2), pp. 243–66.

Gamble, J. (2003) *Shanghai in Transition: Changing perspectives and social contours of a Chinese metropolis*, London/New York: Routledge Curzon.

Garavan, T. (1997) 'The learning organization: a review and evaluation', *Learning Organization,* **4** (1), pp. 18–29.

Gardner, J. W. (1990) *On Leadership*, New York: Free Press.

Garrick, J. (1998) *Informal Learning in the Workplace*, London: Routledge.

Gärtner, J. and Wagner, I. (1996) 'Mapping actors and agendas: political frameworks of systems design and participation', *Human–Computer Interaction*, **11**, pp. 187–214.

Gates, W., with Myhrvold, N. and Rinearson, P. (1996) *The Road Ahead*, New York: Penguin.

Gattiker, U. and Paulson, D. (1999) 'Unions and new office technology', *Relations Industrielles/ Industrial Relations*, **54** (2), pp. 245–76.

Geary, J. F. and Dobbins, A. (2001) 'Teamworking: a new dynamic in pursuit of management control', *Human Resource Management Journal*, **11** (1), pp. 3–23.

Gee, J., Hull, G. and Lankshear, C. (1996) *The New Work Order: Behind the language of the new capitalism*, Boulder, Colo.: Westview.

Geertz, C. (1973) *The Interpretation of Cultures*, New York: Basic Books.

Geller, E. S. (2002) 'Leadership to overcome resistance to change: it takes more than consequence control', *Journal of Organizational Behavior Management*, **22** (3), pp. 29–49.

Genovese, E. (1972) *Roll Jordan Roll: The world the slaves made*, New York: Vintage Books.

George, C. S. (1972) *The History of Management Thought* (2nd edn), Englewood Cliffs, NJ: Prentice-Hall.

Geppert, M. and Williams, K. (2006) 'Global, national and local practices in multinational corporations: towards a sociopolitical framework', *International Journal of Human Resource Management*, **17** (1), pp. 49–69.

Gersick, C.J. (1988) 'Time and transition in work teams: towards a new model of group development,' *Academy of Management Journal,* **31**, pp. 47–53.

Gherardi, S. (1994) 'The gender we think, the gender we do in our everyday organizational lives', *Human Relations*, **47** (6), pp. 591-606.

Giberson, T. R., Resick, C. and Dickson, M. (2005) 'Embedding leader characteristics: an examination of homogeneity of personality and values in organizations.' *Journal of Applied Psychology*, **90** (5), pp. 1002–10.

Giddens, A. (1971) *Capitalism and Modern Social Theory*, Cambridge: CUP.

Giddens, A. (1979) *Central Problems in Social Theory*, London: Macmillan.

Giddens, A. (1984) *The Constitution of Society,* Cambridge: Polity.

Giddens, A. (1985) *The Nation State and Violence: Volume Two of A Contemporary Critique of Historical Materialism,* Cambridge: Polity.

Giddens, A. (1989) *Sociology,* Cambridge: Polity.

Giddens, A. (1990) *The Consequences of Modernity,* Cambridge: Polity.

Giddens, A. (2001) *Sociology* (4th edn), Cambridge: Polity.

Gil, F., Rico, R., Alcover, C. M. and Barrasa, A. (2005) 'Change-oriented leadership, satisfaction and performance in work groups: effects of team climate and group potency,' *Journal of Managerial Psychology,* **20** (3/4), pp. 312–29.

Gilligan, C. (1982) *In a Different Voice*, Cambridge, Mass.: Harvard University Press.

Gilliland, S. W. and Chan, D. (2001) 'Justice in organizations: theory, methods and applications', in N. Anderson, D. Ones, H. K. Sinangil and C. Viswesveran (eds), *Handbook of Industrial, Work & Organizational Psychology, Volume 2: Organizational Psychology*, London: Sage.

Glenn, E. and Feldberg, R. (1979) 'Proletarianizing clerical work: technology and organizational control in the office', pp. 51–72 in A. Zimbalist (ed.), *Case Studies on the Labor Process*, New York: Monthly Review Press.

Glomb, T., Richmann, W., Hulin, C. and Drasgow, F. (1997) 'Ambient sexual harassment: an integrated model of antecedents and consequences', *Organizational Behavior and Hunan Decision Processes,* **71** (3), pp. 309–28.

Godard, J. (1991) 'The progressive HRM paradigm: a theoretical and empirical re-examination', *Relations Industrielles/Industrial Relations*, **46** (2), pp. 378–99.

Godard, J. (1992) 'Education vs. training in business schools', *Canadian Journal of Administrative Science*, **9**, pp. 238–52.

Godard, J. (2005) *Industrial Relations: The economy and society* (3rd edn), Concord, ON: Captus Press.

Goffman, E. (1959) *The Presentation of Self in Everyday Life*, New York: Anchor.

Goffman, E. (1967) *Interaction Ritual: Essays on face to face behavior*, New York: Anchor.

Gold, J. and Smith, V. (2003) 'Advances towards a learning movement: translations at work,' Human Resource Development International.

Goldberg, L. R. (1990) 'An alternative "description of personality": the Big-Five factor structure', *Journal of Personality and Social Psychology*, **59**, pp. 1216–29.

Goldthorpe, J., Lockwood, D., Bechhofer, F. and Platt, J. (1968) *The Affluent Worker: Industrial attitudes and behaviour,* Cambridge: CUP.

Goleman, D. (1998) 'What makes a leader?' *Harvard Business Review,* November-December, pp. 93–102.

Goltz, S. and Hietapelto, A. (2002) 'Using the operant and strategic contingencies models of power to understand resistance to change', *Journal of Organizational Behavior Management*, **22** (3), pp. 3–22.

Goodwin, G. A. and Scimecca, J. A. (2006) *Classical Social Theory*, Belmont, Calif.: Thomson.

Gordon, D. (1976) 'Capitalist efficiency and socialist efficiency', *Monthly Review*, **28**, pp. 19–39.

Gordon, J. R. and Whelan, K .S. (1998) 'Successful professional women in midlife: how organizations can more effectively understand and respond to the challenges', *Academy of Management Executive*, 12 (1), pp. 8–27.

Gorz, A. (1982) *Farewell to the Working Class*, London: Pluto.

Gospel, H. (ed.) (1991) *Industrial Training and Technological Innovation: A comparative and historical perspective*, London: Routledge & Kegan Paul.

Governance Network (2002) *At the Crossroads of Change: Human resources and the municipal sector,* Ottawa: Federation of Canadian Municipalities.

Grabb, E. G. (2002) *Theories of Social Inequalities*, Scarborough, ON: Nelson Thomson.

Gramsci, A. (1971) *Selections from the Prison Notebooks*, London: Lawrence & Wishart.

Granrose, C. S. (2001) 'The challenge of Confucius: the generalizability of North America career assumptions', in J. Kidd, X. Li and F.-J. Richter (eds), *Maximizing Human Intelligence Deployment in Asian Business: The sixth generation project,* Basingstoke: Palgrave.

Gray, R. and Robertson, L. (2005) 'Effective communication starts at the top', *Communication World*, **22**, July, p. 4.

Greenberg, J. and McCarty, C. L. (1987) 'A taxonomy of organizational justice theories', *Academy of Management Review*, **12**, pp. 9–22.

Greenhaus, J. H. (1987) *Career Management*, Chicago, Ill.: Dryden.

Grey, C. (2005) *A Very Short, Fairly Interesting and Reasonably Cheap Book about Studying Organizations*, London: Sage.

Grint, K. (1995) 'The culture of management and the management of culture', in *Management: A sociological introduction*, Cambridge: Polity.

Grint, K. (ed.) (1997) *Leadership.* Oxford: Oxford University Press.

Grint, K. (1998) *The Sociology of Work* (2nd edn), Cambridge: Polity.

Grint, K. (2000) *The Arts of Leadership,* Oxford: Oxford University Press.

Grint, K. (2001) *Leadership and Communication,* Oxford: Oxford University Press.

Grint, K. (2005a) *Leadership: Limits and possibilities*, Basingstoke: Palgrave Macmillan.

Grint, K. (2005b) 'Communications with followers' in J. Bratton, K. Grint and D. Nelson (eds), *Organizational Leadership*, Mason, Oh.: Thomson-South-Western.

Grint, K. and Willcocks, L. (1995) 'Business process re-engineering in theory and practice: business paradise regained?' *New Technology, Work and Employment*, **10** (2), pp. 99–108.

Grubb, N. (1996) *Learning to Work: The case for reintegrating job training and education*, New York: Russell Sage Foundation.

Guest, D. E. (1997) 'Human resource management and performance: a review and research agenda', *International Journal of Human Resource Management*, **8** (3), pp. 263–76.

Guest, D. E. (2000) 'Piece by piece', *People Management*, **6** (15), pp. 26–30.

Guest, D. E. and Conway, N. (2002) 'Communicating the psychological contract: an employer perspective', *Human Resource Management Journal*, **12** (2), pp. 22–38.

Guest, D. E., Michie, J., Conway, N. and Meehan, M. (2003). 'Human resource management and corporate performance in the UK', *British Journal of Industrial Relations*, **41** (2), pp. 291–314.

Guffey, M., Rhodes, K. and Rogin, P. (2005) *Business Communication: Process and product* (4th edn), Scarborough, ON: Thomson Nelson.

Gunderson, M., Ponak, A. and Taras, D. (eds) (2005) *Union-Management Relations in Canada* (5th edn), Toronto: Addison Wesley.

Guthrie, J. P (2001) 'High-involvement work practices, turnover, and productivity: evidence from New Zealand', *Academy of Management Journal*, **38** (3), pp. 171–88.

Guzzo, R. and Salas, E. (1995) *Team Effectiveness and Decision Making in Organizations*, San Francisco, Calif.: Jossey-Bass.

Haart, E. G. O.-de, Carey, D. P. and Milne, A. B. (1999) 'More thoughts on perceiving and grasping the Mueller-Lyer illusion', *Neuropsychologica*, **37**, pp. 1437–44.

Habermas, J. (1970) *Towards a Rational Society*, London: Heinemann.

Habermas, J. (1971) *Knowledge and Human Interests,* London: Heinemann.

Hacker, S. (1991) *Doing it the Hard Way: Investigations of gender and technology,* Winchester, Mass.: Unwin Hyman.

Hackman, J. and Oldham, G. (1980) *Work Redesign*, Reading, Mass.: Addison-Wesley.

Hales, C. (1986) 'What do managers do? A critical review of the evidence', *Journal of Management Studies*, **23**, pp. 88–115.

Hall, E. T. (1976) *Beyond Culture,* New York: Doubleday.

Hall, E. T. (1983) *The Dance of Life,* New York: Doubleday.

Hall, R. H. (1999) *Organizations: Structures, processes, and outcomes*, Englewood Cliffs, NJ: Prentice Hall.

Hambrick, D. C. (1989) 'Putting top managers back into the picture', *Strategic Management Journal*, Special issue, **10**, pp. 5–15.

Hamel, G. and Prahalad, C. K. (1994) *Competing for the Future*, Boston, Mass.: Harvard Business School Press.

Hammer, M. (1997) *Beyond Reengineering*, New York: HarperBusiness.

Hammer, M. and Champy, J. (1993) *Reengineering the Corporation*, London: Nicholas Brealey.

Handy, C. (1978) *Gods of Management,* London: Pan.

Handy, C. (1985) *Understanding Organizations*, London: Penguin.

Hansen, L. L. (2002) 'Rethinking the industrial relations tradition', *Employee Relations*, **24** (2), pp. 190–210.

Hanson, J. (2003) 'Fighting for the union label: the women's garment industry and the ILGWU in Pennsylvania', *Oral History Review*, **30** (1), pp. 143–58.

Hardill, I. and Green, A. (2003) 'Remote working – altering the spatial contours of work and home in the new economy', *New Technology, Work and Employment*, **18** (3), pp. 212–22.

Harding, K. (2003) 'Working with art', *Globe and Mail*, 20 August, p. C1.

Hardy, C. and Clegg, S.R. (1999) 'Some dare call it power', pp. 368–87 in S. R. Clegg and C. Hardy (eds), *Studying Organization*, London: Sage.

Harley, B., Hyman, J. and Thompson, P. (2005) *Participation and Democracy at Work*, Basingstoke: Palgrave.

Harrel, A. M. and Strahl, M. J. (1981) 'A behavioral decision theory approach to measuring McClelland's trichotomy of needs', *Journal of Applied Psychology*, **66**, pp. 242–7.

Harris, S. G. (1994) 'Organizational culture and individual sensemaking: a schema-based perspective,' *Organization Science*, **5**, pp. 309–21.

Harter, N. Ziolkowski, F. and Wyatt, S. (2006) 'Leadership and inequality', *Leadership*, **2** (3), pp. 275–93.

Hartmann, H. (2003) 'Closing the gap amidst ongoing discrimination: women and economic disparities', *Multinational Monitor*, **24** (5), pp. 25–7.

Haslam, S. A. (2001) *Psychology in Organizations: The social identity approach*, London: Sage.

Hassard, J. and Parker, M. (eds) (1993) *Postmodernism and Organizations*, London: Sage.

Hassard, J., Morris, J. and Sheehan, J. (2004) 'The "third way": the future of work and organization in a "corporatized" Chinese economy', *International Journal of Human Resource Management*, **15** (2), pp. 314–30.

Hayes, E. and Flannery, D. D. (2000) *Women as Learners: The significance of gender in adult learning*, San Francisco, Calif.: Jossey-Bass.

Healy, G., Hansen, L. L. and Ledwith, S. (2006) 'Editorial: still uncovering gender in industrial relations', *Industrial Relations Journal*, **37** (4), pp. 290–8.

Hearn, J., Sheppard, D., Tancred-Sheriff, P. and Burrell, G. (eds) (1989) *The Sexuality of Organization*, London: Sage.

Heath-Rawlings, J. (2003) '33% worry retirement finances too scant', *Globe and Mail*, 3 September, p. A6.

Heidegger, M. (1977) *The Question Concerning Technology*, New York: Harper and Row.

Helgesen, S. (1995) *The Female Advantage: Women's ways of leadership*, New York: Doubleday.

Heller, F., Pusic, E., Strauss, G. and Wilpert, B. (1998) *Organizational Participation: Myth and reality*, Oxford: Oxford University Press.

Hendry, C. and Pettigrew, A. (1990) 'Human resource management: an agenda for the 1990s', *International Journal of Human Resource Management*, **1** (1), pp. 17–44.

Herman, B. (2001) 'How high-road partnerships work', *Social Policy*, **31** (3), pp. 11–19.

Herrbach, O. and Mignonac, K. (2004) 'How organizational image affects employee attitudes', *Human Resource Management Journal*, **14** (4), pp. 76–88.

Herriot, P. (1998) 'The role of human resource management in building a new proposition', pp. 106–16 in P. Sparrow and M. Marchington (eds), *Human Resource Management: A new agenda*, London: Financial Times Management.

Hersey, P. and Blanchard, K. H. (1969) 'Life cycle theory of leadership', *Training and Development Journal*, **23**, pp. 26–34.

Hersey, P. and Blanchard, K. H. (2001) *Management of Organizational Behavior: Utilizing human resources* (8th edn), Upper Saddle River, NJ: Prentice Hall.

Hersey, P., Blanchard, K. H. and Johnson, D. (1977) *Management of Organizational Behavior: Utilizing human resources* (3rd edn), Upper Saddle River, NJ: Prentice Hall.

Hertog, J. F. and Tolner, T. (1998) 'Groups and teams', pp. 62–71 in M. Poole and M. Watner (eds), *The Handbook of Human Resource Management*, London: International Thomson Business Press.

Hertz, N. (2002) *The Silent Takeover: Global capitalism and the death of democracy*, London: Arrow.

Herzberg, F. (1968) 'One more time: how do you motivate employees?' *Harvard Business Review*, January–February, pp. 53–62.

Herzberg, F., Mansner, B. and Snyderman, B. (1959) *The Motivation to Work* (2nd edn), New York: Wiley.

Hesselbein, F., Goldsmith, M. and Beckhard, R. (eds) (0000) *The Organization of the Future*, San Francisco: Jossey-Bass.

Highhouse, S. (2001) 'Judgment and decision-making research: relevance to industrial and organizational psychology', in N. Anderson, D. Ones, H. K. Sinangil and C. Viswesveran (eds), *Handbook of Industrial Work and Organizational Psychology. Volume 2: Organizational Psychology*, London: Sage.

Hill, C. and Jones, G. (2004) *Strategic Management Theory*, New York: Houghton Mifflin.

Hinton, J. (1973) *The First Shop Stewards Movement*, London: Allen & Unwin.

Hirsch, B. and MacPherson, D. (2003) *Union Membership and Earnings Data Book: Compilations from the Current Population Survey*, Washington, D.C.: Bureau of National Affairs.

Hobsbawm, E. (1968) *Industry and Empire*, London: Weidenfeld & Nicolson.

Hobsbawm, E. (1994) *Age of Extremes*, London: Abacus.

Hobsbawm, E. (1997) *On History*, London: Weidenfeld & Nicolson.

Hochschild, A. (2003) *The Second Shift*, New York: Penguin.

Hockey, G. R. J. (2002) 'Human performance in the working environment', in P. Warr. (ed.), *Psychology at Work* (5th edn), London: Penguin.

Hockey, G. R. J., Wastell, D. G. and Sauer, J. (1998) 'Effects of sleep deprivation and user-interface on complex performance: A multilevel analysis of compensatory control', *Human Factors*, **40**, pp. 233–53.

Hodgkinson, G. (1997) 'Cognitive inertia in a turbulent market: the case of UK residential estate agent', *Journal of Management Studies*, **34**, pp. 921–45.

Hodson, R. (1999) 'Management citizenship behavior: a new concept and an empirical test', *Social Problems*, **46** (3), pp. 460–78.

Hodson, R. and Sullivan, T. A. (2002) *The Social Organization of Work* (3rd edn), Belmont, Calif.: Wadsworth/Thomson Learning.

Hoel, H. and Beale, D. (2006) 'Workplace bullying, psychological perspectives and industrial relations: towards a contextualized and interdisciplinary approach', *British Journal of Industrial Relations*, **44** (2), pp. 239–62.

Hoeve, A. and Nieuwenhuis, L. (2006) 'Learning routines in innovation processes', *Journal of Workplace Learning*, **18** (3), pp. 171–85.

Hofstede, G. (1984) *Culture's Consequences: International differences in work-related values*, Beverley Hills, Calif.: Sage.

Hofstede, G. (1993) 'Cultural constraints in management theories', *Academy of Management Executive*, **7** (1), pp. 81–94.

Hofstede, G. (1998a) 'Organization culture', pp. 237–55 in M. Poole and M. Warner (eds), *The Handbook of Human Resource Management*, London: International Thomson Business Press.

Hogg, M. and Terry, D. J. (2000) 'Social identity and self-categorization processes in organizational contexts', *Academy of Management Review*, **25**, pp. 121–40.

Hogg, M. A. and Vaughan, G. M. (2004) *Social Psychology: An introduction* (4th edn), Hemel Hempstead: Prentice Hall.

Holland, J. L. (1985) *Making Vocational Choices: A theory of vocational personalities and work environments* (2nd edn), Englewood Cliffs, NJ: Prentice Hall.

Hollway, W. (1991) *Work Psychology and Organizational Behaviour*, London: Sage.

Holman, D., Pavlica, K. and Thorpe, R. (1997) 'Rethinking Kolb's theory of experiential learning: the contribution of social constructivism and activity theory', *Management Learning*, **28**, pp. 135–48.

Hoogvelt, A. (2001) *Globalization and the Postcolonial World* (2nd edn), Basingstoke: Palgrave.

Horwitz, F. M., Chan Teng Heng and Quazi, H. A. (2003) 'Finders, keepers? Attracting, motivating and retaining knowledge workers', *Human Resource Management Journal*, **13** (4), pp. 23–44.

House, R. T. (1971) 'A path goal theory of leader effectiveness', *Administrative Science Quarterly*, **16**, pp. 321–38.

House, R. J. and Mitchell, T. R. (1974) 'Path-goal theory of leadership', *Journal of Contemporary Business*, **3**, pp. 81–97.

Houtenville, A. J. (2003) *Disability Statistics in the United States*, Ithaca, NY: Cornell University Rehabilitation Research and Training Center.

Howell, J. P., Bowen, D., Dorfman, P., Kerr, S. and Podsakoff, P. (1990) 'Substitutes for leadership: effective alternatives to ineffective leadership', *Organizational Dynamics*, **19**, pp. 21–38.

Howells, C. A. (1987) *Private and Fictional Words*, London: Methuen.

Hughes, T. (1983) *Networks of Power*, Baltimore, Md.: Johns Hopkins University Press.

Hulin, C. L. and Blood, M. R. (1968) 'Job enlargement, individual differences, and worker responses', *Psychological Bulletin*, **69**, pp. 41–55.

Hung, D. (1999) 'Activity, apprenticeship and epistemological appropriation: implications from the writings of…' *Educational Psychologist*, **34** (4), pp. 193-205.

Hung, D. and Chen, D. (2001) 'Appropriating and negotiating knowledge: technologies for a community of learners', *Educational Technology*, May–June, pp. 3–12.

Hurst, C. (2005) *Living Theory*, Boston, Mass.: Pearson.

Huselid, M. A. (1995) 'The impact of HRM practices on turnover, productivity, and corporate financial performance', *Academy of Management Journal*, **38** (3), pp. 635–72.

Hutchinson, S., Purcell, J., and Kinnie, N. (2000) 'Evolving high commitment management and the experience of the RAC call centre', *Human Resource Management Journal*, **10** (1), pp. 63–78.

Huy, Q. N. (2001) 'In praise of middle managers', *Harvard Business Review*, **79** (8), pp. 72–9.

Hyman, R. (1982) 'What ever happened to industrial sociology?' in D. Dunkerley and G. Salaman (eds), *The International Yearbook of Organisation Studies 1981*, London: Routledge & Kegan Paul.

Hyman, R. (1991) 'Plus ca charge? The theory of production and the production of theory', pp. 259–83 in A. Pollert (ed.), *Farewell to Flexibility?* Oxford: Blackwell.

Hyman, R. and Mason, B. (1995) *Managing Employee Involvement and Participation*, London: Sage.

Ichniowski, C., Kochan, T., Levine, D., Olson, C. and Strauss, G. (1996) 'What works at work: overview and assessment', *Industrial Relations*, **35** (3), pp. 299–333.

Institute of Personnel and Development (IPD) (1997) *Key Facts: Psychological testing*, London: IPD.

International Labor Organization (ILO) (2001) *World Employment Report*, Geneva: ILO.

Jackson, A. (2000) *The Myth of the Equity–Efficiency Trade-Off,* Ottawa: Canadian Council on Social Development.

Jackson, S. E. and Joshi, A. (2001) 'Research on domestic and international diversity in organizations: a merger that works', in N. Anderson, D. Ones, H. K. Sinangil and C. Viswesveran (eds), *Handbook of Industrial, Work and Organizational Psychology. Volume 2: Organizational Psychology*, London: Sage.

Jacoby, S. M. (2005) *The Embedded Corporation: Corporate governance and employment relations in Japan and the United States*, Princeton, NJ: Princeton University Press.

Jaffee, D. (2001) *Organization Theory: Tension and change*, Boston, Mass.: McGraw-Hill.

Janis, I. L. (1972) *Victims of Groupthink*, Boston, Mass.: Houghton Mifflin.

Jarvis, P. (1985) *The Sociology of Adult and Continuing Education,* London: Routledge.

Jarvis, P. (ed.) (1991) *Twentieth Century Thinkers in Adult Education,* London: Routledge.

Jessop, B., Bonnett, K., Bromley, S. and Ling, T. (1988) *Thatcherism*, Cambridge: Polity.

Jinkins, M. and Jinkins, D. B. (1998) *The Character of Leadership*, San Francisco, Calif.: Jossey-Bass.

Johns, G. and Saks, A. (2001) *Organizational Behaviour* (5th edn), Toronto: Addison-Wesley.

Johnson, D.W. and Johnson, F. P. (2000) *Joining Together: Group Theory and Group Skills* (7th edn), Boston: Allyn & Bacon.

Johnson, R., Selenta, C. and Lord, R. (2006) 'When organizational justice and the self-concept meet: consequences for the organization its members', *Organizational Behaviour and Human Decision Processes*, **99** (2), pp. 175–201.

Jones, B. (1988) 'Work and flexible automation in Britain: a review of developments and possibilities', *Work, Employment and Society*, **2** (4), pp. 451–86.

Jones, T. (1993) *Britain's Ethnic Minorities,* London: Policy Studies Institute.

Josselson, R. (1987) *Finding Herself: Pathways to identity development in women*, San Francisco, Calif.: Jossey-Bass.

Judt, T. (2005) *Postwar: A history of Europe since 1945*, New York: Penguin.

Kakabade, A., Myers, A., McMahon, T. and Spony, G. (1997) 'Top management styles in Europe: implications for business and cross-national teams', in K. Grint (ed.), *Leadership: Classical, contemporary, and critcal approaches*, Oxford: Oxford University Press.

Kanter, R. (1990) 'Motivation theory in industrial and organizational psychology,' pp. 75–170 in M. D. Dunnette and L. Hough (eds), *Handbook of Industrial and Organizational Psychology*, Palo Alto, Calif.: Consulting Psychology Press.

Kanungo, R. and Mendonca, M. (1992) *Compensation: Effective reward management,* Toronto: Butterworth.

Kasl, E., Marsick, V. and Dechant, K. (1997), 'Teams as learners', *Journal of Applied Behavioral Science*, **33** (2), June, pp. 227–46.

Katz, P. (1999) *The Scalpel's Edge: The culture of surgeons*, Boston, Mass.: Allyn and Bacon.

Katzenbach, J. R. and Smith, D. (1994) *The Wisdom of Teams*, New York: HarperBusiness.

Keats, B. W. and Hitt, M. (1988) 'A causal model of linkages among environmental dimensions, macro organizational characteristics, and performance', *Academy of Management Journal*, September, pp. 570–98.

Kelley, H. H. (1973) 'The process of causal attribution', *American Psychologist*, **28**, pp. 107–28.

Kelley, M. R. (1990) 'New process technology, job design and work organization: a contingency model', *American Sociological Review,* **55**, pp. 191–208.

Kelly, J. (1985) 'Management's redesign of work: labour process, labour markets and product markets,' in D. Knights, H. Willmott and D. Collinson (eds), *Job Redesign: Critical perspectives on the labour process,* Aldershot: Gower.

Kelly, J. (2005) 'Industrial relations approaches to the employment relationship,' pp. 48–64 in J. A-M. Coyle-Shapiro et al. (eds), *The Employment Relationship*, Oxford: Oxford University Press.

Kerr, C. (1962) *Industrialism and Industrial Man,* London: Heinemann.

Kersley, B., Alpin, C., Forth, J., Bryson, A., Bewley, H., Dix, G. and Oxenbridge, S. (2005) *Inside the Workplace: First Findings from the 2004 Workplace Employment Relations Survey (WERS 2004)*, London: Department of Trade and Industry.

Kersley, B. et al. (2006) *Inside the Workplace: Findings from the 2004 Workplace Employment Relations Survey (WERS 2004),* London: Routledge.

Khurana, R. (2002) 'The curse of the superstar CEO', *Harvard Business Review*, **80** (9), pp. 60–6.

Kidd, J., Xue, L. and Richter, F.-J. (2001) *Maximizing Human Intelligence Deployment in Asian Business*, Basingstoke: Palgrave Macmillan.

Kim, J. (2002) 'Taking note of the new gender earnings gap: a study of the 1990's economic expansion in the US labor market', *Journal of American Academy of Business,* **2** (1), pp. 80–5.

Kimmel, M. (2004) *The Gendered Society* (2nd edn), New York: Oxford University Press.

Kirkpatrick, D. (1994) *Evaluating Training Programs: The four levels*, San Francisco: Berrett-Koehler.

Kirkpatrick, S. A. and Locke, E. A. (1991) 'Leadership: do traits matter?' *The Executive,* **5**, pp. 48–60.

Kitayama, S., Markus, H. R., Matsumoto, H. and Norasakkunkit, V. (1997) 'Individual and collective processes in the construction of the self: self-enhancement in the United States and self-criticism in Japan',

Journal of Personality and Social Psychology, **72**, pp. 1245–67.

Kitchin, R., Shirlow, P. and Shuttleworth, I. (1998) 'On the margins: disabled people's experience of employment in Donegal, West Ireland', *Disability and Society,***13** (5), pp. 785–807.

Klein, H. J., Whitener, E. and Ilgen, D. (1990) 'The role of goal specificity in the goal-setting process', *Motivation and Emotion*, **14** (3), pp. 181–93.

Klein, J. (1994) '*Maintaining expertise in multi-skilled teams', Advances in Interdisciplinary Studies of Work Teams*, 1, pp. 145–65.

Klein, N. (2000) *No Logo*, London: Flamingo.

Kline, T, (1999) *Remaking Teams*, San Francisco, Calif.: Jossey-Bass.

Knights, D. and Willmott, H. (eds) (1986) *Gender and the Labour Process,* Aldershot: Gower.

Knights, D. and Willmott, H. (1992) 'Conceptualizing leadership processes: a study of senior managers in a finance services company', *Journal of Management Studies*, **29** (6), pp. 761-82.

Knowles, M. (1973) *The Adult Learner: A neglected species*, Houston, Texas: Gulf.

Knowles, M. (1975) *Self-Directed Learning*, New York: Associated Press.

Knowles, M. (1980) *The Modern Practice of Adult Education: From pedagogy to andragogy* (2nd edn), New York: Cambridge Books.

Kochan, T. and Dyer, L. (1995) 'HRM: an American view', in J. Storey (ed.), *Human Resource Management: A critical text*, London: Routledge.

Kochan, T. E., Katz, H. and McKersie, R. (1986) *The Transformation of American Industrial Relations,* New York: Basic Books.

Kocher, M. and Sutter, M. (2005) 'The decision maker matters: individual versus group behaviour in experimental beauty-contest games', *Economic Journal*.

Köhler, W. (1925) *The Mentality of Apes*, New York: Harcourt Brace.

Kolb, D. (1984) *Experiential Learning: Experience as the source of learning and development*, Englewood Cliffs, N.J.: Prentice-Hall.

Kondo, D. (1990) *Crafting Selves: Power, discourse and identity in a Japanese factory*, Chicago: University of Chicago Press.

Konzelmann, S. (2005) 'Varieties of capitalism: production and market relations in the USA and Japan', *British Journal of Industrial Relations*, **43** (4), pp. 593–603.

Kotter, J. P. (1979) *Power in Management*, New York: Amocom.

Kotter, J. P. (1982) *The General Managers*, New York: Free Press.

Kotter, J. P. (1990) *A Force for Change: How leadership differs from management*, New York: Free Press.

Kotter, J. P. (1996a) *Leading Change*, Boston, Mass.: Harvard Business School Press.

Kotter, J. P. (1996b) 'What leaders really do', in *Harvard Business Review on Leadership*, Boston, Mass.: Harvard Business School Press.

Kraft, P. (1977) *Programmers and Managers: The routinisation of computer programming in the United States*, New York: Springer-Verlag.

Krahn, H. and Lowe, G. (2002) *Work, Industry and Canadian Society* (4th edn), Toronto: Thomson Nelson.

Kramer, R. M. and Tyler, T. R. (1996) *Trust in Organizations: Frontiers of theory and research*, Newbury Park, Calif.: Sage.

Kraut, A., Pedigo, P., McKenna, D. and Dunnette, M. (1989) 'The role of the manager: what's really important in different managerial jobs', *Academy of Management Executive*, **3** (4), pp. 286–93.

Kray, L., Galinsky, A. and Thompson, L. (2002) 'Reversing the gender gap in negotiations: an exploration of stereotype regeneration', *Organizational Behavior and Human Decision Processes*, **87** (2), pp. 386–409.

Krippendorff, K. (1985) 'On the ethics of constructing communications', ICA presidential address, Honolulu, Hawaii, and quoted in E. M. Eisenberg and H. L. Goodall (2004) *Organizational Communication: Balancing creativity and constraint* (4th edn), p. 26, New York: St. Martin's Press.

Krippendorff, K. (1995) 'Undoing power', *Critical Studies in Mass Communication,* **12** (2), pp. 101–32.

Kuipers, B. S. and de Witte, M. C. (2005) 'Teamwork: a case study on development and performance', *International Journal of Human, Resource Management*, **16** (2), pp. 185–201.

Kumar, K. (1978) *Prophecy and Progress*, Harmondsworth: Penguin.

Lakoff, R. T. (1990) *Talking Power*, New York: Basic Books.

Lam, A. (2002) 'Alternative societal models of learning and innovation in the knowledge economy', *International Social Science Journal*, March, pp. 67–82.

Landes, D. S. (1969) *The Unbound Prometheus*, Cambridge: CUP.

Lane, H. and DiStefano, J. (eds) (1992) *International Management Behavior* (2nd edn), Boston, Mass.: PWS-Kent.

Latham, G. P. and Locke, E. A. (1990) *A Theory of Goal Setting and Task Performance*, Englewood Cliffs, N.J.: Prentice-Hall.

Latour, B. (2000) 'Technology is society made durable', pp. 41–53 in K. Grint (ed.), *Work and Society: A reader*, Cambridge, UK: Polity.

Lave (1988)

Lave, J. (1993) 'The practice of learning', in S. Chaiklin (ed.), *Understanding the Practice: Perspectives on activity and context,* Cambridge: Cambridge University Press.

Lave, J. and Wenger, E. (1991) *Situated Learning: Legitimate peripheral participation,* Cambridge, UK: CUP.

Lawler, E. E. (1971) *Pay and Organizational Effectiveness,* New York: McGraw-Hill.

Lawler, E. E. (1973) *Motivation in Work Organizations*, Monterey, Calif.: Brooks-Cole.

Lawler, E. E., Mohrman, S. and Ledford, G. (1998) *Strategies for High Performance Organizations,* San Francisco: Jossey-Bass.

Lawrence, P. R. and Lorsch, J. W. (1967) *Organisation and Environment: Managing differentiation and integration*, Cambridge, Mass.: Harvard University Press.

Lazonick, W. (1979) 'Industrial relations and technical change: the case of the self-acting mule', *Cambridge Journal of Economics*, **3**, pp. 231–62.

Lazonick, W. (1993) 'Learning and the dynamics of international competitive advantage', pp. 172–97 in R. Thomson (ed.), *Learning and Technological Change*, New York: St. Martin's Press.

Lee, R. and Lawrence, P. (1991) *Politics at Work*, London: Stanley Thornes.

Lee, S. and Klein, H. (2002) 'Relationships between conscientiousness, self-efficacy, self-description, and learning over time', *Journal of Applied Psychology*, **87** (6), pp. 1175–82.

Legge, K. (2000) 'The ethical context of HRM', pp. 23–40 in D. Winstanley and J. Woodall (eds), *Ethical Issues in Contemporary Human Resource Management*, Basingstoke: Palgrave.

Legge, K. (2005) *Human Resource Management: Rhetorics and realities (2nd edn)*, Basingstoke: Palgrave.

Leidner, R. (1993) *Fast Food, Fast Talk: Service work and the routinization of everyday life,* Berkeley, Calif.: University of California Press.

Leonard, D. and Sensiper, S. (1998) 'The role of tacit knowledge in group innovation', *California Management Review*, **40** (Spring), pp. 112–32.

Leontiev, A. N. (1978) *Activity, Consciousness, and Personality*, Englewood Cliffs, N.J.: Prentice Hall.

LePine, J., Hollenbeck, J., Ilgen, D. and Colquitt, J. (2002) 'Gender composition, situational strength, and team decision-making accuracy: a criterion decomposition approach', *Organizational Behavior and Human Decision Processes*, **88** (1), pp. 445–75.

Lester, S. W., Turnley, W. H., Bloodgood, J. M. and Bolino, M. (2002) 'Not seeing eye to eye: differences in supervisor and subordinate perceptions of and attributions for psychological contract breach', *Journal of Organizational Behavior*, **23**, pp. 39–56.

Leventhal, G. S., Karuza, J. and Fry, W. R. (1980) 'Beyond fairness: a theory of allocation preferences', pp.167–218 in G. Mikula (ed.), *Justice and Social Interaction,* New York: Springer-Verlag.

Lewin, K. (1935) *A Dynamic Theory of Personality*, New York: McGraw-Hill.

Lewin, K., Lippitt, R. and White, R. K. (1939) 'Patterns of aggressive behaviour in experimentally created social climates,' *Journal of Social Psychology,* **10**, pp. 271–99.

Lewis, R. (2004) *When Cultures Collide: Managing successfully across cultures,* London: Nicholas Brealey.

Lieberman, M.D. (2000) 'Intuition: a social cognitive neuroscience approach', *Psychological Bulletin*, **126**, pp. 109–37.

Limerick, D. (1990) 'Managers of meaning: from Bob Geldof's band to Australian CEOs,' *Organizational Dynamics*, **18** (4), pp. 22–33.

Lincoln, J. R. and Kalleberg, A. L. (1990) *Culture, Control and Commitment*, New York: CUP.

Linehan, M. (2005) 'Women in international management', pp. 181–201 in H. Scullion and M. Linehan (eds), *International Human Resource Management*, Basingstoke: Palgrave Macmillan.

Lindeman, E. (1926) *The Meaning of Adult Education*, New York: New Republic.

Linden, M. V. (1995) *Racism and the Labour Market: Historical studies,* New York: Bern.

Lipsey, R. G., Bekar, C. and Carlaw, K. (1998) 'What requires explanation?' in E. Helpman (ed.), *General Purpose Technologies and Economic Growth*, Cambridge, Mass.: MIT Press.

Littler, C. R. (1982) *The Development of the Labour Process in Capitalist Societies,* London: Heinemann.

Littler, C. R. and Salaman, G. (1982) 'Braverman and beyond: recent theories of the labour process', *Sociology*, **16**, pp. 251–69.

Littler, C. R. and Salaman, G. (1984) *Class at Work: The design, allocation and control of jobs*, London: Batsford.

Livingstone, D. (1999) *The Education Jobs Gap*, Toronto: Garamond.

Livingstone, D. and Sawchuk, P. (2004) *Hidden Knowledge: Organized labour in the information age*, Toronto: Garamond/Washington, D.C.: Rowman & Littlefield.

Locke, E. A. (1968) 'Towards a theory of task motivation and incentives', *Organization Behavior and Human Performance*, **3**, pp. 152–89.

Lopez, J. (2003) *Society and its Metaphors: Language, social theory and social structure*, London: Continuum.

Loprest, P. and Maag, E. (2001) *Barriers and Supports for Work among Adults with Disabilities: Results from the NHIS-D*, Washington, D.C.: Urban Institute.

Louli, C. and Bickerton, G. (1995) 'Decades of change, decades of struggle: postal workers and technological change', pp. 216–32 in C. Schenk and K. Anderson (eds), *Re-Shaping Work: Union responses to technological change*, Toronto: Our Times.

Lovell, J. (1977) *British Trade Unions, 1875–1933*, London: Macmillan.

Lowe, G. (2000) *The Quality of Work: A people-centred agenda*, New York: Oxford University Press.

Luff, P., Hindmarsh, J. and Heath, C. (2000) *Workplace Studies: Recovering work practice and informing system design*, New York: CUP.

Lukes, S. (1974) *Power: A radical view*, Basingstoke: Macmillan.

Lyness, K. and Thompson, D. (2000) 'Climbing the corporate ladder: do males and female follow the same route?' *Journal of Applied Psychology*, February, pp. 86–101.

Mabey, C., Salaman, G. and Storey, J. (1998) *Human Resource Management: A strategic introduction* (2nd edn), Oxford: Blackwell.

Mabey, C., Skinner, D. and Clark, D. (eds) (1998) *Experiencing Human Resource Management*, London: Sage.

MacGillivray, E., Fineman, M. and Golden, D. (2003) 'Roundup of employment related news', *Journal of Organizational Excellence*, **22** (3), pp. 83–102.

Macionis, J. J., Jansson, S. M. and Benoit, C. M. (2005) *Society: The basics* (3rd edn), Toronto: Pearson.

Mackie, K. S., Holahan, C. and Gottlieb, N. (2001) 'Employee involvement management practices, work stress, and depression in employees of a human services residential care facility', *Human Relations*, **54** (8), pp. 1065–92.

Macrae, C. N., Bodenhausen, G. V., Milne, A. B. and Jetten, J. (1994) 'Out of mind but back in sight: stereotypes on the rebound', *Journal of Personality and Social Psychology*, **67**, pp. 808–17.

Madsen, D. B. and Finger, J. R. (1978) 'Comparison of a written feedback procedure, group brainstorming, and individual brainstorming', *Journal of Applied Psychology,* **63** (1), pp. 120–3.

Maitra, S. and Sangha, J. (2005) 'Intersecting realities: young women and call centre work in India and Canada', *Women and Environments*, Spring/Summer, pp. 40–2.

Malloch, H. (1997) 'Strategic and HRM aspects of kaizen: a case study', *New Technology, Work and Employment,* **12** (2), pp. 108-22.

Malott, R. (2002) 'Power in organizations', *Journal of Organizational Behavior Management*, **22** (3), pp. 51–60.

Mandel, E. and Novack, G. (1970) *The Marxist Theory of Alienation*, New York: Pathfinder.

Mani, S. (2002) *Government, Innovation and Technology Policy: An international comparative analysis*, Cheltenham: Edward Elgar.

Mann, M. (1986) *Sources of Social Power,* Cambridge: CUP.

Manz, C. and Newstrom, J. (1990), 'Self-managing teams in a paper mill: success factors, problems and lessons learned', in A. Nedd (ed.), *International Human Resource Management Review*, Vol. 1, Singapore: McGraw-Hill.

Manz, C. and Sims, H. (1980) 'Self-management as a substitute for leadership: a social learning theory perspective,' *Academy of Management Review*, **5** (3), pp. 361–7.

Manz, C. C. and Sims, H. P., Jr. (1993). *Business Without Bosses*, New York: Wiley.

Manz, C. C. and Sims, H. P., Jr. (1987) 'Leading workers to lead themselves: the external leadership of self-managed work teams', *Administrative Science Quarterly*, **32** (1), pp. 106–28.

Manz, C. C. and Sims, H. P. (1989) *Superleadership: Leading others to lead themselves*, Englewood Cliffs, NJ: Prentice Hall.

Manz, C. C. and Sims, H. P., Jr. (1993) *Businesses without Bosses*, New York: Wiley.

March, J. G. (1997) 'Understanding how decisions happen in organizations', pp. 9–32 in Z. Shapira (ed.), *Organizational Decision Making*, New York: CUP.

March, J. G. and Simon, H. A. (1958) *Organizations*, New York: Wiley.

Marchington, M. (2001) 'Employee involvement', pp. 232–52 in J. Storey (ed.), *Human Resource Management: A critical text*, London: Thomson Learning.

Marchington, M., Goodman, J., Wilkinson, A. and Ackers, P. (1992) 'Recent developments in employee involvement', Employment Department Research Series, 1, London: HMSO.

Marchington, M. and Wilding, P. (1983) 'Employee involvement inaction?' *Personnel Management*, pp. 73–83.

Marcuse, H. (1964) *One Dimensional Man*, Boston, Mass.: Beacon.

Marcuse, H. (1969) *An Essay on Liberation*, Boston, Mass.: Beacon.

Marglin, S. (1982) 'What do bosses do?: the origins and functions of hierarchy in capitalist production', in A. Giddens and D. Held (eds), *Classes, Power and Conflict*, Basingstoke: Macmillan.

Marsick, V. J. (1988) 'Learning in the workplace: the case of reflectivity and critical reflectivity', *Adult Education Quarterly*, **4**, pp. 18–29.

Marsick, V. and Watkins, K. (1990) *Informal and Incidental learning in the Workplace*, London: Routledge.

Marsick, V. and Watkins, K. (1997), 'Lessons from informal and incidental learning', pp. 295–311 in J. Burgoyne and M. Reynolds (eds), *Management Learning*, London: Sage.

Martin, J. (2000) 'Hidden gendered assumptions in mainstream organizational theory and research', *Journal of Management Inquiry*, **9** (2), pp. 207–16.

Martin, J. and Nakayama, T. (2000) *Intercultural Communication in Contexts* (2nd edn), Mountain View, Calif./Toronto: Mayfield.

Marx, K. (1867/1970) *Capital: A critique of political economy, Volume One*, London: Lawrence & Wishart.

Marx, K. (1973) *Grundrisse*, Baltimore: Penguin.

Marx, K. and Engels, F. (1848/1967) *The Communist Manifesto*, London: Penguin.

Marx, R., Stubbart, C., Traub, V. and Cavanaugh, M. (1987) 'The NASA space shuttle disaster: a case study', *Journal of Management Case Studies*, **3**, pp. 300–18.

Maslow, A. H. (1954) *Motivation and Personality*, New York: Harper.

Maslow, A. H. (1964) *Religions, Values, and Peak-Experiences*, New York: Viking.

Masterson, S., Lewis, K., Goldman, B. and Taylor, M. (2000) 'Integrating justice and social exchange: the differing effects of fair procedures and treatment on work relationships', *Academy of Management Journal*, **43**, pp. 738–48.

Mathias, P. (1969) *The First Industrial Nation*, London: Methuen.

Matthews, J. and Candy, P. (1999) 'New dimensions in the dynamics of learning and knowledge', pp. 47–64 in D. Boud and J. Garrick (eds), *Understanding Learning at Work*, London: Routledge.

Maurice, M. and Sorge, A. (2000) *Embedding Organizations*, Amsterdam: John Benjamins.

Mayes, B. and Ganster, D. (1988) 'Exit and voice: a test of hypotheses based on the fight/flight response to job stress', *Journal of Organizational Behavior*, **9** (3), pp. 99–117.

Mayhew, B. H., Miller-McPherson, J., Rotolo, T. and Smith-Lovin, T. (1995) 'Sex and race homogeneity in naturally occurring groups,' *Social Forces*, September, **74** (1), pp. 15–52.

Mayo, E. (1946) *The Human Problems of an Industrial Civilization*, New York: Macmillan.

McClelland, D. (1961) *The Achieving Society*, Princeton, NJ: Van Nostrand.

McCrae, R. R. and Costa, P. T. (1995) 'Toward a new generation of personality theories: theoretical contexts for the five-factor model', pp. 51–87 in J. S. Wiggins (ed.), *The Five-Factor Model of Personality: Theoretical perspectives*, New York: Guilford Press.

McFarlin, D. and Sweeney, P. (1992) 'Distributive and procedural justice as predictors of satisfaction with personal and organizational outcomes', *Academy of Management Journal,* **35**, pp. 626–37.

McGregor, D. (1960) *The Human Side of Enterprise*, New York: McGraw-Hill.

McIvor, A. (2001) *A History of Work in Britain*, Basingstoke: Palgrave Macmillan.

McKinlay, A. (2002) 'The limits of knowledge management', *New Technology, Work and Employment*, **17** (2), pp. 76–88.

McKinlay, A. and Starkey, K. (1998) *Foucault, Management and Organization Theory*, London: Sage.

McKinlay, A. and Taylor, P. (1998) 'Through the looking glass: Foucault and the politics of production', in A. McKinlay and K. Starkey (eds), *Foucault, Management and Organizational Theory*, London: Sage.

McLean, S. and Moss, G. (2003) 'They're happy, but did they make a difference? Applying Kirkpatrick's framework to the evaluation of a national leadership program', *Canadian Journal of Program Evaluation*, **18** (1), Spring, pp. 1–23.

McMahon, J. T. (1972) 'The contingency theory: logic and method revisited', *Personnel Psychology*, **25**, pp. 697–710.

McShane, S. L. (2006) *Canadian Organizational Behaviour* (6th edn), Boston, Mass.: McGraw-Hill.

Mead, G. H. (1934) *Mind, Self and Society,* Chicago: University of Chicago Press.

Meek, V. L. (1992) 'Organizational culture: orgins and weaknesses', pp. 192–212 in G. Salaman (ed.), *Human Resources Strategies*, London: Sage.

Meijs, M. (2002) 'The myth of manageability of corporate identity', *Corporate Reputation Review*, **5** (1), pp. 20–35.

Merriam, S. (ed.) (1993) *An Update on Adult Learning Theory*, San Francisco, Calif.: Jossey-Bass.

Metcalfe, D. (1989) 'Water notes dry up', *British Journal of Industrial Relations*, **27** (10), pp. 1–32.

Meyerson, D. E. and Fletcher, J. K. (2000) 'A modest manifesto for shattering the glass ceiling', *Harvard Business Review*, **78** (1), pp. 127–37.

Mezirow, J. D. (1981) 'A critical theory of adult education', *Adult Education Quarterly*, **32** (1), pp. 3–24.

Mezirow, J. D. (1990) *Fostering Critical Reflection in Adulthood: A guide to transformative and emancipatory learning*, San Francisco, Calif.: Jossey-Bass.

Mezirow, J. (1991) *Transformative Dimensions of Adult Learning*, San Francisco: Jossey-Bass.

Milgram, S. (1973) *Obedience and Authority*, London: Tavistock.

Milkman, R. and Pullman, C. (1991) 'Technological change in an auto assembly plant: the impact on workers' tasks and skills,' *Work and Occupations*, **18** (2), pp. 123–47.

Miller, N. and Brewer, M. B. (eds) (1984). *Groups in Contact: The psychology of desegregation,* New York: Academic Press.

Miller, S. J., Hickson, D. and Wilson, S. D. (1999) 'Decision-making in organizations,' pp. 43–62 in S. R. Clegg, C. Hardy and W. Nord (eds), *Managing Organizations: Current issues*, London: Sage.

Millett, K. (1985) *Sexual Politics*, London: Virago.

Mills, A. and Simmons, A. (1995) *Reading Organizational Theory*, Toronto: Garamond.

Mills, A., Simmons, A. and Helms Mills, J. (2005) *Reading Organizational Theory* (3rd edn), Garamond.

Mills, A. and Tancred, P. (eds) (1992) *Gendering Organizational Analysis*, Newbury Park, Calif.: Sage.

Mills, C. W. (1959/2000) *The Sociological Imagination*, New York: Oxford University Press.

Millward, N., Bryson, A. and Forth, J. (2000) *All Change at Work: British employee relations 1980–1998*, London: Routledge.

Millward, N., Stevens, M., Smart, D. and Hawes, W. (1992) *Workplace Industrial Relations in Transition*, Aldershot: Dartmouth.

Milner, A. (1999) *Class*, London: Sage.

Mintzberg, H. (1973) *The Nature of Managerial Work,* New York: Harper and Row.

Mintzberg, H. (1979) *The Structure of Organizations,* Englewood Cliffs, NJ: Prentice-Hall.

Mintzberg, H. (1983) *Structure in Fives: Designing effective organizations,*

Mintzberg, H. (1989) *Mintzberg on Management*, New York: Free Press.

Mintzberg, H. (1990) 'The manager's job: folklore and fact', *Harvard Business Review*, March–April.

Mintzberg, H. (1993) *Structure in Fives: Designing effective organizations*, Englewood Cliffs, NJ: Prentice Hall.

Mintzberg, H. (1997) *The Structuring of Organizations*, Englewood Cliffs, NJ: Prentice Hall.

Mintzberg, H. (2004) 'Enough leadership', *Harvard Business Review*, **82** (11), p. 22.

Mintzberg, H., Ahlstrand, B. and Lampel, J. (1998) S*trategy Safari: a guided tour through the wilds of strategic management,* New York: Free Press.

Mishel, L. and Voos, P. (eds) (1992) *Unions and Economic Competitiveness*, New York: M.E. Sharpe.

Mishra, R. C., Dasen, P. R. and Niraula, S. (2003) 'Ecology, language, and performance on spatial cognitive tasks', *International Journal of Psychology*, **38**, pp. 366–83.

Modood, T., Berthoud, R. et al (1997) *Ethnic Minorities in Britain: Diversity and disadvantage*, London: Policy Studies Institute.

Morgan, G. (1980) 'Paradigms, metaphors, and puzzle solving in organization theory', *Administrative Science Quarterly*, **25**, pp. 605–22.

Morgan, G. (1986) *Images of Organization,* London: Sage.

Morgan, G. (1997) *Images of Organization* (2nd edn), Thousand Oaks, Calif.: Sage.

Morgan, N. (2001), 'How to overcome 'change fatigue''', *Harvard Management Update*, July, pp. 1–3.

Morris, J. (2004) 'The future of work: organizational and international perspectives', *International Journal of Human Resource Management*, **15** (2), pp 263–75.

Morris, M. W. and Peng, K. P. (1994) 'Culture and cause: American and Chinese attributions for social and physical events', *Journal of Personality and Social Psychology*, **67**, pp. 949–71.

Morrison, K. (1995) *Marx, Durkheim, Weber,* London: Sage.

Moss, N. E. (2002) 'Gender equity and socioeconomic inequality: a framework for the patterning of women's health', *Social Science and Medicine*, **54** (5), pp. 649–61.

Mottaz, C. J. (1985) 'The relative importance of intrinsic and extrinsic rewards as determinants of work satisfaction,' *Sociological Quarterly*, **26** (3), pp. 365–85.

Mottaz, C. J. (1986) 'Gender differences in work satisfaction, work-related rewards and values, and the determinants of work satisfaction,' *Human Relations*, **39** (4), pp. 359–78.

Mouzelis, N. (1967) *Organization and Bureaucracy*, London: Routledge & Kegan Paul.

Mulligan, T. (1986) 'A critique of Milton Friedman's essay "The social responsibility of business is to increase its profits"', *Journal of Business Ethics*, **16** (1), pp. 265–9.

Mumford, L. (1964) 'Authoritarian and democratic technics', *Technology and Culture*, **5** (1), pp. 1–8.

Munby, D. K. and Putnam, L. L. (1992) 'The politics of emotion: a feminist reading of bounded rationality', *Academy of Management Review*, **17**, pp. 465–86.

Murry, M. A. and Atkinson, T. (1981) 'Gender differences in correlates of job satisfaction', *Canadian Journal of Behavioural Sciences*, **13**, pp. 44–52.

Myers, D. G. (1988) *Psychology*, New York: Worth.

Nadler, D. A. and Tushman, M. L. (1997) *Competing by Design: The power of organizational architecture*, New York: Oxford University Press.

Naisbitt, J. (1982) *Megatrends: Ten new directions transforming our lives*, New York: Warner.

Negroponte, N. (1995) *Being Digital*, New York: Knopf.

Neher, W. W. (1997) *Organizational Communication*, Boston, Mass.: Allyn & Bacon.

Nelson, B. (2001) *Divided We Stand: American workers and the struggle for black equality*, Princeton: Princeton University Press.

Neuman, W. L. (2007) *Basics of Social Research* (2nd edn), Pearson.

Ng, R. (1991) 'Sexism, racism and Canadian nationalism', in J. Vorst et al. (eds), *Race, Class, Gender: Bonds and Barriers*, Toronto: Garamond Press.

Ngo, H., Foley, S., Wong, A. and Loi, R. (2003) 'Who gets more of the pie? Predictors of perceived gender inequity at work', *Journal of Business Ethics*, **45** (3), pp. 227–41.

Nichols, T. (1969) *Ownership Control and Ideology*, London: Allen & Unwin.

Nichols, T. (1980) *Capital and Labour*, Glasgow: Fontana.

Nisbett, R. and Ross, L. (1980) *Human Inference: Strategies and shortcomings of social judgement*, Englewood Cliffs, N.J.: Prentice Hall.

Nkomo, S. M. and Cox, T. Jr. (1999) 'Diverse identities in organizations', pp.88–101 in S. Clegg, C. Hardy and W. Nord (eds), *Managing Organizations: Current issues*, Thousand Oaks, Calif.: Sage..

Noble, D. (1979) 'Social choice in machine design: the case of automatically controlled machine tools', pp. 18–50 in A. Zimbalist (ed.), *Case Studies on the Labour Process*, New York: Monthly Review Press.

Noble, D. (1984) *The Forces of Production: A social history of industrial automation*, New York: Knopf.

Noon, M. (1992) 'HRM: A map, model or theory?', pp. 16–32 in P. Blyton and P. Turnbull (eds), *Reassessing Human Resource Management*, London: Sage.

Noon, M. and Blyton, P. (2002) *The Realities of Work*, Basingstoke: Palgrave Macmillan.

Nutley, S. M. and Davies, H. T. O. (2001) 'Developing organizational learning in the NHS', *Medical Education*, **35** (1) p. 35.

Nye, R. (2000) *Three Psychologies: Perspectives from Freud, Skinner and Rogers* (6th edn), Belmont, Calif.: Wadsworth/Thompson Learning.

O'Brien, D. and Buono, C. (1996) 'Building effective learning teams: lessons from the field', *SAM Advanced Management Journal*, **61** (3), pp. 4–11.

Ogbonna, E. (1992) 'Organization culture and human resource management: dilemmas and contradictions', pp. 74–96 in P. Blyton and P. Turnbull (eds), *Reassessing Human Resource Management*, London Sage.

Ogbonna, E. and Harris, L. (2006) 'Organizational culture in an age of the Internet: an exploratory case study', *New Technology, Work and Employment*, **21** (2), pp. 162–75.

Organization for Economic Cooperation and Development (OECD) (1996) 'Earnings inequality, low paid employment and earnings mobility', *Employment Outlook*, Paris: OECD.

OECD (1999) *The Knowledge-Based Economy: A set of facts and figures*, Paris: OECD.

Offe, C. (1976) *Industry and Inequality*, London: Edward Arnold.

Oliver, J. (1993) 'Shocking to the core', *Management Today*, August, pp. 18–21.

Oliver, M. (1996) *Understanding Disability*, Basingstoke: Palgrave.

Oliver, N. (1991) 'The dynamics of JIT', *New Technology, Work and Employment*, September, pp. 19–27.

Oliver, N. and Wilkinson, B. (1992) *The Japanization of British Industry*, Oxford: Blackwell.

Oram, M. (1998) 'Re-engineering's fragile promise: HRM prospects for delivery', pp. 72–89 in P. Sparrow and M. Marchington (eds), *Human Resource Management: The new agenda*, London: Pitman.

Organ, D. (1990) 'The motivational basis of organizational citizenship behavior', pp. 43–72 in L. Cummings and B. Staw (eds), *Research in Organizational Behavior, Volume 12*, Greenwich, Conn.: JAI Press.

Orsburn, J. and Moran, L. (2000) *The New Self-Directed Work Teams*, New York: McGraw-Hill.

Østerlund, C. (1997) 'Sales apprentices on the move: a multi-contextual perspective on situated learning', *Journal of Nordic Educational Research (Nordisk Pedagogik)*, **17** (3), pp. 169–77.

Overbeck, J. and Park, B. (2006) 'Powerful perceivers, powerless objects: flexibility of powerholders' social attention', *Organizational Behaviour and Human Decision Processes*, **99** (2), pp. 227–44.

Paauwe, J. (2004) *HRM and Performance,* Oxford: Oxford University Press.

Paauwe, J. and Boselie, P. (2003) 'Challenging "strategic HRM" and the relevance of the institutional setting', *Human Resource Management Journal*, **13** (3), pp. 56–70.

Paauwe, J., and Boselie, P. (2005) 'HRM and performance: what next?' *Human Resource Management Journal*, **15** (4), pp. 68–83.

Pahl, R. E. (ed.) (1988) *On Work*, Oxford: Blackwell.

Palys, T. (2003) *Research Decisions: Quantitative and qualitative perspectives* (3rd edn), Thomson.

Parker, I. (1992) *Discourse Dynamics: Critical analysis for social and individual psychology*, London: Routledge.

Parrenas, R. (2001) *Servants of Globalization: Women, migration, and domestic work,* Stanford: Stanford University Press.

Parsons, T. (1960) *Structure and Process in Modern Societies*, Chicago: Free Press.

Passer, M., Smith, R., Atkinson, M., Mitchell, J. and Muir, D. (2003) *Psychology: Frontiers and Applications*, Toronto: McGraw-Hill Ryerson.

Patel, D. (2002) *Workplace Forecast: A Strategic Outlook 2002–2003,* Washington: Society for Human Resource Management.

Paul, A. K. and Anantharaman, R. N. (2003) 'Impact of people management practices on organizational performance: analysis of a causal model', *International Journal of Human Resource Management*, **14** (7), pp. 1246–66.

Paunonen, S. V. (1996) 'The structure of personality in six cultures', *Journal of Cross-Culture Psychology*, May, pp. 339–53.

Pedler, M., Boydell, T. and Burgoyne, J. (1988) *The Learning Company Project Report*, Sheffield: Employment Department.

Pelling, H. (1963) *A History of British Trade Unionism*, Harmondsworth: Penguin.

Penn, R. and Scattergood, H. (1985) 'Deskilling or enskilling?: An empirical investigation of recent theories of the labour process', *British Journal of Sociology*, **36** (4), pp. 611–30.

Penrose, E. T. (1959) *The Theory of the Growth of the Firm,* Oxford: Blackwell.

Perrow, C. B. (1970) *Organizational Analysis: A sociological view*, Belmont, Calif.: Brooks Cole.

Peters, L. H., Hartke, D. D. and Pohlman, J. T. (1985) 'Fiedler's contingency theory of leadership: an application of the meta-analysis procedures of Schmidt and Hunter', *Psychological Bulletin*, **97**, pp. 224–85.

Peters, T. and Waterman, R. (1982) *In Search of Excellence*, New York: Harper & Row.

Peterson, C. (2000) 'The future of optimism', *American Psychologist*, **55**, pp. 44–55.

Pettigrew, A. (1973) *The Politics of Organizational Decision-Making*, London: Tavistock.

Pfeffer, J. (1998a) *The Human Equation: Building Profits by Putting People First*, Boston, Mass.: Harvard Business School Press.

Pfeffer, J. (1998b) 'Six dangerous myths about pay', *Harvard Business Review*, May–June, pp. 9–13.

Pfeffer, J. and Baron, N. (1988) 'Taking the work back out: recent trends in the structures of employment', pp. 257–303 in B. M. Staw and L. L. Cummings (eds), *Research in Organizational Behaviour*,

Pfeffer, J. and Salancik, G. (1977) 'Organizational context and the characteristics and tenure of hospital administrators', *Academy of Management Journal*, **20**, pp. 74–88.

Pfeffer, J. and Salancik, G. (1978) *The External Control of Organizations: A resource dependency perspective*, New York: Harper & Row.

Pfuetze, P. (1954) *Self, Society and Existence: Human nature and dialogue in the thoughts of George Herbert Mead and Martin Buber*, New York: Harper.

Phillips, K. and Lewin Lloyd, D. (2006) 'When surface and deep-level diversity collide: the effects on dissenting group members', *Organizational Behaviour and Human Decision Processes*, **99** (2), pp. 143–60.

Phillips, N. (1997) 'Bringing the organization back in: a comment on conceptualizations of power in upward influence research', *Journal of Organizational Behavior*, **18** (1), pp. 43–8.

Phillips, P. and Phillips, E. (1993) *Women and Work: Inequality in the Canadian labour market*, Toronto: Lorimer.

Piore, M. and Sabel, C. (1984) *The Second Industrial Divide*, New York: Basic Books.

Plotnik, (2005) *Introduction to Psychology* (7th edn), Belmont, Calif.: Thomson/Wadsworth;

Pollard, S. (1969) *The Development of the British Economy, 1914–1967*, London: Edward Arnold.

Porter, J. (1971) *Towards 2000: The future of post-secondary education in Ontario*, Toronto: McClelland and Stewart.

Porter, L. W. and Lawler, E. E. (1968) *Managerial Attitudes and Performance*, London: Irwin.

Porter, M. (1980) *Competitive Strategy*, New York: Free Press.

Porter, M. (1985) *Competitive Advantage: Creating and sustaining superior performance*, New York: Free Press.

Porter, L. W. and Lawler, E. E. (1968) *Managerial Attitudes and Performance,* Homewood, Ill.: Irwin.

Poster, M. (2002) 'Workers as cyborgs: labor and networked computers', *Journal of Labor Research*, **23** (3), pp. 339–54.

Prahalad, C. K. and Doz, Y. (1987) *The Multinational Mission: Balancing local demands and global vision*, New York: Free Press.

Pratt, D. D. (1988) 'Andragogy as a relational construct', *Adult Education Quarterly*, **38** (3), pp. 160–81.

Pratt, D. D. (1993) 'Andragogy after twenty-five years', pp. 15–23 in S. Merriam (ed.), *An Update on Adult Learning Theory*, No. 57, San Francisco, Calif.: Jossey-Bass.

Premeaux, S. (2001) 'Impact of applicant disability on selection: the role of disability type, physical attractiveness, and proximity', *Journal of Business and Psychology*, **16** (2), pp. 291–98.

Price, K. H. and Garland, H. (1981) 'Compliance with the leader's suggestions as a function of perceived leader/member competence and potential reciprocity', *Journal of Applied Psychology*, **66**, pp. 329–36.

Probert, B. (1999) 'Gendered workers and gendered work', pp. 98-116 in D. Boud and J. Garrick (eds), *Understanding Learning at Work*, London: Routledge.

Procter, S. and Mueller, F. (2000) *Teamworking*, Basingstoke: Palgrave Macmillan.

Pugh, D., Hickson, C., Hining, R. and Turner, C. (1969) 'The context of organization structures', *Administrative Science Quarterly*, 14, pp. 91–114.

Pulignano, V. and Stewart, P. (2006) 'Bureaucracy transcended? New patterns of employment regulation and labour control in the international automotive industry', *New Technology, Work and Employment*, **21** (2), pp. 90–106.

Punnett, B. J. (1998) 'Culture, cross-national', pp. 9–26 in M. Poole and M. Warner (eds), *The IEBM Handbook of Human Resource Management,* London: Thomson Business Press.

Purcell, J. (1989) 'The impact of corporate strategy on human resource management', pp. 67–91 in J. Storey (ed.), *New Perspectives on Human Resource Management*, London: Routledge.

Purcell, J. (1999) 'Best practice and best fit: chimera or cul-de-sac?' *Human Resource Management Journal,* **9** (3), pp. 26–41.

Purcell, J. and Ahlstrand, B. (1994) *Human Resource Management in the Multi-divisional Company.*, Oxford: Oxford University Press.

Putnam, L. L., Philips, N. and Chapman, P. (1999) 'Metaphors of communication and organization', pp. 125–47 in S. Clegg, C. Hardy and W. Nord (eds), *Managing Organizations. Current Issues.* Thousand Oaks, CA: Sage.

Raghubir, P. and Valenzuela, A. (2006) 'Centers-of-inattention: position biases in decision-making', *Organizational Behaviour and Human Decision Processes,* **99** (1), pp. 66–80.

Ragins, B. (1991) 'Gender effects in subordinate evaluations of leaders: real or artifact?' *Journal of Organizational Behavior*, **12** (3), pp. 259–69.

Ramachandran, V. S. and Rogers-Ramachandran, D. (2005) 'How blind are we?', *Scientific American Mind*, **16** (2), p. 96.

Ramsay, H. (1991) 'Reinventing the wheel: a review of the development and performance of employee involvement', *Human Resource Management Journal*, **1**, pp. 1–22.

Raphael, S., Stoll, M and Holzer, H. (2000) 'Are suburban firms more likely to discriminate against African-Americans?' *Journal of Urban Economics*, **48** (3), pp. 485–508.

Ray, C. A. (1986) 'Corporate culture: the last frontier of control', *Journal of Management Studies*, **23** (3).

Ray, L. J. (1999) *Theorizing Classical Sociology*, Buckingham: Open University Press.

Reason, J. T. (1990) *Human Error,* Cambridge: Cambridge University Press.

Redelmeier, D. A. and Tibshirani, R. J. (1997) 'Association between cellular-telephone calls and motor vehicle collisions', *New England Journal of Medicine*, **336**, pp. 453–8.

Reed, L. (2003) 'Paternalism may excuse disability discrimination: when may an employer refuse to employ a disabled individual due to concerns for the individual's safety?' *Business and Society Review*, **108** (3), pp. 417–24.

Reed, M. (1989) *The Sociology of Management*, London: Harvester Wheatsheaf.

Reed, M. I. (1993) 'Organizations and modernity: continuity and discontinuity in organization theory', pp. 163-82 in J. Hassard and M. Parker (eds), *Postmodernism and Organizations*, London: Sage.

Reich, R. (1991) *The Work of Nations: Preparing ourselves for 21st century capitalism*, New York: Knopf/ London: Simon & Schuster.

Reinharz, S. (1988) 'Feminist distrust: problems of context and content in sociological work', pp. 153–72 in D. N. Berg and K. K. Smith (eds), *The Self in Social Inquiry*, Newbury Park, Calif.: Sage.

Reiter, E. (1992) *Making Fast Food: From the frying pan into the fryer*, Montreal: McGill-Queen's University Press.

Reskin, B. and Padavic, I. (1994) *Women and Men at Work*, Thousand Oaks, Calif.: Sage.

Richta, R. (1969) *Civilization at the Crossroads*, White Plains, N.Y.: International Arts and Science Press.

Rifkin, J. (1996) *The End of Work*, New York: Tarcher/Putnam.

Rigney, F. (2001) *The Metaphorical Society: An invitation to social theory*, Lanham, Md.: Rowman & Littlefield.

Riley, P. (1983) 'A structurationist account of political cultures', *Administrative Science Quarterly*, **28**, pp. 414–37.

Rinehart, J. W. (2006) *The Tyranny of Work: Alienation and the labour process* (4th edn), Scarborough, ON: Nelson Thomson.

Rip, A., Misa, T. and Schot, J. (eds) (1995) *Managing Technology in Society: The approach of constructive technology assessment*, London: Pinter.

Ritzer, G. (1996) 'The McDonaldization thesis: is expansion inevitable?' *International Sociology*, **11** (3), pp. 291–308.

Ritzer, G. (2000) *The McDonaldization of Society*, Thousand Oaks, Calif.: Pine Forge Press.

Ritzer, G. and Goodman, D. J. (2004) *Classical Social Theory* (4th edn), New York: McGraw-Hill.

Robbins, S. P. (1990) *Organization Theory: Structure, design, and applications* (3rd edn), Englewood Cliffs, NJ: Prentice-Hall.

Robbins, S. P. and Langton, N. (2001) *Organizational Behaviour: Concepts, controversies, applications* (2nd edn), Toronto: Prentice-Hall.

Roberson, Q. (2006) 'Justice in teams: the activation of role and sensemaking in the emergence of justice climates', *Organizational Behaviour and Human Decision Processes*, **100** (2), pp. 177–92.

Robertson, I. T., Baron, H., Gibbons, P., MacIver, R. and Nyfield, G. (2000) 'Conscientiousness and managerial performance', *Journal of Occupational and Organizational Psychology*, **73** (2), pp. 171–81.

Robinson, V. (1990) 'Roots of mobility', *Ethnic and Racial Studies*, **13** (2), pp. 274–86.

Roddick, A. (1991) *Body and Soul*, New York: Crown.

Roethlisberger, F. J. and Dickson, W. J. (1939) *Management and the Worker*, Cambridge, Mass.: Harvard University Press.

Rogers, C. R. (1961) *On Becoming a Person*, Boston, Mass.: Houghton Mifflin.

Rogers, C. R. (1980) *A Way of Being*, Boston, Mass.: Houghton Mifflin.

Rogers, C. R. (1983) *Freedom to Learn for the 80s*, Columbus, Oh.: Merrill.

Rogoff, B. (1984) 'Introduction: thinking and learning in social context', pp. 1–8 in B. Rogoff and J. Lave (eds), *Everyday Cognition: Its development in social context*, Cambridge, Mass.: Harvard University Press.

Rogoff, B. (1990) *Apprenticeship in Thinking: Cognitive development in social context*, Oxford: Oxford University Press.

Rogoff, B. (1995) 'Observing sociocultural activity on three planes: participatory appropriation, guided participation, and apprenticeship', pp. 139–63 in J. V. Wertsch, P. del Rio and A. Alvarez (eds), *Sociocultural Studies of Mind*, Cambridge, UK: Cambridge University Press.

Roper, I., Prabhu, V. and Van Zwanenberg, N. (1997) '(Only) just-in-time: Japanization and the "non learning" firm', *Work, Employment and Society*, **11** (1), pp. 27–46.

Roscigno, V. and Hodson, R. (2004) 'The organizational and social foundations of worker resistance', *American Sociological Review*, **69** (1), pp. 14–39.

Rose, M. (1975) *Industrial Behaviour: Theoretical developments since Taylor*, London: Allen Lane.

Rose, M. (1988) *Industrial Behaviour*, London: Penguin.

Rose, N. (1990) *Governing the Soul: The shaping of the private self*, London: Routledge.

Rosener, J. (1990) 'Ways women lead', *Harvard Business Review*, December, pp. 199–225.

Rosenfeld, P., Giacalone, R. and Riordan, C. A. (2002) *Impression Management: Building and enhancing reputation at work*, London: Thomson Learning.

Ross, J. and Staw, B (1993) 'Organization escalation and exit: lessons from the Shoreham nuclear power plant', *Academy of Management Journal*, **36**, pp. 701–32.

Roszak, T. (1994) *The Cult of Information: A neo-Luddite treatise on high tech, artificial intelligence and the true art of thinking*, Berkeley: University of California Press.

Roth, E. M. and Woods, O. D. (1988) 'Aiding human performance, I: Cognitive analysis', *Le Travail Humain*, **51**, pp. 39–64.

Rothman, H. K. (2000) 'What has work become?' *Journal of Labor Research*, **21** (3), pp. 379–92.

Rotter, J. B. (1966) *Generalized Expectations for Internal versus External Control of Reinforcement*, London: Psychological Monographs, no. 80.

Rousseau, D. M. (1995) P*sychological Contracts in Organisations: Understanding written and unwritten agreements*, Thousand Oaks, Calif.: Sage.

Rowbotham, S. (1973) *Woman's Consciousness, Man's World,* London: Penguin.

Rowe, A. (1970) 'Human beings, class and education', pp. 33–40 in D. Rubinstein and C. Stoneman (eds), *Education for Democracy*, London: Penguin.

Rowley, C., and Bae, J. (2002) 'Globalization and transformation of human resource management in South Korea', *International Journal of Human Resource Management*, **14** (3), pp. 522–49.

Rowley, C., Benson, J. and Warner, M. (2004) 'Towards an Asian model of human resource management? A comparative analysis of China, Japan and South Korea', *International Journal of Human Resource Management*, **14** (4), pp. 917–33.

Rowlinson, M. (2004) 'Challenging the foundations of organization theory', *Work, Employment and Society*, **18** (3), pp. 607–20.

Royle, T. (2005) 'The union recognition dispute at McDonald's Moscow food-processing factory', *Industrial Relations Journal,* **36** (4), pp. 318–32.

Rubenstein, H. (2003) *Women and Leadership: Review of recent studies*, Washington, D.C.: Growth Strategies.

Rubenstein, R. (2001) *Dress Codes: Meaning and messages in American culture,* Boulder, Colo.: Westview Press.

Rubery, J. (1998) 'Employers and the labour market', pp. 251–80 in D. Gallie (ed.), *Employment in Britain*, Oxford: Blackwell.

Rule, J. (1987) 'The property of skill', in P. Joyce (ed.), *The Historical Meaning of Work*, Cambridge: CUP.

Rymer, R. (1994) *Genie*, New York: HarperPerennial.

Said, E. (1979) *Orientalism*, New York: Random House-Vintage.

Sako, M. (2005) 'Does embeddedness imply limits to within-country diversity?', *British Journal of Industrial Relations*, **43** (4), pp. 585–92.

Salaman, G. (1979) *Work Organizations: Resistance and control*, London: Longman.

Salaman, G. (1981) *Class and the Corporation*, London: Fontana.

Salaman, G. (1984) *Working,* London: Tavistock.

Sale, K. (1995) *Rebels Against the Future: The Luddites and their war on the Industrial Revolution – lessons for the computer age,* London: Addison Wesley.

Salgado, J. F. (1997) 'The five factor model of personality and job performance in the European Community', *Journal of Applied Psychology*, **82**, pp. 30–43.

Salgado, J. F. (2002) 'The big five personality dimensions and counterproductive behaviors', *International Journal of Selection and Assessment,* **10**, pp. 117–25.

Salzinger, L. (2003) *Genders in Production*, Berkeley: University of California Press.

Saul, J. R. (2005) *The Collapse of Globalism*, Toronto: Viking.

Sawchuk, H. (2004) *Hidden Knowledge: Organized labour in the information age*, Aurora, ON: Garamond.

Sawchuk, P. (2003) *Adult Learning and Technology in Working-Class Life,* New York: CUP.

Sawchuk, Peter H. (2006) '"Use-value' and the re-thinking of skills, learning and the labour process" *Journal of Industrial Relations*, **48** (5), pp. 589–613.

Sawyer, J., Houlette, M. and Yeagley, E. (2006) 'Decision performance and diversity structure: comparing faultlines in convergent, crosscut, and racially homogenous groups', *Organizational Behaviour and Human Decision Processes*, **99** (1), pp. 1–15.

Sayer, A. (1986) 'New developments in manufacturing: the just-in-time system', *Capital and Class* (30), pp. 43–72.

Sayer, A. (1992) *Method in Social Science: A realist approach* (2nd edn), London: Routledge.

Sayer, A. (2000) *Realism and Social Science*, London: Sage.

Schein, E. A. (1985) *Organizational Leadership and Culture*, San Francisco, Calif.: Jossey-Bass.

Schein, E. A. (1991) 'What is culture?', in P. J. Lunberg and J. Martin (eds), *Reframing Organizational Culture,* Newbury Park, Calif.: Sage.

Schein, E. A. (1992) *Organizational Culture and Leadership* (2nd edn), San Francisco: Jossey-Bass.

Schein, E.A. (1994) 'What is culture?' in P. Frost, L. Moore, M. Louis, C. Lundberg and J. Martin (eds), *Reframing Organizational Culture*, Newbury Park, Calif.: Sage.

Schein, E.A. (1996) 'Culture: the missing concept in organization studies', *Administrative Science Quarterly*, **41**, pp. 229–40.

Schein, V. E. (1973) 'The relationship between sex role stereotypes and requisite management characteristics', *Journal of Applied Psychology*, **57**, pp. 95–100.

Schein, V. E. (1975) 'The relationship between sex role stereotypes and requisite management characteristics among female managers', *Journal of Applied Psychology*, **60**, pp. 340–4.

Schein, V. E., Mueller, R., Lituchy, T. and Liu, J. (1996) 'Think manager – think male: a global phenomenon', *Journal of Organizational Behavior*, **17**, pp. 33–41.

Schenk, C. and Anderson, J. (eds) (1995) *Re-Shaping Work: Union responses to technological change*, Toronto: Our Times.

Scholte, J. A. (2005) *Globalization: A critical introduction*, Basingstoke: Palgrave Macmillan.

Schriesheim, C. A. and Kerr, S. (1977) 'R.I.P. LPC: a response to Fiedler', pp. 51–6 in J. G. Hunt and L. L. Larson (eds), *Leadership: The cutting edge*, Carbondale: Southern Illinois University Press.

Schwandt, T. A. (1994) 'Constructivist, interpretivist approaches to human inquiry', pp. 118–37 in N. K. Denzin and Y. Lincoln (eds), *Handbook of Qualitative Research*, Thousand Oaks, Calif.: Sage.

Scott, R. W. (2003) *Organizations: Rational, natural, and open systems*, Upper Saddle River, NJ: Prentice-Hall.

Scott, S. M. (1998) 'Philosophies in action', pp. 98–106 in S. M. Scott, B. Spencer and A. Thomas (eds), *Learning for Life*, Toronto: Thompson Educational.

Scullion, H. (2001) 'International human resource management', pp. 288–313 in J. Storey (ed.), *Human Resource Management: A critical text*, London: Thompson Learning.

Scullion, H. and Linehan, M. (2005) *International Human Resource Management*, Basingstoke: Palgrave.

Seligman, M. E. P. (1991) *Learned Optimism*, New York: Knopf.

Selznick, P. (1957) *Leadership and Administration*, New York: Harper & Row.

Senge, P. (1990) *The Fifth Discipline*, New York: Doubleday.

Senge, P., Roberts, C., Ross, R., Smith, B. and Kleiner, A. (1994) *The Fifth Discipline Fieldbook: Strategies and tools for building a learning organization*, New York: Doubleday.

Sennett, R. (1980) *Authority,* London: Faber and Faber.

Sennett, R. (1998) *The Corrosion of Character,* New York: Norton.

Sennett, R. and Cobb, J. (1972) *Hidden Injuries of Class,* New York: Anchor.

Sewell, G. (1998) 'The discipline of teams: The control of team-based industrial work through electronic and peer surveillance', *Administrative Science Quarterly*, **43**, pp. 406–69.

Sewell, G. and Wilkinson, B. (1992) 'Someone to watch over me – surveillance, discipline and the just-in-time labor process', *Sociology*, **26** (2), pp. 271–89.

Shaiken, H., Herzenberg, S. and Kuhn, S. (1986) 'The work process under more flexible production', *Industrial Relations*, **25**, pp. 167–83.

Shalla, V. (1997) 'Technology and the deskilling of work: the case of passenger agents at Air Canada', in A Duffy, D. Glenday and N. Pupo (eds), *Good Jobs, Bad Jobs, No Jobs: The transformation of work in the 21st century*, Toronto: Harcourt.

Shang, X. (2000) 'Bridging the gap between planned and market economies: employment policies for people with disabilities in two Chinese cities', *Disability and Society*, **15** (1), pp. 135–56.

Sharpe, A. (1997) *Sectoral Skills Councils in Canada: Future challenges*, Ottawa: Human Resources Development Canada.

Sharpe, S. (1976) *Just Like a Girl: How girls learn to be women,* London: Penguin.

Sheridan, A. (1980) *Michel Foucault: The will to power,* London: Tavistock.

Sherif, M., Harvey, O. J., White, B. J., Hood, W. R. and Sherif, C. W. (1961) *Intergroup Conflict and Cooperation,* Norman, Ok.: Oklahoma Book Exchange.

Sherif, M. and Sherif, C. W. (1982) 'Production of intergroup conflict and its resolution: robbers' cave experiment', in J. W. Reich (ed.), *Experimenting in Society: Issues and examples in applied social psychology,* Glenview, Ill.: Foresman.

Shull, F. A., Delbecq, A. L. and Cummings, L. (1970) *Organizational Decision Making*, New York: McGraw-Hill

Siegrist, M., Cvetkovich, G. and Gutscher, H. (2002) 'Risk preference predictions and gender stereotypes', *Organizational Behavior and Human Decision Processes,* **87** (1), pp. 91–102.

Siltanen, J. and Stanworth, M. (1984) *Women and the Public Sphere: A critique of sociology and politics,* London: Hutchinson.

Silverman, D. (1970) *The Theory of Organizations*, London: Heinemann.

Simmel, G. (1908/1950) 'Subordination under a principle', pp. 250–67 in *The Sociology of Georg Simmel* (ed. and trans. K. Wolff), New York: Free Press.

Simon, H. A. (1957) *Administrative Behaviour*. New York: Macmillan.

Simons, D. J. and Chabris, C. F. (1999) 'Gorillas in our midst: sustained inattentional blindness for dynamic events', *Perception*, **28**, pp. 1059–74.

Simons, D. J. and Levin, D. T. (1998) 'Failures to detect changes to people in a real-world interaction', *Psychonomic Bulletin and Review*, **5**, pp. 644–9.

Singh, V., Kumra, S. and Vinnicombe, S. (2002) 'Gender and impression management: playing the promotion game', *Journal of Business Ethics*, **37**, pp. 77–89.

Sisson, K. and Marginson, P. (2003) 'Management systems, structures and strategy', in P. Edwards (ed.), *Industrial Relations: Theory and practice* (2nd edn), Oxford: Blackwell.

Skinner, B. F. (1953) *Science and Human Behavior*, New York: Macmillan.

Skinner, B. F. (1954) 'The science of learning and the art of teaching', *Harvard Educational Review,* **24**, pp. 86–97.

Sklair, L. (2002) *Globalization: Capitalism and its alternatives*, Oxford: Oxford University Press.

Small, M. and Yasin, M. (2000) 'Human factors in the adoption and performance of advanced manufacturing technology in unionized firms', *Industrial Management & Data Systems*, **100** (8–9), pp. 389–401.

Smart, B. (2003) *Economy, Culture and Society,* Buckingham: Open University Press.

Smircich, L. (1983) 'Concepts of culture and organization analysis', *Administrative Science Quarterly*, **28** (3), pp. 339–58.

Smith, A. (1776/1982) *The Wealth of Nations,* Harmondsworth: Penguin.

Smith, D. (1987) *The Everyday World as Problematic: A feminist sociology*, Boston, Mass.: Northeastern University Press.

Smith, J. W. and Calasanti, T. (2005) 'The influences of gender, race and ethnicity on workplace experiences of institutions and social isolation: an exploratory study of university faculty', *Sociological Spectrum*, **25** (3), pp. 307–34.

Smith, P. (1988) 'The impact of trade unionism and the market in a regional newspaper', *Industrial Relations Journal,* **19**, pp. 214–21.

Smith, R. C. (1993) *'Images of organizational communication: root metaphors of the organization-communication relation',* paper presented at the International Communication Association Conference, Washington, DC.

Snell, S. A., Youndt, M. A. and Wright, P. M. (1996) 'Establishing a framework for research in strategic human resource management: merging source theory and organizational learning', *Research in Personnel and Human Resources Management*, **14**, pp. 61–90.

Soloman, B. L. (1990) 'Understanding industrial relations in modern Japan', *Industrial and Labor Relations Review*, **43** (2), pp. 326–7.

Solomon, N. (1990) 'Culture and differences in workplace learning', pp. 119–31 in D. Boud and J. Garrick (eds), *Understanding Learning at Work*, London: Routledge.

Sorge, A. (1997) 'Organization behaviour', pp. 3–21 in A. Sorge and M. Warner (eds), *The IEBM Handbook of Organizational Behavior*, Boston, Mass.: International Thomson Business Press.

Sorge, A. and Streeck, W. (1988) 'Industrial relations and technical change: the case for an extended perspective', pp. 19–47 in R. Hyman and W. Streeck (eds), *New Technology and Industrial Relations,* Oxford: Blackwell.

Sparrow, P., Brewster, C. and Harris, H. (2004) *Globalizing Human Resource Management*, London: Routledge.

Spencer, B. (1998) *The Purposes of Adult Education: A guide for students*, Toronto: Thompson.

Spencer, B. (2001) 'Changing questions of workplace learning researchers', pp. 31–40 in T. Fenwick (ed.), *Socio-Cultural Perspectives on Learning through Work*, San Francisco, Calif.: Jossey-Bass.

Spikes, W. F. (ed.) (1995) 'Workplace learning', *New Directions for Adult and Continuing Education*, **68**, (Winter), San Francisco: Jossey-Bass.

Squires, G. (2001) 'Management as a professional discipline', *Journal of Management Studies*, **34** (1), pp. 473–87.

Stacks, D., Hickson, M. and Hill, S. (1991) *Introduction to Communication Theory*, Fort Worth, Tx.: Holt, Rinehart and Winston.

Stamps, D. (1999) 'Is knowledge management a fad?' *Training*, **36** (3), pp. 36–42.

Stanworth, M. (1981) *Gender and Schooling*, London: Hutchinson.

Statistics Canada (1999) *Survey of Labour and Income Dynamics*, Ottawa: Statistics Canada.

Statistics Canada (2002) *Labour Force Survey,* Ottawa: Statistics Canada.

Staw, B. and Ross, J. (1989) 'Understanding behavior in escalation situations', *Science*, **246**, pp. 216–20.

Steele, C. M., Spencer, S. J. and Aronson, J. (2003) 'Contending with group image: the psychology of stereotype threat and social identity threat', pp. 102–15 in M. P. Zanna (ed.), *Advances in Experimental Social Psychology*, San Diego: Academic Press.

Steiner, I. D. (1972) *Group Processes and Productivity.*, New York: Academic Press.

Sternberg, R. (1999) 'Survival of the fit test.' *People Management,* **4** (24), pp. 29–31.

Stewart, L. and Ting-Toomey, S. (eds) (1987) *Communication, Gender, and Sex Roles in Diverse Interaction Contexts,* New Jersey: Ablex.

Stewart, R. (1967) *Managers and their Jobs*, Basingstoke: Macmillan.

Stewart, R. (1982) *Choices for the Manager,* Maidenhead: McGraw-Hill.

Stewart, R. (1998) 'Manager behaviour', in M. Poole and M. Warner (eds), *The Handbook of Human Resource Management*, London: International Thomson Business.

Stewart, R., Barsoux, J-L., Kieser, A., Ganter, H. and Walgenbach, P. (1994) *Managing in Britain and Germany*, Basingstoke: Macmillan.

Stiglitz, J. E. (2002) *Globalization and its Discontents*, New York: Norton.

Stiglitz, J. E. (2006) *Making Globalization Work*, New York: Norton.

Stohl, C. and Cheney, G. (2001) 'Participatory processes/ paradoxical practices', *Management Communication Quarterly*, **14** (3), pp. 349–407.

Stogdill, R. M. (1974) *Handbook of Leadership: A survey of theory and research*, New York: Free Press.

Stogdill, R. M., and Coons, A. E. (1957) *Leader Behaviour: Its description and measurement,* research monograph no. 88, Columbus, Oh.: Bureau of Business Research, Ohio State University.

Stohl, C. and Cheney, G. (2001) 'Participatory processes/paradoxical practices', *Management Communication Quarterly*, **14** (3), pp. 349–407.

Storey, J. (1989) *New Perspectives on Human Resource Management*, London: Routledge.

Storey, J. (1992) *Developments in the Management of Human Resources*, Oxford: Blackwell.

Storey, J. (ed.) (2003) *Leadership in Organizations: Current issues and key trends*, London: Routledge.

Strauss, A. (1978) *Negotiations: Varieties, processes, contexts and social order*, London: Jossey-Bass.

Strayer, D. L. and Johnston, W. A. (2001) 'Driven to distraction: dual-task studies of simulated driving and conversing on a cellular telephone', *Psychological Science*, **12** (6), pp. 462–6.

Streek, W. (1996) 'German capitalism: does it exist? Can it survive?', Working Paper no. 218, Department of Industrial Relations, University of Wisconsin-Madison.

Suchman, L. (1987) *Plans and Situated Action: The problem of human–computer communication*, New York: CUP.

Suchman, L. (2002) 'Practice-based design of information systems: notes from the hyperdeveloped world', *The Information Society*, **18**, pp. 139–44.

Sundgren, M. and Styhre, A. (2006) 'Leadership as de-paradoxification: leading new drug development work at three pharmaceutical companies', *Leadership*, **2** (1) (February), pp. 31–51.

Sveiby, K. E. (1997) *The New Organizational Wealth: Managing and measuring organizational wealth*, San Francisco, Calif.: Berrett-Koehler.

Swingewood, A. (2000) *A Short History of Sociological Thought* (3rd edn), New York: St. Martin's Press.

Sydie, R. A. (1994) *Natural Women, Cultured Men*, Vancouver: UBC Press.

Tahvanainen, M. and Suutari, V. (2005) 'Expatriate performance management in MNCs', pp. 91–113 in H. Scullion and M. Linehan (eds.), *International Human Resource Management*, Basingstoke: Palgrave Macmillan.

Tajfel, H. (1978) 'Social categorization, social identity, and social comparison', pp. 61-76 in H. Tajfel (ed.), *Differentiation between Social Groups*, London: Academic Press.

Tajfel, H. (1981) 'Social stereotypes and social groups', in J. C. Turner and H. Giles (eds), *Intergroup Behaviour*, Oxford: Blackwell.

Tajfel, H. and Turner, J. C. (1979) 'An integrative theory of intergroup conflict', in W. G. Austin and S. Worchel (eds) *The Social Psychology of Intergroup Relations*, Monterey, Calif.: Brooks/Cole.

Tan, Joo-Seng (1998) '*Communication, cross cultural'*, in M. Poole and M. Warner (eds), *International Encyclopaedia of Business and Management*, London: Thomson.

Tannen, D. (1990) *You Just Don't Understand: Women and men in conversation.*

Taylor, F. W. (1911) *The Principles of Scientific Management*, New York: Harper.

Taylor, J. R. (1995) 'Shifting from a heteronomous to an autonomous world view of organizational communication: communication theory on the cusp', *Communication Theory*, **5** (1), pp. 1–35.

Taylor, M. S. and Tekleab, A. G. (2004) 'Taking stock of psychological contract research: assessing progress, addressing troublesome issues, and setting research priorities', in J. A-M. Coyle-Shapiro, L. M. Shore, M. S. Taylor and L. E. Tetrick (eds), *The Employment Relationship: Examining psychological and contextual perspectives*, Oxford: Oxford University Press.

Taylor, R. (2002) *Britain's World of Work: Myths and realities,*. Swindon: Economic and Social Research Council.

Tennant, M. (1997) *Psychology and Adult Learning* (2nd edn), London: Routledge.

Tetlock, P. (1983) 'Accountability and complexity of thought', *Journal of Personality and Social Psychology*, **45**, pp. 74–83.

Tharenou, P. (1997) 'Determinants of participation in training and development', *Journal of Organizational Behavior*, **4**, pp. 15–28.

Thomas, A. B. (2003) *Controversies in Management Issues, Debates, Answers* (2nd edn), London: Routledge.

Thompson, E. P. (1967) 'Time, work and discipline, and industrial capitalism', *Past and Present*, **38**, pp. 56–97.

Thompson, J. A. (2005) 'Proactive personality and job performance: a social perspective', *Journal of Applied Psychology*, **90** (5), pp. 1011–17.

Thompson, J. D. (1967) *Organizations in Action*, New York: McGraw-Hill.

Thompson, P. (1989) *The Nature of Work* (2nd edn), London: Macmillan.

Thompson, P. (1993) 'Fatal distraction: postmodernism and organizational theory', in. J. Hassard and M. Parker (eds), *Postmodernism and Organizations*, London: Sage.

Thompson, P. (forthcoming) 'Technological innovation and the office: call centres and the reorganization of clerical and service work', draft chapter in P. Boreham et al. (eds), *New Technology @ Work*.

Thompson, P. and Ackroyd, S. (1995) 'All quiet on the workplace front: a critique of recent trends in British industrial sociology', *Sociology*, **29** (4): pp. 615–33.

Thompson, P. and Findlay, T. (1999) 'Changing the people: social engineering in the contemporary workplace', in A. Sayer and L. Ray (eds), *Culture and Economy after the Cultural Turn*, London: Sage.

Thompson, P. and McHugh, D. (2006) *Work Organizations: A Critical Introduction* (4th edn), Basingstoke: Palgrave.

Thompson, P. and Wallace, T. (1996) 'Redesigning production through teamworking', *International Journal of Operations and Production Management*, **16** (2), pp. 103–18.

Thompson, P. and Warhurst, C. (1998) *Workplaces of the Future*, Basingstoke: Macmillan Business.

Thomson, R. (ed) (1993) *Learning and Technological Change,* New York: St. Martin's Press.

Thorndike, E. L. (1913) *The Psychology of Learning*, New York: Teachers' College.

Thornton, P. and Lunt, N. (1997) *Employment Policies for Disabled People in Eighteen Countries: A review,* York: University of York Policy Research Unit.

Tichy, N. and Devanna, M. (1986) *The Transformational Leader*, New York: Wiley.

Tichy, N. and Sherman, S. (1993) *Control Your Destiny or Someone Else Will,* New York: Doubleday.

Tietze, S. and Musson, G. (2005) 'Recasting the home-work relationship: a case of mutual adjustment?' *Organization Studies* 26 (9), pp. 1331–52.

Tiffin, C. and Lawson, A. (eds) (1994) *De-scribing Empire: Post-colonialism and textuality*, London: Routledge.

Tisdell, E. (1993) 'Feminism and adult learning: power, pedagogy and praxis', pp. 91–103 in S. Merriam (ed.), *An Update on Adult Learning Theory*, San Francisco: Jossey-Bass.

Tomaney, J. (1990) 'The reality of workplace flexibility', *Capital and Class*, **40**.

Tong, R. P. (1998) *Feminist Thought* (2nd edn), Boulder, Colo.: Westview Press.

Torbiorn, I. (2005) 'Staffing policies and practices in European MNCs: strategic sophistication, culture-bound policies or ad hoc reactivity?' pp. 47–68 in H. Scullion and M. Linehan (eds), *International Human Resource Management*, Basingstoke: Palgrave Macmillan.

Touraine, A. (1971) *The Post-Industrial Society: Tomorrow's social history: classes, conflicts and culture in the programmed society*, New York: Random House.

Tourish, D. and Vatcha, N. (2005) 'Charismatic leadership and corporate cultism at Enron: the elimination of dissent, the promotion of conformity and organizational collapse', *Leadership*, **1** (4), pp. 455–80.

Townley, B. (1994) *Reframing Human Resource Management: Power, ethics and the subject of work*, London: Sage.

Trevino, L. K. (1986) 'Ethical decision making in organizations: a person–situation interactionist model', *Academy of Management Review*, July, **11**, pp. 601–17.

Trice, H. H. and Beyer, J. (1992) *The Cultures of Work Organizations*, Englewood Cliffs, N.J.: Prentice Hall.

Tubbs, M. E. (1986) 'Goal-setting: a meta-analytic examination of the empirical evidence', *Journal of Applied Psychology*, **71**, pp. 474–83.

Tubbs, M. E. and Ekeberg, S. E. (1991) 'The role of intentions in work motivation: implications for goal-setting theory and research', *Academy of Management Review*, **16** (1), pp. 180–99.

Tucker, K. H. (2002) *Classical Social Theory*, Oxford: Blackwell.

Tuckman, B. and Jensen, M. (1977) 'Stages of small group development revisited', *Group and Organizational Studies*, **2**, pp. 419–27.

Turnbull, P. (1986) 'The Japanisation of British industrial relations at Lucas', *Industrial Relations Journal*, **17** (3), pp. 193–206.

Turner, B. S. (1999) *Classical Sociology*, London: Sage.

Turner, H. A. (1962) *Trade Union Growth, Structure and Policy: A comparative study of the cotton unions*, London: Allen & Unwin.

Turner, J. (1987) *Rediscovering the Social Group: A self-categorization theory*, New York: Basic Books.

Turner, A. N. and Lawrence, P. R. (1965) *Industrial Jobs and the Worker*, Boston: Harvard University, Graduate School of Business Administration.

Tyler, T. (1990) *Why People Obey the Law: Procedural justice, legitimacy and compliance,* New Haven, Conn.: Yale University Press.

Tyson, S. (1987) 'The management of the personnel function', *Journal of Management Studies,* **24**, pp. 523–32.

UK Labour Force Survey (2003) *In-house Report 109: Employment Retention and the Onset of Sickness or Disability.*

Ulrich, D. (1997) 'Measuring human resources: an overview of practice and a prescription for results', *Human Resource Management*, **36**, pp. 303–20.

Unwin, L. and Fuller, A. (2001) *From Skill Formation to Social Inclusion: the changing meaning of apprenticeship and its relationship to communities and workplace in England*, University of Nottingham, UK (online) www.nottingham.ac.uk

US Bureau of Labor Statistics (2002) *Employment and Earnings,* January (online) www.bls.gov/cps/home.htm

US Bureau of Labor Statistics (2003) *Current Population Survey. Merged outgoing rotation groups with earning data*, Washington, D.C.: Bureau of Labor Statistics.

Vallas, S. (1999) 'Re-thinking post-Fordism: the meaning of workplace flexibility', *Sociological Theory*, **17** (1), pp. 68–85.

Vallerand, R. J. (1997) 'Toward a hierarchical model of intrinsic and extrinsic motivation', *Advances in Experimental Social Psychology*, **29**, pp. 271–360.

van der Heiden, B. I. J. M. and Nijhof, A. H. J. (2004),The value of subjectivity: problems and prospects for 360-degree appraisal systems', *International Journal of Human Resource Management*, **15**, pp. 493–511.

VandenHeuvel, A. and Wooden, M. (1997) 'Participation of non-English-speaking-background immigrants in work-related training', *Ethnic and racial studies*, **20** (4), pp. 830–48.

Vecchio, R. P. (1987). 'Situational leadership theory: an examination of a prescriptive theory', *Journal of Applied Psychology*, **72**, pp. 444–51.

Verma, A. and Taras, D. (2001) 'Employee involvement in the workplace', in M. Gunderson, A. Ponak and D. Taras (eds), *Union–Management Relations in Canada* (4th edn), Don Mills, ON: Addison-Wesley.

Verma, A. and Taras, D. (2005). 'Managing the high-involvement workplace', pp. 134–73 in M. Gunderson, A. Ponak and D. Taras (eds), *Union-Management Relations in Canada* (5th edn), Toronto: Addison Wesley.

Vinkenburg, C. J., Jansen, P. G. and Koopman, P. L. (2000) 'Feminine leadership – a review of gender differences in managerial behaviour and effectiveness', Chapter 9 in M. J. Davidson and R. J. Burke (eds), *Women in Management: Current research issues*, Vol. II, London: Sage.

Von Tunzelmann, G. N. (1978) *Steam Power and British Industrialization to 1860*, Oxford:

Vosko, L. (2000) *Temporary Work: The gendered rise of a precarious employment relationship*, Toronto: University of Toronto Press;

Vroom, V. H. (1964) *Work and Motivation*, New York: Wiley.

Vroom, V. H. and Deci, E. L. (eds) (1970) 'Introduction: an overview of work motivation', pp. 9–19 in *Management and Motivation: Selected readings,* London: Penguin.

Vroom, V. H. and Jago, A. G. (1978) 'On the validity of the Vroom–Yetton model', *Journal of Applied Psychology*, **63**, pp. 151–62.

Vroom, V. H. and Yetton, P. W. (1973) *Leadership and Decision Making*, Pittsburgh: University of Pittsburgh Press.

Vygotsky, L. (1978) *Mind in Society: The development of higher psychological processes*, Cambridge, Mass.: Harvard University Press.

Wajcman, J. (1998) *Managing Like a Man: Women and men in corporate management*, Cambridge: Polity Press/Penn State University Press.

Wajcman, J. (2000) 'Feminism facing industrial relations in Britain', *British Journal of Industrial Relations*, **38** (2), pp. 183–201.

Walker, J. T. (1996) *The Psychology of Learning*, Englewood Cliffs, N.J.: Prentice-Hall.

Wallace, M. and Kalleberg, A. (1982) 'Industrial transformation and the decline of craft: the decomposition of skill in the printing industry, 1931–1978', *American Sociological Review*, **47**, pp. 307–24.

Walters, A., Stuhlmacher, A. and Meyer, L. (1998) 'Gender and negotiator competitiveness: a meta-analysis', *Organizational Behavior and Human Decision Processes*, **76** (1), pp. 1–29.

Walton, R. (1985) 'From control to commitment in the workplace', *Harvard Business Review*, March/April, pp. 77–84.

Ward, L. (1998) 'Ethnic minorities pessimistic over race relations', *Guardian*, 10 September.

Warde, A. (1990) 'The future of work,' pp. 86–94 in J. Anderson and M. Ricci (eds), *Society and Social Science: A reader*, Milton Keynes: Open University Press.

Warren, D. I. (1968) 'Power, visibility, and conformity in formal organizations', *American Sociological Review*, **6**, pp. 951–70.

Watkins, K. E. and Cervero, R. M. (2000) 'Organizations as contexts for learning: a case study in certified public accountancy,' *Journal of Workplace Learning*, **12** (5), pp. 187–94.

Watkins, K. and Marsick, V. (1993) *Sculpting the Learning Organization*, San Francisco: Jossey-Bass.

Watson, A. (2001) *In Search of Management*, London: Thomson Learning.

Watson, J. B. and Rayner, R. (1920) 'Conditional emotional reactions', *Journal of Experimental Psychology*, **3**, pp. 1–14.

Watson, T. (1995) *Sociology of Work and Industry (3rd edn)*, London: Routledge.

Watson, T. (1986) *Management, Organization and Employment Strategy*, London: Routledge.

Watson, T. (1995) *Sociology, Work, and Industry* (3rd edn), London: Routledge.

Weber, M. (1905/2002) *The Protestant Ethic and the 'Spirit' of Capitalism,* London: Penguin.

Weber, M. (1922/1957) *The Theory of Social and Economic Organization*, ed. T. Parsons, Glencoe, Ill.: Free Press.

Weber, M. (1922/1968) *Economy and Society*, New York: Bedminster.

Weber, M. (1947) *The Theory of Social and Economic Organization*, London: Oxford University Press.

Webster, E., Wood, G. and Brookes, M. (2006) 'International homogenization or the persistence of national practices? The remaking of industrial relations in Mozambique', *Relations Industrielles/Industrial Relations*, **61** (2), pp. 247–70.

Weick, K. (1979) *The Social Psychology of Organizing* (2nd edn), New York: McGraw-Hill.

Weick, K. E. (1995) *Sensemaking in Organizations*, London: Sage.

Weick, K. E. (2001) *Making Sense of the Organization,* Oxford: Blackwell.

Weiner, N. and Mahoney, T. A. (1981) 'A model of corporate performance as a function of environment, organization and leadership influences', *Academy of Management Journal*, **24**, pp. 453–70.

Weiss, E., H. (2005) 'The elements of international English style: A guide to writing correspondence, reports, technical documents and internet pages for a global audience', Armonk, N.Y.: M.E. Sharpe.

Wells, D. (1993) 'Are strong unions compatible with the new model of human resource management?', *Relations Industrielles/Industrial Relations*, **48** (1), pp. 56–84.

Wenger, E. (1998) *Cultivating Communities of Practice*, New York: Cambridge University Press.

Wenger, E. (2000) 'Communities of practice and social learning systems', *Organization*, **7** (2), pp. 225–46.

Wenger, E., McDermott, R. and Snyder, W. (2002) *Cultivating Communities of Practice,* Boston, Mass.: Harvard Business School Press.

Wenger, E. C. and Snyder, W. M. (2000) 'Communities of practice: the organizational frontier', *Harvard Business Review*, January–February, pp. 139–45.

Whipp, R. (1999) 'Creative deconstruction: strategy and organizations', pp. 11–25 in S. Clegg, C. Hardy and W. R. Nord (eds), *Managing Organisations: Current issues*, London: Sage.

Whitfield, K. and Strauss, G. (eds) (1998) *Researching the World of Work*, New York: Cornell University Press.

Whitley, R. (1999) *Divergent Capitalism: The social structuring and change of business systems,* Oxford: Oxford University Press.

Whittaker, D. H. (1990) *Managing Innovation: A study of British and Japanese factories,* Cambridge: CUP.

Wiener, N. (1954) *The Human Use of Human Beings: Cybernetics and society*, New York: Avon.

Wiggins, J. S. (ed.) (1996) *The Five-Factor Model of Personality: Theoretical perspectives*. New York: Guilford.

Williams, B. (ed.) (1981) *Computer Aids to Clinical Decisions, Vol. I*. Boca Raton, Fla.: CRC Press.

Williams, R. (1983) *Keywords*, New York: Oxford University Press.

Williams, R. (1977) *Marxism and Literature*, Oxford: Oxford University Press.

Williams, R. and Edge, D. (1996) 'The social shaping of technology', *Research Policy*, **25**, pp. 856–99.

Willmott, H. (1989) 'Images and ideals of managerial work', *Journal of Management Studies*, **21** (3), pp. 349–68.

Willmott, H. (1993) 'Strength is ignorance; slavery is freedom: managing culture in modern organizations', *Journal of Management Studies*, **30**, pp. 515–52.

Willmott, H., (1995) 'The odd couple?: re-engineering business processes: managing human relations', *New Technology, Work and Employment*, **10** (2), pp. 89–98.

Wilson, A. L. (1993) 'The promise of situated cognition', pp. 71–9 in S. Merriam (ed.), *An Update on Adult Learning Theory, No. 57*, San Francisco, Calif.: Jossey-Bass.

Wilson, F. M. (1992) 'Language, power and technology,' *Human Relations*, **45** (9), pp. 883-904.

Wilson, F. M. (2003) *Organizational Behaviour and Gender*, Ashgate.

Witherspoon, P. D. (1997) *Communicating Leadership: An organizational perspective*, Needham Heights, Mass.: Allyn & Bacon.

Witz, A. (1986) 'Patriarchy and the labour market: occupational control strategies and the medical division of labour,' in D. Knights and H. Willmott (eds), *Gender and the Labour Process*, Aldershot: Gower.

Wofford, J. C. and Liska, L. Z. (1993) 'Path-goal theories of leadership: a meta-analysis', *Journal of Management*, **19**, pp. 858–76.

Womack, J., Jones, D. and Roos, D. (1990) *The Machine that Changed the World*, New York: Rawson Associates.

Wood, D. J., Bruner, J. and Ross, G. (1976) 'The role of tutoring in problem solving', *Journal of Child Psychology and Psychiatry*, **17**, pp. 89–100.

Wood, M. and Case, P. (2006) 'Leadership refrains – again, again and again', *Leadership*, **1** (2): pp. 139–45.

Wood, S. (ed.) (1982) *The Transformation of Work?* London: Unwin Hyman.

Wood, S. (1986) 'The cooperative labour strategy in the U.S. auto industry', *Economic and Industrial Democracy*, 7 (4), pp. 415–48.

Woodall, J. and Winstanley, D. (2001) 'The place of ethics in HRM', pp. 37–56 in J. Storey (ed.), *Human Resource Management: A critical text* (2nd edn), London: Thomson Learning.

Woodward, J. (1958) *Management and Technology*, Problems of Progress in Industry no. 5, London: HMSO.

Woodward, J. (1965) *Industrial Organizations: Theory and practice*, London: Oxford University Press.

Wright Mills, C. (1959/2000) *The Sociological Imagination* (40th anniv. edn), New York: Oxford University Press.

Wright, P. M., Gardner, T. M. and Moynihan, L. M. (2003) 'The impact of HR practices on the performance of business units', *Human Resource Management Journal*, **13** (3), pp. 21–36.

Wrong, D. H. (1988) *Power: Its forms, bases, and uses* (2nd edn), Chicago, Ill.: University of Chicago Press.

Yeatts, D. E. and Hyten, C. (1998) *High-Performing Self-managed Work Teams*, Thousand Oaks, Calif.: Sage.

Yoder, J. (2002) 'Context matters: Understanding tokenism processes and their impact on women's work', *Psychology of Women Quarterly*, **26** (1), pp. 1–8.

Yoder, J. and Berendsen, L. (2001) '"Outsider within" the firehouse: African American and white women firefighters', *Psychology of Women Quarterly*, **25** (1), pp. 27–36.

Young, R. A. and Chen, C. P. (1999) 'Annual review: practice and research in career counselling and development – 1998', *Career Development Quarterly*, December, p. 98.

Yukl, G. (2002) *Leadership in Organizations* (5th edn), Upper Saddle River, N.J.: Prentice-Hall.

Yuval-Davis, N. (1997) *Cultural Reproductions and Gender Relations: Gender and nation*, London: Sage.

Zaleznik, A. (1990) *Executive's Guide to Motivating People*, Chicago: Bonus Books.

Zammuto, R. F. (1982). *Assessing Organizational Effectiveness*, Albany, N.Y.: State University of New York Press.

Zersan, J. and Carnes, A. (eds) (1991) *Questioning Technology: Tool, toy or tyrant?* Philadelphia, Penn.: New Society.

Zimbalist, A. (ed.) (1979) *Case Studies on the Labor Process*, New York: Monthly Review Press.

Zuboff, S. (1988) *In the Age of the Smart Machine*, New York: Basic Books.

Glossary

A

Activity theory A view of adult learning that envisions learning as a social process whereby individual and group agency and learning occurs through interlocking human activity systems shaped by social norms and a community of practice. Associated with the work of Russian psychologist Vygotsky.

Adaptive culture An organizational culture in which employees focus on the changing needs of customers and other stakeholders, and support initiatives to keep pace with those changes.

Ageism Prejudice and discrimination against people on the basis of age, particularly when they are older persons.

Agents of socialization Those persons, groups or institutions that teach people what they need to know in order to participate in society.

Alienation A feeling of powerlessness and estrangement from other people and from oneself (a term from Marx).

Analysis The process through which data are organized so that comparisons can be made and conclusions drawn.

Andragogy The processes associated with the organization and practice of teaching adults; more specifically, various kinds of interactions in facilitating/learning situations.

Anomie A state condition in which social control becomes ineffective as a result of the loss of shared values and a sense of purpose in society (a term from Durkheim).

Appropriation The process through which, in capitalist workplaces, a proportion of the value produced in work activities – above investment in raw materials, equipment, health benefits, facilities and so on – is retained under the private control of owners, ownership groups and/or investors. A more critical perception of this process sees it as 'exploitation' of collective activities of the organization for private use.

Aristocracy of labour A term used to describe nineteenth-century trade unions representing craft/skilled workers.

Artefacts The observable symbols and signs of an organization's culture.

Attitudes The cluster of beliefs, assessed feelings and behavioural intentions toward an object.

Authority The power granted by some form of either active or passive consent which bestows legitimacy.

Autonomy The degree to which a job gives employees the freedom, independence and discretion to schedule their work and determine the procedures used in completing it.

B

Behaviour modification A theory that explains learning in terms of the background and consequence of behaviour.

Bottom-up processing Perception led predominantly by gathering external sensory data and then working out what it means.

Bounded rationality Processing limited and imperfect information and satisficing rather than maximizing when choosing among alternatives.

Bourgeoisie (or capitalist class) Karl Marx's term for the class comprised of those who own and control the means of production.

Brainstorming A freewheeling, face-to-face meeting where team members generate as many ideas as possible, piggyback on the ideas of others, and avoid evaluating anyone's ideas during the idea-generation stage.

Bureaucracy An organizational model characterized by a hierarchy of authority, a clear division of labour, explicit rules and procedures, and impersonality in personnel matters.

Bureaucratization A tendency towards a formal organization with a hierarchy of authority, a clear division of labour and an emphasis on written rules.

Business process re-engineering A radical change of business processes by applying information technology to integrate operations, and maximizing their value-added content.

C

Capitalism An economic system characterized by private ownership of the means of production, from which personal profits can be derived through market competition and without government intervention.

Causal attribution process The perceptual process of deciding whether an observed behaviour or event is caused largely by internal or by external factors, and by stable or transitory phenomena.

Centralization The degree to which formal decision authority is held by a small group of people, typically those at the top of the organizational hierarchy.

Change agent A generic term for an individual championing or facilitating change in the organization.

Charismatic authority Power legitimized on the basis of a leader's exceptional personal qualities (a term from Weber).

Class The relative location of a person or group within a larger society, based on wealth, power, prestige or other valued resources.

Class conflict A term for the struggle between the capitalist class and the working (proletariat) class (used by Marx).

Class consciousness Karl Marx's term for awareness of a common identity based on a person's position in the means of production.

Classical conditioning A view of 'instrumental' learning whose adherents assert that the reinforcement is noncontingent on the animal's behaviour, that is, delivered without regard to the animal's behaviour. By contrast, in instrumental conditioning the delivery of the reinforcement is contingent – dependent – on what the animal does.

Cognitive dissonance Occurs when people perceive an inconsistency between their beliefs, feelings and behaviour.

Cohesiveness Refers to all the positive and negative forces or social pressures that cause individuals to maintain their membership in specific groups.

Cohort A category of people who are born within a specified period in time or who share some specified characteristic.

Collectivism The extent to which people value duty to groups to which they belong, and to group harmony.

Common-sense knowledge A form of knowing that guides ordinary conduct in everyday life.

Communication The process by which information is transmitted and understood between two or more people.

Communities of practice Informal groups bound together by shared expertise and passion for a particular activity or interest.

Competencies The abilities, values, personality traits and other characteristics of people that lead to a superior performance.

Competitive advantage The ability of a work organization to add more value for its customers and shareholders than its rivals, and thus gain a position of advantage in the marketplace.

Complexity The intricate departmental and interpersonal relationships that exist within an work organization.

Configurations Defining technology as the combination of social and technical factors. Configurations are a complex mix of standardized and locally customized elements which are highly specific to an organization.

Conflict The process in which one party perceives that its interests are being opposed or negatively affected by another party.

Conflict of interest A condition in which the needs of one party (such as an individual or group) run counter to the needs of another.

Conflict management Interventions that alter the level and form of conflict in ways that maximize its benefits and minimize its dysfunctional consequences.

Conflict perspective The sociological approach that views groups in society as engaged in a continuous power struggle for control of scarce resources.

Constructionism The view that researchers actively construct reality on the basis of their understandings, which are mainly culturally fashioned and shared. It contrasts with **realism.**

Constructivist approach Approaches to technology that tend not to focus on social or political influences but rather see technologies as defined strictly in how they are put to use.

Constructs Abstract ideas constructed by researchers that can be linked to observable information.

Contingency approach The idea that a particular action may have different consequences in different situations.

Contingent work Part-time or temporary work, also known as non-standard or precarious employment.

Contradiction Contradictions are said to occur within social systems when the various principles that underlie these social arrangements conflict with each other.

Control The collection and analysis of information about all aspects of the work organization and the use of comparisons, which are either historical and/or based on benchmarking against another business unit.

Convergence thesis The hypothesis that industrialized societies become increasingly alike in their political, social, cultural and employment characteristics.

Core competency Underlying core characteristics of an organization's workforce which result in effective performance and give a competitive advantage to the firm.

Corporate social responsibility (CSR) An organization's moral obligation to its stakeholders.

Corporation A large-scale organization that has legal powers (such as the ability to enter into contracts and buy and sell property) separate from its individual owner or owners.

Co-variation model Kelley's model which uses information about the co-occurrence of a person, behaviour and potential causes to work out an explanation.

Creativity The capacity to develop an original product, service or idea that makes a socially recognized contribution.

Critical approach Approaches to technology that tend to focus on how the social and political effects are produced through contestation and negotiation.

Critical realism A realist epistemology that asserts that the study of the human behaviour should be concerned with the identification of the structures that generate that behaviour in order to change it.

Cultural imperialism The extensive infusion of one nation's culture into other nations.

Culture The knowledge, language, values, customs and material objects that are passed from person to person and from one generation to the next in a human group or society.

D

Decision making A conscious process of making choices between one or more alternatives with the intention of moving toward some desired state of affairs.

Deductive approach Research in which the investigator begins with a theory and then collects information and data to test the theory.

De-industrialization A term to describe the decline of the manufacturing sector of the economy.

Delphi technique A structured team decision-making process of systematically pooling the collective knowledge of experts on a particular subject to make decisions, predict the future or identify opposing views.

Dependency theory The perspective that global poverty is at least partially attributable to the fact that low-income countries have been exploited by the high-income countries.

Deskilling A reduction in the proficiency needed to perform a specific job, which leads to a corresponding reduction in the wages paid for that job.

Dialectic Refers to the movement of history through transcendence of internal contradictions that in turn produce new contradictions, themselves requiring solutions (developed by Hegel and Marx).

Dialogue A process of conversation among team members in which they learn about each other's mental models and assumptions, and eventually form a common model for thinking within the team.

Discourse A way of talking about and conceptualizing an issue, presented through concepts, ideas and vocabulary that recur in texts.

Discourse community A way of talking about and conceptualizing an issue, presented through ideas and concepts, spoken or written, within a social group or community (such as lawyers or physicians).

Discrimination Actions or practices of dominant group members (or their representatives) that have a harmful impact on members of a subordinate group.

Distributive justice Justice based on the principle of fairness of outcomes.

Divergent thinking Involves reframing a problem in a unique way and generating different approaches to the issue.

Diversity theory The theory that people from different backgrounds will tend to generate a broader range of ideas and solutions when they work together.

Division of labour The allocation of work tasks to various groups or categories of employee.

Divisional structure An organizational structure that groups employees around geographic areas, clients or outputs.

Dyad A group consisting of two members.

E

Economy The social institution that ensures the maintenance of society through the production, distribution and consumption of goods and services.

Effort-to-performance (E→P) expectancy The individual's perceived probability that his or her effort will result in a particular level of performance.

Ego According to Sigmund Freud, the rational, reality-oriented component of personality that imposes restrictions on the innate pleasure-seeking drives of the id.

Emotional dissonance The conflict between required and true emotions.

Emotional labour The effort, planning and control needed to express organizationally desired emotions during interpersonal transactions.

Emotions Psychological and physiological episodes toward an object, person or event that create a state of readiness.

Empathy A person's ability to understand and be sensitive to the feelings, thoughts and situations of others.

Empirical approach Research that attempts to answer questions through a systematic collection and analysis of data.

Empiricism An approach to the study of social reality that suggests that only knowledge gained through experience and the senses is acceptable.

Employability An employment relationship in which people are expected to continually develop their skills to remain employed.

Employee involvement The degree to which employees influence how their work is organized and carried out.

Employment equity A strategy to eliminate the effects of discrimination and to make employment opportunities available to groups who have been excluded.

Empowerment A psychological concept in which people experience more self-determination, meaning, competence and impact regarding their role in the organization.

Enskilling Changes in work, often involving technology, that result in an increase in the skill level of workers. The issue of control is often implicated.

Environment Refers to the broad economic, political, legal and social forces that are present in the minds of organization members and may influence decision making and constrain strategic choices, such as the national business system.

Epistemology A theory of knowledge, particularly used to refer to a standpoint on what should pass as acceptable knowledge.

Equity theory Theory that explains how people develop perceptions of fairness in the distribution and exchange of resources.

ERG theory Alderfer's motivation theory of three instructive needs arranged in a hierarchy, in which people progress to the next higher need when a lower one is fulfilled, and regress to a lower need if unable to fulfill a higher one.

Escalation of commitment The tendency to allocate more resources to a failing course of action or to repeat an apparently bad decision.

Ethics The study of moral principles or values that determine whether actions are right or wrong and outcomes are good or bad.

Ethnic group A collection of people distinguished, by others or by themselves, primarily on the basis of cultural or nationality characteristics.

Ethnicity The cultural heritage or identity of a group based on factors such as language or country of origin.

Ethnocentrism The tendency to regard one's own culture and group as the standard, and thus superior, whereas all other groups are seen as inferior.

Ethnomethodology A sociological perspective concerned with the way in which social order is accomplished through talk and social interaction.

Exchange value The price at which commodities (including labour) trade on the market (a term from Marx).

'Exit and voice' A concept referring to the basic choice that defines an important part of employees' experience at work: they can either exit (leave) or exercise 'voice' (have a say) in how the workplace is run.

Expectancy theory A motivation theory based on the idea that work effort is directed toward behaviours that people believe will lead to desired outcomes.

Explicit knowledge Knowledge that is ordered and can be communicated between people.

Extrinsic motivator Covers a wide range of external outcomes or rewards to motivate employees, including bonuses or increases in pay. The incentive (pay) to increase effort or performance is called extrinsic motivation. Practising a musical instrument to obtain money or an award would involve extrinsic motivation as opposed to intrinsic motivation.

Extrinsic reward see *extrinsic motivator*.

Extroversion A personality dimension that characterizes people who are outgoing, talkative, sociable and assertive.

F

Factor analysis A statistical technique used for large number of variables to explain the pattern of relationships in the data.

Factory system A relatively large work unit that concentrated people and machines in one building that enabled the specialization of productive functions and, at the same time, enabled a closer supervision of employees than the pre-industrial putting-out system. Importantly, the factory system gave rise to the need for new conceptions of time and organizational behaviour.

False consensus effect The tendency to over-estimate the degree to which other people will think and behave in the same way as we do.

Feedback Any information that people received about the consequences of their behaviour.

Feminism The belief that all people – both women and men – are equal and that they should be valued equally and have equal rights.

Feminist perspective The sociological approach that focuses on the significance of gender in understanding and explaining inequalities that exist between men and women in the household, in the paid labour force, and in the realms of politics, law and culture.

Fiedler's contingency model Developed by Fred Fiedler, this suggests that leader effectiveness depends on whether the person's natural leadership style is appropriately matched to the situation.

Flexibility Action in response to global competition, including employees performing a number of tasks (functional flexibility), the employment of part-time and contract workers (numerical flexibility), and performance-related pay (reward flexibility).

Forces of production The human capacities, technology and techniques that are required to produce goods and services (a term from Marx).

Fordism A term used to describe mass production using assembly-line technology that allowed for greater division of labour and time and motion management, techniques pioneered by the American car manufacturer Henry Ford in the early twentieth century.

Formal channels A communication process that follows an organization's chain of command.

Formal organization A highly structured group formed for the purpose of completing certain tasks or achieving specific goals.

Formal work group see *work group*.

Formalization The degree to which organizations standardize behaviour through rules, procedures, formal training and related mechanisms.

'Free-rider' problem The fear that firms have that if they invest in training for workers, these workers might eventually leave the firm for one offering higher wages/benefits thus losing the firm its investment.

Functional configuration An organizational structure that organizes employees around specific knowledge or other resources.

Functional theory A sociological perspective that emphasizes that human action is governed by relatively stable structures. It underscores how social micro and macrostructures maintain or undermines social stability. It emphasizes that social structures are based mainly on shared values.

Functionalist perspective The sociological approach that views society as a stable, orderly system.

Fundamental attribution error The tendency to favour internal attributions for the behaviour of others but external ones to explain our own behaviour.

G

Game theory A social theory premised on the notion that people do what is best for themselves given their resources and circumstances, as in some form of a competitive game.

Gatekeeper A non-researcher who controls researcher access to a research setting, such as an organization.

Gender The culturally and socially constructed differences between females and males found in meanings, beliefs and practices associated with 'femininity' and 'masculinity'.

Gender bias Behaviour that shows favouritism toward one gender over the other.

Gender identity A person's perception of the self as female or male.

Gender role Attitudes, behaviour and activities that are socially defined as appropriate for each sex and are learned through the socialization process.

Gender socialization The aspect of socialization that contains specific messages and practices concerning the nature of being female or male in a specific group or society.

Genre A term to describe the different kinds of writing and reading in the workplace including reports, letters and memoranda.

Gestalt A German word that means form or organization and Gestalt psychology emphasizes organizational processes in learning. The Gestalt slogan, 'The whole is greater than the sum of the parts,' draws attention to relationships between parts.

Glass ceiling The pattern of employment opportunities that disproportionately limits achievement of top administrative posts by certain social groups.

Globalization When an organization extends its activities to other parts of the world, actively participates in other markets, and competes against organizations located in other countries.

Goal setting The process of motivating employees and clarifying their role perceptions by establishing performance objectives.

Goals The immediate or ultimate objectives that employees are trying to accomplish from their work effort.

Grapevine An unstructured and informal communication network founded on social relationships rather than organizational charts or job descriptions.

Group context Refers to anything from the specific task a work group is engaged in to the broad environmental forces that are present in the minds of group members and may influence them. A context may be physical, economic and social such as corporate restructuring, and the national business and employment system.

Group dynamics The systematic study of the human behaviour in groups including, the nature of groups, group development, and the interrelations between individuals and groups, other groups, and other elements of formal organizations.

Group norms The unwritten rules and expectations that specify or shape appropriate human behaviour in a work group or team.

Group processes Refers to group member actions, communications and decision making.

Group structure A stable pattern of social interaction among work group members created by a role structure and group norms.

Groups Two or more people with a unifying relationship.

Groupthink The tendency of highly cohesive groups to value consensus at the price of decision quality.

Growth needs A person's needs for self-esteem through personal achievement as well as for self-actualization.

H

Halo and horns effect A perceptual error whereby our general impression of a person, usually based on one prominent characteristic, colours the perception of other characteristics of that person.

Hegemony A conception of power that includes both conflict as well as consent and leadership by generating a particular world-view, or 'common sense' on relevant and appropriate action.

High-commitment management (HCM) See *high-performance work system*.

High-context culture A culturally sanctioned style of communication that assumes high levels of shared knowledge and so uses very concise sometimes obscure speech.

High-performance work system (HPWS) A term that gained currency in the 1990s, describing efforts to manage employment relations and work operations using a set of distinctive 'better' HR practices. These are intended to improve outcomes such as employee commitment, flexibility and cooperation which in turn enhance the organization's competitive advantage. Also known as high-commitment management (HCM).

Horizontal or 'lean' structure An integrated system of manufacturing, developed originally by Toyota in Japan. The emphasis is on flexibility and team work.

Horizontal tension Tensions and contradictions that emerge in terms of people's participation in group endeavours irrespective of hierarchical institutional relationships.

Hot button Personal sensitivity to a feature of another's behaviour which stimulates an automatic response.

Human capital theory The view that people are worth investing in as a form of capital: that people's performance and the results achieved can be considered as a return on investment and assessed in terms of cost and benefits.

Human relations A school of management thought that emphasizes the importance of social processes in the organization.

Human resource management (HRM) An approach to managing employment relations that emphasizes that leveraging people's capabilities is important to achieving competitive advantage.

HRM cycle An analytical framework that diagrammatically connects HR selection, appraisal, development and rewards to organization performance.

Human rights Conditions/treatment expected for all human beings.

Hypotheses Statements making empirically testable declarations that certain variables and their corresponding measure are related in a specific way proposed by theory.

Hypothesis In search studies, a tentative statement of the relationship between two or more concepts or variables.

I

Id Sigmund Freud's term for the component of personality that includes all of the individual's basic biological drives and needs that demand immediate gratification.

Ideal type An abstract model that describes the recurring characteristics of some phenomenon (a term from Weber).

Ideology Multiple uses but in particular refers to perceptions of reality distorted by class interests and the ideas, legal arrangements and culture that arise from class relations (a term from Marx).

Implicit leadership theory A theory stating that perceptual processes cause people to inflate the importance of leadership in explaining organizational events.

Impression management The process of trying to control or influence the impressions of oneself that other people form.

Individualism The extent to which a person values independence and personal uniqueness.

Inductive approach Research in which the investigator collects information or data (facts or evidence) and then generates theories from the analysis of that data.

Industrial democracy A broad term used to describe a range of programmes, processes, and social institutions designed to provide greater employee involvement and influence in the decision-making process, and to exchange ideas on how to improve working conditions and product and service quality in the workplace.

Industrial Revolution The relatively rapid economic transformation that began in Britain in the 1780s. It involved a factory and technology-driven shift from agriculture and small cottage-based manufacturing to manufacturing industries and the consequences of that shift for virtually all human activities.

Industrialization The process by which societies are transformed from dependence on agriculture and hand-made products to an emphasis on manufacturing and related industries.

Informal channels A communication process that follows unofficial means of communication, sometimes called 'the grapevine', usually based on social relations in which employees talk about work.

Informal group Two or more people who form a unifying relationship around personal rather than organizational goals.

Informal structure A term used to describe the aspect of organizational life in which participants' day-to-day activities and interactions ignore, bypass or do not correspond with the official rules and procedures of the bureaucracy.

Information overload A situation when the receiver becomes overwhelmed by the information that needs to be processed. It may be caused by the *quantity* of the information to be processed, the *speed* at which the information presents itself, and the *complexity* of the information to be processed.

Ingroups Groups to which someone perceives he or she belongs, which he or she accordingly evaluates favourably.

Initiating structure Part of a behavioural theory of leadership which describes the degree to which a leader defines and structures her or his own role and the roles of followers toward attainment of the group's assigned goals. It is associated with early leadership research at Ohio State University.

Institutionalized racism A term used to describe the rules, procedures and practices that directly and deliberately prevent minorities from having full and equal involvement in society.

Instrumentalist or technocratic approach Approaches to technology that are uncritical of its broader social, political and economic significance, viewing technologies as autonomous and positive.

Instrumentality A term associated with process theories of motivation. It refers to an individual's perceived probability that good performance will result in valued outcomes or rewards, measured on a scale from 0 (no chance) to 1 (certainty).

Integrative approach Explains the effectiveness of a leader in terms of influence on the way followers view themselves and interpret the context and events.

Intellectual capital The sum of an organization's human capital, structural capital and relationship capital.

Interactionism A term to describe what people do when they are in one another's presence, for example, in a work group or team.

Interlocutor Participant in a conversation or a dialogue.

International human resource management (IHRM) Refers to all HRM policies and practices used to manage people in companies operating in more than one country.

Interpretivism The view held in many qualitative studies that reality comes from shared meaning among people in that environment.

Intrinsic motivator Covers a wide range of motivation interventions in the workplace, from inner satisfaction following some action (such as recognition by an employer or co-workers) to intrinsic pleasures derived from an activity (such as playing a musical instrument for pleasure).

Intrinsic reward see *intrinsic motivator*.

Introversion A personality dimension that characterizes people who are territorial and solitary.

Intuition The ability to know when a problem or opportunity exists and select the best course of action without conscious reasoning.

J

Job characteristics model A job design model that relates the motivational properties of jobs to specific personal and organizational consequences of those properties.

Job design The process of assigning tasks to a job, including the interdependency of those tasks with other jobs.

Job enlargement Increasing the number of tasks employees perform in their job.

Job enrichment Employees are given more responsibility for scheduling, coordinating and planning their own work.

Job rotation The practice of moving employees from one job to another.

Job satisfaction A person's attitude regarding his or her job and work content.

K

Knowledge management Any structured activity that improves an organization's capacity to acquire, share and use knowledge in ways that improve its survival and success.

Knowledge work Paid work that is of an intellectual nature, non-repetitive, result-oriented, and engaging scientific and/or artistic knowledge demanding continuous learning and creativity.

Knowledge worker A worker who depends on her or his skills, knowledge and judgement established through additional training and/or schooling.

L

Labour power A Marxian term used to describe the potential gap between a worker's capacity or potential to work and its exercise. The indeterminancy resulting from the unspecified nature of labour power gives rise to a range of practices designed to make the employment relationship more calculable and controllable.

Labour process The process whereby labour is applied to materials and technology to produce goods and services which can be sold in the market as commodities. It is typically applied to the distinctive labour processes of capitalism in which owners/managers design, control and monitor work tasks so as to maximize the extraction of surplus value from the labour activity of workers (a term from Marx).

Language A system of symbols that express ideas and enable people to think and communicate with one another.

Leadership Influencing, motivating and enabling others to contribute toward the effectiveness and success of the organizations of which they are members.

Leadership grid A leadership model that assesses leadership effectiveness in terms of the person's level of task-oriented and people-oriented style.

Learning The processes of constructing new knowledge and its ongoing reinforcement.

Learning contract A learning plan that links an organization's competitive strategy with an individual's key learning objectives. It enumerates the learning and/or competencies that are expected to be demonstrated at some point in the future.

Learning cycle A view of adult learning that emphasizes learning as a continuous process. It is usually associated with the work of Kolb (1984).

Legitimacy A term describing agreement with the rights and responsibilities associated with a position, social values, system and so on.

Leverage The use and exploitation by an employer of his or her resources, particularly human resources, to their full extent. The term is often linked to the resource-based HRM model.

Life chances Max Weber's term for the extent to which persons have access to important scarce resources such as food, clothing, shelter, education and employment.

Lifelong learning A view of adult learning that became popular following the election of the 'New' Labour Government under the prime ministership of Tony Blair in Britain in 1997. Adherents believe that adults should be encouraged, and given the opportunity, to learn either formally in education institutions or informally on the job or off the job. It is also associated with human capital theory.

Line manager A manager who is responsible for supervising other employees directly responsible for providing a service or manufacturing goods, such as a production manager. Also known as operating managers.

Linguistic relativity The theory that the language we speak has such a fundamental influence on the way we interpret the world that we think differently from those who speak a different language.

Locus of control A personality trait referring to the extent to which people believe events are within their control.

Looking-glass self Charles Horton Cooley's term for the way in which a person's sense of self is derived from the perceptions of others.

Low-context culture A culturally sanctioned style of communication that assumes low levels of shared knowledge and so uses verbally explicit speech.

Luddite revolts Actions by a group of textile workers, led by General Ned Ludd in early nineteenth-century England, who systematically smashed new workplace technologies because they directly undermined their working knowledge and economic interests as workers.

M

Macrostructures Overarching patterns of social relations that lie outside and above a person's circle of intimates and acquaintances.

Management by objectives (MBO) A participative goal-setting process in which organizational objectives are cascaded down to work units and individual employees.

Matching model An HR strategy that seeks to 'fit' or align the organization's internal HR strategy with its external competitive strategy.

Matrix structure A type of departmentalization that overlays a divisionalized structure (typically a project team) with a functional structure.

McDonaldization (also known as '**McWork**' or **McJobs**) A term used to symbolize the new realities of corporate-driven globalization which engulf young people in the twenty-first century, including simple work patterns, electronic controls, low pay, part-time and temporary employment.

Means of production An analytical construct that contains the forces of production and the relations of production, which combined define the socioeconomic character of a society (a term from Marx).

Mechanical solidarity A term to describe the social cohesion that exists in pre-industrial societies, in which there is a minimal division of labour and people feel united by shared values and common social bonds (a term from Durkheim).

Mechanistic organization An organizational structure with a narrow span of control and high degrees of formalization and centralization.

Media richness Refers to the number of channels of contact afforded by a communication medium, so for example face-to-face interaction would be at the high end of media richness and a memorandum would fall at the low end of media richness.

Mental models The broad world-views or 'theories in-use' that people rely on to guide their perceptions and behaviours.

Microstructures The patterns of relatively intimate social relations formed during face-to-face interaction.

Motivation The forces within a person that affect his or her direction, intensity and persistence of voluntary behaviour.

Motivator-hygiene theory Herzberg's theory stating that employees are primarily motivated by growth and esteem needs, not by lower-level needs.

Myers-Briggs Type Indicator (MBTI) A test that measures personality traits.

N

Needs Deficiencies that energize or trigger behaviours to satisfy those needs.

Needs hierarchy theory Maslow's motivation theory of five instinctive needs arranged in a hierarchy, whereby people are motivated to fulfil a higher need as a lower one becomes gratified.

Negative reinforcement Occurs when the removal or avoidance of a consequence increases or maintains the frequency or future probability of a behaviour.

Negotiation Occurs whenever two or more conflicting parties attempt to resolve their divergent goals by redefining the terms of their interdependence.

Neoclassical management approach A model of management which presupposes that managers have the sole right to shape activities, strategy and organize work and people.

Network structure A set of strategic alliances that an organization creates with suppliers, distributors and manufacturers to produce and market a product. Members of the network work together on a long-term basis to find new ways to improve efficiency and increase the quality of their products.

Networking Cultivating social relationships with others to accomplish one's goals.

Norms The informal rules and expectations that groups establish to regulate the behaviour of their members.

O

Objectification Karl Marx's term to describe the action of human labour on resources to produce a commodity, which under the control of the capitalist remains divorced from and opposed to the direct producer.

Objective culture Refers to the phenomenon whereby institutions, practices and social forms that take on a life independent of their creators and threaten to stifle human creativity.

Objectivism An *ontological* position that asserts that the meaning of social phenomena have an existence independent of individuals; compare with *constructionism*.

Occupation A category of jobs that involve similar activities at difference work sites.

Ontology, ontological A theory of whether social entities such as organizations, can and should be considered objective entities with a reality external to the specific social actors, or as social constructions built up from the perceptions and behaviour of these actors.

Open systems Organizations that take their sustenance from the environment, and in turn affect that environment through their output.

Operant conditioning A technique for associating a response or behaviour with a consequence. Also known as instrumental and Skinnerian conditioning.

Organic organization An organizational structure with a wide span of control, little formalization and decentralized decision making.

Organic solidarity A term for the social cohesion that exists in industrial (and perhaps post-industrial) societies, in which people perform very specialized tasks and feel untied by their mutual dependence (a term from Durkheim).

Organization chart A diagram showing the grouping of activities and people within a formal organization to achieve the goals of the organization efficiently.

Organization design The process of creating and modifying organizational structures.

Organizational behaviour (OB) The systematic study of formal organizations and of what people think, feel and do in and around organizations.

Organizational commitment The employee's emotional attachment to, identification with and involvement in a particular organization.

Organizational culture The basic pattern of shared assumptions, values and beliefs governing the way employees in an organization think about and act on problems and opportunities.

Organizational justice In OB literature, the perceived fairness of outcomes, procedures and treatment of individuals.

Organizational learning The knowledge management process in which organizations acquire, share and use knowledge to succeed.

Organizational politics Behaviours that others perceive as self-serving tactics for personal gain at the expense of other people and possibly the organization.

Organizational structure The formal reporting relationships, groups, departments and systems of the organization.

Organizations Groups of people who work interdependently toward some purpose.

Outgroups Groups to which someone perceives he or she does not belong, which he or she accordingly evaluates unfavourably.

P

Paradigm A term used to describe a cluster of beliefs that dictates for researchers in a particular discipline what should be studied, how research should be conducted and how results should be interpreted.

Participatory design An approach to design and implementation of technologies that is premised on user participation.

Path–goal leadership theory A contingency theory of leadership based on the expectancy theory of motivation, which relates several leadership styles to specific employee and situational contingencies.

Patriarchy A hierarchical system of social organization in which cultural, political and economic structures are controlled by men.

Peer group A group of people who are linked by common interests, equal social position and (usually) similar age.

Perceived self-efficacy A person's belief in his or her capacity to achieve something.

Perception The process of selecting, organizing and interpreting information in order to make sense of the world around us.

Perceptual bias Automatic tendencies to attend to certain cues that do not necessarily support good judgements.

Perceptual set Describes what happens when we get stuck in a particular mode of perceiving and responding to things based on what has gone before.

Performance-to-outcome (P→O) expectancy The perceived probability that a specific behaviour or performance level will lead to specific outcomes.

Personality The relatively stable pattern of behaviours and consistent internal states that explain a person's behavioural tendencies.

Perspective An overall approach to or viewpoint on some subject.

Phenomenological approach A philosophy concerned with how researchers make sense of the world around them whose adherents believe that the social researcher must 'get inside people's heads' to understand how they perceive and interpret the world. For Weber, phenomenological understanding is a prerequisite for achieving *Verstehen*.

Political theory model An approach to understanding decision making whose adherents assert that formal organizations comprise groups that have separate interests, goals and values, and in which power and influence are needed in order to reach decisions.

Positive reinforcement Occurs when the introduction of a consequence increases or maintains the frequency or future probability of a behaviour.

Positivism A view held in quantitative research in which reality exists independent of the perceptions and interpretations of people. A belief that the world can best be understood through scientific inquiry (a term from Comte).

Post-Fordism The development from mass production assembly lines to more flexible manufacturing processes. Also referred to as neo-Fordism.

Post-industrial economy An economy that is based on the provision of services rather than goals.

Postmodernism The sociological approach that attempts to explain social life in modern societies that are characterized by post-industrialization, consumerism and global communications.

Power A term defined in multiple ways, involving cultural values, authority, influence and coercion as well as control over the distribution of symbolic and material resources. At its broadest power is defined as a social system which imparts patterned meaning.

Power-influence approach Examines influence processes between leaders and followers, and explains leadership effectiveness in terms of the amount and type of power possessed by an organizational leader and how the power is exercised.

Primacy effect A perceptual error in which we quickly form an opinion of people based on the first information we receive about them.

Procedural justice Justice based on the principle of fairness of procedures employed to achieve outcomes.

Proletariat (or working class) Karl Marx's term for those who must sell their labour because they have no other means to earn a livelihood.

Psychological contract An individual's beliefs about the terms and conditions of a reciprocal exchange agreement between that person and another party.

Putting-out system A pre-industrial home-based form of production in which the dispersed productive functions were coordinated by an entrepreneur. A major disadvantage of the system for the entrepreneur was controlling the behaviour and the level of output of cottage-based workers.

Q

Qualitative research Refers to the gathering and sorting of information through a variety of techniques, including interviews, focus groups, and observations, and inductive theorizing.

Quantitative research Refers to research methods that emphasize numerical precision, and deductive theorizing.

R

Race A term used by many people to specify groups of people distinguished by physical characteristics such as skin colour; also a category of people who have been singled out as inferior or superior, often on the basis of real or alleged physical characteristics such as skin colour, hair texture, eye shape or other subjectively selected attributes.

Racism A set of ideas that implies the superiority of one social group over another on the basis of biological or cultural characteristics, together with the power to put these beliefs into practice in a way that denies or excludes minority women and men.

Rationality The process by which traditional methods of social organization, characterized by informality and spontaneity, are gradually replaced by efficiently administered formal rules and procedures – bureaucracy (a term from Weber).

Realism The idea that a reality exists out there independently of what and how researchers think about it. It contrasts with **constructionism.**

Recency effect A perceptual error in which the most recent information dominates one's perception of others.

Referent power The capacity to influence others based on the identification and respect they have for the power holder.

Reflexive learning A view of adult learning that emphasizes learning through self-reflection.

Relations of production The social (class) relations of ownership and non-ownership of the forces of production (a term from Marx).

Relationship behaviour A term found in leadership theory that focuses on manager's activities that shows concern for followers, looks after subordinates welfare and nurtures supportive relationships with followers as opposed to behaviours that concentrate on completing tasks. It is associated with early leadership research at Ohio State University.

Reliability In sociological research, the extent to which a study or research instrument yields consistent results.

Resource-based model An HR strategy that views employees as an asset as opposed to a cost and assumes that the sum of people's knowledge and distinctive competences has the potential to serve as a source of competitive advantage.

Rhetoric The management of symbols (such as a language) in order to encourage and coordinate social action. 'Rhetorical sensitivity' is the tendency for a speaker to adapt her or his messages to audiences to allow for the level knowledge, ability level, mood or beliefs of the listener.

Rituals The programmed routines of daily organizational life that dramatize the organization's culture.

Role A set of behaviours that people are expected to perform because they hold certain positions in a team and organization.

Role ambiguity Uncertainty about job duties, performance expectations, level of authority and other job conditions.

Role conflict Conflict that occurs when people face competing demands.

Role perceptions A person's beliefs about what behaviours are appropriate or necessary in a particular situation, including the specific tasks that make up the job, their relative importance, and the preferred behaviours to accomplish those tasks.

S

Satisficing Selecting a solution that is satisfactory, or 'good enough' rather than optimal or 'the best'.

Schema A set of interrelated mental processes that enable us to make sense of something on the basis of limited information.

Scientific management Involves systematically partitioning work into its smallest elements and standardizing tasks to achieve maximum efficiency.

Selective attention The ability of someone to focus on only some of the sensory stimuli that reach them.

Self-actualization A term associated with Maslow's theory of motivation, which refers to the desire for personal fulfillment, to become everything that one is capable of becoming.

Self-efficacy A person's belief that he or she has the ability, motivation and resources to complete a task successfully.

Self-fulfilling prophecy An expectation about a situation which of itself causes what is anticipated to actually happen.

Self-leadership The process of influencing oneself to establish the self-direction and self-motivation needed to perform a task.

Self-managed work teams (SMWTs) Cross-functional work groups organized around work processes, that complete an entire piece of work requiring several interdependent tasks, and that have substantial autonomy over the execution of those tasks.

Semiotics The systematic study of signs and symbols used in communications.

Sex A term used to describe the biological and anatomical differences between females and males.

Sexual harassment Unwelcome conduct of a sexual nature that detrimentally affects the work environment or leads to adverse job-related consequences for its victims.

Situated learning An approach that views adult learning as a process of enculturation, where people consciously and subconsciously construct new knowledge from the actions, processes, behaviour and context in which they find themselves.

Situational leadership model Developed by Hersey and Blanchard, suggests that effective leaders vary their style with the 'readiness' of followers.

Skill variety The extent to which employees must use different skills and talents to perform tasks in their job.

Social capital The value of relationships between people, embedded in network links that facilitate trust and communication vital to overall organizational performance.

Social identity theory The theory concerned with how we categorize and understand the kind of person we are in relation to others.

Social interaction The process by which people act toward or respond to other people.

Social learning theory A theory stating that much learning occurs by observing others and then modelling the behaviours that lead to favourable outcomes and avoiding the behaviours that lead to punishing consequences.

Social solidarity The state of having shared beliefs and values among members of a social group, along with intense and frequent interaction among group members.

Social structure The stable pattern of social relationships that exist within a particular group or society.

Socialization The lifelong process of social interaction through which individuals acquire a self-identity and the physical, mental and social skills needed for survival in society.

Society A large social grouping that shares the same geographical territory and is subject to the same political authority and dominant cultural expectations.

Sociology The systematic study of human society and social interaction.

Span of control The number of people directly reporting to the next level in the organizational hierarchy.

Specialization The allocation of work tasks to categories of employees or groups. Also known as division of labour.

Staff manager A manager who is responsible for supervising other employees in a department or business unit that services and/or supports line managers and their subordinates, such as an HR manager.

Stakeholders Shareholders, customers, suppliers, governments, and any other groups with a vested interest in the organization.

Status The social ranking of people, the position an individual occupies in society or a social group or a work organization.

Stereotyping The process of assigning traits to people based on their membership in a social category.

Sticky floor The pattern of employment opportunities that disproportionately concentrates certain social groups at lower-level jobs.

Strategic business unit (SBU) A term to describe corporate development that divides the corporation's operations into strategic business units, which allows comparisons between each SBU. According to advocates corporate managers are better able to determine whether they need to change the mix of businesses in their portfolio.

Strategic choice The idea that an organization interacts with its environment rather than being totally determined by it.

Strategic human resource management (SHRM) The process of linking the human resource function with the strategic objectives of the organization in order to improve performance.

Strategy The long-term planning and decision-making activities undertaken by managers related to meeting organizational goals.

Stress An individual's adaptive response to a situation that is perceived as challenging or threatening to the person's well-being.

Structuration A concept focusing on balancing the dichotomies of agency, or human freedom, and social organization, or structures where individual choices are seen as partially constrained, but they remain choices nonetheless.

Substantive approach Approaches that tend to see technologies as producing negative social and political effects.

Superego Sigmund Freud's term for the human conscience, consisting of the moral and ethical aspects of personality.

Surplus value The portion of the working day during which workers produce value that is appropriated by the capitalist (a term from Marx).

Survey A research method in which a number of respondents are asked identical questions though a systematic questionnaire or interview.

Symbolic interactionism The sociological approach that views society as the sum of the interactions of individuals and groups.

Systemic racism The practices, rules and procedures of social institutions that have the unintended consequence of excluding minority group members.

Systems theory A set of theories based on the assumption that social entities, such as work organizations, can be viewed as if they were self-regulating bodies exploiting resources from their environment (inputs), transforming the resources (exchanging and processing) to provide goods and services (outputs) in order to survive.

T

Tacit knowledge Knowledge embedded in our actions and ways of thinking, and transmitted only through observation and experience.

Task behaviour A term found in leadership theory which focuses on the degree to which a leader emphasizes the importance of assigning followers to tasks, and maintaining standards: in other words, 'getting things done' as opposed to behaviours that nurture supportive relationships. It is associated with early leadership research at Ohio State University.

Task identity The degree to which a job requires completion of a whole or an identifiable piece of work.

Task significance The degree to which the job has a substantial impact on the organization and/or larger society.

Taylorism A process of determining the division of work into its smallest possible skill elements, and how the process of completing each task can be standardized to achieve maximum efficiency. Also referred to as scientific management.

Teams Groups of two or more people who interact and influence each other, are mutually accountable for achieving common objectives and perceive themselves as a social entity within an organization.

Technology The means by which organizations transform inputs into outputs, or rather the mediation of human action. This includes mediation by tools and machines as well as rules, social convention, ideologies or discourses.

Technology agreements Agreements with legal standing that set in place rules for negotiation over technological selection, adoption and implementation.

Theory A set of logically interrelated statements that attempts to describe, explain, and (occasionally) predict social events. A general set of propositions that describes interrelationships among several concepts.

Top-down processing Perception led predominantly by existing knowledge and expectations rather than by external sensory data.

Trade union An organization whose purpose is to represent the collective interest of workers.

Transactional leadership Leadership that helps organizations achieve their current objectives more efficiently, such as linking job performance to valued rewards and ensuring that employees have the resources needed to get the job done.

Transformational learning A view that adult learning involving self-reflection can lead to transformation of consciousness, new visions and courses of action.

U

Unfreezing The first part of the change process, whereby the change agent produces disequilibrium between the driving and restraining forces.

Urbanization The process by which an increasing proportion of a population lives in cities rather than in rural areas.

Utilitarianism The moral principle stating that decision makers should seek the greatest good for the greatest number of people when choosing among alternatives.

V

Valence The anticipated satisfaction or dissatisfaction that an individual feels towards an outcome.

Validity In sociological research, the extent to which a study or research instrument accurately measures what it is supposed to measure.

Value A collective idea about what is right or wrong, good or bad, and desirable or undesirable in a particular culture.

Values Stable, long-lasting beliefs about what is important in a variety of situations.

Verstehen Method of understanding human behaviour by situating it in the context of an individual's or actor's meaning (a term from Weber).

Vertical tension Tensions and contradictions that emerge in terms of hierarchical institutional relationships.

Virtual organization An organization composed of people who are connected by video-teleconferences, the Internet and computer-aided design systems, and who may rarely, if ever, meet face to face.

Virtual teams Teams whose members operate across space, time and organizational boundaries and linked through information technologies to achieve organizational tasks.

Visible minority Refers to an official government category of non-white, non-Caucasian individuals.

W

Will to power The notion that people are inherently driven to develop and expand power and control in their environments.

Win–win orientation The belief that the parties will find a mutually beneficial solution to a disagreement.

Work The physical and mental activity that is carried out at a particular place and time, according to instructions, in return for money, but exactly what counts as work depends on social values and power.

Work ethic A set of values which stress the importance of work to the identity and sense of worth of the individual and encourages an attitude of diligence in the mind of people.

Work group Two or more employees in face-to-face interaction, and each aware of positive interdependence as they endeavour to achieve mutual work-related goals.

Work organization A deliberately formed social group in which people, technology and resources are deliberately coordinated through formalized roles and relationships to achieve a division of labour designed to attain a specific set of objectives efficiently. Also known as formal organization.

Work orientation An attitude towards work that constitutes a broad disposition towards certain kinds of paid work. The *instrumental* orientation to work is the most researched; work orientations are regarded as socially constructed external to the formal organization, rather than internally from the work experiences within the workplace.

Workplace wellness All HR and health and safety programmes and interventions that can assist an employee to live at her or his highest possible level as a whole person, including physical, social, emotional and spiritual, and expand an employee's potential to live and work more effectively.

Index of personal names

Subject index

Note: major treatments of a subject and diagrams are indicated in **bold**, references to definition boxes in *italics*.

16PF, 166–7
42 Up, 237

A

absenteeism, 54, 150, 263, 279, 358
accountability, 300
accumulation theory, 412
achievement orientation, 138, 145, 253
activity theory, *231*, 232, 521
adjournment stage of groups, 305
adult learning theories, 232–6
affiliation, need for, 138, 253
age issues, 43, 206, 292, 521
agency theory, 88, 90, 112, 235, 337
agent of change, 446
agreement staircase, 198
agricultural employment, 38, 45–7
air transport industry, 93–5, 150, 189, 210–11, 330, 392, 411
Aliant Inc., 330
alienation, 48, *71*, **71–2**, 75, 261–2, 402, 448, 521
    four dimensions of, 261
alliances, 88
Amalgamated Society of Engineers, 50
Amazon.com, 407
American Disability Act (ADA), 285, 286–7
analysis, 521
andragogy, *232*, 232–4, **233**, 521
anomie, *74*, 75, 521
anthropology, 15–16
appraisals, 196, 203, 259, 448, 450, 464
apprenticeships, 46, 229, 231
    cognitive, 229
appropriation, *270*, 521
arena, organization as, 9
aristocracy of labour, *50*, 521
artefacts, 86, *414*, 521
Asian economies, xxxiii, 466–7
    see also China, Japan
assessment, 180, 188
    criteria for, 355
assumptions in decision making, 348

attitudes, 521
authority, *372*, 521
    authoritarian technics, 431
    formal, 108
    function, 83
    legitimate, 79, 376
    Weber's view of, 374
    see also control, power
autonomy of workers, 13, 55, 59–60, 219, 267–9, 310, 312, 313, 521
    responsible, 310

B

bargaining *see* negotiations
behaviour, human, 163
    elements of workplace, 9
    explanations of, 18, 447
    in groups *see* group
    management of, 19, 521
    prediction of, 18
    see also personality, psychology
behavioural approach, 107, 139–41
    to learning, 222–5, **226**
behavioural assessment, 180
beliefs, 415
benefits, employee, 450
best practice, 467
'black box', 223, 225
Body Shop, The, 402, 416
Bombardier Inc., 392
bottom-up processing, *195*, 196, 202, 521
boundary, organizational, 6
bounded rationality, *348*, 521
bourgeoisie, *20*, 73, 521
brainstorming, *362*, 522
    computer-mediated, 362–3
British Airways, 189, 210–11
bullying, **111**, 111–12
bureaucracy, *12*, 39, 78, 113, 398–9, **400–4, 405**, 408, 412, 522
    bureaucratization, *78*, 522
    post-bureaucratic organization, 404–8, **479**, 483
business-level strategy, 118–19
business process reengineering (BPR), xxxiii, 56, 134, 313, 392, *405*, **405–6**, 522

Index of movie titles